CW01500509

ACKNOWLEDGEMENTS

I'm hugely indebted to Dave Brock, Douglas Smith, Kris Tait and Nik Turner for the generosity and patience with which they gave their time and assistance in the preparation of this book.

I'd like specially to mention Simon House, Huw Lloyd-Langton and Marion Lloyd-Langton for their willingness to share some intensely personal memories.

Various other past and present members of Hawkwind have also made extremely valuable contributions. Big appreciation goes to Dave Anderson, Harvey Bainbridge, Tim Blake, Richard Chadwick, Thomas Crimble, Alan Davey, Del Dettmar, Martin Griffin, Lemmy, Terry Ollis, Jerry Richards, Adrian Shaw, Mick Slattery, Jason Stuart, Steve Swindells, Danny Thompson and Ron Tree.

And a big hello to Dave Beal, Buttz, Mike King and Penny Rimbaud, who all gave help beyond any of my expectations.

Others connected to the group have kindly made time to participate: many thanks to Animal, JJ Burnel, Tony Crerar, Ian Davidson, Michael Dog, Sam Fox, Frenchy Gloder, Mike Heath of Rebecca And Mike, Chris Hewitt, Jimbo, Allan Jones, Lin Lorien, Bernhard Pospiech, Push, Rat Scabies, Scouse, Jiana Skinner, Lucy Slane, Margaret Tait, Twink (Paul Noble), Jez Willis and Matthew Wright.

For their friendship and professionalism in helping to research this project, Maria Jefferis and Scott Mckenzie are stars indeed.

Murray Chalmers and Jon Bills from EMI have been particularly helpful. Hi and thanks!

I would like to buy a drink, too, for Ian Abrahams, Rae Harrison, Dave Ling and Debbie Wilson for their practical advice and Barbara Ngah for the understanding.

For the opportunity and patience – cheers, Chris Charlesworth. Thanks also to Robert Smith.

Many websites have been useful for detailed information, but I should single out www.starfarer.net, Hawkeye at myweb.tiscali.co.uk/

hawkwind/ and www.hawkwind.com for their excellent resources, as well as www.hawkwindmuseum.co.uk and The Attic at www.kadu. demon.co.uk/index

Love to Stephanie Jones for the diversional reading, Akiko Kato, Doreen Clerk, Stephen Clerk and Jo Boraston, Colin Clerk and Marsha Sullivan and, as always, to my husband Nigel for his selfless support and help and our daughter Eve, who for months has tolerated a deskbound mother.

Finally, thanks to Choccy for her companionship and for the memories, and hello to Speedie and Elric.

To Nigel and Eve O'Brien

FOREWORD

"I should mention something," warned Nik Turner, talking on the phone from his home in Wales during the first of many interviews for this book. "Everybody who's been in the band, everybody you talk to, will have their own reasons for saying what they say."

It was a puzzling and intriguing remark, an intimation of dark and dubious goings-on behind the scenes of a show that has been on the road for a remarkable 35 years.

And as the weeks went on, as the past and present members of Hawkwind opened up, one after another, about their experiences in the group, it became clear that Nik Turner was right. Everybody did have their own reasons for saying what they said and, mostly, they weren't afraid to state them.

The saga of Hawkwind is more fantastic, more dramatic than anything in their trademark science fiction, and sometimes more *Spinal Tap* than *Spinal Tap*.

It's a story littered with casualties and fuelled by conflict, with a long chain of sackings, arguments, threats and fights producing grudges that are borne to this day.

Some of the musicians claim to have been victimised, bullied or manipulated. Some accuse others of financial chicanery, or musical ineptitude. There have been disputes over women. And there are numerous disagreements about songwriting credits and the rights to old and live material.

Several allegations made by one member against another are too serious to publish.

Close observers have despaired at the ill will and suspicion that has developed over the years, particularly in view of Hawkwind's reputation as "the people's band" – anti-materialistic, anti-establishment, campaigners for good causes and champions of the benefit gig and the free festival.

At the heart of the trouble are the vast ideological and personal differences between former friends Dave Brock and Nik Turner, who has been sacked from Hawkwind twice.

But while their long-running feud may dominate parts of the story, a multitude of clashes were at the same time taking place among the other personnel. With such famously fiery characters as Lemmy and Ginger Baker coming in and out of the line-up, the scenes have been unsurprisingly turbulent.

Somehow or other, founder member Dave Brock has soldiered on through the storms, keeping Hawkwind together in a career that has seen them enter into battle with record companies, managers, agents, promoters, police, security forces, immigration authorities, tax officials, local government officers and, occasionally, audiences.

It's said the road to hell is paved with good intentions, and there have been occasions when this could certainly apply to Hawkwind. Sometimes, hell was the Brixton Academy in London, scene of some of their most memorable catastrophes.

There, in 1989, their benefit concert for Bob Calvert's widow Jill descended into chaos. And it was there, too, on October 21, 2000, that they staged a massive reunion of past and present members playing together under the banner of Hawkestra.

It was a wonderful gift to the fans, and many of the musicians had equally high expectations of the event. Yet on the night, after weeks of rehearsal, it quickly degenerated into what Dave Brock describes as "a nightmare of weird things, skulduggery and deviousness", with the equipment failing onstage and various participants falling out bitterly over the organisation and the financial share-out.

What had started out as a great idea ended up in court, to be followed only a matter of months later by another legal showdown, this time between Brock and Turner.

Still, there is much more to Hawkwind than the cut and thrust of their inter-personal relationships. The originators of space rock, they went on to create a pioneering body of work that directly influenced or at least gained enormous respect from ensuing generations of musicians.

In their early days, Hawkwind attracted a following of hippies and bikers, which broadened considerably as time went on. Their disregard for the trappings of "respectable" society, their antipathy towards the powers-that-be and their consequent status as a threat endeared them to the punks, while their political and environmental crusades won the support of any Left-thinking person.

Hard rock and heavy metal fans, meanwhile, responded to the bass-driven energy first introduced by Lemmy and to the extended soloing that accompanies their most celebrated material.

Veterans of Stonehenge and Glastonbury, Hawkwind became figureheads of the free festival scene and folk heroes to the battalions of crusties travelling the land with their friends, families and dogs. That alliance, however, broke down irretrievably in one dreadful day of violence at an outdoor event in Brighton in 1990.

Hawkwind's early sense of theatre and spectacle was ahead of its time; it set the standard for stage production in the early Seventies. With poetry, fantasy, sci-fi, dancers, costumes, a DJ, electronics, psychedelia and a light-show bringing colour and imagination to their repetitive, hypnotic rhythms and riffs, they arrived at a true multimedia experience that pre-dated dance music – and its drug culture – by a good 15 years. They have since been acknowledged by leading remixers, who have queued up to work with them.

A very English eccentricity about the band has resulted in some curious collaborations, most recently with Page Three superstar turned HM singer and reality-show contestant Sam Fox, TV and radio personality Matthew Wright, hiccupping new-wave vocalist Lene Lovich and The God Of Hellfire himself, Arthur Brown.

Hawkwind's long, vivid and, in some parts, glorious back catalogue stands as a testament to their continuing adventurousness. Clearly unwilling to dwell in the time warp inhabited by sad old hippies, they have paid attention to the successive trends in music and today insist that any new recruit must know his or her way around a computer program.

In conclusion, it must be said that various former members have paid a high price for their lives in music. Some stopped playing altogether, some picked up the bottle, some crashed out on the wrong sort of drugs, some lost their health, some lost their families, some cracked up completely and, in the worst possible outcome, the gifted young designer Barney Bubbles committed suicide.

This is Hawkwind Do Not Panic blared the album title. Certain individuals might have appreciated slightly different advice: "This is Hawkwind . . . approach with caution."

CHAPTER 1

Busking, Blues And
The Seaside Gang

DAVE BROCK was not cut out to be a gas-fitter's mate.

His second job, as an assistant film editor at Larkins Studios, making cartoons and TV ads near London's Berkeley Square, was a good deal more interesting although also short-lived. And by the time he became a despatch manager for the Central Office of Information, he was ready to quit regular work completely.

Dave Brock was always going to be a musician.

He knows this because he recently took a video camera to his parents' home and filmed them talking about his boyhood.

Dave's 97-year-old father Cyril and his mother Beryl, 93, were clear in their recollections of his earliest musical influences. They rekindled memories of his Uncle Maurice, a choir master and a banjo player who gigged around the local village halls in a band with an accordionist and a piano man.

"My Uncle Maurice gave me his banjo and I used to plonk on it when I was 12," says Brock. "He probably set me on this course."

Dave was born in Isleworth, Middlesex, on August 20, 1941 and brought up in nearby Feltham. Cyril was a painter and decorator and Beryl was a dinner lady for BEA, later renamed British Airways, and also for an infants' school.

At Longford Secondary Modern School, Dave's growing interest in music was fuelled by the memorable Mr Dyson. This art teacher, with his big shock of ginger hair, played banjo in a traditional jazz band in his spare time and he talked passionately about New Orleans, and blues, to his pupil.

Inspired, the 14-year-old Dave Brock set about learning to play a

1

guitar his parents had bought for him, and he started a record collection at around the same time, his first purchase being 'Africa Blues' by Sandy Brown's Jazz Band. He quickly built up a varied selection of 78rpm records which he played on his wind-up gramophone. Fats Domino was a great favourite. Then there was Humphrey Lyttelton and 'Bad Penny Blues'.

By age 16, Dave was sneaking off to London with a friend to explore its dens of iniquity – the smoky jazz and folk clubs and coffee bars of Soho. He also became a regular at the Eel Pie Island jazz club in Twickenham, an old ballroom famed for having the best-sprung floor in the south of England.

Dave formed his own jazz band, The Gravier Street Stompers, named after a road in New Orleans' French quarter, in 1959. He was on banjo. "We used to play in the fish market in Brighton," he recalls. "We'd take the milk train out of London at about two in the morning because the tickets were cheaper then, and we'd play during the day. They were beatnik events or 'raves', as they were known. We'd go home again in the late evening.

"We played with Ken Colyer. I met George Lewis, a very famous clarinet player. I used to collect all his records. He had these fantastic, hot bands – a wonderful rhythm section. It was a great moment in my life to meet this man. He was very quiet, very humble."

In the early Sixties, Dave put together a jug band called Dr Brock's Famous Cure, gigging in pubs with a female singer and a guy playing a stone jar in place of a bass.

Dave went on to busk in the streets of London and to sing and play guitar with various combinations of friends, sometimes forming blues duos for appearances in small venues. In one such duo, he went out gigging around the folk clubs with harmonica player Pete Judd, who'd moved from Cardiff to London and had met Dave at Eel Pie Island. They took bottom billing to artists including Wizz Jones and Long John Baldry who were at a similarly modest stage in their careers.

By 1963, Dave was striking up important new friendships as he became a familiar face in the clubs and coffee bars of Soho and also around the Richmond and Kingston beat scene. It was at L'Auberge, a coffee bar in Richmond, that he met budding musicians Eric Clapton and Keith Relf, both in an early line-up of The Yardbirds.

"I was big buddies with them," says Dave. "I used to be better than Eric Clapton on the guitar. I've got photos of us sitting playing together. I went round to see him in Notting Hill Gate in the Seventies. He was a big star by then, and I was a bit overawed by him. It's quite weird how things come round, quite weird that Ginger Baker [Clapton's drummer in Cream] ended up playing with Hawkwind."

And, presumably, quite weird that Brock should have been the one to sack him.

At L'Auberge, Dave also met the curiously named Dikmik, a future member of Hawkwind, who lived locally. Dikmik had played drums in an early incarnation of the band that would metamorphose into The Yardbirds.

Brock was in the habit of leaving for the summer to go busking in Europe with another friend, Luke Francis, a professional wrestler, singer and harmonica player from Newcastle upon Tyne. "I did get around a bit in my youth, and busking was a good way of doing it," remembers Dave. "I went to France, Germany, Holland, Belgium . . . Luke and I normally used to go to Paris and then down to the south of France.

"We used to play with gypsies and all sorts of people. We weren't nice boys. We were quite hard characters, and we had that reputation. Street life isn't an easy old existence. It's hard. You have to put up with a lot of crap from drunks. I wouldn't put up with any nonsense."

One summer, Pete Judd helped to make Dave's busking life in Europe a touch more luxurious. "Pete could drive," says Dave. "He had an old Mercedes and we decided to go off to Europe and sleep in the car. It must've been 1965, '66. We'd be busking and people would come past and say, 'I've got a club. Fancy coming to play?' So we ended up playing in all these clubs and cafés."

By 1965, Dave Brock, Luke Francis and a talented boogie-woogie pianist called Mike King had become a regular fixture at Eel Pie Island, the place where Dave had spent so many nights soaking up jazz and blues as a member of the audience.

"They used to have a major trad band, people like Bob Wallis & His Storyville Jazzmen, playing from 8pm to 10.30pm with a 45-minute break," says Dave. "We used to play the interval. We were the resident blues boys doing our bit. Sometimes they'd have special guests and we'd be invited to play with them as a treat, although it didn't happen very often.

"Memphis Slim played there once and he was fantastic. Champion Jack Dupree was the worst one. He used to change key deliberately, just to fuck us up – 'You white boys never know how to follow anything.' "

Mike King remembers Dave as an uncompromising person from the outset: "When I first met him, he had long blond hair hanging down and he told me once, 'People look at me in the street, but I just feel it's right for me. I don't want to get my hair cut.' This was right at the beginning, before the hippies got going and everybody had long hair."

One evening a couple of years later, Mike and Dave went to a Notting Hill cinema to see DA Pennebaker's Bob Dylan docufilm, *Don't Look Back*. Says Mike: "I was bored, but I didn't dare commit what might be a musical blasphemy by admitting it. Dave did. He said, 'I'm fed up with this, man. What about you?' We all left, and I really admired him for that."

Later in 1965, now operating under the name of The Dharma Blues Band, Dave, Luke and Mike recorded four tracks, two of which – 'Dealing With The Devil' and 'Roll 'Em Pete' – were released by Immediate on a blues anthology. Since reissued many times with a succession of different titles, *Blues Anytime* was noticed, in January 1969, by *Jazz Journal*, which stated: "The Dharma Blues Band have a nice Bluebird sound with unamplified harmonica and Mike King's rolling piano."

In 1971, the double album, by now titled *British Blues Archive Series*, was reviewed by *Rolling Stone*: "The Dharma Blues Band provide one of the surprises of this set with an extraordinarily enthusiastic rendering of 'Roll 'Em Pete'. Pianist Mike King is especially good."

Most recently, in 1998, the compilation was reissued as *White Boy Blues* by Castle. And the Dharma Blues recordings, for the first time augmented by the other two original tracks, 'Come On' and 'My Baby's Gone', were included on Blueprint's *Dawn Of Hawkwind* collection the next year.

"We got some royalties off that Immediate album when it was first released," recalls Mike King. "About £28 each. It came out in Sweden as well, although we didn't get anything for that. I think I was the one who wrote to ask about it and got no reply. When Dave got with Hawkwind, he spoke to his lawyers and they said it would cost more to trace the royalties than what they'd be worth. We didn't get any more."

It was after this that The Dharma Blues Band were offered what they thought might be an important opportunity. Says Mike: "There was this guy Bob, a rather self-important agent who hung around the fringes, and he booked us up at EMI or somewhere to do some demo discs.

"Luke was living on the beach at Brighton with a Swedish girl. We got to the studios and Luke didn't turn up. Dave and I jumped in my minivan and rushed to the beach. We found Luke looking very sheepish and we started swearing at him. He said, 'I can't commercialise my blues to make money.' We couldn't help it; we started laughing. But that was the end of our one chance."

It was also the end of Luke's membership of the band, and of his years-long companionship with Brock, one which had seen them busking and travelling together and even auditioning for *Opportunity Knocks*, eventually coming second.

Dave and Mike carried on gigging round the pub scene in southwest London. "We broke up in a friendly way when Dave decided to go electric," explains Mike. "I said, 'I'm not going to go on electric pianos.' He had his sights fixed on new ideas. He was ahead of his time."

Mike kept The Dharma Blues Band going for a while with different musicians, playing irregular gigs and making a few more recordings but as a working man with a family, it was more of a hobby for him than a career prospect.

Dave Brock found a new collaborator in Mick Slattery, a guitarist he had known and busked with for several years.

Mick was born and brought up in Richmond, Surrey. Leaving Lonsdale Road Secondary School in Barnes, he took "hundreds of jobs" and objected to all of them. "I just hated work," says Mick. "I changed my job every couple of weeks. I'd save up a bit of money and go down to St Ives in Cornwall. I'd live down there all summer, come back for a few weeks, earn a bit more money and go off again. I never wanted to settle down and get a proper job."

By the time he hooked up with Dave, Mick had been in a couple of bands. One, The Compromise, was the first English group to sign to CBS in the UK, and they released a couple of singles. Bob Dylan's producer Bob Johnston supervised the sessions that resulted in 'You Will Think Of Me' and its B-side, a cover of Dylan's 'Love Minus Zero/No Limit'. It didn't make many waves at the time, but it now changes hands for £12 a copy. The second single was 'You Baby'.

The Compromise broke up towards the end of 1966, and Mick and

Dave began jamming together. They played in folk and blues clubs and set up a couple of impromptu groups. "It was a very informal thing," explains Mick. "I don't even think we had names for the bands. We'd just meet up and someone else might come along. There were so many guitar players around, we were all getting invited to play at each other's gigs. It was very loosely structured."

Still, they were exciting days. Dave and Mick were being noticed by the music press, and Dave was getting the opportunity to watch, meet and sometimes play with his great blues heroes. "They had a fantastic magnetism and aura about them," he enthuses.

The other great excitement was acid. "Mick had got to know this guy called Pete Meaden, and it was him who turned us on to LSD," says Dave. "We got invited round to his flat. He had all these arty books and Turner paintings. I'd never taken LSD before. It was put into sugar lumps using eye-droppers. He'd spiked me up in a cup of tea. He said, 'I don't want you getting into a panic – I've just dropped some LSD into your tea.' I had a wonderful trip."

So did Mick Slattery, although it wasn't his first. "Not many people had a stereo system in those days," says Mick. "This may have been the first good stereo system we'd heard. Pete played us Captain Beefheart, The Electric Prunes and Country Joe & The Fish. What I remember more than anything else is Dave sitting there all the way through the trip looking from one speaker to the other, saying, 'What's going on?'"

Pete Meaden was a flamboyant, fast-talking mod publicist, who had worked with The Rolling Stones and, wholeheartedly, with the early Who, often being mistaken for their manager. With his encouragement, Dave and Mick recorded what Brock now describes as a "silly psychedelic single", a cover of Beefheart's 'Electricity'. Dave played 12-string, Mick played guitar and bass, and no one can remember who was on drums.

Dave was by now forming another group. In a nod to his old jug band, he named it The Famous Cure, although this was a blues-based outfit. It comprised Brock on guitar and vocals, Pete Judd on harmonica and tambourine and a guitarist called John Illingworth, who had previously played in jazz and jug bands, and had been involved in folk.

In spring 1967, The Famous Cure took a trip to Holland where the audiences fell in love with their acoustic, folk- and country-flavoured blues. They released a single, 'Sweet Mary', for Dutch label Negram Delta and watched it race up the chart.

However, Dave was interested in creating a harder, more psyche-delic sound, and when the band returned to London, Pete Judd left the line-up. Dave continued on guitar, vocals and harmonica, John Illingworth switched to bass, guitarist Mick Slattery came in and the group played with a succession of different drummers.

Before long, with beads, bells, love and flowers making headlines all over the world, The Famous Cure went back to Holland, this time with electric guitars, to join Tent '67, Psychedelic Psircus, a rock circus tour which was travelling the country in a massive tent from August through to October. "It was like being in a proper circus," remembers Dave. "We were all living in caravans. A very basic lifestyle, really. We had a psychedelic light-show with oil blobs."

Dave, Mick and John eventually got chatting with one of the tour roustabouts. His name was Nik Turner. The repercussions of that fateful meeting are rumbling on to this day but, at the time, it was an unremarkable event for Dave Brock. "Nik was just an English guy who happened to be working putting the tent up," says Dave. "I don't remember that much about him in Holland. He sat there smoking dope and talking."

Nik Turner was born on August 26, 1940 in Oxford. He was brought up in Buckinghamshire until the age of 14 when his parents, Charles and Kate, moved the family to Westgate on Sea, a couple of miles outside Margate in Kent. He went to Chatham House Grammar School and continued his education with a mechanical engineering course at Canterbury Tech.

Nik's early years were filled with the creative influence of relatives from his mother's side. Kate herself was a boogie-woogie piano player. Her sister, Marjory Mason, is still a member of the Royal Shakespeare Company, and has appeared in numerous films. Uncle Bert Mason was a cameraman who worked on a number of high-profile films, later made B-movies, worked on *Thunderbirds* and also played clarinet. Nik's grandfather, Henry Mason, made movies, ran theatre groups and reper-tory companies, and published and wrote reviews in a film critique which was circulated around the country. Indeed, he roped the whole family into the reviewing work – including Nik, whose speciality was B-Westerns.

At 17, inspired by the Dixieland jazz greats, he acquired a clarinet and took lessons from a neighbour, a former bandmaster in the

Marines. Nik was impressed by his neighbour, who played sax in a local dance band, and by other musicians from the area. Having also discovered the joys of Charlie Parker, John Coltrane, Coleman Hawkins and Stan Getz, he bought himself a tenor sax.

Nik's brother Roger had musical leanings too, forming and playing trumpet in a jazz band called The Canterbury Tailgaters while studying at Canterbury Art College. Nik, attending the Tech, joined in on his saxophone. They played one "really wild" gig, an art-school dance at the Chez Laurie nightclub. "I always wanted to play jazz," he declares. "But I found when I attempted it how difficult it was. I can more or less play it now. Or at least I'm still working on it . . ."

While he was still at school, Nik had been hanging out with his older cousins. They were arty bohemians, who had turned him on to trad jazz, taking him to exciting London clubs such as Ken Colyer's and Cy Laurie's, and introducing him to writers including the controversial American Henry Miller. At college, Nik started socialising with his brother's circle of friends, who were beatniks. Together, they took in such legends as Miles Davis, Dave Brubeck, Sonny Stitt and Stan Kenton, and read Jack Kerouac, William Burroughs and the other beat generation writers. The beatnik movement spawned the "ravers", those who grew their hair long, travelled for miles just to go to a party and, in Margate, slept on the beach.

Nik was absorbing still more cultural influences from friends living at the nearby American Air Force base: "I was like a typical American college boy," he laughs. "Just like *American Graffiti* – flat-top hair, Ivy League clothes, Levi's and leather jackets, even a Yank accent on occasions."

In 1962, he joined the Merchant Navy, sailing to Australia and back as an engineer on a passenger ship called *Southern Cross*. The trip was one long booze-up, which was "okay for some". Nik, by contrast, had become an avid reader, interested in Buddhism and mysticism, and he quit shortly afterwards.

Next, in 1963, he took up employment with London Transport. He was a development engineer based in Gunnersbury, west London, where he tested materials on buses.

By night, Nik would be out at gigs watching jazz bands and observing, at first hand, the development of British R&B. He was a regular at the Scene Club, the Marquee Club and the 100 Club. And as his network of friends expanded, he found himself on the fringes of the social scene surrounding The Rolling Stones and The Yardbirds in Richmond, where the Crawdaddy Club was at the heart of the activity. The club had opened at the Station Hotel, shortly afterwards moving to the Athletic Ground.

Yet, if Nik's personal life was exciting, his working days were boring in the extreme. He stuck it out for a year and then headed back to the coast. It had been his second and last "real" job.

Margate was and remains famous for its Dreamland amusement park. It also has a certain military and artistic tradition: Nik's namesake Turner, the great painter, lived there for a time, Van Gogh apparently passed through on his travels and, more recently, Tracey Emin emerged as a resident. Author John Buchan had also lived in nearby Kingsgate.

As for Nik Turner: "I was quite enchanted by the sunsets."

Moving back into his parents' home, Nik immediately realised that while the sunsets were as glorious as ever, certain other things had changed. The mods and rockers had arrived. In the summer of 1964, they fought pitched battles on the beaches of south-coast seaside resorts, including Margate. "I was a friend of everybody," says Nik of his seafront days.

By now, he was spending his summers on Margate promenade selling hats, sunglasses, buckets and spades, saucy postcards and psychedelic paraphernalia to the day-trippers and holidaymakers.

He looked after the rockers' beloved bikes from time to time, even though he rode a scooter and dressed along the smart, sharp lines of the mods. He also helped the mods by stashing their ill-gotten substances [robbed from chemist shops] in his hat stall, all the while chatting politely to any passing plod.

In his usual manner, Nik absorbed the details of the prevailing youth cultures, the clothes and the attendant music, and utilised, stored or adapted whatever elements he admired for his own use. "Margate was a bit of a melting pot," says Nik. "There were a lot of diverse people hanging around. No lines were drawn between the various groups of young people except for the mods and rockers – and their lines were drawn by the media and drugs – and the mods and police. As an influence of the ravers, there were long-haired, beatnik, hippie types hanging out with mods, even though they weren't mods themselves."

And then the hippies came along for real.

As someone who was as passionately interested in modern jazz as in the traditional variety, who had been exposed to all shades of thinking and bohemian behaviour, Turner was excited but not surprised by the advent of psychedelia, complete with its emphasis on musical adventure and individual liberation. He saw it as a natural progression, evolving through a lineage that had included beatniks, ravers, modernists and mods.

"I had a VW car," he recollects. "After I finished work at the sea-front on a Saturday night, I used to pile about eight or 10 people into my car – I don't know how we did it – and drive to London and go to an all-nighter. There were these psychedelic events at places like the UFO and Ally Pally. I went to see Jimi Hendrix at Olympia at some sort of all-nighter. I saw Pink Floyd at The Roundhouse."

Nik's passengers were various "weird and wacky people" from Margate and the neighbouring Ramsgate. One of them was Robert Calvert.

Born in Pretoria, South Africa, in 1945 to English parents, Calvert had relocated to Margate with his family at the age of two or three. He left school with a great love for poets such as Keats, Shelley, Dylan Thomas and Paul Verlaine, and an ear for unconventional music.

At 15, he was playing the local dancehalls with his first band, Oliver Twist & The Lower Third. Then came a satirical group, Mordecia Sludd & The Others (pre-dating The Bonzo Dog Doo Dah Band), although it didn't do too well either: there wasn't much demand for satire in the ballrooms, nor for Calvert's luminous socks.

Nik: "Robert was living in Ramsgate with his wife Pauline and about four kids. His mother was a state registered nurse living in Margate, and she told me that Robert had been having a nervous breakdown every 18 months, from quite a long time before I met him.

"He had a problem with his parents. His father, a building-site manager, was very macho and Robert wasn't very macho. His father wanted him to be a 'real man', and he wanted to be a poet. He used to have a hard time with his dad.

"When I met Robert, he was a poet, doing readings. When we went off to London on Saturday nights, he used to leave his wife at home. Sometimes he would be manic, sometimes he would be depressed and, in between, he used to neglect his wife and family."

Another soul squashed into Turner's Volkswagen was Dikmik. A veteran of the jazz and blues scene in Twickenham and his hometown of Richmond, where he'd met Dave Brock in the L'Auberge coffee bar, he was now spending long periods with Robert Calvert's family in Margate.

Dikmik had endured a brief secondary-school education and had lasted only a few months in art school, but he had an intense and individual imagination which was presumably recognised by the embryonic Yardbirds. Named Michael Davies, he became known in some circles as Dick Davies. Then the two names, Dick and Mick, were put together to denote some sort of dual personality; hence Dikmik.

Nik Turner remembers him as one of the long-haired, post-raver types who had befriended the local mods, possibly because of a mutual fondness for speed. "Dikmik was a mate of mine. He was and is a very nice guy. He had interesting musical and artistic tastes, and he had a lot of ideas. He became a hippie, always talking about going to India."

It was during this period that Nik had his second experience of live performance, stepping on to the back of a lorry to play alto sax with a blues band called Virgin at a local carnival. The group went on to play a series of free gigs in a shop on the seafront, with Nik in the audience.

"It gave me the idea that it was good to be involved and do some good and help people," says Nik. "I realised the value of free music. It was influential in my being happy and positive towards getting free gigs and benefits together when I joined Hawkwind."

This would later become a source of tension between the idealistic Turner and the more pragmatic Dave Brock.

Meanwhile, on either side of the summer season in Margate, Nik had been travelling to Holland to visit friends and work casually. On one such trip, he acted as road manager for a singer called Davey Jones. Nik had come to love the raw, brassy, funky soul of "The Godfather", James Brown, and in Jones, he found an imitator who opened his eyes to some dramatic stagecraft.

In 1967, Turner returned to Holland, this time at the invitation of friends in Amsterdam who were helping to organise the Tent '67 circus tour. "I wasn't playing. I was one of five roustabouts, putting up a different venue every day – a nine-masted tent holding 3,000 people. I worked in the bar too. There were psychedelic bands and a light-show and all that sort of thing going on. The Famous Cure were one of the bands that played there. I met Dave Brock and Mick Slattery, and I kept in touch with them after that."

The Famous Cure were doing rather nicely in Holland – they were stealing the show on the circus tour and receiving major coverage in the Dutch press – so it was a shame that they had to leave so suddenly.

Dave Brock explains: "Unfortunately, we were involved with some people who were dealing in large amounts of hashish, who got busted. We'd put some money up for hash, and the police had found out we were involved. Someone warned us, 'You should get out of the country quick,' otherwise we'd have got involved in a big web of drug-dealing. We had to flee back to England."

Safe in London, the group played a string of gigs at the Middle Earth in Covent Garden and other alternative venues, but eventually ran out of steam. Dave remembers: "I went back to busking, playing in the streets of London, which I did for the next three years."

Brock had long ago learnt to keep one step ahead of the law, although inevitably he copped for the odd hand on the shoulder and an order to "move on" or, at worst, a £1 fine from the local magistrates.

Mike King remembers the point at which Dave was forced to become serious about his incomings and outgoings: "He was on the employment exchange payroll as a guitarist. After some years, they said to him, 'Look, Mr Brock, in all this time we've never had a request for a guitar player. You're a lovable rogue, but I'm afraid we're going to have to cut you off.'"

Dave was working his way up the busking hierarchy. It was a community that operated its own code of conduct, to be broken by the newcomer at his or her peril. Says Dave: "You have to be quite callous and vicious if you want to succeed. I ended up doing cinema and theatre queues. When you start out, you'll be third in line, but you get to the point where you'll be doing your own queues.

"We all had different girls working for us, collecting the money. They were called 'bottlers'. The actress Jenny Agutter was a bottler in her spare time while she was studying drama. My bottler was called Anneke. She went on to become the manager of a restaurant in Soho. She used to be in the queue waiting for me to turn up. No one who knew me ever tried to take my place, 'cos I'd have clocked them one. I've knocked people out."

Dave also acquired a prime pitch in the subway at Tottenham Court Road where he played jazz and blues to the West End commuters. It would also serve as something of a recruitment centre for Hawkwind, with Brock enrolling two new members of the band through chance encounters in the subway.

In January 1969, Dave was one of the performers taking part in The Buskers Tour. It was organised by Don Paul, manager of one-man-band and genuine busker Don Partridge, who had enjoyed surprise hit singles with 'Rosie' and 'Blue Eyes' the year before.

The buskers took to the road in a double-decker bus, a motley crew of old music-hall stars, tap dancers, banjo and spoon players, a toothless woman . . . and Dave. Also on board were Gordon Giltrap, who would go on to a successful solo career, and the star of the show, Don Partridge.

They slept on the top deck as the bus criss-crossed the UK, arriving in London at the end of the month for a glittering, grand finale at the Royal Albert Hall. "There were only about four people in the place," chuckles Brock.

An album, *The Buskers*, followed on EMI/Columbia, and his contribution was a rendition of Willie Dixon's 'Bring It On Home'.

True to form and in keeping with the spirit of the day, Dave had formed another band at this time. Dave Brock & Friends brought together his long-time colleagues Mike King and Pete Judd. Mike Greig, who was appearing on The Buskers Tour, completed the line-up. They played mainly in folk clubs.

On January 29, on the eve of the Albert Hall concert, John Peel presented the band in session on his Radio 1 *Night Ride* show, where they performed six songs including 'Roll 'Em Pete'. They received a princely £32.

Dave was no stranger to the BBC. He had played for John Peel in his own right in 1968 and had also made appearances with Pete Judd.

By now, his musical interests were broadening. He had become intrigued by electronic music. "It was quite an inventive part of the Sixties," reflects Dave. "Psychedelia was going on. The Arts Laboratory in Covent Garden had lots of arty films on, poetry and electronic music. Then there was the UFO in Tottenham Court Road where [pioneers] Pink Floyd and Soft Machine used to play.

"I used to stay indoors and play electronic music with a guitar and echo unit. I used to play slide guitar a lot and make the loops. (The one good thing I learnt to do at Larkins Studios was the loops.) I made weird electronic music, music concrete. I looped Sonny Terry's harmonica so it went, 'Waah, waah, waah'. I used to sit at home doing this with Mick Slattery.

"There were a lot of people doing it. Silver Apples used a bank of six oscillators. They had one guy with a drum kit and another guy playing all these oscillators. You'd think, 'Christ, it's really fucking boring.'"

Clearly, Dave was having better ideas of his own. It was time to form a group that could express them.

After the circus tour of Holland had ended, Nik Turner went back to Margate where the rhythm of life continued as usual. He sold his wares on the beach, and turned his hand to any other odd jobs that came along.

"I was a croupier in a nightclub," he reveals. "A couple of guys I knew had a craps table that we ran every night, but I couldn't cope with it. We just made too much money, and my business on the sea-front was totally exhausting me. It was awful watching all these people *loving to lose*, trying to impress their girlfriends. I gave up gambling after that."

In the winter of 1968, Turner went to Berlin. There, he was invited to sing with a rock'n'roll band that included a drummer friend from Margate, whose mother lived in Berlin and whose grandfather was Franz Hofer, the pre-War German expressionist painter. Nik also met and mixed with free-jazz musicians including Edgar Froese from Tangerine Dream, and was invited to such fashionable haunts as the Blue Note jazz club. He went to parties, gigs and leading squats, where he met many of the influential figures in the city's counterculture and was adopted by them.

Travelling home for Christmas, he was filled with excitement at the idea of playing freeform jazz in a rock band. He was also convinced of the benefits of the underground – a coming-together of people for the greater good.

Unlike Dave Brock who was devoted to music above all else, Turner was inspired by the prospect of a young society in which all of the creative elements, from music to writing and art to fashion, would be interconnected and of equal importance. It was already happening in London.

Early in 1969, Nik bought a van and kicked his heels in Margate for a while as he pondered his next move. He took a freelance job as a sur-veyor for the Westinghouse washing-machine company, scouting out areas that looked as though they could do with a launderette.

He was at the same time continuing his regular visits to London where he went to gigs, strengthened friendships he had established with writers and artists working for the alternative press and kept in touch with two of the musicians he'd met in Holland: Dave Brock and Mick Slattery.

In time, they told him about the new band they were forming and soon invited him to be their road manager and driver. "The van was one of my main assets," remarks Turner. "Transport was something very few groups had. My van was capable of carrying a lot of equipment."

When the summer came, Nik Turner rolled up a sleeping bag, jumped into his van with Robert Calvert and headed for London. The familiar, towering figure on the seafront at Margate had sold his last kiss-me-quick hat.

Dave Brock and Mick Slattery thought the band was complete. With Dave on vocals and guitar and Mick on lead guitar, both – but particularly Brock – were keen to experiment with electronics. They had recruited bassist John Harrison and drummer Terry Ollis. Unusually, the new boys were strangers.

Dave: "When I was busking in the Tottenham Court Road subway, I used to meet all these different characters. One day, this guy came over and said to me, 'The name's John Harrison.' We got chatting, and he told me he used to play bass with the Joe Loss band. I asked him if he'd like to come and jam with us. He turned up and played and he was a knockout, a fantastic bass player, really solid. I put an advert in *Melody Maker* for a drummer, and that's how we got Terry Ollis."

Terry was born on April 11, 1952 in Hammersmith, London, and attended a secondary school in Chelsea, where he enjoyed his morning walks along the King's Road. Leaving school, Terry worked at his parents' scrapyard in the Shepherd's Bush area, and took up drumming – nothing formal, just jamming – with various groups of friends.

Answering Brock's advertisement, Terry went for a meeting with the drummer-less band, and was greeted by John Harrison and a guitar player. He was then invited back another day to meet Dave Brock, on which occasion Dave was accompanied by Mick Slattery. The guitarist Terry had previously met never showed up again. The band got down to work straight away.

It was the summer of '69 and Dave was still living in a cold-water flat in Putney. He'd moved there after separating from his first wife,

Maureen, because "we didn't get on very well" and leaving the marital home in Fulham – which for a short time they'd shared with Mick Slattery, early in the Sixties. Dave had since met and married his second wife Sylvia with whom he would have a daughter, Marti, and a son, Pascoe.

Mike King, a guest at the Wandsworth Register Office wedding, remembers Dave as a nervous if not reluctant bridegroom. "We said, 'It'll be all right, Dave,'" he recalls. "I was very friendly with both of them. Dave was easy to get along with and Sylvia was a very nice person, into science fiction and mysteries and things like that."

As Dave's musical opportunities began to open up, his absences from home weren't always appreciated. "I went off to Holland with The Famous Cure while poor old Sylvia had to look after the baby," says Dave. "I think she used to get a bit lonely."

Mike King adds: "I stayed one night when Dave was playing abroad. He said I was the only man allowed to stay with Sylvia when he was away, the only one he trusted."

Dave often called into a music shop on the corner of Gwalior Road, Putney, the street where he lived with Sylvia. The shop was run by Bob Kerr – he of the Whoopee Band. Hearing about the new group, Kerr invited them to rehearse in the basement. They took him up on his offer.

By now, Nik Turner had arrived. "I was living in squats and the back of a lorry and sleeping on people's floors, and Robert Calvert did the same thing," remembers Nik. "We were hanging out together."

A lot of their hanging out was done in Notting Hill, the nerve centre of alternative London, particularly around Ladbroke Grove and Portobello Road. The area had long been populated by unconventional types and immigrants, including dope-smoking West Indians, and so it offered ideal surroundings for the incoming hippies.

Calvert gravitated towards the underground press and found kindred spirits in the people producing the information, stories and cartoon strips for *IT* (*International Times*), Richard Neville's international magazine *Oz* and *Frendz*. Calvert began to write poetry and fiction for *Frendz*, seeing himself as "a kind of anti-literary establishment guerrilla". He also staged an "environmental poetry" event at The Roundhouse, as part of their *Better Place To Live* exhibition.

Nik was trying to maximise the use of his van to make ends meet. He hired it out to various bands, he carried out removals and he made deliveries of posters, silk screens and other desirable items for the owner of a hippie hang-out called The Dogg Shop in Blenheim Crescent.

He was also spending time with Dikmik, who was back in London and, together, they went to see Dave Brock, Mick Slattery, Terry Ollis and John Harrison. The upshot was that Dikmik, who had known Dave and Mick for years, was offered a roadie's job alongside Nik Turner.

The band were rehearsing intensively in the basement of Bob Kerr's shop and in a small theatre in the Royal College of Art, behind the Albert Hall. A friend had arranged for them to use the hall for free during the summer holidays.

In a typical example of how informally things operated in those days, the group soon invited both Nik and Dikmik to join in for a bit of fun. Mick Slattery remembers: "They started jamming with us. We thought, 'This is great!'"

Dave Brock: "Nik had a saxophone. He couldn't play the thing at all. He used to honk on it, a bit avant-garde jazz. We said, 'Oh, that sounds really good – perhaps you'll have to come onstage with us.' Then Dikmik bought an audio generator and an echo unit. He started playing the audio generator."

According to Nik Turner, "It's a signal generator used for testing radio valves, I think. If you stick it through an echo unit, it creates weird and wonderful sounds, which is what we were doing."

"Dikmik was quite an innovator, even a genius," continues Brock. "He'd follow what we were playing, which is quite difficult to do. He used to have his little card table. He'd stick his audio generator and echo unit on it and off he used to go."

And that's how the roadies joined the band that would become Hawkwind.

The sound changed immediately, of course. Dave Brock recollects: "We used to play a lot of open music. We used to jam a lot, loosely blues, electronic. We had a nucleus of material that included a lot of my old busking numbers which we would jam around. So it was a very open thing."

"Dave was really interested in electronic music, as I was," adds Mick Slattery. "Nik was into freeform jazz and Dikmik just liked making sounds with whatever he could. Through trial and error, we got a few numbers together. And the psychedelic stuff was all happening, so we felt we could experiment as much as we wanted. We just came up with that sound."

Mick looks back on that period in London with great affection.

"It was fantastic," he says. "It was the place to be, just great. There was nothing like it, although it had been even better a couple of years before. Lots of people shared the same ideas and the same goals. There were lots of good drugs, lots of good little shops, lots of things happening. It was really, really exciting with all the psychedelic music we were hearing and all the new venues starting up, The Roundhouse and the UFO.

"We all liked to smoke a bit of dope and take a bit of acid, I suppose. Maybe some of us would dabble in other things. It had a big impact on me as a guitar player. It changed the way I thought about music. It all became very experimental and intuitive."

And as for the band: "There were obviously clashes and disputes, but generally we got on okay to start with."

Terry Ollis seconds that. "We were very much like brothers living in each other's pockets," he says. "There weren't very many upsets."

Nik Turner agrees: "I got on very well with Dave Brock. I used to go and sleep on his floor in the cold-water flat in Putney. I had a soprano sax I was playing a lot, he had his guitar, and we went busking a couple of times at North London Poly."

However, a misunderstanding had already arisen between the two.

Says Dave: "We were a bunch of spaced-out freaks but, really, I was a bit of a band leader in terms of what was going on. You have to have a captain of a ship otherwise nothing could ever be done."

Nik Turner understood a different set-up. "I thought the band was a communal thing, a community project," he contends. "Dave wasn't in charge any more than anybody else was. In hindsight, I wasn't that *au fait* with certain things that were happening."

They were opposite viewpoints that would lead to all kinds of trouble in the future.

CHAPTER 2

Anarchy In The All Saints Hall

THE band with no name were impatient for a gig, and rather than waste time organising one, they decided to play at somebody else's.

Mick Slattery had a flat in Talbot Road, off the Portobello Road, with Terry Ollis living in the back room. It became a gathering place for the group, somewhere to share their drugs while Nik Turner warmed up his baked beans and drank cups of tea before rehearsals. From this vantage point, they noticed a series of weekly gigs taking place at the All Saints Church Hall, which was close by.

On August 29, 1969, Mick called into the hall as preparations were being made for a show. He approached someone who looked important and asked if the band could play a couple of numbers that night. "Yeah, just turn up and play," was the accommodating answer.

Mick later remarked that "he was probably only the electrician," but he may well have been Tim Blake, who was helping with the sound and would himself join Hawkwind 10 years later. The band reacted to the news of their debut gig by skinning up some fat spliffs and deciding to call themselves Group X, in the absence of any better suggestion.

Arriving at the church hall, they again had to ask for permission to perform. Tim Blake remembers that, at some point, he told someone from the group that they were welcome to do a few numbers. Certainly, they had to convince a couple of managerial characters who were now present.

Douglas Smith was a partner in Clearwater Productions, a company with an office in nearby Westmoreland Mews. The other members of his team were Richard Thomas, Wayne Bardell, Kick Van Henkel and Max Taylor. They managed a country-rock band called Cochise who went on to some measure of success, together and individually.

Douglas looked after a band called Trees, Wayne was responsible for High Tide and Richard had Skin Alley.

Kick was their music-business insider, an import salesman at EMI, and Max was "the money", due to an inheritance. Max would much later become chairman of Lloyd's, the insurance brokers. (Legend has it that he kept a guitar in his office and never deleted the line in his CV which described him as a one-time manager of Hawkwind.)

Clearwater was essentially a management company branching out into publishing and gig promotion with the help of some local lighting specialists and an agent called Paul Fenn, now with the leading Asgard agency. Like Mick Slattery, the Clearwater people had noticed the regular gigs happening at All Saints Hall and they had decided, with a trace of rivalry, that they could do the same. They booked a string of dates at the hall, primarily as a showcase for their own bands.

"These gigs were doing quite well," says Douglas Smith. "We were getting probably 250 people in the hall. We were very lucky. We had David Bowie one night. He was running the Beckenham Arts Lab at the time. Wayne got him to perform for us at All Saints as a favour because we supplied bands for his Lab at good deals. High Tide were playing there a lot then. They'd just got a publishing deal, I think with Apple, and they had this new equipment, really good guitars and all the rest of it. We had them booked to do this night at All Saints Hall."

The audience was to include an influential figure. John Peel lived in the neighbourhood, in Stanley Square, and he was a fan of High Tide. Wayne Bardell had known Peel since his days as a plugger for Apple and had asked him along in the hope that he might offer High Tide a session.

Douglas recalls what happened next: "As we were getting everything together, this band turned up in an old, green Morris van driven by Nik Turner. He had this long hair and a beard that was tied in the centre. They wandered in and said, 'Can we play? We're just getting together a band.' I think Wayne asked, 'Have you any equipment?' 'No. Can we borrow some?' 'What are you called?' 'Group X.' "

Douglas and Wayne agreed that Group X could play a short set at the end of the night.

The band had not worked out any songs. The gig had taken them by surprise, and they'd spent the preceding hours in a cloud of dope smoke. But the 15 minutes they played at the All Saints Hall on August 29 are written large into Hawkwind legend.

It was an insane jam, a cacophony of instruments soloing and crashing together around the riff from The Byrds' 'Eight Miles High'. They called it 'Sunshine Special'.*

Mick Slattery later described it this way: "Dikmik was twiddling with his generator, Nik was honking up a storm, Dave and I were getting our guitars to feed back the way we'd seen Hendrix do it and Terry was thrashing his drum kit to within an inch of its life, while the strobes and liquid light-show added to the air of chaos."

The audience in the All Saints Hall was stunned by Group X. Among the wide-eyed observers were three musicians who would later join Hawkwind. One was Thomas Crimble, Skin Alley's bassist. Another was Tim Blake, who was experienced in studio sound and owned some equipment. He had become involved with Clearwater, helping out with all of the bands although his favourite was the "mind-blowing and definitely progressive" High Tide. The third future member of Hawkwind to see their first-ever gig was High Tide violinist Simon House, who was celebrating his 21st birthday that very night.

"I think I was tripping. I must have been," says Simon. "Group X were astonishing 'cos they had a strobe and an audio generator, two things very few people had in those days. They had this complete audiovisual assault."

John Peel was equally impressed.

"High Tide he obviously liked," says Douglas Smith. "He'd been spouting off about them. As he was leaving, we asked him, 'What did you think?' He goes, 'That Group X – *get them.*'"

"We were a bunch of weirdos who turned up at somebody else's gig," marvels Nik Turner. "John Peel saw us a bit like The Sex Pistols of the time, like nothing else that was happening. We were chaotic, undisciplined and wild."

Douglas took John Peel's advice and signed Group X to a one-page management contract with Clearwater. Not only did this give them the prospect of a real career, it also broadened their contact with other bands.

"All the Clearwater acts knew each other," says Simon House. "We

* 'Sunshine Special' has been resurrected recently in live performances by a band containing three of its originators – Mick Slattery, Terry Ollis and Nik Turner, whose Space Ritual group is dedicated to the spirit of Hawkwind.

used to hang out at the office. It was like a big club. We used to go round and smoke joints. We got to know Group X, and I suppose we must have done several gigs supporting each other, although High Tide broke up in 1970. We didn't last very long."

Nik Turner earned a few extra quid roadying in his van for the other groups in the "club".

Douglas' first priority was to find a rehearsal space for his new protégés, and he did this with the help of Tommy, the Westmoreland Mews landlord.

Douglas had recently moved out of the office, where he also lived, while preparing to set up camp in the neighbouring number 13, a former warehouse. During this period of transition, Tommy, who owned a range of properties, gave Douglas a home in Great Western Road, north-west London, for a few weeks.

It was a top-floor flat, complete with leaky roof, in a Victorian terraced house on the canal, next to a bridge. Douglas knew that there were other vacant units in the house, and when Group X came along, he arranged to rent the basement from Tommy.

"There were two basements, one on top of the other," Douglas remembers. "They had the higher one. They decorated it in all these fantastic colours, and they'd get out of their boxes and go down there and just jam for hours and hours – with strobe lights."

Nik Turner remembers the accommodation as "derelict, down at heel", but the band nevertheless persisted in their psychedelic cellar, still firmly engaged in an extraordinary fusion of buskers' blues, electric rock power, electronic impudence and freewheeling, avant-garde solo-ing. But if the futuristic aspect of their sound was undeniable, there was little hint of sci-fi. That would come later.

Nik Turner remarks: "Originally, the thing was very much more inner space, not outer space. It was mind-expanding."

The music was inspired as much by the mood of the times as by the collective influences of the band members. "None of us were fantastic musicians, but as an entity we had a real creative energy," states Dave Brock. "We had a big entourage of people, there was a lot of drug-taking and we were in the hippie lifestyle. We were all into this alternative lifestyle and alternative music, free-flowing music. It was a really liberating atmosphere.

"Lots of things were going on, good arty stuff. Freedom and out-spokenness of the press was happening then. *IT* used to put out news about what dope you could buy, and the prices, and the same with acid."

These publications covered drug busts and court cases, opposed censorship and promoted alternative medicine, protection of the environment, feminism and gay rights – views which have since been widely adopted in society. The underground editors sent copies of their newspapers, magazines and comics to each other, at home and abroad, and allowed their articles to be reprinted free of charge, creating something of an international understanding among the readers.

"There was a big sense of community," continues Brock, "although it all collapsed later on. It was like a reflection from San Francisco in a way, happening in Notting Hill Gate. All the bands around that era, Principal Edwards Magic Theatre, Mighty Baby, The Edgar Broughton Band, were playing a free-flowing sort of music with a lot of improvisation. Numbers didn't finish after three minutes. They went on for 15. We had strobes going.

"When I used to go to Middle Earth, I would wear flowery shirts and take acid and jump around. We had the freedom to dance instead of being stared at. The feeling of freedom was very important."

It was during their rehearsal period in Great Western Road that Group X realised they needed to change their name to something more imaginative, and they came up with Hawkwind Zoo. The "Zoo" part referred to their tongue-in-cheek view of themselves as a menagerie. "Hawkwind" was Nik Turner's nickname, bestowed upon him because of his excess wind and phlegm.

"Nik's thing of farting . . . he used to be terrible," says Dave Brock. "And clearing his throat, hawking. He used to do it quite often."

He still does both, unashamedly.

It may also, perhaps, be pertinent to mention the prominent outline of Turner's nose, and the nature of his former business on Margate seafront, hawking novelties to passers-by. It all tied in perfectly. The nickname was itself an adaptation of the surname of Dorian Hawkmoon, hero of sci-fi writer Michael Moorcock's *Runestaff* books.

Later, as the band came to prominence, Dave Brock would offer a more romantic explanation of the name. The hawk, he said, was an important historical symbol. To the Egyptians, it represented a winged god. And in pagan mythology, it was revered as a strong and single-minded predator, riding on the wind.

As if all that weren't enough, the word "Hawkwind" was loaded with numerological significance, as were the names of the band members.

Surely encouraged that the fates were on their side, Hawkwind Zoo emerged from their rehearsal chamber to record a demo. And that's when Dave's contacts came in handy. He recalls: "Don Paul, who'd organised The Buskers Tour, was working for EMI Records. He said to me, 'I'll arrange a session for you. Bring the boys in and I'll record you.' I could say that if it wasn't for him, maybe Hawkwind would not have happened."

Hawkwind Zoo laid down three songs on a Revox tape machine, courtesy of Don Paul. 'Hurry On Sundown', 'The Kiss Of The Velvet Whip' and a cover of Pink Floyd's 'Cymbaline' were their first-ever recordings.

These were the tracks on a tape that Douglas Smith took to Andrew Lauder, a Liberty Records executive he'd first met in a record shop in Portobello Road. "I went to his office and I took two things," says Douglas. "I had Cochise. Andrew was really taken with them; everybody was big on country rock at the time. Then I played him Hawkwind Zoo. He said, 'Hmmm, I don't know.' I said, 'Let's do Cochise and give the new band a break too. Let's make a single.'"

It was eventually negotiated that Hawkwind Zoo would record more than a single for Liberty. They would be albums artists. In November 1969, Dave Brock, Nik Turner, Mick Slattery, Terry Ollis, John Harrison and Dikmik signed on the dotted line.

Prior to this, Douglas had been to see John Peel, who'd moved from Stanley Square to a mews at Regent's Park. "I think I'd taken something for him to listen to," says Douglas. "I said, 'By the way, Group X have chosen a new name.' I told him what it was. He shook his head and said, 'Drop the "Zoo". It's too Haight Ashbury.'"

They did. They were Hawkwind.

The ink was barely dry on the contract when Mick Slattery left the band.

"I think I must have got out of bed the wrong side," he says of his sudden departure. "I had some people staying round my flat for a week or so who'd just come back from Morocco, telling me what a fantastic place it was. I just wanted to go to Morocco. And I did do.

"I've done that all my life since – I get fed up with something and I just up and leave with my guitar. I must have got a bit bored with

Hawkwind. I think I felt a bit that we'd sold out to a big record company. I thought, 'This is the beginning of the end.' I'd had a record deal before, and I didn't think it meant anything. I never expected them to become so successful. It did make me wish I'd stayed on a bit longer."

Slattery had a marvellous time in Morocco, jamming "crazy" music with the local musicians. "When I came back, I had some acid and I heard the first Hawkwind album and I thought it was just wonderful. It really blew my mind. When I heard it *straight*, I thought, 'It's all right . . .'"

Mick went on to form a band called Laughing Sam's Dice with Terry Ollis, playing mainly festivals and squatters benefits. In the mid-Seventies, he went to Ireland for a holiday, spotted an old gypsy caravan for sale, bought it and lived in it for the next four years.

He returned to London in 1979, busking and playing the odd acoustic gig. "I'd got pretty messed up on drugs," he admits. "I lost it, really. I was doing just about everything, the whole range – lots of speed and mandies [Mandrax], all sorts of shit. This had been going on since before Hawkwind. I got into heroin and downers. I was enjoying it for a long time, playing music and staying up all night, and then it all caught up with me and knocked me for six. I got quite ill. In 1985 I cleaned up. I still have the odd spliff but that's it. I don't even drink any more. My liver's pretty sort of rotten, so I have to stay away from alcohol."

In the late Eighties, Mick took a college course in guitar-making and formed a band with some fellow students. He later teamed up with an old friend from the Sixties and is still playing with him in a bluesy rock band called Fat Finger. "Don't ask!" warns Mick.

Now living in Brixton but planning to move to the country, he also turns out for Nik Turner's Space Ritual and is planning another collaboration with Terry Ollis.

Hawkwind needed a new guitarist and Dave Brock had come across the very person.

Huw Lloyd-Langton, a gifted young player, was between jobs and trudging through the West End when his life changed in the space of a few moments. "I was wandering up Tottenham Court Road and, lo and behold, there was Dave Brock busking in the subway. I knew Dave so I stopped by and said hello. He asked if I knew of a guitarist looking for a job. I said, 'Funny enough, you're talking to one.'

"I was invited along to jam in a little basement opposite the Clearwater offices and it just seemed to click."

Huw joined Hawkwind, subsequently leaving and rejoining more than once in the most dramatic circumstances, and he still turns out for them today on the odd occasion.

He was born in Park Royal, north-west London, in February 1951 and brought up in the nearby industrial area of Harlesden. There, his parents ran the inherited family business, a chemist's shop. As a small child, Huw decided to be a drummer. But his fascination turned to the guitar during his years at St Francis's, a private primary school in Acton – later taken over by Barbara Speake's stage school.

Even though none of the pupils was older than 11, there was a school band. Huw wasn't in it, but he was friends with the lead guitarist, Chris, and the bass player, John. And he was hugely impressed when the second guitarist, John Fiore, showed off a set of rainbow-coloured plectrums. Huw was a coin collector (and still is). In an act of supreme sacrifice, he traded a valuable Roman coin he had been given by his father for one of Fiore's desirable plectrums, despite the fact that he had no guitar.

The Welsh lady from the local fish and chip shop took pity on his plight. She dusted off an old, stringless, ukulele banjo she'd unearthed from her attic and presented it to him. Huw attached four lengths of common-or-garden string and although they would never play music, he bought an instruction book and worked out a series of four-string chord shapes, all the while imagining what they would sound like.

Going up to the private King's School in Harrow – not *the* King's School, but nevertheless an excellent establishment – Huw was upset that there were no girls. Persuading his parents to transfer him on the pretext that he didn't enjoy the curriculum, he arrived at Wembley's Copeland Secondary School to find, disappointingly, that the only young lady he fancied was a foot too tall. "It was an absolutely foul school," raps Huw.

The writing was on the wall from the first moment, when his new form master marched into the class, glared at Huw's proud mod haircut and uttered one damning word: "Chrysanthemum!"

Things quickly went from bad to worse. A promising pupil, Huw nevertheless saw his grades fall steeply from A to C. The self-confessed "lazy little git" was forced into the rugby team. And there was no provision for art, the subject he adored. "I had to petition to get an art class instituted," he recalls. His campaign succeeded but the subject was not taken seriously, least of all by the teacher, and Huw was lucky to emerge with an art O-Level, as well as four CSEs.

But at least he had acquired a real guitar, which was almost unplayable. "It was a Rossetti Lucky 7," says Huw. "The Lucky 7 models had a pick-up and mine didn't. So I think it was an Unlucky 7."

He did eventually get a pick-up, and he put real strings on it, but every time he struck one of the chords he'd learnt from the manual, it sounded awful. The instructions had never mentioned that a guitar should be tuned. Finally realising this, he found a use for the family's white baby grand piano, a beautiful instrument that had never interested him. Now, it was "a great, heavy guitar tuner".

Leaving school, Lloyd-Langton told a youth employment adviser that he was interested in art and electrics and was unimaginatively steered into a job in "electrical contracting". He didn't know exactly what that might be, but it turned out to mean he would spend a lot of time on building site roofs in the middle of winter, "freezing my brasses off". "They paid just about what it cost to get to work and back, and a bread bun at lunchtime," recalls Huw.

He ate that bun in a Jamaican café in Portobello Road where he thrilled to the sound of reggae records on the jukebox, adding to his musical knowledge of jazz and blues.

One day, after his boss had tried to stop him going to the aid of a dog in distress, Huw told him: "Stick your job where the light don't shine. I'm off."

He was indeed. He began work at Ivor Mairant's music shop in Rathbone Place, off Oxford Street. Mairant was a guitar player and tutor, widely respected by the music world and also by casting agents for the British black and white film industry, who would regularly place him in orchestra scenes. "He should've been another Bert Weedon," says Huw. "His shop was excellent, probably the top-notch guitar shop in the whole of town. It was almost more frustrating than working on the building sites. You were surrounded by incredible guitars which you weren't allowed to touch unless you were cleaning or restringing them.

"Any of the top guitarists visiting the country, jazz, classical or flamenco, would pop in and say hello. That's where I met another great guitarist – Dave Brock. Him coming into the shop, that's how I got to know Dave."

The job at Ivor's paid a tiny bit more than electrical contracting. It also came with luncheon vouchers, which meant that Huw could now afford cheese with his bread bun at lunchtimes. He spent these at the Gioconda, a musicians' hang-out in Denmark Street, London's Tin Pan Alley, which is where he met the flamboyant Winston G.

Winston had a band, he had back-up and he looked every inch a pop star in the making. Huw spent the next year touring army bases in Germany and Holland with the group. Its members were convinced of Winston's potential, including Tony McIntyre, who left his old friend Steve Marriott's band to join up. Famously, McIntyre declared: "I can't turn this down. Marriott's never going to do anything."

Through Tony, Huw Lloyd-Langton spent a day with the future Small Faces and Humble Pie legend Steve Marriott, who had agreed to lend him a guitar while his was being mended. "We went over to Marriott's place," remembers Huw. "He loved his dope. He opened a box with a big lump of black stuff in it. We sat there smoking most of the day and I can hardly remember any of it. I remember lots of dogs, and newspaper all over the floor."

The Winston G band, after changes to the name and line-up, fell apart in Europe, and Huw returned to London. Heading to the Gioconda to see if anyone knew of vacancies for a guitarist, he bumped into Dave Brock in the Tottenham Court Road subway and his fate was sealed.

Huw now joined Terry Ollis as one of the "babies" of the band. "We all felt pretty much on the same level," says Terry. "I respected the others for their age and experience."

"They were well into the substances," says Huw, describing his first impressions of Hawkwind. "The original idea of the band was to create a situation that would be a trip in itself without the necessity to take hallucinogenics. But I think eventually the substances took over. The idea went west. Dave used to go on about all sorts of weird things."

Adds Huw's wife, Marion: "Dave was convinced in the early days that Hawkwind would find the lost chord."

"I think we *did* find it," answers Huw. "I think that's when I went completely mad."

There was no time for anything but the band.

As Nik Turner remembers it, "We were rehearsing and working on getting an album out and doing gigs – free gigs and benefits and supporting lame ducks and anything else that was going on. It was just for the fun of it, not to make progress or have a hit record or be superstars."

Hawkwind were beginning to build a reputation as one of Notting Hill's two big freak bands, the other being Pink Fairies – "We were *the* bands," says Dave Brock – and really, they were anti-heroes, men of the people; certainly not superstars. Besides, they were poor.

They played in small venues and student halls, and they performed so many charitable or free shows, outside and inside prisons and on the backs of lorries, that they were usually operating at a loss financially. Still, they kept on doing it, appearing for CND, the drug-rescue organisation Release, the White Panthers, the legalise-cannabis lobby, and any other crusades they deemed worthy.

At least they were *playing*, raising consciousness, charity money and a profile, even if their own income was minimal. Dave Brock kept on busking for his supper, and Nik Turner was still homeless.

Says Nik: "I used to initiate people by sleeping on their floors. I would sleep on a different floor every night so as not to wear out my welcome. It was very insecure but it was quite nice because people would be pleased to see me – 'Come in, have a cup of tea.'"

Certain floors would crop up more frequently than others in the rotation. Dave Brock's was one, Dikmik's another. Pink Fairies drummer Twink was always accommodating, and so was Douglas Smith at the Clearwater offices, where Turner could always roll out his sleeping bag. He also stayed with Barney Bubbles, a brilliant young artist who was working for *Frendz* and *Oz*.

"A couple of the band lived in the van," ventures Huw Lloyd-Langton. "Dave, I know, had to hitch to a few gigs because he'd been out busking, while we drove."

Marion Lloyd-Langton remembers Hawkwind living on their wits back then: "There were no hotels. When they played outside London, we stayed with students if we could. We stayed anywhere. The band were lucky if they got a fiver."

"Being broke and half-starved didn't bother me," says Huw. "I was young and fit enough to cope with it, and I had my parents' home to go back to. But I'd never invite them [Hawkwind] there. My old man was a pharmacist . . ."

Onstage, Nik Turner was dressed according to his poverty: "I had this thing of street cred. I wore a leather jacket and jeans with my arse hanging out. One should wear in performance what one wore normally, I thought."

He would completely change his mind about that in later years as he turned himself into one of the most spectacular showmen in rock, not entirely with the approval of certain band members.

In 1970, Huw Lloyd-Langton and Nik Turner were at opposite ends of Hawkwind's ideological spectrum, although both are certain that the differing attitudes within the group were perfectly workable to begin with; that there was a feeling of democracy.

As Marion Lloyd-Langton says, "It was a unit, and nobody was a particular star."

Huw revelled in the experience. He reflects: "I was just happy to be out doing things. I wasn't thinking about why we were doing them. I wasn't aware we were doing them for any reasons other than the music, getting up and playing. I wasn't aware of any higher reasons at all. I was just a guitarist in a band."

He enjoyed the social side of things too, fondly recalling the Sunday afternoon "happenings" at The Roundhouse in Chalk Farm, London, where Lemmy was one of the regulars.

Dave Brock was also, primarily, a music man, selective about the company he kept. He wasn't particularly interested in hanging out with the Ladbroke Grove literary set, although he appreciated what they produced. "Nik used to have more to do with them," says Brock. "He was more into all that entourage sort of thing. I was married and I had two kids, so I had to alternate the band with going home and all that."

Brock believed in some but not all of the many causes that Hawkwind went out of their way to support.

Nik Turner, however, viewed his membership of Hawkwind as a personal responsibility, one which extended as much if not more to the "lame ducks" and other deserving recipients than to himself or the band. Fully immersed in the counterculture, he felt duty-bound to use his position helpfully, generously and influentially. A great lover of jazz, he was a relative beginner on the flute and the saxophone, his chosen instruments, and enthusiasm, spontaneity and communication were his guiding values.

Brock and Turner agree that music was simply one aspect of the alternative lifestyle, no more or less important than any other aspect. That lifestyle had come together cohesively in Notting Hill even though, in America, the Woodstock generation had already seen their ideals butchered in August 1969 by Charles Manson and his disciples, and again by the Hell's Angels at Altamont four months later.

Determined to keep the faith on this side of the Atlantic, writers, artists, poets, fashion designers, stallholders, shopkeepers and musicians had joined forces to create a world of mutual help and electric colour, essential in the light-shows at gigs. Lime green and vivid purple were typical in the bubbly lettering and swirling artwork of the posters, album sleeves, printed cotton clothes and packaging of everything from herbal cigarettes to henna, replacing the monochrome, pastels and navy blues of bygone eras.

The Portobello Road market and others that followed its example heaved with velvet and cheesecloth, patchouli oil and sandalwood, incense and joss sticks, rich, exotic and inspiring scents and sights that connected to the sounds and textures of the music and the kaleidoscopic audacity of its illustrators. Pot and acid were integral to everything.

A definite commercial exploitation had, of course, leapt into the environment, but some genuinely inspired individuals were at work here, and no one felt hemmed into any one area of activity. Writers could be musicians, could be anything they liked, and vice versa.

Mick Farren, editing *IT* and the comic book *Nasty Tales* (which would land him in court on an obscenity trial), had led a band called The Social Deviants, then The Deviants, before briefly working with Pink Fairies and on to solo work in 1970. A beat fan, Farren had seen The Deviants as an outlet for political and social protest rather than passive purveyors of hearts and flowers, and their Stooges-like music was loud, violent and informed by drugs. He also acted as a mouthpiece for the MC5's revolutionary and politically active White Panther Party, which was dedicated to "cultural revolution through a total assault on the culture".

Later, with other counterculture characters including writer and musician Nick Kent, Farren would help revitalise a tired and out-of-touch *New Musical Express*, and he would go on to forge a career as a novelist, resurrecting The Deviants as and when he saw fit – all of which he still does today, from his home in LA.

At the same time, author Michael Moorcock – "a natural anarchist" – was editing the *New Worlds* science-fiction magazine and writing prolifically, contributing stories and novellas to various publications including *Frendz*, where Robert Calvert also found an outlet for his streams of imagination. Both were performers, Moorcock as a guitarist and banjo player with a succession of bands and Calvert with his readings. Calvert was at the same time coming to the conclusion that "the only way to get through to people is through music."

Frendz art designer Barney Bubbles was setting ingenious new standards in design, while Jonathan Smeeton – known locally as Liquid Len – was emerging as a great psychedelic lighting designer. Photographer Phil Franks was at the same time snapping everything on film for the underground press.

Calvert, Moorcock, Bubbles, Smeeton and Franks would eventually team up with Hawkwind in an explosively creative collaboration that would set them apart from every other band on the planet.

Nik Turner, arriving in London, had already made contacts in the so-called hippie press, but he became more involved through Robert Calvert and made other friends in his daily life with Hawkwind. "I was living in the street, eating out of a paper bag from chip shops a lot of the time and staying in squats and sleeping on floors, and we were playing benefits, so I met a lot of like-minded people.

"There were lots of other bands – Pink Fairies, Help Yourself, Sutherland Brothers and Mighty Baby . . . John Curd [who would become a major promoter] was managing Mighty Baby. He was around and already promoting. There was a cross-fertilisation between the bands and the managers and the media. We were involved with *IT* and with *Frendz* magazine in the Portobello Road. They were the vehicles for a lot of disparate creative energy.

"They were attracted to us 'cos we were available to do gigs anywhere and we played free music. They saw that as quite a revolutionary or alternative thing. The Rolling Stones had done the free concert in Hyde Park, but that was very high-profile stuff. We were just enjoying playing, and the underground press saw us as quite creditable. We were able to help them and they were able to help us without any agenda.

"We distributed *Frendz* at our gigs. Once, we were served with an injunction for doing it. We'd given out copies at a college for the sons and daughters of service people in Europe. It was all pretty innocuous, but they took exception to it at the time.

"People like Barney Bubbles were interested in the band, having spent some time in San Francisco hanging out with The Grateful Dead and people like that. There was this group of people in San Francisco called The Diggers, led by Emmett Grogan, who used to go round supermarkets getting food that had been thrown out and taking it down the park and giving it to people. There was free food, free music and a whole alternative thing going on, and Barney was involved in all that scene. A lot of people saw us as the British counterparts, or something like it.

"We were quite a natural phenomenon. We weren't trying to imitate something that was going on in America. I became aware of the San Francisco situation rather later."

It was rather later, too, that Nik would take tea with Jefferson Airplane and swap stories from the rock'n'roll front line with The Grateful Dead, Frank Zappa, Captain Beefheart, Dr John and Spirit's Randy California.

Spring 1970. Hawkwind went into Trident Studios, off Wardour Street, to make their first professional recordings. They were intent on capturing the unpredictability of their live sets with all of the sprawling experimentation, soloing, acoustic and electric interplay, and mad audio–generator sound effects that arose from their workouts of Brock's bluesy busking staples.

The sessions produced their first album, *Hawkwind*, which was released in a gatefold sleeve by Liberty in August 1970 and the single which preceded it in July, 'Hurry On Sundown' backed with 'Mirror Of Illusion'.

The album caught the ear of *Melody Maker*, which immediately rushed into print with a feature in its issue dated September 5, 1970. The journalist, Mark Plummer, was impressed with this "truly progressive band" and reported Huw Lloyd-Langton's complaints about the studio as a "sterile and inhuman" place to make music.

None of Hawkwind were comfortable recording separate parts or messing about with things like double tracking, and their solution was to play their whole set live two or three times and pick the best versions of the numbers, later adding a smidgeon of spit and polish.

They were lucky to have a sympathetic producer in The Pretty Things' Dick Taylor, who also contributed some guitar. "Pete Judd and me were on the same bill as The Pretty Things once when they played a live version of *SF Sorrow* [arguably the first-ever concept album] at The Roundhouse," remembers Dave Brock.

"He came and played guitar with us on some of the gigs to get a feel for what we were doing. He was a great help in the studio. He directed us. He had a good head on his shoulders and he was creative and he did a good job. He was all right, Dick was.

"It was a good representation of what we were about. If you listen to it, a lot of it is busking numbers, but it was reasonably organised. The early influences of electronic music and blues came out through what we were doing. We had like-minded people who were into free music. We had a saxophonist [Turner] who couldn't play the saxophone. He bought himself a wah-wah pedal, and he used to do runs up and down. It was basically avant-garde sax with an echo unit on it so it would flow.

"It was the most wonderful achievement in my life to actually do an album."

To this day, Brock rates *Hawkwind* among his favourite accomplishments. Terry Ollis believes, "It's the one that probably captures the spirit the most. It was such underground, ground-breaking stuff."

Huw Lloyd-Langton also names the album as one of his favourites, although he has less than rose-tinted memories of the sessions.

"It was quite crazy," he recalls. "A hell of an experience. I was 18, a very impressionable kid smoking too much dope. We were all smoking quite a lot. Being in the studio with the famous Dick Taylor, a very well-known guitarist, made me very introverted. It was a bit intimidating. I was stoned, which caused me to be paranoid and insecure, and this inhibited my freedom of expression quite a lot. Some of what I was playing came through to me as being clichéd.

"But I enjoyed the experience. At one point in the studio, we'd all dropped a tab. Everybody was cracking up laughing, not being able to stop laughing until the engineer suggested he'd record us in this hilarious state. All of a sudden, we completely stopped laughing. This engineer was trying to kick the laughter off again, but failed dismally. Somehow, we did the album and it turned out very well."

There are many who agree that it does indeed sum up the heady atmosphere of its time and place, who enjoy its innocent spontaneity, and who see it as a crucial document of Hawkwind's evolution. Other critics and indeed some fans are less fond of it. Pointing to the fact that only the two tracks from the single are at all conventional, they complain about unremarkable material, condemn the repetitiveness of its rhythms and chords, and criticise the "self-indulgence" of its lengthy improvisations.

"A lot of the cuts were much longer when we did them originally," an indignant Nik Turner told *Melody Maker*'s Mark Plummer. "The cuts were about 15 or 20 minutes each, then they got edited down to seven."

He now says of *Hawkwind*: "This *was* the band. The album captured it well. It wasn't pretentious or over-produced. Although we got a shit deal on it – two-and-a-half per cent, or something."

"It wasn't much better than that," concedes Douglas Smith. "It was about five per cent, but it was actually more money than The Rolling Stones were getting then."

Hawkwind were still plugging away in their Great Western Road basement. They explained to Plummer that they were experimenting with lights and strobes to work out their effects on the audience.

"We want to use a complete environmental thing where all the senses are moved and used," explained Nik Turner. "We want people to get stoned on the show, not on acid and things. We are rehearsing with the strobes turned on us, and it really does get you high."

"Dikmik is working on a thing where sheets of reflecting plastic are put in front of the speakers and they move round with the soundwaves, sending sound and reflected light in all directions," confided Dave. "But one of our troubles is money . . ."

At this time, Hawkwind had yet to embark on the relentless gigging that would become a key feature of their early career. By the time of their *Melody Maker* interview, they had played two memorable free concerts, one at Wormwood Scrubs and the other on the back of a truck at a festival in Bath with Pink Fairies.

"We organised a collection at Bath," revealed Turner. "We received money, acid and loads of other things."

"We don't do too much work," offered Dave Brock. "Most of Britain's progressive clubs won't have us because they say we are too progressive for them."

Turner added, hopefully: "Work is picking up now, mainly because of the LP."

Before the interview had even gone to press, all that had changed. Hawkwind went to the legendary 1970 Isle of Wight festival and suddenly, they were in demand, big time.

By now, bassist John Harrison had departed.

It's a recurring feature of Hawkwind that its many members have different memories, understandings or interpretations of the same events. This is one such instance.

Thomas Crimble, coming in as a replacement in July 1970, states unequivocally that Dave Brock sacked Harrison shortly after the album recordings.

Huw Lloyd-Langton says, "I turned up for rehearsals one day and John wasn't there. I was quite sad. He was like an anchor in the band, 'cos he was so solid when everyone else was usually quite out of it. I presumed he'd been sacked 'cos he was so straight and we weren't."

"We used to take a lot of drugs then, LSD and organic mescaline," admits Dave, contending that John Harrison left of his own accord. "We'd gone off to rehearse in a cottage we'd rented on the moors in Cornwall. John was quite keen on playing golf, and he used to practise his strokes on the moor. We'd all taken this organic mescaline, and we were saying, 'Come on, John, have some of this mescaline.'

"He frowned on our drug-taking. We spiked him up in a glass of milk – we put the mescaline in it. I was running around with no clothes on. I found this blue medicine bottle and it was like I'd found a chalice, this wonderful memento that meant so much.

"And so John had taken the mescaline in the milk. He was all right in the end, but he actually said, 'Look, I don't want to take any more drugs.' It wasn't the life for him, this loony rock'n'roll lifestyle. He wanted a pretty ordinary life. Which is a real shame. He was a wonderful bass player and a nice guy too. A good, reliable bloke, John was. He was a good friend of mine. I've not got a bad word to say about him.

"I would say he was very sad to leave, but I think he had a girlfriend he was in love with and wanted to marry. I heard he got a job van driving after he left the band, and I think he did get married. I believe he went to America in the end."

Nik Turner was, as usual, oblivious to anything being amiss until Harrison vanished. He says: "I was perhaps rather naïvely living in my own world of peace and love and brotherly friendship and trying to use what power we had as a band to help people socially and to raise people's consciousness and try to do it without drugs, ultimately. Consequently, things went down within the band that I wasn't totally aware of.

"John Harrison left and I didn't really see why. In a way, things didn't touch me, not because I was stupid but I suppose I had my own idea of what the band was about. Things used to happen – 'Oh, I wonder why he left?' In hindsight, I became a bit more aware."

Nobody has any idea what became of John, but they do know that to this day, he has not collected a single penny of the small fortune he has amassed since leaving. This is from royalties on every song, since the entire album was credited to Hawkwind/Brock.

Thomas Crimble: "Apparently, it broke his heart to leave the band and he's never been heard of since. He never picked up his royalties for the album. I've never met the guy, I know nothing about him, but he should pick the money up."

Dave: "In 1992, Douglas [Smith] said he was going to split it up between the band. There's about £20,000 there."

Douglas: "Probably more than £20,000. It's kept in a client's account at an accountant's company, protected under the law. EMI [which now owns the first Hawkwind album] sends the royalties out to the respective people. John's are paid into that account, an interest account which has been running for about 30 years. There's no death certificate, so John's not dead, and it's his money."

CHAPTER 3

The Isle Of Fright

THE 1970 Isle of Wight Festival would become one of the most famous events in rock history, a landmark, bringing together the great superstars of the era – even though it was a disaster for almost everybody involved. Jimi Hendrix, The Doors and The Who played there. So did Miles Davis, Jethro Tull, Ten Years After and Joni Mitchell. And so did Hawkwind, the hippies from Ladbroke Grove.

They had not been invited to share the stage with these gods of popular music. Travelling and living in a parcel van dubbed "The Yellow Wart", Hawkwind had turned up to play for free outside the festival perimeter, ready to entertain the 50,000 who had paid their £3-a-head admission and the 450,000 who had arrived without tickets.

Mick Farren, under the guise of the White Panther Party, had previously distributed pamphlets informing music-lovers that they could watch the festival for free if they sat on a hill overlooking the site.

The organisers quickly called in the police, who patrolled the fences with guard dogs, aggressively. The festival was clearly heading for financial trouble, and there were rumours that bands were demanding money upfront before they would play. The toilet facilities and local grocery supplies were woefully inadequate. It wasn't long before the folks on the hill began to assert their hostility towards the police and the bands, demanding that the festival should be made free to everybody and that the artists should play for nothing. The whole event was fraught with problems, largely because too many people turned up. Joni Mitchell was reduced to tears by the unruly rabble.

For Hawkwind, by contrast, it was business as usual. They made impromptu appearances outside the fences throughout the duration of the event, from Wednesday, August 26 to Sunday, August 30 – for the most part in a huge, inflatable dome called Canvas City, held aloft with air pumped by a generator.

On one occasion, just before a Hawkwind show, the tent collapsed. Dave Brock recalls: "The generator conked out and people were holding the tent up while it was deflating. A lot of them were freaking out 'cos they were tripping, and this thing was coming down."

Terry Ollis was trapped inside. "We were just about to play, I walked in first and they shut the doors behind me," he relates. "I was the only one of the band in there. Someone leaped out of the crowd and started whacking the drums."

Terry decided that if anyone was going to whack the drums, it would be him, and he embarked on the longest solo of his life. "It was fucking great," he laughs. "It went on for ages. It must have been pushing an hour. As soon as they got the machinery fixed, the band came in and somebody, I think it was Dave, said to me, 'Keep playing.' So I never got any applause. If I'd stopped, I'm sure they would have gone berserk with applause – my greatest accolade ever. It was a real career highlight, and I felt a little bit robbed."

An exhausted Ollis played on while Hawkwind took their places onstage and delivered a full set.

It wasn't until the fences were dismantled on the last day, and the event finally declared free, that Hawkwind actually entered the festival enclosure and set up their gear.

However, although they were something of a sideshow, they were noticed by a sizeable proportion of the half-a-million fans who had flocked to the island. They were definitely noticed by Jimi Hendrix, who dedicated a song to "the guy with the silver face".

That guy was Nik Turner who, from humble beginnings in ripped jeans, was already warming to the idea of theatrics. "Nik had his face painted half-silver at the Isle of Wight," remembers Dave Brock. "He had his hair and his beard plaited, and he used to have a pair of trousers with silver stars sewn on them. He looked quite eccentric. He was a good frontman in the band, 'cos he used to jump around a lot."

Typically, he qualifies his praise: "If you've got somebody who's very visual, it takes a lot of focus from the other members of the band."

Jimi Hendrix was also in the audience when various members of Hawkwind had an all-night jam. Thomas Crimble was one of them. He remembers: "We went in at about 10pm. It was dark. We came out and it was morning. Everyone was very out of it. Huw Lloyd-Langton and I played all through the night. Dave Brock and Nik Turner wandered in and wandered off and various characters came in and jammed with us, including people I've never met before or since. It was an extraordinarily long set.

"I got this thing going with the echo chamber, which was fairly high-tech for the time. I was playing along with the echo beats, and I got into what I call mantra rock or raga rock or space rock – self-perpetuating sounds driven by the beats created by the echoes. That turned into dance music years later. I was just playing repetitive beats, and then you build something over the top, you keep building up, and it had to stay simple 'cos everyone was so out of it. If you changed the chords, no one would know where the fuck we were. When you're jamming, there's no structure.

"Jimi Hendrix saw some of that set. He was standing at the back of the tent, and he sent his roadie to us later on that day with the message that he really liked what we'd been doing but that if he'd got on and jammed with us, which he'd wanted to, it would have completely spoilt the vibe of the whole thing. People would've been saying, 'What's happening in there?' 'Jimi Hendrix is playing.' And it would have been the end of it. He was man enough not to do that, which was nice."

Crimble had met Hendrix before, while playing bass for another Clearwater Productions band, Skin Alley. "We were playing at the Revolution club in London a month or so before the Isle of Wight. Stephen Stills and Jimi Hendrix came down to the club, and they had a jam. They asked me and Charles Pope to back them for the evening, which was nice.

"Oddly enough, Jimi Hendrix didn't play very well that night, although you couldn't tell that from the audience, which was full of liggers and hangers-on. All he had to do was blow his nose and he'd get a standing ovation. That taught me a lot about the music business.

"I had a nice chat with him later. We were talking about how he could cope with that kind of adulation. If you play a great gig and get a standing ovation, that's fine, but if you play a crap solo with the wrong notes and flat chords and you still get a standing ovation, it makes you wonder what's going on. It was very hard to know if genuinely good playing was appreciated, when bad playing was appreciated at the same level."

Thomas Crimble was born and brought up in Staines, Middlesex, where his father was a car dealer. He was educated in Berkshire at Maidenhead's St Piran's.* Working as a petrol-pump attendant in the school holidays, Thomas went on to Tavistock Kelly College in Devon and, after that, to a college teaching technical and business studies in Guildford, Surrey. By now, he'd joined Skin Alley as their bass player.

Says Thomas: "I was coming home at four or five in the morning having done a gig, and my mum was waking me up at 7am to go to college. The two didn't mix. I was given an ultimatum – either stay at college and live at home, or leave home and do the music. I left home on January 1 – I think it was 1968 – and moved to Ladbroke Grove."

He was present at Hawkwind's legendary first gig at the All Saints Hall and bumped into them regularly after they teamed up with Douglas Smith and Clearwater.

One night in the early summer of 1970, Dave Brock turned up to a Skin Alley gig in Hammersmith. "It was in a big club with a revolving stage," remembers Crimble. "I'd already decided to leave the band. I wanted to add a light-show and the other guys didn't want to 'cos it would cost them money in their wages.

"At that gig, Dave Brock asked me if I wanted to join Hawkwind. It seemed more creative, there was seemingly a much more positive attitude towards that sort of thing, and I was into the artistic potential of the band. With Skin Alley, I couldn't really see that going any further, while with Hawkwind, there was every possibility. Soon after that, I did a rehearsal or two with them. I thought they were really good. They *got off.*"

Only weeks later, Thomas was packing his bedroll into "The Yellow Wart" for the trip to the Isle of Wight, which would become a turning point for Hawkwind in many decisive ways.

The festival brought their first coverage in the mainstream press, with a photograph appearing in *The Observer* colour supplement. Nik Turner, with his bright red hair, starry trousers and silver face, would also see his picture in the *Telegraph Magazine*, *Vogue* and *Paris Match*.

Also at the Isle of Wight, Turner met someone who was destined to play a major role in the success of the band – as a dancer. One freak among thousands, Stacia nevertheless stood out in the crowd at the Isle

* Named after St Piran, the outspoken Cornish saint who was so well regarded in life that his neighbours attached him to a millstone and threw him off a cliff.

of Wight: she was Amazonian. Nik recalls that, "Stacia was impressed or infatuated with this boyfriend of mine, Philippe, who was at the Isle of Wight with me."

It should be pointed out that for anyone to have a boyfriend or girl-friend of the same sex in those days was not specifically a declaration of being gay (although it could have been that too) but a consequence of the Sixties' sexual liberation, of having the freedom to choose a partner or partners without fear of censure.

"I don't think Philippe was gay," says Nik. "He had the most beauti-ful girlfriends. He used to be part of the whole scene surrounding Donovan. I wasn't at all gay, and that wasn't the influence. It was more of a French thing, the Left-Bank, Paris scene – the boho existentialists. It was quite groovy for me. I used to wear make-up and speak camp and hang out with very beautiful girls. It was this camp glamour which I saw as quite an attractive thing. I saw The Rolling Stones go through it, and Bowie, projecting this sort of androgynous image."

To Nik, Philippe is simply a character from his life, as are the various girlfriends to whom he refers in an equally matter-of-fact manner. "We got talking to Stacia at the time, and I think she fell quite in love with Philippe. He used to hang out with all these really groovy people in Paris. He was quite outrageous looking."

Other members of Hawkwind would become less tolerant of Nik's boyfriend as time went on, but at the Isle of Wight, Philippe was prob-ably the least of their preoccupations.

Dave Brock: "I had a really weird trip there. One afternoon, someone spiked up our fruit juice with LSD. Huwie had drunk some of it and he was freaking out in the front of the van. Someone said, 'Don't go in the van because Huw's having a bad trip.' I said, 'Fucking hell, I've had some of that as well,' and as I said it, this rush came over me, a great, huge surge. I went all hot. I was really hard-pressed to keep it together.

"A friend of mine, a girl called Jackie, said, 'Come on, let's go for a walk, Dave,' and she took me to the downs. While we were walking up there, we were trying to wade through all this straw. It was about two feet high. There were helicopters in the sky, and they looked like big dragonflies. My hearing was attuned. The whole thing was quite spectacular. It lasted for fucking hours, right the way through the evening.

"Eventually, I came back to the festival. I was given a Mandrax to calm me down. I know The Moody Blues were playing that night. I'd been hoping to see them, but because I'd taken the Mandrax, I fell asleep and I missed it all."

Huw Lloyd-Langton wasn't faring quite so well after his unexpected dose of acid.

Nik Turner tries to phrase things diplomatically: "He had a trip and saw God or something. The lifestyle was a bit hard for him. He's very sensitive and highly strung, and I think he was macrobiotic or vegan. He had a bit of a nervous breakdown. I can't define exactly what the problem was. It was one of those things where he didn't come back. He didn't feel well or he didn't think the band was right, or he didn't see things in the same perspective as everybody else."

"He went a bit nutty," says a typically blunt Dave Brock.

Huw Lloyd-Langton would be the first person to agree that he "went a bit nutty". An apparently innocent glass of fruit juice on the Isle of Wight sent him literally insane, plunging him into a world of terrifying mental torment from which it seemed there was no escape. Weeks later, he was on his way to the straitjacket, guaranteed, when something happened. "It was a miracle," says Huw. A real one. Like Paul on the road to Damascus, Huw was touched by the hand of God on the A23. Marion was with him, and she felt it too.

Huw had had a bad trip in 1969, not long after joining Hawkwind, and he'd sworn off acid forever. "We were going up to Norfolk," relates Dave Brock. "We didn't take LSD all the time, but on this occasion, Huw had taken some in the van. We stopped off somewhere on the way, and Huw went missing. I went to look for him. He was sitting in a field. He saw me as this wizened old man, like Gandalf, and he suddenly freaked out."

Nik Turner: "I remember him looking awful and frightened and nobody feeling they knew how to help him."

"We were in a cornfield," says Huw. "I was sitting cross-legged and I started hallucinating. It was the first time I'd really hallucinated on it. I saw birds in the sky that formed a circle and were spiralling towards us. All of a sudden, I went into this reverse state, this dead state. Everybody turned into wrinkled old men. Total hallucination. It was horrible. As far as I was concerned, I'd died. It was hell, if anything, but there was no warmth. It was cold. I don't know how long I was in this mental state. Thankfully, I came out of it. I wasn't dead, it seemed.

"But as a result of that, I was completely not taking that stuff. Then I got spiked up at the Isle of Wight. I was not one of those hardened trippers that had taken hundreds of trips. You could count them, including the spiking, on two hands.

"A lot of the time when people did spike someone, they thought they were doing them a favour. I don't think it was malicious. Chances are some people did do it with evil intent – you're messing with the mind. Anything can happen during a trip that can cause it to turn bad. There are people around that have had bad trips and never come out."

Huw was nearly one of them.

"At the Isle of Wight, somebody came round with a bottle of apple juice and passed it round. It was lovely, hot weather and we were all totally skint. I was told some minutes later that there were all sorts of trips in the bottle.

"Half an hour or so later, it started coming on. I was sitting with Dikmik. I was scared, 'cos I didn't want to 'die' again. Dikmik said, 'Don't fight it. You just go negative if you fight it.' Somebody stuck a guitar in my hand and pointed me to the stairs of this big blue top. I can remember taking my gold watch and various other bits of jewellery off and flinging them on the floor in the front of the van."

Eventually, Huw found himself on the stage of the tent for that afternoon's gig, trying to tune his guitar. Since it was Huw who had the tuning fork, the rest of the band always tuned to him. But he couldn't do it.

"I was standing on this slightly soft mattress thing on the floor and I felt like it was ballooning all over the place. I played the note and it went up and down, so it was impossible to tune. There was me, not being able to hear the note, and I was in hell. I was damned to be in this situation for eternity. I was in such a petrified state of mind that I ended up hitting any old chord.

"Then this whole cacophony started. I absolutely dread to think what it sounded like. Definitely the lost chord. There was a very gory light-show and eventually, all around me, there were people freak dancing and turning into devils. It was absolutely horrific. As far as I was concerned, I was literally in hell. I was still playing guitar and I got down on my knees and I was praying. Eventually, somehow, it stopped and I was led out of the place.

"Nik Turner, a couple of days later, said, 'You know what you did on the stage that day – do it in every gig. It looked cool.' But I was *meaning* it. I was on my knees flipping praying.

"Later on, in the evening, we were due to do another gig in another tent in the area. I turned up with my guitar. Thomas Crimble turned up. We started jamming. At one point, there were a bunch of Brazilian percussionists onstage. It was a brilliant sound I was getting somehow, and we had an incredible jam. We literally played all night. I was playing my heart out, playing this rubbish out of my soul, playing the horrors out of myself."

Huw didn't notice Jimi Hendrix standing at the back, listening intently. "We finished at dawn," says Huw. "I went down to the sea front, I took most of my clothes off and I baptised myself in the sea, just to get rid of this horrible nightmare I'd come through. I was cleansing myself."

Hawkwind returned to London, and Huw handed his guitar over to Clearwater, resolute that he was turning his back on the band. He retreated to his parents' place in Harlesden to relax and recover.

"I was sitting at home and I'd rolled this strong joint," recalls Huw. "Frankie Howerd was on telly, and there was a perfect white flower on top of the television set. I was watching this show that was on, and my eyes started flicking between good and evil, the good being this flower and the evil being the crap on the telly. I felt that this flower – a soul – was dying, a horribly frightening feeling.

"That starts off this whole fucking breakdown. A tug of war between God and the Devil was going on in my head. I wasn't brought up a religious person at all. My mum would take me and my sister to church when she could drag us. That was the extent of my religious upbringing, although there was always a spark of belief in me somewhere.

"Now I had this battle between good and evil going on in my head. I didn't know which was which. My mind was in such a blown state. One minute I was all right and the next minute I was completely freaking."

That's when the nightmare really started. And Marion got the phone call.

Huw had met Marion while he was playing with the Winston G band. In 1967, on one of his trips home from Germany, he called to see a close friend called Tim, and Marion was there. She'd met Tim in hospital, where they'd both been having operations, and they'd become friends, living as neighbours in Harlesden.

Marion looked much younger than her age, and was wearing a blue outfit on the day of Huw's visit. He immediately assumed she was a pupil at the local convent school.

"He would not acknowledge me," says Marion. "I thought, 'Who the hell do you think you are?' In actual fact, he was disgusted with Tim 'cos he thought he'd picked up this little kid. He thought I was about 12."

In fact, Marion, who was 18, had been through a "brutal, frightening" marriage and divorce and had a three-and-a-half-year-old daughter, Louise – whose father had been sent to prison for armed robbery.

Huw takes up the story: "The next day, Tim suggested we pop over the road to see Marion. I assumed we'd be going to her parents' place. Instead, we were ushered into a flat where two of her flatmates were kneeling down by a bed counting out rows of pills.

"I was like, 'What? Funny old household, this.' Marion walked in with a long, flowing robe on and this bloody great reefer sticking out of her face. She still looked like a little girl."

Marion moved out soon afterwards. "I smoked a lot of cannabis, but I got so scared when I found out that these two girls were heavy-duty pushers," she reveals. "And one of them had gone off with my boyfriend Gary – a fickle lad."

Marion soon realised Huw was not the arrogant guitar hero she'd imagined, and Huw became aware that she was not an underage temptress. They began a romance, but it was interrupted when Huw went back to Germany with Winston G. Marion started flat-hunting and got chatting with a lady in the pharmacy where she took her hospital prescriptions.

"She said to me, 'My son's away at the moment. Why don't you rent his room for a while?' Within about half an hour of moving into the room, I realised it was Huw's. Jimi Hendrix was painted over the walls. I thought, 'Oh my God, this is *his* room. He'll kill me. I'll move out before he comes back from Germany and he'll never know.' I didn't tell his mother that I knew him."

Marion found a flat right round the corner, and arranged to move in four weeks later. But as chance would have it, Huw came back early because the band had split up.

He recalls: "I arrived home, walked into the living room at the back of the shop, sat down with my bag, rolled a fag, and I was saying hello to my old man sitting there with his pipe when the door opened and

Marion walked in. I thought, 'What's *she* doing here?' I had to move on to the settee 'cos she was in my bleeding room."

Marion: "He called me upstairs. I said, 'I'm really sorry. I didn't know they were your parents.' He said, 'Well, that's fine. We'd better cool it. We'll just be friends.' For the next 18 months, we were just friends and we went everywhere together. We were inseparable. Everybody, even his parents, thought we were an item but by then, we weren't. We were ever such good friends though. I was hoping he would ask me out again but he didn't – not for a long time."

When Huw Lloyd-Langton joined Hawkwind, his best mate Marion travelled with him to lots of gigs, got to know his old friends from Acton (who still had the school band, now called The K-Liffs) and explored with him the alternative lifestyle in Notting Hill.

Says Marion: "Everything was open-door. We went from flat to flat, party to party, and everybody knew everybody. It was the beginnings of that ghetto thing in Portobello Road and Westbourne Terrace. That was the centre in those days. It was very much an open culture, very relaxed. We shared flats, we moved in, we moved out. We used to leave our key on the mat. I loved it. Huw, I think, was a bit lost."

Huw: "I was totally lost."

Marion: "You were quite a fragile character."

"That was all the bloody dope," retorts Huw. "It didn't sit well with me."

Marion was living in Victoria when Hawkwind went to the Isle of Wight. Shortly after they came back, she received a phone call from Tim.

"That's when the shit hit the fan," says Marion. "Tim said, 'You've gotta go and get Huw. He's at home, and he's off the planet.'"

In her capacity as a close friend, Marion tried to nurse Huw through his breakdown and appealed for help from everyone she could think of.

"Nobody really wanted us," remembers Marion. "They couldn't cope with Huw. My father gave me money to put Huw in a hotel 'cos he was freaking the dog out. I went to Huw's parents and said, 'I don't know what to do. Help!' In the end, I had nowhere to go, nowhere to take him. I thought Huw was going to die. He didn't sleep and he didn't eat at all. I do remember Dave Brock ringing me two or three times, really worried about him."

"I was so skinny," admits Huw. "I'd become a macrobiotic, and I was more or less living on peanuts when I was on the road with Hawkwind."

Marion explains: "We'd decided we wanted to clean our bodies out. But Huw decided to do it for more than 10 days. He took it as being a way of life."

Huw: "When I do something, I tend to go the whole hog. Ten days on a rice diet and I carried it on for six months."

Marion drove Huw to hospital in desperation. "We saw two nurses who looked like they had speckles of blood on their uniforms, so we walked out," says Huw. "Then Marion decided to drive me down to her parents' home in Worthing, 'cos her dad had bought her tickets to go to the South of France. She was going to take her daughter there, but because I was in such a bad state, she thought she'd take me."

They were travelling on the A23 in Marion's Mini, heading for the south coast, when it happened. "She had to pull the car over 'cos I was freaking," says Huw. "And we held on to each other and at one point I screamed out, with all the feeling I could muster, 'God! Help me!' A funny thing happened then. When I cried out to Him Upstairs for help, I went into a trance state, and I was aware of Marion being with me. I felt this current of electricity going on between the pair of us. When it started, I was scared stiff, she was scared stiff. There were no drugs involved. Then I was aware of being part of the air. I was aware of being. I was aware of breathing, and that our breath was part of the wind and there was no thought, just awareness of being part of the air and the wind and of us being together. It was totally peaceful."

Marion: "All of a sudden, he was shaking. All I knew was this electricity, this force between us. It was so like a circle but very, very fast and furious. And we became one. I remember we were part of the wind and the air. We didn't have bodies. We were up in the sky."

"I don't know how long this experience went on for," says Huw. "Minutes, half an hour, an hour . . ."

"There was no time," explains Marion. "That was the thing."

"But when I came back to sitting in the Mini with Marion, this whole battle I'd been going through in my brain for so many weeks and months was gone," says Huw. "All the thoughts and fear and paranoia had disappeared. Crying out to Him Upstairs – it was like he'd taken my soul out from this mangled brain and corpse and hung it up on the washing line to dry for a bit. Then he'd put it back in and I came to and I was just normal again – whatever normal is."

Marion: "When we came back down to earth, Huw was next to me. We looked at each other. And Huw was totally, utterly normal. I said, 'What was *that*?' Huw said, 'It was obviously God.' I said, 'Well, I know you cried out.' I was in awe. I didn't stop being in awe. It was a wonderful experience. It was something not earthly. I look back now and I think that because I was with Huw, I experienced it too. For a long time, we told people about it, but I think they thought we were mad."

Huw says: "I think this is something that I would have had to confront sooner or later, but in the natural, human course of experience. Everything that I was confronted with just happened in one fell swoop. As human beings, it takes you years to come to various conclusions. It happened to me overnight.

"I'd never, ever advocate LSD. Many drugs, used under medical supervision, can help mental disorders. Taken for the fun of it, they can cause you to be in that state.

"Without the miracle happening, I would have ended up being institutionalised eventually, or I would have died or killed himself, I don't know. Although at the time, I was far too afraid of death after my acid experiences to have killed myself. I totally believe, and have done ever since, that it was God, whoever God is, that brought me through the breakdown and out of it. Then I went through all the various beliefs, searching for who God was."

That search would take some time for Huw and Marion. It would also be a while before they rekindled the romantic spark in their relationship.

Leaving them to it, Hawkwind too were entering into a period of great change and excitement.

CHAPTER 4

Tripping And Stripping

AS a direct result of their public-spirited appearances at the Isle of Wight, Hawkwind acquired instant and widespread credibility, a ready-made grass-roots following and a sudden flurry of gig offers. Before long, they were playing almost every night, often at free shows and benefits.

Nik Turner admits, "In a way, I was the PR guy, 'cos I was accessible to people and I made them feel part of it. They'd say to me, 'Would you do us a gig, or could you do a benefit for this?' and I'd say, 'All right, fine, so long as we don't lose any money on it,' 'cos we were working on such a shoestring.

"I'd arrange these things half the time without asking the band, because this was what I thought we were about, what we should be doing. As my van was driving the equipment around, it was probably me that was putting the petrol in the tank. If I could afford to do it, then we did it. The rest of the band went along with it. In hindsight, I'm not really sure that they were into it to the same degree."

Terry Ollis was. "We were an ideals band," he says. "We were living those ideals and totally fucking believing them and trying to put them about as much as possible, trying to make things better for everyone. There wasn't a lot of money around at the time. It was the hippie ideal. I think generally we was all up for it, we meant what we were doing, and the audiences believed in us. That's how we got to where we did."

Thomas Crimble was also happy to play benefits and free gigs. Hawkwind were still putting more money into his pocket than Skin Alley had ever done. "We needed a certain amount," he recalls. "When I was in Skin Alley, we were getting fuck all. I was living off two shillings and sixpence a day (12-and-a-half pence), which was enough to get me one meal at a greasy café on Ladbroke Grove. So suddenly to be getting a fiver a night for a gig was a hell of a lot more money.

"We were on the crest of a wave, and we were working about six nights a week. Every gig we played had a standing ovation at the end of it. We knew something was happening, although it hadn't happened enough for us to take it for granted or to start picking and choosing the gigs.

"We toured a lot of universities, and we were playing in the open air in their campuses in the summer. They'd just put up a stage on the grass, put some lights on and we'd turn up and do it. Keele University was a good one for that. Sometimes we played for free. Some others, we'd get paid by the Students' Union but they wouldn't charge the students. There was really quite a feel of people being together, and love and peace and all that.

"Everyone in the band did seem to be into the spirit of it, although as time passed, perhaps Dave Brock was into the money. I think everyone else could take it or leave it."

Dave Brock reasons that while he had goodwill towards the charity gigs, there had to be a happy medium – enough cash coming in to keep Hawkwind going. "We were all about the alternative lifestyle and we were doing lots of benefits," he concurs. "But Nik would say, 'Yes,' every time he was asked, and we'd get lumbered with doing it. He dropped us in the shit loads of times because we had to keep the reputation – and if we didn't do all the things he'd agreed to, it looked rather black for us. Later on, his ego got so big . . ."

Turner retorts: "I didn't see it as some vehicle for me to get egotistical or do anything except enjoy myself in the moment."

In December 1970, Brock broke down the figures as he saw them for the long-defunct *Disc* music paper: "Clearwater need expenses of about £200 a week to keep going. And they get about £140 a week. We realise the necessity of not doing too many free gigs, but we would like to undercut [other] bands.

"We played with Free recently and they were getting something like £800 for doing a series of numbers that all sounded exactly the same. People like that are going out for ridiculous prices. We don't mind getting a lot of bread off universities because they can afford it. Small clubs can't, and we'd like to help them. We'd like to do them for expenses only."

According to *Disc*, Hawkwind were going out at regular gigs for

£70 a time, although they were about to raise their fee to £125 which, it was roundly agreed, was "still cheap".

Their set was a mixture of material from the album and improvised jams, some of which would eventually mutate into all-time Hawkwind favourites.

Crimble: "We were doing creative space rock. Dave Brock used to say, 'Okay, Thomas, start it off,' and I'd start off on a bass riff and it would carry on. We played for an hour and a half in one go. We ran one number into the next, and we got a big dose of applause at the end of the set. I don't think anyone else was doing that at the time.

"At some of the gigs, I was wearing a gas mask from the Second World War that I'd inherited from my dad. I did it as a protest about pollution, car fumes and all that, and it was also an anti-war statement, but it was totally impractical. Have you ever worn a gas mask? They steam up and you can't see fuck all, so I gave that up.

"We were into Ken Kesey and Tim Leary and experimenting with mind-altering drugs, so the consciousness thing was forefront in our minds. I expect Mick Farren and Pink Fairies were into consciousness-changing as well, maybe more tinged with anarchy – which is all very well but unless you offer a practical alternative it's a very destructive thing, and having witnessed Glastonbury go down the anarchist route, I know there's no light at the end of that particular tunnel. The consciousness thing is what The Beatles started. They've done so much, those boys. Our effort was very small-fry after theirs."

It may seem an odd comparison, but Thomas Crimble is not the only one to make it.

Penny Rimbaud, a long-time activist and for many years a member of the Crass collective, states: "Hawkwind were undoubtedly one of the great rocket ships of what was going on then. In many respects, I'd have preferred to listen to The Beatles than Hawkwind, but in a funny way, Hawkwind were probably achieving what The Beatles imagined they would like to do."

He sees a similar relationship between Crass and The Clash: "The Clash were very good at being out there and selling billions of records and that sort of confined them. We did what they said *they* would do."

It was in the second half of 1970 that Hawkwind started something of a tradition by playing free gigs under the arches in Ladbroke Grove.

"We'd run a cable round to a café under the flyover," remembers Thomas Crimble. "We plugged in there, set up and played on Saturday mornings. The café people were up for it. People coming to see the band bought cups of tea."

"They were Ladbroke Grove's favourite freak band," comments Douglas Smith. "Every time anyone wanted them to play, they'd play underneath the arches."

Hawkwind were still appearing on bills with the leading psychedelic bands of the day, including Pink Fairies, who were friends of theirs, and Pink Floyd, who weren't.

Says Douglas: "They had no relationship whatsoever with Pink Floyd. They were so stuck up they wouldn't talk to the likes of Hawkwind. They thought of them as a bunch of dirty hippies. We did a gig with the Floyd in Paris. They were there in their smart new outfits, 'cos they'd had a couple of hit records, and we were like the poor little nobodies. They just ignored us."

Pink Floyd, of course, were former architectural students from upper- and middle-class families who'd been well educated at private schools – not for them the communal life of squatting and spending 2*s* 6*d* on breakfast in a greasy spoon on Ladbroke Grove. Drummer Nick Mason's favourite leisure pursuit was "rebuilding Aston Martins", a fondness for which he's inherited from his father.

By now, Hawkwind were just as often headlining, playing to full houses of a couple of hundred people. And as their following grew, so did the climate of drugs around the band. "It was peace and love, hippies and a smattering of bikers," recalls Thomas. "The audiences used to get terribly stoned. As far as we were concerned, I think it was part of the creative process. I gave it up a long time ago, after Hawkwind, when I started having children. That was about 1973. It just seemed to disagree with me after a certain point. And you can't be responsible for a kid, being out of your face. I even managed to give up nicotine three years ago. It's the hardest thing I've ever done."

"Obviously, there were a lot of drugs being taken," agrees Nik Turner. "Hawkwind gigs were like drug dealers' conventions. Dealers would be there giving away large quantities of drugs, in the audiences and backstage. We tried to break down the barrier between the audience and the band and the backstage.

"People were taking lots of LSD and the idea was to 'open your mind'. There was a great deal of free thinking and peace and love. A lot of people were having a good time and a lot of people were destroying themselves and a lot of other people were making a lot of money, probably. All these acquaintances used to have their own factories making stuff.

"There was a whole drug scene going on around Kensington Market. There was pot and acid, but a lot of other weird things like PCP [the perception-changing phencyclidine] going around. There was speed – sulphate – but that wasn't anything I was ever that interested in. I don't think there was the incidence of heroin and cocaine that there is today . . ."

Heroin and Mandrax, tablets frequently prescribed as sleeping pills, dangerous with alcohol and since banned, were nevertheless present to some degree, not only among the audiences but within the group.

According to Dave Brock: "Terry Ollis was on bad drugs. He was taking downers. We used to call upon Viv Prince [The Pretty Things' outrageous drummer] when Terry couldn't play his drums properly. Terry would be taking his downers and be a bit slow, or he wouldn't turn up, and he once broke his hand, so we'd have Viv playing with us instead. Russell [Hunter] from Pink Fairies at one point too."

Twink, the Fairies' other drummer, would also sit in with Hawkwind from time to time.

Terry Ollis, replying that there were ordinary explanations for his absences, says of Viv Prince: "It's a good job he was there. I can't remember the various reasons I wasn't there myself. I do remember once running out of petrol in somebody else's vehicle. There were occasions like that."

According to other members, Terry would later crash out of the band paralysed by "bad drugs". He admits enjoying the drug culture as much as anybody else, although he gives a completely different account of his departure from Hawkwind.

Mick Slattery, for his part, has freely confessed to taking all sorts of "bad drugs" before, during and after his tenure.

Nik Turner didn't notice any of this to begin with: "I tended to have been rather naïve about drugs, and so everything was really groovy. I didn't know what was going down among people. I've never taken heroin, so I didn't have much experience of that side of things, and I wasn't aware that people were doing it. They're always a rather closed society."

By all accounts, Nik was in a world of his own, certainly onstage. "By the very nature of how things were, you just got on with your thing – 'Wow, that was great!' If somebody else had an awful time, perhaps took too much LSD and had a bad trip, it didn't mar what *you'd* experienced. There were a lot of casualties, I guess, people who went out there, and stayed out there some of the time, people that couldn't cope.

"I've never promoted drugs. I tried to say that what we were doing was a bit more meaningful than just the product of a drugs binge. I've always thought of music as a healing force. It's all about communication to me. You have to take an overview of the social importance of it."

Blissfully convinced that "everything was really groovy", Nik went about his business unaware of any gathering storms, and began actively to seek out gigs for Hawkwind. "It was quite an easy thing to make a few phone calls and promote the band, because of the word of mouth. We'd done benefits and played outside Wormwood Scrubs, we'd been involved with the CND march to Aldermaston, we'd played inside Pentonville Prison and Chelmsford Prison, and we'd played outside the Isle of Wight festival. We'd made friends and associations and contacts.

"One gig I promoted in Bayswater, I actually hired the place. Shep Gordon* was there and so was Larry Parnes, who used to manage Billy Fury, Eden Kane and Marty Wilde. Larry Parnes wanted to manage Hawkwind. I had a real problem taking this guy seriously. He was old-school management, a Don Arden type. I didn't see the music business in his terms. Maybe he should've managed the band. He may have taken us into a very different universe."

Hawkwind carried on in their own universe with Clearwater, and the visual possibilities suggested by their music were beginning to interest such notable Ladbroke Grove talents as Jonathan Smeeton (Liquid Len) and Barney Bubbles.

"Jonathan began working with us around this time," remembers Thomas Crimble. "He used to do the most fantastic lights with a projector and two bits of glass with coloured oil and bits of paint in them. They'd heat up and bubble. That's how it all started. And Barney Bubbles started coming in on the scene too, although most of his work came after this."

Thomas and Nik Turner were among those members who were pursuing their friendships with Smeeton, Bubbles and the underground community, and they were still trading favours. "We used to hang out in the *Frendz* office in Portobello Road quite a lot, talking about

* Gordon would became famous as Alice Cooper's ingenious manager.

things," says Thomas. "*Frendz* and *IT*, they used to give us all their unsold back copies and at the end of gigs, we used to throw 40 or 50 of them into the crowd.

"I wasn't totally convinced by this. I thought it was a bit stage-managed, a bit music-business. But the people were getting the message as put over by *IT* and *Oz* and *Frendz*, so it wasn't a bad thing."

These publications, in return, would write about Hawkwind and print their news.

Thomas Crimble was happy in the band and, like Nik Turner, unaware of any disturbing undercurrents. In December 1970, he received an unexpected and unwelcome Christmas gift: the news that his services were no longer required.

"Thomas wasn't actually a permanent member," states Dave Brock. "He was a stand-in, as far as I remember. He was just sitting in for about five months while we found another bass player. He was a nice, amiable sort of character and a good bass player, although I wouldn't say he was a Hawkwind man."

Thomas Crimble is certain that he was taken on as a full-time member.

"I was really into the band," he says. "I thought they were really good. And I believed all that hippie, trippy stuff, playing music for the people and all the rest of it. I was sacked by Dave Brock, and no reason was given. I couldn't believe it. Every one of the band said that they liked me and didn't want me to leave. I came from a musical background, I did want to have an input into Hawkwind, and I think Dave felt threatened by that."

This suggestion is denied emphatically and incredulously by Brock.

"Prior to this happening, I'd been asked down to Worthy Farm to help get a festival together," carries on Crimble. That turned out to be the first Glastonbury Fayre.

"I'd met some people at the Isle of Wight. We were standing in a sea of Coke and beer cans, it seemed like a foot thick, in front of the main stage after it had all finished. It was a hell of a mess, and we were saying, 'There must be a better way of doing this.'"

Thomas was struck by the idea of organising a big, free festival cleanly and efficiently. His then girlfriend, Jutte Klamer, had met some people in London including one Andrew Kerr, who shared a similar vision with farmer Michael Eavis.

The hippies had been heading to the Glastonbury area every June to celebrate the summer solstice on common land outside the town. A Tory MP called Derek Heathcote-Amery lived in a house backing on to this land, and he hated the annual invasion. In an ironic move – considering what would happen in later years – the police opened up a dialogue with Eavis and Kerr, proposing that the celebrations could be moved to the grounds of Eavis' Worthy Farm.

Andrew Kerr contacted Thomas Crimble, who was by then living in south Wales, and invited him to help set up a festival for 1971. Thomas travelled to Glastonbury for talks, and then returned to Hawkwind. "The next weekend I was doing gigs with them and suddenly I was sacked," he declares. "I did a last show with them, a big Christmas gig in London at The Roundhouse [on December 13], and then I left and I moved down to Worthy Farm."

At the same time, his relationship with Jutte was grinding to a halt and although Thomas was "angst-ridden" about that, he was philosophical about his departure from Hawkwind. "I hadn't actually been looking for a career in music at that time," he asserts. "I thought if I got six months' work out of it, I was lucky. They were really rocking and I was upset to have to leave, but then I had a good thing going at Glastonbury. It wasn't like, 'There goes my career,' because I wasn't aware that one could have one. I thought they'd either kill themselves or be very big. I was reading *Siddhartha* by Hermann Hesse at the time, so leaving the band seemed quite all right on the spiritual side of life."

Of Thomas' dismissal, Douglas Smith remarks: "He was just too nice for them."

And Nik Turner comments cryptically: "Certain people had their own personal agendas."

Crimble went on to spend almost 30 years as Michael Eavis' right-hand man at Glastonbury.

Coming into 1971, Dave Brock was faced with an ultimatum.

Just before Christmas, he'd talked to *Disc* about the problems of being in what their reporter Caroline Boucher described as "the freakiest and most electrifying band doing the rounds at the moment". It was, said Brock, ruining his busking career.

"I didn't always turn up at Hawkwind gigs," Dave admits today. "I was earning more money busking than I was with Hawkwind. My guitar case used to be full up with coins, big old pennies and halfpennies."

Mike King, his old Eel Pie Island friend, had been present when Dave pulled in a record haul on July 5, 1969 – the day The Rolling Stones played their free concert at Hyde Park. "I was sitting in the front row in Hyde Park, next to Dave's wife Sylvia, behind the little fence they'd put up," he recalls. "Dave went up to busk at the Albert Hall where The Who were playing a bit later the same day. I met him afterwards. He said, 'Grab this,' and gave me his guitar case and two socks, all full of money. I nearly dropped it, it was such a weight. He'd had a good day."

Dave: "I didn't turn up at the Marquee once for a Hawkwind gig and Douglas Smith said, 'Look, you'll ruin everything for everybody else. Make the major decision – either you're a busker or you're playing in the band.' So I stopped busking by 1971, and I was playing in the band and turning up for the gigs."

With that small matter sorted out – excepting the occasional relapse on Dave's part – Hawkwind set about changing and expanding the membership, building towards the classic line-up that would conquer the world – or, at least, a good part of it.

First, they needed a bass player to replace Thomas Crimble. They had already met their new man in the corridors of United Artists, the record label that had recently bought Liberty, inheriting and honouring various signings including Hawkwind and Amon Duul II, the pioneering Kraut-rock band.

Flying to London for a press function at the record company HQ, Amon Duul's English bassist Dave Anderson had bumped into Nik Turner.

Anderson subsequently left the group because he no longer wanted to live in Germany, going on to play some sessions for RCA Records, completing a stint with the much-loved white bluesman Alexis Korner and briefly replacing Nic Potter in Van Der Graaf Generator, the experimental British group led by Peter Hammill. After that, chilling out at the Northwood, Middlesex, house where he lived with some old friends – the band Brinsley Schwarz – Anderson received a phone call.

He says: "Hawkwind were looking for a bass player and Nik Turner knew that I was available. I said, 'Oh yes, I'd love to.' Then Dave Brock got in contact and said, 'Can I come for a jam?' We had a jam together at the Brinsleys' place, and I was asked to join."

Dave Anderson was born in Romford, Essex, on November 21,

1949, and brought up in Northwood. He was privately educated until the age of 13, thereafter moving to a grammar school where he formed a band with Nick Lowe – the future pub-rock genius, Elvis Costello producer and esteemed solo artist.

Dave had taken piano lessons at 10, graduating to the acoustic guitar and folk music a few years later. He went electric after the example of Bob Dylan, and by the time he left school, he and Nick Lowe were playing local gigs with their band. Dave left after a while, but he kept up with his friends in the school band, including Lowe, who went on to form Kippington Lodge, later renamed Brinsley Schwarz.

Dave accompanied Kippington Lodge, as a friend, when they went to Munich to play a club residency. On a night off, they returned to the club to check out the "mad German band" who were appearing there, and Dave ended up joining them after a joint-smoking competition loosely masquerading as an audition. Now on bass, he remained with Amon Duul II for three years, appearing on their celebrated albums *Phallus Dei* (1968) and the double *Yeti* (1970).

Joining Hawkwind, Anderson found himself in an inspiring and spontaneous environment. "We believed in all the things that everybody did then: free love, peace, make love not war. We liked giving out incense and fruit at the gigs, and we used to hand out politically orientated information. We were definitely doing things differently from anybody else, but we weren't aware that we were creating any kind of society – which, in the end, I think we did do.

"We were enjoying ourselves, having a good time and making music. We weren't really thinking about how we could change the world. I don't know that we thought we stood for anything, just that we were trying to rebel against the establishment. But because of the way we were living, it was inevitable we had something that people would see and perhaps like.

"We were trying to make some interesting music. It was totally free-form. I took it in its truest sense. I was quite happy to contribute towards band compositions, whereas other members were much keener on getting their own personal identity stamped on things.

"The drug use was phenomenal. Mandies to calm you down, Dexies to get you up, acid to freak you out and pot to keep you grooving. There was no drink, though."

It was around this time that Douglas Smith parted company with Hawkwind for the first time, having been ousted by his partners in

Clearwater. "They were saying I worked too hard," he says. "I was living in the office. I would wake up to the phone calls. All the bookings were coming in via me. It made them look as if they were doing nothing. They weren't coming in until lunchtime. I said, 'Well, fuck it then. Bye bye.'"

Douglas went on to manage Donovan's old band, Open Road. Soon afterwards, just before the release of Hawkwind's second album, he would receive a visit from Dave Brock and Nik Turner. "They came and saw me one Saturday morning and said, 'Clearwater's falling to pieces. Would you be interested in taking us back on?'"

This set the pattern for the on-off relationship between Douglas Smith and Hawkwind which has carried on intermittently to this day.

She's one of the most popular characters in their history, and also one of the most mysterious.

Known only as Stacia, the statuesque dancer with the memorably large bosom stripped naked onstage while Hawkwind played, explaining that she was reaching for the "freedom of expression" attained by her heroine Isadora Duncan, dubbed the mother of modern dance.

Stacia had no training in music or dance. Born in Exeter as Stephanie Leech, she had received a normal education at a convent school and a secondary modern, going on to a variety of jobs: she was a bookbinder, she slaved in a Wimpy Bar, and she worked in a boutique and in the record shop in an Exeter department store.

She had loved music from an early age, particularly the classical composers, and had later fallen in love with The Beatles and with jazz artists including Billie Holiday, Stan Getz and Dizzy Gillespie. The young Stacia was always drawn to dancing and acting, although she considered herself too tall, at six feet, and too majestically built to pursue a career in either. Gravitating towards the freak scene and the festival circuit, she met Nik Turner and his boyfriend Philippe at the Isle of Wight. Later, on a trip to London, Stacia met Hawkwind at the Middle Earth club.

The teenager was living a less than alternative existence as a petrol-pump attendant at a garage in Exeter when Hawkwind hit the West Country in the spring of 1971. She turned up to see them play at the Redruth Flamingo Ballroom, Cornwall, on April 15. "That's when she asked us if she could take her clothes off and dance," recalls Dave Brock. "We all said, 'Oh yes!' And she did."

Stacia later explained that it was "one of those impromptu things that just happened", and reasoned that it was her personal way of confronting the self-consciousness she'd felt for years about her size, often bending over as she walked to try to appear smaller.

She had prepared for the gig by painting her body.

"She was fantastic," remembers Nik Turner.

"In those days, people did discard their clothes," explains Dave Brock. "She was a totally over-the-top character. I liked her."

Dave Anderson relates: "We were doing this gig in Redruth with all the strobes going on and off, so you couldn't see much anyway. Very often it was best not to have your eyes open because of the strobes. I opened my eyes at one point and thought, 'There's somebody up and dancing.' I opened my eyes again a bit later – 'Oh, I'm not too sure, but I think they're naked.'

"Afterwards, she said, 'That was wonderful. That's the most free I've ever been.' We asked her if she'd like to dance every night with the band. We said, 'If you want to do this, we'll come and pick you up at lunchtime tomorrow from wherever you work and you can come to the next gig with us.' She handed her notice in at the garage and jumped in the back of the van."

After a short period making occasional appearances with Hawkwind, Stacia moved to London to be a full-time member. She began to wear costumes, which became more exotic as time went on and, before every gig, she would have her face and body painted with flowers and elaborate patterns. Although there could be a real eroticism about her performances, her intention was never to titillate but to interpret the music as she felt it. Consequently, she didn't always take her clothes off.

Referring to her first gig at Redruth, she commented, rather hopefully: "People watching did not regard it as a sexual thing. Hawkwind don't attract that type of audience. They reacted to my dancing as an expression of freedom."

"She was lovely," says Anderson. "She was very easy-going and bubbly. I was the one who painted her every night. It was a great job. I painted her all over – any colours I'd got."

Stacia wasn't the only naked performer in Hawkwind. Terry Ollis regularly drummed in the nude, as Dave Anderson had discovered to his great surprise shortly after joining the band. "The first few gigs I probably didn't even notice, because you couldn't always tell, with the lights," laughs Dave. "Suddenly, one night I glanced at him and I thought, 'Fuck me, he's doing this naked!' One night he was photographed with no clothes on, and it made all the Sunday newspapers. It was incredible."

Terry Ollis explains: "I just used to get really, really hot and I'd be loading up the van in soaking wet clothes at two in the morning. I wasn't that together to bring extra clothes. Rather than go home in dripping, hot clothes, I used to take them off before I got to the stage, and I'd still end up steaming like a racehorse at the end of it. I'd put my clothes back on when I cooled down a bit. It was the spirit of the age. I was doing it all the time. It was all very hippie. I believed in the lifestyle implicitly, and still pretty much do.

"On one occasion, we did a debutantes' ball, and the dressing room was at the far end of the hall from the stage. We all walked through and I was bollock-naked with a towel over my shoulder. Nobody batted an eyelid. But on the way back, I was dripping in sweat and this fucking great path opened before me."

There was a certain comedown routine at the gigs, says Dave Anderson: "Usually when we finished the main set, someone would come and give us all Mandrax. We'd be spacing out during the encores, and when we'd get back out to the van, we'd instantly fall asleep."

And so there were times when Terry would curl up in his sleeping bag naked.

"I'd crash out. Sometimes I'd wake up and they'd all be in the services, I'd be dying for a piss and I'd be that much out of my head I couldn't be bothered to get dressed . . ."

In these dire circumstances, Terry would find his way out of the van and head for the toilets, or the café.

Dave Anderson remembers one such night. He says, grinning, "We'd been playing in Wales and we were driving back up to London. Terry had fallen asleep. I hadn't. We got to the Severn Bridge services and some of us went to get something to eat. Out of the corner of my eye, I saw Terry getting out of the van and walking into the cafeteria – bollock-naked, apart from a pair of socks.

"He got his tray, collected his food, slid the tray along the rails, and there was a lorry driver paying for his meal at the end of the sliding thing. Terry slid his tray up against this guy's, went to lean on the rail and missed. His hand went right in this lorry driver's meal.

"The lorry driver hadn't noticed Terry until he saw this hand going into his food. He turned round and saw Terry, and he was so shocked he paid for his meal, left it there and walked out."

Ollis did not feel upstaged by Stacia; nudity was nothing unusual. "She obviously got up and got her kit off," he states, matter of factly. "Yeah – fine."

Now Dikmik was threatening to quit the band. The audio-generator ace had been travelling with Hawkwind's road crew in the truck taking the gear up to the north of Scotland when it crashed head-on into a car coming the other way.

"Dikmik got such a fright he didn't want to travel any more," says Dave Anderson. "The rest of us were in a car. We were on the way to the Aviemore Ski Centre to rehearse for the *In Search Of Space* album. The crash happened as Dikmik and the crew were driving through a place called Pitlochry. The guy in the car had his head cut off. Then the truck turned over, and one of the road crew got his arm caught underneath it. He was in hospital for months."

"That was John The Dump," says Dave Brock. "There was another guy called John The Bog, a drug dealer we used to know. He was a larger-than-life character in the Seventies. He supplied us with lots of drugs, and he was working for us. I remember he started this cream-cake fight in a Swiss restaurant once. He was a mate of Nik's, and he died in a car crash.

"I knew another guy who impaled himself on a spiked fence after taking an LSD trip. 'Days Of The Underground' from our [1977] album *Quark Strangeness And Charm* is about these guys."

Dikmik was still talking about going to India, as he had back in Margate, although his new-found reluctance to travel might explain why he didn't actually go. His membership of Hawkwind was hanging by a thread, and they responded by absorbing their road manager Del Dettmar into the band in May 1971.

Del had been recruited to the crew by Douglas Smith, before Smith's short-lived estrangement from Hawkwind. While attending to his duties as road manager, Del also sat out front at gigs, operating a synthesiser and mixing the band. He was the obvious candidate for the impending vacancy, but the complication was that while Dikmik dipped in and out of the group as he pleased, he didn't finally leave Hawkwind for another two years.

This turned out to be a blessing in disguise. Together, Dikmik (audio generators, percussion, oscillators and vocals) and Del Dettmar (VCS3 synthesiser and keyboards) would create a unique musical quality that had them described by one author as "giants of electronic music". They played complementary roles, with Dikmik immersed in his familiar world of sound and Del more eager to explore the advancing musical technology.

Del Dettmar was born on April 20, 1947 in Thornton Heath, Croydon. He attended the private, three-class Aberdeen House school up to the age of eight, moving on to Kensington Road Primary and then to Norbury Manor Secondary.

"I had no ambition," he recalls. "I didn't really want to do anything when I first left school. I got a job in a bank and it was great, giving money away. I took an extended holiday to see the TT racing in the Isle of Man, and after that I got transferred to the surveying department of the bank. Then, I guess, my hair got too long and we parted company."

Del went hitch-hiking in Europe, returning to a job with the Paint And Steam Cleaning And Beading Company, which had outlets in Thornton Heath and Latimer Road. He left in 1967 to live in Jersey with some friends from Croydon: "We heard we could make big money picking potatoes. The only thing that was bigger was the size of the coins . . ."

Then Del moved to Cambridge, where he punted tourists up and down the river and pretended to know the history of the city. By the time he knew the names of the colleges, he had been taken on in one of them as a painter. "I got fired after one day because I was so slow," he admits.

He wasn't too thrilled, either, with his washing-up job in a university centre and in 1969, he headed back to Croydon. That's where he bumped into one of the musical friends he'd made in Cambridge. Charlie Weedon had been working as a roadie for a band called Little Women, which included the future Humble Pie drummer Jerry Shirley and guitar maestro Tim Renwick, later of Quiver. Charlie invited Del to come along and hump gear for The Pretty Things, and so his entry into the music world was "all Charlie's fault".

Dettmar subsequently carried out road-managing duties for The Edgar Broughton Band, Arthur Brown, Juicy Lucy and Pete Brown's Piblokto before winding up with Cochise, who were managed by Clearwater Productions.

Says Del: "I left Cochise 'cos they wouldn't spend money on improving anything. Doug [Smith] asked me to work for Hawkwind and I turned them down. Then he bribed me with more money, so I agreed."

He contends that when he first joined the band, "Dave had a plan to get rid of Dikmik." If that were the case, then it didn't work, at least not immediately. "Dave did the hiring and firing. I told him I wasn't interested in that kind of thing."

Dave Brock speaks affectionately about Del: "He was like a little gnome, a cheeky Cockney gnome. He was a quirky character; quite outspoken. Him and Stacia fell in love."

Del Dettmar admits that he later enjoyed a romance with the towering dancer, a good foot taller than he was.

It would be one of the many unusual things to happen in Hawkwind.

CHAPTER 5

"Lemmy A Quid 'Til Friday . . ."

THEY'D been booked for ages to appear at the first-ever Glastonbury, the free festival being held at Worthy Farm, Pilton, on June 23, 1971. And Dave Brock missed it.

This is a subject which still ruffles Dave Anderson's feathers, and although there is no disagreement over the reason for Brock's absence onstage – he had a tummy upset – they have different memories of what happened that day.

Brock offers a graphic account: "Both Dave Anderson and me had terrible diarrhoea at the festival. They didn't have toilets there. All they had was logs that you sat on. You had to crap into a hole. I had really bad stomach ache and I went home 'cos I was ill. I never actually played, and everybody else did. It was disappointing to me to miss that gig – the magical moment I wasn't there."

Anderson protests: "Dave never turned up at all. He phones up to say, 'I've got terrible diarrhoea.' I said, 'Yes, so have I.' It was just one of those things that was going round at the time, but I still turned up. At that time, Dave was living somewhere in Devon. It was only an hour's drive or something.

"I ended up having to play guitar for the first half, while Thomas Crimble was brought in to play bass. I switched back to bass for the second half. Dave not turning up at gigs was one of the things that used to pee me off more than anything else. To find yourself at Glastonbury Festival having to play guitar was not my idea of fun – I don't like playing guitar onstage – although it was still the most amazing experience.

"But a really important thing like that – to not turn up I thought was awful, really unprofessional and let us all down."

Thomas Crimble, who had been relieved of his duties in Hawkwind and was now a part of the Glastonbury organisation, declares: "They turned up without Dave Brock. He didn't want to do it for free, so the other members said."

Brock, however, insists that on that day, in between dashes to the log-seats, he met fantasy artist and Pink Fairies associate Peter Pracownik, who has since built up an international reputation and is currently responsible for Hawkwind's artwork. "Peter actually gave me some of his old 8mm film," says Brock. "There's some footage from the first Glastonbury – and we all are there."

Hawkwind were by now working new material into their set, including the revered 'Master Of The Universe', and Thomas Crimble was in two minds about being drawn back into the fold, however briefly. "I'd been down there for six months helping organise the festival, and then Hawkwind turned up and said they couldn't do the set without Dave Brock," he recalls. "They asked me if I'd stand in and play bass so that Dave Anderson could move on to guitar. I hadn't seen them since I left the band, and I was still smarting a bit."

He agreed to help. "They taught me 'Master Of The Universe' in about three minutes. That's how complicated it is. I remember being onstage thinking, 'Bloody hell, this is a bit much,' especially doing new songs I'd only just heard. It was a bit of a shock to the system. But there's a hell of an energy with Hawkwind so it was nice from that point of view. It was great to do it just for one afternoon, and it was great to leave it again."

The experience proved to Thomas that his life had become richer since Hawkwind. "When you're in a band, that's all you've got time to do, just going from one gig to the next and meeting a few people. The whole thing of Glastonbury was consciousness-expanding. I realised it was a much bigger universe than I'd previously imagined.

"Everyone was welcome to come and do their thing at Glastonbury. There was every kind of spiritualism and healing, and all the cosmic jokers were there. It opened my head up to all of life's possibilities, so suddenly playing with a rock band again seemed rather limiting. I found the whole rock'n'roll experience to be very self-centred. I was into what I perceived to be a much more expansive consciousness, something much bigger and better, I feel."

Thomas Crimble would remain a part of Glastonbury until 1999, during which time he also opened up the aptly named Mountain rehearsal and recording studios on a peak near Llandeilo, south Wales.

In the Eighties, his clients included Killing Joke, Thompson Twins, China Crisis and Roy Harper. Around 10 years ago, Thomas sold the property and moved his operation into the Towy Valley, still near Llandeilo.

In all of this time, he had no further dealings with Hawkwind as a band, but they would meet up again, tumultuously, in the year 2000 and on occasions afterwards.

Thomas did, however, keep in touch with Nik Turner, a near-neighbour for many years now. "We often talked about maybe getting the old band together without Dave Brock," says Crimble. "And Nik rang me up one day a few years ago and said, 'Let's get it together.'"

Thomas is now a part of Turner's Space Ritual band alongside Mick Slattery, Dave Anderson, Terry Ollis and his son Sam and, occasionally, Del Dettmar. Thomas lives in Wales with his wife Diane and is father to Jasper, Grace, Donna and Boysie.

The two Daves were not at loggerheads after Glastonbury. That conflict wouldn't happen for some time. Despite Anderson's annoyance at Brock for missing the gig, he liked him.

"I thought Dave was a bit of a crafty old crook," says Anderson. "But I don't think there was any bad feeling there, or in the band in general. Nik was sharing my flat with my wife and me, and I felt quite close to Dave Brock; I thought we had a good relationship.

"The only person I had a problem with was Dikmik. He became really aggressive. When I'd first joined the band, Dikmik and I shared a flat with two girls. I met my future wife, Angela, and obviously I left to move in with her, which put him in a bit of a difficult situation. Our friendship just went down from there."

Anderson would eventually storm out of the band in a furious showdown over Dikmik but, for now, he was happy to ignore the simmering tensions: Hawkwind were on a roll, and then some. Dave's girlfriend Angela was working for Clearwater, and booking the band lots of gigs.

And crucially, they were coming to realise that they really could create an extraordinary, otherworldly experience for their audiences through the dramatic union of music, words, performance, lights and packaging. They began presenting themselves onstage with a DJ, Andy Dunkley, who also provided set introductions.

If Hawkwind had been all about "head space" in their earlier, tentative explorations, now they were on the launch pad, about to blast off through the universe. Space rock finally found its real voice with *X In Search Of Space*, their second album and their breakthrough. They only needed to find the money to make Hawkwind the biggest, most extravagant show in town. Eventually, they would find it but, in the meantime, *X In Search Of Space* served as a statement of intent.

And the vital, creative influences that helped to shape the new vision were those of Robert Calvert, Barney Bubbles, Jonathan Smeeton, Michael Moorcock and photographer Phil Franks, whose images adorned the sleeve of this and succeeding Hawkwind albums.

Franks, also known as Philm Freax, had worked for *Rolling Stone* and more recently for *Frendz*. Well known in the underground scene, he became highly sought-after for album shoots by the likes of Frank Zappa, Yes, Daevid Allen and Gong.

Nik Turner invited Robert Calvert to join the band primarily as a songwriter, believing that Hawkwind offered an ideal outlet for his friend's poetry, philosophy and keen interest in science fiction. Calvert, still writing for *Frendz*, also became a vocalist, speaking and singing, although he later told *Sounds* journalist Martin Hayman: "I'm a sound poet rather than a singer. I'm intending to use words not in a conceptual way but as concrete things in themselves."

Hayman was struck by Calvert: "Bob is quietly spoken, articulate, with an obvious dedication to both his own work and his part with Hawkwind."

Like Turner, Calvert could also turn his hand to the flute, but his live appearances with Hawkwind were at first sporadic. He made his debut at a three-night residency at the Seven Sisters Club in London's Finsbury Park on May 26, 27 and 28, 1971, delivering 'Co-Pilots Of Spaceship Earth'. This was the origin of the soon-to-be-famous pronouncement from *In Search Of Space*: "Technicians of spaceship Earth. This is your captain speaking – your captain is dead."

Barney Bubbles, *Frendz* designer, was also "inspired by the band", according to Nik Turner. "He was completely sold on it. He wanted to do all the artwork. I thought we were privileged."

Born Colin Fulcher in 1942 in Whitton, Middlesex, Barney attended Isleworth Grammar School and then Twickenham College Of Art. "He wasn't considered by the tutors to be an illustrator or designer, so he was plonked into the window-dressing department," says Mike Heath, whose company Rebecca And Mike, specialists in unusual art and design projects, staged an acclaimed exhibition of Bubbles' work at a gallery in Clerkenwell, London, in 2001. "If you're slightly radical, people find it difficult to get their head round what you're doing."

Undeterred, Barney kept up his interests privately, and around this time designed a much-admired poster for a band called The Muleskinners, whose Ian McLagan would later join The Small Faces. Memorable for its bold but simple graphics, it was one of the first times Bubbles turned his artistic skills to a musical project.

He was always interested in performance art, not just 2D and 3D work, and would stage "crazy events" with his college friends, even when he had left and started work with a "very straight" typographic designer and then, in 1965, with the Conran Design Group. He once "performed" with an air-guitar band called The Erections in front of a bank of static TVs.

He was also collaborating with friends and colleagues to create light-shows for groups including Gun and Quintessence at such hip venues as The Roundhouse, the Electric Cinema, Middle Earth and the Speakeasy.

"In those days, it was all about collective effort," says Mike. "There was a community-based mentality. It wasn't about individuals."

Barney used all sorts of methods to generate imagery, using oil and food colouring to create zany, bubbling projections (some say that's how he got his name, some say it came from a film, and some believe it was bestowed upon him by Jerry Garcia) or filming scenes around the city to layer over other projections.

Intrigued by the underground, he left Conran in 1968 and travelled to Haight Ashbury where he met such luminaries as Jerry Garcia, Pigpen, Janis Joplin and the poster artist Stanley Mouse. He also had the great opportunity of working with Bill Ham on his legendary light-show at San Francisco's Avalon Ballroom.

Barney's trip was "an awakening, a reinforcement and an inspiration," says Heath, although his life in the counterculture would later unsettle and overwhelm him from time to time. Returning, he moved next door to the *Frendz* office in Portobello Road, began work there, freelanced for other underground magazines such as *Oz*, and consequently met Hawkwind.

By now interested in fantasy illustration (although well versed in art history), the charismatic Bubbles saw the opportunity to create a complete visual identity for the band – an intricate, hippie-friendly blend of

Gothic and sci-fi imagery that perfectly suited their music and concepts. He would go on to design everything from the logo, the letterheads, stickers and transfers to the record sleeves and posters, sometimes in conjunction with photographer Phil Franks, who now has an impressive Hawkwind archive.

"By the planning stages of the album, Barney was obviously going to do the artwork," says Dave Anderson. "He took over a huge great chunk of the visuals – the sleeve, the poster . . . He painted all our equipment."

Bubbles also masterminded the unique, fold-out sleeve – a trick he would return to.

"He was a really major part of what made Hawkwind work," continues Anderson. "He drew it all together visually. Nobody has ever been better than him. And he was a lovely guy, really sweet and as gentle as you could possibly imagine."

"His artwork was wonderful," agrees Dave Brock.

Douglas Smith adds: "He totally created their image."

Barney was a big inspiration to young, would-be designers including Malcolm Garrett who later commented: "The way Bubbles worked with Hawkwind influenced the way I wanted to work with The Buzzcocks, as part of a whole team, in order to present a unified picture."

Barney and Calvert were together responsible for the booklet issued with *X In Search Of Space*. The album is all about a two-dimensional trip in a spaceship, although it focuses on earthbound issues too, particularly ecology, with the rocket-ship visiting Earth in 1985 to find a wasteland of concrete and iron. The booklet is the spaceship captain's log.

Bob Calvert came up with the proposal for the two-dimensional trip, and wrote some of the album lyrics, while Barney introduced the idea of the spaceship. Calvert wrote the words for the log, and Barney designed and illustrated it. "That's what gave the band their direction," concludes Nik Turner.

At the same time, Jonathan Smeeton was becoming involved, along with Sally Vaughan, who lived with him. As time went on and money became more plentiful, Smeeton's Liquid Len & The Lensmen would design some jaw-droppingly spectacular light-shows for Hawkwind. Back in the early Seventies, Smeeton was making his name by using slides rather than kinetic wheels.

Brock: "Sally used to do a lot of the mandalas that we used in light-shows, projections that we used to paint on glass."

Another member of the "creative team", Michael Moorcock was a friend of Robert Calvert's through the underground press. In addition to editing *New Worlds*, he contributed to alternative publications and, like Calvert, he would endow Hawkwind with poetry, lyrics, concepts and vocals.

He had previously been alerted to the group by Bob Calvert and John Trux, a leading light at *Frendz*. They asked him: "Why don't you come along and see Hawkwind? Dave and Nik like your stuff."

"I was reading his books," says Dave Brock. "We all used to read sci-fi books a lot."

Moorcock went to see the band at Shepherd's Bush, and was particularly impressed by the way they embraced technology. He was later quoted as saying, "It was like a mad spaceship with everybody jamming things in to see what would happen. Half of it was Dikmik just finding out what would happen with the synthesiser, and Nik used to have his captain's or seaman's white cap on, and he looked very good 'doing that'."

Michael went to see Hawkwind again, and he was soon asked if he'd like to collaborate with them. However, Moorcock felt that that would be "moving in" on Calvert's territory, so he hung back for a while.

In July 1971, Calvert was off the scene, being treated for one of his regular bouts of psychiatric illness. "Bob went into the loony bin," stated Moorcock, who took the opportunity to debut with Hawkwind on July 23 – the first of three free gigs under the arches at Ladbroke Grove (the others taking place on August 7 and 28).

" 'Sonic Attack' was the first thing I did, and I was the first person to perform it," said Moorcock later. "Later on, Lemmy started doing it and I think it was Lemmy that did the first recorded version. There's no recorded version of me doing 'Sonic Attack'."

Despite this, it remains Moorcock's favourite Hawkwind track, and he wrote the words specifically for the band. "After that first gig, I said to Bob that until he wanted to come back, I would fill in for him, which is basically what I did, and that was how it ran thereafter."

Michael Moorcock was born in Mitcham, Surrey, in 1939 and he was brought up there, on the outskirts of south London. Fuelled by his mother's "lunatic genius", he wanted to be a writer from the age of 10, when he began producing fanzines about music, books and science fiction. Failing the 11-plus, he spent five years at college, learned to type and continued with the fanzines.

At 15, he was listening to Woody Guthrie, and to skiffle and blues music in the coffee bars of Soho. He started playing blues guitar in these venues for a coffee or a whip-round. He also played in a whorehouse because "the girls liked me". In one claim to fame, he taught a friend his first three chords. That friend turned out to be Peter Green, future guitar hero with Fleetwood Mac.

Moorcock went on to play in various blues outfits and, to his embarrassment, was kitted out in a Stetson hat in a semi-pro country band called The Greenhorns. By the time he was 17, he was editing *Tarzan Adventures*, a comic which reprinted strips from American newspapers, but his attempts to make things more interesting by incorporating written stories did not go down well. He was fired.

He became interested in science fiction by reading Alfred Bester, although he wasn't writing much of it at that time. He specialised in general fiction or general non-fiction, and he was providing comic strips for a range of publications, including *Lion* and *Tiger*. But before long, he had invented his famed character Elric of Melnibone, and was seeing the stories published in *Science Fantasy Magazine*. They captured the imagination of the readers, and so Moorcock simply "drifted" into writing science fantasy and science fiction stories and novels. He would go on to win a Lifetime Achievement award from the World Fantasy Convention.

Moorcock was still playing music on and off, hitch-hiking around Europe before ending up in Sweden where he played guitar. Returning, starving, he became caught up in the excitement of the early Beatles and formed a band which did little more than rehearse.

By the mid-Sixties, he was editing *New Worlds*, which consumed all of his time and energy, and he became somewhat dislocated from music – apart from a huge passion for Zoot Money's Big Roll Band – until the night he went to see Hawkwind at Shepherd's Bush.

In Search Of Space was produced and engineered by George Chkiantz, much to the satisfaction of Dave Brock, and the band's creative juices were flowing. "When we did that album, we used to take LSD and play," says Brock. "The engineers were paranoid about drinking anything in case they'd get spiked up."

They had good reason. Dave Anderson: "The first week we were due in the studio, we were put into Air London.* Unknown to us, some of our friends – the Furry Freak Brothers, named after the comic characters – turned up, broke into George Martin's drinks cabinet, pinched all his booze and spiked one of the engineers with acid.

"At the end of the week, we'd spent thousands of pounds in this studio and we hadn't done anything. The engineer had been refusing to work. We later heard that George Martin was really furious. We'd probably been spiked up ourselves, because we just didn't know what was going on. United Artists said, 'We're sending you to Olympic Studios. You've got to get the album finished quickly.'

"It was fantastic at Olympic. We had the Stones in Studio 1. George Chkiantz was the producer there, and he'd done things for people like The Yardbirds."

Anderson was proud of the album, but his already strained relationship with Dikmik was deteriorating fast. "He was a bit of a hard nut," says Anderson. "He was taking far too much speed, even by my standards. I used to like a bit of speed as well, but he'd just do it to crazy levels.

"I remember having a few fights with him, physical fights. I didn't want to be in a band with somebody I was having fights with. I started travelling to all the gigs by myself in my car, and that's when Dikmik started getting more aggressive. I'd really had my fill. Hawkwind didn't want to tour in America at that point – 'Oh, we don't want to go there, it's full of Americans.' I thought touring America was the next logical step."

The band had played their first European tour, two weeks at the beginning of June 1971, but Anderson felt they should be looking at a bigger picture: "All the things I wanted to do within music they were saying they didn't want to do. I was really disillusioned with Dave Brock. I began to doubt what the band really hoped to achieve. It no longer felt like the happy thing I'd got myself into. I decided to leave."

Dave Anderson told the group: "I'm not enjoying it now. Therefore I'd prefer to go and find something else."

They persuaded him to stay on for another six months, but in October, something happened – just as *X In Search Of Space* was released, to a chart placing of number 18.

"Dikmik had a huge great argument with my wife, and she phoned

---

* Air was founded by Beatles producer George – now Sir George – Martin.

me up in hysterics, crying her eyes out. I never asked her what the argument was about. I just said, 'Right, that's it. If you feel that bad about it, take it from me I've left the band.'"

Leading up to this, Hawkwind had been trying to find a manager in Douglas Smith's absence, and Andrew Lauder at United Artists had suggested a possibility. The man involved was prepared to consider the proposition, but he would only liaise with one appointed band member, and that was Dave Anderson. Says Dave: "I went in to see this guy and he's going, 'Oh, it's great, isn't it? The album's gone in the Top 20.' I said, 'Yes, that's great, but I've left the band.'"

Hawkwind accepted Anderson's resignation rather than get rid of Dikmik – "He'd been in it for longer than I had, and he probably had a better relationship with the others. The road crew lived in the flat above me and I told them not to pick me up for the gig that night. I left everything – my amps, two stacks and a bass guitar. Somehow I didn't really expect them to be returned.

"All the equipment had been painted by Barney Bubbles, and my equipment was the most beautiful of the whole lot. My top cabinet had an eagle flapping its wings, and out of the wings came flames which dropped on to the bottom cabinet. Where the flames landed, there was a pond with lots of lotus blossom and ripples going out over the water."

Dave Anderson would not see Hawkwind again for more than a decade. And his bass guitar was picked up by a good friend of Dikmik's, one Ian Kilmister known as Lemmy due to his familiar, desperate cry of "Lemmy a quid 'til Friday" – or so the legend and the T-shirt would have it.

Lemmy had been hanging out at Hawkwind gigs, and Nik Turner regards him as a catalyst for the trouble between Dikmik and Dave Anderson.

"The motivation was probably Lemmy wanting to be in the band," says Nik. "A lot of the problem was drug-related. People get psychotic on drugs, and there are a lot of personality clashes. In retrospect, you can see a certain dynamic that perhaps you didn't see at the time. I was optimistic, and I didn't really notice the negative situations.

"Later on, Dikmik lived with me for quite a long time. My parents died and I inherited their house in Westgate on Sea, near Margate. He came to live there with his girlfriend, and they had a baby. I never saw an aggressive side to him. We had a different relationship. I don't know if he was like that with other people, but I certainly never experienced it."

Dave Brock remarks: "Dikmik was grumpy and he used to threaten to clock people but I wouldn't say he was aggressive and violent. He was all right."

Nik Turner's return to the seaside was still some time away, but various members of Hawkwind were beginning to move out of Ladbroke Grove due to increasing attention from the local constabulary, dispersing to such outer areas as Hanwell in the west and Clapham in the south. Brock and his wife Sylvia relocated to Devon, where Dave has remained.

"I'd lived in the city all my life," says Dave. "I used to think, 'Gosh, I would love to move.' My parents used to come and holiday down here in the Sixties, and I'd be camping with them in a bivouac tent. I used to hitch-hike down to St Ives. I have an affinity with this part of the country.

"I signed a publishing contract with United Artists, I got a £500 advance, and I managed to get a mortgage. Andrew Lauder said he would give me a reference, but I actually ended up writing my own. I got headed notepaper from UA and asked one of his secretaries to type this glowing confirmation that I'd signed a five-year contract and was going to make a lot of money.

"The mortgage company phoned up the secretary. She probably said that Andrew wasn't there. So I was able to get this old, empty police house in Oakford, north Devon, which I did up."

It wasn't always easy for Dave, living so far away from the hub of activity in London and from the majority of the gigs. When he couldn't blag a spare room or a floor for the night, he would have to make the long journey home.

"I'd catch the milk train to Taunton," he relates. "Then I'd have to hitch-hike down from there, carrying my guitar. I used to have to cross this River Exe to save me walking two miles. I'd take my trousers off, put the guitar case on top of my head, wade across the river and go through the woods and up the hill."

Douglas Smith still believes that Brock could have struck a better bargain with the now-dead publisher: "He signed a 50-50 deal with the publisher – for perpetuity – with UA, which is owned by EMI. Still, it did get him his first house."

One of the most difficult Hawkwind dates to pin down is the day that Lemmy joined the band.

He remembers the first time he played with them, at a free concert in Powis Square, Notting Hill, and the only record of Hawkwind appearing there during this period is on September 1, 1971.

Lemmy was a guitarist back then, and Hawkwind had not appointed a successor to Huw Lloyd-Langton after his sudden acid-fuelled breakdown. Dave Brock was taking care of the guitar work, and sharing lead vocals with other members of the band. Dikmik was still coming and going from the line-up.

"He was going to India to be a mystic," chortles Lemmy. "He only got as far as Gloucester Road, so he was going in the wrong direction anyway. Dikmik decided to go to the gig. He was saying, 'Do you want to go and see the band? They've lost their guitarist, Huw Lloyd-Langton.' *He* was a strange person. He still is, in fact.

"I went along with Dikmik to this gig they were doing in Powis Square on the back of a lorry. Dave Anderson hadn't shown up. He didn't do the free ones. He did the ones he got paid for – another accountant in guitarist's clothing. But like an idiot, he left his guitar in the gear truck, like, 'Please steal my gig.'

"The band were saying, 'Does anybody play bass?' Dikmik pointed at me and said, 'He plays bass.' I'd never played one in my life before. Fucking Turner came over and said, 'Make some noises in E.' I did that for a bit. None of this old-fashioned stuff like two verses and a chorus.

"The gig was . . . problematical. I was in a state of sheer terror and panicking, but I was covering very well. I'm good at that – 'Hey, everything's wonderful.' I must have done all right. I eventually got the nod."

But not straight away.

"Some nights I played, some nights I didn't," says Lemmy. Given Dave Anderson's date of leaving, just after the October release of *X In Search Of Space*, that would have kept Lemmy on the subs' bench, sitting it out, for more than a few weeks – which would tie in with Nik Turner's suggestion that Lemmy was in place before Anderson decided to quit.

Anderson also buys into the conspiracy theory: "They'd found Lemmy ages before. He was tailing along with us, learning the set, although there wasn't much of a set to learn. He was in the wings, ready to take over. I think they just wanted him in the band, in whatever role. I don't know what their thoughts were. I was so divorced from them, I was just turning up at gigs."

"They never actually told me I was in the band," sniffs Lemmy, nicknamed "The Lurch". Nevertheless, he "bought" a Hopf bass guitar from Del Dettmar, who just happened to have one in the back of the van, reputedly for £27. Del is still waiting for his money.

"I think about it as being a bit like Duke Ellington," decides Nik. "One of his drummers would leave and the bass player would say, 'My mate plays the drums.' He wasn't a terribly good drummer, perhaps, but Duke Ellington would write songs to highlight his best qualities, and make the drummer sound fantastic. They weren't superlative musicians, but they had creative ideas.

"In Hawkwind, we allowed the same sort of freedom. We didn't really audition people. They just joined and that was it."

The blond and beautiful baby, Ian Fraser Kilmister, was born on Christmas Eve, 1945. Even then, it seems, he was something of a speedfreak, arriving five weeks earlier than expected. He came into the world in Burslem, the hardest area of Stoke on Trent, and his earliest memory is of shouting, so the fates were already, clearly, conspiring in the infant's favour.

Lemmy's mother was a TB nurse, going on to become a librarian and a barmaid, and his father, an ex-RAF padre, left the family three months after he was born. Lemmy moved with his mother and grandmother to Newcastle under Lyme, near Stoke, and from there to the nearby village of Madeley.

His schooldays were characterised by rebellion and truancy while, on the domestic front, his mother married his stepfather George Willis when Lemmy was 10. George was a former Bolton Wanderers footballer and latterly the owner of a factory making shoe stands for shop windows. It went bust.

Lemmy was younger than George's children from a previous marriage, Patricia and Tony, who he claims bullied him. He didn't get on too well with his stepfather either.

The family moved to Benllech on the Isle of Anglesey, where the young Lemmy caused mayhem with his mates by setting off seaside explosions with gelignite belonging to a building firm working on the local drainage.

He has recently admitted that people started calling him Lemmy around this time – "It was a Welsh thing, I believe" – shattering the fondly held myths surrounding the origins of his nickname. However, it would later become quite fitting as associates testify that "Lemmy a quid 'til Friday" turned quickly into a fiver, and a tenner.

Before long, he had discovered horses, sex and rock'n'roll. The animals were stabled at the riding school where he'd taken a job, the girls were there too, and the rock'n'roll – well, that started when he heard Bill Haley's 'Razzle Dazzle' on Radio Luxembourg. Music would become a lifelong passion, more potent and enduring than his commitment to any woman, or horse, he would ever meet.

The first record Lemmy bought was a 78rpm single by British rock'n'roll idol Tommy Steele. The second was Buddy Holly's 'Peggy Sue', released in 1957, and his first LP was *The Buddy Holly Story*.

All fired up by Holly, Eddie Cochran and Little Richard, Lemmy started learning to play the guitar, precociously aware of its mighty pulling power. It was a Hawaiian guitar of his mother's, and it did the trick: Lemmy was instantly surrounded by girls, and has been ever since.

At 15, during a school trip to Paris, he played 'Rock Around The Clock' for three hours one night, all the while bleeding copiously from a finger he'd accidentally cut with a flick-knife. Some time later, back in Anglesey, he was caught bunking off school and summoned to the headmaster's office. Sentenced to two strokes of the cane on each hand, he asked if he could instead have four on one hand so that the flick-knife cut would not burst open. The headmaster wasn't having any of it. With the first spurt of blood, Lemmy snatched the cane and crashed it down on his tormentor's head.

Needless to say, he was expelled, although he kept up the pretence of going to school for his parents' benefit, since he would have been leaving anyway after a few months. He spent his days at the riding school, and went on to a job painting houses. When the family moved away from Anglesey, to Conwy on the mountainous Welsh coast, Lemmy sat on a production line in a factory making washing machines. It was soul-destroying. He grew his hair until they fired him.

By now, he'd exchanged his mother's Hawaiian guitar for a Hofner Club 50 and was playing locally, making his first public appearance with a group called The Sundowners, which later mutated into The DeeJays. Their debut took place in a café in Llandudno, where they performed a selection of instrumentals and Lemmy sang Ricky Nelson's 'Travelin' Man'. They ended up on the wedding and dance circuit, and so it was time to move on . . . into another local band, The Sapphires. Unfortunately, Lemmy couldn't stand the lead guitarist, and it didn't last long.

During this period in Conwy, Lemmy first began smoking dope, shortly afterwards falling in love with speed when he was given an ampoule by a long-haired friend from Anglesey.

It was with another beatnik type, Ming, that Lemmy left Wales for Stockport, Greater Manchester, in pursuit of two young ladies they had met holidaying in Colwyn Bay. Lemmy and his teenage lover Cathy were eventually parted when she became pregnant and was forced into having the baby, Sean, adopted at birth.

With Manchester as his home base, Lemmy would often go on the road with various friends, hitch-hiking around the country wearing an American army jacket, sleeping in railway depots or caves, begging money and living off tins of creamed rice and food parcels from girls he met on his travels.

He was still seeking out bands, now armed and not too dangerous with a sparkly silver and black Eko guitar. He soon traded that for a more macho model and joined The Rainmakers, another band whose name he can't remember, and then The Motown Sect who didn't play Motown at all, but "kick-ass R&B". "We used to get gigs on the strength of the word Motown," says Lemmy. "People would book us into northern dance clubs, and we'd get to the gig with shoulder-length hair and Gibsons. 'Here's a number for all the James Brown fans!' 'Yeah!!!' And we'd play a Chuck Berry song.

"We played for Peter Stringfellow up in Sheffield. That's how long I've known him. I remember once we backed The Pretty Things at Halifax Town Hall, and all four of us were going through one 30-watt amplifier.

"Everybody did it for nothing. You didn't get wages. The drummer usually had the van, because he had to have transport for his kit. He would be running us around, driving, setting the drums up, taking the drums down and driving us all home again. If you got a sausage roll, you'd give him half of it.

"We used to do three 45-minute sets for £6 between the five of us at Middleton, near Oldham, at The Limit. It had zebra crossings, and traffic lights hanging off the ceiling. I still can't work out what that had to do with 'The Limit'. A real cunt used to run it as well, with glasses like a civil servant. 'You boys are late. *Late!*' "

It was 1965. After three years with The Motown Sect, Lemmy wanted to spread his wings. He'd seen a band called The Rocking Vicars at Manchester's Oasis club, and they were, indeed, rocking. They wore Finnish national dress with vicars' collars, they were very loud, and they smashed up their gear onstage.

Learning that they might need a new guitarist soon, Lemmy followed them from gig to gig and, finally winning an audition, covered up his lack of lead guitar skills by turning up the volume and trashing his own equipment plus the piano. He was hired.

The Vicars had a manager, Jack Venet, who set them up in a big flat in Manchester. There, Lemmy entertained the usual succession of girls, some more regularly than others. One frequent visitor was a singer called Tracy, who toured American air bases with a band. She subsequently gave birth to Lemmy's second child, Paul, and brought him up as a single parent. Father met son when Paul was six, and they remain in close contact to this day.

The Rocking Vicars released three singles in the two years Lemmy was in the band and one of them, a cover of The Kinks' 'Dandy', was a Top 50 hit. They were huge in the north of England, they played to adoring crowds in Finland and they became the first British band to play behind the Iron Curtain, gigging across the former Yugoslavia.

It was also in the Vicars that Lemmy had an experience that would certainly go down well on his CV for Hawkwind: he saw a UFO. "That was in 1966. We were driving across the Yorkshire Moors after a gig at either Nelson or Burnley, and I think it was Harry [Feeney, singer] who saw it first, 'cos he was driving. I was dozing off a bit. Ciggy [Cyril the drummer] went, 'What the fuck's that?' Harry stopped the car, we got out, and this thing came over the horizon and stopped dead. We stood and watched it for about five minutes."

It was pink and round, and eventually it shot off out of view as fast as it had approached. "It's like the guy said. Once you eliminate the possibilities, whatever's left, however impossible, is the truth. It was a UFO. We didn't have anything like that, neither did the Russians. Therefore, it was somebody else."

Lemmy left the Vicars because he was looking for something bigger than northern stardom. He moved to London and stayed with a friend called Neville Chesters, who'd roadied for The Who. Also living there was Jimi Hendrix's bass player Noel Redding.

It turned out that the Jimi Hendrix Experience needed another roadie in England, where they were enjoying their first burst of popularity, and Lemmy was that man. He worked for Hendrix for a year, picking up performing tips, swallowing uppers and downers like they were going out of fashion and tripping for weeks on end.

He also developed a lifelong dislike of heroin after witnessing at first hand the ruthless greed of those who would sell rat poison on the streets, claiming it was smack, and the degradation of the junkies who craved not only the drug but the ritual. When his girlfriend Sue died from a heroin overdose at the age of 19, his hatred for it was absolute.

After the Hendrix experience, Lemmy played guitar for singer PP Arnold for a couple of weeks until she realised that the brilliant rhythm guitarist wasn't that good at lead work. In 1968, he recorded an album, *Escalator*, with Sam Gopal, most of which Lemmy wrote in a night under the influence of methedrine. The music, an almost punky mix of psychedelia, blues and Middle-Eastern percussion, didn't cut the mustard with the public, and Gopal's band split.

Lemmy spent the next year loafing around in squats and taking acid before bumping into future Hawkwind drummer Simon King in the Chelsea Drug Store, an eating, drinking and shopping complex which was popular with musicians despite its prices.

Simon was playing with a band called Opal Butterfly, and Lemmy joined them for a few months before they jacked it in. By now, he'd seen Hawkwind playing live, and he'd also met Dikmik socially through their mutual interest in speed.

According to Lemmy, Dikmik was feeling isolated in Hawkwind. They were all into pot and acid. What Dikmik wanted – and got – was a speed buddy in the band.

CHAPTER 6

Lift Off

DESPITE the striking differences in their backgrounds Hawkwind and Pink Floyd were working along parallel lines, pushing the boundaries of swirly, spacey, pulsing, psychedelic rock as creatively as they could. The Floyd were about to unleash *Meddle*, which contained the side-long 'Echoes'. Hawkwind pipped them at the post by a few weeks when they released their visual and narrative concept, *X In Search Of Space*, in October 1971.

Pink Floyd attained a number three chart placing in November with *Meddle*, but Hawkwind, peaking at number 18, believed they had the edge over their rivals in several ways.

They were still, first and foremost, a people's band, supporters of the underdog and leaders by example in the counterculture. They had street cred: they were out and about in Ladbroke Grove, even if some of them weren't living there any more, they were still quite happy to sleep on floors when necessary, and their open-door policy at the dressing room made them accessible to everyone.

The members of Hawkwind onstage also looked a great deal more unusual than the Floyd gang. They had a naked drummer and a naked dancer painted with flowers. They had a lunatic saxophonist and flautist who was now appearing in all kinds of outlandish costumes. They had the unpredictable Robert Calvert dropping in and out of proceedings, and the hip writer Moorcock. With the addition of Lemmy, they had rock'n'roll personified, and basslines that charged and drove. They had two mad professors forcing extraordinary sounds from the synth and the audio generator. They had fantastically painted equipment.

Dave Brock, a more subdued presence onstage, was the musical director, and a unique and highly regarded guitarist and vocalist.

In a nod back to his busking days, the acoustic guitar is still a significant factor on *X In Search Of Space*, and he contributes a short ballad, 'We Took The Wrong Step Years Ago'. The rest of the album is a riot of jamming, squawking sax, electronic swoops and whooshes and oscillations, vocal sound effects and echo, wah-wah and phasing-a-go-go.

The 16-minute opening track, 'You Shouldn't Do That', remains a Hawkwind favourite, as does 'Children Of The Sun' with its acoustic riffing, but the real show-stopper is the insistent 'Master Of The Universe' which is powered by one of the simplest but most memorable rock riffs ever.

"It was an interesting album," says Brock, modestly. "I suppose the cover was good, and we had the book. I haven't listened to it for years. I don't listen to our old albums at all."

Reviewing the LP, *Melody Maker* described the band as "the prophets in our own backyard", balanced certain instrumental short-comings against the "creative use of electronics", complimented the "very uplifting" music and "occasionally thought-provoking" lyrics and concluded that it was all "well worth perusal".

However, none of the music critics realised how influential *In Search Of Space* would become years later. Push, aka Chris Dawes, author and acknowledged expert on rave and dance culture in the Eighties and Nineties, says the electronic accomplishments of Dikmik and Del Dettmar were "really important". "I'm a huge fan," he says. "The first Hawkwind album was the first album I ever bought. I couldn't get my head round it at all. Now, many years on, it would be in my top five albums ever. But, actually, there were three or four Hawkwind albums around that time that were key in terms of the dance stuff.

"A lot of those tracks have a real groove to them. From *In Search Of Space*, 'You Shouldn't Do That' is so long and repetitive, so drum-led, so simple, and it lasts for 15 minutes – pretty much what a lot of the dance stuff was like. You could listen to tracks like that on E [Ecstasy] should you choose to, and you'd pick up on that kind of repetition. That's another important thing with the dance stuff."

Terry Ollis, the drummer responsible, acknowledges: "I do remember hearing certain music and thinking, 'Yeah, possibly *In Search Of Space* has been listened to. I've been an influence on some of these.' It's nice that people have picked up on it."

Push also points to the light-show, the dancer and the DJ as trademark Hawkwind features which would later become familiar, even essential, in the dance world.

Douglas Smith remarks: "Hawkwind have really never had their just appreciation. They were always called a poor man's Pink Floyd or something, but they're an important, seminal British act."

Intriguingly, *In Search Of Space* remains a thorn in the flesh of at least two former members of Hawkwind who claim that it contains tracks they initiated and for which they've never been credited, much less paid. The two tracks mentioned are officially credited to Brock/Turner.

Bassist Thomas Crimble had left the band and gone to Glastonbury before the recordings were made. He says: "When *In Search Of Space* came out, I discovered that some of the jams I'd been responsible for starting had been turned into songs with other people's names on for credits, namely 'You Shouldn't Do That' and a couple of others. The riff from 'You Shouldn't Do That' came from the Isle of Wight. I didn't get any money for that and quite rightly so, although it would have been nice to be credited. It's not a perfect world and Hawkwind are certainly not a perfect band."

Dave Anderson, replacing Thomas on bass, did appear on the album, and he claims to have co-written 'Master Of The Universe' with Nik Turner. At first, Anderson was philosophical about the missing credit, but he has become infuriated over the years having seen the track – a solid Hawkwind classic – turning up time and again on compilations and live albums.

"I wrote some of the musical parts when I was with Amon Duul," declares Dave. "I've got recordings of it from that time. And then Nik and I worked on it in this blue Transit tour bus. We always used to sit in the front two seats and write together. I've always liked writing with Nik. I can write riffs 'til the cows come home, but I don't like writing lyrics. Nik was the opposite.

"We were down at Glastonbury about three or four months before the actual festival, and I remember showing Dave Brock how to play it. He didn't used to play guitar with barre chords, and the only way you can play 'Master Of The Universe' is with barre chords.

"That's the most popular song I've ever written. It's ever so easy. I've never, ever had any credit for it. Dave Brock just claimed it was him that wrote it with Nik. After 30 years of being told I didn't write it, it's funny that they've never come up with anything like it.

"I was quite happy to let this whole thing lie; I've lived for 30 years without getting too worried about it. By the time I left the band, I was so glad to be out of it, I couldn't give a shit. I wasn't interested in the business side of it. But it would be nice to know that the truth can come out now, even if it means damaging the myth of Hawkwind. I don't care about that. I don't need it. I've never needed it. When I've seen what Dave has done to other, weaker members of the band over the years, I think it's absolutely outrageous. And the way that Nik's been treated by Dave is terrible, unbelievable . . ."

But that particular conflict comes later.

Dave Brock is familiar with the complaints of Crimble and Anderson, as well as other similar allegations down the years. "All these little whingeings," he sighs wearily, first addressing the subject of Thomas Crimble and 'You Shouldn't Do That'.

"I don't know . . . it's a big, long jam. I know it goes off at tangents. Where do you draw the line? Writing is quite a difficult thing to draw the line on. If you sit there and write a song and work out exactly how it goes, you can have the credits to it. Over the years, quite a few people like [future drummer] Simon King got credits for writing songs just because the drummer hasn't usually got any credits. It's sharing things out."

Of Dave Anderson and 'Master Of The Universe' he says: "I don't recollect Dave Anderson writing the chords of 'Master Of The Universe'. Well, I don't know but I don't think he did. If he did, then why has he never ever tried to get the credit? I think I wrote the chords and Nik did the words. I know they did 'Children Of The Sun' together, which is very similar.

"It's sour grapes. Well, hard luck. It's a bit late now, isn't it? I would say that if you write a number and it's credited wrongly, you would say so at the time. Logically, you'd speak to the band about it, you'd sort it out with the publisher or you'd tell the record label. You wouldn't wait for 30 years and then start moaning about it. I should say, 'Very strange.'

"On Bob Calvert's [1974] album, *Captain Lockheed And The Starfighters*, I wrote 'The Widowmaker' with Bob. In fact, 'The Right Stuff' I wrote with Bob too, but it's just down as Bob Calvert. Things like that don't bother me so much. Anyway, the evidence is all there if you listen to *Came Home*, a bootleg thing. You'll hear a lot of these riffs in early Hawkwind stuff that wasn't officially released."

Nik Turner says: "I found myself rather in the middle. People would ask me to put some words to a song or a riff. There was friction between Dave Brock and Dave Anderson going on. I ended up writing 'Children Of The Sun' with Dave Anderson, and 'Master Of The Universe' with Dave Brock, by which time he'd commandeered this riff from Dave Anderson. I put words to it."

Douglas Smith sees the situation through a manager's eyes. He remarks: "When they got fed up with Dave Anderson and he left, the publishing probably hadn't been registered, and when it was registered, they probably just said, 'Take Dave Anderson off. Fuck it. He's gone.' That's what it sounds like to me.

"As for what Thomas Crimble says, a lot of people do that, nick ideas and not credit them. That has been a constant accusation over the years, that they jam something and the day comes and Dave Brock has tidied it all up, so he says he wrote it. I think there have been complaints to publishers."

Dave Anderson further alleges: "I've never had a penny in royalties for anything I ever did with Hawkwind, never had anything off *In Search Of Space*, apart from publishing royalties for 'Children Of The Sun'. I never had any publishing from 'Adjust Me', which is credited to the band. And I've never had any record royalties. I know it's ridiculous, but I just couldn't be bothered chasing it up."

Douglas Smith explains that during his period of absence from the band, Hawkwind had entered into the recordings for *X In Search Of Space* without altering the names of the members who were recording it via the original Liberty agreement. Liberty had been taken over by United Artists by then. Hence, Anderson did not receive recording royalties.

"When I enquired about Dave Anderson's departure after returning from absence, I was informed that he had left under a cloud and hadn't signed anything with UA," says Smith. "From that point on, I never heard from Dave Anderson, although maybe band members did. I don't know."

As for 'Adjust Me', Douglas believes it may have been an old song that had been hanging around from before Anderson's era, although he's not sure: "Everyone's got a different story and as to the writing credit being Hawkwind – which Hawkwind?"

He continues: "Dave Anderson never contacted anybody about this. Then, about 12 or 13 years ago, I had a meeting with him because I was told that he had released all this old Hawkwind stuff. At that time, I was only aware of two albums that Dave and Nik told me they had licensed to Dave Anderson.

"At that meeting, Dave Anderson gave me accounts up to the last accounting period of the two albums, both unrecouped. I agreed with him that he would bring the accounts up to date of the records he'd released and, in return, I would try to sort out his situation with *X In Search Of Space*, the band members and EMI, which by then had taken over UA. I didn't get the accounts. Nor did I get another set of accounts since then on anything."

Interestingly, Dave Anderson is now embroiled in a new war of words with Dave Brock, with each accusing the other of making money immorally out of old Hawkwind recordings.

"I'm still really glad that we did *In Search Of Space*," concludes Anderson. "There are at least three songs on it that are not bad at all – 'Master Of The Universe', 'Children Of The Sun', and I love Dave's song, 'We Took The Wrong Step Years Ago'. It all still sounds pretty good.

"I'm very glad that I was on it. I never made any money out of it, I never got proper credits for what I did do on it, and I became part of the Hawkwind mythology, however incorrect it was. But I'm proud of everything I've been involved in."

Dave Anderson would briefly return to Hawkwind in 1984.

Lemmy was immediately thrust into the hurly-burly of a UK tour, promoting an album that he hadn't played on, and he loved it; the road was his natural habitat.

"They were great days," he remembers fondly. "We all used to kip in the van. It was a six-wheel Transit. We took the back row of seats out and we had mattresses in the back, although they weren't that comfortable. You needed two or three to get any kind of bounce."

He would later declare that he didn't really master his bass playing for another two years. But amateurish or not, Lemmy brought a new and urgent, metallic quality to Hawkwind, and they rose to his energy.

Says Nik Turner: "He was interesting, 'cos he used to play chords instead of notes. He'd play bass like he might play rhythm guitar. His contribution was quite simple and solid. The music wasn't very demanding or complex or technical, otherwise I wouldn't have been able to play it. I was trying to find my own way.

"Lemmy fitted quite well 'cos he was primitive. What I liked about early Hawkwind was someone like Terry Ollis who taught himself to play the drums and was completely primitive, very basic and gutsy."

Unfortunately, Terry Ollis was missing, presumed stoned, when *Melody Maker*'s Jim Simpson turned up to review a gig at Birmingham's Kinetic Playground towards the end of 1971. Pink Fairies' Twink had been hastily drafted in, although a string of other "hang-ups" turned the gig into a disaster. Nik Turner, having mislaid his alto sax, was forced to play his usual brassy flourishes on a flute, and a PA failure caused particular problems for Dave Brock.

Still, the band battled valiantly through a set that included 'Paranoia' from their first album, drew heavily on *In Search Of Space* and introduced three new songs, 'Earth Calling', 'Born To Go' and 'Silver Machine'.

Simpson, sympathetic to their problems, was fascinated by the "heavily electronic, repetitive and compelling" sound of Hawkwind but seemed unsettled by the "doomy, gloomy, space-age atmosphere", the painted equipment's fluorescence and the "disturbingly hypnotic strobe directed at the audience".

He decided: "The band's claim that it is specifically aimed at dope freaks certainly seems to be valid – it rather flashes past we Tizer drinkers."

Luckily, Jim wasn't one of the people targeted by a mischievous Dikmik who, in collusion with Lemmy, would allegedly identify vulnerable-looking audience members and use the audio-generator frequencies to try to induce a physical reaction – flopping about, falling over, vomiting, and worse.

The theory was that the highest and lowest sounds could not be heard by humans but were capable of wreaking havoc upon sensitive persons via the inner ear. Whether or not these sonic experiments actually worked, or were simply seen to work by the hallucinating Dikmik and Lemmy, or occurred coincidentally as a result of drugs or drink taken by the apparent victims, is open to debate.

However, asked how Dikmik singled out the likely person, Lemmy explains: "He'd probably see somebody starting to look a bit uncomfortable. Not very PC at all. We used to give people fits with the strobes. They made a regulation in 1971 that you couldn't have a strobe going faster – but it's the slow ones that give you the fits."

Lemmy and Dikmik were the best of friends, whizzing their way through the days and nights with Hawkwind. Now Lemmy was getting used to the personalities of his other bandmates. Some he'd met before, through the gig circuit and the Notting Hill community. He'd known Nik Turner prior to joining the band, inevitably, since they moved in overlapping circles.

Says Lemmy: "I was living around Ladbroke Grove, sleeping at people's houses. I did that for a couple of years. I had a little army knap-case, three pairs of socks, a pair of underpants, a cassette player, headphones, some tapes and my prescription. I got it from a fucking expensive doctor – 'The Night Tripper'. He prescribed me Dexedrine and Mandrax. Then they banned Mandrax and they gave you Tuinal [a much heavier downer].

"It was an all-right era. Hippies are really good a lot of the time. A lot of freaks used to be really inventive and creative in the way they dressed. The women were just dressed a bit more extravagantly. There was a lot of swirling, a lot of pirouetting happening, entrances with the shawls . . .

"It's trendy to look down on it now and go, 'How awful.' These people weren't there. What do they know? It was a lot more fun than dressing up as a businessman, that's for sure, or sticking pieces of metal through your lips and eyebrows. Now people are getting artificial lumps under the skin so you've got a pattern. Your dick becomes a vibrator. They can leave my dick alone, thank you. You can hear it screaming, 'I thought we were friends!' "

During this era, Hawkwind and Pink Fairies were still close allies. Says Lemmy: "We was all in Ladbroke Grove, and we played the same shows a lot. We did collaborative things as Pinkwind. We was all on dope. They was always chaos, them things. When you're stoned, jamming is great. When you're not, it's really fucking tedious. It's all right for the guitar player. But it was more fun with them than jamming nowadays where you get a couple of blues licks and the guitarist plays for four hours and says, 'Great, guys.' In those days, you could improvise on anything. I used to do bass solos."

Within Hawkwind itself, Lemmy would only ever have two real friends – Dikmik and Stacia – although he tolerated the other members and their idiosyncrasies since he was enjoying the music and was thrilled to be in a working band on the rise. "I used to get along half the time with Brock," says Lemmy. "He was an old-school nutter anyway. Nicky [Nik] and Bob [Calvert], as soon as they got together in the band they formed this quorum of two, which had 'culture' on its mind. [Adopts a toff voice] 'Oh, hello. How's the ambience today?' They both played flute. If you've got it – flaut it.

"Bob Calvert wore a little bracelet and a pair of earrings. He was always trying desperately to be a radical, and he was just a suburban young man – 'Awfully cool . . . très cool . . . ciao.' He was a phoney, I always thought. He would be all right and then he would lose his mind, swallowing Valiums, talking a mile a minute, hyperventilating.

"One of his ideas – he was going to go onstage with a typewriter round his neck on a strap and type things and throw them to the crowd. He was a kind of a talent, but he wasn't the great talent that people thought he was. I did that album with him, *Captain Lockheed And The Starfighters*, and he really didn't know what he was doing."

Lemmy had more time for Michael Moorcock. "He was always a very good writer, and he was working on his books all the time. He just made cameo appearances. He'd read his poems in a panic-stricken, high voice, much too high for anybody to understand. Fucking terribly nervous. He got a rock band together as well – Deep Fix."

Then there was Del Dettmar, Dikmik's electronics partner. "Del was just a little nutter," chuckles Lemmy. "He used to run around with his blanket half the time. It was an awful blanket as well – big squares, like you used to get in council houses. He wore it for two years, that I know. He never had it washed or nothing. The fucking thing was alive. You could stand it up and it could become a tepee, and tepees were very popular. But he played a good game of chess . . ."

Del says, politely, "I didn't have any great rapport with Lemmy."

Neither did Nik Turner. Although Lemmy and Nik were both genuinely involved in the alternative lifestyle, they were really worlds apart. Turner was interested in literature, the avant-garde and the idea of social responsibility. Lemmy was more earthy, a dyed-in-the-wool rock'n'roller. Nik had been brought up on Charlie Parker, John Coltrane, Stan Getz and Miles Davis, although they did find some common ground in Hendrix and, later, punk.

If Lemmy was cool, all black leather jacket, Nik Turner was going more and more over-the-top with his stage wear.

"I became more interested in theatricality when Stacia joined the band," explains Nik. "I had a good time with Stacia. We enjoyed ourselves. I had weird ideas about costumes and style, and I got help from people like Barney Bubbles. I thought that rather than just playing a musical instrument, why not make it more of a total performance, visual and theatrical as well as musical? Performance is about having a good time.

"I had this costume I designed myself in conjunction with Barney. I got this body stocking and I got him to paint these cosmic images on it of planets and stars and supernovae. It was inspired by this character from *Dr Strange* called Eternity, this all-powerful being that was beyond good and evil, a very nebulous character made out of the fabric of the universe."

Dave Brock recalls Nik experimenting with make-up around this time.

"He used to wear lipstick and eye make-up when he was with Philippe, his boyfriend," says Dave. "We had the blue Transit van then. In the front, there was a driver's seat and a double seat. Nik and Philippe were in the front kissing each other. Dikmik said, 'If you don't stop doing this, I'm going to smash your heads together.' Lemmy said the same. Lemmy threatened to clock Philippe once.

"Nik and Philippe were having their little scene together, but if it used to overlap into our area, it used to piss everybody off, fondling each other in front of everyone. We all had a freak-out over it. Calvert had a go at it. There's lots of things. Lemmy used to say, 'The geese are flying south tonight,' 'cos Nik couldn't play the saxophone properly. Bob called him 'an expensive clown'."

It's unlikely that Nik Turner would consider himself to have been a clown, but he was certainly accident-prone and at the centre of some unexpected theatrical displays. "We once played a Gay Liberation Ball at St Pancras Town Hall," remembers Nik. "I used to wear this shirt with bits of metal, sequins, on it. I had this saxophone with a pick-up, and it went through a 100-watt amplifier and a big speaker cabinet or two.

"I went up to the microphone to say, 'Good evening,' and I was blown over backwards by the full force of 10,000 watts of power coursing through my body. I don't think my amplifier had an earth on it. The microphone stuck to my hand, the saxophone stuck to my chest. All I could see was this huge big flash I was in the middle of. I could hear people in the distance – 'Turn the fucking power off!' I could hear my heartbeat going 'ba-doom' and getting slower every time.

"I had really bad burns all over my hands. I was rushed off to the hospital, and I came back to finish the show. I just thought it was a laugh. I didn't say, 'Oh, fucking hell, I nearly died.' It was more like, 'Oh, that was all right. That was good acid.' "

Nik, in fact, has escaped death several times, in different parts of the world. "I missed my footing at the top of the highest waterfall in Scandinavia," he reveals. "The side of the waterfall was 200 or 300 feet, and I nearly fell off the cliff.

"Another time I set myself alight in America doing some fire-blowing with lighter fluid and a gas lighter onstage. When the big fireball had gone down, the only thing that was left was my hand, which was still alight. Excruciating. I got it dressed, and I don't think I came back to finish that show."

Lemmy's favourite moment involves Nik Turner and the PA. "He skidded on some red wine he'd spilt himself, and it crashed on to him," grins Lemmy. "All you saw was the hand sticking out with the saxophone."

Michael Moorcock recounted another anecdote for an interviewer recently: "We did a free gig at Harlow," he said. "Nik and I were late getting onstage, Hawkwind had already started, and we both ran forward. But Nik had this frog mask on and he actually missed the edge and fell into the audience. It was great . . ."

Terry Ollis was still appearing naked at the drum kit.

"He used to go on wearing a pair of ladies' pants," says Lemmy. "They'd be gone after one song. A lot of people get their dicks out these days, but he was one of the ground-breakers, the pant-snappers. He was just blasted out of his head and he wanted nothing hanging on to him. He used to tap his todger with the stick – death by stick mastur-bation. But he fucked up so bad he couldn't play."

Towards the end of 1971, all of Hawkwind were concerned about Terry's drug consumption.

"He was a bit hooked on heroin or he was dabbling or something," says Nik. "I found myself giving him a talk about stopping taking drugs: if he wanted to stay in the band, he'd have to clean up his act."

It seems there followed a period of stability, but then, according to Turner, "He got bored or lost interest. A lot of people were taking Mandrax and he got a bit hung up with Mandrax, ultimately."

Terry Ollis still takes the view that what is a problem to one person might simply be a recreation to another. "I was into Mandies, although not at the start of Hawkwind, and never continuously," he says. "One Mandie was the equivalent of about four pints. It was a lot easier and cheaper to just do a Mandie, and it was fairly social. That was my social choice. At the same time, there were liberal amounts of acid and speed and all the rest of it, but no, it was not at all a problem, except from the point of view of accidentally ODing, which did happen to me. I did come a bit close a few times, and that was a bit scary. I don't think it really interfered with my playing. Maybe once or twice."

By now, drummer Simon King was on hand to step in, in case Terry was out of action for whatever reason. Sometimes they both played. Nik describes a London gig where Simon and Terry played together: "It might have been under the arches," says Nik, uncertainly. "What I do remember is this awful, horrible, monstrous machine grinding to a halt. One drummer was playing in time and the other was getting slower and slower."

The final straw came in Scotland at the turn of the new year. Dave Brock: "We were going up to Glasgow in our van. People who take downers and such suffer from constipation, so Terry had taken his Senokot and he asked to stop the van 'cos he wanted to go to the toilet. He didn't come back.

"Dikmik went off to look for him, and under one of the doors, he could see Terry's jumper and some of his stuff from his bag, a toilet roll, and Terry was on the toilet. We had to hang around and wait for him. He got back in the van and off we went, and he took these Mandrax."

Lemmy takes up the story: "We arrived in Glasgow, and he got out of the van at the lights, thinking we were at the gig, and just crashed to the ground."

"It was one of these gigs where he couldn't play his drums," adds Dave Brock. "It was terrible. He fell off his drum stool."

"Then he just sat with his sticks crossed on the snare drum for the whole show," says Lemmy. "We were playing with Nazareth that night, and they were at the side of the stage going, 'Funny drummer – when's he gonna start playing, like?' It was the last gig we did with him."

Terry Ollis doesn't remember it quite like that, believing that while the story is based on an element of truth, it has subsequently been exaggerated many times in the retelling. "I did make a really big boo-boo. We was woken, Lemmy and I, and I stupidly took a couple of Mandrax thinking we had a day off. Then I realised they were talking about a gig. As we drove off, I was hoping this would wear off by the time we had to play.

"I came to in the van and everyone had gone. I didn't know where the fuck I was. I could hardly walk properly. I did the gig really poorly, but I don't think I actually fell off the drum stool. There are numerous accounts of me falling off drum stools, but I think it might have only happened once or twice."

Terry says that by this time, he had decided to leave Hawkwind. "We seemed to be going down the business road – 'We can't do this benefit, and we can't play there. We've gotta do *this*.' It was coming from a management, Dave-ish direction. The fun started going out of it. More than half the band wasn't interested in the money aspect, but there were some people who were getting really money-minded.

"I remember rehearsing 'Silver Machine' – a much better version – down in Covent Garden. I remember thinking, 'This has a good chance of cracking it.' It was poppy-rocky, a bit rock-starry, businessy fucking bollocks. And we had such an underground reputation as well. I chose to opt out.

"I enjoyed the time I was in Hawkwind, it was great. You can't buy that. I was never in it for the money, and I have no regrets about leaving. Who knows what might have happened if I'd stayed on? I might've been dead. As it is, I have two smashing kids."

They are Sam (30) and Tom (11). Terry split with their mother, his wife Jane, after 26 years together and now lives a bachelor life in Ealing. After Hawkwind, he hung out with the Furry Freak Brothers for a while, and went on to play with a succession of people. First was Laughing Sam's Dice, the jamming group which reunited him with guitarist Mick Slattery, touring festivals and staging benefits.

He was then lured into a covers outfit, which was "absolutely crap", leaving after a year to form a five-piece blues band, Raw Dogs, with a bunch of friends.

Also in the Seventies, he played with Auntie & The Men From Uncle alongside The Pretty Things' Dick Taylor and an extraordinary frontman known in punk circles as Auntie Pus (a friend and protégé of The Damned's Captain Sensible).

Terry kept on playing drums, his passion, whenever and wherever he could. He joined a blues group based in Greenwich, which developed into the jump-jive band ID Crisis, and stretching further into the

Eighties, teamed up with a Scottish rock band called Downtown Fliers.

By now, he was a house husband, "just enjoying being a family man," and he went for long periods without playing music. "I used to have my missus out working," he says. "It was quite nice, a social, family time and lots of friends and all that."

Now a school caretaker, Terry Ollis is a fully paid-up member of Nik Turner's Space Ritual along with his son Sam and other early members of Hawkwind and is "loving every minute of it". He may be launching a new project with Mick Slattery in the near future.

Terry keeps his clothes on in public these days.

Simon King, his successor in Hawkwind, was born in Oxford in the early Fifties. His earliest musical memories are of jazz, listening to the great drummers that would influence his playing in later years. "I always really wanted to play jazz," he told one interviewer, "but I never really got around to it."

Rounding out his record collection with Chuck Berry, Elvis, The Velvet Underground, Hendrix and The Beatles, he began playing in local bands when he walked out of a painting and decorating apprenticeship after four months. Simon played around Oxford with a seven-piece soul outfit, which he hated, and soon afterwards moved to London in search of a decent group.

Countless unsuccessful auditions later, he put together a series of short-lived bands with friends. In the late Sixties, he began playing with Opal Butterfly and met Lemmy, who then joined the band.

Simon had stopped drumming after Opal Butterfly and was following in his father's footsteps, running a small antiques business, when Lemmy spotted him getting out of a taxi in London. With Terry Ollis becoming disillusioned in Hawkwind, and with the other members adamant that Terry was not functioning at full speed, Lemmy mentioned to King that a vacancy might be coming up and introduced him to the band. Simon was happy to become involved, while making it clear that, "There's nothing cosmic about me – all I'm interested in is racing and football."

His friendship with Lemmy would not survive Hawkwind. Eventually, they would find themselves in opposing "camps" in a vendetta which would culminate in Lemmy being sacked.

No such issues were on the horizon when Simon took his place on the drum stool and the band got ready for a gig at London's

Roundhouse on February 13, 1972. By now Douglas Smith had returned as manager, and he had liaised with promoter John Curd to present the Greasy Truckers Party with Hawkwind, Man, Brinsley Schwarz and Magic Michael. The show was being recorded for release as a live album – and it would prove to be Hawkwind's ticket to success.

"By this time, people were turning up in truckloads to see them live," says Douglas.

Lemmy and Dikmik made extensive preparations for the gig. They stayed up for the three days leading up to it taking drugs: Dexedrine, Mandrax, acid, mescaline, more Mandrax and more speed. At The Roundhouse, for good measure, they accepted cocaine, eight Black Bombers [uppers] each, and some more acid. "That wasn't particularly over the top," says Lemmy, a man with a cast-iron capacity for pharmaceuticals and blood so toxic that doctors say today it would kill a normal person.

Nevertheless, the road crew had to help Lemmy and Dikmik onstage, where the band delivered a blinding set. Lemmy describes it as one of the best live gigs they ever taped, with some inspired jamming between himself and Dave Brock.

The double album, *Greasy Truckers Party*, released two months later by United Artists, includes Hawkwind's 'Master Of The Universe' and 'Born To Go'.

Around the same time, they were invited to contribute to a limited-edition triple album called *Glastonbury Fayre* alongside Grateful Dead, David Bowie, Pete Townshend, Marc Bolan, Pink Fairies, Gong and other leading acts. The interesting thing about the album, released by Revelation in June 1972, is that very little of it was recorded at Glastonbury. Hawkwind supplied 'Welcome To The Future' and 'Silver Machine', recorded live at the Greasy Truckers Party and sung by an out-of-tune Robert Calvert.

"His vocal was fucking hopeless, but he never realised it," asserts Lemmy. "That's how mad he was. It sounded like Captain Kirk reading 'Blowing In The Wind'. Fucking atrocious."

Douglas Smith, mixing down the tracks with Dave Robinson,* agreed. However, 'Silver Machine' – Calvert's spoof on space-travel

---

* In 1976 Dave Robinson would become the co-founder of Stiff Records with Jake Riviera, manager of Elvis Costello.

songs – had all the potential for a great single. Eventually, it was decided to use the backing track from The Roundhouse with a new vocal on top.

"They tried everybody singing it except me," says Lemmy. "Then, as a last shot, Douglas said, 'Try Lemmy.' And I did it in one take or two."

Smith explains: "Lemmy had a high voice but it was just very much more powerful, he had a gruffness with it, so we decided to use his vocal."

"Lemmy was the one that could do it the best," Brock concedes.

But Robert Calvert knew nothing about it.

"Just at that particular moment, he'd had a 28-day section," remembers Douglas. "He was a manic depressive and he'd disappeared into hospital. Certainly, he wanted to kill me afterwards because I'd taken his voice off, but he did forgive me eventually."

"Robert was having a nervous breakdown at the time," expands Nik Turner. "He'd be great for a while and then he'd suddenly freak out at a tangent, foaming at the mouth and expressing all these ideas at break-neck pace. He got very excited, and it was difficult to keep up with.

"People that are manic-depressive go completely wild and stay up and don't go to sleep for a couple of weeks. They get burnt out and get to the point where they have a nervous breakdown, and that's the time they admit themselves to a loony bin. They see it not as a threat but a haven, safe and secure. They come out on medication, a bit like vegetables.

"I remember taking Robert to places like this a couple of times. At one place, we did spend quite a lot of time with the head doctor, who was quite sociable and also dictatorial in his way, which was good. I've taken other friends too. I got the impression after a while that I tended to attract manic-depressives and schizophrenics, or perhaps I'm attracted to *them*. Michael Moorcock and Barney Bubbles were manic-depressives too."

There has never been any disagreement over the authorship of 'Silver Machine'. Dave Brock composed the music and Bob Calvert wrote the words. However, when it was released it was credited to Calvert and Macmanus, the maiden name of Dave's wife Sylvia.

"It was a nom de plume," says Dave. "When Calvert and I signed our publishing deals, we signed 50 per cent of our earnings away for perpetuity. All we got was 25 per cent each, with United Artists [and now EMI] getting 50 per cent. What we got on the records themselves was one per cent, which is really nothing. That was the reason I did it as a nom de plume. I wanted to put pressure on them to give me an advance, and when I got paid an advance, I changed it back to my name."

'Silver Machine' streaked up the British singles chart, peaking at number three in July 1972, and several things happened.

Hawkwind, amazingly, received invitations to appear on such mainstream TV programmes as *Top Of The Pops* (they were represented by a live clip), and were frequently heard on BBC radio.

Thomas Crimble, their former bass player, was astonished when he first heard 'Silver Machine'.

"I was in Staines High Street," he recalls. "And it was coming out of a radio in the pet shop. Jimmy Young was playing it. He said, 'Here's a new song by a pop group called Hawkwind, and I think the singer sounds like Andy Fairweather-Low.' I thought, 'This is so incongruous. Why is Jimmy Young playing Hawkwind?' They were well known for being anti-establishment and taking drugs.

"I developed a theory then that this was one way you could control unruly blokes. Make them successful, they'll earn lots of money and blow it, and then they've got nothing to complain about so they'll stop rocking the boat. Maybe I'm reading something into it that wasn't there, but it works. Give these guys who are kicking against the system a lot of money – end of problem, isn't it?"

Nik Turner and Dave Brock had different concerns to deal with.

Turner was satisfied with his efforts to stay "down with the people", despite the glittering hit single: "Hawkwind really maintained its street cred when we became big with 'Silver Machine'. I kept up my connections with people, personally.

"We were invited to play a concert at the Oval cricket ground. Frank Zappa's Grand Wazoo and Jeff Beck were on, and they hadn't sold many tickets. Hawkwind were invited to play as special guests and we packed the place out. This was after 'Silver Machine' had been a hit. But we still had this credibility and this following as 'the people's band'."

Nik is quick to add: "Most people couldn't stand 'Silver Machine'. I've known this at gigs. 'Shall we play "Silver Machine"?' 'Nooooo.' "

Brock was delighted to have made a success of the group he'd founded, but he was anxious about losing the respect of their natural audience due to the influx of younger pop fans who'd loved the single. Almost a year later, he was still confiding his disquiet in interviews, telling one music journalist that the atmosphere at gigs was "crushing and uncomfortable" and to some extent driving away the band's "cool" followers. He complained, too, about his embarrassment at being asked for autographs and treated like "some great hero".

To Dave's relief, Hawkwind would soon recapture their constituency, and expand it.

One effect of 'Silver Machine' was that Lemmy became a national hero, widely perceived to be the frontman and lead vocalist of Hawkwind. As such, he was pictured alone on the front cover of *NME*.

"They hated it," says Lemmy of his bandmates. "New boy, new speedfreak, sings song in two takes. Three weeks later, the front of the *NME* – and it was just me. Gnashing of teeth. 'The speedfreak upstart – how dare he? Why isn't it me?' I never got offered to sing another single."

Not that Lemmy was upset. "I was all for it! I loved being on the front of the *NME* on my own. Are you kidding?"

Dave Brock doesn't remember any rampant jealousy, and neither does Nik Turner. He says, "It might be true if Lemmy says that, but I don't recollect it as being, 'I want to be doing that, what's he doing it for?' I thought, 'That's the way it goes.' Perhaps call me naïve. I didn't really see a lot of the undercurrents. I was still just doing my thing and thinking, 'Isn't it groovy?' I was having a nice time and thinking everybody else was."

Douglas Smith, on the subject of envy towards Lemmy, ventures: "The thing is . . . there probably was a little bit of that."

But the single most important result of 'Silver Machine' was the cash it generated. Hawkwind invested all of it into the grand production of their dreams, and it paid off handsomely. The Space Ritual was born.

CHAPTER 7

Fear And Loathing In East Finchley

IT was a year of big shows for Hawkwind, and now they were being paid for them.

One of the first was the Bickershaw Festival, taking place outside Wigan, Lancashire, between May 5 & 7, 1972. Hawkwind appeared on the opening night with Dr John and Wishbone Ash. The following nights starred Captain Beefheart, The Kinks, Family and Cheech & Chong (May 6) and Grateful Dead, New Riders Of The Purple Sage and Country Joe (7).

It was one of the last officially approved all-night festivals, if not *the* last, with MPs already scrabbling to introduce legislation that would curtail late music outdoors.

Lemmy was especially disappointed by the event: "I was really excited to see the Grateful Dead. I thought their records were boring, but I was hoping that live they would be different. I stood there for an hour, and they were fucking tedious and noodling. I thought, 'These guys are fucking garbage.' We played a few festivals with Jefferson Airplane, and they were 10 cuts above the Grateful Dead."

Nik Turner was more appreciative. He'd turned up wearing a motorcycle jacket that Barney Bubbles had customised with a painting of Thor coming out of a flying saucer and the words Thunder Rider, Bubbles' nickname for Turner, emblazoned across it. Nik was happy to meet the Dead's Jerry Garcia and pass on Barney's regards.

In June, Hawkwind appeared at Glastonbury, which was still a free festival. Only weeks later, they finally realised what a massive draw they were when they headlined London's Rainbow Theatre on August 13, 1972, accompanied as usual by their DJ and presenter Andy Dunkley and supported by the Welsh band Man, themselves inveterate devotees of the 20-minute jam.

Not only was the concert sold out, but up to 2,000 people turned up without tickets and, of those, hundreds stormed a side door to gain free entry. They must've considered themselves lucky, witnessing what *Melody Maker* decided was "probably the best performance Hawkwind have ever put on".

Noting that Calvert had returned to the group with a short haircut and shades, *MM* reviewer Andrew Means, who would become an important supporter of the group, waxed lyrical about his experience: "Hawkwind played what they always play, but for once the full extent of their wailing guitars and spewing synthesiser was actually heard. For one rare performance lights sliced through hard shapes, walls melted, and a seven-tier sound wrecked all sense of balance. Like falling asleep on a night drive, one regained awareness of self after split seconds of suspension."

Pictorially, he informed the readership that, "Stacia heaved from side to side like a ship's figurehead in a moderate gale . . ."

Sounds' Mike Reeves was equally awestruck, although his appreciation of Stacia was slightly earthier: "There they were – the biggest boobs in the business!"

Declaring that "this was one of their greatest sets" and that Hawkwind "had everything", Reeves enthused: "Unlike Floyd, who reflect the mysteries of space, Hawkwind seem to draw straight from the powerful life forces flowing through the universe. With Del Dettmar and Dikmik supplying the electronic thrust, the Rainbow seemed to power on into space."

This is something close to the reaction that the band had been aiming for, and Lemmy is keen to emphasise their importance at this moment.

He says: "A lot of stupid shit has been written about Hawkwind by people who never heard them. To understand Hawkwind, you had to be in London in 1972 in the freak scene. We were fucking huge."

Contrary to the band's avowed mission to create a psychedelic experience through music and not substances, Lemmy insists: "The drug culture was absolutely crucial to Hawkwind. They could have existed without it, but they wouldn't have been the same band. We hadn't got on to the shit drugs. We had the good quality stuff. You could get 20 Bombers for a quid. I used to take meth – the liquid stuff in the ampoules. Ticket-to-the-moon time. I used to get three of them for a shilling and ninepence [less than 10p today]. That's what the slogan 'Speed kills' was coined in connection with – methedrine. It certainly wasn't pills or powder.

"Speed didn't change anything in me. It just made me want to stay up longer and go onstage when I might not have wanted to, so it was a utility drug. Acid changed me completely, like it was a new religion or a sacrament. When you think how straight we'd been and then *that* showed up. The first trip I took, I was out for 18 hours.

"At festivals, we used to spike everybody's food and drink with acid. We'd drop a little, and we'd throw it on people. If it got on your skin, you'd trip out. A bit irresponsible, you could've said. On the other hand, there was a lot of free acid. I used to go to Middle Earth before I joined Hawkwind, and a chick used to stand at the top of the stairs. She'd give you a tab of acid free as you went in. Nice times, though. They've been slowly tightening up the harness ever since."

Hawkwind were at Rockfield Studios in Wales, recording their next album, when they took a break for Frank Zappa's Grand Wazoo gig at the Kennington Oval, home of Surrey County Cricket Club, in London on September 16. It was a big crowd, albeit probably less than half the 35,000 that The Who attracted to the same venue the previous year.

News of their appearance created a stir in the music press, with *NME* and *Disc* taking the opportunity to catch up with the band. It was announced that Hawkwind would be closing the concert, in line with Nik Turner's understanding that they had really been brought in to save it. However, promoters the Foulk Brothers diplomatically explained that Hawkwind needed darkness for their lights and visuals while Zappa wanted to play earlier anyway. Tickets were £2.

By the time Hawkwind took the stage, the show was running more than two hours late. In customary fashion, they played continuously, without a break between songs, and after 35 minutes, they had completed 'Born To Go', 'Master Of The Universe' and 'Seven By Seven' when they were informed that the power would be cut in four minutes' time. The audience greeted this announcement with hisses and boos, but Hawkwind were forced to wrap things up quickly with 'Silver Machine'.

As they did, officials dashed to the stage, ordering Stacia to cover her nakedness.

Sounds' Steve Peacock, a Zappa fan, stayed on, professionally, for the closing moments of the concert, even though Hawkwind's "policy of total assault" had previously left him cold as often as it lit his fire. He admitted that, this time, "it had its effect".

Not a bad result, in the circumstances.

Things were getting a little crowded in the Clapham flat that Del Dettmar shared with Nik Turner. Dikmik was in the habit of crashing there, and so was Dave Brock when he was staying in town.

Hawkwind decided that they wanted a communal home, like Brinsley Schwarz's, with a bedroom each and all the equipment set up in the living room. "What we got was this stupid little house with a box room for each person," says Del Dettmar.

The stupid little house, a rented property in Long Lane, East Finchley, was home to Nik Turner, Del Dettmar, Lemmy, Dikmik, Stacia and, from time to time, Bob Calvert. There was no bed for Dave Brock, since he had a home in Devon, but it was such a convenient crash pad that he soon improvised a sleeping space of sorts. He was used to dossing down in people's flats, often waiting up until four or five in the morning to grab the settee, or sleeping on the floor in studios where he could make use of the toilets and the kettle.

"It wasn't a luxurious lifestyle, that's for sure," he grins. "When the band rented the house in Finchley, I used to sleep in the corner of the kitchen. I had this space under a sheet which was propped up by a ladder, for a bit of privacy. The rest of them all had rooms."

Del Dettmar was the resident handyman. "People would forget their keys and have to break in," he says. "I was continuously fixing windows."

It was an eventful household.

"The time I ate the 50 Blues, that was pretty fucking interesting," suggests Lemmy. He'd been travelling back to the house in East Finchley with Hawkwind's driver, John The Bog, at the wheel. They'd just shared out about 100 Blues – pills that combined speed with downers – when they were stopped by the police. This had become a regular occurrence, given the band's high profile in the counterculture. Both Lemmy and John The Bog quickly ate the evidence, foaming at the mouth while they somehow managed to fob off their inquisitors.

Dave Brock and a frantic Stacia saw Lemmy stumble in through the front door. "He'd overdone it," says Dave. "He was all over the place, falling over. We had to tie him to the bed, and then we phoned a mate of his and said, 'We're sure he's going to die. Should we take him to the hospital to get his stomach pumped?' His friend said, 'No, no, he'll get over it.' We were afraid he might try to get up again, or vomit and choke on it, so we left him tied to his bed, and the next morning he was right as rain."

Lemmy remembers hearing the exclamation, "Aaaagh! He's dead!" He continues: "I was thinking, 'These fuckers are noisy. Can't they see I'm trying to get some sleep?' I was lying there with my eyes half-open, but I used to sleep like that all the time."

"The problem with Lemmy," reflects Nik Turner, "was that he'd take speed and stay up for a week, and he always had to be *right about everything*. Then he'd take some downers and go to sleep for a week. You end up living on a different timescale. There's a problem of communication, really. We don't understand what he's into and he doesn't understand what we're into.

"I'd known Dikmik before. I knew he was into speed and we got on very well. I lived at his place, slept on his floor quite a lot, so I didn't have the same kind of problems with him. Lemmy, by the nature of the drugs he was doing – and I'm not saying this in a derogatory sense – was on the make. He probably saw it [Hawkwind] as, 'Wow! This is great! Take more speed, go further out,' and I didn't see it in those terms."

Lemmy was happy enough in East Finchley; he was used to crowded houses.

"I'd lived in a lot of squats by then. I lived in one squat where there was two fridges with padlocks on them. It sort of defeated the idea – 'I don't want you to eat my sardines.' Not very communal.

"'Cos a lot of upper-middle-class people were getting into squatting by then, and they didn't have the mental equipment to do it properly. They'd go home to daddy and the expense account. They always became the leading lights of the scene, which was unfortunate. They were always the ones with the biggest crash pads, the best shawls and the decorated sandals.

"East Finchley was all right. Stacia was living there. She was fun. We used to share a room on tour. She'd get these little boys that had been at the gig and bring them back, and I'd go out discreetly for half an hour. She was a spectacular girl. She had a 52-inch chest, she was six feet two in her shoes, and she would wear spike heels."

Stacia had once declared that, "I regard them [Hawkwind] as brothers and they treat me like a sister." However, she made an exception for the well-liked Del Dettmar, causing much hilarity in the house at Long Lane because of the difference in their heights. "It's true," says Del. "We went off to bed together. She was a big girl from where I stand. I'm five feet three and shrinking. I think I scaled the left breast . . .

"It's a vague bit of my life. Somewhere, we had a love affair. We weren't together that long. It was just one of those things. It was the age of free love. We made free love and then we went off and made free love with other people."

Among Stacia's ardent admirers was the esteemed *Melody Maker* photographer Barrie Wentzell who had a flat on Carlisle Street, conveniently placed for Soho's nightspots. Another of her conquests was Arthur Kane, bassist with The New York Dolls.

Dave Brock: "She had all these girlfriends, and she had scenes with different people, romances with famous rock stars. I've discovered photographs of her with Alice Cooper. She had a fantastic time. She was an unusual woman, actually. Quite a nice, easy-going character too. I got on wonderfully well with her."

Perhaps unsurprisingly, the landlady did not get on so wonderfully well with her tenants. She complained endlessly until, eventually, the great communal experience was over.

Nik Turner moved to a flat in Paddington with his girlfriend Corinthia. Through her family connections, they were able to find a home in Devon for Barney Bubbles and his partner Jiana. Six months later, Nik and Corinthia split. She went on to romance Mick Jagger, also adorning the cover of Robert Palmer's *Pressure Drop* and appearing in The Beatles' spoof film *The Rutles*. Nik moved to a flat in Gloucester Road where he would have some less glamorous experiences.

Later, he would spend a summer in a caravan in East Anglia with some friends of Jonathan Smeeton (Liquid Len) before returning to Margate in 1973 after his father's death. His mother became ill and died shortly afterwards, and Nik stayed on in his inherited family home.

Hawkwind kept up their hectic gigging schedule throughout 1972, incorporating three short European trips in May, September and October. They booked dates in and around the Rockfield recording sessions for their next album, *Doremi Fasol Latido*, including two which would have a monumental impact on their career. One was at Liverpool Stadium on September 30.

Dave Brock says: "I'll always remember that. When we drove down, there was a queue of people about a quarter of a mile long, and we were like conquering heroes arriving into the amphitheatre. People were cheering and applauding us and we were all sitting there waving like royalty, turning up at this boxing stadium with its rickety old stage."

The Stadium gig, and one at the London Brixton Sundown, were recorded for a live album, *Space Ritual Alive*, which would brilliantly realise everything Hawkwind had been working towards.

The self-produced *Doremi* came first. It was released by UA in November, halfway through the band's winter tour, climbing to its highest chart position of 14 in the week before Christmas.

The reviews were encouraging. *Melody Maker*'s Andrew Means was still intoxicated by Hawkwind, praising their ambiguity, their use of contrast and their "varied spacescape" while noticing, "The group's musicianship is catching up with its visionary thought."

Sounds also saw progress, reporting that the band were more ably capturing their live sound on record. Pausing to congratulate Barney Bubbles' "magnificent" cover art, the review stated that while the music was "technically brilliant at creating an impression of a continuous rush", it was "thicker, fuller, more convincing than ever before."

However, both reviewers complained that they couldn't make out many of the words (which were influenced by Michael Moorcock's book *The Black Corridor*).

The album opens with Nik Turner's 11-minute epic 'Brainstorm', which would become a favourite along with Dave Brock's shorter 'Space Is Deep', 'Lord Of Light' and 'Time We Left This World Today'. It also includes Lemmy's first contribution, the ominous 'The Watcher', and Del Dettmar's 50-second 'One Change'.

Nik Turner is still fond of *Doremi*, describing it as "quite creative". Dave Brock and Lemmy are not so sure. "I can't remember too much about it," says Brock. "It got near the Top 10, so it must have been all right."

"It was my baptism into the band," says Lemmy. "Fair play, they gave me quite a bit of input. I played guitar as well as bass on some tracks ['The Watcher' and 'Space Is Deep'], but not that well 'cos I was a really mediocre fucking guitar player.

"It was very much cobbled together in the studio. Dave had his ideas for it and, of course, he wouldn't tell anyone else what they were 'til we got there. We were rehearsing and recording at the same time. Dave or Bob or Nik would have the basics of the song, then we'd jam. I always figured it was badly produced. 'The Watcher' was really fucking thin. Onstage, we did the songs much better.

"There were a lot of fuck-ups on the album, unfortunately. On 'Space Is Deep', the bass and drums come in half a beat late. I didn't protest at the time because I was the new guy – 'Shut up, new guy!' I wasn't always this confident."

Huw Lloyd-Langton, recovered from his breakdown, was still avoiding Hawkwind. To listen to them, even to think about them, brought back terrifying memories of acid trips. Huw wasn't in search of space; he was in search of God.

He and Marion had gone to the south of France with one-way tickets paid for by her father. Laden with bags of brown rice and muesli, Marion's old Spanish guitar that had no case, a box of oil paints and a pad of paper, they arrived at their accommodation, a swish apartment in Cannes, intending to stay for a month.

The money, muesli and brown rice ran out after two weeks, as did the tolerance of the *concierge*, and Huw was perhaps a little frustrated to discover that people were not queueing up to own his "silly", crinkly paintings. He hadn't realised that artists using oils should work on canvas, and the few francs a day that buyers gave to Marion, seemingly out of pity, weren't enough to keep them in bread and cheese.

Flat broke, they hitch-hiked home, and still they remained devoted companions, not lovers. To Marion's disappointment, they had still not re-ignited their early romance. She sighs: "When we got back to England, I hoped he would ask me out again, but he didn't." They would go through a great deal more together before the old spark flickered back into flame.

Marion came across a former Salvation Army brigadier who had been shunned by the organisation for being too radical. The two women made an instant connection, they chatted about the hand-of-God experience in the Mini, and the brigadier suggested a meeting with Huw.

"She thought what had happened to us was a miracle," relates Marion. "She said, 'That's wonderful.' We sat down with her and started talking about Jesus and everything slotted into place."

"She was like a light bulb," agrees Huw. "She was so bright. She told us about the old Christian way. It was basically aimed at anyone on the planet, as opposed to people who sit about in monasteries and meditate. I had been reading a lot of books, but the old way is the one that made sense."

Huw and Marion were invited to a gathering.

Says Huw: "A whole bunch of Christians travel the world talking to people at meeting halls. They explain the connection between the Jews and the Christians and the Muslims – it's old Jesus Christ and his father."

"We were listening to an hour lecture," adds Marion. "The leader said, 'If any of you would like to stand up and accept this faith . . .'"

"We both automatically stood up," says Huw. "It just made so much plain, simple sense of everything. Hence, we took to that particular faith."

They still follow it.

Meanwhile, Huw was returning to the music business, joining a band called Salt at the invitation of an old drummer friend, John Lingwood. They had originally tried to headhunt Huw while he was still in Hawkwind, before he "went all over the shop".

Marion now abandoned all hope of a real relationship.

She says: "Huw was so well that he didn't want to be tied down. Having been through all that experience, he wanted a bit of freedom. I decided to go back and live with my parents in Worthing. It had been a traumatic couple of years. I'd had enough of it. I didn't know what to do with my life.

"Then Huw went to Germany with Salt and I decided that was it. I wasn't going to answer any letters. I thought I'd close that chapter in my life and start again. I got a job in Worthing working for a carpet wholesaler as a secretary.

"One day my boss said, 'You've had a call from Germany. He's going to ring back.' And it was Huw. He said, 'Why haven't you replied to my letters?'"

"I was with Salt in Munich," Huw remembers. "Eventually we got back together and Marion came and stayed at my parents' gaff in Harlesden."

Marion: "I thought, 'Maybe he *does* want me.'"

Some time later, the couple were dealt one of their many strokes of bad luck. Marion contracted jaundice.

"I asked her to marry me because I thought she was on her death-bed," says Huw. "She was, by all outward signs, dying. And a couple of weeks later, she'd fully recovered and had organised the wedding."

Huw and Marion were married on October 23, 1972, in a church which has since closed. John Lingwood lent them money to pay for the ceremony. The brigadier footed the bill for Huw's suit. And guests arriving for the reception at an Indian restaurant paid for their own meals.

Among them was former Hawkwind bassist Dave Anderson who had by now formed a band called Amon Din with Huw and John Lingwood. They had a full datesheet, and the Lloyd-Langtons organised a honeymoon in Scotland so that Huw could fulfil the gigs. Eventually, the group would fall out.

"Mainly over money," says Huw.

Dave retreated to the Foel Recording Studios he'd bought in north Wales to become an engineer and producer, which he still is.

It was undoubtedly intended as a promotion for *Doremi Fasol Latido*, but Hawkwind's November/December UK tour was a thing of much greater significance.

This was where the Space Ritual came together, the long-planned "opera" that for the first time achieved a seamless, imaginative and inspiring blend of psychedelia, science fiction, science fantasy, cosmic travel, inner contemplation, social comment, theatre, dance, mime, performance, poetry, singing, lights, effects, visual surprises and a vigorous and colourful musical triumph.

For many people, this was Hawkwind at the very height of their creativity.

The Space Ritual was Robert Calvert's idea, and the band had been talking about it to anyone who would listen for at least a year. Calvert himself, preferring Michael Moorcock's term "speculative fiction" to "science fiction", had told *Melody Maker* in November 1971: "The basic idea is that a team of starfarers are in a coma, a state of suspended animation, and the opera is a presentation of the dreams that they're having in Deep Space. It's a mythological approach to what's happening today.

"It's not predicting what's going to happen. It's the mythology of the space age, in the way that rocket ships and interplanetary travel are a parallel with the heroic voyages of man in earlier times."

Calvert continued: "Even when the band started, it had a very spacey sound. Now the image has become more concrete, although a lot is still implied rather than explicit. Perhaps there's a bit of hypnosis in it too, with the electronic sound and the flashing lights."

"It's something to do with drones as well," elaborated Dave Brock in the same interview. "You know that each note has its own colour, and it's just a matter of finding the right combinations. The opera is intended to reach the audience on a very deep level, and we'll be using techniques that haven't been used in this way before."

Nik Turner today emphasises Barney Bubbles' "wonderful creativity" in the stage design and presentation of the tour. Barney had always been about more than mere design. His influence extended into costumes, lights, effects, film, choreography, concepts and even titles.

"It was very mixed media," says Nik. "It was like a rock opera but a bit nebulous as well. It was evocative of many things. It's actually about somebody going further than the moon and achieving nirvana or total enlightenment. It was really weird and influential. We were reading books like *The Psychedelic Experience Manual* by Timothy Leary and *The Doors Of Perception* by Aldous Huxley, and it was all coming out in what we were doing."

There was something else too: *Pythagorean Music Of The Spheres* by William Wilde Zeitler, a collection of 12 pieces of music inspired by the ancient Pythagorean conception of the universe.

"The positioning of the planets in the solar system is similar to the notes in the Western scale," explains Nik. "And the space between them is similar to the space between the notes. So the planets are the notes in an octave. Between the third and fourth notes, and the seventh and eighth, you have only a semi-tone. Hendrix had that song called 'Third Stone From The Sun'. The Earth, that was the third note.

"The Space Ritual, when it was originally mooted by Robert, was based to a large degree on the theories of the *Pythagorean Music Of The Spheres*."

For this reason, Barney Bubbles had worked out where every member of the band should stand onstage to be in astrological alignment. It didn't matter that the audience might not pick up on this. The important thing was that thought rather than mere style underpinned the production.

"I wish I'd been in the audience," says Turner. "It was a schoolboy's dream. The whole thing was fantasy. It wasn't only science fiction. It was metaphysical as well, verging on sword and sorcery – madness!"

Dave Brock explained at the time: "We play extra-terrestrial music in which we try to get the audience involved. Participation creates energy and through the energy it is possible to make experiments. We are working on all kinds of sound developments, because sound has different points which can either make you feel good or bad. It's a matter of getting them sorted out."

"Barney Bubbles had a theory that at a certain volume, the band could generate enough energy for the stage to lift off and take them into space," remarks Mike Heath, his exhibitor.

This was one feat that Hawkwind, disappointingly, couldn't manage to pull off.

They had invested heavily in the tour. They'd bought their own PA and transport for themselves and their gear, and they'd spent a lot on the visuals.

"It was probably the first time we'd been able to do what we wanted on that grand scale, with Jonathan Smeeton and all those lights," says Dave.

Smeeton had turned Liquid Len & The Lensmen into the leading British light-show, with the help of Molten Mick (Mike Hart) and Astral Alan (Alan Day). Smeeton had provided two miles of fairy lighting at the 1970 Bath Festival, and had worked with Traffic, Free, Mott The Hoople, Black Sabbath and Frank Zappa's Grand Wazoo.

However, he told *Disc* in January 1973 that the Space Ritual represented everything he had wanted to achieve for the past two years: "We've really reached a point, from working with Hawkwind, where we can do something serious to expand the whole scope of lighting . . ."

To this end, the Lensmen travelled with more than a ton of equipment, designed and built by themselves and John Perrin, who also constructed sound systems, and employed Britain's first lighting roadie, John Lee.

Among the innovations were front projections (projecting images on to the front of the stage), a low-wattage laser which could project 3D images on to a flat surface, and a mirror ball controlled remotely by a 61-key colour organ, creating what Astral Alan described as "a direct relationship between colours, light and shade, and sound".

Disc concluded: "Aside from Joe's Lights' collaboration with the

Grateful Dead, this is the first time that light and sound have fused as a whole, each a part of the other."

The gigs were starting to take on the feeling of primeval gatherings. Encouraging the all-inclusive atmosphere, Hawkwind provided each member of the audience with a joss stick and a printed sheet titled *An Extract From The Voyage Of Doremi Fasol Latido*. It contained a fantasy story about Hawkwind on a space trip interspersed with the lyrics from the show.

Two more dancers had joined the entourage – the petite blonde Miss Renee, who had previously danced for Quicksilver Messenger Service and Jefferson Airplane, and a male mime artist, Tony Crerar. Adding to the spectacle was Nik Turner's extraordinary frog suit.

"It metamorphosed from an archbishop into a frog," says Nik. "Quite a quantum leap. The mitre turned into a frog's head."

Robert Calvert came out on the road too, his recitations an integral part of the Space Ritual.

The press reviews were overwhelmingly positive, recognising the power and glory of this musical and theatrical amalgamation. All round, it was a remarkably satisfying period for Hawkwind.

"We were playing bigger venues, there were more people, we were earning more money and everything just got better," says Dave Brock. "Things were jolly fine. But it does affect people's egos, and there were problematic things. Bob was doing interviews where he never said 'we', he always said 'I', and he liked to have dramatic pictures taken, which used to piss everybody off. Nik Turner had an inflated ego as well, walking around with his entourage. The funny thing with Nik, he was quite a good friend of mine, but he used to love adulation.

"Instead of having one captain of the ship, there was about four captains – Lemmy, Bob, Nik and me. It was an experience, really.

"It was difficult for Stacia 'cos she was travelling in the van with a lot of blokes. She'd be saying, 'Stop the van 'cos I want to go for a wee wee,' and we'd be saying, 'Oh, for fuck's sake – carry on.' She did find it quite hard sometimes putting up with everybody. Then Renee came along, and Renee and Stacia used to argue. They had terrible scenes."

However, the real tension was building up between Dave Brock and Nik Turner.

"So many times we'd told him not to play his saxophone when we were singing," grumbles Dave. "He ignored us. We used to have huge rows after it – 'You've done it again! You played your sax again, out of tune!' When you listen to the *Space Ritual* album, you can just hear the saxophone very faintly in the background. Vic Maile [producer] took him out 'cos it was out of tune.

"Half the time he wouldn't listen to what we were doing. One of the gigs, he went honking on his saxophone and he just didn't stop. I was so pissed off. I had a can of beer and I threw it across the stage and it hit him on the head. It knocked him sideways a little bit."

According to Brock, Nik didn't complain. "I don't think he would have said, 'That was a naughty thing to do, Dave.' I'm quite a volatile character. I might clock them one."

Nik Turner declares that he has more respect for other musicians than deliberately to play over their solos or vocals, and he had already admitted to *Sounds* that, "I don't have any illusions about my technical ability."

He added: "I tend to use it [the saxophone] as an electronic medium rather than an instrument. It's the overall feel rather than the individual parts of the music that we're interested in."

More recently, Nik talked to *Classic Rock* about *Space Ritual Alive*, the album, stating that, "I don't like my playing very much, although that doesn't mean it isn't a very powerful album, not only the music, but the cover, the graphics."

The double album was released by United Artists in May 1973, and Barney Bubbles did indeed excel himself with the design of the fold-out sleeve. As usual, it encapsulated everything that was alluring, mysterious and dramatic about Hawkwind. Nik Turner has never thrown out the trousers he's pictured in, complete with rising flames.

It was their highest-charting album ever, reaching number nine in the British chart in June. Recorded live at Liverpool Stadium and Brixton Sundown, it roved from the heads-down rock power of 'Orgone Accumulator' to Calvert's recitals of Michael Moorcock's 'Sonic Attack', set to a chant, and an excerpt from the opening of the Moorcock novel *The Black Corridor*, which Nik Turner remarked "says all there is to say about space".

A mighty, multi-faceted body of work that never once loses context or continuity, a bona fide masterpiece of heavy-duty space rock, the album was accorded some rapturous reviews.

Writer Nick Kent, who had been part of the Ladbroke Grove under-ground scene, declared in *NME*: "On this album, Hawkwind have achieved the feeling of space, of creating a total environment which has been their vision from the beginning. They're still Britain's best psychedelic band and a great combo to take cerebral depressants to."

And he advised: "After *Space Ritual*, everything else is just horse tranquilliser."

Melody Maker said it was "this strangest of strange electronic journeys".

"That was *the* Hawkwind album," whoops Lemmy. "Vic Maile captured it completely. Fucking brilliant. The artwork was so cool too. Catch a record company doing that now . . . Barney Bubbles was fucking brilliant."

"That's how I got my gold disc," grins Dave Brock. "The one and only. It was jolly exciting."

CHAPTER 8

Angels And Demons

DAVE BROCK thought Nik Turner had an inflated ego. Nik Turner thought everything was fine and dandy.

"My inflated ego . . ." muses Nik today. "Anybody that doesn't want to do things Dave's way, that's probably how he sees it. How can you tell if you've got an inflated ego? I wouldn't say I have or I haven't. If that's how Dave saw me, then using what I call the 'Dave Brock formula' – because he says it of me, it's probably more true of himself.

"I sang most of the songs and I did a lot of the interviews, but only 'cos most of the band didn't want to, so I was seen as the front image of the band. I was always pushed into a leadership role by people who were inarticulate or didn't have anything to say or weren't bothered. I'd do several interviews in a week with different papers and tend to say the same thing. I'd think, 'I'm really boring.'

"My whole motivation and stimulation within the context of the band was spreading peace and love. I got into it with Barney; we were like brothers and we were just into that. We were the keepers of the flame. I've also been quoted as being the conscience of Hawkwind in other situations."

Turner had more in common with the band's so-called creative team, the literary and artistic characters he had been attracted to in his early days in London, than he did with the other musicians. "I approached Hawkwind as a lifestyle and as an ideal," he reflects. "It wasn't just a musical thing. It was a whole concept, it was about raising people's consciousness, and that was helped by people like Barney Bubbles and Robert Calvert, Michael Moorcock and Jonathan Smeeton. It was a communal thing, and it ended up being a melting pot rather than any one person's idea. No one can go round saying, 'I take the credit for the success of Hawkwind.' We were successful because of what we represented to people, and because of the disparity between us.

"Robert Calvert was very literary. He turned me on to [playwright] Samuel Beckett and a lot of science-fiction writers. Barney Bubbles had really interesting ideologies, metaphysical things. I've just written a song about Barney, about the ideas he gave me – *The Secret Teachings Of All Ages*, which is a book about magic by somebody called Manly Palmer Hall. The Seal of Solomon . . . Egyptology. I became interested in Egypt, and I later recorded in the King's Chamber in the Great Pyramid.

"Visually Barney, presenting the Space Ritual, had a different angle from what Bob had, and what Michael Moorcock had, and I was very stimulated. We were surrounded by these sorts of things going on."

Other cracks were beginning to appear within Hawkwind. Del Dettmar was friends with everyone, he worked especially well with Dave Brock on sounds and production, and Simon King hadn't upset anybody (yet) but the gulf was widening between Nik Turner and Lemmy. He would later describe Nik as "one of those moral, self-righteous assholes, as only Virgos can be".

"I was a bit disappointed by that," says Turner. "He talks as though he thinks I've got my head up my arse. I never really felt I fell out with Lemmy. The drugs he took put him on a different plane. That's the thing about people that take amphetamines. Everything is very much in the now, and you say things that come into your head and forget them the next minute.

"I was always on at Lemmy about taking speed because I felt it was detrimental to his relationships with people. It was only ever for his own good. I never had any big hobby horse about it. I'd seen people go down the pan on it, people who were permanently damaged, and I didn't want him to go the same way.

"He took it as a personal criticism of his character, so we had these dramatically opposed points of view, compounded by the fact that we used to get Hell's Angels at the gigs, self-appointed stewards, and they were all out of it on amphetamines and were sometimes completely unreasonable.

"We did get involved with the Hell's Angels, I certainly did, although I think Lemmy got more involved. Lemmy never had a motorbike. I had a motorbike. I was probably more of a biker than Lemmy was. I had a big chopper – a silver machine.

"But the whole essence of Hawkwind was that it was an ideal, a spirit of love and awareness. It was wonderful playing in the band. We had the power to help people and to be acknowledged and respected. Maybe Lemmy approached it as a musician, thinking it was a musical opportunity. How I saw the band and how he did are very different animals."

At the same time, Lemmy realised that the speed factor was alienating him and Dikmik not just from Nik Turner but from the entire group.

"It completely separated us," says Lemmy.

"Dikmik could be grumpy having a speed comedown and piss people off occasionally, making mountains out of small things," affirms Dave Brock. "He's grumpy and Lemmy's grumpy – 'Fucking miserable cunts.'"

"They were on their own trip," agrees Turner.

But the "speed division" would only become a problem with Dikmik's eventual departure, leaving Lemmy in a minority of one.

Nik Turner's charitable inclinations were starting to cause dissension in the ranks. Hawkwind were now so big, and it cost so much to transport them from one place to the next and to put on a show, that they were sometimes losing more money than they raised for the designated causes.

Lemmy remarks, caustically: "That was Nik Turner's big thing. He wanted to be seen to be a hippie, a good guy. He's a bit better now. He's had a few more kicks in the ass. Hawkwind were products of the south, and the south has always been a bit soppy. You come out of north Wales and Liverpool – no such illusions.

"We'd make what would've been good wages for three or four shows, say in Cornwall. But two of them would be benefits, and that would fuck the whole thing up 'cos you had to chip in for the gasoline. We ended up with fuck all, just to make Nik feel better.

"And there were always cons going on. You make £10,000 for charity. You've gotta pay for the hall, this, that and the other. The charity itself gets £5,000. The people [beneficiaries] get £2,000. Sometimes the money never gets to them at all."

However, Lemmy was always happy to play for Friends Of The Earth. "We did a gig at the top bit of Cornwall once," he recalls. "There was all these sheep and cows dead in the fields 'cos of leakage from the atomic power plant. It had got into the earth, into the grass, and nobody ever heard about that. Friends Of The Earth were pretty good. They always had lots of dope. If you had no wages, at least you could get wrecked."

Del Dettmar takes an objective view.

He remembers: "At one time, we'd do a benefit for anybody, for any stupid reason. But at a certain point, we realised we wouldn't make any money if we carried on like that.

"We did one in Scotland. The plan was to take an overnight train and get some sleep. The gear van went up there, and our expenses were £274. The people we were playing for had already spent money on the advertising and stuff like that, and it worked out that even if we took all the proceeds, we'd have made a loss of £4. You can't carry on doing benefits like this.

"After that we had a meeting. We said, 'What we'll do is go through all the requests for benefits and decide which ones are worthwhile.' By that time, we'd learnt how to put ourselves on at a gig and make money. So we'd put ourselves on, make money, cover our expenses and divide the rest among the different charities we'd chosen. That's how it was up until I left the band. I don't know what happened afterwards."

Hawkwind spent 1973 intensively touring the Space Ritual. They crossed England, Ireland, Scotland and Wales headlining major venues, they played in February for the inmates of Wandsworth Prison where Stacia wisely kept her clothes on, they observed the summer's free festivals, and they also launched a huge assault on Europe, including Scandinavia. At the end of the year, they went to America for the first time.

But there were wobbles along the way.

"Upheaval in Hawkwind" warned the *NME* news pages on May 12, reporting that Lemmy had seemingly quit, Dikmik was about to leave and Dave Brock had gone into hiding, "uptight and refusing to play with the band".

The next week brought brighter news, delivered on the paper's front page under the headline: "Hawkwind: Problems Resolved".

It was stated, with relief, that the group were back to full strength for their concert at the prestigious Wembley Empire Pool on May 27. Dave Brock was on top form and writing new material, Lemmy had only missed the first three gigs of the recent German tour because he'd been ill, Dikmik going AWOL was par for the course, and Robert Calvert had just returned to the fold after a short period of writing for his solo album, *Captain Lockheed And The Starfighters*.

The story was apparently accurate with regard to Dikmik and Calvert. But the real gen was that Brock had sacked Lemmy and then reinstated him.

Says Lemmy: "He fired me because I missed the plane to Germany. Two days later, he came on the phone. He always used to do 'Um, um,' [throat-clearing noise] when he was embarrassed. 'Um, um, do you wanna get your bass and come over?' Off I went, then."

This was all happening around the release of *Space Ritual Alive*, but the band patched up their differences for the time being and they did appear together at Wembley.

Lemmy remembers: "Bob Calvert showed up dressed in this long cloak thing with moons and stars and a witch's hat and a trumpet and a sword. A couple of verses into the third number, he came over and started poking me with the sword. I batted him off. You were kind of tolerant with a loony, and it's very hard to punch somebody out when you're playing a bass guitar. I could have whacked him with the bass, but I was afraid I'd break it."

The concert that night was taped – and its appearance on a number of albums released since is still causing fierce arguments among past and present members of the band.

The classic line-up of Hawkwind hung together for a few more weeks, shakily, until Dikmik and Robert Calvert both left around the same time. Calvert, never a reliable presence, once again committed himself for psychiatric treatment, having recognised the onset of his manic symptoms. This set the scene for a series of appearances by Michael Moorcock. Calvert would take a long time out, working on his own music, although in time he would return to Hawkwind. Dikmik would not. After all of his to-ings and fro-ings, it seemed that the prospect of an American tour was too daunting for someone who didn't want to travel any more.

This was a particular blow to Lemmy, who was such close friends with Dikmik that he was the only person able to wake him in the morning without risking a punch on the nose. "If he didn't want to wake up," says Lemmy, "he'd go for the sound of the voice like *that* [slamming fist into palm], but he didn't do it with me. I remember when he first moved in with this bird in Greenwich. I rang up and she said, 'He's asleep.' I said, 'Could you wake him up?' All I could hear at the end of the line was, '[very gently] Dikmik . . . Dikmik . . . and then [very loudly] 'Uuuuuuh!'

"He was one of them restless fellows," continues Lemmy, offering a different perspective on Dikmik's departure. "He was sick of Nik Turner and Brock and Bob Calvert. I wasn't sick of them 'cos I'd only just joined. Dikmik had left twice before I met him, and that time he took me with him, he only went back 'cos he needed the bread. And he enjoyed playing with me."

Dikmik remained in touch with the members of Hawkwind, living with his wife and baby at Nik Turner's house in Westgate on Sea, outside Margate. After leaving there, parting "sort of friends" with Nik, he was busted, as a result of which he served a short prison sentence.

"It took a lot out of him, that jail thing," says Lemmy, shaking his head. "He was a real fucking tearaway before that. He came out and he'd gone quiet. I didn't keep in touch with him after that."

At the time of writing, Dikmik was recuperating from a serious illness, having been hospitalised with pleurisy and pneumonia.

There was an atmosphere of unease around Hawkwind. They owned their equipment and transport, they'd been able to stage the Space Ritual, but now the money had run out. They needed a quick fix of cash to be able to keep progressing.

"We've been forced to bring out another single because we need the bread to advance," grumbled Dave Brock in June 1973. "It's not from choice. I mean, who wants to be a pop star?

"It seems terrible that money determines the future of a band. On the road we just about break even, which means that we have to rely on our record sales to finance any new projects. 'Silver Machine' saved the band once and it looks as though another single is going to have to save the band again."

It never got the chance.

'Urban Guerilla', by Brock and Calvert, was released at the end of July, complete with lyrics that declared, *"I'm an urban guerilla/ I make bombs in my cellar."*

"We once did a benefit for the Stoke Newington 8," says Lemmy. "They was anarchists of some sort – *The Anarchist Cookbook*, making bombs in your basement and all that. 'Urban Guerilla' was about that. That's what Calvert was like. 'Fuck off, Bob.' "

"It was a major political statement," says Douglas Smith.

Unfortunately, in its first week of release, the IRA began a bombing campaign in London, and the single was banned by the BBC and then withdrawn. It was a blow to the band, since 'Urban Guerilla' had started flying off the shelves, entering the singles chart at number 39.

"It would have gone Top 10," says Brock.

The fact that Nik Turner's flat was raided by the bomb squad around this time was probably not a coincidence.

" 'Urban Guerilla' wasn't seen as being a very groovy thing to sing about," Nik admits. "It wasn't politically correct. It wasn't like 'God Save The Queen' by The Sex Pistols. It was more like 'Fuck Everybody' by The Nihilists.

"We were just rather naïve and we had a free hand. We were probably feeling fat with the success of 'Silver Machine', and so we thought anything we released would be successful. And it wasn't really true. One became aware one wasn't in control of the situation. The record companies were, the accountants were in charge of the record companies, and they weren't interested in 'Urban Guerilla'.

"Robert Calvert used to dress up as an urban guerilla. He wore jackboots and combat clothing quite a lot, khaki stuff. His influences were people like Lawrence of Arabia. He was really into military uniforms. One nervous breakdown he was having, he dressed up as a soldier, marched for 25 miles and admitted himself to a loony bin. A lot of these things merge into some sort of vague imagery.

"My flat was raided by the bomb squad. They tore the floorboards up looking for bombs or guns or something. I remember going to Holland with the band where we got pulled up for a day at Dover because of the terrorist thing. We were seen as, I guess, *agents provocateurs*. My brother-in-law was a policeman who worked for the Special Branch and ended up as personal bodyguard to Princess Anne and people like that. At certain times, he was also a customs officer, which was the other side of the coin."

Turner's support for the White Panthers, for whom Hawkwind had played benefits, and such linked organisations as the morris-dancing Blackheath Foot And Death Men had probably been noted too. And then there were his entanglements with the Hell's Angels.

"I had an American Hell's Angel staying with me for a time," explains Nik. "He'd come over from California with another Angel who'd been arrested at Heathrow – his fingerprints were found on a gun that had been used to kill an FBI officer. He hadn't been allowed into the country."

There had always been a loyal biker element in the Hawkwind audience, going back to their earliest days in Ladbroke Grove, and the band appreciated those supporters, but now things were getting troublesome.

Turner had become pretty closely involved with the Angels through his friendship with Jamie Mandelkau, a writer and the author of 1971's biker book *Buttons: The Making Of A President*. He had also been involved with The Deviants and in setting up Pink Fairies, reputedly bringing Canadian guitarist Paul Rudolph over to London to join the band. In another claim to fame, Mandelkau had set up home with Joy Farren, wife of Mick Farren.

"The Hell's Angels started coming to gigs and they were pals of mine because of my association with Jamie," reveals Nik. "They became interested because it was a groovy scene. The Oakland Angels were the marshals for the Grateful Dead and then Altamont, so there was an association between the Angels and the underground bands. They became self-appointed guardians."

Eventually, things turned nasty at one of London's three Sundowns – Nik believes it was the Mile End venue – where Hawkwind were running a mask competition. "Young kids in their masks were getting beaten up by these great big thugs. One of the Angels got his glasses trodden on accidentally by a fan, it was some sort of misunderstanding, and he beat up this fan. We drew the line at that. It was 'Fuck off.' It was all to do with amphetamines."

Nik also had to extricate himself from the Angels in his personal life. "They used to come round to my flat in Gloucester Road. One day they said, 'Here, we want you to invite the president round, and then we want you to go out.' I said, 'What you going to do when I go out?' They said, 'We're going to shoot his legs off.' I wouldn't do it. I said, 'You're friends of mine, but I'm not interested in your club politics.'

"They once asked me to invite Jamie Mandelkau round so they could shoot *his* legs off, claiming he owed them money from that book about Buttons. I wouldn't do that either. I just found it rather boring eventually. I had to fuck them off. You have to tell people they're not really welcome, although I don't think Lemmy ever got around to that. He stayed in with them."

Douglas Smith adds: "I've always had a rumbustious relationship with the Angels and the bikers. I was usually able to keep things in order, but there were a few incidents that got out of hand."

"We used to know lots of them when we were younger and they all started taking LSD," recalls Dave Brock. "There's one I remember who saw the light. He started writing this really wonderful poetry when he was in jail for some misdemeanour. When we go over to Dublin, a few of them still pop up and say hello to us, but they don't come to the gigs to the extent they used to.

"Back in the Seventies, they did become problematic a few times because of their names always being on the guest list. We knew the old boys. We didn't know all the new boys, but they'd just turn up and they'd be eating all the food and drinking all the booze. There was this weird vibe. No one dared say anything."

The guest lists, in general, were causing bad feeling in the band. Says Brock: "We'd have huge guest lists. They got unbelievably stupid sometimes."

The person responsible for this was Nik Turner. He admits: "Hawkwind were a community band, but as we became more success-ful, it was difficult to walk down Portobello Road the day before a gig. I'd be inundated with requests to put people on the guest list, which I found very difficult to refuse. I seem to remember having a guest list of about 300 people, I think for the Rainbow, and insisted they were all let in before we would go onstage."

The people's band were clearly having problems on the home front. Hassled by the authorities as a "subversive threat", compromised by Hell's Angels and besieged by fans who expected free admission to their gigs, they jetted off to America in November 1973 with excitement and relief.

"Wow!"

Every single member of Hawkwind was blown away by the United States, by the size of the venues and the warmth of the reception.

They were not a band who would ever sell truckloads of records in America, but they packed out concerts from the very first.

For Nik Turner, it was the moment he realised just how far the band had come: "I'd never had any aspirations about being successful or famous. It was quite amazing."

He was "overjoyed" by the scenes at the gigs, by the record

company's enthusiasm, by the chance of giving four or five syndicated radio interviews a day, with Douglas Smith and Andrew Lauder, to promote the band.

"They had such a profile in America at that time," agrees Douglas.

Lemmy was thrilled by the grandeur of the scenery, the huge scope of the landscapes, the palm trees of California – and the women.

"This chick came up to me, dressed as a cowgirl," chuckles Lemmy. "She was one of them corn-fed blondes. She was lovely. She said, 'I've been waiting for three years for you to come through town, and the truck's outside. I'm taking you home.' "

" 'Yes, you are,' I said."

The ladies would soon make Hawkwind feel very welcome in America.

They had arrived with a bongo player, Al Matthews, who had formerly played with Richie Havens (and would remain with Hawkwind for a couple of years), and another dancer and mime artist called Phyllis, recruited just for the tour. As always, Andy Dunkley was in tow to play records before and after the set, and to make the introductions.

Their first gig, at Philadelphia's Tower Theater, was an unqualified success. In New York two days later, they attended a party at the Planetarium along with Stevie Wonder, Alice Cooper, Status Quo and Focus, hoping to observe the crossing of the comet Kohoutek.

"We couldn't see it for clouds," bemoans Lemmy.

The dates progressed through Chicago, Akron, Detroit, St Louis, Denver, Santa Monica and San Francisco. And although Hawkwind returned to the UK for The Ridiculous Roadshow Tour that started before Christmas and stretched way beyond it, they would soon fly back across the Atlantic for a longer visit.

Hawkwind now consisted of Dave Brock, Nik Turner, Del Dettmar, Lemmy, Simon King and Stacia, with performers and collaborators coming in and out as required.

In the new year of 1974, Del Dettmar – who had recently married – started talking about emigrating to Canada, and Hawkwind decided to bring in a new member. Simon House would not only take over Del's role on synthesisers and mellotron but, as a violinist, he would open up new musical vistas.

Simon had known the band since their earliest days, having been part of the Clearwater gang as a member of High Tide. Indeed, he'd witnessed their first gig, as Group X, at the All Saints Hall. They invited him to bring his violin to the Edmonton Sundown where they played two shows on January 25 and 26, 1974. It was an audition, of sorts.

"I never actually played a note," remembers Simon. "We were hanging around backstage getting stoned. There were the dancers, the light-show and everyone wearing funny costumes. Simon King was a lion. Nik was a frog. It was totally bizarre. Complete chaos. I got the job – I knew everybody anyway."

Simon was born in Nottingham on August 29, 1948. He was a pupil at High Pavement Grammar School on the outskirts of the town, and went on to Reading University where he studied maths, physics and psychology.

Although Simon had received formal violin lessons, reaching Grade Seven, he fancied being a bass player, and he took on that role after meeting guitarist Tony Hill, the leader of High Tide. He later switched to violin, and the band found a new bassist.

When High Tide broke up in 1970, Simon played violin and VCS3 synthesiser with Third Ear Band for a couple of years. Also with them at the time was Paul Buckmaster, who arranged David Bowie's 'Space Oddity' and was also Elton John's arranger. Third Ear Band spent three months in Air Studios recording the soundtrack for Polanski's *Macbeth*.

"I was totally ripped off," sighs Simon. "I never got any money for that. Over the years I would've made a fortune from it if I'd got a fifth of the royalties."

Simon went to work in a boilerhouse, which he loved: "I was on my own for most of the time. I took my guitar or violin down there, or just read a book. I was getting lots of money – £75 a week. I'd been there for a year or less and then Hawkwind phoned up."

The group were aware of House's accomplished musicianship. "I had a pretty thorough classical training," he confirms. "I suppose it does give you solid ground for the technique, being familiar with your instrument, although there was a lot of head-getting-off, and I plead guilty to that as well. I made lots of mistakes. Musically, Hawkwind weren't demanding compared to something like High Tide. Some of their arrangements and tunes were incredibly complicated, and I could do them because I had a classical training."

Simon House was eventually called into active service when Hawkwind returned to America in March 1974, with Del Dettmar still in the line-up. By now Dave Brock was also playing synth onstage, in addition to his trademark powerhouse strumming.

It was called the 1999 Party since one of the themes involved Nostradamus' prediction that the world would end in that year. The six-week tour, with Welsh band Man supporting, was later immortalised on the album *1999 Party: Live At The Chicago Auditorium.*

Again, there was tremendous interest in the shows, with up to 6,000 people flocking to the venues, and it was a memorable trek. In Nashville, their hotel was hit by a tornado. In Berkeley, California, Hawkwind played a benefit for jailed acid guru Timothy Leary (as they had in London), but this time managed to contact the famous prisoner on the phone and broadcast the conversation to the audience. Nik Turner also visited Leary, who had been incarcerated as a psychiatric case for possession of marijuana.

Melody Maker despatched Geoff Brown to report on the tour from Kansas City and St Louis. He was surprised that without much record company promotion, album sales or positive press reviews, Hawkwind were selling "inexplicably large numbers of tickets". He decided that they were being admired as anti-heroes.

It must be said that Brown wasn't the band's biggest fan. He remarked on the paucity of new material in the set, but also complimented the Lensmen's lights, noted the musical chemistry between Dave Brock and Lemmy – "that frantic simplicity, that basic earthy drone and tumble" – and admitted that in St Louis, the atmosphere Hawkwind created was sizzling, electric.

That is, until someone attacked Stacia. Halfway through her second dance an assailant ran across the stage and put his arms around her. He was flung into the crowd by a roadie. "Five seconds, maybe 10, the guy is back again and now, Jesus Christ, it's clear what he's doing," reported Geoff Brown. "Two hands closed round her neck, this nutter is out to strangle Miss Stacia and that is The Truth."

The nutter was thrown off more forcefully, this time by three roadies, and didn't make his hat trick.

Stacia ripped off her blonde bubble-wig and dashed from the stage, returning later to finish the show somewhat unenthusiastically. Hawkwind responded to the outrage with "power and vengeance", finally finishing the concert to the sight of thousands of lighted matches.

Violent attacks àpart, it was a tour that Simon House remembers fondly, and if there were stressful undercurrents running between Dave Brock and Nik Turner, and between Lemmy and almost everybody, particularly Nik, then they weren't serious enough to be noticeable.

"The show in those days, the lights, the band as they were – Hawkwind were years ahead of their time," he declares. "It was just one big happy family, the band and the road crew and the light-show guys. There were little squabbles now and again. It's inevitable on the road. But this camaraderie did build up, especially when we were flying to the States and then travelling Europe and going through all kinds of adventures together. We had some great times. We did get on well most of the time.

"I think Stacia liked it. She was one of the lads, although she did used to piss people off in the morning on the way to the airport, talking when everybody was hung over – 'Oh, shut up.'"

Geoff Brown had detected an element of homesickness, certainly within Dave Brock. But as the band began to strike up friendships with some of the American women they met, they would soon start to feel quite at home in the United States, Dave included.

Hawkwind went into Olympic Studios in May 1974 to work on their next album, emerging in June for a trip to Germany and the Netherlands.

This would be Del Dettmar's last outing with Hawkwind, by choice, and his departure to Canada gave rise to one of the most colourful and enduring legends in Hawkwind mythology.

It's described, in part, in Lemmy's autobiography, *White Line Fever*, and remembered as fact by other members of the band.

Dave Brock: "Del fell in love with this girl who became pregnant. She went across to Canada, I think. Del followed her over, and when he got there, he discovered the baby was black. He was really upset. I don't think he stayed with the girl, but he did stay in Canada. He went off and worked as a lumberjack in the Canadian backwoods, and he built himself a log cabin."

The details change a little in Lemmy's version. Dettmar, he says, went to Canada and built the log cabin with his bare hands for his wife, who was pregnant in England. When she later came out to Canada with a mixed-race baby, it was "very bad news".

"I don't think he immediately put her right back on the boat," writes Lemmy, "but it was words to that effect."

An amused Del Dettmar sets the record straight: "I had a lot of reasons for leaving Hawkwind. I wasn't unhappy in the band, and I didn't have any arguments with anybody, but I was never a great fan of the real loud noise, and we were getting louder and louder. That's one of the reasons. Also, I felt like I'd done the band thing."

Usually gracious and diplomatic about Hawkwind, Del also ventures, "It's a band that thrives on the mushroom syndrome, which is being kept in the dark and fed bullshit."

He continues: "Definitely, I was in love with my wife. She was English, although she's Canadian now. We were emigrating. I never built a log cabin in Canada with my bare hands. There was never any log cabin. Someone once asked Bob Calvert what had happened to me and he made that up.

"My wife and I had already lived together in England for a year. She was pregnant and I knew it wasn't my baby. She had a beautiful child who was Pakistani. I felt all right about it. I don't think I was in the state that people have said. My wife and I went on to be happily married for 10 years, although we didn't live together all that time. Unfortunately, the child got killed when he was 11 years old."

Del, who has never remarried, began his working life in Canada – in the Kootunai or Kootenay area where he still lives – as a cone-picker. He went on to plant a million trees for the Forestry Service, leaving in protest that rather than reforesting areas burnt down by fires with their native trees, shrubs and plants, the authority simply wanted to establish plantations using one or two species of tree that grew quickly.

In 1977, he started building a post-and-beam house – long after the story of the log cabin had been circulated by Bob Calvert. And it went up in flames. "I never did really finish it," says Del. "As soon as I could read a book in comfort, I stopped building. It was standing five years. By the time it burnt down, I was living in the studio."

That's the studio he bought with his Hawkwind record royalties.

Del had bumped into Paul Rudolph, a native Canadian, who had played with Pink Fairies and, by now, had been in and out of Hawkwind. Rudolph gave Dettmar the details of a solicitor who would chase up his due payments, and the legal eagle duly obtained "a whole bunch of money".

"Funny nobody ever wrote and said, 'You've got a gold record,' or 'You've got money owing to you,'" jokes Del, pointedly.

His studio went into insolvency in the mid-Eighties because the musicians didn't pay their bills. He was also, at this time, hiring out a circus tent.

In 1987, he made one of his regular trips back to England. He would always look up old friends in Hawkwind, and even succeeding band members he hadn't met before. On this occasion, he went to see the group in Croydon. They were "terrible, too loud, with a big, booming bass".

In the same year, Dettmar hooked up with Nik Turner and has been playing with him in various groups ever since. He also once returned to perform at the ICA with Twink from Pink Fairies, Hawkwind's occasional mime artist Tony Crerar and Miss Renee the dancer. Del and Twink provided the musical accompaniment for a show called An Exploration Of The Human Body, with Tony and Renee putting on the visual style.

In 2003, Del was forced to take a year off when his eyesight failed. "I had cataracts," he explains. "I didn't know I had them until I went blind. I couldn't even see the strings on my guitar – which I thought might make me a better musician! It was the worst case of cataracts my eye doctor had ever seen. I can see again now, although I'm still using eye drops, and it's a modern-day miracle. I've been *looking* at stuff ever since, just enjoying using my eyes."

While Hawkwind were playing their last tour with Del Dettmar in June 1974, they also said goodbye, temporarily, to drummer Simon King, who'd bust a rib or two playing football after the American trip. They drafted in a temporary replacement, Alan Powell, who had previously played with Chicken Shack and Vinegar Joe and was a friend of Simon King's. Alan loved it all so much that Hawkwind decided to keep him on when King returned for the last few dates in the Netherlands.

"He's a fine drummer and a nice guy," nods Dave Brock.

Now there were two drummers. And that's when it all started going wrong for Lemmy.

CHAPTER 9

Let There Be Drums

HAWKWIND had cast off the long, shapeless jams of yesteryear and were harnessing their power, paying more attention to arrangement and contrast. Dave Brock's insistent, scrubbing guitar welded to Lemmy's amphetamine bass wallop and a big drum sound created the drive, the metal, the solid ground from which the flute and sax, the fiddle and the synths could sweep and spiral and soar off on fantastic intergalactic journeys. The combination of hard-rock energy, dreamy, trippy, trancey soundscapes and futuristic sci-fi effects had gradually become more thoughtful and structured, more melodic.

Stacia, too, had advanced her artistry, no longer writhing around on a whim but incorporating mime and dramatic interpretation.

However, it was the total experience, the whole world of Hawkwind, which really gripped the fans and kept them hooked. They were in that spaceship with the band, and many would spend hours pondering the lyrics, writing streams of Hawkwind-inspired poetry and prose, and painting their own Bubbles-style tableaux.

One such fan was Ian Davidson from Belfast, a place where Hawkwind were held in high esteem due to their willingness to play there at the height of "The Troubles" when other English bands would not.

The first album Ian ever bought was *X In Search Of Space* and he went to see them live when they next rolled into town, performing the Space Ritual. Prior to this, he had written a book which he intended to present to Nik Turner. "There was an inspirational booklet in *In Search Of Space*," says Ian, referring to the Calvert/Bubbles creation. "It was this far-out thing. Most of the bands back then were doing rock music with wah-wah pedals blasting away. Hawkwind inspired so many thoughts in me. They taught me that you can put music and poetry together to make a story.

"I was into semi-occult stuff, pyramids, astral and psychic things. They didn't call it New Age then. My book was based on an LSD trip. It was all about psychedelic warlords, space and Atlantis and things like that. It was triggered by Hawkwind, but it was all that I was into at the time. It was handwritten, 30 or 40 pages in a wee, hardback school book, and it was called *The Psychedelic Warlords*. Then they brought a track out called 'The Psychedelic Warlords'. I don't know if that had anything to do with it.

"The book was all my ideas and feelings written down – a teenager in Belfast, under the influence and inspired by Hawkwind, sitting in my bedroom listening to their records. Dreams, taking you away. It was freedom, a sense of freedom through space and through music and through your dreams."

Ian was blown away by the show. He still has the Space Ritual leaflet that was circulated at the gig. "To me, it was the first musical," he says. "It was a space musical. It was a visual, sound and poetic experience in the void that was Belfast. If you remember the Space Ritual, it was a form of musical, sexual, teenage experience. You had the orgasmic build-up, and 'Brainstorm' was the orgasm and in between those, you had the bits of poetry to keep you in the right direction.

"Everything was quiet and the lights went out. Robert Calvert came on with this helmet and jackboots, and he guided you into the next level of this big musical rush, and at the very end, you came back down to reality. They took you away and they brought you back. And then you went back home to Belfast's version of reality. But you'd had a two-hour glimpse of the other world."

Ian was thrilled to discover that you could simply walk into the dressing room after the concert, no problem. There, the band members were milling around, greeting fans in a down-to-earth manner. "Hawkwind came to Belfast, they brought a totally new experience of music, and they had time for the ordinary punters," says Ian. "A lot of respect to them. They didn't lock the doors. They didn't act like big, famous rock stars, and they talked to us as people.

"Dikmik said to me, 'All I do, mate, is just flick the switches.' Lemmy was out of it on speed. He looked stressed, and I gave him a bottle of Mogadon, thinking it would be cool to help him. Nik Turner was the main man for me. He was as straight as a die. He was so approachable. And I went over and I sat and talked to him, and he listened. It was just awe-inspiring. He was really appreciative and he thanked me for giving him my book. He could have been a rock star and said, 'Fuck, I'm not taking that.'"

Turner is pretty sure he still has Ian's book stored away at home in Wales. He also, that night, gave Ian an address for Hawkwind feedback.

"I wrote to it," remembers Ian. "And they sent me a transfer. No one else in Belfast had one. I got my mother to iron it on my Wrangler jacket, and I wore that jacket until it fell off me. That Hawkwind transfer walked around Belfast for years and years."

Ian remained devoted to the band: "They were the biggest part of my teenage life."

Now a family man with two children, Ian Davidson still follows Hawkwind's career today, and he continues along a path they championed decades earlier: "I'm still asking questions, still wanting to know, 'Why?'"

Some fans, however, took their worship of Hawkwind to outrageous extremes. "The freaky ones – they were everywhere," guffaws Lemmy. "They were fucking maniacs, people who think the earth is inside a block of ice. Hawkwind still get them now. They always had a lot of dope. You need a lot of dope to sustain that bullshit."

Lemmy was getting pissed off with the drummers, Simon King and Alan Powell. He called them "The Drum Empire".

Their equipment was gradually becoming more elaborate, and he reckoned they were starting to get too big for their boots, too dominant in the band. Lemmy, on the other hand, having already lost his partner-in-speed, Dikmik, was feeling increasingly sidelined, although he met the challenge head on.

Says Lemmy: "It was great for a while. Then 'The Drum Empire' took over the stage. They got all these gongs and an anvil, tubular bells and fucking chimes and all this shit. It was fucking hopeless. All the rest of us were pushed up on the side of the stage, so that wasn't a good idea. I used to be over, urging them on – *'Come on, you cunt!'* – to stop them being slow. I'd always be up the front chasing it, trying to get a break. If we're onstage together, I will upstage you. That's how good I am. I can't help it. I want to be a rock star. That's what I am. I'm good at it.

"Simon King was beginning to be a pain in the ass with me. He wanted me out 'cos I was the one that hired him. He didn't want to owe me anything. He couldn't ever say shit to me about my behaviour, whereas the new guy [Alan] . . . he wanted to be a tree surgeon, but he couldn't stand the sight of sap.

"Then they got more and more clout. Simon used to hang around with Dave and butter him up. Alan was a great butterer. I was always the one that was keen to be in on the discussions on songs, but they just used to shut me out. Simon House was a very quiet guy. He didn't want to make any waves. He was an excellent fucking musician, and he was always nice to me, but he was part of 'them'."

Nik Turner was typically unaware of Lemmy's problems with "The Drum Empire". "I'm quite amazed," he says today. "I never saw it as being anything other than people playing drums. I don't know what Lemmy expected, really. Maybe he thinks it detracted from his bass. I wouldn't say that having two drummers who were interested in experimenting with gongs and all sorts of stuff was detracting from anything. I'd see it as another dimension of the music, a broader potential."

Dave Brock, for his part, has come round to Lemmy's viewpoint, confirming that the two drummers "probably" hogged the stage. "There were a lot of percussion things all over the place," he agrees. "They'd have the gong and only use it once on one number. It got a bit silly. We had a few percussionists – Al Matthews was one, coming along to play congas. He was a nice, over-the-top character. But Lemmy was probably right. It was just one of those things."

Brock is less sympathetic towards Lemmy's complaints of being cut out of the musical decisions. "Maybe that was true, although Lemmy did write a lot of things," he responds. "I think you'll find that he never used to turn up at meetings, nor did Dikmik when he was in the band, 'cos they'd gone to bed – 'Well, they're never here.' The other thing was I was living down in Devon, trying to organise rehearsals."

As far as Lemmy was concerned, one thing outweighed the negative aspects of his life in Hawkwind. "Onstage, it all vanished," he states. "It was all right. I've never had a rapport like I had with Dave Brock. We could face different ways and I'd change when he changed. I don't know what it was. I knew where he was going and when he was going to do it. We were really fucking good at that.

"I loved playing his stuff. I don't know what the genius with it was. It was only as long as those people were together. I was the driver behind them, and Dave was driving and he was singing too."

Brock confirms: "We were very close musically. It's one of those magical things that, luckily enough, was recorded."

"He had a schoolgirl fantasy," rattles on Lemmy, warming to the topic of Dave Brock. "He'd be hanging out the window if he saw a bunch of schoolgirls, going 'Spank, spank, spank.' Dirty old acid-fuelled fucking busker. One day we rang up for Dave. His old lady said, 'He took some mescaline and went out for a walk and I haven't seen him since.' He used to go out with a loincloth on. He'd get out there frothing at the mouth and walk around the fields carrying a staff."

"It was a stick," corrects Dave.

"And he didn't show up for the gig," continues Lemmy. "We got Twink [Pink Fairies drummer] to do the gig on a guitar with two strings on it. It was pretty loose, Hawkwind. But Dave did write a lot of good songs for them. Let's not forget that."

The album, *Hall Of The Mountain Grill*, was named after a favourite café in Notting Hill and released in September 1974, with artwork by Barney Bubbles, working again in collaboration with photographer Phil Franks. It was preceded a month earlier by a single, a Dave Brock song called 'The Psychedelic Warlords (Disappear In Smoke)', which didn't trouble the chart. The album, produced by Hawkwind and Doug Bennett, reached number 16. Two Brock compositions – 'You'd Better Believe It' and 'Paradox' – were taped live at the Edmonton Sundown in January the same year. The rest of the album was recorded at Olympic.

"I was sleeping on the studio floor yet again," remarks Dave.

Hawkwind had been working quite a few of the songs up live, including 'The Psychedelic Warlords', Nik Turner's 'D-Rider' and Brock's 'Web Weaver' as well as 'Paradox' and 'You'd Better Believe It'. The album also includes the departed Del Dettmar's charming, one-and-a-half minute 'Goat Willow' and a contribution from new-comer Simon House who wrote the title track, an instrumental and another short piece at just over two minutes.

Hall Of The Mountain Grill is a very well regarded album among Hawkfolk. While serving up the requisite obstinate riffing, swishing space sounds and extended experimental passages, a new scope and a fresh life spring from the keyboards, synths and violin of Simon House, not without some classical overtones.

Hawkwind had been round the block a few times by now. Indeed, at this early stage in their career, they were viewed in some quarters as dated, with Allan Jones of *Melody Maker* suggesting they had the standing of a "psychedelic music hall joke".

The reviews, where they were positive, offered grudging or defensive praise. Geoff Brown, for *Melody Maker*, decided the album was as visionary, as inspirational as a plate of egg, sausage and beans in the Mountain Grill café, and accused Hawkwind of being "stuck in a time-warp hippie image, [with] passé optics and recording techniques". At the same time, he commented on the wider range of sound, rather grumpily allowing that it was their best album to date and admitting: "In their own way, 'Wind are a tremendously charismatic bunch of itinerants and were, arguably, one of the biggest draws among British bands. The greatcoats would gather in force at the drop of a tab."

In fact, the greatcoats – the collective term for a particular rock audience who dressed in these dull garments – were still turning out in force at the drop of anything.

Charles Shaar Murray, a veteran of the Ladbroke Grove scene and a friend of Mick Farren's, suggested in *NME* that Hawkwind should be writing soundtracks for cheapo sci-fi movies. He berated them for their "persistent habit of bashing their riffs around for several minutes on end with no appreciable textural variation (except a sheepish mellotron three quarters of the way through)".

He did, however, confess that "I have a sneaking fondness for this album," especially 'Goat Willow' and 'Lost Johnny', which Lemmy co-wrote with Farren. These were the two least characteristic tracks on the LP.

Shaar Murray adored 'Lost Johnny' for its "appealingly slipshod guitars and a gorgeously damaged hoarse vocal".

Lemmy was less impressed with his only contribution to the album. "I really didn't like it much," he says. "It was crap, the Hawkwind version. Only Del Dettmar and Simon King stayed in the studio with me. I did all the bass and guitars and vocals myself.

"But *Hall Of The Mountain Grill* is the best studio album I did with Hawkwind. I was quite to the front. I think it stands the test of time. I like that piano track with Simon House on it [the title track]. It was brilliant to hear that violin going. He was really good on that. He made it bigger."

Lemmy would only be happy with 'Lost Johnny', and 'The Watcher' from *Doremi*, when he re-recorded them with Motorhead.

Dave Brock, who wrote the majority of the tracks on *Hall Of The Mountain Grill*, isn't too bothered about it, sniffing: "Some of it's all right and some of it isn't. It's a bit of both, really."

Hawkwind were in America when the album was released. After a quick sprint round the August festivals in Harlow, Bristol and Windsor, they jetted back to the States for two months of dates, breaking for a fortnight at the beginning of October when they came home for interviews to promote the album.

The US tour started out well. Hawkwind, their trusty DJ Andy Dunkley and bongo man Al Matthews were averaging crowds of 3,000 a night, still without a chart placing to their name. A 21-strong crew – more than three times the number normally attending a band of this stature – were in place to see that the workings and the synchronisation of sound and lights were perfect.

A central feature of the visuals was the acclaimed "tree sequence" slide show. Screened during 'Hall Of The Mountain Grill', it was picked up for the first time in live reviews, although Dave Brock believes "the tree" has its roots in the Space Ritual period. "It doesn't seem that fantastic now," says Brock. "First in the sequence is the tree and then there's a cottage and then a village. Roads appear, then a town and skyscrapers, and the tree becomes a little tree in a small park. It was all painted up by Sally Vaughan. Years later, I think it was Rush did the same thing with their light-show, and it was a pinch from us."

In an environmentally happy ending from Hawkwind, the tree fought back, and won.

Three weeks into the tour, on September 21, the group played what had seemed like another normal gig in Hammond, Indiana, and were walking offstage when they were ambushed by a gang of Internal Revenue Service officials, physically seizing their instruments from their hands.

Melody Maker's Chris Charlesworth, based in New York and reporting on the tour, was right on the spot to file the news story unfolding before him. *MM* readers were informed that the IRS were demanding several thousand dollars in unpaid taxes from Hawkwind and that their gear was impounded in the venue, the Civic Center. Every item was stickered with the words, "Property of the US Government".

In the turmoil, Chris was virtually ignored by everyone except Douglas Smith but he was still outraged on the band's behalf. Back at the group's Holiday Inn that night he wrote his story in a notebook and later dictated it over the phone back to the paper's offices in London: "Hawkwind are a modern-day equivalent to the travelling circus, a closely knit community whose means of supporting themselves suits them admirably and entertains a growing following wherever they go. Taking this line of thought, it was a particularly odious act by the IRS to impound their instruments. Would they confiscate a carpenter's hammer or a painter's brush in similar circumstances?"

Manager Smith had enough problems of his own without this development. Earlier in the tour, he'd severely damaged a nerve in his right arm, according to Charlesworth, by "making his point" in an argument, with the plate glass window coming off worse. His arm was in a sling as a result.

Douglas recalls: "The whole tax thing was all to do with red tape. Hawkwind were innocent. They hadn't done anything wrong at all. On their previous tour, they'd set up a company to take care of their withholding tax. Their accountant thought he'd set up all the paperwork, and it was completely kosher.

"The IRS started with Simon House, grabbing his violin. I said, 'You can't take that. It's his personal property. It doesn't belong to the band.' I lost my temper."

So did several other people, not least Simon. "Simon wanted to clock this IRS guy," says Dave Brock. "He was furious. And Higgy the tour manager was stepping in there."

Douglas continues: "At the time, I had paralysed my arm and it was all bound up in these peculiar leather straps to stop it going into crystallisation. I thought, 'I'll get out of this – I'll show them I'm a spastic, that'll do it.' One of the officers pointed me to the window. The gig was in a hall right in the middle of a town green, and all the way round it were police cars with their lights on, pointing at the venue.

"They confiscated everything and insisted we had to pay the withholding tax. I said, 'Here's the paperwork for your IRS people,' and they took it."

This all happened on a Saturday night. There was no gig booked for the Sunday, which gave Douglas some breathing space to find a solution. Meanwhile, a couple of roadies peeled the offending stickers off the equipment.

A meeting was arranged for the Monday, when the IRS would be expecting payment. Until then, Douglas and the band were kept under house arrest at the hotel, banned from driving anywhere. But the roadies could come and go, and they went out to get the sticker images printed on to T-shirts. Douglas made a series of frantic phone calls to United Artists representatives in London and LA, and he eventually managed to raise the required, substantial sum.

"Monday came and we went back to the venue to pay the money and collect the equipment," says Douglas. "When the Treasury men arrived, the roadies were standing there with their T-shirts on. Nik and others were taking photos of them, telling these officials they were going to publish them in magazines when they got back to England. They were winding them up like nobody's business.

"I paid them the money, but one official said they wanted another $550. I started being really very rude, very mouthy. Two or three guys were standing behind me in suits and sunglasses, and I thought they were going to do me a little bit of knuckle massage. At that moment, Andy Dunkley literally fell in through the door and the whole atmosphere changed. He jumped up from the floor and said, 'Don't worry, I've stashed $540,' so we paid and we left."

It took Hawkwind's accountant three years to achieve the reimbursement of a sum of money for which they had not been liable in the first place.

The tour continued without any further serious incident. Their old friend Mick Farren checked them out as they wound up in New York in November. He reported in the *NME* that, "The addition of Alan Powell as a second drummer has produced a percussion interplay that is a whole new source of interest and dynamics."

He noticed nothing of Lemmy's antipathy towards "The Drum Empire", but remarked upon how dextrously he played with them: "His bassline wove in and out of the double drum pattern like the star quarterback in the afternoon's TV ball game."

Farren also complimented Dave Brock and Simon House who, he said, "have emerged as a melodic top line, far in advance of anything they have done previously. The clanks, honks and tweets of the early band have been resolved into sweeping harmonies . . . reminiscent of the Floyd's 'Careful With That Axe' period."

He was impressed with Nik Turner's more rounded role in the band, cutting down on the flute to sing more and working with Stacia "in a series of strange Living Theatre pas de deux".

These weren't the only *pas de deux* that were taking place. The band members had been getting used to the wide, open spaces of America and beginning to take advantage of the freedoms it offered.

Lemmy, a young gun going for it, had always welcomed the attentions of young ladies he met on the road. Now, one by one, the others were giving in to temptation. "We all had our American girlfriends," confesses Dave Brock. "When we used to go across the States, it was like we were with our American wives as opposed to our English wives. It was jolly nice, really. Every time we used to go there, we'd have the same girlfriends. They used to travel around with us.

"Mine was called Vicky. She used to meet us at the airport in her red Mustang. Actually, Vicky became a Doctor of Archaeology, teaching in one of the universities over there. Another member of the band had this girl Donna, who made all this wonderful leather clothing. We used to go to America quite a lot then, and it was very nice that we had our regular girlfriends. In the lifestyle we were living, it did keep us reasonably together."

"Yeah, it was a bit like that," confirms Simon House. "We were only young, you know."

Asked if keeping two relationships alive, one on either side of the Atlantic, made life complicated, Dave replies: "It did when we went back to England. It was quite difficult sometimes. I was married as well, and some of the other boys were. It wasn't very loyal, I'd say.

"That lifestyle – huge amounts of drugs and staying in hotels and flying from one place to another . . . unfortunately you become so involved in what you're doing, nothing else matters. Quite a few people I know have said the same. It's like saying, 'I was the problem,' because of the lifestyle I was leading.

"You're back for two weeks at home and then you go away again. You're not yourself any more. You've got jet lag and the phone is non-stop and all these different things are going on, and you're living in hotels and everything's done for you. You're cosseted when you're on the road. It's not a real world, and consequently your nice, stable relationship with your wife and kids goes down the drain, and you can't see it 'cos Hawkwind is more important. I can look back and see it."

Dave's marriage would survive another nine years and when it finished, it wasn't anything to do with rock'n'roll. "I didn't actually split up from Sylvia. She died. Unfortunate circumstances and all that."

His old friend Mike King remarks: "It was the Sixties and Seventies and Dave was the spirit of the time, and it was freedom, you know. He just wanted to play his music and be free, and as he got more successful, obviously he expanded outwards, like they all do. I think it may have led to some unhappiness in his marriage. But he's told me that the old days are gone. He seems to have found himself with Kris.* He's calm and quiet."

Brock himself asserts that he's a different man these days. He enjoys a monogamous relationship, he drinks the odd glass of wine and he's choosy when it comes to drugs.

"Yeah, I still smoke a spliff," he shrugs. "We've been trying to bring about the legalisation of cannabis for years. But acid? Nothing like that. Not for years now."

Nik Turner had equally indulged in pot and acid in the Seventies while insisting that, in his life, drugs should be a relaxation and not an occupation or a distraction. He now leads a healthy lifestyle in Wales as a teetotaller, telling one interviewer about the chaotic touring of the Seventies: "It was very exciting and I enjoyed it. I found it a bit of a strain in some respects. I was doing a lot of meditation and stuff like that to keep myself straight. And I was drinking a lot at the time, and I just found that a bit boring, really. I was glad when I stopped doing it."

December 1974, and Hawkwind were back to play in Britain. They had set up a tour which once again would carry on after Christmas and, with major venues selling out almost immediately, would confirm the band as one of the biggest live draws in the country.

They managed to snatch some recording time over the festive period to produce a new single, 'Kings Of Speed', which was backed with 'Motorhead' – another term for a speedfreak – and released in March. It didn't chart.

Melody Maker's Allan Jones, turning up at Birmingham Odeon in January, found Dave Brock having less than a happy new year. Perhaps it was tour fatigue: Hawkwind had hardly been off the road since the Isle of Wight.

The Birmingham gig had been a storming success yet Brock, after-wards, "looked no more than an exhausted counterfeit of his dramatic space-warrior stage persona and there was a shadow of confusion behind his tired eyes".

* Kris Tait, his long-time partner.

Around the same time, Jones visited Dave at his isolated country home in Devon for an interview. There, Dave confided that he was struggling with the impersonal nature of the huge audiences he was playing to every night. He missed the intimacy of the small gigs, and he regretted that because of the sheer scale of things, Hawkwind could no longer work for and in the community as they had done when they were genuinely "the people's band".

Jones says today: "I remember sitting in Brock's lovely old farmhouse getting incredibly stoned. We went out for a walk at sunset and he was leaning against a big wooden fence, chatting away about God knows what. This horse trotted up behind him and started munching on his hair. He was too stoned to notice and I was so stoned I couldn't speak. I just stood there opening and closing my mouth trying to tell him that the fucking nag was chewing away at his billowing locks."

Dave told Jones that he was finding it more and more of a strain being away from home. He loved the land and the rural society he belonged to, undoubtedly he loved the hair-eating horses too, and he was starting to hate the city. It made him edgy. Cooped up in the van on tour, he could find little in common with his fellow band members. Interestingly, he felt a greater empathy with Nik Turner than anyone else.

Lemmy was definitely on the shit-list that week. Asked about Lemmy's identification with the Hell's Angels, Dave shot back: "That's a complete fantasy trip. Lemmy lives that fantasy. It's what he'd like to be but he can't."

He went on to describe a backstage atmosphere of rows and temper tantrums and complained about Nik Turner playing sax over his vocals: "Some nights I've unplugged my guitar and marched across the stage to sort Nik out."

Lemmy, too, had been screwing up onstage, according to Dave. He'd been staggering into Simon King's cymbals, he'd thrown his bass on the stage at a recent gig because the strings kept coming out of the bridge, and at Hammersmith Odeon, he didn't notice that his lead had come out of the amp.

"He carried on playing," said Brock to Allan Jones. "He plays so loud, man, he can't hear a thing we're playing. That's what annoys Simon House. We were all shouting to Lemmy, 'Your fucking lead, man,' and he still didn't understand. Then somebody plugged his lead in. I told him, 'You cunt. If you do that again, I'll fucking kill you.'

And sure enough, he did it again. We were all freaking out about that.

"Lemmy's quite a good frontman, though. He can put it about a bit. Likes to pose a lot. Simon House is the complete opposite, a very quiet boy."

Hawkwind called off the final dates of their UK tour to get down to another album, *Warrior On The Edge Of Time*, which they recorded over February and March at Rockfield Studios in Monmouth, Wales, with the mixing completed at Olympic.

Another conflict then arose, this time between Lemmy and Nik Turner. Says Nik: "Lemmy didn't really like the direction I thought the band ought to go in. There was a disparity of ideals. What Lemmy thought the band was and what I thought were very different things."

The disagreement erupted over the artwork. "I wanted the album cover to be an Eastern, mystical sort of thing, more allegorical and not so literal as some warriors on the edge of time. Lemmy might have wanted these heroic warriors, so he put his foot down and demanded his mate's artwork to be used."

As a result, Barney Bubbles was elbowed off the cover, and his work appeared only on the inner sleeve.

Douglas Smith and Dave Brock remember only that United Artists took charge of the cover artwork, which is credited to Comte Pierre D'Auvergne (thought to be UA's Pierre Tubbs) and Eddie Brash who, presumably, was the artist commissioned.

Two important things happened in May, 1975. *Warrior On The Edge Of Time* reached a UK chart position of 13. And Lemmy was busted, then sacked from Hawkwind.

CHAPTER 10

Goodbye And God-speed!

THESE were busy days for Michael Moorcock.

Warrior On The Edge Of Time was based on his *The Eternal Champion* series of books, and he contributed three songs: 'Standing At The Edge', which was performed by Nik Turner, and 'The Wizard Blew His Horn' and 'Warriors', both delivered by Moorcock himself.

He told an interviewer: "*Warrior On The Edge Of Time* was a concept of mine. What Dave tends to do is he says, 'Do us a concept,' or, 'I've got this rough concept, can you work it out?' I do it, then Dave has a different idea and the whole thing shifts away, so that's the way it works. It's a perfectly good way of working . . . I was only in the studio about an hour to do the stuff I did, and it was one of those weird things I didn't get the session fee either."

Moorcock had also been collaborating with writer and film-maker Iain Sinclair, and he had recorded an album of his own. Not that he'd planned to. Through his associations with Hawkwind, he'd ended up at lunch one day with the A&R man from United Artists.

"He asked, 'When do you plan to deliver the album to us?'" explained Moorcock. "I didn't know he wanted an album. So I did him one – *The New Worlds Fair* – and we took a band out [Deep Fix]. And I was going out with Hawkwind when Calvert was in the loony bin, and there's nothing sweeter than going in front of an audience of several thousand people who are really, really glad to see you!"

Deep Fix were called after the title of a short story written by Moorcock in the Sixties and later used as a band name in the "Cornelius" series. The real group found Moorcock on guitars, mandolin, banjo and vocals, aided and abetted by Steve Gilmore and Graham Charnock, both on guitars and vocals. Gilmore also produced *The New Worlds Fair*.

It was released in May 1975, as was *Warrior On The Edge Of Time*, and it was inevitable that certain editors would not be able to resist reviewing them together. At *Melody Maker*, the task fell to Allan Jones to compare and contrast the two albums.

Allan had become the resident Hawkwind expert somewhat despite himself. He says today: "I used to be asked to do them because Michael Watts [assistant editor] thought that because I had long hair, I must be a fan. I was very friendly at the time with Richard Ogden, who did press for them and a lot of dodgy bands, but he was good fun and wasn't afraid of shooting the bar or coughing up for a good nosh. Hawkwind's music didn't mean much to me, but they always had great drugs!"

He wasn't converted by the new album. Dismissing the Moorcock contributions as "aural dandruff" and 'Kings Of Speed' as "the thoroughly idiotic single", he declared that although there was a new clarity about the group's own production and an improvement in their technical proficiency, Hawkwind had become predictable.

He wrote: "Simon House's contributions shouldn't be underestimated here, but compositions are still firmly constructed around standard Hawkwind traditions of sweeping synthesiser passages contrasting ethereal space with the violence of monotonous bass and rhythm guitar."

Jones did, however, mention Dave Brock's 'The Demented Man' and Simon House's 'Spiral Galaxy 28948' as diversions from the "predominant formula". He also conceded that this was the most professional record of their career and an "unqualified masterpiece" compared to Moorcock's efforts with Deep Fix.

The years have been kinder to *Warrior On The Edge Of Time*. It's now considered a semi-classic, and tracks such as 'The Golden Void Part II' and 'Magnu' are enduring fan favourites.

A grouchy Lemmy argues, "The album was a fuck-up from start to finish. That 'Opa-Loka' is a lot of fucking rubbish. I wasn't even on that. That was the drummers' thing, that track. That was the genius of Simon King there. Judge not lest ye be judged! Him and Alan Powell made their mark – 'The Drum Empire'.

"We were kind of complacent anyway. If you have a hit album, you're complacent, and if you have two you really are in trouble. With them, they had four, 'cos they had *In Search Of Space* before me. They were still trying to write a hit single, which they never could do except by accident with 'Silver Machine'.

"There's great stuff on all them albums. 'The Golden Void' was a beautiful track, but by then I was well out of favour."

Dave Brock had written most of the songs, with Nik Turner represented only by 'Dying Seas'. Brock defends the album: "It's me on the bass on 'Opa-Loka' and not Lemmy – 'cos he was fast asleep. There was some good stuff on that album, *Warrior On The Edge Of Time*. I think we peaked then, in 1974/75."

The album marked the end of one era in Hawkwind's history. Perhaps it was because they felt they really had peaked and needed to move on, perhaps they were listening to the critics, or perhaps it was a combination of both, but they would now turn their backs on outer space, at least in the studio.

If Dave Brock was alienated and homesick for the countryside, Nik Turner was also feeling disillusioned, and compromised. In an interview with *Maya*, published in June 1975, he poured out his frustration that Hawkwind were being absorbed into the industry and could no longer work for the community as much as he would like. He talked of quitting the group, or starting a second band which would exist to play benefits and informal gigs where anybody who wanted could join in.

The focus of his growing dissatisfaction had been a Hawkwind show at The Roundhouse on February 16. It was a measure of the group's popularity that they had already played two sold-out tour dates at the old Hammersmith Odeon.

The Roundhouse concert had been scheduled as a benefit for Radical Alternatives To Prisons (RAP). Nik told *Maya*: "Some of our equipment had been stolen, and we were faced with the problem of having to buy a new set of drums and things like that. Subsequently, the equipment was found but that still didn't alter the fact in some people's minds that we were in a financial state."

The upshot was that the benefit turned into a normal commercial gig. "I and Douglas both donated our share to RAP," said Nik. "But the rest were just into it being another gig to help the band get by, which I understand as well. But I think it's a drag, 'cos in spite of our financial state, we're better off than a lot of people and one gig doesn't make that much difference . . .

"That's the sort of situation that I very often find myself in – torn

The classic early-Seventies line-up of Hawkwind featuring, left to right: Nik Turner, Del Dettmar, Dikmik (bending over), Simon King, Lemmy and Dave Brock. "To understand Hawkwind, you had to be in London in 1972 in the freak scene," says Lemmy. "We were fucking huge." *(LFI)*

Dave Brock at the turn of the Sixties, playing Eric Clapton's guitar at a fair in Twickenham, possibly showing him a few licks. "I used to be better than him on the guitar," says Dave. Note Clapton's feet, bottom right. *(Dave Brock Collection)*

Formed in 1959, Dave's jazz band, The Gravier Street Stompers cut their teeth at beatnik raves in Brighton fish market. They are, left to right: trombonist Dave Butler, Dave Brock on banjo, a trumpeter remembered only as Pete, and Tony Chesters on clarinet. *(Dave Brock Collection)*

Dave onstage at the Eel Pie Island jazz club in Twickenham in 1966 with his lifelong friend, pianist Mike King. "We used to play the interval," says Dave. "We were the resident blues boys doing our bit." *(Dave Brock Collection)*

Brock in cheerful mood during a newspaper interview in north Holland in April 1967. His latest band, a blues-based three-piece called The Famous Cure, made the Dutch singles charts with 'Sweet Mary'. *(Dave Brock Collection)*

The second line-up of The Famous Cure comprising, left to right: Mick Slattery, Dave Brock, John Illingworth and Humpty. Slattery and Brock would go on to form Hawkwind together.

In 1970, Hawkwind had become one of London's top freak bands. "We were doing free gigs and benefits and supporting lame ducks," says Nik Turner. They are, left to right: Thomas Crimble, Nik Turner, Dikmik, Huw Lloyd-Langton, Terry Ollis and Dave Brock.
(Peter Sanders/Rex Features)

The band were widely hailed as people's champions after their appearances at Canvas City, outside the legendary Isle Of Wight Festival, in August 1970. But it all spelt disaster for Huw Lloyd-Langton who was spiked with a massive dose of acid: "I went completely mad," he said.

Nik Turner in the crowd at the Isle Of Wight – "the guy with the silver face" to whom Jimi Hendrix dedicated a song. Hendrix also caught some of a Hawkwind set. "He sent his roadie to us with the message that he really liked what we'd been doing," says Thomas Crimble. *(Barry Plummer)*

Barney Bubbles, captured by leading underground photographer Phil Franks. Barney masterminded a complete visual identity for the band. "He was a really major part of what made Hawkwind work," said bassist Dave Anderson. Barney later committed suicide.
(Phil Franks)

A fully dressed Terry Ollis, otherwise known as "the naked drummer", and (inset) in a more characteristic, fleshy pose with Nik Turner. "I used to take my clothes off before I got to the stage," reveals Terry.
(Main pic: Phil Franks)

When Lemmy joined towards the end of 1971, he brought a harder, more urgent quality to Hawkwind.
"I was the driver behind them, and Dave was driving and he was singing too," says Lemmy.
(Jorgen Angel/Redferns)

In 1972/73, Hawkwind were at the top of their game. Pictured in a carefree moment are, left to right: Simon King, Nik Turner, Lemmy, Del Dettmar, Dikmik, Dave Brock's unnamed roadie (without Dave) and Stacia. *(Jorgen Angel)*

By 1974, Hawkwind's line-up had changed again. They were, top left to right, Del Dettmar, Dave Brock and Nik Turner and, bottom left to right, Simon King, Lemmy and Simon House. A classically trained violinist, House comments: "There was a lot of head-getting-off, and I plead guilty to that as well." *(Michael Ochs Archive/Redferns)*

Stacia's naked dancing was one of Hawkwind's major live attractions early in the Seventies. "In those days, people did discard their clothes," explains Dave Brock. "She was a totally over-the-top character." *(Jorgen Angel/Redferns)*

Problems were always stewing within the band, but Simon House took an unusually sunny view of things: "Hawkwind were years ahead of their time. It was just one big happy family, the band and the road crew and the light-show guys." *(Barry Plummer)*

Alan Powell (left) and Simon King - "the drum empire" – had become the bane of Lemmy's life by 1975. "They got all these gongs and an anvil, tubular bells and fucking chimes and all this shit," complains Lemmy. "It was fucking hopeless."
(Richie Aaron/Redferns)

Nik Turner (left) and Michael Moorcock share a joke during a joint music-press interview about the release of new albums by both Hawkwind and Deep Fix in May 1975.
(Barry Plummer)

between what I really believe in and what is the reality of the situation, and the realities of other people that are involved."

He concluded: "It really is heavy."

Trying to set aside their private disenchantments, Hawkwind left for a tour of the States and Canada, opening in St Louis on April 29, 1975.

But the resentments were festering beyond their control. Dave Brock and Nik Turner were individually losing patience with Lemmy who, in turn, was at the end of his tether with drummers Simon King and Alan Powell. And he was still isolated by his speed habit.

Hawkwind played a gig at Chicago on May 7, and it was after that that the first crisis occurred. "We were travelling through Michigan," relates Lemmy, "going from Chicago to Detroit. I was with Nik and Dave and somebody else in a car. We stopped off at a roadhouse to eat. I didn't want to eat, 'cos I'm a speedfreak. We don't eat. I went out for a walk and a look around. I came back and they'd driven off without me."

Douglas Smith remembers, "He disappeared and they waited for hours. He fucked everybody off."

"We thought that perhaps he'd gone off with somebody, that he'd been offered a big bag of drugs or a lift with a pretty girl," says Nik Turner. "We left the service station without him. What had happened was that because of what he used to take, he went off to the toilet and went to sleep. Nobody knew where he was."

Lemmy would not be the last member of Hawkwind to be left stranded for being unpunctual. "I hitch-hiked overnight, tripping, in trucks and VW vans," he recalls. "I got there at seven in the morning, arrived at the hotel and there was a cripples' convention. I'm coming down off acid and there's all these fucking wheelchairs and gimps around. I get into my room, go to sleep . . . and then I'm called for the soundcheck."

Lemmy was not the most popular person in the world that day, although he did the Detroit gig and the trouble blew over.

But a much greater trauma lay ahead. Setting off in one of two cars to Canada, where Hawkwind were due to play a gig in Toronto on May 18, Lemmy was busted at the border for possession of cocaine. In fact, it was speed, which was a much less serious offence, but he couldn't prove it straight away: the on-the-spot vial test couldn't tell the difference between the two substances. It simply turned a certain colour, and that was enough to have Lemmy charged and carted off to jail on remand.

There were, apparently, two ways of entering Canada if you were travelling from Detroit – the easy way, over the bridge, and the hard way, under the tunnel, where the border police were more scrupulous.

"They spotted Lemmy with his mouth open, head lolling back," says Dave Brock, who had been with Lemmy in the car taking the more problematic tunnel route. "We were quite a shady-looking lot. The annoying thing is we'd already been waved through. Then we all had to get out of the car. They searched Lemmy, and they found some speed which they thought was cocaine. We didn't know it was speed at the time."

Lemmy was dragged off by the Canadian police and the rest of Hawkwind carried on to Toronto.

Douglas Smith was in New York when it happened. "I wasn't going to Canada," he explains. "I was due to fly back to London the next day. I got a phone call, probably from one of the band, who said, 'Lemmy's been arrested and they confiscated a white substance.'

"I think I contacted someone in New York, who organised a brief to represent Lemmy the next morning when he came to court. But as far as I remember, the brief was told there was no point in seeing the client 'cos the case was going to be chucked out. They'd thought they were going to get him for coke, and they'd realised it was amphetamine sulphate."

Lemmy was quickly released from prison when the band arranged his bail. And since, according to his understanding, he couldn't be charged again for the same offence, he was therefore a free man. He was whisked off to the airport at lightning speed, and as he flew to rejoin Hawkwind in Toronto for the gig, he believed that they had been doing their utmost to help him since his arrest.

He sums up what happened next in a few loaded words: "Get off the plane, do a soundcheck, do a really good show . . . and get fired."

Gathering their thoughts in Toronto while Lemmy was inside a jail cell, Hawkwind held a meeting.

Nik Turner recalls: "It was collectively decided that everybody had had enough of the ups and downs of Lemmy and the difficulty of working with him at the personality end. It was decided that he would leave the band. This was one of the only collective decisions the band ever made.

"The bust was the last straw. We didn't know at the time that he only had speed, but whatever it had been, it was such a lot of hassle, and who fucking needs it, really?

"I didn't have anything personally against Lemmy, but I found it very difficult to work with him. It's regrettable that it should have come to that sort of pass. Previously, I had allowed or accepted things – 'Oh well, that's Lemmy.' But then it got to the point where we were getting attention we didn't really want from the Drug Enforcement Agency.

"We felt he'd actually drawn that attention to us. He probably didn't think he was doing anything wrong and was just carrying on as normal. But it had become too much for people. Were we supposed to be revolutionaries, confronting the authorities? I don't think that's what we were trying to do, but it was the stance that Lemmy wanted us to take."

Dave Brock agrees: "We all discussed it in a hotel room – 'He's let us down too many times in the past . . . He's always late . . .' Prior to this, it had always been hard to get Lemmy out of bed. It wasn't just one person saying these things. It was a joint band decision."

Simon House says: "I remember the meeting. Dave and Nik were saying he had to go. I'd only been in the band a few months, so I wasn't really in a position to voice an opinion. I did think it was a shame because he was such a nice bloke but, at the same time, he was habitually late for things. In retrospect, it was the wrong decision. It was a terrible, terrible decision. I think Lemmy had power and a really big charisma, he writes good songs and he's a good musician."

Having made the fateful decision, Hawkwind urgently needed someone to step in on bass. Paul Rudolph, formerly lead guitarist with Pink Fairies, was the popular choice since he knew the band's material already through his gigs with Pinkwind over the years.

Douglas Smith had arrived back in London and had just gone to bed when the first phone call came through. "It was Dave. He said, 'We've sacked Lemmy. Get Blackie [Rudolph] over here as soon as possible.' All the moves, the motivations about Lemmy came out of all of them, but were specifically pushed along by Dave. He was the person who rang me up."

Two or three hours later, Douglas woke again to the sound of the phone.

"It was Lemmy. It really put me in a difficult position because I already knew they'd thrown him out of the band. I thought it was going to be temporary. I thought they were teaching him a lesson. On numerous occasions, Lemmy wouldn't turn up until they were about to go onstage – 'Where the fuck is Lemmy? He's doing it again.' And there were threats of chucking him out."

Dave Brock and Nik Turner each claim to have been the one to break the news to Lemmy, with Nik believing that, "It seems to be something that Lemmy has always held against me, the fact that I sacked him. To me, I was just voicing the consensus of the band."

Lemmy may well believe that Nik was instrumental in the decision, but his memories of being sacked are as follows: "I did the show in Toronto and I was quite happy. I was all right with them [the rest of Hawkwind]. I'd got used to all the bollocks. The show was a sell-out and it went down a storm.

"We were in the hotel after the show, it was 4am and I was summoned to one of the other rooms. I think it was Nik Turner's room. Dave and Nik and Simon [King] were together, and Alan Powell. It was Dave who actually spoke. I was fired. I went straight back to my room, 'cos I had two chicks there.

"The only reason they'd let me do the Toronto show was 'cos Paul Rudolph couldn't get out there in time. They already had Paul on his way, apparently. I didn't find that out until after I'd been fired."

Dave Brock says of the sacking: "I remember a billboard flashing outside the window. I was the one who actually had to say, 'We've all made this decision.' Quite upsetting, it was. Lemmy was very upset, 'cos it was his life."

Nik Turner adds: "I think he was very stunned by it, and very remorseful, but he probably couldn't see the reason for it because he was always *right*."

Some believe that certain individuals had wanted to get rid of Lemmy long before he was apprehended at the border.

Nik claims: "I don't know, in hindsight, if there was a personal agenda going on as well. I was told that Dave Brock had been talking about sacking Lemmy six months earlier. *I* hadn't been talking about sacking Lemmy. I hadn't been talking about sacking anyone. I just accepted the way things were. At the end, when he was leaving, it wasn't me that said, 'I don't want Lemmy in the band.' I wasn't a driving force more than anybody else was. Everybody had agreed it. It was increasingly difficult to work with him because of the drug situation and because he always had to be right."

Brock rejects the suggestion that he had been planning to fire Lemmy, counter-claiming that Turner had threatened to leave if Lemmy didn't – an allegation vigorously denied by Nik.

Douglas Smith does not go along with any of these theories. He declares: "I can't remember anything going down before this, or that this was a conspiracy. I think that when they sacked Lemmy, it was a hot-headed reaction to what had happened on the tour and at previous gigs. It was such a shame. I just could not believe it. I thought they were completely mad.

"There was always the evil side to Hawkwind, the wicked side that the public wouldn't see. They weren't very nice to each other . . . chucking Lemmy out of the band because he got busted. 'Hey, wait a minute – you're supposed to be supporting this guy.'"

"They fired a guy 'cos he got busted for the wrong drugs," snaps Lemmy.

In one interview published on the internet, Lemmy revealed that he felt looked down upon by the other members. "They weren't doing speed, and it was just like the caste system in India. 'Well, we'll take these drugs because they're cool and we don't take those drugs because they're not.' It was very strange – anybody who does take those 'lesser' drugs must be a fucking pariah. Unmentionable."

The "speed division" had claimed its remaining victim.

Lemmy returned to England as Paul Rudolph arrived to take up his unexpected post in Hawkwind. They finished up one or two gigs in America and not much more than a week later, set off on a European tour.

But Dave Brock wanted Lemmy back.

Says Lemmy: "He agreed with my sacking at the time, and then he realised what a horrible fucking mistake they'd made. He didn't think he was to blame. It was already in his head he hadn't been even part of it. Paul had arrived and it didn't work, and Dave asked me to rejoin. He was the only one who did. He was most embarrassed. In those days, he got on very well with Nicky [Nik], although he doesn't now, but it's always been Dave Brock's band. So I said, 'Okay.'"

On this occasion, however, the captain was unable to garner any support for having Lemmy back, and the invitation was withdrawn without apology. "Dave's not good at that shit," acknowledges Lemmy. "He's not good at 'sorry'. The others wouldn't let him go through with it – 'We think you should stand by the decision.' The two drummers were really vocal about it. They wanted a 'real' bass player, one who stands still at the back and lets them play their gongs. Dave never really lost his grip of the band, but there are periods when he coasts along."

Dave confirms: "I didn't withdraw the offer. The others did. They decided 'no'. The trouble was, Lemmy and me used to play together and then I had to start working with a bass player I'd never played with. There he was playing bass and I felt, 'God . . .' I knew Paul could play better lead guitar than I could, and my confidence went a bit down the drain. He started playing lead guitar and I'd switch to bass on some of the numbers.

"Del had gone, and things were changing anyway. I used to get on very well with Paul. He was a nice enough character and I used to share a room with him on tour but, yeah, I missed Lemmy. We'd been playing together for four years. It was a wrong decision to get rid of him. We should have written things more together, we should have done lots of things differently, but that's the way it is. We're all involved in egos, don't forget. Some people felt more important than others."

Lemmy ventures: "I always say I would never have left Hawkwind if I hadn't been fired – or I might have. If 'The Drum Empire' had carried on, I would have left, but it obviously was not going to carry on because they fired Alan Powell later.

"It was great – they fired me and their career immediately went down the toilet, although it wasn't 'cos they fired me – it was 'cos they didn't get the right replacement. I was the driver. I wasn't indestructible, but you can't replace me with somebody who puts their leg up on the drum riser and plays a jazz solo."

Perhaps surprisingly, Dave Brock agrees with Lemmy's assessment. "It did go down the drainhole after Lemmy had gone," he affirms. "That was the start of the decline of that era, the start of the empire changing. Three years later, that was the end of it all."

But only for a little while.

Douglas Smith was coming to terms with the fact that Lemmy had gone for good. He was still appalled. "It was such a silly thing," he says. "That was *the* successful band, *the* live gig. The personae onstage were just awesome. If you look at the period from the Space Ritual to

Lemmy leaving – that was their peak. That's when they sold more albums and tickets than they'd had hot dinners. That really was the magic band and everybody since has just really lived off that era of success.

"Lemmy's front-of-the-stage persona was one of the strongest that the band had apart from Nik Turner who basically went over the top, which was great. And Stacia – every little boy's fantasy, of course. I don't think any of them ever realised what size of a draw she was in Hawkwind. She was enormous.

"As far as the show went, Nik, Lemmy and Stacia were really the key people, and Calvert when he was there. The trouble about Robert was that he never got recognised for what he really was in that band. Going back to *In Search Of Space*, there's a lot of influence from Calvert – and Barney."

In terms of personal politics, Douglas cites a different combination of characters: "Dave and Nik and Lemmy and Simon King were the most powerful people within the band, and Dave and Nik were the two main contenders for power."

Smith believes that Hawkwind should have hung on to Lemmy no matter what their problems with him, admitting to having his own difficulties with the reckless bass player. "I had Lemmy up to here [points to neck] all the time," says Smith. "He was constantly ahead of himself financially. Near the end, just before he left the band, we were having a real desperate time. Financially, we didn't have tuppence. I was just trying to keep Hawkwind afloat.

"They cost a lot of money. We had so many people being paid to go out and do a show – three people to do lighting, an out-front sound engineer, a monitor engineer, virtually a roadie for every member of the band. We were carrying, on any given night, maybe 13 to 15 people. We bought visuals for Hawkwind, and lighting equipment.

"One day I was going to borrow money from this less-than-salubrious East End character. I remember telling Lemmy, 'I don't have any money. I'm going to have to go and see Alan today.' He said, 'Big Al? Oh, well, maybe you can borrow £50 for me as well.' And there was me trying to raise five or 10 grand . . .

"He used to spend hours on slot machines at gigs and clubs, and he used to try and tap people for a couple of quid. I remember seeing him once counting out poor old Magic Michael's pennies. Everybody used to go, 'I've got no more money.' We couldn't get a bank manager to give him a loan. They'd say, 'Look at his bank account. You put it in, it goes out.' He spent money that was unbelievable on a weekly basis. You put £1,000 in his pocket and he'll spend it.

"Lemmy didn't have money. He just spent it. And he was living in hotels. He got very comfortable in this hotel in the Edgware Road. He'd ring up and want to borrow £30. He'd say, 'Put it in a cab.' Then he'd ring back – 'Has the cab left yet? Can someone pop down to the off-licence and get me a bottle of Jack?' The bottle of Jack would go in the cab, and the £30 had suddenly become a tenner because he'd have to pay for the cab and the off-licence.

"Dave Brock knew what money was. Nik Turner was peace and love most of the time. Simon King and Alan Powell were okay. Lemmy has never understood what budgeting is. But at the same time, if you look at record sales and changes in personnel, you can see how quickly it started to go downhill after he left."

Nik Turner begs to differ.

He states: "Lemmy probably felt that he was the main cause of the band's success, but I wouldn't really say that was true. He probably says that the success trailed off after he left because he felt he was quite contributory and instrumental to that success. It escapes me how. The only thing he did was sing on 'Silver Machine'.

"He probably was a good frontman, but I don't remember whether he was a good frontman any more than Robert Calvert was, or I was, although I've never seen myself as a frontman. I saw Robert and Barney Bubbles as really being the people that created the band's success.

"Lemmy says it was Dave's band. I thought it was everybody's band. Obviously, Lemmy had his own slant on it. I saw it as a community project with everybody involved and we were all hippies together. Lemmy discounts that as a lot of rubbish, lacking in any relevance or value. He saw it as a vehicle for him and Dikmik to take speed and be on big ego trips, although Dikmik wasn't like that.

"I don't know that we were criticised for getting rid of him. Obviously, people wanted to know where Lemmy was. I can't remember anybody saying, 'Oh, the band isn't the same without Lemmy,' although they probably did."

Devastated though he was to have been chucked out of Hawkwind, Lemmy has not been too proud to return to the band every now and again for guest appearances. "You can't bear grudges all your fucking life," he says. "Life's too short. I'm not going to spend my life thinking about how I hate somebody. I got a lot of funny shit to do, and none of it involves that."

Which is not to say that he didn't exact his revenge at the time.

He confided, in *Classic Rock*: "By the time they got back to England, I'd fucked all their old ladies except for Dave Brock's wife, because she lived in Devon, too far away, and besides, I didn't fancy her."

Lemmy is slightly more evasive today.

He admits: "I didn't fuck all of them. Some of 'em were butt ugly.

"I was back and all their geezers were away. I went around and saw these women just as a 'courtesy thing'. It was all done in the best possible taste. Some people will believe anything . . .

"I'm not going to say which ones I did, because it would lead to terrible sideways glances next time I see them. I like to keep them on their toes – 'I wonder if it was mine?' "

Just a while later, Lemmy managed to find a way into Hawkwind's storage space to sneak out his equipment with an accomplice.

He was quoted in *Classic Rock*: "We had just gotten my stuff into the van when Alan Powell caught us. He was shouting, 'Yeah, ya cunt, you thought you'd steal your stuff back!' We drove off laughing . . ."

Lemmy went on to form Motorhead, which he still fronts, remarking: "The first Motorhead album, you can still hear a lot of the stuff I did with Hawkwind. Eddie ["Fast Eddie" Clarke, guitarist] would just play on E and I'd go all around him."

It was like history repeating itself with a slightly different twist, echoing back to Nik Turner asking Lemmy to "make some noises in E" those years earlier at Powis Square.

Refusing to give up on Lemmy's potential, Douglas Smith took up the reins of Motorhead with Richard Ogden, who left his press officer's job at United Artists to work in a managerial capacity with Smith at his office – another premises in Great Western Road, north-west London, close to the house in which the early Hawkwind had painted the basement and rehearsed with strobe lights.

Douglas and Richard kept Lemmy on salary, signed Motorhead, and then licensed them to United Artists.

It was troublesome from the beginning, according to Douglas. "Lemmy didn't want to make the move to set up his own band. He was playing with it. He'd had rehearsals and at one point it was even a five-piece. He wasn't maturing into it, and every week we were paying him wages. Sooner or later we needed to make an album, get him out on the road.

"I remember Richard saying, 'That's it, I've had enough.' We did a deal for Motorhead with UA and, of course, we hadn't told Lemmy. I said to him, 'Lemmy, you're probably going to get a few phone calls from journalists today about your new band. I've told them you're called Motorhead.'

"He said, 'Oh, you fucking shit, man. I wanted to call it Bastards.' "

News of Lemmy's sacking from Hawkwind was printed in the June 7 issue of the *NME*, along with the announcement that Motorhead had been formed.

"The first gigs they did were terrible," says Smith. And the first tour was supporting Hawkwind.

"I didn't mind supporting them," recalls Lemmy. "We needed a tour. We didn't see much of them on the road, although I'd see Dave Brock now and again. We were too busy being Motorhead for the first time. Later on, they supported us at Wembley . . . ha, ha, ha!"

A few years after his sacking from Hawkwind, Lemmy would inspire Nik Turner more than he ever had when he was in the band.

Says Nik: "I went to a Motorhead gig at Hammersmith Odeon. The whole of the back of the stage was Hell's Angels, really giving people black looks. Jesus Christ, what a fucking horrible place. And the band were so loud I had to wear earplugs.

"I met Rick Parfitt from Status Quo and he said, 'What do you do, then?' I said, 'I'm a roadie.' He said, 'I know Hawkwind. One of their songs made a big impression on me.' He told me it was 'You Shouldn't Do That'. I said, 'I wrote that,' and then I told him who I was.

"Driving home, all I could hear was this fucking ringing in my ears, a roaring noise. Out of the noise, I could hear a tune, and out of the tune I could hear these lyrics, which were all about this girlfriend I had who became a junkie, about her world and my world. I went home and wrote it all down and it turned into 'Two Worlds', a song I recorded with my band Inner City Unit. It was on our second album, *Maximum Effect*. So that's one thing Lemmy did – he inspired that song."

Douglas, meanwhile, went on to expand his management company, also taking in Girlschool – big friends of Motorhead – but in time his problems with Lemmy would escalate. Amid serious arguments, legal threats and accusations of stealing money, all of which ended with

Douglas being cleared by accountants of any wrongdoing, he would terminate his management of Motorhead.

But back in 1975, in the aftermath of Lemmy's departure, Douglas was happy to handle both Hawkwind and Motorhead. At the end of the year, though, he gave up on Hawkwind completely. At the same time, they lost their record deal with United Artists.

CHAPTER 11

Astounding Sounds, Amazing Music, Astonishing Troubles

WITH Lemmy gone and Paul Rudolph in place on bass, Hawkwind spent June 1975 touring Europe with a package that also included Gong, Man, Henry Cow and a curious vibes player called Robert Wood.

Melody Maker's Allan Jones was once again sent into the fray to gauge their progress and he reported that, "None of the bands seem to be enjoying the tour to any great extent."

They certainly didn't enjoy the riot that broke out in Paris at La Gare De La Bastille during Man's set. According to Jones, "The stage doors are violently flung open. There's some kind of explosion. Tear gas. Your reporter gets a face-full, catches sight of Stacia reeling back, and heart stops, dozens of maniac French *musique libre* guerillas . . . well, very stoned lunatics . . . swarm through a breach in the ranks, smashing equipment as they hurtle onwards."

The French security guards were quick to respond, whipping out lengths of wood from their combat-jacket sleeves and lashing out indiscriminately. "There are a lot of cracked heads," reported Allan.

Hawkwind took the stage when the gig had returned to some semblance of normality, although Allan Jones felt that the tension added an extra dimension to the band's set. More than that, though, he proceeded, "They actually are sounding much better.

"The sound is cleaner, more efficient," he wrote. "And whatever one's essential antipathy, they do sound impressive at times."

Jones especially appreciated Simon House's increasing contributions on keyboards and violin. He added: "Rudolph clings more to the careering rhythm machine of King and Powell, which means that Dave Brock can ease back a little. The overall sound, then, is not so distractingly dominated by his surrogate Sterling Morrison guitar vamps."

Paul Rudolph was born in Canada where he grew up and, as a schoolboy, was friendly with Jamie Mandelkau. Leaving school, he performed around nightclubs until 1969 when Mandelkau – by then in London managing The Deviants – invited him over to join the band as their guitarist.

The Deviants spent a few hungry months on the west coast of America, playing only a handful of gigs. "We were starving," Rudolph told Allan Jones. "We eventually moved back to Montreal where we spent Christmas . . . hot dogs and Coke for Christmas dinner. Boy, were we hungry. But I believed that we could pull through."

They couldn't. Rudolph was in the line-up when the band plotted to get rid of frontman and prime mover Mick Farren, and did so in Vancouver, Canada. In a second act of perceived treachery, Mandelkau had taken up with Farren's wife Joy.

The former Deviants then returned to England where they re-grouped as Pink Fairies with one-time Pretty Things drummer Twink. When the Fairies finally ground to a halt, Rudolph found himself out of work for a while. He played occasional gigs at the London watering hole Dingwalls in Chalk Farm, and served briefly with Uncle Dog, a band led by the talented soul-influenced rock singer Carol Grimes.

In the meantime, he was trying to put a band together with some friends from May Blitz, but gave up after auditioning something like 100 drummers.

Fate intervened when Uncle Dog played what would be their penultimate gig at a pub in the Portobello Road. The audience included Brian Eno and John Punter, Bryan Ferry's guitarist and a friend of Rudolph's. Eno was struck by Paul's playing, and invited him to join the sessions for his forthcoming album, *Here Come The Warm Jets*.

Then came the distress call from Hawkwind.

Now they were seven: Dave Brock, Nik Turner, Stacia, Simon House, Simon King, Alan Powell and Paul Rudolph.

After Europe and a few selected UK shows, Hawkwind called in Al Matthews, on congas, for a prestigious appearance at the Reading Festival on August 22, headlining the Friday line-up over Dr Feelgood, UFO and Kokomo. Robert Calvert also made a surprise guest appearance on vocals and percussion, having completed work on his second solo album, the Eno-produced *Lucky Leif And The Longships*. Released the next month, it failed to chart.

The Reading set was largely built around *Warrior On The Edge Of Time*, with renditions of 'Assault And Battery', 'The Golden Void', 'Opa-Loka', 'Spiral Galaxy 28948' and 'Magnu', although every other album was represented too, apart from the first. Hawkwind played 'Master Of The Universe', 'The Awakening', 'Sonic Attack', 'Welcome To The Future', 'Brainstorm', 'The Psychedelic Warlords', 'Wind Of Change' and finished with 'Silver Machine'.

By contrast, the next night's gig was filled with freeform jams, just like the old days, with 'You Shouldn't Do That', 'Brainstorm', 'Paradox' and 'Magnu' forming the recognisable parts of a set performed at the Watchfield free festival by Dave Brock, Nik Turner, Alan Powell and Paul Rudolph.

They were without Stacia. In fact, they would be without her from now on. Quitting on a high after Reading, she left the band to get married. Says Lemmy: "We were the freaks in the band and they were gradually getting rid of us. Stacia was the top freak, and the most visible. When she left, they should have realised that something was seriously wrong. She was the ultimate live-and-let-live girl. She went off with Roy Dyke, the drummer from Ashton, Gardner & Dyke, and they moved to Hamburg where, for all I know, they still are."

Actually, Stacia was last heard of in Ireland pursuing artistic interests including painting – a tranquillity she would not have found in Hawkwind.

Dave Brock remarks: "When we did these tours of America, she had these idolising groupies, men and women, following her around. It was quite a strange entourage. The travelling was very difficult for her, being the only woman in the group. She also injured her foot onstage at some point. There was one of those iron weights they put on scenery to keep it down. She kicked that and fractured a bone in her foot. And then falling in love with Roy Dyke . . . Maybe it was a combination of all these things that led to her leaving the band."

Stacia has a grown-up daughter, keeps her life private and, by all accounts, is not mad keen on talking about her old days in Hawkwind. It's believed that she has separated from Roy Dyke and that he relocated to Germany.

It was in the aftermath of Reading that Jonathan Smeeton – Liquid

Len – also took a break from Hawkwind, although he would soon return in spectacular style.

And there was yet another personnel change when, after an autumn tour of Europe, Douglas Smith decided that his on-off management of the band was definitely off. This coincided with their United Artists contract coming up for renewal. "The ticket and album sales were still okay at that particular moment," he says, "and I had worked out a deal with UA where they would support the band and the crew for a year to allow us to rebuild a new stage show and do something like Floyd did – stand back, look at what we'd done and then go at it again.

"I was watching things starting to go down a little, and we had to get the band back up again. They looked out from the stage, they'd see 500, 600 people there and they'd go, 'That's pretty good.' They didn't realise the people had four feet between each other. They'd say, 'It was full, man.' 'Oh, so the promoter's ripping you off?'

"And so this thing was going down and I'd got this deal with UA all sorted out and I got a phone call. I think it was Simon House that called me: 'Man, it's like this. We're a gigging band and we just want to go on gigging.' I said, 'But you've just been offered a year off to put something nice and new together.' 'Oh, but you know, man, we're a gigging band.'

"I said, 'There's not much we can do then.' "

Douglas Smith – who only a year or two earlier had rented out a room in his Acton home to Dave for use when he was in London – also claims that he started feeling uncomfortable about other aspects of Hawkwind at this time. "At the beginning, there was a very equal attitude among everybody. We lived as a family, a large collective in many ways. What came in went out. When large sums of money rolled in, they were shared among everybody. I never took my commission, whatever it was. I just paid myself salaries, which were probably less than what my commission would've been at the time. It was very much one for all and all for one. And then one day it quickly changed, which is when I left the whole thing."

Two or three years later, Douglas would once again be persuaded back to the group. But in the meantime, they took on new management in the shape of Tony Howard, whose Wizzard Artists looked after T Rex among other acts.

Nik Turner was instrumental in securing the management deal with Howard, who had strong links to Steve O'Rourke and Pink Floyd's management. Howard and O'Rourke were old buddies who had offices in the same Bond Street building.

Jeff Dexter – perhaps the most influential club DJ of the Sixties and early Seventies – was part of Howard's set-up, frequently acting as a road manager for Hawkwind. Nik Turner also "wangled" a place in the touring operation for Jamie Mandelkau, who had originally suggested he approach Howard.

Tony Howard negotiated a record deal with Charisma, with the returning Bob Calvert assigned to lead vocals – a role which had previously been shared out. Now he would apply his unique monotone to the actual songs rather than the usual recitations in between them.

Come 1976, Hawkwind had a new management, a new record deal and a new album on the way. Yet, for Dave Brock, the captain, it was all going seriously wrong. And it would get worse.

Brock, who was already confronting a couple of major insecurities, was unhappy with the way things were heading with the new album, *Astounding Sounds, Amazing Music*, which the band were recording in The Roundhouse Studios, Chalk Farm, during February and March. Moving right away from the concept of time and space, the universe that Hawkwind had made their own, it sought a more contemporary approval, and Barney Bubbles' cover art confirmed the change of direction.

Says Nik Turner: "Barney and Robert and myself devised it. We intended it to be a cheesy Fifties pulp-sci-fi sort of thing, 'cos I'd grown up on comic books where there were adverts for all these wonder cures and hypnotism and Charles Atlas, stuff like that. We used all these images characterising the band members in different roles promoting different products – Monsieur Nik's French Lingerie Company, Doc De Brock's Atomic Pile Remover . . ."

Robert Calvert told *Melody Maker* that the album aimed for "a kind of meeting between intellectual thought and Marvel Comics."

Tellingly, Turner loved it as much as Brock disliked it. "I think it was a very good album," says Nik. "There was a lot of input from everybody in the band, which hadn't hitherto been apparent. In the past, Dave probably wrote about 90 per cent of what was on the albums. I wrote seven per cent. I wrote a few songs with Dave, and Robert Calvert wrote quite a few songs with him, but I would say that Dave dominated most of the output.

"On *Astounding Sounds,* most of the people in the band got credited for writing. We had very much more variety in the musical input and creative ideas."

Dave Brock retorts, "Some of the songs were Nik's. They were really boring. Rather than standing up and saying, 'These numbers are fucking awful,' we felt like we had to play on them. I didn't like that album. We'd gone funky, and I didn't like the sound. I felt I was being given the elbow – which I was."

In March 1976, the group went out on a short UK college tour to introduce some of the new material, usually 'Reefer Madness', 'Kerb Crawler', 'Steppenwolf' and 'The Aubergine That Ate Rangoon'. They were joined on the road by dancer Rikki Howard, who had previously worked with such diverse talents as Alex Harvey and Des O'Connor, and would go on to play Betty in the BBC sitcom *Hi-de-Hi!*

Dave Brock chuckles: "She had a sense of humour, Rikki did. She used to be onstage for 'Kerb Crawler'. Bob Calvert was quite a stickler for things being right. He'd be singing, *'Excuse me, lady, are you looking for a lift?'*, and she used to have little high heels clicking, like the song says, and she minced across the stage with him following, singing this song to her. He'd have his back to the audience.

"One night at Preston Guildhall, she grabbed his bollocks and made him choke. He was furious and he went bananas. After the show, he was shouting, 'Don't you ever do that to me ever again.' It was quite funny."

It was a quiet summer for Hawkwind on the live front, although they ventured out for a couple of gigs, one at an all-day music festival at Cardiff Castle on July 24 with Status Quo, Strawbs, Curved Air and Budgie.

NME declared the band to be "shit hot" and appreciated the theatrics, with Brock and Turner affecting World War I aviator goggles and Robert Calvert, in black leather jodhpurs, riding boots, a headscarf and a flying helmet, coming on "like a cross between Biggles and Lawrence Of Arabia with definite S&M overtones".

At the same time, Hawkwind released 'Kerb Crawler', which was mixed by Pink Floyd guitarist Dave Gilmour, as a single. It bombed.

The album, released by Charisma a month later, reached its top chart position of 33 in September – only one place higher than the UA compilation *Roadhawks* had managed in April.

Despite the reservations of Brock and an apparent portion of the

Hawkwind audience, *NME* pronounced that with *Astounding Sounds, Amazing Music*, Hawkwind were "back on form". Reviewer Dick Tracy urged readers: "On the strength of this album, all those who stopped listening after 'Silver Machine' should tune into this wavelength again immediately." He was particularly impressed by the high-powered 'Reefer Madness' and 'Kerb Crawler', by the "nice surprise" of 'The Aubergine That Ate Rangoon', with its tricky drums and convincing instrumental work, and by the "other lazy, spacey electronics".

Sounds' Geoff Barton was less enthusiastic, feeling that it was "good enough but failing to match the greatness that was, for example, *Doremi Fasol Latido*".

The album would not survive the years as a Hawkwind classic.

The Astounding Sounds tour, a massive extravaganza, began in September 1976, just as punk rock was exploding all over the media. Unlike many of their contemporaries, the members of Hawkwind were interested and excited by the new cultural phenomenon. They certainly didn't feel threatened since although they had little obvious musical connection with the rising, noisy young upstarts, they shared a deep and healthy disrespect for the status quo.

The great punk-hippie divide was never completely convincing: the apparent enemies, if they were serious about their ideologies, had more similarities than differences. Later, many of punk's leading lights would avow their admiration for the example set by Hawkwind with some, including the Sex Pistols' John Lydon, confessing a more direct influence.

Liquid Len had returned to Hawkwind in collusion with a lighting designer called Larry Smart to create a spectacular stage set called Atomhenge for the tour. Dave Brock: "The idea was that it was Stonehenge made to look like crystals. We had a Cornish theatre company working with us with lots of dancers and mime artists. It was a very good, very visual, very exciting stage show. It cost quite a lot of money to run. We probably had 30 people with us."

Geoff Barton described Atomhenge to *Sounds* readers this way: "The construction not only took up the width of the stage but also towered imposingly above the audience. It looked like some vast blow-up of the structure of an atom, central 'crystals' joined at various points by translucent 'bridges' . . ." And then the object "blazed into life".

"The device is every bit as impressive as Ritchie Blackmore's

Rainbow, even though it only cost about £3,000 as opposed to Rainbow's £40,000. Atomhenge is full, it seems, of multi-coloured bulbs. Throughout Hawkwind's show, it pulses on and off quite dramatically, and when slides are projected on to the screens behind it, the 3D effect is startling."

Barton reported that the Birmingham Odeon was packed to capacity and that the band themselves were "revitalised", professing his relief that they had, for the most part, left the Space Ritual behind. He enjoyed the theatrical exchanges between Robert Calvert and Dave Brock during the "stole my stash" chant in 'Reefer Madness'. Indeed, he seemed completely fascinated by Calvert – "a most compelling onstage figure", who appeared in a sinister black coat and black top hat for 'Steppenwolf' and, later, was even more literally dressed to kill, brandishing swords with which he battled invisible enemies. Eventually, he assumed his increasingly familiar Lawrence Of Arabia persona.

The next day, Calvert told Barton that the band were hoping to move towards a more spontaneous theatre supplied by the musicians and not their stage show, while insisting that it must arise naturally from the music. "We're trying to get the visual side of the band focused on individuals rather than on screen projections," he said. "Nik, Dave and myself are, in some parts of the show, playing the parts of actors . . . what we're striving for is a true science-fiction show.

"Take 'Brainstorm', for example. In the middle of the number, we all do three different chants that merge together. What happened last night was that first of all Nik was playing this sax solo wearing a big pair of lenseless spectacles, looking totally insane. I used my megaphone like an eyepiece and examined him – I could've been a galactic psychiatric inspector or something.

"Then I went over to Dave who was wearing a gas mask with a big hole in it and the trunk hanging down, looking extremely sinister, and I examined him and then accused them both of brainstorm. 'Brainstorm! Brainstorm!' I yelled into the microphone. Nik denied it with his 'Brainstorm!' and Dave went, 'Brainstorm – What's he say? What's he say?' "

Calvert also talked about his onstage characterisations. "The main character I play is someone called Aubrey Dawney. He's a sort of 1914 fighter ace, plus a bit more. He has connections with the Far East and also opium smoking. At the end of the show, I'm a sword-and-sorcery character wearing a silver horned helmet and inscribing runes with my blade."

As an interesting aside, Geoff Barton remarked on the lack of drugs around the Hawkwind camp and his surprise at finding Nik Turner and Paul Rudolph extolling the virtues of health food.

The tour wound up at London's Hammersmith Odeon on October 5, with Del Dettmar – visiting from Canada – appearing on synthesisers as a special guest. The band continued telling journalists about Del's "log cabin".

During the year's live concerts, Paul Rudolph had been taking lead guitar spots while Dave Brock or Simon House stood in on bass. Both *NME*, reviewing the Cardiff festival gig, and *Sounds* at Birmingham were effusive in their praise for Rudolph's prowess.

"My confidence was really waning then," confesses Dave Brock, who remembers an attempted coup. "Paul Rudolph was the catalyst for that," he asserts. "I knew Paul could play better than I could. Behind it was Nik's manipulation. He was a big buddy of Paul's. I could see how the situation developed into them trying to get rid of me."

Interestingly, Rudolph would end up being instrumental in Nik Turner's sacking from the band. But to begin with, the crisis was Dave's.

"I was sacked," Brock reveals. "When you look back over all this, I'm quite an easy-going character. I don't think I'm a difficult person. They'd got rid of Lemmy, and Nik had got Paul Rudolph in the band. Nik was very buddy-buddy with him. I'd probably say my guitar playing was a bit wishy-washy at the time. You go through bad patches.

"But you get cliques within the band, and I felt I was being edged out by Paul Rudolph, Alan Powell and Nik Turner. Bob [Calvert] was at a meeting with them and he rang me up and said, 'Nik Turner's decided you're sacked from the band.' 'What? I'll punch him in the mouth . . .'

"I phoned up our manager Tony Howard. He said, 'Perhaps we should meet up.' Bob Calvert said, 'Let's go to London and sort them out.' We went to Tony Howard's office, and I think Simon King was there. Basically, it was decided: 'Turner goes 'cos he can't play the saxophone properly.'"

Nik Turner emphatically denies any plot to oust Dave Brock. "I was really good buddies with everybody," he insists. "I thought Paul Rudolph was a good guitarist. But I didn't have any conspiracy with him, or any meeting to sack Dave. No, but I wish I had. Nobody else would remember this because it isn't true. I didn't engineer or manipulate a situation like that. It's a fantasy in Dave's lurid imagination. Warped."

Nik's recollection of events is being suddenly presented with an ultimatum. "I was put into what I considered to be an untenable position where I was told by certain people – Paul Rudolph, Simon King and I can't remember who else – that if I didn't leave the band, they would. In which case one would end up with no band, which would have been a terrible outcome.

"Dave evaded the issue. His stance was, 'I don't mind, but it's everybody else.' But I'm sure he instigated it, Dave. I think he engineered the situation. It was quite ironic, really. I was at one point involved in getting the band a management deal with Tony Howard. Then I saw how he operated with, for instance, Marc Bolan. He just dealt with Bolan, the main man, and sacked or manipulated the rest of the band. They weren't a band any more. They were just guys that did tours and got wages for them, and probably got a session fee for recording. The lion's share was owned by Marc, or his manager and Marc.

"That's how I saw Tony Howard retrospectively. I felt that Hawkwind went down the same path. Tony Howard saw Dave as the person he could deal with, that they spoke the same language, and the band were all expendable. I felt that was how I came to leave.

"It may be rather a naïve viewpoint, but I felt I'd contributed to a large degree to the band's success. I was very happy it was a community thing I was able to take part in. I contributed PR. I did most of the interviews for quite a while and I was on the front pages of all the music papers periodically.

"I hadn't seen it [his own sacking] coming. I should've been a bit wiser, I guess. I was just very trusting. When I realised what was happening, I think I was quite disgusted and happy to leave because, quite honestly, I didn't want to be involved with these people, a bunch of shits that had no loyalty or regard or respect for my role in the band, which I feel was contributory to its success.

"Lemmy always saw it as Dave's band. I later discovered that Dave considers it to be his own band, and he was in control of it. That made me aware of the fact that he was actually behind the scenes and had his own agenda."

Douglas Smith was not working with Hawkwind at the time of this upheaval, although he would later have many dealings with the band and its ex-members. He doesn't remember hearing about the uprising against Dave Brock, although he sees the situation that arose in November 1976 as the outcome of a leadership struggle between Dave and Nik.

"Not at all!" protests Turner. "I never wanted to control Hawkwind. I wanted to maintain the spirit of the band, what it represented to me and to people like Barney Bubbles, Robert Calvert and Michael Moorcock, this thing which was initially brilliant for positive action, doing good things for people. I used to organise lots of benefits, I'd drive the van a lot of the time and I'd get the band there. I never saw this as my being the leader.

"You may say Dave and I were the strongest personalities or images in the band, but we were sort of opposites as well. I tend to be positive and spread a little happiness. Dave is totally self-interested."

"I think there was a rivalry between the two of them," insists Smith. "If not a rivalry, Nik had a view of life that was very different to Dave's. It's difficult. Sometimes Nik can't relate to other people's emotions and feelings, and that might have been more what the relationship was. He was a very strong go-getter. He was very much into working hard, building a show, creating something. Dave was as well, but he wanted it to go his way."

Brock, who has always seen himself as the captain, agrees that he and Nik may have been equally single-minded in their differing ambitions for the band.

Responding to Dave's criticisms of his saxophone playing, Turner says today: "That might have been true. Lemmy said the same thing. But I'm improving . . . I don't know, really. I just enjoyed playing, and a lot of people enjoyed what I was doing, and quite often other people had their own agendas."

Of the charges that he played over other band members' efforts, he ventures: "I don't know if it's true or not. I wouldn't say it wasn't true. I wouldn't say it was either. I've heard records which I'm not credited with being on which I obviously am on, and I wouldn't say I'm playing over anybody else. I don't try to impose myself or play over someone else's solo or try to block people out in any way. I'm a great fan of John Coltrane, Charlie Parker . . . I just like the saxophone."

The shock and drama surrounding Nik Turner's departure was

compounded by other exits. Alan Powell left at around the same time and after a short December tour, so did Paul Rudolph. Their sackings had been agreed at the same meeting with Tony Howard that had sealed Nik Turner's fate. Rudolph told the *NME*'s Dick Tracy that Nik was turfed out because he was "one chap spoiling the fun for the rest of the chaps" – only days before himself leaving the fun and the chaps.

Turner, Powell and Rudolph were the three people Dave believed had tried to remove him from the band he had founded. And although he thought that Powell and Rudolph were great musicians and that Alan was "a nice character", Dave had not been happy with *Astounding Sounds, Amazing Music*, which he reckoned had taken the band "off at a tangent". It was time for a change.

The double-drummer experiment – Lemmy's hated Drum Empire – was over, not to be repeated. Simon King was powerful enough on his own to carry Hawkwind into their next incarnation, and Rudolph was soon replaced on bass by Adrian Shaw, a musician the group had known for quite some time.

Powell and Rudolph then teamed up to form an outfit called Kicks. Rudolph was most recently thought to be running a bicycle shop in Vancouver, while Powell has continued to play, notably experimenting with something called "croonabilly", according to Nik Turner.

Adrian Shaw, the incoming bassist, says, "I know that Paul Rudolph and Alan Powell wanted to go in a very different direction. They were slicker musicians. They wanted to be funkier, which was missing the point of the band. I have to go along with Dave on that one. There again, it didn't return to the old Hawkwind we knew, but for different reasons."

Nik Turner's absence was the most keenly felt of the three, certainly among the fans. They had become very fond of the gangly, outrageously dressed sax and flute player who always had time for a friendly chat.

He reflects: "At the time, Robert Calvert was in the band and I would've thought he'd fill the gap, but maybe he didn't. Perhaps I was something to the people that I wasn't aware of, or maybe I just didn't think of what I did as being anything other than normal. I didn't think about any of that when I left. Retrospectively, I should have used it as a springboard. Instead, I went into a spiritual situation and recorded flute music inside the Great Pyramid."

That particular project would go under the name of Sphynx, resulting in an album titled *Xitintoday*, released by Charisma in June 1978 and produced by Steve Hillage who also contributed guitar. The assembled musicians included Miquette Giraudy of Gong, Tim Blake on keyboards, Andy Anderson and Malcolm Ashmore on drums, Mike Howlett on bass, Harry Williamson on guitar and a zither-like instrument, and a bunch of friends collectively known as The Lost Bongos Of Atlantis.

Sphynx would eventually mutate into Inner City Unit, with Nik collaborating once again with former Hawkwind bassist Dave Anderson. And it was during a difficult time with Inner City Unit that Nik would finally return to Hawkwind for a second troubled term.

In the meantime, Turner sold the family home outside Margate and moved to south-west Wales, near Fishguard in Carmarthen, where he still lives, now with the benefit of a studio at his house.

As 1976 gave way to a new year, Robert Calvert looked back over the arguments, the comings and goings, and stated simply: "It was the worst year for us."

Things could only get better. Or maybe not.

CHAPTER 12

Quark Strangeness And Punk

IT looked like it was jinxed, the bass player's job in Hawkwind.

But Adrian Shaw was no wide-eyed novice when he took up his post early in 1977 alongside Brock, Calvert and the two Simons, King and House. He'd played with a variety of professional bands, including The Crazy World Of Arthur Brown, and he'd supported Hawkwind in Magic Muscle. He was a bikers' friend and favourite. He was a good, solid replacement for Paul Rudolph, and he wouldn't out-dazzle Dave with displays of fabulous lead-guitar virtuosity. Brock was back in charge, and Calvert was his right-hand man.

Adrian was born on the stage at the Gracie Fields Ballroom in London's Hampstead in January 1947. In the post-war years, the building was being used as a nursing home. Then, every available space was being utilised for medical care, and Adrian's mother had been sent to the ballroom from her home in Tottenham for the birth.

The young Adrian attended the strict Wembley County Grammar School, and was expelled for some trivial misdemeanour at age 15. He doesn't remember what it was, but he can still hear the headmaster's voice telling him that he had brought "more shame on the school than anyone in its history".

He went on to an annexe of Harrow Tech, in Pinner, where children were given a second chance at doing GCEs, and was expelled from there a few months later after an accident on his motorbike, a 500 Twin Matchless. "I went for a spin and a van pulled out in front of me and knocked me into a bus stop," he says. "I had a bad fracture of the right arm and leg and I was in plaster for three months."

Returning to college, Adrian was way behind in his coursework and was advised to leave. Interestingly, it was his accident rather than his education which secured his future. He spent his compensation money on a 1962 Gibson EB3, which he plays to this day.

Adrian had started learning guitar at the age of 12. Driven by early Elvis, Jerry Lee Lewis and Little Richard, then The Beatles and later classic soul and the psychedelic sounds of San Francisco, he joined his first real group in 1967, giving himself the chance to quit the succession of jobs he'd tried since college. He'd done everything, from fridge-building to lorry-driving. He was a trainee estate agent and a Corona salesman, but he hadn't found anything he enjoyed.

The band, JP Sunshine, were funded by a drug dealer who fancied investing a bit of cash, although by recruiting Adrian, they found themselves with three guitarists and no bass player. He helpfully switched instruments to fill the gap.

The group split before it ever got off the ground due to a series of drug busts, but it had already introduced Adrian to two musicians who would figure in his future.

He and his wife Maureen were sharing a flat in London with JP Sunshine's Andy Rickell and wife Pat when Adrian joined another group called Dobbin. Rickell soon accepted an offer to join The Crazy World Of Arthur Brown, who were living in a Dorset farmhouse in Puddletown, at the heart of Hardy country. Shortly afterwards, in 1970, Adrian was invited to move down to help out with the band. He did their lights for a while, worked Arthur's siren, and lit the flames on his helmet before strapping it to his head. He was subsequently asked to join the band on bass.

Arthur and the group parted company after Andy "Android Funnel" Rickell and the drummer Drachen Theaker "turned into egomaniacs". The group then recruited JP Sunshine's Rod Goodway, who had moved to Bristol, and became Rustic Hinge And The Provincial Swimmers.

They carried on living in the farmhouse, which had been used as the setting for Hardy's *Tess Of The D'Urbervilles*, and a BBC film crew, shooting a documentary about the novelist, copped some footage of them performing in the front garden.

Some of the Swimmers were not enthusiastic about gigging, preferring to write and record, and so Adrian and Rod Goodway moved to Bristol to form a "people's band", which was Magic Muscle.

They were already friends with High Tide, the Clearwater group which included Simon House. And they came to know various other members of Hawkwind really well as they bumped into each other at countless benefits and festivals, including Windsor and Bickershaw.

"The house in Bristol we were living in was a notorious centre of depravity," said Adrian. "We were adopted by the west-coast chapter of the Hell's Angels. For some reason, the Angels liked us and seemed to think of us as kindred spirits, which in a way I guess we were."

Among the visitors to this den of iniquity were Hawkwind, whose Dave Brock says: "We used to stay there. They were nice characters, Magic Muscle."

Adrian and Maureen later relocated to Somerset, moving in with Keith Christmas. Adrian played sessions for Christmas and other folkies in addition to his Magic Muscle shows, and during this period he received an unexpected proposition.

"Nik Turner and [surprisingly] Dikmik came up to ask me to join Hawkwind as Lemmy was misbehaving – unusual for him! – but I turned them down out of loyalty to Muscle," he recalls.

All the while, Shaw was learning as he went along, teaching himself keyboards and drums to augment his skills on guitar and bass, and he is able to say today that, "I've never had a music lesson in my life. I'll get a tune out of anything!"

Magic Muscle gave Adrian Shaw a thorough grounding in drug management.

"We had a little gig ritual of some acid, speed and a huge hash pipe," he recently told one interviewer. "We wouldn't go onstage without this cocktail. Of course, it didn't help that at that time, we were doing the Space Ritual tour with Hawkwind and kept getting busted by various local police forces who always thought we were them."

A few months after the first Hawkwind offer, Magic Muscle split up, and Adrian and his wife moved back to London where he recorded some songs with Andy Rickell and Simon House. He then formed Reds, Whites And Blues with Canadian guitarist Richard Moore, who'd been playing with The Troggs, a second guitarist called Mike Rogers and a succession of drummers, including Ducks Deluxes' Tim Roper and Roy Dyke, Stacia's future husband.

They gigged around the club circuit, then split, and Adrian went on to play with a host of different musicians including High Tide's Tony Hill, Atomic Rooster [once], The Nice's David O'List and Steve Peregrine Took, who formed a band that also included drummer Dave Bidwell from Chicken Shack and Japanese guitarist Hiroshi Kato.

That line-up fell apart due to the difficulties of working with band leader Took, who was drinking very heavily at the time – although he would later become notorious for his drug problems.

Adrian then depped in Hawkwind for a couple of German dates – almost certainly the occasion in 1973 when Dave Brock sacked Lemmy, temporarily, for missing the plane. He also did some recording with Arthur Brown, Simon House and Android Funnel, and with Keith Christmas, whose band he joined.

Coming out of that, he formed an outfit called Zarabanda, who played around the clubs and cabaret scene for a couple of years, all the while dreaming of one day becoming a great prog-rock act.

In 1977, Simon House called Adrian, asking him to join Hawkwind. This time he said yes.

"Adrian's a very fine bass player and a nice character," declares Dave Brock. "We always got on wonderfully well."

January brought another unsuccessful single, 'Back On The Streets', but the band put it behind them; they were moving on. In February and March, they set up home at Rockfield Studios, surrounded by idyllic, peaceful countryside, to record a new album, *Quark Strangeness And Charm*.

Adrian Shaw remembers this as a "really good, fun time". "Everyone got on well, and it was really happening," he adds. "The band were very much back on track. Bob [Calvert] was really buzzing, in a good way. Simon King was a great drummer and a great guy. He was a football fan like myself, which was very uncool at the time."

"Bob was going on one of his wobblers," recalls Dave Brock. "I can't remember what number it was, but he recorded eight tracks of vocals, each time a little bit different. He couldn't make his mind up between them, and he went on and on for hours on end, jumping from one to the other. It ended up that Dave Charles, the engineer, called in Kingsley Ward [co-owner of the studio with his brother Charles] to decide which one was best."

Spirits were still high when the band broke for a short European tour in March, and headed back out for a few more dates in April.

The album was released by Charisma in June 1977, with the title track issued as a single in July. The LP improved slightly on the performance of *Astounding Sounds* by charting at number 30, and it received a cautious welcome from the weekly music papers. Most reviewers reckoned that the band were heading in the right direction but that there was room for improvement.

In line with this, Dave Brock was still not satisfied that Hawkwind were fulfilling their potential, despite a pointed message on the inner sleeve of the album informing listeners that "we are back on course" following "the sacking of Nik Turner, Paul Rudolph and Alan Powell".

Melody Maker's Brian Harrigan complimented the clever hilarity of Robert Calvert's lyrics, particularly enjoying the romantic problems of the android in 'Spirit Of The Age'. He also praised Simon House's violin playing on 'Hassan I Sahba' and 'Damnation Alley', a vivid post-nuclear vision.

On the negative side, Harrigan proposed that it was time Hawkwind reined in their long instrumental rambles, finally concluding: "They're sharper and more direct than they've been for a long time, and it only needs them to match their trimmed-down personnel with an equally trimmed-down approach to song structure and they could well be on the way to a new and refreshing lease of life."

Monty Smith in *NME* enthused about Calvert's "psychotic sense of humour" and summed up the record: "It's all battering ram riffs and monoplane synthesised drones, with Dave Brock occasionally cutting loose on guitar (rather than just providing frenetic rhythm) and Simon House contributing some hypnotic violin solos. But Calvert remains the dominant force. He's a clone, flawless . . . Hawkwind reckon they are Back On Course. They are. This is a very funny album."

Sounds' Geoff Barton picked up on the humour too, and he liked the LP although he felt the production was a little too clean, suggesting that Hawkwind would do well to return to the "magnificent mugginess" of his beloved *Doremi*.

All three critics addressed the crucial problem that the band were perceived to be facing in 1977, which was to do with public opinion: "That is," declared Barton, "that Hawkwind are outmoded, outdated and should, for their own good as well as for the current punk-styled listening public's, retire to a commune in Cornwall or somewhere as soon as possible."

The punk-styled listening public was one thing. But nobody had asked the punk stars.

John Lydon asserted in his 1994 autobiography, *Rotten – No Irish, No Blacks, No Dogs*, that as a teenager, he was into Hawkwind and Alice

Cooper and he listened to their albums in his bedroom. Decades later, when The Sex Pistols re-formed in 2002, they opened their London Crystal Palace show with 'Silver Machine'.

In an interview with a Pistols-dedicated website, Lydon explained: "'Silver Machine' was a great start. If people didn't get that, well, they're ignoring punk. That's the beginning of rave! And we're giving a nod and a wink to it. People have got to get off this snobbery . . . they've got to get away from it. If anyone makes a record, then it's done for your entertainment. It's not a threat to your lifestyle, unless your lifestyle is fake."

Lydon was not too snobbish or fake to turn up at a Hawkwind gig in London – one of two they played at the Camden Music Machine on June 10 and 11, 1977, in support of *Quark Strangeness And Charm*.

Adrian Shaw confesses: "I wasn't a huge fan, initially, of punk rock. When The Sex Pistols came out, I remember slagging them off to Bob Calvert. We were sitting in the dressing room at the Music Machine and Johnny Rotten came in with a cohort. I thought I'd have a chat. He was really nice. He told me he'd been a Hawkwind fan. Suddenly I was aware of a presence looming. It was Bob, just listening in.

"He tapped Johnny Rotten on the shoulder and said, 'I don't know what he's talking to you for. He thinks you're absolute shit.' *Oh, great, thanks Bob.* Johnny Rotten looked Calvert straight in the eye and said, 'Well, we are.' He handled it beautifully. He let me off the hook. Bob was a bit deflated.

"I think there was a certain connection between Hawkwind and punks, even though Hawkwind were a bunch of long-haired, hippie gits. Partly it was attitude. Hawkwind had two fingers up to the establishment. And a lot of the time, they were pretty basic musicians. The *Quark* period was as complicated as it got. Calvert loved punk. And I revised my opinion of it once I really listened to The Sex Pistols."

The Stranglers' bassist JJ Burnel remains an ardent admirer of the title track of *Quark Strangeness And Charm*, a tongue-in-cheek dig at Albert Einstein, and he has been playing it in solo and informal collaborative shows right up to date.

JJ says: "There's a crime – *a murder* – been committed, and it was committed in the glorious year of '77. And in that glorious year of '77, the baby was thrown out with the bath water. To my mind, it was 'Quark Strangeness And Charm', which is a song I really fucking wish I'd written. *'Einstein was not a handsome fellow . . .'*

"It's punky as hell, it's really clever, and I'm still trying to talk The Stranglers into playing it. I like the energy of it, the fact that it was just three chords and yet it made a bloody great racket . . . and the very intelligent lyrics, and they were fun and sexy as well. I was born in Notting Hill but I'm French, and I can see 'sexy' in things that others might not."

Burnel has covered the song in solo acoustic performances, and also with Three Men And Black – a loose, occasional, acoustic combo that usually includes Jake Burns from Stiff Little Fingers, Pauline Black from The Selecter and Bruce Foxton from The Jam and, later, SLF. Also coming in and out of the shows have been The Selecter's Nick Welsh and The Buzzcocks' Steve Diggle.

Says JJ: " 'Quark' is dead easy to do, and Jake and Pauline Black have played it as well. In fact, we started the set with it. And if anybody wants any royalties off us, I've got a fiver in my pocket. I think that'll cover it."

Nik Turner played with The Stranglers in April 1980 at London's Rainbow Theatre (the month after the band's singer/guitarist Hugh Cornwell was sent to prison for drug possession) alongside Robert Smith, Ian Dury, Wilko Johnson, Steel Pulse and other luminaries. A live album of the event, *The Stranglers And Friends*, was released in the early Nineties by Sanctuary.

The Damned, for their part, became friendly with Nik Turner and Robert Calvert. Original drummer Rat Scabies explains: "We used to bump into Nik Turner quite often. We've got the same publisher [Peter Barnes] so there was always a bit of a Hawkwind/Damned connection.

"I used to think they were boring hippies. They were taking much better drugs, I think. Much as I never bothered with them very much, they were anarchy and chaos in their own little way. It was all right to have an association with that disruptive influence. A punk band can't go on about Hawkwind's [lack of] musicality. They did their own thing, and it was for a lot of people taking acid with a different view of the world."

The Damned and Turner would bump into each other quite often at gigs and festivals.

In June 1978, Nik staged a Sphynx concert at The Roundhouse which included former Damned guitarist Brian James' Tanz Der Youth, Lightning Raiders, punk poets John Cooper Clarke and Patrik

Fitzgerald, Roger Ruskin Spear, Steve Took's Horns, Blood Donor, Magic Michael and Michael Moorcock's Deep Fix, with Adrian Shaw on bass. Titled Nik Turner's Bohemian Love-In, it was a "complete disaster" for Moorcock, coming on after Tanz Der Youth – who'd turned everything up treble. The aptly named Deep Fix couldn't work out how to moderate the sound, and Moorcock was heckled by audience members calling him an "old hippie fart". It was the last time he played live with his own band. For Steve Took's Horns, it was their first and last gig.

Nik's own Sphynx line-up brought together Harry Williamson and David O'List on guitars, Mike Howlett (bass), Steve Broughton (drums) and former Hawkwind player Alan Powell (percussion).

In 1979, Nik Turner started jamming with The Damned onstage. "There would be merciless piss-taking with the saxophone," laughs Rat Scabies. "Somebody, I think it was [bassist] Paul Gray, put oranges in it in the dressing room. Nik wasn't happy about it. The thing about him was that once he was onstage, you couldn't get him off. But he was always a really nice geezer. He came and played with us a few times."

In 1981, Scabies' Foxes And Rats band played at Glastonbury, where they came across Turner. "He owned a pyramid stage," says Rat. "And I remember he put it up at Glastonbury and Foxes And Rats played on it."

Rat met Calvert for the first time at Dingwalls: "He was wearing jodhpurs and boots and he came up and said, 'Hello, I'm Bob Calvert from Hawkwind.' I remember saying, 'I don't want to talk to you 'cos you dumped Lemmy, you rotten bastards.' He said it wasn't his fault, and he was very convincing. He was actually a total gentleman."

Scabies would go on to spend quite a lot of time hanging out with Calvert, drinking tea at his home in Notting Hill Gate, round the corner from where Brian James was living.

Rat went on to play drums at one of Calvert's theatrical productions in a West End theatre, which included songs from *Hype* and *Captain Lockheed*. They performed one show for the press. "I did this big drum roll," says Scabies. "I saw this journalist down the front take his pen out and start writing. So, of course, I did a few more drum rolls. And then I saw the article – 'I find Mr Calvert's backing group to be over-percussive.'"

The show opened to the public and closed after one performance. "Then Calvert got into a fight with some Arabs on his way home. It involved him and the tube train and the doors and getting on and getting off," says Scabies.

In the Eighties, The Damned would create a spoof psychedelic group called Naz Nomad & The Nightmares and they would end up supporting Hawkwind – the real thing – at an outdoor concert in Finsbury Park.

Jon Savage, author of *England's Dreaming: Sex Pistols And Punk Rock*, wrote about Hawkwind as an inherent part of the squatting movement of the Seventies, which found more than half of the country's squatters in London – a number that would grow to include large groups of punks. Savage comments: "Squatting was then an ideological choice . . . as well as a practical solution to the most basic need of housing. This was the harsher version of the hippie dream, with a soundtrack by the group Hawkwind."

They played the festivals over the summer of '77, notably Stonehenge in June and Reading in August. In September, they made a rather unusual appearance – on Marc Bolan's TV show, *Marc* – only days before the T Rex leader was killed in a car crash on Barnes Common. Dave Brock didn't turn up for the filming, probably because he felt the whole thing was too poppy.

"He didn't want to do it," says Adrian Shaw. "The rest of us did. We had to re-record the track at Granada on the morning of the show, and I played guitar as well as bass. We all just wanted to be on the telly. I'm glad we did it."

Robert Calvert had been buzzing as loudly as ever over the summer in one of his typically frantic bursts of activity. Not only was he holding down a full-time role in Hawkwind, and writing for them, but he also had three literary projects on the go.

He had completed work on his second play. The first, about Jimi Hendrix, had been staged a year earlier. Its follow-up concerned The Rolling Stones' late Brian Jones and the lone sailor Donald Crowhurst, who had mysteriously died during the *Sunday Times* marathon yacht race. The play, which dealt with the pressure brought to bear on individuals by major organisations, ended with Jones and Crowhurst having a conversation in the afterlife.

Calvert had at the same time completed a book of poems titled *Centigrade 232* – "the temperature at which writing paper burns" – in reference to an author or poet destroying their rough drafts.

Finally, he was halfway through writing a science-fiction novel.

Michael Moorcock, at the same time, was disowning a novel for which he was prominently credited as being the co-author. Michael Butterworth's *Time Of The Hawklords* stars members of Hawkwind as "the only potential saviours of the human race otherwise doomed to extermination in an apocalyptic battle between the forces of good and evil," according to the promotional material. The tale also namechecks a string of Hawkwind songs.

While the saga was based on concepts of Moorcock's, he vehemently denied being involved in the writing and fell out with the publishers.

Robert Calvert was becoming a worry. Experience had taught his bandmates that when he got hyper, filled with ideas, brimming with enthusiasm and leaping from one project to another, he would generally become more wildly manic until he was so burnt out he'd have a nervous breakdown.

It was with this possibility on the horizon that Dave Brock, Simon King, Simon House, Adrian Shaw and Robert Calvert embarked on a six-week tour of Britain and Europe. The gigs in the major UK venues went well, but in Europe, Calvert started to become unmanageable.

"He was really mad at the time," remembers Adrian. "He was pushing it. It was at the time of Bader Meinhof [the terrorist gang], and he was in a full combat outfit with a replica pistol. He had it in his mind he was some kind of urban guerilla.

"At four o'clock in the morning, there'd be a knock on your hotel-room door and there's Bob with black foam in the corner of his mouth. He had some weird chemical imbalance which meant that he couldn't sleep. He wasn't doing any drugs of any description, although the rest of the band were, which made it all the more puzzling. It was purely a clinical condition.

"I remember he and Simon King getting into a fight in the dressing room. I don't know what it was about, but suddenly fists were flying and I had to get in between them. A bit later, I had to threaten to punch Bob if he didn't calm down. He was trying to get a point across during a soundcheck and he made the mistake of scragging me round the neck to pull me closer. I grabbed him by the throat and said if he ever laid a finger on me again, I'd kill him."

The situation came to a head when the band arrived in Paris for a gig at the Palais Des Sportes on October 26. Dave Brock recalls: "Bob was overexcitable at the time, but he was really good onstage. On this night, he grabbed Adrian Shaw's hair and drew his sword across his throat. We thought he was going to decapitate Adrian. He threw the sword; it stuck in the wooden floor really hard. The audience loved all this. We left the stage and got three encores. It was one of those successful nights."

It was not so successful later. "We were doing interviews in the dressing room," says Brock. "There were these guys from *Le Monde*, or one of those famous European newspapers. Jeff Dexter, who was tour managing, said to Bob, 'Please do an interview with this arts correspondent.' The guy started talking and Bob says, 'He sounds like a homosexual,' and slapped him round the face with his glove – 'I challenge you!' The journalist had this major freak-out, saying, 'I've never been so insulted!' and stormed out. Bob said, 'I fucking won't have homosexuals in my dressing room,' in his very clipped accent, like a colonel in the army.

"The rest of us packed up and said, 'We're off now.' Jeff Dexter walked back to the hotel with Bob and he tried to strangle Jeff in the street. He'd gone mad. Jeff said, 'I had to try and talk about other things to get his mind off things.' Back to the hotel and Bob was so excited he couldn't go to sleep.

"As part of the show, we used to have a replica pistol. There was an empty cartridge in the gun. Bob would spin it round – 'I will now see if I can play Russian roulette.' The gun would go 'click'.

"I had this gun in my suitcase at the hotel, and Bob was in the bar holding court. Jeff was keeping him there. He was drinking all night, and at some point, a plain-clothes policeman came in. Bob was probably talking about urban guerillas and the usual things, and somewhere along the line he must have said something loudly about me being upstairs with a gun in my room. The Bader Meinhof gang were at large at the time, and they were supposed to be in Paris.

"The policeman called some back-up and about six in the morning, there was a knock on my door. I opened it and all these police suddenly burst in. They had me up against the wall in my underpants with my hands in the air. They said, 'We know what's going on here. You're a terrorist.'

"They searched my bag and they found the gun. I said, 'Ring our fucking tour manager.' Jeff was with Calvert – and we only later found out he'd caused this mayhem.

"We were at the end of our tether. Jeff Dexter said, 'I'm going to take Bob back to London and put him in a hospital. I suggest you cancel the next gigs.'"

The handful of remaining dates, in the Netherlands, were duly called off.

Adrian Shaw doesn't recollect his threatened decapitation onstage, but he does remember high-tailing it out of Paris as quickly as possible. "Dave got us all together and said, 'I can't deal with this any more. I want to go home.' We all went along with it. We had this plan that we'd meet in the lobby in a quarter of an hour, get in the car and go home without Bob. And so we were sat with our bags packed in the lobby waiting for someone, I can't remember who it was, and Bob suddenly arrived. He said, 'What's going on?' We said, 'We've decided we're going.' 'Oh, right, I'll go and get my bag.'

"Whoever we were waiting for arrived, we got in the car and we were just about to drive off when Bob appeared clutching his bag."

Dave Brock describes what happened next. "We had this golden Mercedes estate we'd hired. We'd just put our bags in the back when Bob walked out wearing a pair of jodhpurs and a pistol belt. Someone said, 'Drive off.' So I drove about 10 yards down the road and got stuck in a traffic jam. Bob saw us – 'They're going without me!' Simon said, 'Quick, go up the kerb.' I went round this little traffic jam and Bob was chasing us."

"We pulled away and left him there," says Adrian Shaw. "I felt terrible about it. I feel even worse now. You don't leave mentally ill friends abandoned in a foreign country just for your own convenience. Jeff Dexter said that when he got Bob to the airport, he had to hit him over the head with a stick. Bob had grabbed Jeff by the throat and was getting really violent."

Dexter must have been getting used to the feeling of Calvert's hands around his neck by this time.

Back in England, Bob made enough of a recovery to get married almost immediately. Having become estranged from Pauline and the children he had left behind in Ramsgate when he jumped in Nik Turner's van bound for London, he was ready for a second shot at wedded bliss with writer Pamela Townley.

The ceremony took place at the Caxton Hall register office in London's Victoria on November 5, with Simon King as best man. Calvert, dapper in a Noel Coward-inspired outfit, had clearly forgiven

King, if not the rest of Hawkwind, for their great escape from Paris.

NME reported the marriage in an article written by wedding guest Jamie Mandelkau. Due to his proximity to the band, Jamie was perfectly placed to fill in the background from every perspective, and he did. He relayed that it had been "rumoured" Calvert had broken down in Europe, had become "crazy, manic, dangerous", had tried to strangle Jeff Dexter and had insisted on dressing in combat gear, all of which had resulted in the rest of the band "fearing for their lives".

Mandelkau also gave Bob the opportunity to reply. "Dave Brock convinced the others that I was having a nervous breakdown," retorted Calvert. "What nonsense! They dumped me and my bags on the street in Paris. If I had been ill, what kind of mates are they to leave me? Call themselves human beings? I was a bit high-spirited. After all, I was going to get married. The truth is that Dave Brock didn't want to do the extra gigs. He wanted to go home to his wife. He was tired."

Calvert also told Mandelkau: "You know, given a KGB interrogation, only me and Simon King would survive. Inside I'm ice and steel. The rest of you would cop out, fail. *Weaklings . . .*"

Hawkwind had already started thinking about their next album. Some of the material they had played on their autumn UK shows would be included on *PXR5* – 'Robot' and 'High Rise', recorded at the Leicester De Montfort Hall, and 'Uncle Sam's On Mars', from the London Hammersmith Odeon.

And despite the dramas that had unfolded in Europe, the band regrouped at Rockfield in January 1978 where they recorded 'Death Trap', 'Jack Of Shadows' and 'PXR5'.

The line-up included Bob Calvert, who seemed willing to overlook his abandonment in Paris. Adrian Shaw remembers: "It all got forgotten, miraculously, and everything went back to normal, recording and touring again. I think Robert had probably had some treatment, and he forgave us. He was heavily involved in the album. The atmosphere wasn't as good as it had been before, but it was okay. There were some tensions and certain chemical problems creeping in which I'd rather not go into. But there were no big problems. It was a creative atmosphere.

"The general opinion was that *PXR5* wasn't as good as *Quark*, which is probably true. It was a bit patchy, but there were still some good things on the album like 'High Rise' and 'Robot'. It had its moments."

In the event, the release of *PXR5* would be held up by more than a year.

Dave Brock, though, had other things to think about. There was a month-long tour of America coming up in March. And then there was his occasional band, Sonic Assassins, which he'd formed with Bob Calvert.

By now, Calvert was living near Dave in north Devon. "I was in High Bickington," says Dave. "Bob was living in a place called Chittlehamholt about three miles away. I was on top of the hill, and he was on the opposite side of the River Taw valley. He had a thatched cottage he was renting there. He was there for a few years. We used to write lots of stuff together."

Harvey Bainbridge was a teacher in north Devon, playing bass in his spare time with a local band called Ark. They had a keyboard player, Paul Hayles, and a drummer called Martin Griffin. Ark soon bumped into Calvert and Brock, who was known for his helpfulness in the community. "He lent an amplifier or two to some people," remembers Harvey.

Martin Griffin, who was running a recording studio in Roche, Cornwall, recalls: "I met these guys who had a band called Ark and I sat in with them occasionally. I sat in on a couple of sessions with Dave Brock too."

Dave and Bob put Sonic Assassins together with Harvey Bainbridge, Martin Griffin and Paul Hayles. The idea of the band was to play charity gigs and free festivals and to recapture the space-rock spontaneity that Brock felt Hawkwind had rather lost. "It was a bit of fun," says Dave. "We used to rehearse at my place."

According to Harvey: "The rest of Hawkwind didn't want to do the festivals 'cos they wouldn't get paid. We said, 'Yeah, sure, we don't mind.' We were into doing free festivals."

"Bob thought I was very wonderful at the time," chuckles Martin Griffin. "He said I was 'God's own drummer'. Simon King was out of favour then. Hawkwind were going through some funny times. I got on well with Bob Calvert. We all had a good time."

Sonic Assassins did turn up at a couple of festivals in the summer of 1978, but before that they played a memorable gig at Barnstaple Queen's Hall, north Devon, just before Christmas 1977. Five of the numbers – 'Magnu', 'Angels Of Life', 'Death Trap', 'Over The Top' and 'Freefall' – would appear as live tracks on the band's only album, augmented by six Dave Brock compositions.

The album, *Sonic Assassins/Dave Brock*, was eventually issued in March 1980 on a previously unheard-of label called Weird Records. It was the first in a series of cassette-only releases which have since become known as The Weird Tapes. The series, along with releases on Flicknife Records and other small labels, features live and studio recordings by various incarnations of Hawkwind, which have now been released on CD by a company called Voiceprint. Many former members of the band are furious at this, alleging that Dave Brock has been releasing streams of material for years without informing or crediting the musicians involved.

Most are now receiving regular cheques from Voiceprint, but Nik Turner for one is refusing to cash his, claiming that the money sent represents only a small percentage of what is owed.

"The album was wonderful," says Brock of *Sonic Assassins*. "But that's when Calvert goes totally nutty again. He was working himself up to a big peak for about three or four days. He'd been like a loony. He couldn't sleep. He'd been full of brilliant ideas. He was very excited about the Barnstaple gig, and he had some magic moments onstage there. He ad-libbed this fantastic poem on a number called 'Over The Top'. It was similar to going over the top in the trenches in the First World War.

"Around this same time, he wanted to buy Pamela a car, an old Vauxhall Cresta that this guy had in Barnstaple. He didn't drive, and he asked me to run him in to have a look at it. He said he'd have it and that he was going home to pick the money up. In the meantime, I think this guy sold it to somebody else, and Bob went bananas. He walked up to our place, he had his blank firing pistol, and he demanded I drive him into Barnstaple to shoot this bloke. Sylvia drove him off in her little two-door Morris Minor, and she calmed him down.

"Eventually, he learnt to drive. I sold him a Rover. He was coming to Rockfield one day, which has a dual carriageway running past. He missed the turn-off, so he reversed madly back along the dual carriage-way and smacked into this lamp stand. He arrived at Rockfield all hyperactive and shaky.

"Bob was difficult sometimes and wonderful other times. He got into all sorts of scrapes and we'd have to bail him out. I remember once when they all lived in East Finchley, he went off to see [the famously barmy] Viv Stanshall of The Bonzo Dog Doo Dah Band.

"Viv had this house full up with junk and Bob went round there. They were drinking wine and I think they'd taken a Valium or something like that. Bob was lurching round the place, and Viv had this doll that looked like a baby. Bob sat down on the doll. Viv was screaming, 'You've sat on the baby, you cunt!' Bob said, 'But it's not real.' Viv yelled, 'It's real to me. Get out of my house!' And he was throwing things at Bob as he stumbled down the stairs. They were very similar characters.

"He was a clever bloke, Bob. We fell out lots of times, but I always liked him."

Douglas Smith was still "dabbling" in Motorhead. He was also representing Leber Krebs Inc – the near-legendary American management team of Steve Leber and David Krebs – for their acts in Europe. It was a role that Douglas fulfilled for more than five years, and the artists included top rock attractions Aerosmith and Ted Nugent. He would continue as an associate of Krebs for another 20 years.

One day at the beginning of March 1978, Douglas was due to jet to New York for a meeting with Krebs about an upcoming tour.

He says: "I missed the flight, which I was disappointed about because I'd particularly booked a 747. All the other flights were 707s which I didn't like. They were skinny, narrow-bodied – too claustrophobic. I had to take the next available flight and it was a 707. I boarded, walked up towards the back of the plane where my seat was, and sitting in the rows behind me were . . . Hawkwind.

"The first person I spotted was Simon King. Then I saw the rest of the band, plus Jeff Dexter and Jamie Mandelkau. I hadn't had any communication with them since we'd parted company. They were very friendly, jumping over, sitting next to me, chatting. We all had a few drinks and a good flight.

"We arrived in New York and we went through customs and immigration together. I was expecting to take a cab, as I'd missed my original flight and the car that I knew Mel Baister, David Krebs' assistant, had booked for me into town. The band offered me a lift.

"As we came into the arrivals hall, I noticed a limo driver holding a card with my name on it. I think I turned to Simon King and said, 'Oh my God, they've sent a limo for me.' It was such a funny sight. There was their roadie waiting for them with a minibus, and there was my chauffeur waiting for me. Dave Brock and Simon King looked at each other. They went, 'Can we get into town with you, Doug?' "

Hawkwind spent the night in New York, prior to their first date in Boston on March 4. Douglas turned out to see them at New York's Bottom Line club, where they played two shows a day on March 6 and 7.

He relives the experience: "Calvert's with them. He's on there in this tiny little club swinging his sword around, and I'm sure someone is going to get their head cut off. Things had really dipped for them by this point. The last time I had them in New York, they'd played the Academy to three-and-a-half-thousand people."

Adrian Shaw estimates attendances of 500 or 600 people a night on the tour, much smaller than the band's UK and European audiences, although the American fans who did turn out were dedicated Hawkwind followers, and they would reliably be there in years to come.

However, it wasn't a happy period for Dave Brock who recollects: "Bob was really quiet and subdued. He was on a downer. I'm sure he'd been in a sanitarium and was taking the medication to calm him down. Sometimes he'd say, 'I don't like taking this.' He realised how these things affected him, and he knew that when he didn't take them, he became quite a genius. It was very, very difficult."

To add to the problems, Simon House, the ace violinist and keyboard player, left mid-tour to join David Bowie's band. Simon explains: "David Bowie phoned me very early in '78 and asked how I felt about playing violin on a world tour and some recording. I explained my position with Hawkwind. He said, 'Think about it and call back in a couple of days.' I thought about it and I knew there was no way I was not going to do it. Apart from the money and everything – what an experience! I couldn't refuse.

"I told Dave Brock. Everyone said, 'I suppose you've got to do it.' The rehearsals for the Bowie tour started halfway through the Hawkwind tour of the States, so I went over and did the first half with a stand-in keyboard player [Sonic Assassins' Paul Hayles], showing him the ropes, and when the time came, I buggered off down to Dallas to start rehearsing with David Bowie.

"David goes back to High Tide days. He had the band called Hype before he was well known. Before that, he was in a musical mime group, Feathers, which Tony Hill, the guitarist from High Tide was in. That's how I met Bowie, through Tony. High Tide and Hype did a couple of gigs together.

"There was a Brian Eno connection as well. We were doing some sessions with Robert Calvert, and Eno took my number. When Bowie and Eno were planning their tour and album, my name must have come up."

Simon would become a sought-after session player, appearing with some of the biggest names in music. "The most demanding thing I ever did was playing with Mike Oldfield in 1983 on a tour to celebrate the 10th anniversary of *Tubular Bells*," he recalls. "It was the most technically demanding gig as regards key changes and time changes and fiddly bits. He's like a petulant little boy, Mike Oldfield. If you make a mistake he gets incredibly upset. His pet name is Spike. He writes brilliant music, but he's a wanker."

While Simon House was down south starting to find his way with the Bowie band, Hawkwind were missing his expertise and instrumental leads. Says Adrian Shaw: "The music suffered when Simon left, and that's when the rot really set in. But even though it was going against my own interests at the time, I was one of the ones who told him he should take the gig with Bowie. His money went up tenfold. One never made a huge amount out of Hawkwind. It paid okay at the time, but it wasn't going to put us in the lap of luxury."

Dave Brock was becoming more disheartened as the tour progressed. "Calvert was depressive, awful really," he says. "Then Simon House left. All of us were verging on a nervous breakdown."

Adrian Shaw wasn't. "Nothing could be further from the truth," he says. "That was one of the best months of my life. I've done America countless times since, and I'm bored to tears with it, but at that time, I was really enjoying being relatively young and it was the epitome of what I wanted to do as a musician, plus all the things that one probably shouldn't do but did – the drugs and so on. I had a great time."

He appreciates that other members of the band were not sharing the great time and that Calvert was in some sort of decline, although he adds: "Bob was still performing well."

The tour wound up with two days at San Francisco's Old Waldorf, on March 27 and 28. Dave Brock remembers: "A couple of guys from Jefferson Starship came to see us and they said, 'God, it's like a shell of a band.' I was disenchanted and down in the dumps. We were staying in this famous Chinese hotel in San Francisco, and I felt, 'Calvert's on a downer, Simon's left us in the lurch. This is the end.' I sold my guitar to a fan, Marc Sperhauk, who'd been following us around. I looked out of my bedroom window and I saw Adrian Shaw walking down this street, doing shopping or something. I didn't see him again for years."

Adrian stopped off in New York for a short holiday, and had no idea Dave had disbanded Hawkwind until he returned home. "I got a phone call from Tony Howard saying Dave had split the band and that I should look for another gig. I thought, 'Easy come, easy go.' I've always been fairly relaxed about these things."

Hawkwind had split, although Brock found another guitar before too long, and called in Simon King to help him complete two final tracks for *PXR5*. 'Infinity' and 'Life Form' were recorded in June 1978 at Week Park Farm in Devon with Brock on bass, guitar, synthesisers and vocals.

The big challenge for Dave Brock now was to build "a totally new band". He was doing this in partnership with Robert Calvert, and the incoming musicians would be paid a wage.

Brock and Calvert booked rehearsal and recording time, and Hawklords began to take shape.

CHAPTER 13

Hawklords: An Industrial Evolution

HAWKLORDS were really Sonic Assassins (minus Paul Hayles) under another name, which was handy for Dave Brock because it meant that the band were all living close at hand in Devon. However, it took a little while for the line-up to stabilise.

They were ensconced in a rehearsal studio at Langley Farm, north Devon, from June to August 1978, having hired Ronnie Lane's mobile for the recordings. The studio had something of a musical tradition, at one time being used by Yes and then bought up by one of the members of Seventies rock band Lone Star.

Hawklords at first recruited Simon King on drums, and he's credited with performing on four tracks on the ensuing album, *25 Years On*.

For Brock and Calvert, though, it was a case of out with the old and in with the new. Harvey Bainbridge, Martin Griffin and keyboardist Steve Swindells were soon summoned to the farmhouse.

Harvey recalls: "I had a phone call from Bob Calvert saying, 'We're recording up here, and we'd like you to come and play the bass.' Dave and him were going to be The Hawklords and hire us to play. For me at the time, yeah, that was okay. I just got paid as a session musician."

Harvey Bainbridge was born on September 24, 1949 at an army camp in Dorset, and he spent his first 11 years living in military camps and relatives' houses around the north of England.

He began his secondary education at Ormskirk Grammar School in Lancashire, later moving to Bentley Grammar School in Wiltshire where he became involved in music. He was in a school band, and with the encouragement of his "excellent" music teacher, he became a cathedral chorister. "We did operas instead of school plays," he remembers. "The teacher put together a little choir called The Tudor

Choir. There were six of us. We sang at competitions and at Radio 4."

Harvey then attended St Luke's College Of Education in Exeter from which he emerged as a qualified teacher. Despite this, he was forced to take odd jobs from time to time to supplement his musical earnings. He was a builder's labourer – and a sheep-catcher.

"It was quite a tough job chasing bloody sheep, especially when they didn't want to be caught," he laughs. "I had to bomp them on to their back ends and sit them up so the shearer could take over without any stopping."

Harvey was teaching in north Devon while he played around the local area with Ark – which led to Sonic Assassins, Hawklords and, ultimately, Hawkwind.

Drummer Martin Griffin was born in 1950 and schooled in Devon. He read English at Keble College, Oxford, but found it dull compared to the music scene: "Oxford wasn't keen on my dope enthusiasm and I wasn't keen on Oxford's Anglo Saxon. We parted company."

He put together a promotions company, staging gigs with the likes of ELO, Caravan and Can, but found it "edgy financially".

Meanwhile, he'd been playing in a student hippie outfit called Half Human Band, and they decided to go pro. He picked up an HGV Class 1 licence at this time so that he could finance his fledgling career as a musician by driving. The Half Human Band gigged prolifically around the pub-rock circuit and at the free festivals – Windsor, Watchfield, Stonehenge and Trentishoe – where, of course, they came across Hawkwind.

Picking up a following in France, Half Human Band eventually played with Hawkwind in Grenoble. "Then," says Martin, "Nik got us into their show at Paris Olympia and we went back with them to the Château Hérouville, the 'Honky Chateau' of Elton John fame."

When Half Human Band split, Griffin – a keen scuba diver – returned to the West Country, thinking about taking up commercial diving.

Instead, he ran into Gerry Gill, a former DJ and manager who was operating the Roche recording studio in Cornwall. Martin played a couple of sessions and grew friendly with Simon Fraser, the producer there. After joining the studio band, Diesel Beaver, he became increasingly involved at Roche, and took it over when Gerry Gill left and Fraser moved to the esteemed Sawmills Studio.

Martin began building up Roche, and at the same time put on a run of gigs as Great White Shark with a friend called Min Jackson. "We did a Christmas show at Plymouth Poly and one of the bands playing was Ark," says Griffin. "We seemed to click. They hadn't got a regular drummer and asked me to sit in. So I did a few gigs with them."

Ark, of course, included Harvey Bainbridge and Paul Hayles, Martin's future bandmates in Sonic Assassins.

Keyboardist Hayles, having taken over from Simon House on Hawkwind's last, ill-fated American tour, was not called up for Hawklords. Neither was Martin at first. He finally received the invitation when the band were some way through the album.

Simon King later explained his abrupt exit from Hawklords to *Melody Maker*'s Steve Gett. "I didn't want to do the tour even though I'd played on the album," he said. "It was just like Bob and a backing band, which had little to do with the real essence of Hawkwind where essentially there are four or five musicians, all of whom are fronting and backing the show. If ever the guy wanted me to do some work for him in the studio, I would – but I couldn't go on a tour."

Steve Swindells, a keyboard player, arrived in the line-up through the recommendation of his friend Caroline Guinness, who'd been working with Douglas Smith. Douglas had agreed to take on Hawklords, perhaps as a result of the *entente cordiale* established on the 707 flight to New York.

Swindells was born on November 21, 1952 in Ipswich, Suffolk. He grew up in the Bath/Bristol area and attended Sexey's Grammar, a boarding school in Bruton, Somerset. He boarded until he was 14, and then switched to the Bristol Cathedral School where he stayed until A-Levels.

Going on to art college in Bristol, he dropped out after three months, briefly joining a band with James Warren and Andy Davis who would later play together in Stackridge and The Korgis. That group didn't do a lot, and Steve went on to join a classical rock band called Squidd, playing such standards as 'The Planet Suite' while smashing toilet bowls onstage and burning effigies of skinheads. Squidd supported major acts including Wishbone Ash, Deep Purple, David Bowie and Jack Bruce, and their drummer Rodney Matthews went on to great success as a fantasy artist designing album sleeves and posters.

One of their more significant gigs was a gay liberation concert at Fulham Town Hall. There, Steve met Mark Edwards, his future manager and nemesis.

For a time, Swindells lived in a wood, and then he moved to Glastonbury with a huge marquee he'd stolen from the Women's Institute. He shared it with 39 other people.

Busted for being in possession of two joints, Steve was fined £120 and he legged it to London in 1973 hoping he wouldn't be found. He lived in a squat in Camden with his brother Frank, and they formed a band to play around the free festivals. Later, he squatted in a slaughterhouse in Oxford.

In London, Mark Edwards came back into the picture. He'd produced the first Curved Air album, *Air Conditioning*, a Top 10 hit which had caused a stir in 1970 because it was the first LP to be released on multi-coloured vinyl. Edwards became Steve's manager and secured him a solo deal with RCA which resulted in an LP, *Messages*, in 1974.

Says Steve: "It was produced by Mark Edwards. He was in love with me. We had King Crimson's drummer, Elton John's guitarist, a full orchestra, and he completely screwed up the production. I recorded a second album, *Swallow*, which was mastered, printed and manufactured in small quantity but never released. Mark Edwards swept everything off the managing director of RCA's desk in a drunken rage, thereby losing me my deal with them after the first test pressings had been made.

"In the end, I had to be rescued from Edwards. It was a nightmare. We were recording at Ramport Studios with Elton John's musicians and members of Roxy Music and he was threatening me with a whisky bottle. I was 'kidnapped' by my friend Caroline Guinness and her then boyfriend, Tim Clark, who used to be a chauffeur for [Culture Club's] Jon Moss' dad, *maitre d'* at the Joe Allen restaurant, executive editor of *Arena* and, later, the *Wallpaper* group. Mark Edwards then fled to LA."

In the late Eighties, Steve was fronting a bar called Franklins when Mark Edwards walked in one night. "I told him to piss off because he'd ruined my life," says Steve. "He went on to become a lighting designer in LA."

It was something of a relief for Steve, after his tumultuous solo career, when he was offered a "regular" job in the Scottish glam-pop band Pilot, taking the place of his friend Billy Lyall, a former Bay City Roller. The group had already enjoyed two smash-hit singles, 'Magic' and 'January', around the turn of 1975, and Steve recorded an album with them, *Two's A Crowd*, before they split up.

He was sitting around wondering what to do next when Hawkwind invited him to come and have a play. He'd seen them twice before, once at the Isle of Wight 1970, outside the gates, and then at an alternative Bath festival.

Says Steve: "It was in an abandoned hotel which had once been very grand. There were wonderful velvet curtains and chandeliers. Hawkwind played in the lobby, and this grand staircase was absolutely packed. It was the most incredible atmosphere. That's when I realised what a driving, original musical force they were. It was the generator synthesisers and that Dave Brock guitar that really got to me. No one plays guitar like Dave Brock. It's just so powerful.

"I was driven down to this farm they were renting near Barnstaple. They were probably a little cynical about my past, but it gelled and I got the job on the spot. I came back to London, grabbed a few things and was taken back down by Les the roadie. I stayed at the farm for six weeks with my pregnant dog, who subsequently gave birth to six puppies on my bed at the farmhouse."

At the time, Steve was into Steely Dan, Little Feat, black music, jazz and jazz-funk, but he was ready to jump into the unknown, albeit on a session basis rather than as an equal partner. "I liked the idea of something totally different that would be a challenge and fun. I knew if I joined Hawklords, it probably wouldn't involve a great deal of work in terms of musicality, tricky chord changes and time signatures. I imagined there would be lots of jamming going on, although that wasn't necessarily true."

He also imagined the band as their reputation had painted them: "'Are they a bunch of drug-crazed hippies?' I thought there would be lots of drugs around the band. No. Almost none. It was a drug-free zone. Simon King liked a bit of puff, and I think Dave had the odd secret toot, but that was it."

Swindells was disappointed when King left "'cos I really liked him". But he got on just as well with the new drummer Martin Griffin, and they remain good friends today.

Dave Brock, Harvey Bainbridge, Martin Griffin and Steve Swindells remember the sessions for *25 Years On* as harmonious and productive.

Dave, the captain, was firmly at the helm, and Calvert was genuinely inspired, coming on all Rolf Harris with wobble board and didgeridoo as well as jumping in on Jew's harp, guitar, percussion and vocals.

There was a very open and willing exchange at play in the recordings, with Brock contributing guitar, vocals, keyboards, synthesisers and bass, and session player Henry Lowther came in to blow some trumpet.

The album blends a typical sense of experiment with a stylish, dynamic onslaught that seems to have been inspired by punk and new-wave influences.

"Maybe it was a response to all that," muses Dave. "I can't remember. I never saw any of those things as a threat. Same as dance music. Some of it I really liked. It's the sort of music we'd been playing for years, that aggressive three-chord stuff. Our songs were quite political too. Bob was very political. Bob and me used to like a lot of punk music. 'Death Trap' – that's a real punky number.

"We'd gone away from the big, spacey, epic stuff like *Warrior On The Edge Of Time* into that funky thing that I didn't like and then into heavier, space-metal music more. It's quite punkified if you listen to it now. Aggressive songs, short and sharp. It was something totally different yet again, and it was quite successful."

Harvey Bainbridge remembers that, "Bob Calvert was in a heavily imaginative frame of mind, just coming to the end of a really, really fruitful period."

"Calvert was in great form during the making of that," agrees Steve Swindells. "I bonded with him. We all had great fun making the album. Dave was always a bit distant, but he could be quite charming.

"There was some really interesting experimental stuff on there, like 'Free Fall', which does have time signature changes and an outrageous keyboard solo that I did. They had this fabulous Yamaha early polyphonic synthesiser – huge. It weighed a ton. It was the same model Vangelis used, a fantastic instrument and a joy to play.

"The album had more than a hint of a punk influence going on and a lot of the input was Calvert. It was based on *Metropolis* [Fritz Lang's classic, futuristic silent film]. It was kind of arty and it had a lot of that punky energy going on in there, which was great."

"I recall Julie Burchill coming to interview Bob when she was an angry young punk journo and grumbling about rock stars in their country mansions," adds Martin Griffin. "'What are you on about?' Bob demanded. 'I've got a 15-year-old car and I live in a rented house.'"

Martin found the relationships within the band slightly difficult to understand. "It was a little weird," he says. "Simon King had been involved, but something was going down and he'd gone. I went away for a day and Simon King came in, did two tracks and then went back to London. Simon House came in for a couple of tracks. The politics of the set-up were bewildering. Maybe they are with all bands, but I just kept out of it."

When *25 Years On* was released by Charisma in October 1978, along with the single 'Psi Power', press opinions were mixed, and views of the album conflict to this day, although it charted at number 48.

NME's Bob Edmands was particularly grumpy. His review, accompanied by a photograph of a foppish Calvert, opened with the pronouncement that, "Old hippies rarely die, they just bland away." And having said that, he went on to lambast the band for modernising their approach.

Not only, in his opinion, had they been stealing from Spirit and Pink Floyd, but they had also been pilfering from "the art school glitter days of Roxy Music", XTC and "any intellectual new waver".

He ended by huffing that Hawkwind's original fans, from just nine years earlier, were "well on the way to becoming grandparents by now".

Adrian Shaw, meanwhile, was wondering why he hadn't been invited to join Hawklords.

Reflecting on what may have been going on behind the scenes during Hawkwind's last American tour, he says: "I know that Dave had these problems with Charisma and he wanted to get out of the deal. This is why Hawklords sprang up. Hawkwind were sort of dissolving anyway. Bob was mad at the time, Simon House had left, Simon King had a couple of problems and Dave was disillusioned with the whole thing.

"He may have thought that changing the name and getting a new deal would get him out of the Charisma contract. I'm sure Charisma said, 'You owe us an album,' and then *PXR5* came out."

Douglas Smith counterclaims that Charisma had wanted to get rid of Hawkwind "because they weren't selling enough records to make it worthwhile. I suggested to the boss at Charisma that they make an album under this different name, Hawklords."

The Hawklords album, which did not sell particularly well, came out on Charisma. Hawkwind's *PXR5*, issued after it in June 1979, would be the last studio album on the label, peaking at number 59.

Adrian Shaw continues: "I've got this theory that Dave at that point wanted total control of the band. It had always been a collective, and there had been a lot of strong characters, and immediately after the American tour, he tended to be replacing them with locals from down his way in Devon. I'm sure they're all nice guys and worthy musicians, but he could pay them a wage and tell them what to do. He could call all the shots. He thought, 'I don't want to argue the toss about creative and financial matters. It'll be easier if I take over the band completely.' It suited him down to the ground.

"I really think that's the answer to a lot of questions – why he didn't want me to carry on, and why he didn't want Simon King, a great musician revered by Hawkwind fans, to be part of the line-up. It's a shame because, in my opinion, the band really suffered as a result.

"I think in many ways the *Quark/PXR5* line-up was the best of all the line-ups there have been down the years, so naturally I'm pleased to have been part of that."

Dave Brock says: "I've no idea why Adrian wasn't invited to join Hawklords. Probably 'cos we were down in Devon. I can only assume it was because the band we had down there, Sonic Assassins, just meandered into Hawklords, with Simon King joining up again for a while. There was no idea of 'getting rid' of Adrian or anything like that. I always got on well with him. One thing I remember is he always used to smell of aftershave, and his plimsolls were always spotlessly Blanco'd, immaculately white."

Adrian was philosophical about it: "When it came to the end, I didn't explore the whys and wherefores. I just accepted it. I had other things going on in my life."

Returning from America, Adrian discovered not only that Hawkwind had split but that his wife Maureen was pregnant with their son, Aaron. Since he was also buying his first property at the time, he retreated from music temporarily and stopped taking drugs. "It did me the world of good," says Adrian. "I'd been doing a lot of speed and prior to that, I'd been on psychedelics. I got myself back into a normal frame of mind, which I was glad to do. I was fed up with speed comedowns. I didn't stop everything, though. To this day, obviously, I still smoke a bit of dope, but I'm nothing like I used to be."

He was persuaded out of retirement to play with Michael Moorcock's Deep Fix at The Roundhouse concert organised by Nik Turner, thereafter returning to DIY and home improvements at his new house in Barnet. He still lives there with Maureen and Aaron, who's 25 at the time of writing, although they are planning a move to Dorset.

Having spent some time out of the business, Adrian met a Canadian guitarist, Dave Rutchinski, who moved in across the road and was playing solo gigs around London. The two formed a duo, The Vox Bros, and played for a couple of years in venues such as Break For The Border, where they had a twice-weekly residency.

Then Magic Muscle came back into the picture with the opportunity to release a retro and a new album, and play a tour. A line-up which also featured guitarists Rod Goodway and Huw Gower, Simon House on violin and Pink Fairies' Twink on drums was quickly assembled, and the resulting album, *100 Miles Below*, was released at home and in America in 1989.

In the same year, Magic Muscle were invited to support Hawkwind at a special 20th anniversary gig at Brixton Academy. The band decided to drop Twink, who had become "a little difficult", and they also needed a guitarist to replace Gower, who'd moved to New York.

Adrian was friends with guitarist and singer Nick Saloman, who was recording under the name of The Bevis Frond, and although Nick was known to dislike live gigs, he agreed to stand in at the Hawkwind show along with his old drummer Martin Crowley.

The band, including Saloman, enjoyed it so much that they continued playing, at first under the Magic Muscle name, then as The Magic Bevis Muscle Frond and finally as The Bevis Frond. In 1998, they were thrilled to accompany Country Joe McDonald in London and Aberdeen, with Adrian's son Aaron – "a fine guitarist" – playing second lead. The Frond are still touring Europe and America at least once a year with varying line-ups headed by Nick and Adrian, who together run the Woronzow record label.

In other noteworthy achievements, Adrian played bass with Mick Farren's Deviants at a couple of gigs in America and appeared live and on record with Pearls Before Swine's Tom Rapp, releasing his album, *A Journal Of The Plague Year*, on Woronzow.

Barney Bubbles had left Hawkwind around the same time as Nik Turner, apparently in solidarity with the axed saxophonist.

Sticking solidly to the street cred he had observed, sometimes puritanically, in the early days of the counterculture, Barney continued to live in "incredible austerity", he was extremely prolific, he charged very little for his commissions, he paid scant attention to paperwork, and he never sought recognition or fame: he almost never signed his work.

Yet, he went on to create some of the new wave's most memorable images, having been absorbed into independent and then mainstream culture via labels such as Stiff and F-Beat who appreciated the wit, cheek and originality of his art. He was responsible for the Stiff and Radar Records logos, he deliberately placed a photograph of Eddie & The Hotrods on the back of The Damned's first album, thus creating an instant "collector's item" and duplicate sales, he produced 52 different covers for Ian Dury & The Blockheads' *Do It Yourself* LP, each with its own wallpaper, he worked extensively for Elvis Costello, providing both the simple but striking cover for *This Year's Model* and the herd of stampeding elephants on the sleeve of *Armed Forces*, which also featured lots of complicated, unfolding flaps, and he devised Billy Bragg's *Life's A Riot With Spy Vs Spy* sleeve.

He also turned his hand to books, posters, T-shirts, advertisements and backstage passes.

Pauline Williams, a colleague at Stiff, said of Barney: "He really embraced the punk philosophy. He was quite into nihilism and existentialism."

Chris Morton, the Stiff art director, added: "He was suffused with the idea that this was a new start, and he was basing a lot of what he did on Russian art just after the revolution."

Barney was passionate about his work but at the same time refused to take it or himself too seriously. Anything but snobbish, he took his inspirations from all over the place, seeing as much value and potential in an everyday household item as in a master painting. And he was just as happy to work with Nik Turner as with any of the latest bright young things in punk.

Nik and Bubbles collaborated on a succession of ventures, the first being the Sphynx project. Then, as later, Turner stayed over with Barney, who was living in London again, rather than commuting from Wales.

Says Nik: "We were still very close. I thought he was wonderful. As a graphic designer, he just seemed to make something fantastically interesting out of pretty well nothing. He treated me very nicely, with a lot of respect. He'd done me lots of favours and done very creative things in which I was involved. I said, 'Would you design my album cover?' He said, 'On two conditions. That I can use it as one of my own concrete poetry pieces. And that when you put a stage show together, you let me choreograph it.'

"I said yes to both. To me, Barney did things as acts of love. They were all done with heart, and I was flattered that he would work with me, and I felt myself very lucky. We organised a free concert at the Roundhouse in June 1978 as a promotion for the album, on the same night that Bob Dylan was playing at Earls Court."

This was the gig which included performances by Brian James' Tanz Der Youth, Lightning Raiders, John Cooper Clarke, Patrik Fitzgerald and (catastrophically) Michael Moorcock's Deep Fix.

Turner says: "Several of Barney's performance-artist friends were there too, injecting eggs with hypodermic syringes before they stuck them in their eyes or something. It was fantastic, actually.

"Certain friends of Dave Brock's from Devon were involved in my show, and I think Dave was impressed by the choreography and wanted to do something like it. Hawklords had done their album, *25 Years On*, and Dave wanted Barney to design the artwork and choreograph the show. I helped talk Barney into it. He was doing for them what he'd done for me. He did an enormous amount of work.

"He used all my dancers. He got involved with this girl Frances Griffin, a photographer. They coordinated thousands of shots on to a film-led light-show. It was built around what the stage show was supposed to be, a very futuristic, industrial scene with all these photographs of dancers in bizarre industrial and avant-garde costumes. It was influenced by Mao Tse Tung and stuff. At the last minute, Dave phoned Barney and said he'd changed the order of the songs."

"I don't know if I did or not," says Brock. "I couldn't tell you."

Dave describes the concept for the show: "We had this wonderful idea of doing a 'Metropolis', and getting workers wearing grey, drab uniforms onstage. There were six dancers. Barney had designed a wonderful album cover, and he was involved in a lot of the ideas for this. We thought it would make a change.

"It all revolved round a factory society – Pan Transcendental Industries Inc. We had workers with berets sweeping the stage, doing mundane tasks, and there were four towers and a spotlight, a bit like a concentration camp. Bob Calvert was quite on the case with this too. He was playing guitar on some numbers, and audio generator.

"But the whole thing started losing money. We were on the road with about 30 people, and what we were getting per night didn't cover the costs. October 25, 1978 at Bradford was the day we had to sack three of the dancers, 'cos they were costing a fortune, along with the sound engineer, Dennis Smith. It was quite sad, we didn't want to do it, although it was done diplomatically. I know Barney was upset."

"Barney had been working on this thing for fucking months," rages Nik Turner. "First Dave changed everything, then he started getting rid of the dancers, and it completely pissed Barney off 'cos it fucked up the stage presentation he'd designed for it with Frances Griffin.

"Barney then vowed he'd never work with Dave again. I just thought it was very sad Dave didn't really respect the guy, who I saw as having been very instrumental in the success of the band. He helped put the whole thing together. He did lots of things, with love. He never came on to the band for anything, really."

Steve Swindells, on the other hand, was not sorry to see the back of the three dancers. "They were a bunch of arty prima donnas and they were totally unnecessary," he declares. "They were a bit prissy, and the atmosphere improved after they'd gone. We settled into being a good, tight unit with good relations. We became a much leaner, meaner machine. It all got very powerful. We'd been wearing these ridiculous boiler suits sprayed with paint, but I ended up wearing a Hell's Angel original jacket with cut-off sleeves which the Angels had lent to me. It made me feel very butch."

Martin Griffin recalls: "Dennis Smith, who co-produced the album, was mixing front of house. And Alistair Merry, the percussionist with Ark and the male figure on the Hawklords album cover, was fronting a trio of grey-uniformed dancers.

"The rehearsals had gone okay, although Bob was a little more fraught and dictatorial than I'd known him before. We did final production rehearsals at Shepperton. They were shooting the movie *Alien* in the next-door studio, and we got to wander around the set, which was a huge, amazingly elaborate structure.

"At some stage, we were staying in a Novotel somewhere up north. I don't like Novotels. They make tea with UHT milk. I mean, really! Something happened overnight and come the morning, Alistair, his two other dancers and Dennis Smith left the hotel to go home. There was gossip that Dave had been listening through the wall with a glass to his ear and had heard talk to his detriment. It seems unlikely. But it became known as 'the night of the long knives'."

It was a huge UK tour, running through October and November 1978. And while Douglas Smith comments that "they did reasonably well on the road, but there were places where the sales were down," all of the band feel it was a successful enterprise.

"It was quite an intensive show," says Dave Brock. "The set was very successful."

"It was probably 90 to 95 per cent sold-out," says Steve Swindells. "Calvert and I got on particularly well. He was on top form on that tour, very compelling to watch. Martin Griffin and I had a lot of laughs, just dressing up and being daft. It was all rather exciting, and we had fun. We had a nice tour bus.

"I had 3,000 watts of monitoring at my side onstage. It was so loud. Dave didn't have much in the way of synths going on. He had a few, but he was really concentrating on singing and guitar playing. He was just driving. I was providing this gothic wall of sound and lots of spacey synths. The whole thing was a spectacular visual experience and it went down really, really well. There weren't any ructions on that tour except between Dave and Calvert."

Of those, Dave explains: "It was just the pressure of the tour. Bob and me were supporting the whole thing, and it was probably just due to the stress and worry. We always wanted things to be right."

Harvey Bainbridge remarks: "Bob was constantly getting a bit over-excited and having to go and calm down. He fell out with Dave on the road. Bob's imagination ran away with him lots. He got himself wound up and ended up having to go into some sanatorium again, I think."

Martin Griffin has memories of a "disconcerting" sequence of events. He says: "The front end of the tour was distinguished by the fact that either the PA, or more likely the lights, blew the main circuits at every venue, every night, more than once. There's a live multi-track recording from Brunel University, and you can hear us break off in the middle of 'Death Trap'. I had never before and have never since come across that happening on a major tour."

Bradford is the date that everyone remembers, not just because of the sackings that happened but because yet another leading punk rocker stepped forward there to offer respect. Dave Brock: "We were in the hotel bar after the gig when Pete Shelley of The Buzzcocks came over and shook my hand and said, 'I've been a fan of Hawkwind for years.' "

This was a particularly exciting meeting for Steve Swindells, who recalls: "I immediately bonded with Pete Shelley, with him being gay as well. He was thrilled to meet Brock. The funny part was that Pete and I were playing pool in a very butch fashion while our respective road crews were smashing up the restaurant of this gruesome hotel. It was quite a good spectacle."

Martin Griffin adds: "Mick Smith of The Softees, who were supporting on this part of the tour, was ludicrously strong. He'd been a Para somewhere in Africa. In the battle of the crews, he had to restrain – apparently gently and affectionately – one of our lighting guys, Curly, who was getting a bit carried away. The following day, Curly's whole upper arm was black."

Not even Lemmy, joining the band onstage at the Hammersmith Odeon on October 13, could top that for drama.

And when the tour was over, says Dave Brock, "We decided we'd go back to being Hawkwind again."

It was 1979, they had no record deal, and they were broke. They spent what money they had holing up at Rockfield's Mill House, one of the various buildings at the expanding studio complex. They would not appear onstage again until November, apart from a special one-off in September.

One member of the band was not present.

Martin Griffin recalls: "We came to the end of the Hawklords tour and we were supposed to be going to America after that. Calvert called me up and said, 'You're not coming to America.' I was slightly taken aback. I will never know what that was actually about.

"Bob originally having been very enthusiastic about my style of drumming – 'God's own drummer' – I assumed that was what they wanted me to do. But they must have wanted me to be Simon King. Actually, Simon had turned up at the Hammersmith Odeon gig and I'd told him this. He said he'd had the same situation when he joined: they wanted him to be Terry Ollis.

"Simon is Simon, very laid-back, very Hawkwind, a very cool guy. I imagine he's a lot of fun to be on the road with, which obviously I never was. If you listen to Hawklords' live stuff, it's not as vibrant as Hawkwind, but I thought the drumming was rather good. It was pretty much what they'd insisted on, but there you go."

Perhaps unsurprisingly, then, the group sent for Simon King, who returned to the fold.

"It was mildly disappointing," remarks Griffin, "but I threw all my energies into the studio, upgraded the gear and started recording some good stuff. We had acts through from Elvis Costello to The Wurzels."

He continued playing sessions, and had the pleasure of drumming on a CBS album that reached number one in France. Then he joined forces with Richard "Kid" Strange, former mainman of Doctors Of Madness, a cool, cult new-wave outfit. Martin raised the cash for Strange to record a single, a cover of 'Maggie's Farm', which was timed to coincide with the looming general election and the prospect of Margaret Thatcher becoming Prime Minister. The band brought together Strange on guitar, TV Smith on backing vocals, Steve Swindells on keyboards, Dave Winthrop (Supertramp) on sax, Paul Martinez on bass and Martin on drums.

Later, Strange decided to tour America with backing tapes on a Revox. He brought a band of musicians down to Roche where they recorded a whole set's worth of tracks. Thus, Martin has the distinction of playing on a *Live In New York* album without ever leaving Cornwall.

There were more recording sessions with Strange, and occasional gigs where Strange needed a live band. Then, Martin was invited to take up the drum stool on a European tour. He had a "bloody wonderful time", and he would return in the summer of 1981 to a phone call inviting him to join Hawkwind.

The band, meanwhile, were jamming for hours at Rockfield, trying to work up material for a new set.

Steve Swindells remembers: "It was lovely at the farmhouse. It had this wonderful, former chapel attached, where we rehearsed and jammed and wrote, and a big lawn running down to the river. We were renting it for a pittance because it was little better, condition-wise, than a squat. We were in abject poverty. We had zero budget for food. I was cooking for everyone – vegetarian food, because that's all we could afford.

"The line-up then was Dave, Calvert, Simon King, Harvey and me. Calvert was suffering definite mental problems when we were there. I think he was going through a divorce from his novelist wife, Pamela, and he was very unstable."

It was obvious Bob was going to leave.

Harvey Bainbridge says: "We took a tape machine down and just played. Doug Smith was trying to interest a record company with the stuff we were getting together."

"That's when I wrote 'Shot Down In The Night'," states Swindells. "I presented it to the band and they liked it. Then Brock asked me if I'd be lead singer when Calvert left. There was no money there, there was no record deal, so I said no."

Calvert did indeed leave, and returned to his solo career.

Huw Lloyd-Langton hadn't been short of a gig since his marriage to Marion in 1972.

He played a two-year acoustic stint in a London vegetarian restaurant called Pastures. For six months of that time, he was joined by singer John Butler (Diesel Park West), and for another year by Rattles vocalist Eddy Klima. He taught guitar at a comprehensive school in Streatham for a year, played numerous sessions and toured the UK and Europe for six months with Leo Sayer.

There was a succession of bands. He joined Gallery, which included bassist Rich Driscoll from Kenny. Then there was Magill with Pete Scott from Savoy Brown and Rob Rawlinson from Ian Hunter's Overnight Angels. Then a tour of Yugoslavia with Alekzander Mezek.

One of Huw's favourite bands was the Trinidadian Batti Mamselle, who played Latin-American flavoured music and were fronted by singer Jimmy Chambers from London Beat. They made a brief appearance in the film *Alfie Darling*, starring Alan Price, having refused to perform without Huw when the director said he wanted an all-black band.

In 1974, Huw joined Widowmaker, a supergroup of sorts which brought together Steve Ellis, the former singer of Love Affair, guitarist Ariel Bender, ex of Mott The Hoople, bassist Bob Daisley from Rainbow and drummer Paul Nichols from Lindisfarne. John Butler took over on vocals after Ellis left.

Four years of international travels later, Huw was back in London, trying to get a band together with Simon King, who had yet to be invited back to Hawkwind. "It was a three-piece called Jawa," says Huw. "We couldn't actually find a suitable bass player. It was a period of time when the old jazz rockers were flying quite high. It was almost impossible to find a bass player that could just lay it down. We did find one bass player that we liked. Nic Potter [ex-Van Der Graaf Generator] fitted in well, but he was very busy working with Peter Hammill quite a lot at the time. Simon and myself, we couldn't pay him anything. Doug Smith was vaguely in the picture and he was paying for the rehearsal studios we were using, but he wasn't paying *us* anything. Nothing much was happening."

It was during this period that a small-scale Hawkwind reunion was proposed.

Says Nik Turner: "It was being put together for a concert at the Electric Ballroom, and it was to be called the Kitty Hawks. I went to a rehearsal and Lemmy turned up. We were there for about half an hour and then Lemmy said, 'I don't think I wanna do this gig.' I can't remember what reason he gave."

"We were all gathered in Ear rehearsal studio, where Simon King and myself had been rehearsing," elaborates Huw Lloyd-Langton. "There was Lemmy, Nik, Simon and myself, and a couple of faces I didn't know. We started playing something and then it all fell apart. Everybody started disappearing. The whole thing disintegrated into nothing. It was a non-reunion. At the end of it, there was just me and Simon sitting there wondering what had happened. And Dave didn't turn up, which was ridiculous."

Brock replies: "It was nothing to do with me."

Jawa didn't last much beyond the Kitty Hawks.

"Eventually Simon was asked to come back into Hawkwind," says Huw. "So that put a stop to the whole project for that period."

The trio were brought back together again by Steve Swindells, who was recording demos after departing Hawkwind.

"I was whizzed off to New York in October 1979 by an Italian count who turned out to be a closet case," reveals Steve. "He owned half of Rome, and he had this incredible apartment in New York with a Greek temple at one end. He'd financed the demos and Simon King, Huw Lloyd-Langton and Nic Potter were paid for the sessions.

"We took the demos to New York and I got a solo record deal in three days. I was signed to Atko/WEA by Doug Morris, who is president of Universal. My friend Caroline Guinness had moved from Douglas Smith and was running the office of Bill Curbishley of Trinifold, The Who's management. So I got my deal, I was taken on for management by Bill Curbishley and I made a solo album, *Fresh Blood*."

Once again, Steve was accompanied by Huw, Simon and Nic Potter and photographed for the sleeve by Bob Carlos Clarke.

"I produced it myself. David Bowie offered to produce it but Trinifold inexplicably decided it wasn't a good idea," says Steve, ruefully. "Still, the album came out to quite a lot of acclaim and great airplay, especially in America, in 1980. It reached number three in the *Billboard* airplay charts two weeks after its release in the US."

One of the album tracks was 'Shot Down In The Night', the composition that Steve had presented to Hawkwind at Rockfield, and it was released as a single in the summer of 1980. Hawkwind, for their part, were including the song in their live set, and on exactly the same day – Swindells thinks deliberately – they too released it as a single.

The Hawkwind version of 'Shot Down In the Night' won the contest, creeping into the chart at number 59 in July. It would be their last-ever registered chart single, except for a reissue of 'Silver Machine'.

"It was ironic that their version nudged into the chart while Huw and Simon were playing on my version," says Steve. "And that's where my adventure with them ends."

Despite the early promise of his solo career, Swindells saw his record deal terminated due to lack of sales, a result, he believes, of the company's failure to capitalise on the interest in the album.

He recorded a series of new demos at Pete Townshend's studio, and Roger Daltrey recorded four of his songs over three albums, with Steve playing keyboards on some of them.

"I had two extra songs on the *Best Bits* album, which was Top 10 in the States, and one on the *McVicar* album, although it didn't appear in the film."

Steve went on to pursue a hugely successful career as a club promoter and party organiser in the Eighties. He formed the Pure organisation, set up parties for the likes of Prince, introduced club nights to such prestigious venues as Heaven, and created Jungle, the first house club in London, giving Fat Tony his first-ever gig as a DJ.

In the Nineties, Swindells branched into journalism, writing an internet column for *Time Out* using the alias Spyder from 1995 to 1999. He also edited *Attitude Interactive*, the online version of *Attitude* magazine in 1997. At this time he was suffering from a mystery illness which first struck in 1994.

"It just got worse and worse and I had every test under the sun," he confides. He was then diagnosed with granular cell tumour, a rare form of cancer, and at the time of writing had just had lumps removed from his chest. Luckily, the lumps turned out to be non-malignant and a CT scan was normal, but Steve is still consulting a variety of specialists and the mystery illness remains just that: a mystery.

Most recently, Steve has formed a band called Emoticon with former Culture Club drummer Jon Moss, Winston Blissett, the Massive Attack bassist, Dale Davies (another bassist) and ex-Hawkwind guitarist Jerry Richards, playing "intelligent, soulful, passionate rock with a quirky edge".

He is also writing material with his best friend Shanks, of Shanks & Bigfoot.

Steve lives in Willesden Green with his cat. And what of the Italian count?

"The second time he took me to New York, he declared his undying love for me after five years of not declaring anything. I hopped on a plane and went back home. I never saw him again."

CHAPTER 14

Cream Crackers

THEY used to call him Gollum, after the character in *Lord Of The Rings*.

"My precious . . ."

Tim Blake had been around since the earliest days, when he'd off-handedly assured Group X that they could certainly crash the stage at the All Saints Hall.

A familiar face around Ladbroke Grove and the Clearwater offices, the ultimate hippie, he was from an extremely well-to-do family.

Douglas Smith recalls: "He got to know everybody and he would come into the office and hang around, and he just carried on hanging around. He used to get under my feet. I've never been a huge fan of Tim, but at the same time, I'm congenial with him. He knows the rules of how to be polite."

"He spoke in this very public-school accent," remembers Huw Lloyd-Langton. "I knew him from the early Roundhouse days. We used to think he was a little hanger-on or something."

"He was always under your heels," adds Marion Lloyd-Langton, echoing Douglas Smith's early memory. "He drove you nuts. He rabbited on and on about music. But he's a damned good musician."

By the summer of 1979, Dave Brock, Simon King and Harvey Bainbridge had waved goodbye to Bob Calvert and Steve Swindells, and they needed musicians to complete the new Hawkwind line-up. They contacted Tim Blake who, in the interim, had built a reputation as a real keyboard wizard.

Tim was born in Queen Charlotte's Hospital in Hammersmith, London, on February 6, 1952, exactly one year after Huw Lloyd-Langton's arrival in the world. Tim's family moved to Northwood, Middlesex, and that's where he grew up.

"I'm a Cranleigh schoolboy," he reveals. At Cranleigh, he was taught classical trumpet, and he played harmonica and slide guitar in a school band. "Then I was a drama student, and even when I was in drama school, I spent my holidays working as an assistant engineer in a studio."

After living and breathing the Ladbroke Grove experience in 1969 and 1970, making particular friends with Dikmik due to their mutual interest in signal generators, Tim moved to France, where he became increasingly absorbed by electronic music. "I did some musical jobs," he relates. "Variety and things like that. Then Gong."

Tim had met Gong's leader, Daevid Allen, some time earlier. He had gone to London's Marquee Studios to help Allen mix his solo album, *Banana Moon*. When Gong eventually regrouped at their French HQ, Tim was invited to join as a sound mixer and general helper.

He subsequently left after buying an EMS synth, which he revamped to his personal specifications and called the Crystal Machine. This was the name also given to Tim's pet musical project, which took in gigs and recordings.

Daevid Allen heard a tape of Crystal Machine and invited Blake back to Gong in 1972, this time as a full-time member primarily playing synthesiser but also contributing trumpet, percussion and some vocals. In his alter ego of Hi T Moonweed, Tim was involved in some of the band's most valued albums, namely the "Radio Gnome" trilogy formed by *Flying Teapot*, *Angel's Egg* and *You*, and he was working towards achieving a perfect correspondence between the synthesiser and the light-show.

The progress of the trilogy was interrupted in 1973 when Allen left Gong for a short while, and Tim joined a splinter group, Paragong. The line-up included Steve Hillage with whom Tim formed a significant friendship. Upon Daevid Allen's return to Gong, Blake and Hillage had already forged an intuitive partnership which, with *You*, gave rise to a phenomenon dubbed "om rock".

In 1975, Tim left Gong, having been "castigated by the group". Daevid Allen followed him 10 days later, and Hillage led the band for three months before splitting to form his own band. Tim worked on his acclaimed album *Fish Rising*.

Virgin, Gong's label, terminated Tim's recording agreement but maintained a control of his publishing "in order to recuperate on the massive passive in the Gong accounting".

He had also, during the Gong period, become involved briefly with Cyrille Verdeaux of Clearlight, travelling to England to do some recordings.

Tim reactivated Crystal Machine and began playing live performances in Paris. His accomplices now included Patrice Warrener, an inventor who helped Tim bring laser shows to the city for the first time.

Taking a short break for a project with the Saratoga Space Messengers, Tim returned to Crystal Machine and they made their debut UK appearance at the Seasalter Free Festival outside Whitstable, Kent. They played a few more British dates in February '77, and attended a massive, 12-hour Gong reunion in Paris which saw Tim playing three different sets, with Crystal Machine, Steve Hillage and Gong. Crystal Machine then played at Stonehenge where Hawkwind, headlining, had installed their spectacular Atomhenge stage set. An album of live Crystal Machine tracks was released in France by Egg Records in November 1977.

Tim took part in Nik Turner's 1978 Sphynx project, appearing on the album *Xitintoday* alongside a host of other musicians including Steve Hillage and his girlfriend, Gong singer Miquette Giraudy.

Blake also began working on his first studio album, *New Jerusalem*, with a second synthesiser player called Jean Philippe Rykiel. The two musicians toured France, Spain and Japan with Patrice Warrener in 1978 and during rehearsals for more dates, recorded sessions that would much later be released as *Waterfalls In Space* by Ottersongs.

New Jerusalem was released in November 1978 and Tim set out on a major tour to promote it – but by mid-1979, he was getting fed up. "I'd been all round the world touring with *Jerusalem*," he recalls. "Since Gong, I'd been working as an independent, trying to deal with the record company, trying to deal with tours. It was getting a little bit too big for me to manage.

"I played at Glastonbury in June 1979, and they told me I was going to have to go on after Peter Gabriel. After this experience, I finished the world tour and came back to Paris. Jean Michel Jarre was starting up with some of the people who worked with me. All sorts of things were happening, telling me that whatever was going to happen next, I wasn't capable of handling it."

By something like divine intervention, what did happen next was that Tim joined Hawkwind. He reflects: "It was very, very simple. It was a very strange set of circumstances. Sometimes one's destiny makes itself clear, and this was one of those times.

"I was in Paris, and I said to my girlfriend, 'Look, really, despite the success we've been having with the *Jerusalem* tour, it's so hard for me to handle that if a group with a management phoned me up and said, "Tim, come and play," I would do so immediately.' I said this to her in her house which, in principle, is a place where no one could get hold of me. At that very instant, the telephone rang and it was Douglas Smith asking me if I wanted to play with Hawkwind."

Tim learnt that they were planning to proceed as a four-piece, which would have put him into the position of a lead instrumentalist.

"Nowadays, I'd feel very happy in the virtual guitarist role, but at the time, I wasn't sure if it would work," recalls Tim. "I suggested that we call Huw Lloyd-Langton in. It was the right thing to do."

Huw was doing a bit of session work when Simon King phoned to ask if he'd like to rejoin Hawkwind.

"I didn't know whether I wanted to or not," says Huw. "I really didn't want to go back to Hawkwind as it had been when I left. The whole drug thing still frightened me. At the same time, I quite fancied joining a band that was working a lot, which they were."

He agreed to give it a go. "I went along to Rockfield with Simon," he says. "I really liked Simon; we got on very well. And I certainly had no adverse feelings about going back and working with Dave. I'd never fallen out with him, and I'd always respected him as a writer, singer and musician.

"Simon said this guy Tim Blake was coming along to play keyboards, and he insisted I knew him. I didn't know the name. We had to pick him up from the airport. As soon as I saw him, I recognised him – 'It's Gollum!' He was always a very likeable person, even if he got up your nose a lot, and he was a very talented musician."

Huw met Harvey Bainbridge for the first time at Rockfield. "Lovely chap, Harvey. I was totally happy to be a part of it all, and more than happy that they were going out and doing big gigs and playing to lots of people. It meant getting paid as well, which is a fairly rare experience in the music game."

The dates were originally set up to celebrate Hawkwind's 10th anniversary but are more widely remembered as the Live Seventy Nine tour, since that's the name of the live album that ensued.

The new line-up of the band played a one-off at the Leeds Futurama Sci-Fi Festival early in September, where they were joined onstage by a surprise guest, Nik Turner, for a rendition of 'Brainstorm'. They followed on with the tour proper in November and December, taking with them Tim Blake's working partner Patrice Warrener and his lasers.

It was a brave and ambitious undertaking, a major tour of big venues staged without any record company backing, since they didn't have a deal, and with a minimum of advertising and promotion. Still, the public rallied to the cause and all but four venues sold out, with the result that the venture paid for itself.

Hawkwind took the opportunity to debut new material which would appear on their next studio album, slotting 'Motorway City', 'Who's Gonna Win The War?', 'World Of Tiers' and 'Levitation' in among the more familiar fare: 'Urban Guerilla', 'Prelude', 'Spirit Of The Age', 'Brainstorm', 'PXR5', 'Master Of The Universe' and 'Silver Machine'.

Also new to the set were two Tim Blake songs – 'New Jerusalem' and 'Lighthouse', presented together as a 15-minute solo slot, giving Tim a showcase for his dramatic marriage of electronics and light. "It gives us a chance to go off and get our heads straight," Brock told *Melody Maker*.

However, there were teething problems. "The lasers never used to be used until Tim did his solo spot," says Brock. "We got very disgruntled with all this. We were paying Patrice a large fee for these lasers. We wanted them on a bit earlier."

"We ran into a bit of trouble with various health and safety people around the country because of the lasers," says Harvey Bainbridge. "In one venue, a health and safety officer really thought it was going to be like something from *Star Trek* where you push the button and half the wall gets blown out. We'd been demonstrating it to him all afternoon at the City Hall. He was wandering around with his clipboard up to his face, shielding his eyes as if he was going to get obliterated at any minute.

"He was determined we weren't going to use the lasers, and he was going to use any means to stop us playing. So in the end, we said, 'You're going to have to speak to our manager about this – he's in here.' We ushered him through a door backstage, which was a cupboard. We locked him in the cupboard, just to get him out of the way for a while, and we let him out once the show had got going.

"The upshot was that several days later, the same guy turned up with two bigwigs from London. He was most aggrieved. We demonstrated the whole thing in the afternoon for the two main guys and they said, 'That's perfectly fine.' They gave the other guy an earful and they all marched off."

It was, by all accounts, a happy and friendly tour for Hawkwind, with Dave Brock declaring to Steve Gett that, "I haven't enjoyed myself so much for at least three years. It was really fun. We had our little holiday earlier in the year, but now we're getting back into the swing of things. We'll definitely progress from here."

Tim Blake comments: "I always considered Douglas Smith to be one of the great members of the creative team. Every time he has looked after the group, he has done interesting things. The atmosphere in the band was very satisfying, because they'd been through a lot – being Hawkwind, 'Silver Machine', then not being Hawkwind, Hawklords . . . from being an original structure with several lines of direction at the same time to personality conflict to becoming very much Robert Calvert's group and then back to Hawkwind. There's a certain satisfaction in that. Going on the voyage from Group X through to Hawkwind 1979 had been a bit of an adventure. A complete cycle had been done over 10 years, and there we were, together. I probably got on best with Dave. I like playing music with Dave."

Huw Lloyd-Langton states: "Brocky, as far as I'm concerned, has always been the main man, the brains behind the whole thing, the ideas man. When I rejoined in 1979, he was still the motivating force behind it. Me, I'm just a guitarist although, obviously, every musician adds their part."

It was a particularly rewarding tour for the fans, with Hawkwind rediscovering their original strengths after the period of experiment and with Huw Lloyd-Langton, their ever-popular guitarist, giving forth in his inimitable space-rock fashion.

A couple of familiar faces turned out to support the band. Dikmik showed up at one of their two Hammersmith Odeon gigs, and Lemmy joined them onstage on December 29 when they played their second night at the Camden Electric Ballroom.

It was an especially significant tour for Dave Brock who met his future life partner at Newcastle City Hall on November 19. Kris Tate, born and brought up in Newcastle upon Tyne, was working with the venue's stage crew. "We all met up after the show in the dressing room for a drink," she says. "I didn't know who Dave was. I thought he was one of the roadies."

The two struck up a conversation, at the end of which they exchanged phone numbers.

"What did I like about him?" wonders Kris. "His accent. I liked his accent. He went off and did more gigs, and then he phoned me up and we started calling each other. I went to see Hawkwind in Bridlington quite a long time after that, and we met up in London."

Dave and Kris became friends and confidantes, although there was no romance for the time being. She would later take on various duties in the Hawkwind organisation and onstage too, as a dancer and then a fire-eater. These days, Kris manages the band and lives with Dave at their farmhouse near Exeter.

Hawkwind, meanwhile, had taken a mobile out on the road to record the 1979 concerts. "We played a show at St Albans City Hall [on December 8] and we didn't think much of it at the time," remembers Harvey Bainbridge. "Doug Smith thought we'd better have a listen to the recording. It was a lot better than we'd thought it would turn out. We went off and mixed it at Eel Pie Studios."

Douglas took the tape to Bronze Records. "I thought there was an album there," he says. "I suggested to Bronze that they take the album, with an option for a second album, so Hawkwind did *Live Seventy Nine* and *Levitation* with Bronze."

Released in July 1980, *Live Seventy Nine* charted respectably at number 15, and it remains a great fan favourite.

Despite this, the band were not rich.

"Harvey was teaching on and off on the side, and I used to get by sometimes by doing up old cars," says Dave. "I had a friend who used to buy up all these old Rileys and old Austins. I used to get them going and make a bit of money out of that. We only played one tour in 1979 and one tour in 1980, and the amount of money from one tour doesn't keep us going for a whole year."

Hawkwind made their traditional appearance at Stonehenge in June 1980, and they took time out the next month to play a handful of gigs. However, July and August were largely spent recording *Levitation* at Bronze's Roundhouse Studios in London's Chalk Farm.

There was no big concept planned for the album; possibly there wasn't enough time for anything like that.

"There was no lack of material but we were backs against the wall," explains Huw Lloyd-Langton. "We only had a short period in which to do the album. There wasn't a particular theme. The idea was just for it to be a darned good album, with a tour to follow. Luckily, it just happened."

Harvey Bainbridge agrees: "I never thought there was a musical brief other than it was rock music with a psychedelic influence. It was a space-rock band. I felt that we ought to be as non-commercial as we possibly could. In hindsight, Dave likes to go for the outrageous, but he really wants to be commercial as well. The typical hypnotic, trancey drum beat kind of thing is what Dave likes. That's what the album was, really. Everybody putting in their thruppence worth, like a collection of one-man-bands."

They had at their disposal in the studio some of the most modern equipment that then existed, and this was one of many examples of Hawkwind actually being ahead of their time, embracing new technology rather than stagnating like the bunch of old hippies certain journalists still believed they were.

"We were one of the first bands to be recorded digitally," says Dave Brock. "Bronze had this state-of-the-art digital gear. *Live Seventy Nine* had done very well. Everything was looking jolly rosy. And then, all of a sudden, our drummer was failing us."

Simon King was about to make his final exit from the band.

"He couldn't play his drums properly 'cos of taking bad drugs, unfortunately," carries on Dave. "He was taking heroin. He couldn't hold the drumsticks properly. It was a sad moment. He was a Chelsea supporter and a jolly good friend of mine, but there was a lot of tension in the studios."

Simon was having his touchy moments at the time. Douglas Smith recalls: "He walked into my office one day, really angry about something, and he knocked two or three boxes full of Nolan Sisters cups on to the floor." A surreal scene by any standards.

Douglas' wife Eve had a successful merchandising company – Holy T-shirts – and the cups were part of the stock she had left over from a Nolans residency in Blackpool. "Simon took his anger out on the cups," chuckles Douglas. "He only broke about 10 or 15 of them. He was a great guy most of the time. He came from a very good family in Oxford. I think he and Simon House may have dabbled in heroin, but I can't remember any times at all when it made any difference to the life of the band."

Harvey Bainbridge corroborates Dave Brock's diagnosis.

"Poor old Simon was having a few problems with various substances," he agrees. "We were in the studio playing and Dave was freaking out 'cos he wasn't keeping perfect tempo. He brought in a drum machine – 'This is the tempo. You've gotta play to this.' I suggested that everyone should go away for a day, calm down and come back. I said, 'Why don't you let me and Simon put down some backing tracks?' Dave said, 'No, no, we'll use the drum machine.' Simon was really, really upset by it. He went off – and that was it with him."

Brock says: "There was a new Steinberg drum machine in the studio. Ashley Howe, the engineer on that album – I think he suggested that we used this drum machine. None of us knew how to use it. Nor did Ashley."

Huw Lloyd-Langton was there when Simon left the building. "I went out for a bag of chips," he recalls. "I came back to the studio and Simon was coming out almost in tears as I was going in. He said Brock had told him he wasn't cutting it, and he walked off up the road. This was a week into recording the album."

"The Live Seventy Nine tour had been fantastic," points out Huw's wife Marion. "Simon had been playing brilliantly."

Harvey Bainbridge declares that King was "edged out" of the band, although Simon himself told an interviewer years later that he was not sacked: "I simply wanted to get away. I was very heavily into drinking and had become a danger even to myself. My split with Dave and the boys was amicable, and my days after *Levitation* were fixed on getting my family life together."

There would later be one aborted attempt, in 1982, to return Simon to Hawkwind.

For a while, Simon rehearsed with Simon House in a London-based band called Turbo, but it didn't come to anything.

By 1985, he had sold all of his drums and has not played since. He spent some time in social work, then moved into buying and selling, and is now a local authority manager dealing with waste and recycling, joking to friends that "I've got a degree in rubbish." He is "just living a normal life away from the madding crowd", although his experiences in Hawkwind have clearly left their scars.

"Simon has remained a good friend of mine," says Douglas Smith. "He won't talk to anyone in the band. My wife Eve and I see him. He's got a lovely house in Richmond. He's gone through a lot of changes in his life, but he's still exactly the same person."

Simon has two children. One is a son by his ex-wife Jackie. They had at one time lived in a flat in Kensington above Alan Powell, who would join Simon in Hawkwind as the other half of The Drum Empire. The other is a daughter by his ex, Izzy, who had previously been Dikmik's partner.

Some of his former Hawkwind bandmates would love to see Simon again, but they confirm that, to this day, he resists any contact.

The Hawks were flapping. They had an album to make, and they'd lost their drummer.

"It was panic stations," says Huw. "I seem to remember that Simon's drum roadie George was a good drummer in his own right. They tried him out, but they weren't happy."

Marion Lloyd-Langton suggested Cream legend Ginger Baker. At the time, she was a press officer for Baker's management company Oak Productions (having previously worked as an assistant PR for several years at Robert Stigwood's RSO).

"We discussed it and put it to Dave that we could ask Ginger to come and do the album," says Huw. "Dave was totally up for it. Ginger agreed to do it. We offered him three times the union rate, although he did the whole thing in two days anyway. A lesser player, it would have taken three weeks at least, and it would probably have cost more than it did paying Ginger the triple session fee.

"Ginger was a saviour in a way. It took him no time at all to play any of the numbers. One track I wrote, 'Space Chase' – he came in and breezed through it straight away. I don't think Simon could've played that. With Ginger, his style is very percussive. And funnily enough, Terry Ollis' style was very percussive in the early days. Ginger fitted the band like a glove. His style was just totally right for it. Very percussive but far more advanced and knowledgeable in a music sense than Terry had been.

"The Ginger Baker situation was inspiring, I thought, 'cos he's such a good player, but I was unhappy at the same time with the suddenness of Simon leaving. I hadn't expected that to happen at all. His playing was a little bit erratic, but it's horrible when people fall out and disappear."

Dave Brock remembers the excitement surrounding the arrival of the notoriously explosive Baker. "We thought, 'Cor blimey, here we are with a world-class, famous drummer!' He was all right, actually.

He's another Leo. I'm one. Kris is one. Simon King's one. Ginger was a professional musician and a fantastic drummer – 'Here am I playing with Ginger Baker! What a fantastic thing to happen!' "

Marion: "Ginger always said that apart from the *Blind Faith* LP, *Levitation* was one of his favourite albums of his whole career."

The former *Melody Maker* journalist Chris Charlesworth says today: "I do remember the astonishment that greeted the news that Ginger Baker had joined them. It was a bit like Ringo joining The Sweet, though I suppose Baker's wayward lifestyle was not incompatible with Hawkwind's."

The public supported *Levitation*, which would reach number 21 in November, although over time, it has come to be considered one of the band's less inspired albums, despite Lloyd-Langton's well-regarded lead work and the presence of a famous drummer.

With the album almost finished, Hawkwind ventured out of the studio to talk to the press and defend themselves against accusations of "old fartdom". Dave Brock told *Melody Maker*'s Ian Pye: "I don't think we're outdated. Rock theatre, the show side, is still strong. We get people coming from all over the country to see us . . . A bloke came down to see us, from *Record Mirror*, I think, and he kept going on about us being old farts. I nearly punched him on the nose."

The band were also asked to comment on "the failed aspirations of the Woodstock generation". Harvey Bainbridge replied: "People were changed by it all, but there was probably more optimism than was warranted. The thing is that the media and the system in general has this amazing capacity to absorb threatening movements, sometimes even repackaging them and selling them back to people."

Stopping off to pay tribute to Robert Calvert, and mentioning that Bob was currently in the middle of writing his music-business novel *Hype* (he also released an album of the same name), Dave Brock had the last word: "Next thing up is a British tour because that's it when it comes down to it. To play, man, that's the point of a band. To play and have fun."

Before the fun, though, Hawkwind and Douglas Smith fell out again. "I got the tour together," says Douglas. "And what happened was that Ginger Baker's manager Roy Ward – he was into polo horses – was around at the time, and he was a madman, a complete lunatic. Marion Lloyd-Langton said, 'I can work with him. Why don't I do that and you stay in the background?'

"Once it got to the planning and budgeting, arguments started about how much was going for this and that. The usual thing happened. *Hawkwind know best.* They always thought they knew the right and wrong thing to do. I said, 'This is ridiculous. Why am I doing this?' I just had enough, and I left them with Roy Ward."

At the same time Danny Betesh at Kennedy Street, the tour promoters, was taking an interest in Hawkwind for management. Douglas: "Danny asked me, 'You let them go and we'll take over.' I know there's a legal document around on it."

Marion recalls: "Because of Doug's departure, everything was in a mess. Thus, I picked up the remnants of the tour, working with Kennedy Street, who were promoting the gigs, doing the deals with lighting, trucking and so on, as well as all the PR for the band.

"Roy Ward joined the tour as acting personal manager and I ran the office acting as manager and PR coordinator. Roy was always more of a figurehead. He left it all to me. But, really, publicity had always been my main thing for Ginger. I wrote half the articles at gigs 'cos the journalists would turn up drunk. I toured with them to do publicity."

Huw Lloyd-Langton says: "The time came when we got fed up with earning so little. We were playing long tours and big gigs and we were getting a fairly paltry amount of money, maybe about £200 a week. I don't recall exactly, but it didn't seem to match up with the size of the gigs and the capacity crowds we were playing to.

"There have been all sorts of fall-outs and making-ups with Doug and the band over the years. And it's usually about money somewhere along the line."

Tim Blake adds: "I think Douglas costs a lot, but he's very good and we'd gross a lot of money. I imagine that all Douglas' working expenses came out of the band too. I personally have made more money out of Hawkwind with Douglas handling the band than with Douglas not handling the band.

"There was a management change going on. It wasn't who they were going to that was important, it was who they were going away *from.* They were going away from Douglas, via Ginger's manager Roy Ward.

"When Douglas is involved, it's very well organised, very big. He controlled Hawkwind better than anybody else. But there's unease between him and Brock. And every time it got off the ground, Dave put it in the hands of somebody else who handled it and then stopped it."

There was definitely some unease when Roy Ward became involved.

Says Huw: "Dave and co weren't particularly keen on Roy. I don't think they saw eye to eye very much."

As a result, Dave liaised directly with Danny Betesh and Kennedy Street who eventually did take over Hawkwind's management.

Meanwhile, Kris Tait had been invited to join the tour, which was taking place over October, November and December 1980, with a few weeks' break between the Irish dates in November and the second leg, starting in Scotland in December. She was helping out with the merchandising stall and the catering, and running errands. "I was somebody Dave could trust to do things," she says. "Also, I knew a lot about printing."

Kris joined the band at Rockfield's Mill House where they were rehearsing for the tour and where they first saw a fairly startling side of Ginger Baker's personality. "He'd been all right during the recordings, really calm and nice," recalls Kris. "One day at Rockfield, he drank this bottle of Bacardi. Then he stood on the table with the bottle in the air, going, 'Yeah! It's going to be a great tour, boys!' We thought, 'Oh, God.'

"When Ginger turned up at Rockfield, he had this horrible dog called Toerag. It looked like a small Doberman, with similar colouring. I had my dog, Kickstart. He was a curly-haired mongrel. Kickstart was really friendly. Ginger said to me, 'Keep your dog in the bedroom. My dog will rip your dog apart.'

"Poor Kickstart used to wander round all happy. Ginger had a young girlfriend, and they'd gone off for this long walk. Me and Dave were playing pool when they came back, and Kickstart saw Toerag. He ran right beneath Dave's legs and we were trying to get the two dogs apart.

"Toerag turned out to be a complete coward and ran off to his room. There wasn't a great deal of damage to the dogs. But Ginger started laying into Kickstart, kicking him. The only thing I had in my hand was a pool cue. I started hitting Ginger over the head with it. He yelled to Dave, 'Get her off me.' He stopped kicking my dog. Kickstart was all bruised and upset. I think Ginger would have killed him. He was a big man and this was a little dog.

"He was volatile, but there were times when he was all right. His roadie, Phil, was really nice. He's dead now. Everybody had their ups and downs, but people didn't have to leave because of it. I never really didn't get on with Ginger except for when he kicked the dog which really annoyed me. He wasn't a person who carried resentment, and neither was I. I think it was a case of having a screaming row with each other. That's what Leos do."

Kris had another memorable run-in with Baker. "I used to cook food for everybody," she recalls. "One day I'd cooked everybody pancakes. Ginger came in late and said, 'Make me a pancake.' I said, 'No, I've put everything away.' He rang up Danny Betesh and told him I wouldn't make him a pancake. He was getting paranoid. There was a lot going on."

The tour went on the road, complete with Kickstart and Toerag.

"Kickstart used to have a little laminate pass round his neck with his name on," laughs Kris. "There was a ton of Pedigree Chum on the rider. He'd get to the gig, sniff out where the kitchen was and come back out with his Pedigree Chum in his mouth. He'd get it off the catering girls. He loved all that, Kickstart did.

"Toerag used to bite people all the time. He used to bite the fans. People had to go to hospital and get tetanus injections and stitches or whatever. Ginger used to go, 'You can bite *him*, he's not important. You *can't* bite *him*, he's the promoter.'

"People coming into the dressing room – Ginger would throw bottles at them. He used to be really pissed, but we thought he was just putting it on. One day, he fell in the shower and cut all his back open. We realised, 'He's not joking. He really is out of it.'"

Dave Brock adds: "Ginger, of course, had a drug problem. We tried to wean him off that. He used to have these weird characters turning up at gigs, heroin dealers we wouldn't allow in the dressing room. He started drinking then. After the day he fell in the shower in the dressing room, we realised he was drinking a lot, a bottle of Bacardi a day.

"This camaraderie we used to have – we used to try and get these people off these drugs and support them. It used to be a waste of time sometimes, but we'd try."

At the same time, according to Dave: "What Ginger could do with one hand, other drummers would have to do with two. And he was a very, very amusing character."

The first critical tour problems didn't involve Ginger. They concerned Tim Blake.

Dave Brock recounts the irritations that were building up as the tour carried on. "Tim had this partner, a beautiful model, a lovely girl. She was French and she used to wind him up something rotten – 'I'm going to a party tonight, ha ha.' She'd really wind him up into a state of mania and he'd spend huge amounts of money on phone bills. We'd always be waiting for him because he'd be on the phone. He smashed a phone when we were in Southampton in the hotel lobby in front of all these people. It fell in pieces on the floor. Our tour manager said, 'Oh, very sorry, he's under terrible stresses and strain.' Then I think he threw an ashtray through his hotel window in a fit of rage.

"He was always causing scenes, Tim was. He's just one of these characters. He's an old friend, but he's hard to work with. He gets on his high horse, very uppity. Next day it's all back to normal.

"I remember once we knocked at his room and he came to the door with a green face mask on. I've got a photo of that. Another time, Tim and Harvey had a fight in a car down Charing Cross Road, just past Foyles bookshop. Tim was wearing green lamé sparkly trousers. He used to wear glam-rock clothes. He had a shiny cloak. They'd had an argument and he'd grabbed hold of Harvey round the neck. At that point, Tim opened the door and he fell out on to the road. We were only going five miles an hour. He slammed the door and ran off."

"I've no recollection of that," says Tim Blake. "It doesn't sound quite logical, but it's the stuff legends are made of."

Harvey Bainbridge confirms there was an argument in the car. He says: "I can't remember any physical fight. Dave had got pissed off with Tim. I think Tim was asking to be paid. There was a huge row about money and I probably yelled at him, 'Why should you have money if I haven't got any?' I think I was probably the one who was wound up by Dave to tell him he couldn't have any. I do remember we got him out of the car, that's for sure. Whether he went of his own accord, I can't honestly remember.

"It's probably true about the green lamé trousers – without underpants. It was a standing joke at Rockfield. He'd be on the phone and the cleaning ladies would say, 'Doesn't he ever wear underpants?' Tim was quite a flamboyant man in those days, with his long, long hair and his big Parisian shades."

Everyone in the band tells the same story of the day that Tim was dumped by Hawkwind. They were in Hanley, Stoke on Trent, and they'd played a gig at the Victoria Hall on October 17.

By this time, the group were travelling in two rented cars. There was the "early car", for Dave Brock, Harvey Bainbridge and Tim Blake, who liked to be up and about early, and there was the "late car" for Huw Lloyd-Langton and Ginger Baker, whose nights ran rather late. "We were the morning boys," confirms Tim Blake. "We would get up and have breakfast and then we'd drive off and we'd stop for a spot of lunch. And the only thing that was wrong with this – as soon as we were on the motorway, where Dave had a virtually captive audience, he'd say, 'Now, look, I want to talk about Douglas and the money.' And that was his main preoccupation."

On the morning that Hawkwind were leaving Hanley, Dave and Harvey were sitting outside the hotel in the early car, waiting as usual for Tim. Says Harvey: "I ran in to see where he was. I said, 'Tim, are you ready?' He wasn't. I went back – 'He's not ready yet.'"

There were flurries of swearing from Dave Brock who himself went back into the hotel to hurry up the keyboard player. "Then his partner rang him back," says Brock. "I said, 'If you're not at the car in five minutes, we're going to leave you here.' He wasn't, so we drove off and left him there. That was it."

Tim had not told anyone in the band that he had a particular reason for phoning home to France so frequently during the tour. He reveals: "Obviously there was something going on in my private life. I hadn't actually wanted to go on tour at that particular time. My partner was pregnant and having trouble with it. The night before this incident, we lost our baby.

"Effectively, when you're on the phone talking to your wife who's just lost a child the night before and your mates drive off and leave you, that's the time when you think your place is somewhere else."

CHAPTER 15

Ginger's Last Stand

TIM BLAKE had not wanted to leave Hawkwind.

"In that situation, you get out, don't you?" he reasons. "But I was very frustrated 'cos the band was sounding right. I was leaving a version of Hawkwind which I personally enjoyed. *Levitation* was rather good. With Ginger on drums, it wasn't a 100 per cent success on the album, 'cos he wasn't driving. He came along and he was being driven. By the time we got on to the stage with Ginger, he was driving.

"I thought everything was really positive at that time. It was quite annoying to have to leave. I took a plane home to France and I wasn't very interested in music for a little while. I turned down an offer to go to Glastonbury."

"It was pretty unfortunate about Tim," says Huw. "His performance in the band was quite strong."

There was more misfortune in store for Tim, too. He states it carefully: "My separation with Hawkwind was very prejudicial to my equipment."

Harvey Bainbridge explains: "The codicil to the Tim story – and I'm not very proud of myself for my part in it – was that at the end of the tour, all his equipment was in England, and he lived in France. Dave reckoned Tim owed us money 'cos he'd been paid for the tour and hadn't done the whole tour. He was on session fees. Dave says, 'We'll take Tim's equipment because he owes us money.' We parked up at Ginger Baker's manager's studio in Acton and we took the equipment.

"At this time, being fairly new, I hadn't a fucking clue what was going on. All this stuff was happening. I thought Dave was just wanting to hang on to the gear until we got the money back.

"I took most of it to my place in Devon. Then Tim Blake was trying to get the stuff back, and he'd been in touch with Danny Betesh and

Kennedy Street. Eventually, Danny Betesh phoned me up and said, 'I hear you've got Tim's equipment and you're holding on to it.' I said, 'Yes.' I was really bamboozled into that one. I fell for it. When it came down to it, Dave washed his hands of it, and it was all down to me. We took the equipment back to London and it was picked up.

"By that time, it was all a question of, you kill someone before they kill you. Very 'peace and love'. From then on, Dave made it out that Tim was just money-grabbing all the time."

Dave comments: "Tim got paid for the whole of the tour. He wanted session fees, and he got twice as much money as we did. We were still trundling round the country. What Harvey is saying is true – Tim did get all his gear back in the end."

Dave, Harvey and Huw had all signed a legal business agreement, but Tim had been getting paid on a session basis because he was still signed to Barclay Records.

"We have a long-standing *litige*," says Tim. "I couldn't sign any record agreement with Hawkwind. At one point, Douglas sent me to see a lawyer in Paris with my contracts. They were saying, 'Let's try and get him out of these contracts,' when what they should have been saying was, 'Let's try and collaborate with Tim's record company.'

"An arrangement was agreed but not respected. It was made by the then management – Douglas' company. But Hawkwind were changing managers, so finally no agreement was made. As a result, there's a disagreement about those two records [*Live Seventy Nine* and *Levitation*]. I was paid a £750 advance for *Levitation*, and that was it.

"That being said, it doesn't stop me from being very good friends with Dave. If I was invited to go on tour with Hawkwind today, I would go – even though they are very, very naughty people sometimes – because there's still something likeable there. But there was a very difficult time when I left or was thrown out. I was not a director of the company because of this Barclay thing, simple as that."

Douglas remarks: "One of the band accused me of never paying him an advance on one particular album. I had had a letter from Harvey, Dave and Huw Lloyd-Langton telling me they were the company and Tim wasn't. I followed my instructions."

Blake alleges that, furthermore: "A very important part of my equipment vanished. I picked up my equipment from Roy Ward's rehearsal studio. I got it all but one part back, the polyphonic part. It was quite an expensive piece of equipment.

"At the same time, it became clear that there was a lack of revenue from the Hawkwind time. I must say playing with them was definitely good business in those days, but afterwards there was a lack of royalties coming in from them. One way or another, I had to find more money to live.

"There was no way I was able to invest in my equipment. The cheapest way I found of getting polyphonic again was a small computer. I was on the edge of computers coming in. EMS built a PolySequencer for their Polysynthi with a computer."

However, Tim continues, he found the programming very laborious, and he took to writing bursts of interesting music 30 seconds long. Which led him into a new career in 1981, writing jingles for radio stations. With the advent of non-State-run FM radio in May the same year, following the election of François Mitterand, he then found an outlet for his talents as a sound expert running a production studio for a radio station. He stayed there into the Nineties before returning to music.

He made tentative steps back into live performance, playing a few shows in France in 1988. In the early Nineties, he began work on *Magick*, his first solo album in years, and in 1991, he toured Britain and the States. There, he bumped into Hawkwind again. He opened for them at a few shows in north America, and thus began a series of sporadic guest appearances which have continued down the years. Tim has continued to record and play live concerts in his own right.

"I'm a musician now and I write music," he states. "I live in a windmill in the countryside in south Brittany. I live alone and I have one daughter, who was born in 2001."

Hawkwind were still only in the first month of the tour when they left Tim Blake behind in a cloud of dust in Hanley, and they urgently needed a replacement keyboardist. Tim's roadie Twink, also a keyboard player (not to be confused with Pink Fairies' Twink), took over.

Dave Brock says, "I'd known him before through doing festivals and things and so he guested with us. That's the idea of music, isn't it, really? Like a jazz band . . ."

Twink, whose real name is Paul Noble, had roadied for Steve Hillage, Planet Gong and Gong, with whom he'd also performed. He'd played synthesiser with Here & Now and was a close friend of Zorch, reputedly the first all-synth group in the UK.

So when he was asked to take Blake's place on the tour, he wasn't fazed. But disaster struck after only a few dates. Twink winces: "I was travelling with Ginger Baker's drum roadie, and the truck turned over in a ditch. I broke my foot, and that was the end of the tour for me."

He went on to become involved in dance music in the Nineties and is now working with computers and occasionally playing with the original drummer and guitarist from Here & Now, rechristened *Ici Maintenant*.

Hawkwind, meanwhile, had to find the tour's third keyboard player. Eventually arriving in Kris' hometown, Newcastle upon Tyne, for their City Hall gig on October 22, they recruited Keith Hale to the job. Says Brock: "We had to run through the numbers on this little organ in Kris' living room. Keith used to be in Blood Donor, a very good little band a bit like Soft Machine. He'd actually sent us a tape. I'd kept it, because he's a good musician, and I found his phone number."

It's believed that Keith may have known Ginger Baker prior to this. If not, he was by all accounts a major fan.

Huw reckons: "He only joined because Ginger was in the band. He was like Ginger's roadie and lapdog as well as being a keyboard player."

Now Ginger had a supporter and the band began to separate into two factions, with Baker and Hale eventually mounting a challenge to the status quo – and getting fired themselves.

There were certainly some memorable Ginger moments along the way. Kris Tait recalls: "I had a friend called Val who used to have a catering studio behind Hammersmith Odeon. All the bands that came to play there, Val would cater for them. I used to stay with her. She got a company together and came out on the road with us. It was her first catering tour. And she had this terrible bad scene with Ginger Baker. He wanted to sack them off the tour.

"He'd lost his stash [believed to be cocaine]. He had it in a matchbox when he'd been in the catering area. Later, he discovered he had a matchbox with matches in it and he realised he was without his stash. He went absolutely bananas. He went in and caused a huge scene and said they'd stolen it. Somebody came up to him and said, 'Is this yours? I've got the wrong matchbox.' He had to back down and apologise.

"Ginger was also responsible for one of the key tour personnel having to leave. He didn't trust this person. Ginger did his own books every night. He'd been a millionaire twice and lost it twice. He was quite embittered, very suspicious. I remember Dave saying to me, 'If I start getting like that, please tell me.' And a few times I have had to say, 'Look, Dave . . .'

"What happened was Ginger said that £2,000 had gone missing, and he unfairly accused the guy of stealing it. I don't believe for one moment he had stolen it. He was a really nice chap, and his wife was nice too. I wouldn't have thought that anybody would blow their whole career for £2,000 when they were handling a lot more money than that. Why steal £2,000 when he could have stolen £20,000? He seemed to me to be a very honest bloke anyway, and he believed in karma."

Ginger was also at the centre of much gossip over his magnetic appeal to females. Marion Lloyd-Langton says: "Ginger, old and decrepit as he was, always picked up these young, beautiful women. He had this entourage of women, but he wasn't a womaniser. He was a one-woman man."

"I don't think his first wife would say that," retorts Huw.

Marion adds: "He married his daughter's best friend . . ."

Despite all of Baker's unusual behaviour, Huw greatly admired his musicianship. He says: "The drum solo he did on that tour came about via one particular number we played which had a very percussive section in it. It wasn't initially a drum solo, but he got so technical that everybody else thought, 'What's the point of playing with it, 'cos it's so good?' We all just stopped playing. A lot of fans didn't like it. A lot of them didn't like the fact that Ginger Baker was in the band anyway."

Harvey Bainbridge was starting to agree with them. "I'm afraid I'm not into drum solos," admits Harvey. "We used to give him a solo in the middle of 'Brainstorm', and he would go into strange rhythmic patterns and then bring it back to the ordinary rhythm of the song.

"Anyway, we were at Hammersmith Odeon and the drum solo went on and on, and we were standing on the side of the stage. I could tell when he was coming back to the main rhythm and I joined in on my bass guitar from the side of the stage. It took him by surprise. He didn't like it very much. There probably were words spoken afterwards. He probably did have a go and I probably said the solo shouldn't have carried on so long."

Huw Lloyd-Langton recalls: "I wasn't in the dressing room when this discussion happened, and it wasn't important enough that I can even remember what it was about. It was over some musical point or other. I seem to recall that Ginger was almost definitely right, but Harvey being a bit of a proud old sod wouldn't stand down.

"It got a little bit heated. Harvey was on his high horse. So from that point onwards, Ginger sort of blanked Harvey. Prior to that, he was prepared to work with Harvey, to get on with him, help him. He'd worked with the best musicians. He's a bit of an old hard-head, Ginger."

Marion agrees: "He's very unforgiving."

"So from that point on," continues Huw, "the relationship between Harvey and him deteriorated."

There was another disagreement between Ginger and Harvey, stemming from a meeting held with Danny Betesh. "Ginger wanted to cut back on the light-show so that we could all earn more money," says Harvey. "I'd signed a contract with Bronze and I was part of it, not just an employee, and I felt I was entitled to my opinion. I was the only one who argued against him. It would have made a mockery out of the Hawkwind show: it's an *event*. He lost on that one, and I think his argument with me really started then."

The relationship between Huw and Marion was also suffering a little due to her duties on behalf of Roy Ward. "Huw and I were arguing 'cos I was so close to Huw and trying to be a manager at the same time," confides Marion. "I had some argument with the management at Hammersmith Odeon to do with not paying the full percentages we were due – just the normal problems you get with gigs. We went to a restaurant afterwards and something snapped. Huw and I had a row, and it was nothing to do with Huw, but he was the nearest and dearest.

"Harvey said, 'Don't do this. Don't give Huw a hard time. You're really a good manager. Come on.' I said, 'You're absolutely right,' and I apologised."

Huw nods, "It's quite a hard thing for artist and management to be partners and living together under one roof. Business and art are two different things."

Marion concludes: "It was a relief for me, and for Huw, for me not to be doing it after that tour. It was a natural progression. I love Hawkwind. They've always been my favourite band whether Huw's in or out. Huw's always said to Dave, 'Marion loves the band.' But if you're involved in the management, it takes away from the magic.

"I wanted to do my best and I did my best. The publicity side of it was not a problem. You have to have an angle, there has to be a reason why a paper wants to print a press release, and with Hawkwind I always found there was."

Dave Brock and Harvey Bainbridge both remember a band meeting in a Dublin hotel room in November, following an incident involving a wedding reception. Harvey thinks the wedding was in Dublin, and Kris believes it was Belfast. However, the outcome was the same. The group got together in their Dublin hotel, having ordered tea and snacks for the meeting. After a long delay, they were brought a plate of sandwiches and a pot of tea so enormous that it would have served two football teams. It also tasted like treacle. Someone from the band counted the tea bags inside: there were almost 30.

Says Kris of the wedding drama: "Ginger and Roy Ward got drunk at the hotel, and there was a wedding going on. They were told they couldn't go in, but they gatecrashed and went in and caused a kerfuffle at the wedding party."

Harvey says: "We talked about Roy Ward at the meeting, and I have a feeling we told him we didn't want him to have anything more to do with things."

But as long as Ginger Baker was in the band, Roy Ward was still in the picture somewhere. He wasn't only Ginger's manager; he was his best friend.

Michael Moorcock had made two appearances in Lancashire during the tour, at Preston Guildhall on October 20 and Lancaster University on December 16.

He'd moved to the neighbouring county of Yorkshire following the break-up of his marriage to Jill. In fact, Jill had fallen in love with Robert Calvert – who had split from his wife Pamela.

Nik Turner sketches the background to the rather messy love tangle: "Michael Moorcock was this established, underground science-fiction writer who'd been living with his wife, Hilary. He decided to move round the corner, in with this girl Jill who he subsequently married. That relationship broke up and Robert Calvert moved into the flat around the same time. It disturbed things between Mike and Robert and Jill, although they all became friends in the end. They forgot their differences."

"Robert Calvert went off with my wife as well," volunteers Douglas Smith. "It was before he married Pamela. I was married to Ellie Smith. I didn't complain about it, though. I encouraged it in a funny sort of way. I thought that Robert needed someone to do his press, and I suggested Ellie. It was me giving Ellie something to do.

"Al Matthews was a character who used to be on the road with Hawkwind [as a percussion player], and he recorded and released a song called 'Nobody Told Me', which was all about Ellie having an affair with Bob while I was on the road."

Ellie went on to forge a great career in PR, becoming head of press at CBS Records, then moving to Sire and on to Virgin and Virgin Radio.

Michael Moorcock, coming to terms with the situation in the north of England in 1980, would turn out to be more distraught than Douglas had been. One day in October, Moorcock picked up a newspaper, saw that Hawkwind were playing in Preston and decided on a whim to turn up unannounced.

Dave Brock immediately invited him to join the band onstage.

"Well, I haven't done anything for a long time," replied Moorcock. "But I could probably fake something."

He did a couple of numbers and enjoyed them, turning up two months later for the Lancaster gig where he performed again. Dave invited him to Rockfield for the next official Hawkwind album.

Prior to this, the band and Michael Moorcock repaired to Battle Studios in Hastings at the end of 1980 where they recorded three tracks, later included on the *Zones* compilation. Moorcock contributed vocals to 'Running Through The Back Brain', a favourite of Brock's.

"It was quite daring and unusual," says Dave.

Moorcock had just released his own Deep Fix single, bringing together 'Dodgem Dude' and 'Starcruiser', on the Flicknife label. The recordings had long been a source of worry to him, as well as the root of some major problems with United Artists and Douglas Smith, allegedly.

Later, Moorcock told a journalist that he'd earmarked the two tracks as a single for United Artists, to be released in 1975 at the same time as *The New Worlds Fair*. After a series of arguments, UA chose not to release the single, leaving Michael infuriated. The tapes then remained at Douglas Smith's office for a long time, according to Moorcock.

Eventually, he bumped into Flicknife's mainman Frenchy, who asked if he had any material that would suit the label. "If anything comes up, I'll let you know," promised Moorcock.

He said: "I then went up to Douglas' office. I was on the edge of bankruptcy and I just needed to have some idea of how much money was owed me, even if I didn't get the money, and he started bullshitting me. I mean, loads of bullshit. I couldn't take it; it was too much.

"So then I got shoved out and, waiting around in the front office, I looked at the tapes that were in the office and I saw my tape, which I'd been asking Douglas about for years. He [had] said, 'Oh, can't find it, can't find it.' There was nobody there, so . . ."

Having slipped the tape out of the building, Moorcock gave it to Frenchy and it became one of a series of releases on Flicknife.

Douglas responds: "Michael did have financial problems. He had always signed to book companies that went down the toilet and since they had retained the copyright, it went to the receiver.

"I tried to do a deal for him with Warner Brothers for films and books. I got a million dollars on the table for him and he wasn't interested. All Michael wanted to do was get an album out . . . *any* album. But he didn't want to give away the rights to his books. Warners, of course, weren't interested in a Michael Moorcock album, but they were prepared to do it as part of a package that included books and films.

"Michael must've come in and asked if he could get tapes for Frenchy. I seem to remember saying, 'Well, get Frenchy to get paperwork over and we'll go for it,' because the tapes belonged to my company, Western Productions. He may well have taken a tape from the front office, or from the basement where the tapes were stored."

Moorcock's hostility towards Smith would worsen in time.

Hawkwind broke for Christmas after the December dates and recordings, and flew out to Baden-Baden in Germany on February 14, 1981 for a TV show.

Harvey Bainbridge recalls: "We opened and closed the show [with 'Motorway City' and 'Who's Gonna Win The War'], and Bonnie Tyler and Alexis Korner with Jack Bruce were on it too. It was the first time Ginger Baker and Jack Bruce had been in contact since Cream. They weren't speaking to each other.

"Alexis was beautiful, a really lovely man. He actually was instrumental in getting them to speak to each other during the course of that TV recording. They did speak, but then Ginger went off to his hotel room for an assignation, so they didn't actually talk very much."

Still, the ice was broken, and this would be significant for Dave Brock before many days had passed.

Harvey continues: "There was a funny moment at the end of the show. We finished the last number and Alexis Korner and Jack Bruce crouched behind Ginger's drums and started lobbing balloons and blowing bubbles, leaping up and down like little kids.

"When filming stopped, we were packing up and we were going to be taken for a meal by the production company. Jack Bruce walked straight up and said to me, 'He's a bastard, isn't he?' I realised what he meant. Ginger likes changing times. You just have to go with it. I said, 'Well, yeah, he can be.' When I was a teenager, Jack Bruce was one of my heroes, and it was rather nice that he spoke to me about it all. He said, 'Don't worry. You did really, really well.'

"Hawkwind music isn't that difficult. The thing is, you can make it as complicated as you want to. Ginger was doing all sorts of things to liven things up. I understood what was going on.

"That evening, we were all in the tavern and Jack got really pissed and ended up face down on a pool table. Myself, Huw and Alexis had to carry him back to the hotel. He had a young girlfriend, and she was most concerned. I haven't seen him since."

Harvey saw Ginger Baker, though, all too soon. Hawkwind gathered again at Rockfield, where tensions between Ginger and Harvey began rising dangerously.

Huw Lloyd-Langton describes how the trouble began on what had started out to be a normal day of rehearsals. "Ginger went into town with Keith Hale," says Huw. "Obviously, they hit the pub. Ginger had a few Bacardis, no doubt. I'd just got up and I was watching whatever it was on the telly. Dave was in the back room playing table tennis with Kris. I heard the front door being kicked open and a loud crash, and I heard Ginger shouting at Dave – '. . . Besides which I can't work with that fucking bass player.'

"It's hit the fan. In the old Mill House, it didn't matter where you were: if somebody was having a large conversation somewhere, you'd hear it. Harvey obviously heard the shouting. Ginger and Keith, backed up by this roadie, wanted Harvey out. Me and Dave were shell-shocked. We were like, 'Oh my God! What do we do?' We didn't know what to say. Harvey had been in the band for a long time before Ginger, and Harvey was a friend.

"I got on all right with Keith, but it was clear that Keith was on Ginger's side, backing him up against Harvey. Harvey eventually came down, and he'd heard what was going on. He said, 'It seems we've got something to talk about.' It was almost agreed without even talking about it that Harvey was going to have to go."

Harvey says: "Dave came to my room and said, 'You'd better come downstairs 'cos something's going on.' We went downstairs and Ginger Baker and Keith Hales reckoned that I was useless and that I should go. I said, 'Oh, well, if everybody thinks like that, I'd better go.'

"I'd had no idea he felt that way. When we were arguing about who was going to go, Ginger's comment was: 'Jack Bruce is the only other bass player to argue with me like this, and he was a giant.' Huw Lloyd-Langton thought the whole thing was disgusting. Dave was wondering what to do. I phoned Kennedy Street and I said, 'I don't want any bad things. I'll go.'

"Dave said, 'Just hang on and we'll see what's going on.' It boiled down to whether he wanted Ginger or me to stay. With Ginger Baker in the band, it opened up doors to all sorts of things, because of who he was."

Says Huw: "That whole day was absolutely awful. Harvey was broken. He was moping around for the rest of the day."

"I spoke to Harvey," adds Marion. "He was just distraught."

Huw continues: "Those of us that like a pint went out to the pub. Ginger and Keith were on top of the world, and had been all day, thinking they were getting their way. I was getting a bit miffed with them. Dave was back at the ranch, obviously, thinking about the whole thing. We'd not all sat around together and talked about it."

Dave takes up the story: "Ginger and I walked round the lawn at Rockfield. He put this proposition forward. We'd done the TV show with Alexis Korner and, of course, Jack Bruce. Then Ginger suggested getting a band together with Jack Bruce, Huwie and me."

"I remember walking along the river at Monmouth with Dave," continues Kris Tait. "He didn't know what to do about this superband. Dave was going, 'What should I do? What should I do?' I said if he betrayed his mate over money, he'd never be happy. He'd always told me never to let him get like Ginger. Money and fame or sticking with your mates? He was wrought with indecision. He shot it backwards and forwards and talked about it for ages."

"We got back from the pub," says Huw. "We were in the front room watching telly, and Ginger and Keith were ranting on. Keith was going, 'Yap, yap, yap.' At one point I snapped at him. I said, 'Why the whatever did you join the band if you thought what you seem to think about it? Shut your damn mouth. You've only been in it for a couple of months.' And all this crap's kicked off.

"Ginger said something. I shouted something at him. I just saw red. I told them both to shut up. They ended up storming out of the room. I went to my room and there was a knock on my door – Dave. I was totally pissed off. Dave said, 'I think we should let them go and keep Harvey on.' I said, 'I totally agree.' "

Dave reflects: "People having a go at you, it undermines your playing. Especially for Harvey. He weren't a bad bass player, he's an emotional character and I've known him for years. I don't know what would have happened with the band Ginger was proposing. It wouldn't have sounded too much like space rock. It probably would have been quite a successful venture, but I stuck by Harvey. He was a very good friend of mine."

Harvey recalls: "Dave said he'd much rather be a big fish in a small pond than a small fish in a big pond. So he felt that Ginger had to go. I told Ginger. He swore a bit and shuffled off.

"Huw didn't like Keith joining in with Ginger Baker and trying to renegotiate the situation with the band. Huw said to Keith, 'If you're with him you can fuck off too.' Huw never used to swear that much, so he probably didn't say exactly that, but it's what he meant."

Kris is sure that Dave also spoke to Ginger Baker. "Dave came back and he said, 'That's it. Sacked.' I remember Ginger being really shocked. He was confident it would be him who would stay."

Huw says: "I was watching telly again when Ginger walked in, and they were obviously going to leave. He said to me, 'I've blown it, haven't I?' I said, 'Yep.' "

Ginger Baker and Keith Hale left the band and, at the same time, the backdrop disappeared.

"Ginger and Keith went off to Italy under the Hawkwind name," marvels Brock. "We were pissed off."

The "alternative" band didn't last too long.

With Ginger's departure from Hawkwind, Roy Ward left too, and Marion realised that, "My role wasn't there any more."

She adds: "Ginger stayed more or less with Roy, who rented stables and a farmhouse near Acton. Ginger I think had changed his number, and I called Roy and I said, 'Have you got Ginger's number?' Roy said, 'He's sitting here.' I said, 'Has he told you what happened? You tell him from me I'm so disgusted, I can't believe the way he's behaved towards Harvey. You don't do that to a dog.' Roy said, 'You can't mean that.' I said, 'I never want to speak to him again.' And I didn't speak to him for about five years.

"Then Roy rang and said, 'Ginger's really upset. He wants to make friends.' I spoke to Ginger. He was living in Italy by then. We made peace and I stayed friendly with him. Ginger did say sorry. He didn't to Harvey, though. I think that would have been nice. He then went to the States, he lived there for a few years, he did Ronald Reagan's anti-drugs tour, and we lost touch again."

And as for Roy Ward: "He was a lovely fellow, married to Gilly who ran a hairdressing salon in Barnet for many years. They retired to Spain a few years ago."

Meanwhile, back in the Hawkwind camp, there was one final post-script to the Ginger Baker saga. "The worst bass player in the world sacks the best drummer in the world!" screamed the headline in *Melody Maker*.

Unfortunately, the reporter got the facts slightly muddled: Huw Lloyd-Langton suffered the indignity of being named as the bass player.

CHAPTER 16

Science Friction

MARTIN GRIFFIN was in two minds about returning to Hawkwind.

They'd been trying out different drummers and keyboard players without any success and had decided to invite Martin back. Dave Brock and Harvey Bainbridge would handle the keyboards themselves.

Martin got the call in the early summer of 1981, after returning from his European adventures with the Richard Strange band. He recalls: "I'd been to see Hawkwind on the Live Seventy Nine tour, and then in 1980. I didn't get on very well with Ginger Baker. They practically had to stop us fighting in the dressing room.

"They'd got rid of Ginger, they were in Rockfield and there was a phone call. They said: 'Why don't you drop by?' They asked if I'd like to rejoin. It was a difficult decision. I'd been quite peed off being thrown out of the band."

That was in the perplexing call from Robert Calvert, who'd previously expressed his admiration for Martin's playing.

Harvey says Dave Brock was behind the sacking but didn't want to be seen as the "bad guy": "Bob always thought Martin was a good drummer. Thinking back to Hawklords, Dave wound Bob up to tell Martin he was no good and he didn't want him there any more."

Martin had other considerations: "My studio really was beginning to cook, we'd recorded some early tracks for ABC, I was in the process of recording an album for Secret Affair, and my people weren't awfully keen on me joining Hawkwind. But I really wanted to because it's a turn-on playing a big stage with Hawkwind, and I always enjoyed playing with Dave's guitar."

By now, the band were out of their deal with Bronze Records, which was having financial problems. It would close down a couple of years later, a victim of declining record sales and the ballooning costs of promoting artists and financing videos.

It's alleged by various members of the band that at the time it went out of business, Bronze still owed Hawkwind in the region of £100,000.

"Bullshit," snaps Douglas Smith. "It was probably a few thousand."

"Gerry Bron [label founder] used to fly around the world, living an expensive lifestyle," maintains Dave Brock. "His sister is [actress] Eleanor Bron. Bob Calvert had a crush on her – 'Oh, what a lovely woman! Delightful! That's the sort of woman I'd like.'"

Marion Lloyd-Langton says: "For the first time, they would have had lots of money in their pockets if they'd been paid what they were owed by Bronze."

"But as normal," adds Huw, "the business side of things let us down. So it was almost, but not quite, back to the drawing board."

It wouldn't be the first time, or the last.

Kingsley Ward, co-owner of Rockfield, quickly came to Hawkwind's rescue. He had a record label, Active, which was distributed through RCA, and it was through him that the band signed to RCA Active.

Dave Brock wouldn't get on brilliantly with everybody at the new company. He recalls: "I was actually refused entry to the company offices by the fucking doorman. There was a write-up in the paper later which said I wasn't allowed in 'cos I looked 'scruffy'. I suppose they expected their bands to come in wearing dinner jackets. I had a big row with the guy. You know how people scratch their head as if they're going to hit you? I said, 'If you do that once again, I'll clock you one.'

"He wouldn't have it. He said, 'If you don't go, I'm going to call the police.' I went round the corner and called up Sean Greenfield, an A&R man. He said, 'Oh, outrageous.' He had a big freak-out and said, 'Come back right now.' The doorman wasn't there when I came back."

Hawkwind rehearsed and recorded their next album, *Sonic Attack*, at Rockfield, breaking for appearances at Stonehenge on June 19, 1981 and Glastonbury the day after.

"Stonehenge was a big turn-on for me," says Martin Griffin. "I'd played there before, but Hawkwind were the kings of the free festival, and to do it with them was fabulous. It was possibly my best gig ever. Glastonbury, again, was a big turn-on."

"We got to Glastonbury and we were ferried to the gig in a Land

Rover," Harvey remembers. "We were looked after by Michael Eavis and his family. We had such a fantastic view from the Pyramid Stage. We had a laser show out of the pyramid, and we were gobsmacked when it came on. After the set, I remember being carried to the vehicle 'cos it was so muddy."

"My partner, Sall, had got her car stuck deep in the mud," says Martin. "Lofty, our enormous roadie, lifted it out as though it was a toy and we set off to a very nice hotel in Bath. My daughter still sneers at the idea of staying in a hotel after a festival, but it was a great, great luxury."

Dave Brock remembers that Hawkwind, headlining, followed a performance by New Order. "They went well over time with their set," says Dave. "We'd got lasers and fireworks all set up for the grand Saturday night finale. We didn't go on until 11pm. It got to midnight and behind me I could see Michael Eavis waving his hand at me. This superintendent from the Somerset police was with him. I had to go round the back of my gear to see what they wanted. He said, 'Really sorry, Dave, but you've got to finish it because of the curfew.' Of course, we had the fireworks and so on, and we never had the chance to use them. He said, 'We'll put you on again in a couple of years.'

"We had to make this announcement that we were having to stop the gig. People started smashing the front of the stage up. They smashed the pyramid stage [which had now been installed as a permanent feature]. That was it, really. They never booked us again. We did go on to play twice in the travellers' field, which caused real bad problems for them. They could hear us playing at five o'clock in the morning.

"Three or four years ago, they approached us about booking us. We said we'd do it and told them we wanted to put on a real good space-age show. We wanted to have Lemmy, and we were going to get Michael Moorcock and Buzz Aldrin to recite some poetry, which Buzz Aldrin said he'd do as long as the proceeds went to a charity. It would've been fantastic, something totally different.

"Lemmy wanted to fly first class, so that was £5,000 for a start, and other costs started mounting up, so in the end they didn't want us to do it. We asked them for too much money, although I didn't think it was too much for the show we were planning to put on. They wanted us to do a smaller show for a lesser fee. We thought, 'If we're going to do something, we either do it big or not at all.'"

Glastonbury was no longer a free festival. In 1981, it was held as a fund-raiser for CND, and Michael Eavis and CND shared the organising.

Thomas Crimble, who'd joined the Worthy Farm organisation after being sacked by Hawkwind more than 10 years earlier, says: "There were a few, spontaneous free festivals in the Seventies. Nik Turner had a little pyramid stage on the back of a lorry. We'd run a cable into the back of a caravan and we'd be feeding 50p bits into a meter to run the festival. Those festivals weren't payers. It was at one of those we had a double rainbow over the site. They're nice things.

"The Year Of The Child festival in 1979, that was a payer, and from then on, it was a paying event. I sort of turned into what might have been termed as 'the management' at that point and after 1981, Hawkwind did free gigs in the corner of the site somewhere. We didn't pay them. I'd hear they were playing somewhere in the travellers' field, and people didn't have to pay to go there. I never got over to see them 'cos I was busy working."

Hawkwind returned to their recording sessions for *Sonic Attack*. It was a creative time, and a memorable one for Martin Griffin who went down with German measles.

That unfortunate episode apart, Martin recalls: "It was pretty much a case of learning the material in the studio. After Huwie's 'Rocky Paths', we just kept jamming and that became the track 'Psychosonia'. I think I had a co-writing credit, but that seemed to disappear over the years . . .

"I loved the whole thing. We were just a four-piece and were getting on really well. The sun shone. The people of Monmouth were hospitable. Our favourite pub even had exclusive lock-ins as long as you drank the landlord's favourite tipple, Woods full-strength Navy rum."

Michael Moorcock took Hawkwind up on their earlier invitation to join in. 'Sonic Attack' was the number he'd performed all those years ago when he first appeared with the band under the arches in Ladbroke Grove – his series of instructions to any listener who should chance to come under the dreaded sonic attack. He also provided lyrics for 'Coded Languages', 'Psychosonia' and 'Lost Chances'.

The band recorded a new version of 'Sonic Attack' with Moorcock at the microphone, although in the end, they used Harvey Bainbridge's vocals.

Moorcock later said: "I just wasn't getting the timing right. If you look at the stuff I did, it was all about sound and language [communication being a personal obsession of his], so that's what my contributions to the album are all about."

He also recorded lead vocals for 'Coded Languages', and this time his performance *was* included on the album.

Sonic Attack, released by RCA Active, was hailed by many as a return to form, a hard-assed take on space rock with none of the fanciful diversions that had coloured their work from time to time since the mid-Seventies. Dave Brock still thinks of it as a "pretty good album". Other observers professed disappointment, calling it dour and mediocre. It charted at number 19 in October 1981 while the band were out on a major UK tour.

John Perrin had returned to Hawkwind to take charge of the lightshow, which was spectacular, spacey and fluid with blobs and spirals. Liquid Len had departed for pastures new, going on to work with major-league artists such as Rod Stewart and lighting Ronald Reagan's Presidential campaign.

"A lot of our crew went on to great heights," remarks Brock. "Our tour manager Higgy brought rock music to south America, and he worked with Queen. You know, the funny thing was, about three years ago, a friend of ours who's a Chelsea fan invited us to go to see Newcastle against Chelsea. We'd just sat down and two seats behind me was Higgy. I hadn't seen him for about 15 years. Him and Simon King used to go and see Chelsea together. Strange coincidence."

The Sonic Attack tour, stretching through October, with a clutch of extra dates in December, was a memorable one for several members of the entourage.

Martin Griffin looks back: "Just at the end of the tour rehearsals at Rockfield, we were partying a bit at a local venue with various members of Budgie when Huwie got a bit of aggro and had his nose broken. Come the day of the first date, Huw was in St Mary's Hospital with bits of padding stuffed up his nose to stop the blood flow. No way was he playing. I assumed, no way were we playing either. But I drove down to Reading anyway to see Dave and Harvey. Everything was set up onstage and they were looking at their watches. We were going to do the gig as a three-piece. Hawkwind a three-piece?

"It was actually really good. Somehow knowing it couldn't be perfect made for a lack of inhibition. Dave announced to the audience that Huw had slipped on a banana skin, and we got into the whole thing. After one more date, Huw had recovered and we carried on as a four-piece."

Dave Brock won't forget in a hurry what happened in his hotel room in Liverpool on October 4. He says: "We were playing in the Empire, and the hotel was just across the road from the stage door. Kennedy Street were managing us, and I had these old contracts from Douglas. There was some sort of thing I disagreed with. I tore them up and put them in a tin rubbish bin in my room. I decided to set fire to them. It was some sort of ritual burning that I was doing. They'd all gone out when I left the room, although it was smoky. I opened the window.

"I went out to the gig across the road and after a while, the tour manager said, 'Cor blimey, the hotel's on fire.' All these people were milling around outside. There were some strange scenes going on, young girls in their dressing gowns with old blokes. It was like a scene from a *Carry On* movie. I thought, 'I want to go and get my bag.'

"Nobody stopped me walking in, and I went up the stairs. As I came round the corner into the corridor, this fireman came down with this bucket. He said, 'Somebody has thrown a fag into the bin.' It was my room! When I'd opened the door to go out, the draught from the window blew the smoke down the corridor after us, and the smoke alarm went off. What a silly thing to do."

Despite his earlier misgivings about rejoining Hawkwind, Martin Griffin thoroughly enjoyed the outing. "It was my favourite tour," he reveals. "Way back when I started getting involved in bands, the turn-on for me was to be a part of something that was a little bit stimulating and entertaining. On a good night with Hawkwind, we knew we were doing that, and the high is absolutely incomparable."

Again, the band were travelling in "early" and "late" hire cars. "Dave and Harvey were in one car," says Martin. "Huwie and I were in the other. We liked to party after gigs. We would start late the next day and shamble gently on to wherever the next town was. It was a great tour, the album went Top 20, all the gigs sold out, and there was a good buzz around."

There wasn't such a good buzz on the night that Hawkwind arrived at London's Rainbow Theatre on December 18. They'd already played two nights at Hammersmith Odeon during the October leg of the tour, and were a big enough live attraction to be able to add a third major gig only two months later.

"It was so cold that the guys on the trucks left the engines on tick-over to prevent freezing," shivers Martin Griffin. "We went into the gig and, unusually, there was a safety curtain. Normally, we walked out to the intro music and then we'd start the set. Here, the curtain was going to go up and we would be there already.

"Our monitor guy had already been booked for another tour and so we had a replacement. Just as the curtain started to move, there was a ghastly shriek from my monitor. I got 2,000 watts of high-frequency feedback, and I was completely deafened. I couldn't hear a thing. I could see Dave's right hand playing the pattern, I guessed where to join in and all I could do was think, 'Right, chaps, you'd better follow me because I can't hear *you*.' Calvert and Moorcock both turned up to perform."

Michael Moorcock had taken up with a new girlfriend (now his wife), an American called Linda who would eventually sort out his business affairs. Clearly, though, there were still some unresolved issues surrounding his ex-wife Jill's defection to Robert Calvert.

Dave Brock says: "He kept losing his houses to wives. He lost two houses. It wasn't the women he was upset about, it was the houses."

On stage the band suddenly became aware that Moorcock and Calvert were coming to blows.

Says Dave: "Michael was about to come on and do a poem, and I looked across the stage to give him a cue. Michael and Bob had their hands at each others' throats. The curtain at the side of the stage was bulging with this struggle. More and more people were rushing round there to stop this scene."

Marion Lloyd-Langton was one of them. "There was this almighty fisticuffs," she says. "I remember getting between them and holding on to one of them, I think it must have been Mike, and saying, 'Stop it!' I assumed it was over Jill. I suppose they hadn't seen each other since that happened."

"They were really going at it hammer and tongs," says Huw Lloyd-Langton. "They were both poets and they both worked with Hawkwind. There was definitely friction there, but whether it was all over the lady, I don't know."

"It started off with an argument," says Kris Tait. "It was quite an intellectual argument. Then there was a fight. It was a classy fight, not a girlie, hair-pulling sort of fight."

Brock: "One of them fell over on the ground and the other one was pulled off. Bob came rushing on to the stage all triumphant. He'd cut his hand. He got wildly excited. Michael Moorcock left."

"Mike and Robert had a lot of respect for each other eventually," remarks Nik Turner. "I think at the time Mike felt he was being pissed on by Robert, which I suppose he was in some ways."

"He was a big, lovable bear, Mike," says Huw.

Martin Griffin agrees: "I found Michael Moorcock very charming. I liked him very much. Historically, Calvert was a remarkably good lyricist. I don't think he was a particularly nice man. He was stunningly egocentric, which is not the same as egotistic. His thoughts and feelings didn't go much beyond Calvert. But he could be very charming and his works were very clever. Generally speaking, he avoided the first person. He adopted an objective poet's view."

Huw Lloyd-Langton: "There was a power cut that night too, which added to the dramas. I remember thinking, 'Oh, God. What more?'"

There was one final misfortune, this time for the crew. "When they loaded the gear and tried to pull off, they couldn't," says Martin Griffin. "The trucks stalled because the diesel had frozen in the pipes, except for where the trickle to maintain tick-over had been flowing."

There were almost immediately more sessions, this time for *Church Of Hawkwind*, a predominantly electronic affair. Recorded in collaboration with Rockfield's Kingsley Ward, it was essentially a Dave Brock album, although Harvey Bainbridge did some of the writing and all of the band members played.

"I wrote most of it," explains Dave. "Harvey did some as well. It was the pair of us, really. Harvey has written some good numbers over the years that we've done. He was progressing from playing bass to going into keyboards and electronics."

The final stages of the album were completed in adverse conditions. It was early in 1982, and people were being warned to stay indoors because of the Arctic weather. "I used to have this old rambler, an estate car that came from Canada," says Dave, the man of a thousand vehicles. "I drove through these huge snowdrifts and I managed to get to Rockfield. We finished the album that week without Harvey. He couldn't make it at all, 'cos he was snowed up."

Marc Sperhauk – the fan who bought Dave's guitar when he split the band in America – is credited with guest bass. And the mysterious guest vocalist Madam X is in fact Kris Tait, "crying".

For what was more or less a side project, *Church Of Hawkwind*, released by RCA Active, would fare remarkably well, reaching a chart placing of 26 in May that year.

Prior to this particular triumph, Hawkwind had been in Europe, theoretically in support of *Sonic Attack*. They got on the plane in March 1982, expecting to be welcomed and fully promoted by RCA's representatives.

"It was silly," scoffs Martin Griffin. "We were told it was going to cost us X amount of money to do it. We'd got an album out there and RCA would make a buzz. We were going out with this band Krokus as co-headliners. The first night, the German RCA guy took us out for a Chinese dinner in Hamburg. He said, 'Ve did not vant you to come.'

" 'Why?!?' "

" 'Ve haff not released ze album yet.'

"I mean, heavens above! That was a bit of a downer. To make it worse, there was no synergy between Krokus and us or our audiences, and the co-headlining looked to me an awful lot more like us supporting them. We had some fun, but it was a disappointment after the highs of the UK tour."

By now, Kris Tait had moved to Devon through a sequence of events.

She had attended the Sacred Heart Grammar School in her native Newcastle upon Tyne and as a teenager had been naturally gifted in the dramatic and creative arts.

Kris would work tirelessly to develop her skills, taking one college course after another to emerge as an accomplished dancer, actress, model, circus performer, printer, photographer, writer, teacher and stage manager. Eventually, she was employed as a freelance floor manager by both the BBC and Tyne Tees Television, where she also worked as an assistant editor. And all this while touring with Hawkwind!

She moved away from home for the first time at 18.

Says Kris: "I was getting away from Newcastle because all the work seemed to be down south. I moved to Bristol first. I was doing screen-printing."

In Bristol, Kris was drawn to the alternative culture, and she made friends with a singer called Claire, who had moved to Bristol from Bath and made appearances with an anarcho acid-punk band called Smart Pils. The drummer was Richard Chadwick, who would later join Hawkwind – and is still with them today.

Someone on the fringe of things back then in Bristol was Bridget Wishart, who was away studying at the art college for most of the time. She would subsequently become Hawkwind's one and only female singer.

"Claire was living in a squat in Bristol," says Kris. "We just did the usual things you do when you're that age. We were on the festival scene, and I used to go helping the fox-hunt saboteurs."

Claire subsequently went back to Bath, moving into a squat where Richard and his friends hung out, and Kris spent time there too. Later, the musicians would reorganise themselves into an all-girl group called The Hippy Slags, with Claire moving to bass.

However, outside of this small community, Kris found her new life pretty isolating. She recalls: "I got fed up with living in Bristol 'cos nobody used to speak to me. I was living in Clifton, the posh area, and it's incredibly snobby, very cliquey. I got quite lonely there. I didn't like it at all.

"A lot of the hippie people I was mixing with were living in the country. I was meeting more and more people to do with Hawkwind, who lived down in Devon. I thought, 'I'm down this far, I might as well move.' So I moved to Bideford."

Arriving there not long before she turned 20, Kris found a more welcoming environment. "I was doing dancing with this guy in Bideford, Devon, at the local artists' centre," she says. "We did some busking on the streets. I was doing some mime stuff, and I collected money for him."

Kris was in regular contact with Dave Brock and Hawkwind, having already been on the road helping out with merchandising, catering and odd jobs. Now she was about to make her first stage appearance with the band.

She was invited to dance at Stonehenge on June 20, 1982 and it turned into a full-blown performance, offstage as well as on. "I had a white skirt with silver tassles and my face made up," says Kris. "I had a little satin waistcoat, with a tie under the boobs, made up from the drapes that they used for the Space Ritual. We made bedspreads and cushions and all sorts of things from them. They had the signs of the zodiac at the bottom.

"The festival was big in those days. People were doing paragliding from the back of a Land Rover, and none of the band would do it. They were all cowards. I was the only one that went up. You have to keep your hands up – you can't let go of the things on the two sides.

Everybody watched. As I came round, the strap of the waistcoat came up above the boobs and my top was right up. I couldn't let go with my hands to fix it. The whole queue was watching, clapping and cheering. It was very embarrassing."

If Stonehenge marked Kris' first gig with Hawkwind, it also saw the beginning of Nik Turner's re-entry into the group.

Dave Brock says, casually, of this momentous event: "When you're doing all these festivals, inevitably we'd bump into Turner and he'd come and jam with us. He's always doing festivals. We probably invited him to come and play with us . . ."

Nik did, indeed, take the stage with the band at Stonehenge, and he would remain a permanent fixture in Hawkwind for more than two years. However, he wasn't involved in the sessions for their next album, except for a little guest flute playing.

Stonehenge apart, Hawkwind spent June and July tucked away in Rockfield recording the album, *Choose Your Masques*. A great deal of thought was going into the LP, which would translate into a fabulous stage show by the autumn.

Concept king Michael Moorcock was back in the fold, writing both the title track and 'Arrival In Utopia', although he was credited as Steele – the maiden name of Linda, the girlfriend he had taken up with after parting with Jill, and later married.

Moorcock later told an interviewer that he used a nom de plume because of a financial dispute with Douglas Smith.

Michael added: "When we got the cheque, we were astonished at how much it was. I've never had anything like as much money . . . [and] off just two numbers."

Douglas Smith says: "There was a time when Michael was complaining that he was on the verge of bankruptcy. I went to my partner in publishing and suggested, 'Why don't we sign him on a publishing deal? If he writes a few more lyrics for Hawkwind, we'll get it back when the records come out.'

"Michael was desperate for £2,000, which at that time was the equivalent of about £10,000 – quite a lot of money for a small publishing company. We did the deal, he signed the contract and we gave him the money. Then, about a year later, his luck changed and Blue Oyster Cult decided to record two lyrics of his. He signed the songs to Blue Oyster Cult's publishing company.

"My partner said, 'Well, fuck him, he doesn't have the right to do that.' So he sued him, and Michael lost. That's why Michael doesn't like me."

In a further twist, Douglas became friendly with Michael's ex-wife Hilary and their children, and regularly invited young Max Moorcock to tea as a guest of his eldest son.

Michael Moorcock, in his interview, also contended that the concept he'd worked up for *Choose Your Masques* became diluted as work continued: "It was the idea of people wearing masks to hide their real selves but, in the end, there wasn't that much of it left. Dave made the final selection, and he had other [songs] he wanted to put in."

The recording sessions were, meanwhile, turning into an ordeal for Martin Griffin. He had been led to believe that there would again be a lot of jamming in the studio, leading to the same sort of creative possibilities that had produced 'Psychosonia' on *Sonic Attack*, which had been produced by Ashley Howe with Pat Moran and Paul Cobbold engineering.

"But the atmosphere had changed," he says. "We had a different producer who was less enthusiastic about that sort of thing. I got on really well with Ashley Howe, who'd worked on the previous albums, but I don't think Pat Moran [producing with Hawkwind] really liked me very much.

"A lot of the material was coming in part-recorded with drums either to be over-dubbed or looped and, frankly, that's not my bag. I liked being my own man. In the end, there's not that much money playing in Hawkwind, so it's gotta satisfy some aspects of art or craft. There wasn't enough money to make it worth going out and being a moron.

"That's not to criticise anyone else or the material – there's some fine stuff on *Choose Your Masques*. But as we finished the album, I said it was time for me to quit and get back to Roche. They said, 'Fine.'"

Huw and Marion Lloyd-Langton remember some rather more turbulent scenes. "Martin wasn't particularly keeping time," reports Marion. "Dave is a perfectionist. He doesn't like anything sloppy. He tends to record all the rehearsals and gigs and listens to them afterwards. Huw doesn't think it's too healthy to do that all the time – 'over-analysis causes paralysis.'"

"You're not getting the whole picture," confirms Huw. "You're only picking up on the parts of it that are going through the desk."

Marion continues: "On the other hand, when someone is so glaringly out of time, that's when they have to go. Dave spoke to me one morning and said, 'Is Huw up yet?' 'cos Huw's not an early bird. Dave said, 'Well, I wanna see him. Tell him I'm with Harvey.' We went to Harvey's room a bit later and Dave said, 'I'm fed up with it. Martin's not cutting it. He's all over the place. I think we should try out Rob Heaton.' "[*]

Rob was Martin's drum roadie, although he would shortly make a name for himself as a founding member of New Model Army.

"They were having a jam with Rob one afternoon and Martin turns up," relates Huw. "He saw that Rob was on his drum kit playing with Dave and Harvey, and he blew up quite badly. He was incredibly miffed."

Harvey Bainbridge says: "It was me that had to ask him to go. He was unhappy, probably very upset. I've spoken to him about this since then. Dave got me to do it. Martin was an old friend of mine, and I should have said no."

Dave Brock comments: "Perhaps I said, 'Harvey, it's your turn to do the deed.' It probably was about time-keeping. Going back to *Choose Your Masques*, 'Solitary Mind Games' was a drum-machine number. Martin hated drum machines. He could not play in time with one. He spent about six hours doing a small bit he couldn't keep in time with.

"We were getting more into electronic music. I had an MS20 analogue sequencer, and we were using Jupiter 8s [synths]. Martin wasn't wearing headphones or anything. He didn't have a click track. It would be blasting out really loud out of his speaker cabinet. We decided we'd have to get somebody else."

Martin claims he jumped, others claim he was pushed, but he did believe his last performance with the band would be at a Castle Donington Monsters Of Rock special on August 21, also starring Status Quo, Gillan, Saxon and Anvil.

The rehearsals for the gig took place at Rockfield, and Martin particularly enjoyed making friends with Bad Manners, the popular ska band led by the big, bald Buster Bloodvessel, and meeting Robert Plant, who was recording *Pictures At Eleven* with Martin's old mate from the Richard Strange band, bassist Paul Martinez.

"Perhaps we should have questioned management decisions a little more closely," says Martin of the Donington gig. "We were meant to have equal billing with Gillan and Saxon, and we didn't. While it

[*] Sadly, Rob Heaton died suddenly in November 2004.

was fun to be there, we really weren't right for the crowd, or them for us."

Kris Tait had once again been invited to participate, and this time she decided to put in some serious preparation rather than rely on the freestyle dancing she had performed at Stonehenge.

She says: "I got this girl Louise who was living locally in Bideford and we took some dance classes. We got what we were doing choreographed. We got these amazing stage clothes made by a dressmaker in Bideford, android costumes made from gold and silver lamé. We had silver swimming caps on with holes in and our hair coming out. Both our bodies were painted silver.

"We had to wear silver knickers with little ties on the side, and as we stepped forward on the stage, we could see all these photographers taking pictures of the silver knickers. We were second on, and there were 65,000 people there. We were just looking out into this sea of faces. We had these massive, silver Flying V guitars made using tinfoil, and we were doing robotic walks, 'cos we were androids. We'd walk across the stage towards each other and do this headbanging, like Status Quo. We looked across and Status Quo were watching from the side. They didn't look like they were enjoying it too much."

The gig was memorable for some of its offstage adventures too. Dave Brock got to drive his old Granada round the racetrack before security chased him off.

And, Kris says, "Martin Griffin, I'm sure, had some kind of bad scene, a scuffle, with one of Saxon."

Saxon found the backstage amenities somewhat lacking, according to Kris. "They came in the dancers' room because, for some reason, they had no mirrors in theirs. We had one with mirrors 'cos we were putting all this make-up on. Saxon had to have their hair curled and dried. 'Can we borrow your hairdriers?' 'Can we borrow your mirrors?' No one else was doing that – certainly not Hawkwind."

The Choose Your Masques tour was coming up in October, and the band were trying unsuccessfully to find a permanent drummer.

Martin Griffin: "The management [Kennedy Street] phoned me up and said, 'Would you do the tour?' I said, 'I've left.' They kept coming back to me. Danny Betesh said eventually, 'What are the terms on which you'd do it?' I said, 'If you make me an offer I can't refuse, then obviously I can't refuse.' He came back and he made me an offer I couldn't refuse.

"I wasn't keen to go back, but sitting in on the rehearsals felt good. I knew most of the material and I enjoyed playing it. I got my cash up front for the tour, and it was more than anybody else was being paid. I didn't deserve it, I've gotta say."

This time, it really would be Martin Griffin's last tour with Hawkwind. And as he was on his way out, someone else was coming in. Nik Turner was back, in a big way.

CHAPTER 17

Behind The Masques

HARVEY BAINBRIDGE was all for it. The way he saw it, Hawkwind needed a bit of visual excitement at the front of the stage, and they didn't come more colourful than Nik Turner.

Dave Brock invited him back into the band, while warning Harvey: "You've got to keep tabs on Nik. He'll play over everything, and play cross-things."

Despite having been sacked by Hawkwind, Turner was willing to make a fresh start with them. He explains: "At that time my band Inner City Unit was going through a bit of a rough period. We were doing really well on one level, but some of the band got involved with heroin, and I couldn't cope with it. It seemed like a nice alternative to go on a tour with Hawkwind, and I needed the money, basically.

"It felt fine, actually. I thought, 'Well, all right, I've been fucked over sideways and upside down already, but I need the gig.' I'm a pretty charitable sort of person – I don't bear grudges against people. I'd forgotten all that thing. I got on the phone with Dave and he asked me if I'd like to come and play with the band again."

Nik had continued to work closely with Barney Bubbles after the Sphynx project. It was Barney who came up with the name of Inner City Unit, taking unlikely inspiration from Islington and Haringey council offices, and he was "very enthusiastic" about the group.

Barney, who would never abandon what he saw as the important principles of hippie culture, supported Inner City Unit's gigging policy, which insisted upon benefits, festivals and squat parties.

Nik and Barney had also recorded an LP together with Robert Calvert and members of Inner City Unit under the name of Imperial Pompadours. In fact, *Ersatz* was less of an album and more of a free-for-all. The A-side, a collection of unrehearsed, one-take rock'n' roll covers, was produced by Barney "like graphics". There was also a definite industrial emphasis, with one solo played on an angle grinder.

"It was nerve-wrenching stuff," says Nik. "Steel scaffolding and stuff like that making an horrendous din, which we slowed down to half speed. We were making all these noises like sticks and iron bars on railings, bashing on the side of a big lorry, smashing up milk bottles.

"We'd record the song, cut the tape into one-yard lengths, throw it up in the air and stick it all back together as it came. Things were going backwards, forwards, upside down, all over the place. It was completely recorded and mixed and we chopped it all up and stuck it together again. That was the A-side."

The B-side, produced by Turner, was no less controversial: "It was the life of Hitler."

Barney told Nik: "I want to do this theatre piece which will involve four people. They will be Hitler, King Ludwig of Bavaria who was the patron of Wagner, Wagner himself and one woman." She stood for the woman in all of their lives.

"We just swopped around the instruments and recorded about three or four hours of everybody playing different things," says Turner. "We used that as the backing track and we recorded the rest of it on a four-track tape machine at my flat in Belsize Park.

"Barney had collected this wad of quotations and different dialogues from Wagner, all the German philosophers, religious philosophers of the 16th Century, *Mein Kampf*, Ludwig of Bavaria and so on, and I chose the most interesting. All the friends who visited me, I'd say, 'Oh, here you are. Hold this microphone a minute and read this.' Girlfriends of mine would be reading quotes from Eva Braun about how Hitler made her crouch on top of his face to examine her genitalia in minute detail."

The album was released on the Pompadour label by F-Beat via Warner Brothers in 1982 once Warners had established that the intention was to protest at Facism, not embrace it.

Hawkwind's *Choose Your Masques*, released by RCA Active in October 1982, seemed positively normal after that. A solid, satisfying if not yet triumphant Hawkwind offering, it reached number 29, complete with "guest vocals" from actor Ian Holm.

"Naughtily, we pinched him from the radio," confesses Dave. "A wonderful little speech."

And so to the tour.

Kris' dancing partner Louise, having taken all the classes and studied the choreography, was at the last minute unable to take part, having somehow torn her stomach lining after Castle Donington.

A replacement, Jane Isaacs, was rehearsed and fitted for costumes, and she joined Kris for the dates which ran from mid–October to mid–November 1982. The women were dressed as robotic androids wearing Chinese god masks.

"It was pretty similar to what we had for Donington," says Kris. "We had these masks on sticks that were popular at the time – see-through ones that made your face look weird. They were courting masks. You bow and drop the mask and there's another one underneath.

"We were on these strange podium-like things. They had lights all the way round the bottom, like aircraft landing lights, and when they put them on, it looked like you were dancing in tubes of light."

Chameleon Lights staged a breathtaking display which incorporated a backdrop of TV screens all connected to video. "It was a fantastic, really weird 3D stage set," says Dave. "Colin from Chameleon Lights had gone around buying up all these second-hand TV sets and, one by one, they started going wrong. He was always looking for another television. But it looked very good onstage."

Hawkwind set the scene from the outset by opening with 'Choose Your Masques', going on to intersperse their more familiar material with a batch of new songs: 'Waiting For Tomorrow', 'Utopia', 'Arrival In Utopia', 'Solitary Mind Games' and 'Dream Worker'.

By now, they were spoilt for choice for favourites to round out the set. 'Magnu' was usually still there. So were 'The Golden Void', 'The Psychedelic Warlords', 'Brainstorm', 'Shot Down In The Night' and the compulsory 'Master Of The Universe', alongside a selection of more recent material such as 'Coded Languages' which followed 'Choose Your Masques' every night.

It was a popular production with the audiences and a memorable one for the band members, some of whom look back today with a personal rather than a musical eye.

"I have a few outstanding memories of the tour, one of which Huw won't find very amusing," laughs Nik Turner. "Huw Lloyd-Langton is like one of those people who live by the Old Testament, a Jesus freak really. It was a bit of a joke. He's holier than thou, a rather puritanical sort of person, although he drinks a lot. On that tour, the guys doing the lighting had a real sense of humour. There would be a multiple image of the same thing on seven or eight of the TV screens, and while Huw was doing his fabulous guitar solo up there, Colin had all these really hard-core porn movies on the TV screens for the duration of the solo."

If Nik was taken on to fill up the empty space at the front of the stage, he was certainly making the most of his opportunities. For the Choose Your Masques tour, he wore a suit that had once belonged to the early-Sixties pop star Eden Kane and topped it off with a Rasta wig.

"I used to dress up all the time in these bizarre things," he recollects. "I used to go and hire costumes. One time I was dressed as a jester, and one time as a knight templar, and another time I was an astronaut in a spacesuit. We had medieval costumes. It's all off-the-wall stuff but fun, really.

"I never got into any controlled choreography. I used to make things up as I went along, do mime things, and I don't know if anybody ever really understood what I was doing. It was all part and parcel of the show. I'm still the same. I've still got all these things I like to do to enhance the image and the presentation so that it's exciting and mixed media."

Nik was provoking differing reactions from the other band members.

Harvey states, "I thought he added to it. He did have a tendency to play over things, but Nik just enjoys himself."

"He was as atmospheric a frontman as he always was and is," agrees Martin Griffin.

Huw says: "When Nik came back, it just became noisier, slightly crazier. He's a character, a showman, so I think he's enjoyable to an extent. It had always been a band as opposed to one member with a backing band, which it vaguely became with Nik's presence here because he was so forceful and outrageous. It got annoying musically because he'd be honking about left, right and centre. He'd honk all over everything."

Nik: "I've had a certain similarity in my opinion of Huw Lloyd-Langton. He gets really drunk, he'll stand right in front of his amplifier with it really loud, and he can hardly hear what anybody else is playing.

There are times when he thinks nobody's playing and he'll carry on."

For Kris Tait, Nik took a bit of getting used to.

"I got on all right with him on that tour," she says. "He was a bit overbearing. And he used to do things to me with his saxophone . . .

"There was a number where me and the other girl dancer, Jane, would be doing quite an erotic dance together. She'd be lying on a podium, and I was lying over her. It was meant to be ambiguous; it was a rising weirdness.

"Nik used to come and join in, 'cos the rhythm was going, 'Doo, doo, doo . . . ' and he had this big light coming out the end of his saxophone. He'd come up behind me and he'd be parping his saxophone and having his light going off, which probably looked disgusting. I had bruises where he'd not just been pretending to push the saxophone up my bum, he actually had been. He used to get carried away. He's like one person offstage and quite reasonable. But people do get into character onstage, and they can get more rough.

"As the music went on, he'd get more and more excited and out of control, and you could feel it go 'Parp!' – 'He's doing it again.' "

"It's very likely I did that," admits Nik. "Just being onstage, it's totally improvised. It was all just very tongue in cheek. The road crew used to make me all these things. One night they gave me a big neon light stick – Darth Vader's sword. The guy doing the sound would pan it as I swung this thing around. They gave me the light that flashed on and off inside my saxophone. When I bought the sax, I painted all these fluorescent flames coming out the front of it. There were flowers and mushrooms all over the side of it. I painted around the scroll work."

Asked about Kris' bruises, Turner replies: "I never checked. You should ask Dave."

Dave and Nik were getting along all right on the tour, or so it seemed. Martin Griffin formed the impression that Nik was feeling protective of Dave in light of the fact that, "Dave had things going on in his life, very heavy pressure for him."

Dave and his wife Sylvia had become estranged, although they were continuing to live in the same house.

Says Martin: "Nik tended to agree with what Dave thought about things."

Harvey Bainbridge didn't notice quite that level of companionship.

He remarks: "They were getting on okay-ish. I don't think Nik took much notice of Dave, and Dave was getting angry about a couple of things."

The one person who did feel ill-at-ease on the Choose Your Masques tour was the normally sunny Martin Griffin.

He confides: "I was travelling with Huw again, and we enjoyed ourselves again, it was a lovely period, but some of the magic had gone for me. I'm extremely fond of Dave, but he didn't really like the fact that they'd had to get me back, and I didn't like the fact that I'd gone back when I'd already left. I probably shouldn't have done it. I felt uncomfortable. After the tour, it really was time to leave."

Martin's diplomacy is again challenged by other band members.

Harvey Bainbridge: "There was a bizarre moment onstage one night when Dave pulled a starting pistol out, pointed it at Martin and pulled the trigger. Luckily, nothing came out . . ."

"I didn't fire a starting pistol at him," retorts Dave. "Martin used to get nervous. He used to knock back two or three tequilas just to steady his nerves. Sometimes we'd watch his legs – they'd be really trembling. I used to say, 'If you play off time tonight, I'm going to shoot you in the leg.' I produced this starting pistol halfway through the show and I said, 'I told you so!' It was just a bit of fun."

Griffin is bemused: "I don't recall any starting pistol, but then again, would I have noticed?"

Nik Turner warns: "You have to remember that Dave was the person in charge of the band and I think he saw Martin as someone who had to have a drink before he went on. Martin had played with Dave and Harvey in Hawklords and Sonic Assassins, and he's a nice guy. He's always had a big handlebar moustache, and he's very 'Awfully, awfully.' He's a friend of mine."

"At the end of that tour," says Harvey Bainbridge, "Dave got me again to tell Martin he had to go. Dave had been moaning that we were speeding up all the time, and poor Martin got the blame. I was well ensconced in the Dave Brock view of things, and I had a go at Martin as well. Since then I have apologised to Martin for that."

Asked how Dave had managed to persuade grown men to think, say and do things that they didn't really believe in, Harvey replies: "He's very good at pointing out the down side – how 'bad' it is for all of us."

Martin remains philosophical. He declares: "Everybody who's been through the band has a love/hate relationship with Dave. There were times when we hated each other. But now I go to Dave's birthday party and he comes to visit me. I'm very fond of Dave."

Returning to Roche, Martin had plans to upgrade the studio equipment and develop more outbuildings for accommodation. Before he could do this, he was unexpectedly sidetracked into a new career.

He says: "An old friend of mine who was MD of a specialist agency approached me with the idea of using music in marketing. I put some ideas to his client, Bacardi and, while developing them realised the potential of music sponsorship. It was a greater challenge than running the studio. So we put together a team of fairly high-powered professionals, raised some capital and launched a company called Music Link, of which I was MD.

"Our first project involved a brief from Cadbury. Cadbury's Crunchie sponsored the pop group 5 Star on tour. They sold 1.2 million albums and Cadbury sold an extra 225 tons of Crunchie. Funnily enough, 5 Star were signed to RCA and the marketing team there found my involvement most amusing. They even dug out some hairy old promo pictures."

Martin went on to link ITT televisions with Chris de Burgh's European tour, C&A with A-Ha and Foster's lager with the Montreux Festival. In the Nineties, Martin became MD of Benson & Hedges Music, operating worldwide outside of the UK and US. The company ran festivals and a record label featuring such diverse talents as Robert Plant, The Stranglers, Bob Geldof, Iggy Pop, James Brown and Fleetwood Mac.

Martin is now living in Devon with Sall and his drummer son Jack, whose band Relentless played at the last Hawkfest. "I see Dave and Kris every so often socially and am in touch with Harvey and Huw," he says. "I'm working in London to develop a project to expand the raft of venues offering live, original music, a cause that I feel strongly about. If I can use sponsorship to make that happen then I'll be very pleased.

"I'm a rock'n'roller. I've loved pop/rock since I first listened to Radio Luxembourg under my bedclothes and I love it now. I have nothing on CD with Hawkwind where I am particularly proud of my drumming and some where I'm a bit embarrassed; I've played better elsewhere. But being in the live band was the high point of my playing career. It was and is a great thing to have been part of. I have tremendous respect for the band and all its members past and present."

It was almost like a reflex reaction: call for Simon King! And that was exactly what Hawkwind did when Martin Griffin left for good at the end of 1982.

Simon was chauffeured to rehearsals by none other than Animal, lead singer of the Anti-Nowhere League – a band of leather- and chain-clad bikers whose brand of tuneful and outrageously obscene punk rock had been taking the country by storm.

He'd been recruited to driving duties by promoter John Curd, an old friend of Hawkwind who was also the League's manager and label boss.

Says Animal: "Curdy phoned me up one day and said do I want to earn £50 for a day's work, picking up this drummer in our old van with his kit and taking him to meet with the rest of the band. Well, seeing as I was fucking skint as usual, and in those days £50 would keep me in substances for a whole week, I said yes. I always liked Hawkwind from my 'bikey' days, so I picked him up and we set off."

Animal entertained his passenger with a tape of his band's debut album, the immortal *We Are . . . The League.*

"He listened to it and said, 'Yeah, it's okay,'" says Animal. "I played him 'Nowhere Man' a couple of times and he never batted an eyelid, which I was very chuffed about seeing as it's a complete rip-off of 'Kings Of Speed'. Well, you gotta start somewhere, ain't you!"

Nik Turner comments: "Simon was supposed to be going to play with the band. Animal from the Anti-Nowhere League brought him down to Dave's house in Devon, and Dave decided he didn't want him in the band after all, which I thought was shit."

Dave: "Simon couldn't keep the time. He didn't have any stamina. Two numbers on the trot, he'd start waning. We had him there for a couple of days and we knew then what was going on really. He knew he couldn't do it. He was a nice character, Simon. I don't think he came back at all after that."

Simon later told an interviewer: "I wanted to go home. I was sick and just tired. My family needed me and I needed the rest."

With a week's worth of major dates written into their calendar for February 1983, giving the band the chance to spread a little more Masque action around the country, it was imperative that they find a drummer quickly.

Andy Anderson, it was unanimously agreed, was a fine musician and a great bloke, although he was much sought-after as a session player and would only ever be a stand-in. "The black, one-eyed drummer," muses Dave Brock with admiration. "Now, Andy could play along with any synthesiser click. He was a very good drummer."

Andy had briefly worked with Nik Turner's band, Inner City Unit, and he had appeared on the Sphynx album, *Xitintoday*. Prior to that, he had drummed with Here & Now. During the Sphynx sessions, producer Steve Hillage had taken a shine to Andy's playing, and Nik Turner told Hillage: "He's a fantastic drummer, he's a good friend of mine and I don't want to halt his progress. So I'm happy if you invite him to join your band."

Anderson then moved on with Steve Hillage, and in 1982 played with former Killing Joke bassist Youth and Jimmy Cauty, later of The KLF, in their band Brilliant.

Come 1983, he was ready to take to the road with Hawkwind. It should have been a great new year for everyone.

But the band, unknowingly, were about to enter the darkest days of their career.

CHAPTER 18

Back In Black

IN January 1983, Dave Brock's wife Sylvia took her own life at home in north Devon.

The family had by then moved from High Bickington to an old vicarage in Abbots Bickington. It was a gothic, stone building which Dave re-roofed himself, and its grounds were memorable for a monkey-puzzle tree which eventually blew down.

To the shock and horror of Dave and the children, Sylvia one day climbed into her car and drove into a barn, where she gassed herself. A frantic Dave later found her, dead from carbon monoxide poisoning.

"It was a terrible thing," says Dave. "Awful. Tragic. I think basically it was a bit of my fault for not paying attention. Sylvia got depressed and I never saw it. People in this situation – you always blame yourself to a certain extent. You never get over it."

Sylvia had never participated in the life of Hawkwind, preferring to pursue her own activities. In one project, she had helped to compile a monthly local listings magazine, incorporating articles on alternative lifestyle topics such as natural healing and meditation, with friends of Anne Bainbridge, Harvey's ex-wife.

"I was going away a lot, touring," explains Dave. "The thing with this band is you become blinkered. It's like being a horse. You get brought out of your stables and off you jump, over the next hurdle. You *forget*. Band members had their private girlfriends touring in America, we were staying in hotels . . . We became focused on Hawkwind.

"At the time, I didn't actually want to go home after being on tour because of the re-roofing. Such a lot of work needed doing to the place. My daughter Marti at the same time – and I'm not making excuses – had become pregnant. She was quite young, 15 or 16. She wanted to be a punk, she was a rebel, and her boyfriend was a punk as well. She did have the baby – my granddaughter Trish. I was off touring, I wasn't there all the time, and it all wore Sylvia down. It was fairly isolated at the vicarage."

Dave believes that Sylvia's suicide was a cry for help that went too far. He reflects: "I think it was like saying, 'Here, look! I'm going to go out to my car and kill myself. Pay attention to the situation,' and it went wrong. It shouldn't have happened.

"I became very ill afterwards. It takes you ages to get over things . . . driving along in tears. I hit my hand through a window and nearly cut my finger off. All sorts of strange things occur that you wouldn't normally do. I had a kidney stone just, really, because of what happened and the aftermath of it all."

To this day, Sylvia is remembered with great warmth by all those who knew her.

"She was a fabulous woman," says Douglas Smith.

And Mike King, a loyal friend to both Dave and Sylvia since the Sixties, recently visited her resting place while on holiday in Devon.

"I picked some flowers and put them on her grave," he reveals. "And I took a picture of her stone."

Dave was still feeling raw when Hawkwind, complete with Andy Anderson on drums, took to the road just a few weeks later for their dates in February.

"Dave and I were the best of friends at that point in time," recalls Nik Turner. "He admitted he was really glad I was on the tour 'cos he didn't have anybody to talk to. He didn't like anybody, and nobody liked him, he said. I tried to talk to him about his wife because I thought he might feel the need to talk to somebody about it, but he didn't want to. I think he went off me after that."

Dave: "Everybody would say, 'Oh, I'm sorry to hear about this.' It was awful. Some people thought I should have paid a bit more attention to what was going on."

Choose Your Masques would be Hawkwind's last studio release by RCA Active. Their option on their contract had come up, and it wasn't renewed.

By now, a stream of Hawkwind material was emerging on two other labels. Dave's *Weird Tapes* series had been continuing, with its selections of live material, out-takes and demos from Hawkwind, Hawklords, Sonic Assassins and Dave Brock solo recordings.

At the same time, Flicknife Records had been issuing singles, EPs and full-length albums.

In 1981, there was the *Hawkwind Zoo* EP, the 'Motorhead' single (considered better than both the original Hawkwind version and the Motorhead rendition) and the *Sonic Assassins 1977* EP.

The next year brought the *Hawkwind Friends And Relations* album, the first of a trilogy which turned into a series that continues to this day. The album includes performances by Hawkwind, Inner City Unit and Michael Moorcock's Deep Fix. A single, 'Who's Gonna Win The War', was also released.

Early in 1983, Flicknife released a compilation EP, *Your Last Chance*, and *Hawkwind Friends & Relations: Twice Upon A Time* which includes live material and tracks by Martin Griffin, Harvey Bainbridge, Dave Brock, Nik Turner and Uncle Nik & The ETs ('Call Home Elliot').

By his own admission, Dave Brock was supplying Flicknife with material for these releases from his extensive tape archives, while other members of the band were contributing tracks of their own.

It was in the spring of 1983 that Hawkwind discovered they were being dropped by RCA. Harvey Bainbridge says: "We were in a meeting with the MD and he said that Hawkwind records were coming out on independent labels and they couldn't handle that. Dave was sitting there quietly, not saying anything. The guy was asking me what our next plans were. I was mumbling on and on when he suddenly dropped this bombshell: he wasn't going to pick up the option.

"After that, I had a long, long phone call from Bob Calvert. Bob was really fed up. He said he was suing Dave Brock because he'd been selling tapes on the quiet while we were signed to other record companies. He wanted me to join him in suing Dave.

Douglas Smith remarks: "Bob Calvert was amassing all this documentation to prove that songs had been released which he'd written and was never credited for. He was going to take action against the band. I do know lyrics have been used for which permission was never granted, and the person who'd written the lyrics has created a stink about it."

Considering the release of material on other labels while Hawkwind were still signed to RCA, Nik Turner comments: "This has been a problem all the way down the line. The band's credibility became pretty well nil with the record companies. Dave thinks the music business is something to be abused and exploited to his own gain. Basically, you end up with the situation where no company wants to sign the band."

Says Dave: "*The Weird Tapes* were old stuff going back to the Seventies. Any money we made from them we used to finance our fanzines. A guy called Brian Tawn used to do one called *Hawkfan*. This money kept our magazines going. All these fanzines had to be financed somehow. A fan who's keen enough to run and write a fanzine – he has to have a means of paying for printing it up and posting it out."

Nik Turner comments: "Brian Tawn's fanzine was a labour of love. It was like a Xeroxed newsletter, and I wouldn't say it cost very much at all to produce. I wouldn't say the ongoing cost was commensurate with what Dave was taking on the tapes.

"Dave may be saying, 'I put all this stuff out to finance a fanzine,' but how was he to judge whether I felt that was a good reason for putting out bootleg tapes that I was on? There's an argument that in the long run these releases would perpetuate the name of the band, which would create demand for other records we're on, but that doesn't give Dave the right to cavalierishly do things on his own without consulting people or asking their permission. *The Weird Tapes* would certainly form a part of any complaint I have about material coming out without my permission."

Turning to the Flicknife releases, Dave continues: "Harvey knew what went on with Flicknife 'cos he was involved. All the stuff on Flicknife everybody got paid for, 'cos it's a proper company." This is not contested by Nik Turner.

Asked if the Flicknife releases had compromised the RCA deal, Dave replies, "No, I don't think so. RCA was losing money and they got rid of loads of their bands, us being one of them. This new guy came over from America and he wielded a big knife. They didn't renew our option. It wasn't to do with other records coming out.

"I've no idea if RCA minded *The Weird Tapes*. They didn't interfere with the sales of records. You're talking about cassettes, and the money was on such a small level. It was only a mail-order thing for fans. It wasn't done on a gigantic scale.

"We did a few things with Flicknife. That was Frenchy and Gina. It was a really good label, like a punk anarchic label. They had all these weird, really obscure bands."

Frenchy Gloder and his then wife Gina "Wild Thing" had become involved with Hawkwind through their connections to Michael Moorcock and Robert Calvert.

Says Frenchy: "I met Michael Moorcock at the Marquee. I went up to him, 'cos I was a great fan of his books and all the work he'd done with Hawkwind. They were one of my favourite bands as a kid. I said I had this little label, and he said he had two tracks left from his album, *The New Worlds Fair*. They were 'Dodgem Dude' and 'Starcruiser', and we put them out as a single.

"Then Bob Calvert gave me a ring and said, 'I got your number through Michael Moorcock. Would you like to do a single?' That was [1980's] 'Lord Of The Hornets'. Then one day Dave Brock rang me up. He said, 'We're currently signed to Bronze, but there's a lot of archive material that could interest the fans if you want. So we met and we decided to do a 12-inch, which was the *Hawkwind Zoo* EP."

It contains 'Hurry On Sundown' and two other early recordings: 'Kings Of Speed (Live)' and 'Sweet Mistress Of Pain'.

"I thought that would be a lot of fun," says Frenchy, who began working with Dave on a campaign of releases. "Dave has always been Hawkwind, and what he says goes. He doesn't care if he's signed to Bronze or RCA or whatever.

"When RCA signed Hawkwind, they said that what material they didn't want, we could do on Flicknife, so everybody was happy. There was no problem with us releasing archive material. We never had any trouble."

Of the Flicknife and *Weird Tapes* releases, Brock says: "They are like interesting old jazz recordings where people have their magic moment. I wouldn't put anything out that's scrappy. Nik Turner tried to stop all this. He had a big bee in his bonnet. People can still get a lot of this stuff. The tracks were all released and re-released lots of times, and some of them have been on the Voiceprint label."

Voiceprint is still issuing old Hawkwind recordings, including the *Weird Tapes* series, on CD. The participating musicians receive cheques and statements from Voiceprint and all but Nik Turner are accepting them.

If Calvert was the first to raise his voice against Dave Brock's programme of archive releases on various small labels, more voices would be heard in time, and they would get louder. But Brock wouldn't be the only person under fire . . .

After RCA, Hawkwind would not work with a major label again and Huw Lloyd-Langton, for one, found this turn of events disconcerting. He says: "Most of the albums that we'd done with the major record companies were quite enjoyable 'cos the financial aspect was taken care of. Without the financial pressure, the worry of that, you can concentrate more on the artistic side – even though you are never sure whether those companies pay you fairly or not. After the RCA situation, it got harder."

Hawkwind then officially teamed up with Flicknife, working on a one-album basis with each release, according to Frenchy.

They emerged on June 4, 1983 to play a one-off gig at a Motorcycle Action Group bikers' festival at the Cricket St Thomas Wildlife Park. It was Andy Anderson's last show with the band – and the first for keyboardist and violinist Dead Fred, who had previously played in Nik Turner's Inner City Unit.

"I always try to get good people playing with me," says Nik.

Andy Anderson went on to join a live line-up of The Cure, drumming on their worldwide Top Tour in 1984, but he didn't go any further with Robert Smith and co. According to Turner, "He became an alcoholic."

Nik invited Andy to play drums at an Inner City Unit reunion gig in 1990.

"We rehearsed for a couple of days," says Nik. "Then there was this thing where he went off to the pub with the guitarist and didn't come back. We had to abandon the rehearsal. I got in touch again and I said, 'We'll rehearse tomorrow. I'll come and pick you up.' I went to his house and he wasn't there. I had to get another drummer to fill in, the drummer who'd played with the band previously and could do the gig without rehearsing.

"I didn't see Andy Anderson again then for several years. He got in touch with me. He said, 'I've got to apologise to you for my mistreatment and disrespect for you in the past.' It wasn't really something I'd taken to heart. At Alcoholics Anonymous, part of their format is they make people redress the indiscretions they've made in the past."

Rob Heaton sat in on drums for Hawkwind's annual appearance at Stonehenge on June 22, joining Dave Brock, Nik Turner, Harvey Bainbridge, Huw Lloyd-Langton and Dead Fred. It was their last gig of the year. They would spend the rest of 1983 working on a new concept. First, there had been the Space Ritual. Now the Earth Ritual was coming together.

There were rehearsals and recordings from October to December, and Lemmy was invited to participate.

Frenchy claims that Lemmy agreed as a favour to him and not to Hawkwind. "Lemmy had always said he wouldn't work with Dave any more," says Frenchy. "Because Lemmy and I were really good friends, he said, 'I'll do it for you, not for Dave.' It went really well."

Lemmy played and sang on 'Night Of The Hawks', which would be released as a seven-inch single backed with 'Green Finned Demon' on March 2, 1984. Simultaneously, a 12-inch EP was issued. *Night Of The Hawks: The Earth Ritual Preview* featured the same two tracks plus 'Dream Dancers' and 'Dragons And Fables'. A *Night Of The Hawks* video, on Jettisoundz, followed in July.

Dave remembers: "I got Lemmy to come and stay at our place down in Devon. It was jolly fine. We got our photographs together, singing away. He brought his girlfriend with him. He had a Sunday dinner and he promptly fell asleep in the chair. It was the home-made hash cakes . . . His girlfriend was a bit peeved that his attention wasn't focused on her, and she went home the next day. Kris had to take her to the station. Probably Lemmy wanted to get rid of her anyway."

Lemmy recollects: "We did the single in this caravan that belonged to Harvey Bainbridge. It was just one day. Very badly mixed, too."

Asked if he had been granted any say in the recording, he replies: "You don't have any choice when you hire me. I'm me. Dave knew that too. That's why he asked me down there. He knows we had that amazing thing. He's never had it with anybody since."

It wasn't the easiest situation for Harvey, who saw Lemmy stepping into his bass role. "Dave had got fed up with my bass playing by then," says Harvey. "We were recording at Dave's place, way out in the middle of nowhere. I went along to do some recording. Lemmy turned up to do some and Nik turned up, and Dead Fred. I remember getting very pissed about something and storming off. There was no animosity with Lemmy or anything silly like that. I'd met Lemmy before anyway. Dave was all, 'My buddy Lemmy . . .'

"I didn't like that song 'Night Of The Hawks', it's a silly song, but I was pleased with the video. We'd only ever had in-house video cameras at the back of the hall, and this was our first professional one."

Dave and Kris have since branded Harvey "a big grumpy old Hector".

Huw Lloyd-Langton enjoyed the session with Lemmy. "I got on well with him," says Huw. "He always called me Huwie Bach, or Little Huwie, because I'm Welsh. Bach is 'little', which is what my mum always called me."

Also playing on the recordings was John Clark – Huw's long-time drummer in his own band, Lloyd Langton Group.

However, the general excitement surrounding the EP and the forth-coming spring tour was shattered with the news that Barney Bubbles had committed suicide on November 14.

"That was very sad," says Dave Brock, shaking his head. "Poor old Barney. He was a strange character. It's difficult to explain what he was like. He was a very humble, shy sort of guy, and he had wonderful ideas."

Barney had not worked with Hawkwind for some years. In his absence, Dave had decided to commission artwork from "good artists that were struggling rather than record company people" – individuals such as John Coulthard and Jimmy Mountjoy.

Nik Turner had remained close to Barney up to his death, and was "heartbroken" when it happened. He had been the only member of Hawkwind to witness at first hand the terrifying transformation dealt by Barney's manic depression.

"There was an incident where he was freaking out," relates Turner. "His girlfriend phoned me and said, 'I don't know what to do. Barney's threatening to kill everybody.' I went round and he was there with a big knife. I said, 'Come on, don't be silly. Give me the knife.' He said, 'I'll kill you.'

"I've actually got quite a lot of experience with people who are in that dark state. I don't take any bullshit. I take the view that they won't do it, that probably the reason they're like this is because they want attention or something.

"I said again, 'Look, Barney, give me the knife.' He said, 'I'm going to stab you.' I said, 'Go on – I'm here.' He dropped the knife and ran out of the room and into the street, distraught. I went out looking for him and I couldn't find him. I heard a couple of hours later he commit-ted himself to a loony bin – a sanctuary."

Barney had met his girlfriend, Bee, during a trip to Australia. She had moved back with him to live in his house in Islington, London, but according to Turner, "They were going their own ways, rather."

Nik continues: "I became involved with Hawkwind again and took off, writing new material and recording, and I thought, 'Well, Barney's great. He's a really good producer and I'd like him to be involved.' I don't think I mentioned it to Dave. I think I just invited Barney to come down. I didn't think Dave would object.

"We were rehearsing in Dave's house in Devon, a vicarage. Barney had come back from Australia. He'd been very depressed. He'd spent a lot of time with aborigines there and gone walkabout. It was at the time of the Cold War as well. At this particular time, he was rather dark.

"One day we were rehearsing and apparently Barney phoned up to speak to me. But he spoke to Dave, and Dave was very non-committal and offhand with him and said, 'What do you want, then?' Barney said I had invited him to come down. Dave said something like, 'Well, we don't want you down here. We don't want you to do that; we don't want you involved in it.'

"According to Barney's girlfriend, he was actually phoning me to ask if I could let him have a bit of money towards the fare. I thought it was absolutely shocking."

Brock says: "I don't even remember speaking to Barney. I can't remember any of that. Barney had never produced an album, but we wouldn't have minded him coming down. I can't remember him phoning, but if he did, I probably wouldn't have known what he was talking about and I would have said, 'What?'

"Nik used to do a lot of this, inviting people to do things. I'll give you an instance. We were at Rockfield Studios around this period and he invited a lot of his buddies to come and stay at Anchor Hill. The main studio at Rockfield is in a square, and the outbuildings have been converted into studios. Opposite the farm is Anchor Hill, a cottage. The Mill House is separate, about a mile down the road, by the river.

"We ended up with about 10 people sitting around Anchor Hill smoking joints. They seemed amiable characters. This girl said, 'I'll cook dinner tonight for everybody. I'll go and buy the food.' She took our money for the whole week and spent it on one meal. She cooked the meal and they ate it all while we were in the studio. When we came back, they'd had the dinner, they'd had a jolly fine old time, they were sleeping on the floor downstairs, we were trying to do an album, and there was no food and no money left. The next day we said to Nik, 'Get rid of them.'

"Nik said to them, 'Why don't you pop down into the quadrangle?' Bad Manners were down there. They stayed with Bad Manners, and after Bad Manners left, they still stayed on. Kingsley Ward phoned me up and said, 'Who are all these people?' I said, 'I don't know. Nik

Turner brought them down and we slung them out.' They were hangers-on."

Not that Dave or anybody else in Hawkwind would ever accuse Barney Bubbles of being a hanger-on.

Douglas Smith says: "I would say his suicide was a combination of lots of things. Barney did become very, very bitter about Hawkwind. Previously, I'd asked him to come back to the band and do some artwork and he'd said no. But he wasn't involved with Hawkwind at the time he died. He was one of the top men in London for design at that point. He'd gone to Australia and he'd met someone.

"I heard lots of different stories. It was an accumulation of, just, despair. He had a big tax problem. He probably had problems in his relationship. Loads of things. For whatever reason he put the bag over his head, he would have been the only person who could ever tell us. When he killed himself, the first person Jake Riviera rang was me. He suggested I should arrange a wake. I said, 'No, I don't want to do that.' "

Douglas was of the firm opinion that anyone feeling so desperate about their life that they should end it would not want to be celebrated by crowds of people at a party.

There is some indication that Barney felt his time in the music business was coming to an end. In 1981, he'd talked to *The Face* about the new young breed of designers, saying: "They're so creative – the kids that do the sleeves – it makes me feel so staid and boring, and I think, 'I've got to get out. It's time for me to go.' "

Barney's exhibitor, Mike Heath, confirms this, and speculates that Bubbles had come full circle in his art.

He says: "Towards the end, Barney just wanted to become a painter. He got disillusioned with getting shafted by the industry. In 1982, '83, just before he died, he did private paintings and he was returning to his Sixties and Seventies style of work."

There is, too, an untold human tragedy in Barney's death: he was just about to build a new relationship with his son, and had been decorating his house in preparation for this.

Jiana Skinner, Barney's former partner, and the mother of their son Aten, met the talented young designer when she was an impressionable 18 and he was 26. By the beginning of 1969, they were living together in a commune in Portobello Road.

"It was a very exciting time," she recalls. "Barney was just great. He was all love and peace. He was very self-effacing. He was modest about his work, he never liked a fuss made about it, but at the same time he was very confident. He was very much a leader. He liked to get everyone organised, and he was the heart and soul of every occasion. He had a very strong personality.

"I remember him saying, 'There's going to be a band practising in the basement,' and it was Hawkwind. I was a bit in awe of them. Every now and again I'd sneak down and listen to them. Everyone was so much older, I felt a bit out of my depth. But the three or four years we were there, we were really happy. Barney was a lovely, lovely person."

The baby was born in 1972 and named Aten. "We wanted something unusual for him," says Jiana. "He's named after an Egyptian sun king, because he's a Leo."

Everything was wonderful until the couple decided to live in Devon. Aten was just four months old when they set off – but Barney never actually moved in. He returned to London, leaving Jiana with Aten and another couple they had intended to share with.

Jiana was miserable. She didn't get on with the male half of the couple, and the household had no electricity or gas, no hot water and no bathroom. But most of all: "I was fed up living there and hardly ever seeing Barney. He was working really hard. I kept saying, 'When are you moving down?' He did come and visit us, but it emerged he had no intention of staying in Devon, because of his work. I said to Barney, 'If you're not moving down, I want to come back.' "

Mother and child returned to London in 1974. Barney was living with his parents in Whitton. Jiana went to stay with her parents near Orpington, Kent.

"We were on opposite sides of London," she states. "We'd meet up. I'd stay at his parents' and he'd come and visit me. That went on for a couple of years. We never could get it together to be together."

Jiana met and married another man. "Barney was very upset about it, but he seemed to get over it," says Jiana. "He had all these other girlfriends and he seemed quite happy."

Eventually, Jiana moved to Ireland and kept in touch with Barney by letter. Gradually, Barney's correspondence began to include "strange" qualities that Jiana didn't recognise. She had never seen any sign of Barney's illness in their years together, perhaps apart from his reaction to her marriage.

"He was having, I suppose, his depression," she reasons now. "He said he attacked Nik once. It was really unlike him. I didn't know why he was doing all this strange stuff. He didn't say he had manic depression but, apparently, he went to hospitals and I think he was on medication. I didn't know any of that at the time."

Meanwhile, Jiana was feeling guilty that Barney was missing his son growing up. She took Aten for a trip to England when he was about 10, and they met up with Barney. It was later agreed that in the next year, 1983, she would come back from Ireland and they would work towards Aten living full-time with Barney.

"He was happy about all that," says Jiana, who by now had a young daughter as well. "I really wanted them to get to know each other. I felt 'cos Barney had missed out on so much, he should have Aten."

Jiana confirmed the date with Barney and duly returned to England after three and a half years in Ireland. Within a week of her arrival, Barney was dead.

She remembers: "We got back and I thought, 'I must phone Barney. I'll phone him next week. There's plenty of time.' And of course there wasn't plenty of time. It was very, very, very upsetting. It took me years to get over it."

Jiana had to cope with one of Barney's family accusing her of being responsible for his decline. "That was ridiculous," she says. "We'd been split for quite a few years, and he'd had other girlfriends. He had a girlfriend living with him at the time he died."

If Barney had been upset about any problems related to Hawkwind, he never mentioned them to Jiana. He was, however, very depressed about his financial situation. "He was hopeless with money. He was a very trusting person and he got conned as well. He lost all his money somehow. It destroyed him. He was in an awful mess with his tax, and it was still hanging over him when he died. It was a real, real shame.

"In other ways, he seemed to be doing really well. He had lots of work, he had his house, and he was looking forward to seeing Aten. He was getting his house ready. He knew we were arriving that week, and that's what makes his suicide seem so very odd."

Jiana now lives in Tonbridge, Kent. Aten, 31 at the time of writing, has inherited his father's artistic talent and is currently designing computer games in Leeds.

Zones, released by Flicknife in October 1983, had reached number 57, and it would be Hawkwind's highest-charting album for some time. It brought together the tracks recorded at Hastings in December 1980 and a selection of live material from the Ginger Baker line-up and the Nik Turner/Martin Griffin incarnation of 1982.

There were high hopes for 'Night Of The Hawks: The Earth Ritual Preview' when it followed in March 1984, but it flopped. Says Frenchy: "It was a great 12-inch, it got a lot of radio play and good reviews, but the chart position it got was lower than it should have been because of the way they were doing the charts at the time. You had your chart returns and then there was the 'weighing', a panel which weighed it all up."

This panel decided how well or how badly a single was doing not just through sales but with consideration of the artists' stature, their established following and their chart history, and also in relation to the performances of other bigger and lesser acts.

There was no such confusion surrounding the accompanying tour. It was one of the most outrageous of Hawkwind's career, and none of the musicians will ever forget it. For better or for worse, Nik Turner made sure of that.

CHAPTER 19

Costume Drama

"WHEN Nik came back in 1982, it was all right," reflects Dave Brock. "It wasn't an unpleasant time in the band. Everybody got on. Nik was quite a good frontman. You've gotta think of the fans too – they like these odd things going on. Nik was out the front again, playing the saxophone, wearing his weird clothes and doing weird things. With Nik, there were all these over-the-top theatrical stunts which were really good fun. He was good at doing them. It was fine. It made everybody laugh. He was 'an expensive clown', as Bob Calvert used to say.

"But his ego . . . the attention he'd receive used to make him go even further over the top. It reached the point in 1984 where he got into the idea of having his clothes ripped off . . ."

The tour that was set up to promote 'Night Of The Hawks: The Earth Ritual' was a bit special.

Hawkwind, still assured of a big live following, played five weeks of gigs taking in the Apollos, Empires and city halls of the UK, and their customary two nights at London's Hammersmith Odeon.

Opening at Slough Thames Hall on February 16, 1984 and finishing up at Plymouth Skating Rink on March 23, the band were joined by various guests along the way. Dave Anderson, an old face from the days of *X In Search Of Space*, performed in Dunstable (March 8), Reading (10) and Leicester (11). Lemmy and Michael Moorcock both turned out for the Hammersmith shows on March 13 and 14, while Moorcock also appeared at Oxford Apollo a few days later.

"Dave Brock was trying to re-establish Hawkwind as a force," suggests Harvey Bainbridge. "One of his big notions was for us to be like a circus act with [well-known] people coming on and going off."

275

Dave Anderson had been invited on to the tour by Nik Turner. He explains: "I got a phone call from Nik one day: 'We're just starting a tour, we've announced that we're having a guest, and we haven't invited any. Would you be our guest?' I hadn't played bass for 10 years. I'd hardly been to any gigs let alone played at any."

Indeed, his last venture had been with Huw Lloyd-Langton and John Lingwood in Amon Din, and he had spent the intervening years working at the desk in his Foel Studios in north Wales.

"I was really peed off with working in the studio all the time," he recalls. "The idea of touring with Hawkwind really appealed to me. I much prefer the studio although it's a very isolated existence. There's another complete world of live music and I miss it when I'm not actually part of a group of people in a band. I'm quite happy living my life, it's very solitary down here, but I really like playing and meeting the fans."

Anderson found things had changed since he last performed with Hawkwind. "Dave Brock by then was in his own changing room by himself," he explains. "And everybody else was in the other changing room having a really good time. I bumped into Dave from time to time and he was perfectly polite, but he obviously wanted to be at arm's length from everybody. It was the first time I realised there was the Dave Brock camp and the 'rest-of-the-band' camp. That's what's so lovely now about playing with Nik's Space Ritual band. We're all so pleased to see each other all the time."

While Dave Brock was delighted to welcome Lemmy on to the stage at Hammersmith, he asserts, with the benefit of hindsight, that the Motorhead maestro was so struck by the stage show he later duplicated it.

Michael Moorcock, meanwhile, was typically nervous about his performances although it must be assumed that, as usual, he also thoroughly enjoyed them.

Dave Brock, Nik Turner, Huw Lloyd-Langton, Harvey Bainbridge and Dead Fred set out on the tour with drummer Rick Martinez.

Rick had previously jammed with the band at Rockfield, and they knew his two brothers equally well; one is a guitarist and the other, Paul [Martin Griffin's old friend from the Richard Strange band], is a bass player who also worked with Robert Plant.

Says Harvey: "I remember him coming back with lots of money and buying a house. The other brother is working with Showaddywaddy.

He used to hang around. They were a nice family."

Unfortunately, Rick didn't last the tour, bowing out early in March. "It was probably drugs and egos," says Harvey, succinctly.

Nik Turner elaborates: "I think he took too many drugs and never slept and put himself in a very bad state."

"He was a very good drummer, he was a nice character and he did a lot of session work at Rockfield," remarks Dave Brock. "But he had a bit of a cocaine problem and he got bronchitis too, which didn't help. I remember that Rick's girlfriend had a big freak-out at a hotel in Nottingham and accused Harvey of hitting Rick."

Harvey denies all knowledge of this.

Rick was replaced by Clive Deamer, a respected session player. According to Harvey, Clive had been one of the musicians originally auditioned. "He was a temporary stand-in," explains Dave. "He was a great player, and he told us he wanted to go on doing his own stuff. He was working with bands around Bristol. He went on to play with a jazz quartet, and he worked with Portishead too."

Clive has indeed been a versatile drummer with a CV encompassing Jeff Beck, Van Morrison and Roni Size Reprazent. With the advent of drum'n'bass, he found his forte.

Nik Turner had been making elaborate preparations for the tour. He'd decided to adopt the persona of a "space clown" and, as a simple preliminary measure, he'd had his head shaved leaving a tuft of fluorescent pink hair at the front.

Dead Fred's wife, Claire, tended to Nik's make-up on the road, and she took on the old role of Stacia and Barney Bubbles, collaborating with him on ideas for his costumes.

Says Turner: "I made that body stocking that I'm wearing on the *Night Of The Hawks* DVD [filmed at Ipswich Gaumont on March 9] and Elaine bought me this skateboard helmet. I was performing on roller skates. I would whizz around the stage looking as though I was on ice.

"I did other things as well. I made suits out of dustbin liners, and they looked fantastic. I'd cut arms and legs and stick them together with gaffer tape. It looked quite awesome in the light, like real high-fashion, flashy designer clothing – like Pierre Cardin. I had a silver one that I made out of Melinex, and the lights projecting on it made it look like rainbows."

How this all fitted in with Brock's stated concept of the Earth Ritual as "coming back to the planet and getting involved with the Earth spirits" is anybody's guess. But Huw Lloyd-Langton was anxious from the outset.

He describes his worries: "Nik had acted very normally during the rehearsal period. We turned up to do our first gig in the two hired cars again and he had a shaved head and this pointy bit of hair that looked like a carrot sticking out, unicorn-ish. I thought, 'What are we in for? What's he gonna get up to?'

"He always organised his own dressing room for make-up and whatever. He liked space around him. The plan was that we would do the first couple of numbers and then Nik would make an appearance on the third or fourth number, but we didn't know what he was going to appear like.

"We started the number and he just flew on in a stocking suit painted in luminous colours and roller-skated all across the stage, honking to his heart's content. 'Oh my God!' He continued to honk throughout most of the gig."

The honking, which Nik had promised to tone down, turned out to be the least of Huw's problems.

Says Nik: "One particular thing I did as well . . . I bought all these old suits from Oxfam, about 20 of them. I slashed the seams, and the suits would fall apart when they were pulled. Just before the encore, I'd go off and change into one of these suits. Then I'd go down to the front of the audience, get people singing 'Silver Machine' and encourage somebody to pull my sleeve, pull the leg of my trousers, pull my jacket . . ."

Dave Brock chuckles: "Bit by bit, he'd get nearer to the fans. He'd shake their hands, they'd pull his coat and the arm would come off. He'd wiggle his leg in front of them and his trouser leg would come off. He was a man wearing one half of a pair of trousers. It was a comedy; it was funny. The audience would be reduced to hysteria."

Nik continues: "The first time I did it, I ended up naked. I was trying to recreate the mass hysteria of Johnny Ray, making women wet their pants – a Tom Jones sort of scene with all the girls throwing their knickers. I thought I'd instigate this situation where people tear my clothes off. It was just a bit of cheap theatrics."

No one, however, was prepared for the strength of Huw Lloyd-Langton's objections. "Huw was actually a real prude," declares Nik. "I did this for the first time and I didn't have anything on underneath. I'm suddenly standing there naked onstage and Huw was absolutely shocked, disgusted and traumatised by it. I just thought it was funny. He had a go at me afterwards. He called me 'absolutely immoral', probably things like 'heathen'."

Harvey says: "Huw was very moralistic. He was thankful that his life was saved at some stage or another and things like that he didn't really go for. He said, 'If that's going to happen again, I'm not coming out any more.' It was just hilarious."

"Huw tried to hit Nik," Dave Brock recalls. "He said, 'If you do that again, I'm going to leave the band. You're just an old pervert.' He smashed everything in the dressing room later on."

"I was disgusted," confirms Huw. "I don't like nudity onstage. I was never attracted to that, particularly. I had a go at Nik afterwards. I was pretty angry with him. I thought it was in really bad taste and I let him know that. I think I shouted something, threw something and stormed out of the dressing room.

"We weren't enemies, Nik and I. It was only that that I found offensive. I don't like that sort of thing. I don't feel it's necessary in any circumstances, male or female. I was quite happy not to have been there while Stacia was in the band."

Dave Brock takes up the tale: "Nik apologised to Huw and said it wouldn't happen again. The next night, he put another of his suits on, and the same thing occurred. His trousers got pulled off – but he'd been to the government surplus shop and bought a leather thong thing. In America, they wear leather belts with lots of holders for tools. He had a holder for a hatchet that dangled down. There was no hatchet there but a banana.

"Huw went bananas himself. He tried to kick Nik up the bottom into the audience because he felt Nik had really taken the piss out of him. They had another huge row: 'I wasn't naked!' 'Yes, but you're taking the piss out of me by having a banana stuck in a leather thong thing.'"

Things eventually calmed down. "I started wearing a bit of gaffer tape shaped like a cross," says Turner. "I covered up the offending penis. That was all that Huw was worried about."

Some way into the tour, Hawkwind acquired a coffin, and Nik immediately took it onstage so that he could appear in it.

But even with his pink unicorn hair, the coffin and a nightly debagging from the audience, Nik wanted more spectacle for the

Hammersmith Odeon shows: he wanted to fly.

The setting for his flight was an operating theatre, complete with nurses brandishing syringes, staged for 'Silver Machine'. This time the silver machine was not a spaceship and it was not Bob Calvert's bicycle, which had been the original inspiration for his spoof song. The silver machine was an iron lung.

Nik recollects: "I was wheeled on in a big silver iron-lung thing, and the stage was an operating theatre. I had all these drip-feed things and a liver flying about. I had a straitjacket as well. I was wearing a bin-liner suit, and underneath it, I had a harness with balloons attached to it. There was a compressed-air nozzle on the back of the suit. You pressed it, the balloons would inflate and I would get fatter and fatter."

At this point, the flying rig would lift the swollen Turner into the air – and at any time he liked, he could burst the balloons under his suit. "It all fitted together properly," says Nik of the balloon mechanism. "Dead Fred devised it."

The flying apparatus was not quite so reliable. "Nik was onstage at Hammersmith about to fly on the wire," says Harvey. "Off he went. He got a few feet up in the air and got stuck. He was just literally flopping around like a beached whale. We were taking turns in spinning him. It was like something from *Spinal Tap*. When he came down, he's taking his bin-liners off and doing his standing-naked-in-front-of-the-audience routine."

Dave Brock elaborates: "The flying rig got stuck six feet off the ground and Nik was hanging there. At the same time, this roadie next to me had the gas container for the dry ice machine and his hand got stuck to it. I was right in the middle of singing this number. Nik was stuck in front of me, he couldn't get to the microphone to sing, and he was swinging backwards and forwards. Some of the crew came to the aid of the roadie with his hand stuck to the gas canister – it looked like they were carrying a baby off. We got the roadie off the stage and then Nik suddenly collapsed down from this flying thing. It was all a bit chaotic."

"Things like that happen," says Nik, sagely. "You just make use of them and carry on."

Dave adds: "Lemmy was there, he was playing, and he saw all this. When Motorhead did a tour a couple of years later, they copied it – the nurses, the iron thing, everything."

The set varied from one night to the next, although it spanned Hawkwind's entire career, sometimes including Hawklords' 'Psi Power' and highlighting at least three of the *Earth Ritual* tracks, primarily 'Dream Dancers', 'Dragons And Fables' and 'Night Of The Hawks'. Inner City Unit's tuneful and punky 'Watching The Grass Grow' was also a staple in the performance.

"Dave didn't actually go with that one very well at all," says Harvey Bainbridge. "Some strange events were going on. I was too spaced out to know what was really happening. The only thing to do was get spaced out . . ."

As is usual on a tour, various small tensions were erupting and were just as quickly resolved. "Clive Deamer lost his rag with Huw," recalls Harvey. "I think it was in Leicester. Huw has a very funny way with him. He can wind people up, mumbling and muttering when he gets on one. Clive was in the back of the car and Huw was sat in the front. He wound Clive up to the point where Clive might've *leaned forward* . . . It was just a question of Clive not really understanding Huw's way of digging at people. It calmed down."

More seriously, a deep chasm was once again opening up between Nik Turner and Dave Brock, who was now strongly supported by Kris Tait.

Dave and Kris had become closer. Their original friendship had been almost exclusive, based on a watertight, confiding trust in each other and an exchange of musical, visual and, increasingly, commercial ideas for Hawkwind. Now their partnership was also solidly romantic, and it still is. Somewhere around this time, they moved in together.

Both express their unhappiness with Turner in 1984.

Says Brock: "He liked adulation. He had this weird thing about exposing himself."

Kris adds: "He always wanted his own dressing room. He used to wander round eating raw garlic with his little towel wrapped round him. At any given moment he'd turn round and let the towel drop."

"It was really quite insulting," insists Dave.

"He had all these girls and blokes outside the dressing room waiting to come in," continues Kris. "He'd say, 'I want the girls in but not the boyfriends.'

"At the Manchester Apollo gig [February 19] two girls were standing there and one of them was pretty and one of them wasn't so pretty. But they were both Nik Turner fans. He turned round and he said to the nice one, 'You can come in 'cos you're pretty, and she's ugly, so she can stay out there.'

"The stupid 'pretty' one went into the dressing room and left her friend outside in tears. I took her into the main dressing room to meet the rest of the band. You see someone go from being really excited to crumbling, like they've been dealt a blow. How can a man do that?"

Nik Turner denies this strenuously.

"What awful things people say about me!" he marvels. "I don't recall doing any of that. I might have eaten garlic. I do eat quite a lot of raw garlic. I keep it in my pocket; it's fantastic, brilliant for the blood.

"But trying to lure young girls into my power by dropping my towel in front of them . . . it makes me sound like some sort of paedophile or dirty old man. No, that isn't true [laughing]. Kris may have perceived something like that. They might be totally paranoid; they might see any action to be a threat. A movement of the hand can be seen as a threat. Why should somebody say something like that about me? I think, 'Well, fuck off, it's not true.'

"As for not inviting boyfriends into the dressing room, I don't have any memory of that sort of thing, really. And inviting a 'pretty' girl in and not an 'ugly' girl – I would never say anything like that. How bizarre. How people can possibly misinterpret something . . .

"I suppose everyone has their own perspective. Kris is welcome to her opinion. It's quite a damning thing to say. There's no truth in her allegation. I try to understand why people act in a particular way. I don't hold things against people. I feel rather sorry for them, really."

But whatever the problems, says Dave Brock, "We got through that tour."

There were a couple of one-off gigs before Stonehenge. On April 22, Dave Brock, Harvey Bainbridge, Huw Lloyd-Langton and Bob Calvert played a Brighton show as Sonic Assassins. And on May 28, Hawkwind, plus Calvert, appeared at Ramsgate Marina.

Stonehenge, in June 1984, was a momentous occasion. It would turn out to be the last free festival at the site – the next year's event would break up in violent scenes at the notorious Battle Of The Beanfield. It was also a landmark gig in Hawkwind history, launching a major line-up change that came as something of a shock to Harvey Bainbridge, who had been playing both bass and keyboards in the band.

Harvey had no reason to suspect that he would not be playing bass at Stonehenge and that Clive Deamer would not be drumming. He says: "We were all going to meet up at Stonehenge. Clive didn't turn up. Dave had told me there was no need to bring the bass. He said, 'I've got a bass player and a drummer here,' and presented Alan Davey and Danny Thompson. I was a bit gobsmacked – 'I might as well go home then.'

"They'd been rehearsing at Dave's place for a week, and I'd been talking to Dave on the phone over that week's build-up to Stonehenge and he hadn't even mentioned it. Not once. Alan walked round Stonehenge with me, saying, 'It wasn't me . . .'

"We were going to play on the second day as well. We were going to get up early and play at the sunrise. I thought, 'I'm not going to bother now. I think I'll wait 'til the sun comes up, hang around for a while and then go home.' Then Dave said, 'You've gotta play synthesisers.' So I did."

This is how Harvey, rather reluctantly, switched from being Hawkwind's bassist to their synthesiser player – although he would leave briefly before accepting the role full-time.

Huw Lloyd-Langton reveals: "I was quite shocked. Harvey had rung me up that morning to find out what was going on, 'cos he was confused about the whole thing. Dave had told him to bring his keyboards because, 'There'll be lots of bass players there anyway.' I turned up and there was Alan on bass and Danny on drums. I was quite surprised about the whole thing myself.

"Alan and Danny knew all the material. They were quite big Hawkwind fans prior to joining the band. I knew no more than Harvey did about it. I was living in ignorant bliss. But Stonehenge was always fairly free and easy. As it turned out, it did work pretty well. A couple of young 'uns had turned up, and it was a positive thing for the group. I didn't know what Harvey felt about it, especially after the Ginger thing when he thought he'd been ousted and then everyone was horrible. I was a bit concerned that maybe Harvey would have been extremely hurt. I got on with Alan fine. I was just a bit confused about the whole situation. Harvey definitely was."

Dave Brock insists that Harvey was not in the dark about the arrangements.

"I think he did know that Alan and Danny had been rehearsing," he says. "Harvey only lived a few miles away from where I lived. Harvey wanted to have a go at doing keyboards. We had talked about all these things. He was getting fed up with playing bass all the time. This seemed to be the obvious thing.

"Alan had written to me saying he should be the bass player in Hawkwind. He sent me a cassette. It sounded really good. And Danny – his father is *the* Danny Thompson."

Danny Thompson Sr was one of the big guns in the Seventies' folk-rock scene. He played bass with Pentangle and he was in huge demand as a session musician for the big folk-rock bands and singer-songwriters of the era. He had also been an early boyfriend of Sandy Denny, the Fairport Convention singer, solo artist and undisputed leading lady of the movement.

"I thought these were two young guys who were really keen and enthusiastic," continues Dave. "Stonehenge was the right moment to try it out. They'd come in and rehearsed with us.

"Harvey did know he was going to be doing keyboards. He liked the idea because it gave him more scope to wave his arms around and sing a few numbers. He was quite a good stage presence. He progressed upwards when he started doing all this."

Alan Davey describes his memory of events: "We arranged to play for a couple of days before we did the first gig at Stonehenge. Clive Deamer was the drummer at the time. He did session work too and he couldn't do some of the things. He was in the band but he was usually able to fit his work around it. Sometimes it clashed. Rather than do a free festival, he'd go off and do a session and earn some money. I said I knew Danny Thompson."

Alan and Danny saw Stonehenge as their "initiation".

Says Alan: "Me and Harvey went off for a walk. Harvey didn't know I was coming. I was a little bit embarrassed 'cos I liked Harvey. I liked his synth playing. No one else plays synth like Harvey. I thought that he was going to be moving on to keyboards anyway. There's no way they could chuck him out. Things like 'Dream Worker' [from *Choose Your Masques*] are stunning pieces of synth work.

"When we went off for the walk, I realised what a nice guy he is and I felt so bad. But it was great for the band that Harvey could concentrate on the keyboards. You can't play bass and keyboards properly at the same time. You have to play the keyboards with your foot, and you do lack in your bass playing slightly. Stuff like that.

"The gig was strange anyway, 'cos I think me and Harvey had had a big piece of hash cake each. I hadn't done anything like that before. I was clean when I joined the band. Harvey sorted me out . . .

"So I was out of my brains and the gig was quite unnerving at first. There were thousands of people there, and I was only 20 years old. 'What if they don't think I'm any good?' After about six numbers, Dave came over and he said, 'I think you're in the band.' He could see I was a good player, and tight. I was bringing back that old Seventies sound they had with Lemmy. I suppose Dave thought he'd never experience it again. And so all of a sudden, the mood changed. I realised I was fine and I just got into it and enjoyed it. It's what I was born for, it seems.

"I did have a few people come up to me and ask if I was Lemmy's roadie, and was Lemmy there? I had a white Rickenbacker, so they thought, 'Lemmy's here,' and they got me. But they accepted me straight away."

The gig itself was fairly chaotic. Dave Brock remembers: "We had the sacred rituals and we had vestal virgins dancing. Turner was there. He'd been given a big piece of dope for the band. He swallowed it and became comatose, collapsed. He just knelt down and fell over. His girl-friend really hit him hard. It was hilariously funny. She was so pissed off when he flopped on the floor in a coma, she started really whacking him with a stick."

"I still had my pyramid stage then," says Nik. "I performed with Hawkwind on that. I think I had it built in 1978. It was constructed out of aluminium, scaffolding and canvas. I used it at Glastonbury '78 or '79. It had a great big cannabis leaf on the front of it – a symbol of my enlightenment or freedom or fun. Then I started lending it to various people. I thought it would be nice for others to have the use of it. They took it round the festivals in the summer, and I insisted they brought it back so I could look after it for the winter.

"At one point I lent it to somebody who had a group that did raves and stuff like that, I lost sight of it and I don't have it any more. I'm still on the track of it. I'd like it back some time if I can . . ."

Returning to the topic of Stonehenge, Nik comments: "I played at most of the Stonehenge festivals in one way or another. I knew a lot of the people that were prime movers in the Stonehenge movement.

"In 1984, Hawkwind did two shows, one at night and one at dawn – the 'death' and the 'rebirth'. It was a thing that I devised of Celtic sym-bolism, mythological, Druidic. I seem to remember The Enid were there as well, and Robert Godfrey (Enid leader) was dominating the PA. Every band except The Enid were really quiet.

"One memory is of me and Roy Harper sitting on a toilet together. We were having a crap. And another is of my playing with Alan Stivell, the Breton folk exponent.

"When Hawkwind were playing at dawn, the Druids were doing their thing and somebody told me that the Arch Druid was [actor] William Roache, Ken Barlow in *Coronation Street*. I got this mantra thing going on the stage – 'Ken Barlow, Ken Barlow . . .'"

"The stage was facing the stones," adds Dave. "We could see all the druids coming round in the mist, blowing their horns. All you could hear was 'Ken Barlow' echoing across the field."

For Kris Tait, Stonehenge was a frantic experience.

She says: "Nik was supposed to get these girls together for the vestal virgins dance routine. I made all the white costumes for them in the sizes he said. He got to Stonehenge and he hadn't got any dancers. I had to go round the festival looking for girls that would fit into the dresses and propositioning them – 'Excuse me, would you like to be a vestal virgin, mate?' Some of the boyfriends got really angry."

One of them was the Rt Hon Philip Harvey, an aristocratic friend of Kris and Dave. "He didn't want his girlfriend Jenny to do it at first," carries on Kris. "She used to play guitar and sing in a psychedelic group called Agent Beartrap. He thought it would be degrading for her to do dancing with Hawkwind when she should be singing and playing in her own right.

"Nik's girlfriend Maggie did it. I had to do it. We got this other girl. We didn't know she was only 15 and she'd run away from home and the police were looking for her. Then we got two other girls who still keep in touch with us. They turn up quite often.

"None of them could dance. I tried to choreograph it. I said, 'Just follow me.' I remember we were going round in a circle and, like kids, when you stop, you all bump into each other. But the spirit was there.

"After the first gig, we went to Philip's tepee and he had this big spaghetti. Someone threw a bottle on the fire in the middle of the tepee, trying to get the bottle on fire. In the meantime, someone broke into his Land Rover or his van and stole his new stereo. Then the police were looking for the young girl."

"I thought the vestal virgins looked silly," grumps Harvey, "although they did bring a bit of a focal point to the whole thing, and lots of people enjoyed it."

"It was the usual Stonehenge, quite enjoyable and quite mad," says Huw Lloyd-Langton. "I think I had too much to drink at the end of it. I remember being invited to Philip Harvey's flash tent and accidentally knocking over the bolognese that Jenny had made. It was all over the floor. They were over the moon about that . . ."

By now, other members of Hawkwind were raising eyebrows at Huw's drinking habits.

"It wasn't a problem as far as I knew," says Huw. "It could have been at times. I know Dave doesn't like pubby-type people, and certain members of the band liked going for a pint – Griffin, myself or Simon King. It's just socialising, basically, and Dave has always been a bit of a keep-to-yourself sort of person. He's never too keen on people going off to the pub, which is understandable. You get some unsavoury people hanging around in pubs.

"I don't think I was particularly the flavour of the month for doing that at times, with various other people. Dave enjoys alcohol himself, but not pubbing it. I think over the years, Dave has had some problems with people going out drinking. You get talking to people and certain people have talked to fans or roadies under those sort of social conditions. I'm not naming myself, but if you're socialising, certain things can be said that are not very discreet. That's why Dave doesn't like the pub, socialising things. Whereas I like a pint and a game of pool before I do a gig because it relaxes you."

Some parts of Hawkwind's shows on June 20 and 21 are captured in the Jettisoundz video, *Stonehenge 1984*, which was released that November. They are seen performing 'Ghost Dance', 'Angels Of Death', 'Watching The Grass Grow', 'Utopia', 'Social Alliance' and 'Brainstorm'.

When the festival was over, Harvey Bainbridge decided it was time to quit the group. He recalls: "By this time, Kennedy Street had dropped us. I'd had a phone call from Danny Betesh telling me that the band were unmanageable. Whatever anyone tried to arrange, Dave would rearrange it.

"After Stonehenge, I went home and I said, 'That's it. Goodbye.' Then Frenchy from Flicknife was phoning up saying, 'They want you to play keyboards.' I said, 'I'm not a keyboard player.'

"The summer went by, and I'd left. Then Dave said, 'Would you come and play synthesisers on the tour as a guest?' I said, 'Okay, if I get paid for it I'll come and do it.' During that tour he said, 'Why don't you join the band again as a keyboard player? We'll start up a new partnership.' I quite enjoyed it so I thought, 'Okay.'"

Interestingly, Harvey's transition to synths is regarded by many people as the start of a great return to form for the group. Hawkwind would soon make their best album in years.

Alan had immediately become a permanent member of the band – which he still is – and after a short period of transition, Danny Thompson took over from Clive Deamer. Nik Turner was setting Hawkwind up with a new manager, Jim White, who had worked with Uriah Heep and Nazareth.

By now, the band had been around for 15 years and they had long since given up expecting lengthy album reviews in the music press. However, features editors were aware that Hawkwind still made for exciting copy, and so Dave Brock and Huw Lloyd-Langton stepped out for an interview for *Sounds* in July 1984, following the release of a 10-inch compilation mini-album titled *Independent Days* and a Brock solo LP, *Earthed To The Ground*.

Dismissing 1983's *Zones* as "an unkempt, ratsass bootleg of an album which should never have seen the light of day", writer Steve Keaton was more complimentary about the two more recent albums and he said of Hawkwind: "My schooldays live on in their shadow. The legend is nothing short of daunting." Such declarations are still frequently heard today.

Asked how it felt to have become an institution, Dave declared: "It doesn't matter to us at all. We just carry on regardless. All we want to do is put on a good show and enjoy ourselves. That's the prime objective. We don't make a lot of money out of this. We're not fantastically rich or anything. Most of our money goes back into shows."

"Or other people's pockets," added Huw, drily.

Only a few months later, in November 1984, Flicknife released yet another live Hawkwind album. *Stonehenge: This Is Hawkwind Do Not Panic*, despite its title, includes only two tracks recorded at that year's festival – 'Stonehenge Decoded' and 'Watching The Grass Grow'. The rest of the material dates back to December 1980 when Ginger Baker and Keith Hale were in the group.

Melody Maker responded with a downpage review accompanied by a large photo of a smiling Nik Turner. Mark Jenkins' assessment was mixed, criticising 'Space Chase' for tunelessness and 'Psi Power' for falling short of its potential while praising 'Levitation' as a "superb anthem", 'Circles' for summing up "everything Hawkwind have ever been" and 'Angels Of Death' for its guitar/synth duet.

It didn't chart.

Meanwhile, Kris Tait had written a book titled *This Is Hawkwind Do Not Panic*. She had become an increasingly active member of the entourage, having graduated from running errands and helping the caterers and stallholders to taking over the merchandising herself. Now it was in-house.

On the November tour which was set up to promote the album release, Kris sold copies of her book as well as T-shirts and all the other paraphernalia that the fans flocked to buy. She was learning about the lights, sitting in with the crew and covering for anyone who had to nip out to the toilet. Kris was making the most of the live experience, starting to figure out exactly what it took to keep the show on the road and running smoothly.

Dave and Kris were now living in a house right at the edge of a cliff in Seaton, a resort in south-east Devon. Idyllically placed, it would later become a bit of a nightmare when the cliff started crumbling, taking with it the public footpath encircling their garden.

All things considered, Kris was in just as much of a dangerous situation as her clifftop home. She had become indispensable to Dave, she was his partner in life and in Hawkwind, and that simply was not sitting too well with certain people in and around the band.

There were, she says, concerted efforts to split her up from Dave Brock.

CHAPTER 20

Three Walnuts, A Hazelnut And The Head Of Yuri Gagarin

"I'VE been as happy as Larry since day one," says Alan Davey of Hawkwind.

"We play real music. There are no gimmicks or flashy edges. Everyone can appreciate real music, like jazz was appreciated in the Fifties by everyone from rich businessmen down to poverty-stricken black people. It's the only time you'd see all these people in the same room. Like the old Charlie Parker stuff, his gigs being full of the most amazing mix of people. He played for real, no gimmicks. None of us are what you would call shit-hot technical musicians. All my fingering is wrong on the bass. Technically, it's very badly played bass. But it doesn't matter. And Dave doesn't know music. None of us can read it or write it. It's all about feel."

Alan was born on September 11, 1963 in Ipswich, and brought up there. He attended Nacton Heath Comprehensive – "a very rough place at the time" – and grew up with a great liking for Chuck Berry, Little Richard, Elvis, Bill Haley & The Comets and all the other great Fifties rock'n'roll stars.

At 14, he was given a guitar by his parents, but he showed no interest in it. And then, a year later, he became fascinated by his elder brother Andy's copy of *Quark Strangeness And Charm*. Alan, a huge *Star Trek* and sci-fi addict, loved the "spacey noises". But it was when he heard Andy, a confirmed Hawkwind fan, playing *Doremi Fasol Latido* that Alan became an instant convert.

"'Time We Left This World Today' came on, with Lemmy's bass solo in the middle," he says, "and something switched on – 'I want to make this noise, whatever it is.' I was such an idiot, I didn't know what the instrument was. This guy I knew had a guitar shop and I played it to

Robert Calvert, the vividly imaginative if turbulent writer who had inspired and helped to shape Hawkwind from the outset, joined them at the 1975 Reading Festival in a soon-to-be familiar outfit described by *NME* as "a cross between Biggles and Lawrence Of Arabia".

(LFI)

After sacking Lemmy in 1975, Hawkwind were, left to right: Nik Turner, Simon House, Alan Powell, Dave Brock, Simon King and new recruit Paul Rudolph. Says Lemmy: "I wasn't indestructible, but you can't replace me with somebody who puts their leg up on the drum riser and plays a jazz solo." *(Tony Russell/Redferns)*

Paul Rudolph left the band at the end of 1976 – in part because he was too good. Dave Brock admitted feeling intimidated by Paul's musical proficiency, while both Brock and Nik Turner believed he was conspiring against them individually with other members.
(Dave Brock Collection)

Hawkwind asked an old friend, Adrian Shaw, to replace Paul Rudolph early in 1977. "Adrian's a very fine bass player and a nice character," declares Dave Brock. "We always got on wonderfully well."
(Dave Brock Collection)

In 1978, Dave Brock formed the Devon-based Hawklords with Robert Calvert. Dave, pictured (left) on the road with Caroline Guinness, friend and rescuer of keyboard player Steve Swindells (right), says: "It was quite an intensive show. The set was very successful."
(Steve Swindells Collection)

All out of funds but catching some rays and flexing their muscles (or not) at Rockfield's Mill House in 1979 are, left to right: Dave Brock, Harvey Bainbridge and Simon King.
(Steve Swindells Collection)

Martin Griffin on the Hawklords tour bus in autumn 1978. He says, "The front end of the tour was distinguished by the fact that either the PA, or more likely the lights, blew the main circuits at every venue, every night, more than once."
(Steve Swindells Collection)

Harvey Bainbridge, snapped on the bus, was at the beginning of a decades-long association with Dave Brock and Hawkwind. His abiding memory of that tour is that, "Bob [Calvert] was constantly getting a bit over-excited and having to go and calm down."
(Steve Swindells Collection)

Robert Calvert (left) with Steve Swindells
who contends that, "He was on top form on
the Hawklords tour, very compelling to
watch. Calvert and I got on particularly well."
(Steve Swindells Collection)

Dave Brock breaking out of the "pressure,
stress and worry" of the Hawklords tour.
When it was all over, he says, "We decided
we'd go back to being Hawkwind again."
(Steve Swindells Collection)

Robert Calvert on stage with Hawklords. As the tour progressed, said Harvey Bainbridge,
"He got himself wound up and ended up having to go into some sanatorium again, I think."
Calvert's marriage to novelist Pamela Townley, which had taken place a year earlier at
Caxton Hall, on November 5, 1977, was already starting to hit the rocks.
(left: Stevenson, right: Hulton Archive)

Hawkwind were one of the first bands to use digital technology when they recorded their *Levitation* album in London's Roundhouse Studios in the summer of 1980. Engineer Ashley Howe (left) and Harvey Bainbridge mull over the possibilities. *(Dave Brock Collection)*

The eccentric keyboardist Tim Blake – nicknamed Gollum - joined Hawkwind in 1979. He confides: "It was a very strange set of circumstances. Sometimes one's destiny makes itself clear, and this was one of those times." *(Fin Costello/Redferns)*

For more than a year, until the autumn of 1980, the five-piece Hawkwind line-up was, left to right: Tim Blake, Harvey Bainbridge, Dave Brock, Simon King and Huw Lloyd-Langton. *(Fin Costello/Redferns)*

Ginger Baker had already left Hawkwind when he was snapped at Glastonbury in 1981, strolling the grounds with two dogs including the ever-present Toerag – the larger, dark companion by his leg. *(Dave Brock Collection)*

Lemmy has frequently returned to Hawkwind for special events, and in 1983, he joined Dave Brock in Devon to record 'Night Of The Hawks'. Dave: "It was jolly fine. He brought his girlfriend with him. He had a Sunday dinner and he promptly fell asleep in the chair. It was the home-made hash cakes... " *(Dave Brock Collection)*

Kris Tait made her tour debut as a dancer and theatrical performer with the Choose Your Masques outing. She says, "We were on these strange podium-like things. They had lights all the way round the bottom, like aircraft landing lights, and when they put them on, it looked like you were dancing in tubes of light." *(Dave Brock Collection)*

Nik Turner, with his "unicorn" tuft of hair and black eye mask, and Dave Brock, front right, meet cross-armed magician Paul Xenon backstage at the Liverpool Empire in February 1984 on the Night Of The Hawks tour. Xenon would go on to TV success in America. *(Dave Brock Collection)*

Stonehenge 1984 was a memorable occasion for everyone involved with Hawkwind. Harvey Bainbridge (left) made a sudden but permanent move from bass to keyboards, and vestal virgins were hastily plucked from the crowd and dressed in white for the solstice performances. *(Dave Brock Collection)*

Dame Vera Lynn cosies up with Dave Brock and smiles for the (blue) birdie at an anti-heroin festival held at the Crystal Palace Bowl in August 1985. Harvey Bainbridge comments: "She still had an amazing voice." *(Dave Brock Collection)*

Hawkwind take to the stage in the winter of 1985 with the Black Sword tour – a spectacular, costumed dramatisation of Michael Moorcock's Elric stories. "It was a marathon of organising," recalls Dave Brock.
(Dave Brock Collection)

him. I said, 'What's that instrument?' 'Well, it's a bass.' That was it . . ."

Alan acquired his first bass after doing a deal with his mum. She bought it on HP and he paid it off, week by week, with money from his first job as a butcher's delivery boy, taking food to housebound customers.

Alan started thrashing along to Hawkwind LPs and by 1981, was playing bass in a band he formed with his cousin Nigel Potter. They dallied with several names – Stallion, Stormbringer and Chainsaw – before settling on Gunslinger and setting up gigs for themselves. "We used to play in Ipswich," recalls Alan. "Just about every gig we played we got banned from 'cos it was too loud and raucous. We did six gigs or so, and that was about it, really."

Nevertheless, Gunslinger nearly got a break through the weekly music paper *Sounds* who had teamed up with Neat Records in New-castle to launch a talent search.

"We banged up a demo and sent it off," says Alan. "We got right through to the last two. There was us and Raven [New Wave Of British Heavy Metal band from Newcastle]. Neat Records offered us both a record deal. And then our drummer bottled out. He didn't want to give up his job to go off, and we couldn't find another drummer in time, so they didn't pick us up."

Despite their setbacks, Alan and Nigel persevered in the local area. "It was only a little place for gigs, Ipswich, at the time, and we ended up changing the name of the band just to do gigs," says Alan. "We became Merchants Of Sorrow very shortly before I left, and Nigel carried on with a different bass player."

Meanwhile, Alan had been training as a joiner making pub fittings. "All that moulded wood on bars, mahogany doors, rails . . . I got a City & Guilds in that. Then I gave that up and tried my hardest to get into Hawkwind."

It might have seemed like a fan's impossible dream, but Alan approached his mission practically and optimistically. "My other brother Steve encouraged me to write to Dave," he recalls. "He said, 'Every time I come round here, you're playing along to Hawkwind records.' Fate was controlling it. Brian Tawn was doing *Hawkfan* magazine at the time. I sent him one of the tapes that I'd done with Gunslinger and with this tape, I sent a letter to Dave. Brian sent it on to him.

"I'd seen all the great gigs – Hawklords, the tours for *Levitation* and *Sonic Attack*. Then I saw them in March 1984 and I thought it was the worst band I'd ever seen. Nik Turner and Dead Fred were in it, people who were not really Hawkmen. It was horrible, awful. I thought, 'What's happened to them?'

"In this letter to Dave, I said, 'Hawkwind should be going in a direction where you use the technology of *Church Of Hawkwind* and mix it up with the old *Warrior*-type music – the typical, chuggy rock but using technology.' Dave phoned up and totally agreed with me."

Alan was invited for a jam at Dave's house, and then came Stonehenge, and all of a sudden he had joined the band to the surprise of Harvey Bainbridge. "I remember speaking to Dave and saying, 'It's so good what Harvey does. He shouldn't really be out of the band. He should be playing keyboards. He's perfect for this idea of mixing the old with the new.' Dave said, 'Are you all right with that?' I said, 'Of course I am.'"

In time, Alan's role would expand to that of bassist, synth player, singer and songwriter. It wasn't long after he joined that he also set in motion an occasional band called Snorkwind, usually with Danny Thompson and Huw Lloyd-Langton.

"That was when Danny and I were still living in Ipswich," says Davey. "Huwie was only an hour and a bit away. When Hawkwind weren't working, we'd go out and do the odd gig here and there. We did Hawkwind numbers, a couple of Huwie ones and just jam. We did some nice little gigs. We did one in Ipswich, a couple in London somewhere. We did free festivals that Hawkwind couldn't make."

Huw had already been playing in his free time with his own Lloyd Langton Group, which he describes as "a bit of a fluke".

He explains: "Originally, I was asked by Flicknife if I had a track to contribute to one of the first *Friends And Relations* albums. I said I had various songs I'd written over the years that weren't really Hawkwind material. I was quite keen to put a track down so long as I could get the go-ahead from RCA and everybody. But the management at the time didn't want to go against contracts and whatever else. By the time I'd been given the go-ahead, the album had been done, so Frenchy suggested I do an album of my own. Then so much Hawkwind stuff was coming out, it was agreed eventually to just put out a single, which went into the old heavy metal charts."

Lloyd Langton Group would go on to release a string of albums and singles through the Eighties and Nineties. Huw continues: "With Hawkwind at that point I was twiddling my thumbs for a lot of the year. I went out and did a few gigs of my own and it just built from there. Knowing that I did this, Alan used to ring me when a Snorkwind gig came up. We played a mixture of stuff, leaning towards Hawkwind. We did two or three gigs in East Anglia."

"You did one up in Birmingham as well," Marion reminds him. "Overall, there were only five or six gigs."

Kris Tait was in an unenviable situation. On the one hand, she was living a happy domestic life with Dave, she was forging her own identity within the Hawkwind organisation and she was contributing uniquely to the theatrical, administrative and business interests of the group. There are past and present members who are devoted to Kris. Martin Griffin remains a caring friend, despite his personal experiences with the band. And Alan Davey sees Kris as "the sister I never had". He says, "She is passionate about Hawkwind. She works so hard with us, and she deserves appreciation for it."

On the other hand, Kris was thrust into the time-honoured female roles once held, however unwillingly, by Yoko Ono (the "interfering wife") and Linda McCartney (the "undeserving participant"). Accordingly, she was treated with suspicion and hostility by those at odds with Dave Brock. Suddenly, Dave had an ally, *an accomplice*, and this was a disturbing development.

Harvey Bainbridge has referred to Kris, rather dismissively, as Dave's "little girlfriend", and he's not above slipping the odd dig into his personal recollections.

"I think that Kris saw herself as the power behind the throne," proposes Nik Turner. "So she instigated things that she wanted to do and that probably helped to create an isolating atmosphere. It was suddenly not 'Dave and the band'. It was suddenly him and her with their own agenda and with her own ambition about wanting to be a dancer or a performer or whatever, some sort of vehicle for her to perform and a platform for her sort of talent, whatever that might be."

Kris responds: "I could have had a well-paid job now if I'd not got involved with Dave. Performance-wise, I've given up more for this band than I've taken from it. At one [later] point, when I had to do all the management stuff, I was getting lots of work as an assistant editor at Tyne Tees and I had to turn down a six-month contract working with Robson Green. A lot of what I've done I've had to do because I've had to jump into somebody else's breach."

Asked how she dealt with dislike and criticism from people involved with Hawkwind, Kris says: "It was more difficult when I was younger. It used to upset me. It's been there from day one. Dave's always been a very solitary character. He never used to go to the pub with them all and be part of their group, and he was quite disliked 'cos he had to make the decisions. They didn't like making decisions themselves, but they didn't like the people that had to do it.

"So when I turned up and I befriended Dave, I became his confidante. He was telling me things. They didn't like that, and they thought they could be closer to Dave if I wasn't around. Other people, for nastier purposes, thought that when Dave was with me, he was quite strong. If they got rid of me and split us up, he'd be an easier target.

"Nik tried to split us up quite a lot. He kept saying to me, 'It's not healthy for you to be with one man,' and that I should get around a bit more. This was in 1984. He tried to set me up to go away somewhere with his girlfriend, and he tried to get Dave to go off with all these girls.

"It was a very definite attempt to split us up. Dave is quite susceptible to people. He's easily wind-up-able. These things did happen. Nik was encouraging him to go and meet people, and he managed to kind of close me out. Not for long. He was trying to get the boys together and detach the girls – 'We can all be boys, have more fun together.'

"It was a worrying period and it was quite upsetting. I could see what was happening but I couldn't do anything about it. Dead Fred's wife Claire told me what was going on. She did a bit of dancing onstage as well. She used to be in a band in her own right. She used to do the *Rocky Horror Show*, just before Fred joined Hawkwind.

"We did go through rough patches, me and Dave. Other people tried to split us up for whatever reasons, but none that I can talk about without affecting the relationships we have with them now.

"It's hard. As you get older, you're not so insecure and upset about what people say. When you're young and vulnerable, in your early twenties, things do upset you. You think, 'Why does nobody like me?' You do."

"Goodness gracious me!" gasps Nik Turner, in response to Kris' allegations. "I've never heard such a story. I'm incredulous, really. I'm amazed. I'm trying to think what that could allude to. I can't imagine how anybody could have thought of something like that. I'm trying to think where such an idea or inference or implication or inspiration could have come from.

"If people go round saying blatant lies about me . . . it's not even as if they're hurtful particularly, but just completely misleading. I just wonder what their motivation is for that. I never suggested she went off with my girlfriend, and I never would have done.

"And then to actually say I was trying to break up their relationship and encouraging Dave to go out having affairs with other women – it's beyond my comprehension. It's not something I could ever imagine thinking up. Nik Turner says it's total rubbish!"

Turner continues: "Maybe they're going round saying these things because they're guilt-ridden. This may be caused by the denial of some reality that they don't want to confront – transfer the facts on to somebody else. Transference mixed with paranoia."

Whatever it was that was in the mix towards the end of 1984, one thing was certain: Nik Turner was about to be sacked. Again.

In December, Hawkwind were working on a new and ambitious project inspired by Michael Moorcock. They were preparing a concept album based on Moorcock's most famous fantasy character, the weak, albino emperor Elric of Melnibone, whose story continues over a series of books.

So popular and so compelling is Elric that Moorcock has dropped and then revived him over the years, notably bringing the character back in *The Dreamthief's Daughter* because it was the only way he could persuade his publishers to release another, edgier novel, *King Of The City*.

"So Elric pays for Danny Dover, hero of *King Of The City*," Moorcock told an interviewer.

Elric has been described as "an heroic anti-hero". He represents Moorcock's idea of the Eternal Champion, continually being reincarnated throughout the "Multiverse". Elric manages to struggle along using drugs and magic until he finds a sword, Stormbringer, which gives him strength by sucking up the life force from people he kills with it. The story follows Elric's journey from treacherous beginnings, in which he murders his true love, collaborates with the demon lord Arioch and invades his own homeland of Melnibone, to his eventual rejection of Chaos in favour of Law.

Michael Moorcock commented: "My characters are just like me. They are as at home with Chaos as they are with Law. They are happier with a bit of both."

He added: "Elric is Pierrot. Under every tragedy sneaks a farce."

It was Hawkwind's intention, with *The Chronicle Of The Black Sword*, to tell the main story of Elric as it existed then, and to perform it onstage when the time came to tour.

Clearly, this was the most significant Moorcock-related project Hawkwind had ever attempted, and the author himself contributed one song, 'Sleep Of A Thousand Tears'. He would also write some original poems especially for the stage production.

Hawkwind, meanwhile, were individually settling down to read the Elric saga thoroughly so that they could coordinate their lyrical, musical and theatrical ideas. "I hadn't read the books before that," admits Harvey Bainbridge. "I sat down and read them, we took the key points of the story and just tried to work on those. We made extensive notes and went from there."

"I suffer from dyslexia," confides Alan Davey. "But I did try to read as much as I could. I did read 30 pages of one part of the story, and I got some lyrics from that. Dave gave me all his comic books with the pictures in, the cheeky sod that he is. It's like the old *Carry On* films. Good job I can take it." (Elric had enjoyed a renaissance in the Eighties as a comic-book star.)

Huw Lloyd-Langton recalls: "A lot of thought went into the album. I went through all six books to get ideas for the songs, and I was a bit miffed at the end to find out you could get a synopsis of them."

"I read that lot, I did," remembers Dave Brock. "I read all the books. We all did, and we condensed them down. Lots of Michael's books go off at tangents, it goes on for ages, and then they come back to the main storyline again. Over five or six books, trying to do a stage show is quite difficult . . . how Elric managed to find the sword and became addicted to the sword and how it took all his loved ones away – the story of the sword. But you could condense it down into one quite exciting story. It was written by all the members of the band. If you look, you'll see that everybody's written stuff on this."

That is, everybody except Nik Turner. Says Nik: "We were rehearsing at Rockfield preparatory to recording an album based on one of Michael Moorcock's characters, Elric, and in order to put the thing together, we were writing songs and I was reading all of his books. I said to Dave, 'Have you read the books?' and Dave said, 'Oh, I can't be bothered.'"

Brock obviously contests this.

"Huw said he thought they were really boring," continues Turner. "I was précising the books and writing songs based on them. I wrote about six songs. I went home and while I was away, I was phoned to say there was a meeting with the management [Jim White]. I thought, 'I don't need to be there. I'm reading all these books.' The next phone call I got from the manager was saying I'd been sacked.

"I think then I phoned Dave and Dave said, 'Oh, the band have sacked you.' I said, 'Why's that, then?' He said, 'They've all got their reasons. It's not me.' Then I thought I'd like to talk to these people, so I went to see them at rehearsals and had a little meeting.

"They had all these angles they'd decided on using as reasons. Huw Lloyd-Langton said, 'I think you're trying to turn Hawkwind into a punk band.' I said, 'Well, what's wrong with that, exactly? What do you mean by punk band?' I'd been wearing make-up and I had a big spike of fluorescent hair. It was a wacky sort of thing. I envisaged this as being some sort of alien from outer space. But I was 'turning Hawkwind into a punk band'.

"I think Harvey was okay. He didn't seem to be perturbed by me being in the group. Alan Davey said, 'Oh well, my mate thinks you're not what Hawkwind should be about.' I didn't get out of him what he thought himself.

"I'd sussed this out before in a conversation with Clive Deamer who said, 'Quite honestly, I think it's great that you're in the band.' He said, 'Dave phoned me up and said, "What do you think about Nik being in the band? Don't you think he ought to leave?"' Clive said, 'Not really. What's the problem?'

"That's how I saw the light. I put two and two together with the management company. It's exactly what had happened with Tony Howard, which was another deal that I'd instigated. It's a pattern of how managements manipulate. They want an easy life and lots of money. I feel that they saw me as a bit of a loose cannon. I wasn't predictable or controllable, and I wasn't kowtowing or arse-licking. I would question everything. I would say, 'What's that for? Why are you doing that?'

"Because I'd helped to set up the management situation, I had some sort of position of authority and I was not susceptible to all the bullshit that people were trying to impose upon us. So I was sacked for a second time. I thought it was about time I learnt my lesson, really.

"It gave me an insight into the whole scenario. It's Dave that's in control of it, and that's all there is to it. His role model is probably someone like Don Arden.

"Don Arden was described to me by Viv Prince. One musician went to Don and said, 'Can we have a look at the books?' He said, 'Do you want to look at them before I break your fingers or after?' That's the kind of ethos that I see as being quite a common thing in the music business. Col Tom Parker was a role model for the lot of them."

And finally: "They didn't use any of the lyrics that I'd written for the *Black Sword* album."

Dave Brock wonders: "Why did we get rid of Nik in 1984? I can't remember. 'Cos he was a naughty boy. I honestly couldn't tell you. That was Jim White. I would think it might have been because he was playing out of tune all over the place and we just had enough of it. The trouble with Nik, his playing's not fantastically good sometimes. He might look good jumping around onstage, but at the end of the day, we formed the band because we wanted to play music.

"Then he went off with Gerry Cottle's Circus. He went off to be the ringmaster where he could honk on his saxophone and dress up like a clown. We went up to Clapham Common to see him when he was doing it. There was hardly anybody there and it was rather wishy-washy, really."

"I was the musical director," corrects Nik. "It was a big, proper circus in the park and it was interesting learning other sorts of music, circus music."

Huw Lloyd-Langton ventures: "I don't know exactly why Nik was asked to leave Hawkwind. I think certain people got a bit fed up with his antics and just honking over things. Mind you, *I've* been told off for playing over things in the past – by Dave, normally.

"Nik definitely caused the band to be far more punky. I didn't particularly like it myself. It was too raucous. He definitely leans to being the grandfather of punk. I never saw Hawkwind as being that. As a part of the group, he was great, but I just felt at times that he was almost trying to take over, and I didn't really want to work in the 'Nik Turner Band'.

"I think there was a certain amount of power-tripping or ego-tripping going on. There was a gulf between Nik and Dave anyway."

Both Nik and Dave have attested that when Turner rejoined Hawkwind in 1982, there were no particular problems between them.

However, Marion Lloyd-Langton is sure she sensed an undercurrent even then.

She says: "It started going wrong between Nik and Dave from day one. Nik thought he *was* Hawkwind, and he wanted to control the band. He gave that impression to everybody. There was a lot of enmity, certainly more from Nik's point of view. Nik kept going on and on about the original Hawkwind. But without Dave, there wasn't a Hawkwind. I didn't think Nik had earned the right to be so forceful.

"Like Ginger, he blew it, even though he was liked within the band and, don't forget, he's talented. But it was a democratic band. And there was one member who was not even consulting the group and ending up with the most outrageous costumes which didn't fit with anything else really. It wasn't part of a lovely theatre where you're all dressed up. It wasn't something they'd all agreed. Nik had his own audience and he always has had. Inner City Unit – now, *that* was Nik."

Alan Davey, never a fan of Nik Turner, shares his feelings about the sacking: "We'd done a tour [for *This Is Hawkwind Do Not Panic*] and I'd spoken to a lot of Hawkwind fans. I was out wandering about and meeting people and everybody I spoke to thought, 'Why is Nik in the band? It makes it look stupid.' I used to like it when there was hardly any chat at all and the atmosphere was going all the way through from start to finish. The fans didn't like this clowning around. It spoilt the whole mood. I didn't like it. We weren't a cabaret. We were a deep space-rock experience.

"Nik had been wearing these silly things like dustbin liners. He used to get people to rip them off so he could expose his three walnuts – but we won't go into that . . .

"There were endless bum notes. That's what shocked me the most. We were playing with really good musicians like Harvey and Huwie, a great lead guitarist, but Nik I couldn't believe. There were so many bum notes all night every night that it was embarrassing. It put you off. You're playing and getting into the space and just enjoying it, and it really ruins the atmosphere."

Alan remembers being confronted by Nik Turner. He says: "I told him no one I spoke to wanted him in the band any more. He didn't say anything; he just walked off. I've never done anything bad to Nik, I never slated him in public, but he's hated me ever since. I remember someone told me Nik had said something about me being a 'hazelnut', whatever that means. But we all thought he was spoiling Hawkwind. It wasn't working at all."

Nik was not without his supporters. There were and are many fans who insist that he was crucial to their enjoyment of Hawkwind, there are ex-members who believe that musically and ideologically he personified the spirit of the band (including Dave Anderson, who still refers to Nik as "my captain") and there are industry associates including Frenchy from Flicknife who are convinced that Hawkwind were insane to shed so readily such a popular and charismatic figure.

Harvey Bainbridge declares: "I've been over to America twice in the past three or four years, and Nik has joined in on my set, which is good. Nik's all right. An awful lot of things are said about his sax playing and how he would honk across everything, which he did have a tendency to do. But I can remember him rehearsing quite intensively during the day when Hawkwind were getting ready for an album or a tour. He works hard. He does a lot. He keeps going. More power to his elbow, really."

It's called *Bring Me The Head Of Yuri Gagarin*, and it has caused more trouble than any other Hawkwind album.

Named after Russia's Gagarin, the first human being in space, it was released in January 1985 by Demi Monde Records and it captures live recordings from the Hawkwind gig at Wembley Empire Pool on May 27, 1973 with tracks including 'Orgone Accumulator', 'Urban Guerilla', 'Master Of The Universe', 'Welcome To The Future', 'Sonic Attack' and 'Silver Machine'.

The man behind Demi Monde Records was the former Hawkwind bass player Dave Anderson. And today, nearly 20 years after releasing *Gagarin*, he is still under attack from band members who have not seen any cash from the album, despite the fact that it has since been re-released in various guises on different labels. Anderson replies that it has never recouped the costs and that no royalties are therefore payable.

So controversial has it become that Hawkwind website Starfarer recently published an article purporting to list all known versions of the album under the heading, "Bring Me The Head Of Dave Anderson".

This enraged Anderson, who insists that if anybody's head should be served on a platter, it's not his. And he vigorously rejects allegations that he is linked to a host of other bootlegs.

He explains how it all began: "*Bring Me The Head Of Yuri Gagarin* was the third Hawkwind licence I did. I licensed it from Nik. Previous to that, I'd licensed two albums from Dave Brock, who gave me a whole lot of tracks. I really can't remember what the albums were called. Also, after I'd done the *Yuri Gagarin* album, I licensed from Dave *Space Ritual Volume 2*."

That album features live material from the London Brixton Sundown in December 1972. Dave Anderson also owned the rights to *The Text Of Festival*, an album of really early recordings. "It only came out for a very, very short time," says Anderson. "So that's the entire selection of licences I had. *Bring Me The Head Of Yuri Gagarin* I only did as a favour to Nik."

Nik Turner says: "I had this tape of Hawkwind which I'd had recorded on my own machine in 1973. I was seeing all these bootlegs going out that I wasn't getting anything for. I thought the gig was a monumental event and I'd like to release a record as a bit of an occasion. I instigated the release of *Bring Me The Head Of Yuri Gagarin* on Dave Anderson's record label, Demi Monde. I think I got £1,000 up front to cover my expenses. I never received any royalties for it.

"I did an album, *New Anatomy*, with Inner City Unit in Dave's studio in Wales and that was also put out on Demi Monde. Later, I discovered that Dave Anderson had cross-collateralised *Yuri Gagarin* against my share of *New Anatomy*. I was quite pissed off – this is not something I'd agreed to at all. Consequently, I never got any royalties from it. I had been expecting royalties, which I could pass on to Doug Smith to distribute among the band members who'd been involved. I released it with good intentions of accounting to everybody who was on it – it wasn't some private deal I had – but I never got any accounts.

"Dave Anderson sub-licensed the album. And I had no control or dealings with it after it was released originally. Had I known what was going to happen, I wouldn't have allowed it. But I wasn't consulted. It's something I'm trying to sort out with Dave Anderson, and we're trying to keep things on an amicable level rather than any sort of recriminations or, 'Fuck off, you ripped me off.'

"I'm working in a band with the guy [Space Ritual] and I'm not all the time being suspicious. Life's too short. I just assumed people would do the decent thing. There are certain things I'm not happy with, but there's not a lot I can do without taking my friends to court. And 'friends' may take advantage of the fact I don't really want to take them to court. Justice is for the rich. I just pass it all back on to karma."

Anderson says of the cross-collateralisation: "That's just normal music-business policy. In Nik's case, he had advances, he had Hawkwind and Inner City Unit albums, so they got bundled together. You can't have a separate account for every artist for every single release. And the albums didn't recoup the advances."

Dave Brock says: "*Bring Me The Head Of Yuri Gagarin* has been issued 24 times. That we know. It's come out under 11 different titles. They repackage it, and fans keep buying it thinking they've got a new one. It's been issued with up-to-date pictures of the band, with Alan Davey. It's had pictures of the 1989 line-up with Harvey. It's been licensed all over the world. When we were trying to get a record deal, they'd say, 'But you've got one out.' And it's awful. It's a bootleg. Dave Anderson has never paid out a penny. He keeps saying, 'It's nothing to do with me.' "

Dave Anderson begs to differ. Further, he declares that he wants to nail the whole argument once and for all.

He states: "I do legally own the rights to the albums I've mentioned, for which Dave Brock and Nik Turner signed contracts and received payments from Demi Monde. These contracts stated that Dave and Nik had the legal right to sell the material and if there was any dispute, they would be sued by Demi Monde for compensation.

"The albums were legitimately released on the Demi Monde label and later licensed in various ways to Charly Records, Illuminated Records, Magnum Records, Spalax France, New Millennium and, finally, Cleopatra Records USA to whom I only licensed *Space Ritual Volume 2*. All of these licences finished years ago and now only the Cleopatra contract is current. It's all legit, all above board.

"It's said I put lots of albums out. I know exactly who I've done licensing deals with, and I don't know half of the companies I've been accused of being involved with. To go out and physically try and license 100 or more bootlegs is just ridiculous."

Given Brock's assessment of *Yuri Gagarin* being released 24 times under 11 different names, Anderson responds: "I think that's Dave exaggerating. I've already named the companies that had the rights to it. They don't have the right to license it further on. Each was a one-off licence just to them. Any version of the album that hasn't come through those labels I am absolutely not responsible for.

"I am not responsible for releases by *any* other labels. In fact, I'm taking steps to establish who supplied those recordings so that I can take legal action against them."

Talking about the contracts drawn up with Brock and Turner, Dave Anderson continues: "I didn't do that much with Dave compared with Frenchy from Flicknife, although I worked with much heavier contracts than Frenchy did. They were signed and witnessed. Douglas has got copies as well."

Dave Anderson adds that he supplies the accounting to both Nik and Dave for the albums they made available to him, although he admits that the statements are "somewhat infrequent".

"There are no sales anyway," he states. "The most these albums ever sold was a couple of thousand. *Space Ritual Volume 2* has probably done the best. Even then, it sold a maximum of 5,000 copies. I account to Nik for *Bring Me The Head Of Yuri Gagarin*, and he actually comes here and looks at the accounts whenever he wants, but likewise, I have accounted to Dave for his things, and Doug Smith at exactly the same time, because they work very much together.

"Doug got the accounts sent to him by recorded delivery. If he hadn't got them, he'd never have left me alone. It was always Doug who would approach me. I've still got the correspondence, and the recorded delivery stickers too.

"I don't account regularly, but any time they have asked me for accounts, they've had to give me 30 days' notice to produce whatever it is they've been complaining about. I've done it every time. It's also in the contracts with Dave and Nik that they can have any accountant they want come and go through our books with 30 days' notice.

"There wasn't any money out of those albums. On 2,000 copies, how are you going to recoup? How much did albums used to sell for? £3.90? You've gotta recoup thousands to pay for the manufacturing. The distributors take their cut. You get about 20p a copy."

Anderson says that although Demi Monde received advances for the various licensing deals, these were still not enough for the albums to recoup – "'cos you go on to half-royalties."

"With Demi Monde, only one out of 10 albums actually covered its costs. I stopped doing Demi Monde real bloody quick. I did it for probably four years as a secondary thing to my main business, the studio. It was a way of filling up dead time with friends that couldn't get deals with anybody else. My accountants always called Demi Monde my 'charitable organisation' and reckoned I should apply for charity status."

Anderson says that since he signed the deals exclusively with Dave Brock and Nik Turner, it was not his responsibility to pay any other members or ex-members of the band.

Asked if it had then been up to Dave and Nik to split their advances with their bandmates, he answers: "Maybe we should have done it that way round so that everybody got accounted for, but that's not how it was done in those days."

Turner regards his £1,000 advance as an expenses payment. He explains: "On one level, I could say it was taken up by the expense of having the album mastered and recorded. I had to pay for quite a lot of stuff. I was involved in producing it. On the other hand I could say it cost me nothing 'cos it was recorded on my tape machine, I bought the tape and I got a friend of mine to record it from the audience. You could scale it down so it looks as though I'm making £950 profit. How do you quantify what things cost or what they're worth or what your time is worth? What do you consider justifiable expenses? I don't feel guilty about taking the money, and I don't feel I was ripping anybody off either."

As for publishing, Dave Anderson says: "The people who wrote the songs get accounts from the Mechanical Copyright Protection Society and the Performing Rights Society. When you apply for a licence to manufacture, you have to tell them the songs and who wrote them, and they charge you before issuing a licence, so already, you've paid out almost 10 per cent. Nobody from any of the line-ups can say they didn't get publishing money. They all got it."

Anderson agrees that *Yuri Gagarin* might not be the finest Hawkwind album in existence: "I think all the bootlegs are really, really bad. The best that I had was *Space Ritual Volume 2*. The worst of them is actually *The Text Of Festival*. The only reason I released it was that I wanted a share of what was going out. I put one out, Nik put one out and Dave put three out."

Clearly, there's no love lost between the Daves. But Anderson says of Douglas Smith: "I've always liked Doug. I can imagine he'd be a bastard to be on the wrong side of, but he's okay. He's never done any-thing to me. He's said to me in the past, 'I really think we ought to try and sort everything out [over his lack of royalties from *X In Search Of Space*].' I could actually take them to court, 'cos it is now regarded as being illegal, what they did."

Douglas Smith retorts: "It would depend on who the judge believes. Did Dave Anderson get paid a session fee for *In Search Of Space* or was the agreement that he was to sign into an agreement? I have heard two stories."

Smith was not involved in any capacity with either Nik Turner or Dave Brock when they licensed *Yuri Gagarin* and *Space Ritual Volume 2* respectively to Dave Anderson. He only found out about these albums later when he renewed his relationships with Hawkwind and Turner. Douglas claims no knowledge of *The Text Of Festival* or of Brock's alleged initial two licences, saying: "I have only seen one agreement for one album of the three Dave Anderson says Dave Brock licensed him." Dave Brock also does not remember these two licences.

Douglas says of *Yuri Gagarin* and *Space Ritual Volume 2*, the two albums he was aware of: "No royalties have been paid. The last time I heard from Dave Anderson, he said the albums hadn't recouped. I haven't had a royalty statement from him for more than 12 years, and I don't think Nik and Dave Brock have either."

He is almost certain he's never received any accounts by recorded delivery, stating that, "The only accounts I remember getting were from Dave Anderson himself when he visited me," although he allows that, "Maybe there was another set on the next accounting period, but they were still unrecouped.

"He's a funny one, Dave Anderson," continues Douglas. "Although he has agreements with Nik and Dave, his rights to this product, if challenged by one of the other members of the band at the time of release, could be questionable. I'm not aware of any agreements that Dave and Nik have with any of the other members at the time, but Dave Anderson is completely in control unless challenged by an ex-member on the agreements he has.

"But, in turn, Dave Anderson would have a case against both Dave and Nik as they warranted that they had the rights in the recordings from the other members. Dave Anderson knows that the initial cost to mount a case is a few thousand, which many of the ex-members do not have.

"Even if he's licensed the album on to other companies, they'd still have to account the royalties, or Demi Monde has to, whether it's a credit or debit account. A contract works both ways, and the label has an obligation to account."

Douglas asserts that he received copies of the Brock and Turner contracts with Anderson only "many years" after they were signed. He says that Anderson's "somewhat infrequent" accounting – more than 12 years at the last count – is a "material breach", and that he gave up demanding information because Nik and Dave Brock "were never prepared to put up the money to fight him, or didn't have it".

Considering the idea that the albums have not sold enough to recoup, Douglas proposes that, "The publishing royalties might possibly tell a different story."

He suggests that inviting Nik Turner to look at the books is hardly an ideal check – "Sure, he's an accountant!" – and agrees that Anderson's provision for an auditor to examine the books would be a great idea, adding: "It would put all the suspicions to rest finally – but which of them is going to pay an accountant £150 to £200 an hour to get it done?"

Smith insists that, in his experience, 95 per cent of labels like their contracts to be "straight and honest and with the correct stream of rights, which is the basis of any agreement that is straight. That is why there is a warranty clause in the agreements." At the same time, he disputes Anderson's MCPS licence figure of almost 10 per cent, saying that it's 8.5 per cent today and was "much less" then.

Finally, Douglas says of the recordings contained on *Bring Me The Head Of Yuri Gararin*: "Whether done on Nik's machine or any other machine, they come under the terms and the time of the Liberty/UA contract." And *Space Ritual Volume 2* also comprised material controlled by UA.

Nik Turner answers: "I was not actually aware that UA had exclusive rights to all recordings during the period of their contract. I thought that as the band was no longer signed to UA, that one could release product without reference to them."

Dave Anderson and Nik Turner remain friends. Says Dave: "Nik and I have our disagreements on our ways of living, probably. He lives his life one way and I live my life another way. I'm a hippie in my heart of hearts but I run a business. I have to keep myself together, I have to do lots of stuff. I'm not as free a spirit as Nik is able to be because I've got commitments. I just think, 'For God's sake, how come you're in this situation? You've worked your heart out all your life and you're still really scrimping and having a hard time and fighting with Dave Brock.' I do sometimes get frustrated by it, but I love the guy. He's my captain."

Nik Turner says of Dave Brock's objections to *Yuri Gagarin*: "I will counter-claim that he has put out several albums with Dave Anderson, a number of which I'm on and for which I've never been accounted to by Dave Brock.

"His claim that I've put that out and pocketed all the money is a standing joke, but it's something he wants to make people believe. I had a letter from him at one point claiming I owed everybody lots of money from this album. There never was any money. He probably thinks I've got a little business going on with Dave Anderson. But like Jill Calvert, Robert's wife, once said: everything Dave Brock accuses everybody else of is what he does himself. I have done the 'terrible thing' of putting out one album recorded at the Empire Pool, Wembley. There have been 200 or 300 Hawkwind albums out there which I don't get any money for. And the record companies didn't want to touch the band because of the way they'd been ripped off in the past. It's all crap."

Says Dave Anderson: "I fully expect that Dave Brock's name will emerge as the link to all of the unknown bootlegs that have been referred to in the Starfarer site and I feel that their heading should more appropriately have read, 'Bring Me The Head Of Dave Brock'."

Dave Brock would be quick to retaliate . . .

Despite their differences, band members from various line-ups gathered at a hotel in Manchester on February 10, 1985 for a Hawkwind convention.

It had been set up by a long-standing fan called Trevor Hughes, who to the best of Nik Turner's recollection, was running a record shop in Liverpool at the time.

Turner and Dave Anderson had been working on an Inner City Unit album at Foel Studios, and they travelled to Manchester together in Nik's Volkswagen van. Harvey and Dave Brock made the trip in Dave's car. Huw Lloyd-Langton and Alan Davey also arrived, and in Clive Deamer's absence, Danny Thompson went along. Danny had yet to join the band, but he regularly accompanied them on their various outings. From early Hawkwind days, Mick Slattery, Thomas Crimble and Terry Ollis put in appearances.

People had travelled from all over Europe for the convention, with some setting up stalls alongside their British counterparts. The merchandising was a Hawkwind fan's wet dream, incorporating rare records, magazines, posters and photographs. Nik Turner personally took up a pile of T-shirts and items of memorabilia.

The Hawkwind members strolled around meeting fans and signing autographs for several hours. Alan Davey remembers: "It seemed like the hotel might have been hired out for the convention, because there were no 'real' people staying there. It was sold out. At the end, we had a jam in the hotel foyer, which was a really odd place to set up a gig. Mick Slattery was playing. He's a nice guy. I didn't really know much about him at the time."

Mick says: "Trevor Hughes invited me along and made sure I had transport, got me a hotel. When we started playing, the only person I knew from the past was Nik. Dave didn't appear."

"It was quite hectic answering questions for four or five hours," reflects Brock. "It was the first and only big convention until we started doing the Hawk festivals ourselves. There was a jam at the end, but I didn't do that. I'd had enough of it all by then."

Dave Anderson recalls: "I got the chance to meet and talk to the people. Dave Brock followed me round everywhere I went. I did some interviews and he sat in the chair right behind me listening to every word I said. He was vibing me the whole time. He was very, very paranoid. It was unbelievable. And after the convention, that was it for me with Hawkwind."

Anderson had joined Inner City Unit on bass after becoming interested in the recordings they were making at Foel. After a year or so with ICU, he would begin working with Robert Calvert in his Krankshaft band – Krankshaft becoming an umbrella term for various Calvert projects, including the short-lived theatrical venture that involved Rat Scabies.

In 1986, Dave Anderson joined The Groundhogs, remaining with them right up to the time of writing when, dramatically, they decided to call it a day. He is now devoting all of his musical energies to Space Ritual while still running Foel Studios. He lives outside the Welsh village of Llanfair Caereinion with his girlfriend. He has had three children, one of whom was quite recently killed in a car crash. His son has a PA hire company and his daughter is a doctor.

Hawkwind, meanwhile, were about to enter into a period of creativity and unusual harmony in 1985, thanks to Elric of Melnibone and his bloody sword.

CHAPTER 21

Free Spirits

THE British dance music scene was in its infancy, and Hawkwind would be directly inspirational in several ways.

Stalwarts of the free-festival circuit, they represented many of the qualities held dear by a new generation of audiences, promoters, DJs, producers, remixers and musicians. They could be relied upon to support people's right to gather and to hear free music. They were seen as environmentally, politically and socially enlightened, campaigning for causes ranging from the legalisation of cannabis to saving the black rhino.

Harvey Bainbridge affirms that despite their personal differences and financial squabbles, all of the band held firm to these allegiances.

They had walked it like they talked it; they had experienced life in communes and squats, and now they were champions of travellers' rights to roam the country freely, living in their vehicles as they moved from one festival to another. As such, they were held in high regard by the travelling community, including the crusties, who would form a solid part of the dance audience. Indeed, Dave Brock, Kris Tait and former member Nik Turner had become closely involved with itinerant groups such as the Peace Convoy and the "tepee people".

Musically, Hawkwind had pioneered techniques which would reappear in various strands of dance music. Their earliest trademarks were the repetitive, hypnotic drumbeats which underpinned their instrumental excursions, and their use of electronics and technology. They had made deliberate efforts to induce a state of trance, or a natural hallucinogenic high. They had experimented with sound effects and samples and, later, they would move into ambient territory.

With Hawkwind had come dancers, a DJ and an emphasis on lights and spectacle, all to become regular sights in the dance arena.

Finally, both parties were closely linked to a specific drug choice. Hawkwind represented pot and acid, visually expressed by the cannabis leaf that appeared on everything from T-shirts to tents and by the psychedelic imagery of their early stage shows. Rave culture had E, symbolised by the ubiquitous smiley-face logo.

Partners Bob and Michael Dog opened the esteemed Club Dog in north London in 1985. For the first two years of its life, the weekly club was held in a TU Centre in Brabant Road, Wood Green. Then it moved to the Sir George Robey in Finsbury Park where it remained until it closed in 1992, giving way to the bigger, monthly Megadog shows in the Rocket, Holloway Road.

Michael Dog comments: "The scene that Hawkwind encompassed was the scene that we came from. Our original inspiration for setting up Club Dog came from going to Stonehenge and an array of other free festivals in the late Seventies and early Eighties. The space-rock scene was part of that, so inevitably, our paths crossed. To a greater or lesser extent, our audiences were the same people who would go and see Hawkwind, and they and space-rock music generally figured as part of the soundtrack, what I and other DJs would play. Our mainstay was a mixture of space rock, dub and avant-garde electronica.

"We put on a lot of bands from that scene – Ozric Tentacles, Here & Now, Third Ear Band – but at the time we may have wished to put Hawkwind on, they were too distant, too expensive and too difficult to book.

"We were meeting with a hard-line brick-wall attitude from the management or agents or whatever: 'If you're not willing to pay this much money, you can't have 'em.' Sadly, that projects an image of a band. I would not point the finger solely at Hawkwind with this. Plenty of the bands we worked with over the 14 or so years we did Club Dog and Megadog achieved a certain degree of success and in the process made themselves inaccessible. I never knew anybody in Hawkwind personally, so I don't know if they were aware of being represented by people who had a hard-nosed business point of view. I was always a big Hawkwind fan, they were a big inspiration to me in my younger years, and I would've loved to work with them."

Michael Dog would later be able to book Nik Turner into Club Dog several times with one of his post-Hawkwind ventures, the Fantastic Allstars, and he comments: "Nik was fantastic to work with. The band were playing jazz and ragtime standards. It indicated the eclecticism of

Club Dog that we could put them on and they would completely tear the place up. I worked with Nik at a much later date at a little stage I ran at Glastonbury. It was the year it absolutely chucked it down. I don't think he was happy with the circumstances of the gig. It was a sad way to end my working relationship with him, 'cos we'd got on really well at Club Dog. It was the complete opposite of trying to work with Hawkwind."

As Club Dog became more popular, bringing in visual performers and off-the-wall acts, a broader demographic section of people began crossing its threshold – hippies, Goths, students, squatters, crusties and "a very wide range of people who were all exposed to the festival headspace, 'cos of the general mayhem and madness of the nights we promoted".

Michael Dog decides: "I think that we brought the free-festival scene and the psychedelic music scene to a much wider audience. It exposed a lot of people to the scene Hawkwind came from and were proponents of."

He adds, as an aside: "I went to score dope from a guy who had a flat in Portobello Road, a few doors up from the Mountain Grill restaurant. He made a great deal of pointing out that some members of Hawkwind used to live in that flat and that a ley line ran through the living room."

Dance writer and author Push confirms: "I heard Hawkwind records at Club Dog, and I was such a fan. It wasn't a dance club particularly. You'd hear some club music and a lot of American stuff, you'd hear Zappa and Beefheart, and Hawkwind were thrown in there as well.

"When the whole crusty thing started to cross over into indie-dance with the Mondays and the Roses and God-awful bands like The Soup Dragons, when people started listening to guitars a bit more – at that point the influence of Hawkwind, which may have been at the back of people's minds, really began to emerge, certainly with bands like The Drum Club, who came out of Club Dog and Megadog.

"By 1990, the whole thing had started to fracture. A lot of the kids may have been into rock music beforehand. They slowly got turned on to dance music a bit more. They didn't want to go down the dance/disco route. They found their own route and it was through bands like Hawkwind.

"A lot of the dance bands did retrospectively recognise that influence and were happy to play with Hawkwind. Hawkwind fans were likely to enjoy a lot of the dance stuff and they needed to hear it in the context of a Hawkwind gig.

"Hawkwind were legends. It was the free-festival thing, the noises, electronica, psychedelia. The idea of playing in a field for nothing, the whole Glastonbury-type connection – Hawkwind were kings of it. That's what people like Spiral Tribe would look at and say, 'Oh, they were the pioneers of what we were trying to do 20 years later.'

"I don't think Hawkwind ever conformed. The dance people, especially the crusty dance people, like to think they're non-conformist, and most of them probably are, and that's where Hawkwind come in. They never were like Led Zeppelin. They were always arguing with each other and changing line-ups. It was a fluid thing.

"I think most of all they were a cultural and political influence, especially on the free rave scene. They were making a statement because they wanted to party and they wanted to party all night and they wanted to party all night for nothing. And that's all right – definitely."

Dave Brock considers Hawkwind's influence on dance culture: "We were always an alternative band, and that keeps on. We always stuck to our space-rock music, which is our niche in the music world."

Dave likens Hawkwind to a jazz band which keeps on going for years with different characters coming in and out, adding fresh ideas to the basic blueprint. "A few years ago, Harvey Bainbridge was doing lots of very dance-orientated stuff by himself, and he had the opportunity of doing a solo tour. He hummed and ha'ed and thought about it for three months and he lost out. He could have done really well in major dance venues. Really, he could have been one of the great, glowing lights, with drum machines and things all running. It was cool, but he never pursued it. He is very talented, but he lacks the initiative to persevere. He needs somebody to prod him."

"A lot of the stuff Harvey and Dave did together is very pulsey," adds Alan Davey. "A lot of these bands like Astralasia and The Chemical Brothers say Hawkwind influenced them. Dave is never afraid to experiment. All the Hawkwind albums are different to each other, and that's what keeps people's interest, but they've still got Hawkwind stamped all over them."

Penny Rimbaud is well known to music fans as a member of the anarchist punk group Crass, a collective who lived together in a commune in Essex. His primary objective has always been to make possible an alternative lifestyle and to fight for the ideals embedded in its culture. He still lives in the commune, which continues to welcome all-comers.

He remembers: "When we first opened up this place in the late Sixties, a lot of the young kids were playing Hawkwind here. In those days, the cult of personality hadn't started. People didn't see each other as being separate. We were all just mucking in, and I don't think music was seen as having any greater significance than anything else. It was something one person could do, and another could make cakes. Music was a part of the whole. You just did things and you didn't really think about what might come of them or what you could make of it. That wasn't the issue."

Penny was not a particular fan of Hawkwind's space-rock, but he admired their attitude. "I helped set up the first Stonehenge festivals, me and a guy called Wally Hope, and inevitably, Hawkwind were always going to turn up or did turn up," he says. "Everyone always used to half-expect them at any of the festivals, and there was a bloody good chance they would arrive there. Their willingness to do people's gigs was inspiring."

This respect continued even after Penny's political outlook became more extreme. "Wally Hope died after the second Stonehenge festival," says Rimbaud. "That had a pretty profound effect on me. It was largely that experience which drew me away from the gentle side of things into becoming more of an activist."

When punk came along and Crass were formed, the band were not interested in aligning themselves with the tabloid capers of The Sex Pistols. Rather: "People like us were a cross between Hawkwind's ideology and punk ideology. Everybody worked together, and we were perfectly willing to get on with things without any money and without any thanks. In my opinion, that's where Hawkwind belonged. They were not part of the industry but part of alternative culture, like Crass later."

Penny only ever came to know one member of Hawkwind, and that was Nik Turner. He believes that Nik has kept the flag flying for the alternative society, and comments: "He stuck at it and he didn't change. As far as I know, he's still at it. I've bumped into him on and off over the years, and certainly by the early Eighties, I felt what he was doing was very much the soft edge of things and what we were doing was the hard edge. Essentially, we were trying to face the same issues in different ways."

He concludes: "There have been an awful lot of people who have paid lip service to alternative culture but were just working their way towards becoming another David Bowie. He was a classic example of someone who shat in the face of alternative culture. I think that's un-utterably detestable.

"It's a long, hard battle which will last until the end of mankind, but we have a culture and it's viable and Hawkwind certainly contributed greatly to that."

Hawkwind were in Folkestone when it happened. If they hadn't been booked for a gig at the Leas Cliff Hall on June 1, 1985, they would have been there too.

Earlier in the year, the Association Of Chief Police Officers, the National Trust, the English Heritage Commission, Wiltshire County Council and other landowners had decided to obtain High Court injunctions to stop the annual gathering at Stonehenge.

Despite this, Stonehenge regulars joined forces to travel in convoy to the stones, where they intended to hold their usual musical celebra-tions. Their numbers included peace activists and travellers from Greenham Common and its "sister", Molesworth Common in Cam-bridgeshire, another proposed missile base where a peace camp called the Rainbow Village had been established and then evicted in Febru-ary. The Bristol-based Peace Convoy also joined the procession.

The events of June 1 were many and ugly. As the three main strands of the convoy came together and drew closer to Stonehenge, they were subjected to a series of road blocks and checks by police. Closer still – between six and seven miles from their destination – the vehicles drove into a trap created by road blocks and were ambushed, close to the A303 and the Hampshire/Wiltshire border. Lines of police ran the length of the convoy, smashing windscreens, showering the families with glass, and arresting and assaulting random occupants.

Meanwhile, other officers were physically attacking a couple of hundred people who had walked to the Stonehenge festival site and peaceably occupied it.

For the travellers in their mobile homes, things got worse when they tried to escape the onslaught by driving off the road and through a hedge into an adjacent field. By the time the Battle Of The Beanfield kicked off at 7pm, all of the travellers' attempts to negotiate a settle-ment had met with threats of arrest. Police reinforcements had arrived in riot gear, and an estimated 1,600 officers from five or six counties, accompanied by military police and, some say, army officers in police uniforms had descended upon the field.

A stand-off exploded into violence which led to travellers, including a pregnant woman, being beaten with truncheons, mothers and babies being dragged through broken windows and children being whisked off into care while their parents were either arrested or rushed to hospital. Estimates put the arrests at anywhere between 500 and 650. The vehicles – the hippies' homes – were looted and smashed.

The day's developments were reported with horror by journalists, photographers and cameramen from *The Observer*, *The Guardian* and ITN news, all accompanying the convoy, along with the Earl of Cardigan who was secretary of the Marlborough Conservative Association and who later attested to the "unspeakable" and "grotesque" police violence he had witnessed.

ITN's Kim Sabido said on camera: "What we have seen in the last 30 minutes here in this field has been some of the most brutal police treatment of people that I've witnessed in my entire career as a journalist. The number of people who have been hit by policemen, who have been clubbed whilst holding babies in their arms in coaches round this field, is yet to be counted."

Nik Davies, home affairs correspondent for *The Guardian*, wrote: "There was glass breaking, people screaming, black smoke towering out of burning caravans and everywhere there seemed to be people being bashed and flattened and pulled by the hair . . . men, women and children were led away, shivering, swearing, crying, bleeding, leaving their homes in pieces . . . Over the years, I had seen all kinds of horrible and frightening things and always managed to grin and write it. But as I left the Beanfield, for the first time, I felt sick enough to cry."

Many are sure that the confrontation had been planned weeks or months in advance by the police. Photographer and convoy member Alan Lodge, known as Tash, declared afterwards: "The berserk nature of the police violence drew obvious comparisons with the coercive police tactics employed in the miners' strike the year before. Many observers claimed the two events provided strong evidence that government directives were paramilitarising police responses to crowd control.

"Things have never been the same since the Beanfield. Throughout the rest of the year, whether in small groups or at events, travellers were continually harassed."

Dave Brock and Kris Tait knew many of the victims of the Beanfield, and they immediately began collecting money to help them, as did Nik Turner with Inner City Unit. A particular friend of Dave and Kris was Lin Lorien – later dubbed "Decker Lin" when she replaced the single-decker bus in which she lived and travelled with a double-decker.

Lin was a veteran of Molesworth, she was involved with the School Bus project for travellers' children and then she became treasurer for the Travellers' Aid Trust, which grew out of Festival Welfare.

She still has the double-decker. It doesn't go too fast these days, but it passes its MOT every time, although Lin has given up the road for a conventional home in Dulverton, Exmoor.

Lin was arrested and had her bus trashed at the Beanfield, an event which was televised on the early evening news. She says, "It wasn't on the next news bulletin. But they had more phone calls about that item of news than anything else that night."

Kris Tait recalls the broadcast: "Lin came running out of the bus with her child, shouting, 'There are babies on this bus!' "

Lin continues: "It was a lovely sunny day, and there was a real carnival atmosphere. Everybody was happy and jolly, and there was music playing. We came across a road block, we pulled into a field, and the police started trashing the vehicles. I sat there all afternoon trying to negotiate and the Chief of Police was not going to negotiate. I think there would have been more serious damage done to people if we hadn't had the TV cameras in there.

"Some of the children who were taken away from their parents went into care in Hampshire and some in Wiltshire. Wiltshire Social Services were really brilliant, but Hampshire were really, really bad. I was released the same night."

Lin then joined forces with other women to claim children they knew, whose mothers had not yet been released: "We reckoned they would be better with friends if they couldn't be with their mums. A girl called Sue had a three-day-old baby at the Beanfield. When we all got arrested, they were trying to take the child from her, and I was shouting, 'Don't let them take the baby!' She said afterwards it was the best advice she ever got."

Dave Brock believes that the idealism of the free-festival scene had already been destroyed. While Tash declared that it died with the Battle Of The Beanfield, Brock contends that it was all over bar the shouting with the festival at Molesworth in the summer of 1984, only months before the resident Rainbow Village had been forced to move on.

He says: "Free festivals were like medieval fayres, with people selling their wares. There was a great camaraderie. As the years went past, it became corrupted. There were lots of bad drugs and people getting out of it. The whole thing was turning sour, just like the Roman empire. A lot of people in the cities realised they could make money selling drugs at festivals. Instead of a free and easy lifestyle, the whole system went wrong. At Stonehenge the year before [1984] there were all these characters sitting on top of buses selling heroin."

And at the same time: "You're trying to keep this wonderful lifestyle but, of course, the Thatcher government didn't want that to happen."

"They didn't understand how it worked," says Decker Lin. "They couldn't understand that people could spontaneously come together and do things."

Harvey Bainbridge remarks: "Over the years we'd done lots of things. We played for Greenpeace, and we were very anti-atomic power when the power stations were being built around the country. But the main thing was the freedom to gather at festivals, which the Conservative government in the Eighties really worked hard at putting a downer on, culminating in the big fight at the Beanfield.

"Things did get a bit more aggressive after that incident. It was quite an intriguing period of time. Everything suddenly turned very political. The powers-that-be were not going to allow travellers to have the life-style that they wanted. A lot of them did work around the country wherever they went, so it was a real shame that everybody got lumbered with this reputation for 'sponging off the state'. Hawkwind at the time were all very passionate about it."

Dave carries on: "It used to be quite easy just to make contact with a few people – 'Right, we're going to go and do a festival on such and such a piece of common land.' Everybody would turn up and someone would get a bit of a stage together, get a tarpaulin up, bring a generator. People would be organised but disorganised in a sense. They came together with a camaraderie. Bands would turn up and play, somebody would put up a bit of money to get diesel, you met similar-minded people and so on. But like I say, it went down the drain, really."

This didn't stop Dave Brock from continuing to support free festivals in the coming years. Together with Kris, he would keep up his network of underground contacts, attend meetings that they held, help to organise festivals and play at them, either with Hawkwind or with friends, often including Harvey and Alan Davey.

Kris says of the Beanfield disaster: "The authorities didn't want to allow the festival because it would have been the 12th year. If you've had a festival on the same place for 12 years with no objections, it becomes like a medieval festival, a right. If we could've had this 12th year, we would have had it forever."

Nik Turner adds: "Whether governments would have actually allowed tradition to overrule what they consider to be the corporate good, not the communal good, is another matter. Squatters' rights are one thing when you don't mind people squatting there, but if you do, you can suddenly take their rights away.

"I was actually very heavily involved in the whole Stonehenge campaign for quite a number of years in a rather peripheral way, and I was allowing my facilities to be used to publicise and promote the whole thing. I was always involved in Stonehenge meetings with English Heritage, but there were things I didn't totally agree with as well.

"I do know that they wanted a representative to speak for the people that wanted the festival and no representative was found. The tepee people were all for enlightenment and groovy peace and love and then there was the Peace Convoy, who had their own agenda of funding their operation with drug-dealing.

"The tepee people were more peaceful, into Red Indian-style principles and spirituality. Smoking a peace pipe – that isn't taking heroin. There weren't a lot of tepee people that took heroin; maybe one or two. There were a lot of very positive people.

"You can make a generalisation in terms of lifestyle. Living in a tepee isn't the same as driving a truck, getting off your face and falling asleep at the wheel. A lot of people in the convoy lived in 'benders' – a similar sort of style to a tepee, but more random in a way. Tepees were usually set up in a circle as a social thing. The convoy's benders and broken-down vehicles were set up in a circle to protect them from police.

"I'm not saying all of the Convoy people were like that, but there was a big drug-dealing operation. I was actually on the Peace Convoy, and there *was* a peaceful, well-meaning element, some very decent people too among the new-age travellers. I wouldn't say everybody was a crusty and a junkie and a Special Brew fanatic, but heroin was openly on sale at Stonehenge and Greenham Common.

"The people involved with the Convoy wouldn't have the tepee people representing them and vice versa, and so there was this disparity between the groups. There wasn't any unity. I was told at this time that the police had said that if there was somebody they could talk to, somebody who would respect their views and probably, as far as they were concerned, respect what the stones purportedly represented, then they didn't mind the festival going on. Because they couldn't find anybody to talk to, they weren't going to allow the festival to happen any more."

Kris Tait doubts this. She says: "I wouldn't say that having a spokesperson would have stopped the police beating people up with truncheons. I'd actually quite like to be an idealistic hippie, to live in Nik's world where everything is simple. I don't remember a big divide between travellers and tepee people either. I remember people in tepees doing drugs as well."

Turner contends that without any agreement being reached with the authorities, the perceived threat from free-festival-goers could not be contained or controlled, particularly in the light of previous incidents: "The police station had been burnt down at the car park in Stonehenge and there were people who went to Porton Down [a military centre near Salisbury, researching chemical weapons] and pulled the fences up. There was a lot of anarchy and revolution in the air and that was too much for the police and English Heritage. They didn't want all that sort of stuff going on. Margaret Thatcher used that whole situation to change the law. She claimed the travellers were drug-crazed hippies and a threat to the youth of the country."

Simultaneously: "I know people who sent out a million leaflets to people all over the country encouraging them to go to Stonehenge in 1985 in the sure knowledge there was going to be a confrontation with police. A lot of people came down in buses and suddenly realised the police weren't going to allow it. The laws had been changed, they gave police the inalienable right to do whatever they wanted to, and they used these laws to justify smashing up people's buses. They used the same laws to stop the miners striking and picketing. That's how they broke the unions."

"After the Beanfield," says Kris, "we collected at the next four or five gigs. We raised about £2,500. The money was needed to repair the buses. People couldn't get their kids out of care because they didn't have anywhere to live, and they didn't have anywhere to live because their vehicles had been taken off them. They had to get the windscreens repaired to get the buses out of the pound."

Hawkwind sent their money to the travellers via a trusted friend, John Pendragon – a leading free-festival campaigner and a prime mover at Wandsworth Eco Village. John had hot-footed it from the Beanfield to a Hawkwind gig with his eye-witness report of the carnage. He has since passed away, from pneumonia, on Easter Monday 1998.

There was an "alternative Stonehenge", of sorts, held in torrential rain at Westbury White Horse Hill three weeks after the Battle Of The Beanfield. Various members of Hawkwind braved the weather and the police presence to perform a set on June 21.

Decker Lin remembers: "They played in the direst circumstances you've ever seen, 'cos the police had taken everything at the Beanfield. What vehicles we'd got back had been stripped. We had very little equipment. We made a stage out of everybody's spare wheels, and put boards on top. We tarped [tarpaulined] over the top of that. It rained and rained and rained. It rained some more."

John Pendragon and his friend – remembered by Kris as a "fat biker type" – arrived at Westbury before Hawkwind did. There, they met up with Nik Turner who was bringing a donation raised by Inner City Unit.

Lin was called to a tepee for a meeting involving Nik, John Pendragon and Brig Oubridge, another important figure in the free-festival scene.

She says: "They were deciding what to use this money for. We'd also got some from Lord Cardigan and an ex-traveller who'd gone to live abroad, who put about £500 in my hand. I was called into the meeting because I was a fairly good judge of what was needed, which was windscreens."

However, the whereabouts of the Hawkwind donation remains a mystery.

"I never saw anything like £2,500," recalls Lin. "There was a lot of confusion at Westbury. Everything was happening so quickly, and it was so wet. We didn't see very much of anything that was going on. There were quite a few different groups within the travellers and the festival scene at that time and it may well have been given to one lot that I would never have known about."

Kris Tait comments: "We just assumed the money got to where it should go. Thinking back, John and the fat guy should have found the Travellers Aid representatives and given it to them to distribute. They may have gone round personally giving money to the people."

Huw Lloyd-Langton didn't make it to Westbury, and neither did drummer Clive Deamer. However, Hawkwind had taken the precaution of alerting Danny Thompson to the event.

Says Danny: "I got a phone call from Alan [Davey] at three o'clock in the morning. He didn't know whether Clive was going to get there. He said, 'Come down here and see if you can get in and play.' The police weren't letting anyone in. I remember driving my car through the blockade 'cos I wanted to play. I think that's what got me into the band, actually. I got on to the site, and it was only us and Roy Harper who were there. It was all very miserable. It was pouring."

Alan recalls: "I was phoning Danny to ask where he was, and the police pulled me out of the telephone box and wouldn't let me use the phone."

"In those days, there were no mobile phones," adds Kris. "We had two-way radios in the convoys, and we had to use phone boxes. They couldn't have stopped us if we had the technology we have nowadays. We used to have certain codes, and we'd ring a number to find out where we were all meeting."

Alan Davey enjoyed Westbury as much as Danny disliked it. He says: "That was a wild weekend. Everyone was happy on that one, jolly and having a really good time. A lot of people had survived the Beanfield and had moved on and we still had a place to do a festival. We'd won again. It was euphoric."

Decker Lin remembers the band arriving. She says: "They were camped just behind my bus, and they were playing at dawn. A bunch of people went and played right by the White Horse early that morning. After that, from Westbury, a lot of people split up into different groups going to different places. A bunch of people entered this place called Stony Cross where the police impounded them all for being illegal. They moved out of Stony Cross, took all their kids and everybody else and walked to Glastonbury – a long way. Michael Eavis was on television saying these people were welcome."

And that is when Eavis set off a chain of events that would lead him into serious conflict with the travellers at Glastonbury.

Nik Turner, meanwhile, was having his own problems at Westbury in June 1985.

He says: "I arrived in the middle of the night. The police said, 'You can't go up there.' I thought, 'Oh, well, I'll risk it.' I wasn't involved with Hawkwind at the time. I'd distanced myself because of my last experiences with them. I didn't even know they were playing there, but when I realised they were, I crashed the stage and started playing with them.

"At the end of the song, I said, 'Me and Dave thank you very much. We have decided to bury the hatchet.' A second later, I heard Dave behind me saying, 'In your fucking head, you cunt.'"

CHAPTER 22

Elric: The Enchanter

VERA LYNN, the forces' sweetheart . . . and Hawkwind. It's hardly the most natural pairing, but it came to pass at an anti-heroin festival held at London's Crystal Palace Bowl on August 24, 1985.

Hawkwind, headlining, had laid on a grand finale of their own, with Lemmy joining them onstage at the end of the set for 'Silver Machine'. After that, however, Dame Vera took the stage along with Hawkwind and many of the other bands who had been supporting at the festival – The Armoury Show, Spear Of Destiny, Balaam & The Angel, Doctor & The Medics, The Comsat Angels, The March Violets and The Enid. Everyone linked arms and sang heartily along to Lynn's classic 'We'll Meet Again'.

Disappointingly for the rest of the group, Dave Brock was the only person permitted to have his photo taken with the great lady.

Harvey Bainbridge comments: "Jim White was managing us then, and he arranged for Dave to have the picture taken. We were a bit miffed – 'Why not the whole band?' Vera Lynn didn't really take much notice of anybody that day. She came out and did her bit. She still had an amazing voice."

Once again, Danny Thompson was at the drum kit, having officially replaced Clive Deamer. Danny was born on November 13, 1963 in London, where he lived until the age of 13 when the family moved to Clopton, near Woodbridge, in Suffolk, and he attended an all-boys private school, Everton House, outside Ipswich. Leaving school, he didn't bother with further education or routine employment: "I wanted to get out and get playing as soon as possible."

Danny had grown up in a musical family, with his father enjoying a fine reputation as the double bass player in Pentangle and as a much respected session musician, working with some of the country's biggest talents, most recently Paul Weller and Elvis Costello.

At 14, the young Danny played cornet in a brass band. Then he tried trombone, but he really fancied being a drummer. "My mum got me a little second-hand drum kit when I was about 16," he remembers. "I was into the New Wave Of British Heavy Metal."

Danny played around the local pubs with a couple of bands, including Traitor's Gate, and it was through them that he met Alan Davey. Alan was in Gunslinger at the time, and was known in the Ipswich area as a massive fan of Hawkwind and Motorhead. They became friends and sometimes jammed together.

In 1984, Alan received the life-changing phone call from Dave Brock, inviting him to play with Hawkwind at Stonehenge. "I think Dave said to Alan, 'Do you know any drummers?' because Clive Deamer didn't usually do free gigs," he says. "The only one Alan could think of who would be able to pull it off was me – instead of his Gunslinger drummer, who I don't think has ever forgiven him."

Soon, Alan and Danny were rehearsing with Dave Brock, preparing for the Stonehenge gig at which they would so surprise Harvey and Huw. "Harvey wasn't very keen on us 'cos he didn't know what was going on," says Danny. "I think he was thinking, 'Here we go again – I'm getting pushed out and someone else [Alan] is coming in.' Huwie was really drunk and he was giving us the evil eye all night. We didn't know all that was going on. I thought Dave was great, a character, really funny. He can be really moody too. He's a one-off. An original.

"I found it all a bit strange. There I was at this festival in front of 30,000 people all totally out of it. It was exciting. It was great fun. I knew none of the songs, but I jammed my way through it all with Alan giving me nods for starts and finishes."

Alan joined the group immediately, but Danny remained in the wings for another year. "I had to do my apprenticeship, show my enthusiasm," he explains. "Clive was still in the band but when they went out on the Do Not Panic tour, Dave would say, 'We're playing here, come and bring your drums.' Clive didn't know what was going on with me setting up my drums beside his drum kit. Maybe I'd go on for the encore. And I used to do the free festivals with them. So I was following them around."

In the summer of 1985, after a string of gigs that included Westbury and Crystal Palace, Hawkwind checked into Rockfield Studios to record *The Chronicle Of The Black Sword*. "I got a phone call saying, 'Turn up at Rockfield,' and I did that," says Danny. "Clive was there. He said he wanted to speak to Dave, he went off to see him, and next thing he'd gone and we were going to record an album."

Some tracks, such as 'Needle Gun' – a fast rocker incorporating the band's signature swishes and swooshes – already existed; Hawkwind had been playing it live for some time. Other songs came together in the studio, and everyone was contributing.

Dave, as usual, was armed with a bunch of compositions, and Huw arrived with three songs. Of those, 'The Sea King' made it on to the album and 'Dreaming City' appeared on the live LP which would be Hawkwind's following release. Alan had written 'Elric The Enchanter (Part II)', 'Arioch' (which would be released as the B-side of the 'Needle Gun' single) and 'The Pulsing Cavern', a co-write with Harvey Bainbridge.

"Me and Harvey got stoned in rehearsals one day and just started playing this thing. Dave came in and he liked it. He said, 'What's that? What's that?'"

Alan had already come forward as an important part of the song-writing team, a role for which he is given great credit, and he established a rapport with Dave Brock from the outset. "Me and Dave, we've always been on the same wavelength," he declares. "If we're mixing or something, we'll have ideas at the same time. We'll look at each other and say them. We think the same things and want the same things for the band. It's very intuitive to work with Dave. You can just jam with him. He can go off leading, and he'll do chords under me, and vice versa. Onstage we don't even have to look at each other.

"He's very funny too. If you sneeze loudly, he'll blow a raspberry at exactly the same moment so people think you're sneezing and farting at the same time. It still makes me laugh today."

Aside from the pranks and the hilarity, Alan concludes: "I'm quite passionate about Hawkwind, probably more so than anybody else who's been in it."

Harvey, meanwhile, was starting to like the idea of specialising in synthesisers. He says: "It was an interesting move. I think I'm a frustrated keyboard player anyway. I enjoy making noises with synthesisers. It's good fun. There's an awful lot you can do. It's another learning curve. I can remember being in Wales trying to find a synthesiser noise that we could use for the sword. I can remember Dave and myself working out routines for moving the story on when there weren't songs."

For Danny Thompson, Rockfield was an eye-opening experience. He says: "Being 21 years old and going into a proper studio and recording with Hawkwind . . . it was fantastic. Some people don't like touring and others don't like recording. I love all of it."

But he had his reservations about *The Chronicle Of The Black Sword*.

"I didn't like it," he admits. "That's when the push-button drumming was all new. The engineer said, 'You don't have to actually play the drums.' Some of it was done like that; they sampled the sounds. I'd rather go in and play the drums. So I don't like that album very much. I like the live one [*Live Chronicles*, the successor]."

Released by Flicknife in November 1985, *The Chronicle Of The Black Sword* attained a chart placing of 65, even though it was and is considered by many to be the product of a revitalised and vividly imaginative Hawkwind.

Frenchy Gloder is adamant: "It was their best album in 13 years. I wouldn't say it was as good as *Doremi*, but it wasn't too far from that. It was much better than the Hawklords, better than most of the Bronze stuff. It was probably one of their all-time five best albums.

"If it hadn't been for the weighing system, I'm sure we would have gone into the Top 30, maybe the Top 10. It sold about 20,000 in a week. The next week it sold another 10,000 and it went down. Another band which I don't want to name sold 10,000 in the first week and they were 10 places below us. They sold another 3,000 and they were three places above us.

"I rang up the people compiling the chart at the time and said, 'How?' The weighing system had worked out that Hawkwind, having many albums out and having an established following, were not in fact doing as well as this new band. The chart positions we got were always lower than they should've been."

The Black Sword tour, which travelled the UK in November and December, was probably the most extravagantly theatrical production of the band's career. Music, lyrics and spectacle came together powerfully in the dramatisation of Elric's story, with performance artist Tony Crerar in the role of the weakling emperor with the cursed sword and Kris Tait playing the part of his lover Zarozinia. They and the group were surrounded at any given time by an all-action army and/or the "creatures of chaos", with Alan Davey's then-girlfriend Sally French also dancing at various gigs.

This was a full-scale extravaganza of pyrotechnics, costumes and elaborate sets and lights – a "marathon of organising", according to Dave Brock. To what extent Hawkwind and their entourage could indulge the spectacle each night depended on the size of the stages. Sometimes they down-scaled, sometimes they pushed it to the max.

Tony Crerar, a Caledonian and a graduate of Australia's IDA – "the best drama school in the English-speaking world" – had known the group since the late Sixties, when both were performing at The Roundhouse. He would later join them onstage at occasional gigs before retreating to Wales to grow vegetables. Later, he was persuaded out of retirement for Hawkwind's Space Ritual tour, their first major presentation, and he went on to collaborate with Nik Turner on his live Sphynx project.

Crerar has extraordinary memories of early Hawkwind, of the live music bouncing back off the pillars in one auditorium so forcefully that the band had to play in the wings, where Stacia also sought shelter, because the sound was disturbing their personal sense of balance. On that occasion, Tony's daughter – who was six or seven – took centre stage in her tutu and held the entire show together visually, small enough to dance her way beneath the disorientating bombardment.

Tony tells stories, too, of the band playing on after worried venue managers had long since pulled the plug. The "straights" were often terrified by the physical onslaught of the music, and police and ambulances were sometimes called to gigs when the volume raised health fears. Tony was once thought dead onstage when one of his mimes was mistaken for a heart attack brought on by the overwhelming barrage. "By God they played well," he laughs. "It was utterly hair-raising."

He was therefore more than happy to take part in the Black Sword tour, although he told Dave Brock he had one condition: he wanted complete control of who was on and off the stage at any given time so that he could rely on the complicated choreography to work. The deal was done.

"The 'Elric' show had been very well prepared," he asserts. "Dave had taken the best visual aspects – which were also the heart of the tale. I came along afterwards and said, 'By damn, I couldn't have done it better myself.' We had about 48 hours to rehearse it."

Crerar "managed to screw a few hundred quid" out of Hawkwind to assemble the fire, clothes, paint and other essentials, and he spent a good deal of it on diesel, driving for miles to try and find people and props. He was greatly helped by the network of "dress-up fantasy people" belonging to clubs all over the country. Up to 20 of these enactment enthusiasts volunteered their services for free as members of the army, and one – who specialised in the Vikings and 14th Century Spanish armour – provided some "gorgeous articulated armour" for Elric. Another few were "very experienced, good costume people and real fighters".

"It took a fighter to learn the dance steps quickly enough and be safe and look as though they knew what that thing in their hand was," explains Tony. "Three or four of them came at different times. On a rock stage with a heavy electronic band whose very expensive gear is everywhere, we didn't want anybody wrecking the keyboards with a sword, smashing the stage or chopping Dave's guitar up. We were on there with real weapons.

"I gave these people my hotel room when there was a pack of them. I found petrol money out of my pocket for the cars pulling in the 'army', and I gave them their supper and a case of beer. I did the tour, myself, for virtually nothing."

The road crew, too, were dressed up and put to work as creatures of chaos or corpse-carriers, and Alan Davey's girlfriend Sally was "brilliant", according to Crerar. "I needed a really powerful female dancer, ideally a Martha Graham type. A martial artist wouldn't do. This girl turned up, she had lovely costumes of her own, she was determined and she was a Hawkwind fan. She was a gorgeous woman. She got on very well with Alan, which was very convenient because I wouldn't have been able to afford her otherwise."

Alan elaborates: "Sally was a contemporary ballet dancer. She did two or three of the big shows. Tony wanted her to dance, and he kept bugging me. I didn't really want to be drawn into it. I didn't think it was my place to start getting involved with the dancers and stuff. I didn't know what the politics were, and I tried to stay out of it. Tony wanted to get her into the show full-time. She'd have been well happy to do it, and I wouldn't have minded either, but it didn't really happen. I didn't want to push."

If Tony Crerar was working on a shoestring to bring parts of the production together, then Hawkwind were also making sacrifices. Just as they had invested their 'Silver Machine' earnings into the Space Ritual stage show, they were now ploughing most of their money into the Black Sword.

Says Alan: "We didn't earn much out of the tour because we spent so much on it. We thought it was worth cutting our wages in half because the fans got a better show. They appreciate it. That's why they come back."

The fans definitely did appreciate it. The enactment enthusiasts who were turning up as a result of the buzz in their clubs, the comic collectors immersed in the cult of Elric, the Moorcock readers, the metal fans and the loyal Hawkwind following were appropriately enchanted, and Tony Crerar was quite unprepared for the cheers that greeted his first unmasking.

He recalls: "I appeared on the stage in my black cape, staggering about almost dying on my feet with a spear in my hand. I pulled my hood off and there was a hell of a roar. I thought, 'They can't remember me . . . they must think I'm Nik Turner.' I didn't know that Elric was a big star in the comic books. I only knew the Moorcock novels. So I was a cult figure. No wonder they'd been shouting – they'd been waiting for Elric."

As time went on, Crerar occasionally found himself becoming possessed by the character he was recreating every night, and it defied all his teachings and better judgements. He confesses: "It's the thing one has to watch out for. One night, one of the chief roadies said, 'You were trying to get past me and you kicked me out of the way.' I said, 'I'm terribly sorry. That wasn't me; that was Elric.'"

Kris Tait, dancing the part of Zarozinia, is amused to relate that Tony took his role as her love interest beyond the stage: "He started putting his arm round me and calling me Zaz instead of Kris, behaving like a husband. He'd be sitting at the table next to me talking to me like I was his wife and ordering me around. I was thinking, 'Tony, I'm not your wife.' He was much more in character than he should have been.

"In the show, we had to hug and be all in love. I fell asleep on his arm with a long, white dress on. The creatures of chaos came on and kidnapped me. Elric went on a quest looking for me and it was a trap. He got weak. I was turned into a slug, although my beautiful face was still there. He'd defeated all these armies and he was going to die. He said, 'I still love you,' but he could never love me, and I jumped on to his sword 'cos he needed another soul, and he saved the world.

"At one show, Tony [Elric] stabbed me right through my hip with a four-foot, pointed wooden sword. It went right through my skirt, my leotard and my leg. I suppose that's how things develop when people start playing the role, they get excited sometimes and don't take care with what they're doing, but I've seen it more in Hawkwind than I have in other theatres I've worked in."

Even Dave Brock was not immune to the magnetism of the albino warrior. He confided to *Kerrang!*'s Dave Dickson at the time: "I find it very easy to actually put myself in the position of Elric. You can draw a lot of parallels between the character and this band. Hawkwind is like the sword, Stormbringer – it sucks the life out of you, it really drains you. I found it very easy to relate psychologically to him and how life shifts from one side to the other."

He also took the opportunity to co-credit Robert Calvert for the idea of performing the Elric story onstage. "When Bob was in the band, we used to talk about doing it but we never got round to it," said Dave. "I suppose we were too side-tracked by science fiction, going off into the future. But now I suppose we've decided to do sword and sorcery for a change – be different!

"We'd been working on the Earth Ritual thing, a projected Space Ritual Part II, the return to Earth, but we didn't have enough money to do that. And in the meantime, I'd been working on the S&S stuff because Michael Moorcock had sent me a lot of his lyrics, and then I thought, 'Maybe we can do Elric instead.' "

Michael Moorcock appeared in person to recite some specially penned poems at the Hammersmith Odeon gigs on December 3 and 4, namely 'The Chronicle Of The Black Sword', 'Dead God's Homecoming', 'Dragon Song' and 'The Final Fight'.

It was a fat set: Hawkwind had also been filling it out with older songs they considered pertinent to the adventures of Elric of Melnibone, including 'Master Of The Universe', 'Angels Of Death' and 'Dragons And Fables'.

This was a generally happy and productive time for the band.

"I'm so pleased I was part of that era," says Danny Thompson. "It was really very good."

Danny, who is unusually tall, was given the opportunity to come out from behind his drums and beat the crap out of Elric, night after night.

Tony Crerar chuckles: "We hung a black nightgown on him and got him to wear Chinese warrior's make-up. I gave him this great club with which he came and battered the stink out of me."

Danny's only restriction was that he mustn't hit Tony on the side of the head for fear of sending his wig flying off into the wings. "I was the Lord Of Chaos," remembers Danny proudly. "I was laying into him. Tony was brilliant. He's a really, really nice guy. That whole thing was such good fun. Everyone got on really well. We were still a big live draw, the Elric saga seemed to go down well, and the atmosphere was great.

"Dumpy [leader of Dumpy's Rusty Nuts] supported us throughout the whole tour, and he was a great laugh. He used to wear his bright green socks and his tutu. On the last night, we were all in a hotel room having an after-tour party and Dumpy was standing in a doorway crying his eyes out 'cos it was all finished."

Danny quickly found his place in the two-car set-up: "Half the band were taking their hot chocolate and going to bed early. I was in the late car with Harvey and Huw 'cos we used to like staying up all night."

Even Harvey enjoyed the Black Sword tour, and he had long ago put a Hawkwind survival plan into action: "It was very difficult, in the mid-Eighties, to keep tabs on what was really going on. It was getting to the point that if I asked Dave something, I'd also ask everybody else about it, and then I would try and piece together what was happening from what everyone had said. In the end, it just gets impossible. You think, 'Oh shit, I'll just get spaced out and let them all get on with it.' That's what I ended up doing. It gets very demoralising after a while.

"I think Dave was disillusioned. We weren't all Frank Zappa. I think that was his problem. If he could have had clones of himself, he would have thought it was the best band in the world."

A harsh suggestion, perhaps – but one that Brock himself has made in Kris' book, *This Is Hawkwind Do Not Panic.*

But the Black Sword tour was, for Harvey, "quite a good phase, actually".

"I was in my element during that tour," enthuses Alan Davey. "I was loving it. It was just, 'Wow!' It was what I always wanted to do and we were doing it seriously, properly. When you get to this level it really hits you. We had two nights at Hammersmith to a full house. I've dreamed of this. A kick beyond all known kicks."

Tony Crerar says: "The tour sold out on word of mouth. We didn't have any posters or big interviews, and this was at a time when big bands were cancelling tours and variety shows were cancelling tours. The promoters or the managers or whoever were too thick to see what this was. It was superb. We knitted together very well. Everybody thought what they were doing was very new and special."

It was Tony's last collaboration with the band. Asked if he'd work with them again, he replies from his home in mid-Wales: "It's very difficult. It was hellish hard work. It's highly athletic. You've got to be superbly fit to keep up. Their numbers would go on for 13 minutes, 20 minutes sometimes, at a hell of a pace. You'd have only a minute, two minutes, to draw breath. It's difficult to find other people who can keep up. But I'd love to see Dave and Kris again."

One person who would not love to see Dave and Kris again is Frenchy Gloder.

Danny Thompson remembers hearing Jim White and Frenchy "arguing and shouting" backstage at Hammersmith on the Black Sword tour.

Frenchy asserts that he became the manager of Hawkwind in 1985 and retained that position for two years. Dave Brock opposes this, stating that Hawkwind's management by Jim White's company Irate didn't finish until March 1986. He adds that while Frenchy was their label boss at Flicknife he was never their manager, although he may have helped out unofficially in that capacity and also acted as tour manager on occasion.

Harvey Bainbridge supports this, adding: "Frenchy did put himself in a manager's position for a while. He took it upon himself. He did put a few gigs together, but it was only for a brief period. There were never any papers signed."

Frenchy says: "Kennedy Street were still promoting Hawkwind gigs. It was more a case of me helping them while they had no manager. Then Dave asked me to do it. I should have said no. Obviously."

While complimenting Brock for keeping Hawkwind going for three and a half decades, Frenchy suddenly declares: "As a person, he left a lot to be desired. He's a real bourgeois, capitalist cunt who plays at being a hippie because it makes more money."

A stunned Dave Brock, who was not aware of any existing bad blood, responds: "It's a very strange thing for Frenchy to say. When we were working with him, we put out the Travellers Aid Trust album, which I got together for him, and all the proceeds went to Travellers

Aid. Lots of things that Frenchy did were good. I haven't got any complaints about him or Flicknife, to tell you the truth.

"His attitude — it's a shame, really, because what he did with Hawkwind was all really positive. He was on the case. He paid the bills at Rockfield. He paid Lemmy for the 'Earth Ritual'. He helped us with the merchandising, writing into the contracts that we didn't have to pay any money to the places that usually took 25 per cent.

"I really can't fault him for anything. I look back over that period of time with quite fond memories. It was only when he started going off the rails in his personal life, when he started taking bad drugs, that things started falling apart . . ."

Frenchy has made a series of allegations about Dave Brock which Dave has chosen to answer.

Frenchy: "Managing Hawkwind, you've got no power. What Dave says goes. If you say black, he's white and that's the end of it. You've got no way you can manoeuvre the band other than by the way he wishes. You can do nothing. It's like being a secretary or a glorified roadie. And what you're supposed to get out of the deal, your percentage, you very seldom see. Dave always managed to get his hands on the money first."

Brock: "He never complained at the time. It wasn't just me doing everything. When we had *The Chronicle Of The Black Sword*, we all wrote parts of it. And when we had the tour, we were all involved in organising it. It's not just Dave Brock. It's Hawkwind. I didn't say, 'We're going to do this now.' We'd have a meeting about it. When we had to make a major decision, we were all aware of it, although with some band members, their attention would wane after 15 minutes. This is the other thing — everybody gets paid by the record company or the publishing company direct. No one else's money came directly to me. Nobody would have allowed that. So it would've been impossible for me to get my hands on the money first. Kennedy Street were promoting the gigs, and we had a tour manager through Kennedy Street. They do all the tour accounts, and this goes through the fucking books. Then it's paid to the tour manager who pays the wages. During the period when Frenchy was helping out on management and tour managing, all the money would have gone through him. And he was perfectly fine."

Frenchy: "Dave has done a lot of licensing to us for full-blown Hawkwind albums such as *Zones*, *Out & Intake* and *Stonehenge: This Is Hawkwind Do Not Panic*. We might have done 25 or so albums [including LPs of archive material]. There were ex-Hawkwind members who didn't know about the releases, let alone getting any money out of them. From time to time, I'd get a letter from one of them and I had to say, 'I've got no address for you. I gave money to Dave Brock in different envelopes with different names on them.'"

Brock: "He might have given me money in envelopes, but if they had people's names on them, each one would have got given their envelope. I'd pay everybody. We all have to sign for these things. You have to account for your money as you do for your tax. People don't just give you envelopes stuffed with cash without you having to sign for it. Who does he mean?"

Frenchy: "Last year at Guildfest, I met Terry Ollis for the first time in my life. We had a long chat and he said he never saw the royalties. Dave wouldn't go out of his way to give money to anyone. It was in cash. Dave always insisted on being paid in cash."

Brock: "Terry ... then he's talking about 1969, 'Hurry On Sundown'. Well, I thought Frenchy was paying them direct for that material. I didn't even know where Terry Ollis lived. Flicknife would have had to pay the royalties direct to the others, not to me. The only thing Frenchy paid me for personally was producing a couple of albums – cutting things together, editing stuff, cleaning it all up and remixing things. He gave me £2,000. That's fair enough."

Frenchy: "We used to give Dave £20,000 up front for a brand new Hawkwind album. That's a good advance for a band like Hawkwind. Dave was making money and he wanted a bigger slice than anybody. He would ask me beforehand, 'Should we do a new album?' We were working pretty closely. On full-blown albums, all the group members were signed, and they had to agree to it. With Jim White, I used to give him the money and what he did with it I don't know. When I was doing everything, I used to give the money to Dave in an envelope."

Brock: "No one would give me a big wad of money like that – 'Oh, here you are Dave, old chap.' I can't remember the band being paid £20,000 up front. They pay you half on completion. Frenchy would have all the figures written down in his accounts. I'm sure he didn't give us that, but you don't know. We sold quite a lot of records around that time. I'm sure that every time we got any money, everybody got a split out of it. Everybody was always moaning about never having any money anyway. We'd work for about two months and then we didn't do anything for six. You had to live on what you got out of those two months. We were at Rockfield Studios a lot, that all had to be paid, and it was paid directly to the studios. It's about £800 a day and then about £1,000 a week for rehearsals at the Mill House. So most of our money would go to Rockfield for the Mill House and recording time."

Frenchy: "Basically, there isn't such a thing as Hawkwind. It's Dave Brock. It could have been a massive band if Lemmy had stayed in, if Nik Turner had stayed in. They could have curbed Dave's money-hunger and shown him that money would come from being a big band. They could have been 10 times bigger than they were."

Brock: "Money-hunger! [Laughs] Well, I wouldn't say that's the case. Money is the root of all evil half the time. It seems like Frenchy has got the obsession with money, not me. There were five of us in the band, but he's focusing on me, same as people focus on Lemmy in Motorhead, because the person they deal with is the band leader."

Frenchy: "Nik Turner was great, Lemmy was great. It's only Dave that's an asshole, which is the reason they all left. Ginger Baker turned out to be an asshole as well."

Brock: "Oh dear! Have I mentioned that Ginger and I are both Leos?"

Frenchy: "The perfect idea of Hawkwind for Dave is Dave and five clones of Dave."

Yet again, Dave Brock's own quip has been borrowed and fired back at him as an insult, although there is little jollity among the former members who continue to accuse him of plundering Hawkwind's history for his own gain or in the solid resistance of the musicians who support him. And as for Frenchy – he has a lot more to say, eventually.

Douglas Smith had gone into partnership on a new label, GWR Records, and Hawkwind decided to forget their differences with him and put some records out. It was a period that would also see a series of releases on Flicknife, and Frenchy remains outraged at their return to their first manager.

He rages: "For years and years, Dave had been slagging Doug Smith off. He was supposed to be the biggest shit on earth. Then Dave goes back to Doug Smith."

"Better the devil you know," counters Brock, shrugging off the criticism.

"It got the finances going again," comments Harvey.

Douglas had rekindled his relationship with Hawkwind simply as a label boss, although he couldn't help slipping back into his old advisory role: the band members knew that they could go to him for guidance when they needed it.

"He was someone we could talk to, we all felt," Harvey explains. "If anything else failed, you'd ask Douglas."

Hawkwind had decided to immortalise the Elric tour. It would be captured first on a video, *The Chronicle Of The Black Sword*, released by Jettisoundz in July 1986, and then in November on a double album, *Live Chronicles*, on GWR.

Says Douglas: "I was a 25 per cent shareholder. David Simmons [his music-publisher friend] owned 25 per cent. The people who owned 50 per cent had bought into the music business. They own CD plants and a packaging company. They had a son in the band Boys Don't Cry, who'd had a hit with 'I Wanna Be A Cowboy'. The father, Ray Richards, had a label with his son, Legacy Records. Ray is also the father of Kim Hurd, who married Douglas Hurd's son.

"Leading up to all this, David and I had been managing Motorhead and Girlschool. Gerry Bron had major financial problems and wasn't doing anything for Motorhead as a four-piece. Nobody was getting anything for it. Both Motorhead and Girlschool were heavily in debt, they weren't selling records and we weren't recouping our money from them. One day Gerry called and said he was under pressure financially. He suggested that if we could raise the figure he needed urgently, he would assign the Motorhead contract to David and myself. We scraped this sum together and within 48 hours, and after 18 months of the dispute, we had got Motorhead off Bronze.

"When Gerry collapsed [financially], Ray Richards purchased the Bronze catalogue. He called to say he was now the owner of Bronze and asked me in for a meeting concerning Motorhead. I told Ray, 'You may have bought the Bronze catalogue, but that does not include Motorhead's future.' As far as we were concerned, Motorhead were in dispute with Bronze and had left the label. Ray asked if David and I would still come in for a meeting, and at that meeting he asked if we would like to set up a label with them that would include Motorhead and others. We thought it was a great way to get the bands re-established and clear their debts."

And so GWR was born.

"Initially, Motorhead received advances which helped them clear their debts and make the first album for GWR," continues Douglas. "Later on Hawkwind brought in an album to me – *Live Chronicles*. I thought, 'This is good. We can release this.' I gave them a very good deal for it, a very good advance."

Later, Douglas would be ousted as a managing director of GWR by the Richards family. The label would be absorbed into the Legacy organisation and run by Kim Richards (Hurd).

Live Chronicles, meanwhile, would be hailed as one of the band's great albums. Dave Brock, who is not easily satisfied, calls it "a good one", Harvey Bainbridge still regards it as "a kind of Hawkwind landmark" and Marion Lloyd-Langton feels, "It's on a par with *Live Seventy Nine*, which was a brilliant album too."

On its original release, it contained none of Michael Moorcock's recitations. The compilation consists of material which was almost all recorded at the Hammersmith Odeon, but Moorcock – still smarting at being taken to court by David Simmons over the Blue Oyster Cult farrago – refused permission for his tracks to appear on *Live Chronicles*, telling Douglas Smith: "No. I'll never do anything for you again."

"The tracks were taken off for the sake of Douglas and his little war," remarks Dave Brock. Douglas prefers to think of it as "Michael's little war".

Harvey adds: "The poems weren't a very big part of the stage show. It would have been good to have them on the album but, at the same time, if you can't get everything you need you have to carry on."

Moorcock's contributions were returned to the album when it was re-released by Griffin Records in 1994.

They may not have been a big-hitting chart act any longer, but in their audience's estimation and in their own rising morale, Hawkwind were riding the crest of a wave.

CHAPTER 23

The Story Of The Support Band

HAWKWIND didn't do a lot of live work in 1986. They played one or two gigs a month, if that, before the big Chaos tour in November and December, which coincided with the release of *Live Chronicles*.

But some of their infrequent summer appearances were especially memorable. There was the British Custom Bike Show on August 23, and then there was the Reading rock festival the next day which found them joined for 'Silver Machine' by Lemmy, who was becoming something of a regular guest, and Dumpy.

"Dumpy had these big motorcycle handlebars," laughs Danny Thompson. "If you blew in the end, they made a funny noise. If you ever hear that version of 'Silver Machine', you can hear this big noise that's Dumpy blowing his handlebars."

It was the year after the Battle Of The Beanfield, and Dave and Kris, followed by Danny Thompson in his camper van, had tried to reach Stonehenge in June in the belief that a festival of some sort might be happening there.

Says Kris: "We thought the authorities might've just stopped it for one year in 1985 because of the 12-year thing. As we got closer, we realised it wasn't to be. But we kept going for a few years anyway. Everybody did. We used to go in the Spring Equinox as well. It was habit. We all went to Stonehenge in the hope something would be happening. Something used to happen somewhere, usually. The police would be trying to split everybody up, and everybody else would be trying to coordinate people and get them to one place."

As they approached Stonehenge, they saw that the police had blocked off the road. "There was a mile-long convoy of vehicles," says Dave. "The police were arresting people for obstruction and handcuffing them – but they were the ones who'd caused the obstruction in the first place. I turned the van round and escaped in the other direction. Nobody stopped us, but a helicopter followed us down."

Kris adds: "I was standing in the back making cheese and toast for lunch, and I'd just picked up a hot kettle when Dave did this U-turn. We pulled into a lay-by that had trees growing over it to get out of sight of the helicopters."

"Dave was a bit shaky and panicky," remarks Danny. "We all had our equipment on board."

It was in the lay-by that Dave, Kris and Danny met another group of travellers for the first time – the band Screech Rock, who were involved in the free-festival scene.

Dave and Kris were fond of their lay-bys. They think it was in 1987, although it might have been 1988, when, accompanied by Alan Davey, they once again had to abort their journey and pull into a lay-by, this time on the A36 at Hanging Langford. There, the three played an impromptu gig on a makeshift stage along with other musicians who were in the entourage.

Dave recalls: "It was a big lay-by. There were only a few vehicles, toilets and a hot-dog van in the lay-by, but all the travellers within a 10-mile radius, when they heard we were playing, they all walked across. There must have been 100 people on the bank watching us."

"I was fire-eating as well," says Kris. "Two police vans came driving in and stopped behind the stage. They started pulling their riot gear on. They thought that because there were only a few vehicles in the lay-by, there were only a few people there. There were eight police. When they saw all these other people standing up, they got back in the vans and drove off.

"Around this time, we made up a board game based on police and travellers. You would go one way and the police would be coming another way; you could go to prison for two days."

Kris had spent part of the year taking a three-month course at a school of mime in London. During this study period, she stayed in Brixton at a big house – The Vicarage – owned by her friend, the Rt Hon Philip Harvey.

"Jimmy Page and Wurzel from Motorhead used to stay there as house guests," says Kris. "Philip was an amazing guy. He'd dine with Fergie, and have dinner parties with butlers, lords and ladies. He also had fabulous hippie festivals. He had a horsebox for travelling in. He liked all the different cultures. We used to call him Lord Crusty. He just didn't fit in at all. And he could get you into all sorts of trouble."

Lord Crusty had gone to school with Peregrine Elliott, and he owned the ground at St Germans, Cornwall, where the Elephant Fayre was held every year. Through these connections, in 1986, Hawkwind were invited along as guests, not performers, into the private backstage area next to the house.

"In this were all the lords and ladies, and they had their picnic tables out, with tablecloths," says Kris. "It was very plush. I remember there was a wicker elephant. There was champagne, hams and all these wonderful things."

"We were like the black sheep of the family," grins Dave. "There was this big cooked ham on a private table. We saw our dog Bilko run over, knock the ham off the table, and come running back over to our van. Nobody had seen him go. He was under the van panting over this ham, swallowing it as fast as he could, and this lady was going, 'Who's taken the ham?'"

"There was a marquee in this private area," continues Kris. "As usual, Philip was shouting his mouth off. He kept hassling Harvey to play, and eventually, at about midnight, Harvey set up his gear and speakers and played a set and he kept playing. He played and played all night, and people were really pissed off the next day. That blew over."

The next afternoon, Dave passed Harvey a tape of Frank Zappa and The Mothers Of Invention. It was their infamous, obscenity-strewn album *Live At The Fillmore East*.

"Harvey put in on and played it through the speakers," says Dave. "Then he hid behind a tree. And the album went on and on, and we could see everyone's faces. They couldn't work out how to turn it off."

"Philip was all cross with us," relates Kris. "He was saying, 'My friends, they don't like you any more.' He shouted at Harvey, and Harvey said, 'Well, Dave gave me the tape.'"

"I didn't realise it was going to offend anybody," says Brock, rather unconvincingly. "We did the same thing on a Plymouth rock radio programme. It was a live afternoon show. They asked me to choose my favourite 10 tracks and one was from *Fillmore East*. The presenter was playing it and she turned the sound down 'cos we were talking. She didn't realise what she was broadcasting. The phone rang and it was the boss of the station – 'Take that thing off immediately.' He gave her the sack there and then. She was really upset. I wrote a letter of apology saying it was nothing to do with her and that I hadn't realised it would cause offence. She was reinstated."

Outside the private area with its lords and ladies, some of the campers at the Elephant Fayre were having a terrible time.

Danny Thompson recalls: "We heard all these horrible stories. People were getting stuff stolen out of their tents, and a couple of girls got raped at the gates."

Philip Harvey committed suicide in 1997, having gone into a downward spiral, allegedly involving heroin.

Hawkwind and The Babysitters, their support band on the Chaos tour, were clearly incompatible.

The Babysitters belonged to the young, glam-trash scene that had erupted with the Finnish band Hanoi Rocks two or three years earlier and was later turned into dollars by American bands such as Poison and Mötley Crüe. The Babysitters' take on the essential rock'n'roll music at the heart of the movement was wacky: they out-striped and out-sparkled any and all of their contemporaries, their lyrics were naughty and usually silly, their tunes were high on singalongability and their songs were rarely more than two minutes long.

The Babysitters' manager Dave "The Wheel" Beal explains how it all happened: "We'd got as far as we could at the time. We'd done an album but we didn't have great record sales, so the next stop was to tour. We'd already toured with Hanoi Rocks and Cherry Bombz. We were doing some work with The Agency at the time, I looked at the tours that were coming up and Hawkwind and Bon Jovi were the biggest ones. My partner Louise's dad Peter Mobbs paid the three grand buy-on."

Amusingly, singer Buttz also claims to have raised the buy-on money from a relative.

"The second night [at Birmingham Odeon], there was a heated row 'cos Buttz would only do 20 minutes," says The Wheel. "I told him, 'If you're not interested in doing more than 20 minutes we're going home.' He was used to the chaos that The Babysitters caused at smaller gigs like the Marquee, and these were really big, seated theatres. But I have to say that he rose to the occasion. It was a learning curve.

"The stages were completely blacked out while we were playing. There were no light-shows whatsoever. Every venue we went to, I had to try and get the house lights on, get as much brightness as possible, 'cos the 'Sitters were a visual band. The tour manager wouldn't let us onstage after we'd finished our set. It was because of the blackness that Jimbo [guitarist] managed to get on to the stage towards the end of the tour before Hawkwind went on. I'd been expecting some wind-ups . . .

"But I must say the whole crew and the Hawkwind guys were great. Dave Brock was fine. There was lots of booze kicking around, and it was well purloined. Our only problem was transport. We had six different vans in 30 days as well as a converted bus. We did three dates with the bus. It was a catalogue of disasters.

"I remember the boys' constant mooning at old people's coaches. I remember Jimbo falling out of the van pissed when we arrived at one of the gigs. And I remember the wheel falling off the van I was driving home down the M1. I thought we had a puncture, and as I pulled on to the hard shoulder, the wheel fell off."

Jimbo recalls that Dave Beal's efforts to shed some light on the matter weren't always successful. "These lank-haired smelly hippies went on the road with nothing more than a couple of liquid wheel projectors, some four-feet fluorescent 'black' lights and a couple of smoke machines, maaan! A couple of gigs we played in complete darkness. On one occasion, five bars into the very first song, I ran across the stage right into [bassist] Boo and nearly broke my nose. It's amazing how much nodding and pulling faces at each other it took to get to the end of a 'Sitters gig. I usually had no idea whether we'd played one verse or seven in a song, and this kind of communication was what kept our show the slick, tight and predictable event we became known for."

According to Jimbo, the unwanted food they picked up from the tour caterers took on the proportions of a feast to The Babysitters. "There were a couple of chicks cooking food for the band and crew daily," he recalls. "Not for our band, of course, but there were leftovers. Some of us had not ever eaten that well.

"This led to a 'longest-turd' competition. The contest took place for several weeks in any toilet. The fear of being photographed, along with the inaccuracy of measuring a log in a toilet bowl, forced us to collect plates from the very cooks who were feeding us. These were to be used as bowl substitutes.

"I remember we were all in the dressing room with The Wheel, Louise and many other normal people when [drummer] Stik burst into the room with a plate. There was a huge skid mark on the plate, with a piece of corn stuck on it. He said his log was so big it slid off the plate and then was trying to claim the whole length of the skid as his competition entry. Way back in the mix, behind the laughter, I heard someone scream. They were not amused."

Singer Buttz later wrote a vividly disrespectful account of the Chaos tour from a Babysitter's perspective, as below.

"We were offered a buy-on to the tour. None of the band particularly liked Hawkwind or what they stood for. Indeed, I, like the general public, was only aware of 'Silver Machine' from the Stone-Age chart. Everything else I'd heard sounded like one song droning on and on through the ages. Nevertheless, my Uncle Rod lent us the £3,000 deposit money to secure the spot and so it was up to us to sell enough T-shirts and patches to reimburse him at the end of the 30-odd shows.

"Off we went in a leaky old van, complete with livestock in the bed and rain falling on to the on-board TV. On arrival at the first show, I remember being overwhelmed by the size of the gig, and . . . who the fuck was going to pay £10 to come and see this? But in their hundreds, from out of nowhere, came . . . hippies. Maybe thousands of the bastards. Every night for what seemed like months, the same type of smelly, dreadlocked, bearded bastards. Every night, the type of blokes that you wouldn't want your sister to bring home, and the type of women whose necks you'd wring if only they'd wash them.

"Before each gig, the soundcheck. We managed about half a song on average, after the hairy bastards had spent hours tweaking and fiddling about with their slide show, an endless barrage of drawings of whales and spirals and witches and fucking demons that sent my head spinning. This seemed to be the anchor for their show. The Babysitters were basically a punk band in home-made, glam clothing and this tour was obviously a mismatch of the highest order. I'm quite sure that no members of Hawkwind ever saw us play a note either during a show or at a soundcheck.*

"After the initial shock at the size of the tour, it gradually dawned on us that it was getting quite boring. We were from the 'rock'n'roll' camp, and the routine was painful. At the time, I was 24 years old and we had just finished a tour with Hanoi Rocks and Johnny Thunders. It was the closest thing we knew to the Sex Pistols' Anarchy tour. I didn't want to say so, but it *was* sex, drugs and rock'n'roll. We all became closer friends on the tour, the instruments were swapped around and it

---

* This appears to be true.

was basically just . . . 'rock'n'roll!' That's the way to do it.

"Dave Brock was introduced to me on one of the first Hawkwind shows, just as he was heading out the main door with a can of petrol and a box of matches, as he'd heard of some bloke on the corner selling bootleg T-shirts. '*Blimey!*' I thought. 'Maybe he has to pay *his* Uncle Rod as well.'

"It was the first time I realised that this was a business, and the Hawkwind entourage took it all very seriously. I suppose when you have all your eggs in one basket, you tend to look after them. So we went to buy some eggs . . .

"Our guitarist Jimbo was pretty good with a catapult, and we did manage to fire a few stink bombs on to the stage from the upper circle during Hawkwind's first song. Jimbo was adamant that 'the earlier the better' was the order of the day. After a while, his tactics became more astute. By pretending he had 'equipment problems', he'd slip on to the stage 10 minutes before Hawkwind and gaffer tape a couple under the drummer's stool. I almost died laughing one night in an upper circle when Jimbo came running up to me shouting, 'Watch the drummer's face!' He'd done all three legs of the stool.

"Hawkwind never partied after the shows. I thought that Lemmy had ultimately made the right move. This is when we started to rehearse 'Overkill' and 'Ace Of Spades'. We put 'Overkill' in the show, and nobody seemed to care or even notice.

"We had a small group of fans following us about on the tour. Our tour manager Chief, who was seven feet tall and nuts, pulled one of the girls, only to find that her golden locks were superglued on, and she was totally bald underneath. He came running down the corridor shouting that, 'Tonight's the night for a fight with a hippie!' and he spent the night asking the masses during the Hawkwind show if anybody 'wanted some'. The next night, he wanted to strangle one of the students in Leeds because he didn't know where the refectory was. It was getting like that . . .

"Before one show, I remember watching *The Dambusters* on the in-bus TV with the rain pouring down on to the aerial thinking, 'Jesus, £3,000 for this.' Usually after a show, you go to a party with a few birds at least, but these people were totally from another planet. I suppose you have to take your top hat off to Hawkwind for that.

"We eventually arrived in London for two shows at the Hammersmith Odeon. This was the main reason I borrowed the money for the tour in the first place. I just wanted to say we'd played there. We'd already successfully played the Lyceum, Edinburgh Playhouse, the Camden Palace, which were big gigs for a little band. I kept thinking, 'Thin Lizzy played here – *the Odeon! Cool!'*

"Jimbo and I found ourselves under the stage five minutes before Hawkwind appeared above it. Our gig had been awful, with 80 per cent of the audience at the bar when we played, so we ended our set with trousers down in the kind of military manoeuvre that *Dad's Army* would've been proud of.

"There was an old piano just sitting there . . . under the stage . . . Jimbo and I pissed, with not a care in the world, singing 'When I'm cleaning windows' . . . tinkling away . . . apparently just audible as the Hawkwind projector fired up with its Tolkienesque images of mystery and fantasy. I couldn't breathe – it was one of those magical moments that you wish was on video.

"I remember thinking how young the audience was. I'd been to see The Rolling Stones a few years before and the St John Ambulance people were there, not just because of government regulations: the crowd were the same age as the band and I'm sure a few hip replacements were undertaken during costume changes. Hawkwind audiences were young and I wanted to shake them – 'Why do you only go to see Hawkwind?' They were the same age as us (with the odd embarrassing uncle and aunt dancing like octopi) but from another dimension.

"It's as if we weren't in the gang and had no chance of joining. Whatever Hawkwind had then, I missed the point entirely. I found them really dated, whereas the audience loved them. Again, top hats off to them. No one will remember *my* band.

"A kind of banquet was arranged backstage at one of the last shows. We were permanently pissed by this time, and it was in this room that we examined the 'Turin-Shroud-like' skid mark left by Stik's stool when it slipped off the plate. Giggling, we legged it onward to our next tour."

As a postscript to all this, Dave Beal insists that Jimbo's stink-bomb sabotage campaign extended to all of the foot pedals as well as the drum stool and he remembers being "in tears of laughter at the side of the stage". In conclusion, he tells the tale of an encounter with Huw Lloyd-Langton in The Ship, the pub nearest to the old Marquee in Wardour Street.

Says The Wheel: "Huw was playing at the Marquee as a one-off and

Jimbo, Buttz and I went down to see him. In The Ship, we bumped into Max Splodge [of Splodgenessabounds], who was out of his brain as usual. He took Huw to one side and convinced him and another member of Hawkwind that Stacia was his mum and that he was trying to find out who his father was."

Disappointingly for The Babysitters, no one in Hawkwind noticed either them or their stink bombs. To add insult to injury, Hawkwind appeared onstage throughout the tour with some rather unusual props – rubber chickens – oblivious to the fact that the rubber chicken was a long-established symbol of The Babysitters, along with an infant's dummy and a massive pair of knickers. The Babysitters only had one rubber chicken; Hawkwind had dozens.

Danny Thompson recalls: "On the Chaos tour, we used to go and hit all the joke shops and buy up all these rubber chickens and silly string. The shop assistants must have thought something weird was going on. Harvey would occasionally let out his farmyard animal noises, and we used to get out the chickens."

It didn't take long for the craze to catch on.

"We'd throw a rubber chicken at the audience and we'd get 20 back," continues Danny. "After about a month on the road, you start to go a little bit mad, and things like that help you get through. Harvey had his own personal rubber chicken which he used to keep on his synthesiser. One of our roadies, Alan Arthurs [who went on to become Hawkwind's resident artist/designer], drew a suspender belt and stock-ings on it one day. Harvey came walking out on to the stage that night and found the rubber chicken with its suspender belt and stockings and he stood there and he shouted, 'Who's done this to my chicken?' He was really serious."

As was becoming usual, Danny had his moment at the front of the stage. On the Chaos tour, he wasn't required to beat up any albino emperors, but he did come out from behind the drums to play a balloon solo during 'Flight To Maputo'.

He says: "It was one of a couple of new tracks we'd done for *Out & Intake* [an album released by Flicknife a couple of months later]. We re-did 'Ejection' and there was 'Flight To Maputo', mucking about hitting things and letting fire extinguishers off. I play the balloon, blowing it up and letting the air out. I remember during the Chaos tour that I'd walk around to the front of the stage and try and play my balloon solo. Huwie used to come over and burst it with a cigarette."

Danny's most colourful memory of the tour involves Alan Davey. "He took magic mushrooms for the first time," says Danny. "He wanted to see what it was like. We made mushroom tea in the dressing room and we made sure Alan had most of it. We went onstage. Alan would be playing away and every now and again I'd be flicking silly string at him, and orange juice. He thought his bass was made of orange juice all the way through the gig."

Out & Intake followed hard on the heels of *Live Chronicles*, in February 1987. Mainly comprising live material, it was released largely to generate some money.

In its defence, Danny Thompson ventures that, "There were a couple of all-right tracks on it, remixes of stuff the band already had."

Dave Brock admits: "I think it was bits and pieces we had hanging around, weird things like 'Turner Point'. Harvey had 'Cajun Jinx'. It was really just to finance us all and keep the whole thing going."

With their enforced move from major to independent labels, it might have seemed that Hawkwind were in an ideal situation, one suited to their free-spirited sense of adventure where they were more at liberty to be creative and prolific without feeling the weight of corporate dictatorship.

Brock sees the pros and cons of both. He says: "We would have loved to have a major label sign us up and invest some money into us and push us, and we still would. We always did have freedom, even with the major companies. With independents, you do earn more money, but you don't sell as many records.

"The whole record industry is geared to putting bands into studios the labels have deals with. We rarely used to see any money at all. We'd get expenses for food and so on but once we'd left Rockfield, that was it. We wouldn't earn any money until that record had been sold and the money had been recouped and reinvested. We were probably selling more records with the majors, but I don't think we were earning lots of money."

Hawkwind were now sharing their output between GWR and Flicknife, and a great deal of archive live material was appearing at home and abroad on other small labels – for which Dave Brock continues to be blamed.

In May, Hawkwind embarked on a short tour in Europe, mainly Germany. There would be no major UK tour this year, although the band did venture out for bunches of gigs around the country, and they appeared at a selection of festivals, free and otherwise, during the summer.

"We'd turn up and do really obscure small festivals with only about 100 people there," says Dave Brock. "We were still keeping our hand in, keeping our finger in the pie."

Sometimes Dave would arrive without the full Hawkwind line-up. Says Harvey: "Every summer, Dave and I went to as many festivals as we could. Huw wouldn't come. He wasn't the outdoor type, really. Alan used to turn up and Danny did occasionally. I was going to these festivals anyway, before I was in Hawkwind. We'd take our instruments, turn up with our gear, and if everything was kosher, we'd set up and play. It was all very informal."

"It was like being free to do what we wanted," remarks Dave. "I did things with other bands too. Every time I turned up at a free festival, people would immediately want to know, 'Are Hawkwind coming?' It became a bit boring. Sometimes I just went to enjoy myself. At that time, it seemed like I couldn't go anywhere without having to play because people expected it."

Harvey continues: "We went to the Rollright Stones, an old stone circle in north Oxfordshire, in the Cotswolds somewhere [in July 1987]. A whole lot of travellers turned up and it just poured with rain. Dave sat in his van and I sat in my van and we didn't bother setting up. The weather was so bad we went home again."

However, the Rollright Stones trip was worth it, because it was there that Dave and Harvey (somehow or other) met a young guitarist called Jerry Richards who played with Tubilah Dog, which was more of a cooperative than a band. Jerry confides: "The ethic really was, 'We've got some time on our hands – you're a mouthy git so you can be the singer, I've got a guitar so I'll be the guitarist, you like bashing things so you be a drummer.'

"We thought, 'There's no point trying to do any gigs, 'cos nobody will have us. Let's just go to free festivals, get ourselves a little light-show with a projector, and go out and play and put festivals on.' It was our PA, our light-show and our amplifiers at the Rollright Stones. That was one of the festivals we actually played at. By this time, we didn't usually play ourselves. We'd get things together and whoever had a band came up and put their name on the blackboard. When one finished, the next went on. We just did that as much as we possibly could. I spent pretty much two years living on the road and being at festivals."

The meeting between Jerry, Dave and Harvey led to their formation of an occasional free-festival band known sometimes as Hawkdog and sometimes as The Agents Of Chaos. It was a flexible group, including other members of Tubilah Dog. Harvey, a regular member of the first line-up, was later replaced by a keyboard player called Crum, a friend of Dave's. Alan Davey and future Hawkwind drummer Richard Chadwick were among other musicians who played at Hawkdog gigs, which would be regular festival occurrences through to the end of the Eighties.

Jerry remembers: "We played Hawkwind stuff that hadn't been given an airing for years, Hawklords and unusual album tracks. We'd pick numbers that hadn't been played live ever. I was interested in the Calvert stuff. We'd do a lot of Tubilah Dog numbers as well, Frank Zappa numbers, bits and pieces. We probably did a few Gong numbers too, anything with a festival flavour or groove. We'd play for hours at festivals, although we did do some paid gigs as well."

Much later, Jerry Richards would join Hawkwind as their guitarist.

Probably the most extraordinary gig of the year was at the World Science Fiction Convention at the Brighton Conference Centre on August 28. There, Hawkwind revived their Black Sword show for one night only, complete with Tony Crerar, dancers and props, in front of an audience dressed as aliens, including quite a few impersonating Elric.

The event was organised by Marion Lloyd-Langton, who was living with Huw outside Brighton at the time. She had taken over the arrangements after receiving distress calls from the town hall, which had originally been putting it together. The Mayor and the publicity department told Marion that the whole thing was shaping up to be "a nightmare, a mess".

"It was completely disorganised," she agrees. "I took it over and organised it properly. It was a great gig."

"That was really strange being out of your head, walking around with all these people dressed as aliens," laughs Alan Davey. "It was good fun. I bought a couple of *Star Trek* T-shirts I wouldn't have been able to get otherwise."

"We had to pick the best-dressed people," remembers Dave.

"People at these science-fiction conventions are very odd," comments Harvey. "They'd taken over two hotels on the sea front, the Grand and the Metropole. A bunch of Americans had dressed themselves up as Elric, and they had their pictures in the *Mail On Sunday* magazine. They won the competition. They had a party in their private suites. Everyone was parading around in outfits."

Hawkwind had originally met and befriended some of the sci-fi enthusiasts at a gathering in a hotel in Liverpool, close to the Empire. It was the same hotel where Dave Brock caused the fire alert, although that was possibly on a different occasion.

"We'd gone to check into this hotel," says Huw, "and the place was packed with all these people walking around with science-fiction things on. They were holding their convention in this hotel this particular year."

A natural liaison sprang up. Says Huw, simply: "Hawkwind is basically sci-fi rock," and as an aside, "Me, I like thrillers."

Hawkwind were still also indelibly associated with the LSD and psychedelia of their early hippie days, and in the latter half of 1987, they headlined a pair of concerts under the banner of Acid Daze with a bunch of bands who, to a greater or lesser degree, had psychedelic connections.

The first show, held in a tent in London's Finsbury Park on August 23, boasted support from Doctor & The Medics, Gaye Bykers On Acid, Pink Fairies and, in an inspired booking by promoter John Curd, Naz Nomad & The Nightmares.

Naz & The Nightmares were an alter-ego band of The Damned, freakishly dressed and made-up. They were a Sixties spoof, a mix of garage and psycho-movie soundtrack, but at the same time, they and their audiences enjoyed the covers and original music that they created for the project. They had invented a whole history for themselves, the bottom line being this: "We were pretending to be the band that influenced Hawkwind."

Rat Scabies, aka Nick Detroit, says: "It was all about being precursors to that whole hippie thing. Dave Vanian [singer] used to *become* Naz. He used to age himself. He used to look like Nik Turner's dad. It was a lot of fun. It wasn't like being in The Damned. To be honest, at Finsbury Park, we just arrived, played, smashed the gear up and went home again."

Hawkwind were joined onstage by Lemmy and Dumpy, and all

concerned agree it was a good night's work.

"I think we were peaking at that point," says Alan Davey. "That type of music was all coming back in and we were still doing it and still at the top. Wonderful times, really, they were."

Hawkwind played a clutch of gigs in September, after which Kris Tait put on a backpack and went travelling. This was nothing new for Kris. She had been coming and going regularly, if not to college or to mime school or to circus school, then to festivals or other countries. This time, her destinations were Pakistan, China, Tibet and Hong Kong. Two years later, her wanderlust would see her travelling to Brazil where she would run into Motorhead.

She returned in time for the second Acid Daze concert which took place at Leeds Queen's Hall on December 12, with Doctor & The Medics, Suicide, The Enid, Pink Fairies, Spacemen 3 and Tubilah Dog in support – along with Robert Calvert & The Starfighters.

Calvert was quietly making his way back into the Hawkwind fold. "That was the first and last time I met him," says Alan. "I spoke to him before the gig for two or three minutes. I do know that at that time, we were planning to get him back in the band. We'd talked about it. He was right on form again. It was all ongoing. We were putting it together and there were lots of plans, strange things. He looked fine, healthy. I was lucky to have seen him."

Sadly, Robert Calvert didn't live to rejoin Hawkwind.

Dave Anderson was living in Wales and receiving phone calls from Frenchy.

"He sent some of his Flicknife bands up here to my studio," says Anderson. "He used to phone me up when he was at the end of his tether with Dave Brock."

By the end of 1987, Frenchy had renounced his managerial duties with Hawkwind. "I stopped because there was nothing I could do," he says. "Dave Brock was in charge. It was more work for no money, and it was taking all my time. I had other bands to look after – Alien Sex Fiend, Barracudas, Inner City Unit . . ."

Frenchy continued with his schedule of Hawkwind releases on Flicknife, including the *Friends And Relations* series, and it wasn't until the dawn of the new decade that he cut completely his personal ties with Brock.

"Dave and I fell out really badly," reveals Frenchy. "I had a motorbike crash in the summer of 1990. I injured my leg, and I just bandaged it myself. Then it got infected, and I ended up going into hospital on January 4, 1991. I was there until the end of August. I got gangrene. I'm okay now, but I was fighting for my life for the first three months. I was between dying and not dying.

"Somebody who was supposed to be a good friend – Dave – put the word around, for some reason, that it was all drugs-related, which it wasn't at all. He was saying I was taking this and taking that. I wasn't an angel, I used to go to clubs and get completely out of my head, but I knew where the line was. Then I started getting solicitor's letters. I was in hospital. Dave was demanding that I give him the rights to all the albums that had gone out on Flicknife. I said, 'No way, they're mine.'

"After the first letter, I wrote back to Dave. I said, 'I can't believe you sent me a solicitor's letter.' I got another letter back from the solicitors saying not to get in touch with the client but to speak to them.

"When I came out of hospital, I needed 18 months of physiotherapy, so I licensed Flicknife to Cherry Red. I carried on putting out *Hawkwind Friends And Relations*. We had plenty of Hawkwind tracks we could put there that we had the rights to."

The series also included material supplied by ex-members and groups who had supported Hawkwind, and Frenchy sees no reason why even now he should not continue releasing such tracks under the banner of *Friends And Relations*. He is also currently running a label called Skydog, primarily to launch new acts but also incorporating releases from such rock'n'roll veterans as Iggy Pop and New York Dolls.

Dave Brock retaliates: "The unfortunate thing about some people who haven't got heroin habits any more is that when you mention that they did have, they're really upset about it because others might assume they're the same now. Maybe they are in denial. Frenchy did have a bad heroin habit, although I'm sure he's totally clean now. Back then, lots of people told me what he was up to, and I've personally seen him in states.

"We were told that when he was in hospital, the doctors couldn't operate on his leg because the veins had collapsed, due to him injecting heroin. They were worried he was going to have to have his leg amputated. Someone we knew had heard this from someone who'd been to see him in hospital.

"I don't think we were sending letters to his hospital bed. I think our solicitors sent a letter on our behalf at some point or other. Frenchy was in hospital a long time. As far as I remember, what we were asking for was accounting, which had gone up the creek since his drug addiction. That was happening at around the time he split up with [his wife] Gina, and it had been getting difficult to work with him. There was tension between the pair of them. They had been a really good team, but she wasn't actively involved in the office so much then. She was spending more time looking after the kids.

"This is what happens when people get drug problems. You put up with it for so long to try and support them, but sometimes you reach the point where you realise you can't help them."

Later, according to Kris Tait, there was a possibility of court action relating to Hawkwind's contracts with Flicknife and the subsequent licensing of the label to Cherry Red.

She says: "Frenchy wrote a long letter to Dave asking him not to take action because he was a ruined man – he'd lost this, he'd lost that, he'd lost everything. He didn't want things getting any worse, and he asked Dave to call off whatever was happening to him. There was a lot of Hawkwind money involved, and we'd been trying to see the accounts to find out if we were due money back, and if so, how much. It wasn't us handling it, it was whoever was representing us. In this letter, Frenchy was saying there was no money there but he was very sorry. I remember Dave saying, 'Frenchy was a mate. What can we do? If it's not there, it's not there.' I think it was called off then."

Brock clarifies the current situation: "We do get accounts from Cherry Red, although we don't get lots of money."

Kris relates another episode involving Frenchy, just a few years ago. "He turned up at a gig in London," she says. "It was either the Shepherd's Bush Empire or the Astoria. A guy from the gig brought this note up to the dressing room. He said this guy outside – Frenchy – had been hassling to come and see us because he wanted to apologise. It was quite near the end, after the gig, and I thought maybe I should go down and see him, but I hadn't really got time. There was an awful lot going on, there was some sort of meeting, and we hadn't allowed anybody into the dressing room. It wasn't that we didn't want to know Frenchy. I remember thinking that I would like to see him. It was a shame, really. But I'm quite surprised that he remembers everything so badly and that it has ended up like this for him."

Douglas Smith, Hawkwind's then label boss, asserts that whatever their problems with Frenchy at this time, he was not involved. Later, however, he did take steps to retrieve what albums he could for the band after Cherry Red had taken over the Flicknife catalogue, some time after Frenchy's release from hospital.

Says Douglas: "The contracts were very shaky on a couple of the albums, there could be no arguments about them, so in the end, they were given back to Hawkwind. Cherry Red were able to keep the rest. I think Dave had been trying to get the accounts prior to that and had created a scene. Maybe he instructed a lawyer, maybe he didn't."

But at the end of 1987, all this was some years away. As Hawkwind looked to a new year and a new album, two people were beginning to feel uneasy in the band. One was Danny Thompson. And the other was the loyal and long-standing guitarist Huw Lloyd-Langton.

CHAPTER 24

Dead Poet's Society

THINGS were a little strained in the studio when Hawkwind were recording *The Xenon Codex* in February and March, 1988. For one thing, they didn't like to be rushed, and this was a fast one. They were moving from one studio to another, they were strapped for cash and personal tensions were rising between various members.

"We had about three weeks to do the album," says Alan Davey. "We'd had a phone call from Douglas and Higgy, who tour managed Hawkwind at one time. All of a sudden, we've got a tour booked and we've got to get an album ready to go in three weeks – 'Oh, Christ!'

"We all went to this place in Bournemouth with our pieces of music and did them really quick. It's the biggest rush-job I've ever done with Hawkwind. It reflects the whole mood in the studio at the time. We all went mad. After a week, we had to move to a studio in Monmouthshire [Loco Studios in Caerleon] because Bournemouth wasn't suitable for some things. The engineer in Wales was a keyboard player who'd been with The Bay City Rollers.

"We were working from 12 noon to 12 midnight every day, and sleeping in the studio. We had to get it finished 'cos this tour had been booked. Guy Bidmead was producing it. He'd done stuff for Whitesnake and Motorhead. He was a nice enough guy but he just sat there and smoked his fags. He didn't really put much input in. We had much stranger ideas than other people do, and he got lost. He still got paid, of course.

"We went on strike for a while 'cos we weren't getting paid. You should get a retainer when you're doing an album, money up front, even just expenses, and we didn't get it. I ended up phoning GWR and having a big freak-out. We all stopped working. I said, 'If you don't get some money sent by the bank today, we're all going home. Fuck your tour.' Course, we got it then. I don't normally do things like that but this Higgy, he realised that this was serious, and he reported back that we were on the phone freaking out. It was the first time I'd ever stuck my neck out, and everyone seemed to be pleased I'd got the money."

Alan remains proud of the album, despite the fact it was recorded so quickly. He says: "It seemed to be a very popular one. I liked it. There's some really good stuff on it. Not bad for three weeks."

"It was Douglas' idea," agrees Dave Brock. "I thought it was quite a successful album, and the tour we did to promote it – The Mad Professor's Laboratory tour – was quite successful too. A comic book came out of it by two good artists – John Coulthard and Bob Walker. It was quite an innovative year."

Douglas Smith isn't sure that he pressured the band to the extent described. He says, "We probably didn't. Our association with them at the time was through GWR. We were the label, not management."

For his part, Danny Thompson was noticing changes in the band: the warm and creative atmosphere he had enjoyed in the days of *The Chronicle Of The Black Sword* and *Live Chronicles* had largely disappeared. He suddenly started feeling that he was in a darker environment, and he didn't like it.

"There wasn't a lot of enthusiasm for *The Xenon Codex*," he begins. "After being on such a high with the whole Black Sword thing, this was rushed. We were trying to write songs when we were actually in there recording them. We went into one studio, then into another one. Dave was getting into that again, computer drumming, although I actually played all of *The Xenon Codex* live, as opposed to *Black Sword*.

"There were a lot of politics going on between the record label and the band. Business problems and politics were spoiling everything. We were supposed to be in Rockfield writing songs, but we weren't getting any money to rehearse. They weren't paying us. We didn't have any money. They were holding back money instead of letting us get on with the album."

Huw Lloyd-Langton was also feeling the strain. He had opted out of the band's legal business partnership around the time of the 1986 Reading Festival and he felt that he was being cold-shouldered because of this.

He confides: "*The Xenon Codex* is the last album I did with Hawkwind before I left. It had all gone a bit strange. I felt vaguely like an outsider, partially because I was no longer a partner. To them, I should imagine, I was a traitor or something. The feeling was fairly uncomfortable between me and the rest of the band from the point that I resigned from the partnership.

"I just didn't want the yoke of the business thing, and so I went on the Musician's Union fee. Basically, I wanted everything to carry on as usual and get paid my fair cut as a session musician."

Huw and Marion had previously been harassed by the taxman for two years over a financial issue in which they had been entirely innocent, and Huw had been getting increasingly worried that he could become embroiled in more problems through his membership of the Hawkwind partnership.

He explains: "Dave, Harvey and, I think, Alan and Danny were in it at that point. We were partners. The reason I wanted out of it wasn't anything to do with not wanting to be part of the band. It was the financial worry of the whole thing. If you're a partner and somebody does something naughty, disappears with a lot of money or whatever else, you as a partner become liable. Marion and I had a house at the time, a mortgage. Harvey didn't, Alan didn't, Danny didn't. It was only Dave and me. If anything had gone wrong, we'd have been jumped upon because we were the householders, we had the assets. It was unbearable, the worry of it, the thought that if anything did go wrong on the financial front we could be collared and severely hammered."

Marion adds: "Every three months, I'd get a letter saying we were going to be sued because the VAT hadn't been paid. I was company secretary, so I resigned. We wanted to get rid of that terrible worry. Huw wanted to get back to the music."

Asked why he'd signed up in the first place, Huw replies: "It was almost thrust upon us. It was the businessmen that we were involved with at that point suggesting that we formed a partnership for whatever reasons. It was just a nightmare. If you're not a businessman, it's the last thing you want to be involved in."

Dave Brock confirms that, in time, he would face the very problems Huw had dreaded. Meanwhile, Huw kept his nerve, recorded *The Xenon Codex* and remained with Hawkwind, despite his discomfort, for another year.

The album, released by GWR, reached its highest position of number 79 in May. While the band members and significant pockets of fans claim a certain fondness for it, it hasn't weathered critical opinion quite so well. *Classic Rock* commented on its reissue: "While *The Xenon*

Codex undoubtedly has flashes of the psychedelic brilliance of old, most notably on 'Swords Of The East', the lifeless production leaves one reaching for the off button well before the final yawn of the finale of 'Good Evening'."

Hawkwind could no longer look forward to Top 50 albums and their singles had long stopped bothering the charts, but their status as a live act was still assured as was their determination to keep the faith while moving steadily into the future.

The Mad Professor's Laboratory tour occupied all of April, with the band again playing two nights at Hammersmith Odeon and winding up on May 1 at Lincoln Drill Hall. Hawkwind introduced a fair amount of new material from *The Xenon Codex* including 'The War I Survived', 'Wastelands Of Sleep', 'Tides', 'Heads', 'Mutation Zone', 'Lost Chronicles' and 'Sword Of The East', although old set staples survived: 'Master Of The Universe', 'Brainstorm', 'Urban Guerilla', 'Sonic Attack' and 'Shot Down In The Night'. Also included were 'Levitation' and 'Needle Gun'.

Danny Thompson got his usual chance for a spot of role playing, coming out from behind the kit to appear as Frankenstein while the rest of the band were in lab coats. "But after the Black Sword tour, nothing was as good and it wasn't as much fun," he asserts.

On May 30, Hawkwind played a one-off benefit for the endangered black rhino at the London Town & Country Club, with Lemmy in tow. "We saved four-and-a-half black rhinos," says Dave Brock.

"They sent us a letter," adds Harvey. "I was quite impressed that they got back in touch with us. In those days, it was unusual to hear back from the charities. Greenpeace never told us what they were going to do with the money or anything. It's quite nice to have a follow-up." (Happily, in June 2004, it was announced that for the first time in decades the black rhino population was once again on the increase.)

Danny Thompson says of the gig: "Dave was moaning and going on at everybody and being horrible. And I just had had enough of it. It's more about integrity with me than pretending to be a rock star. And that was it; time to leave. It was a real spur-of-the-moment decision. It wasn't planned at all. I'd had no intention of leaving the band. I was still enjoying it and having a good time.

"I decided, 'I'll play my guts out tonight and just fuck off.' I remember doing a great gig. Then I remember leaving the hotel and thinking, 'That's it. Fuck it, I'm going home.'"

As good as his word, Danny went off home to Tiptree, Essex, without stopping to mention his decision to Hawkwind.

Dave Brock proposes: "It was his girlfriend. She gave him an ultimatum – 'It's either me or the band.' And he went with her. Then they got married and then they got divorced."

By this time, Hawkwind had produced their "board" game, which had been printed out in the April tour programme. "You threw a dice and landed on different squares," recalls Kris. "Get stoned, miss a gig . . . Alan [Arthurs], the artist, had drawn caricatures of the band in different squares, not necessarily related to them. On this square, 'Meet dodgy groupie, go straight to clinic,' there's a caricature of Danny with this blonde girl. And she looked exactly like Heather, his girlfriend. It was a complete coincidence. We didn't even know her at the time we did it. He wasn't going out with her then.

"Heather was good fun. She came on the road for a while. She was a rock chick, leather jackets, tight skirts, her hair all puffed up. Me and Heather got on really well together, but she and Danny hadn't been getting on on the tour."

Dave: "He'd been smashing things up a lot, because they were arguing. It was a rocky relationship."

Alan Davey ventures: "He made a big mistake leaving the band. Only a while later, we went off to America, which he would have loved."

"My partner at the time was giving me a lot of grief about being away," admits Danny. "There was all that going on. But I left because I was fed up with the politics within the band, more to do with Dave Brock than anybody else. There was a big thing about turning up at free festivals. I'd gone to a festival somewhere else and he was moaning at people, 'You should turn up at this one.' And you never knew where the money was going. You never knew what was really going on. Some of them were getting stoned all the time and didn't know what was going on anyway. Harvey was always going to leave, but he never did. I liked Harvey, and Huwie. I liked Alan too. You can trust him. He was always on Dave Brock's good side, though.

"I still admire the band very much. It's just a shame that dark sides seemed to take over. We could all be playing together now and getting on. Certain people cut their noses off to spite their face. They just ruined and spoilt the band. But I look back with fond memories."

Harvey suggests: "I think Danny saw Hawkwind as it was, really, and decided he wasn't going to put up with it, and left."

When Danny quit, he intended to work with Dan Priest, a producer he knew who had previously worked with Ozzy Osbourne. Priest was putting a band together involving a guitarist who'd worked with Tygers Of Pan Tang, Gary Moore's guitar roadie and a singer who went off to join a new incarnation of ELO – putting paid to the proposed band.

Danny also played sessions and formed an industrial metal band, Stranger Than Fiction, in the early Nineties. "We were trying to get a record deal," he says. "We got someone interested and then the guys didn't want to do it. I don't think they really wanted to go out on the road and do it properly."

After this, in the mid-Nineties, Danny teamed up again with Alan Davey, who had left Hawkwind and was assembling a band called Bedouin.

"We did Bedouin for six years," says Danny. "It was hard work. We had no management so we were doing it all ourselves. I used to do all the driving and Alan used to make the phone calls. We were sleeping on floors."

Alan continued with Bedouin after returning to Dave Brock and co, and he still runs it as a side project. Danny is available for any future Bedouin projects, infrequent though they may be, and there are plans for the release of a live album in the near future.

Danny rejoined Hawkwind in July 2002 but thought better of it almost immediately. At around the same time, he began a new career, helping to rehabilitate people with head injuries at a centre in Bexhill-on-Sea, near his home in Hastings. He says: "You just have to be able to listen to people, to be good with people. A friend of mine here at the rehabilitation centre thought that I would be. I didn't have to do any special training. You get all the training while you're doing the job. We've got 10 residents and we have to try and help them to cook and clean, everyday stuff, so that they can go back out into society and live independently."

On June 1, two days after the Town & Country gig at which Hawkwind raised enough money to save four-and-a-half endangered animals, they set off for a free festival at Wick quarry, near Bristol.

There they ran into Richard Chadwick, drummer with the acid-punk band Smart Pils.

Says Richard: "I'd bumped into Dave over the years at various festivals. Harvey tapped me on the shoulder while I was playing, in between songs, and said, 'Do you fancy playing for us 'cos our drummer's not turned up?' I said, 'Well, yeah, but you'll have to let another band play in between us.' Then Harvey got some sort of illness and went home, so the band didn't play anyway."

It would turn out to be Smart Pils' last gig, with their line-up having shrunk to a three-piece. But after his rather non-eventful brush with Hawkwind, Richard would later become their full-time drummer, and he has never left.

Meanwhile, Alan Davey had suggested a replacement for Danny Thompson. Alan had taken advantage of some time off from Hawkwind, with Dave's blessing, to play bass with Dumpy's Rusty Nuts, a popular live draw. They had lost their bassist just before a UK tour, and Alan stepped in to save the day with only two days to learn the set.

He recalls: "Mick Kirton was Dumpy's drummer at the time. He'd played in Marmalade before that. In Dumpy, Mick was a great drummer to play with. He was technical, fast, flash."

Alan told Dave Brock: "He'd suit Hawkwind." And so Mick was invited to rehearsals. "When he turned up and played, he froze," recalls Alan. "I can only assume it was nerves. I felt really stupid. Luckily, Dave being the understanding guy that he is, had probably seen it before. Mick then played a couple of gigs with us and he just looked like a bag of nerves. He'd been going to join Hawkwind, but he didn't."

Hawkwind went on hold for a couple of months. Dave and Kris had decided to spend the summer travelling around the free festivals with the more informal Hawkdog, and Mick Kirton played with them occasionally during this period. Silchester, Burghfield Common, the Brecon Festival, Barnstaple Armada Rock, Mithian Blowinghouse Fayre, Ribblehead Viaduct and Bodmin Moor were among the ports of call. But for more than one reason, the most important date in the diary was the Aktivator festival held at Tewkesbury, Gloucestershire, on August 14, 1988.

It was here that Richard Chadwick played his first gig with Dave Brock. He recalls: "Dave had said to me, 'Come along to the Aktivator festival and have a go with us if you want.' I took my drums along and their drummer at the time, Mick Kirton, turned up too. He was a good drummer, really professional, much more together than me. I started setting my drums up. Mick said, 'I really want this job.' I said, 'That's okay, you can have it. I'm just doing this for a laugh,' and so we played together."

It's been reported that Nik Turner, who was at Aktivator with his Fantastic Allstars, also took the stage with Hawkdog and that Dave Brock subsequently pronounced, "It was just like a Pinkwind gig that we used to do years ago." Turner doesn't remember this particular collaboration, but he was at the festival and he agrees it's perfectly possible.

What Nik will never forget about Tewkesbury is that while he was there, he received the news that Robert Calvert had died the same day from a heart attack.

Dave Brock recalls: "I was at the festival. The sun was shining and I was sitting outside on my chair with my plate on my lap, just about to have my dinner. Nik came over and said to me, 'I've got some bad news.' He told me that Bob had died – 'Oh, fucking hell.' I couldn't eat my dinner. I'd worked with Bob on and off for years. We'd had our arguments, of course, but I remember him with great affection.

"I think back to things like his *Lone Yachtsman* play. This was at the time we were living across the river from each other in Devon. I had a caravan and he asked me if I could tow it up to the top of the hill. We rigged up a battery and lights and he came and lived in it because he wanted to be buffeted by the wind. He wanted to feel like he was on board a yacht. He wanted to get right into the situation. He stayed there for about a week and he wrote the whole play.

"When he played the last gig with us – Leeds Acid Daze – he'd put a bit of weight on. We were talking about our new project together. I think the tablets he was taking were the cause of him having a heart attack. He used to go off and have one of his breakdowns and he'd come back on downers for a while, some sort of tablets to keep him calm. This is probably what ended up with him dying."

Nik Turner agrees with Dave's assessment: "Robert was a manic depressive. When they get manic, they are totally off the wall, using up all their energy, foaming at the mouth, going off at a tangent and not sleeping for a week or two, going for a 20-mile march in the middle of the night. They reach breaking point, having a nervous breakdown. Then when they get depressed, they put a lot of weight on and they're incapable of doing very much. They get stuck on medication which turns them into vegetables, non-creative and very fat. The thing about Robert was that he went through these swings all the time. I was always on to him to stop taking drugs and to take up meditation.

"I think Robert, at the time he died, had been depressed but he was getting manic and his heart, which was the heart of a fat man, was trying to function in a rapidly becoming thin man's body. His heart couldn't cope with it, and I think that's how he had a heart attack. He didn't live any particularly decadent lifestyle, over-indulging in things that weren't good for him, giving him fatty tissue or cholesterol. He might have done, but I don't think so.

"His death was very sad. I was always a very good friend of his. I spent lots of time with him. We had a good relationship. He'd disentangled himself from the Hawkwind situation because he'd felt exploited and patronised.

"I used to go and stay with him just before he died, after he moved back down to Ramsgate with Jill [reputedly because the Calverts were fed up with their home in Notting Hill Gate being burgled]. They had a son, Nicholas, who they named after me."

Huw Lloyd-Langton reveals: "I was sad. I think most members and fans would agree that Robert played a large part, adding to the band in various ways."

And Alan Davey confesses: "A friend of mine called Steve Hibbert, who's been a fan for years, phoned me up and told me that Calvert had died. I'd only met him once, but I started crying. It was such a big loss. I was shedding a tear for someone I didn't know, latching on to the sadness of it all."

Frenchy from Flicknife, who'd had a legal dispute with Robert, nevertheless comments: "He was such a lovely bloke and a talented guy, not only a good musician and a good frontman but an incredible storyteller. I went to see his Krankshaft cabaret. That was for a week. It was just him singing with a tape and Pete Pavli from the Third Ear Band playing cello. I've never laughed so much in my life."

Contrary to popular legend, says Frenchy: "Bob never did injunct us. He sent us a letter that was 'without malice', meaning that they want to put a legal point across but they don't want to sue you. That was concerning the 'Lord Of The Hornets' single. He sold 3,500 or 4,000 copies, but Bob thought he'd sold a lot more. I said, 'You can inspect all the books, all the pressing plant figures and all that,' and that was the end of it."

A "Hawkfrendz Exhibition", commemorating Bob Calvert, was assembled and displayed at Agents Of Chaos club gigs later in the year.

On October 1, Richard Chadwick went to Bilbo Baggins' Birthday Party, a free festival at Hay-on-Wye. "They were tricking the authorities by calling it a party for someone who didn't exist," he explains. "Things were getting hard for the travellers. I went to see Hawkwind, and in the evening, I bumped into Huw and Dave. We were up all night. Somebody was making speed coffee, and everybody was awake. There was one of those moments where you're standing staring into the fire – 'How's it going?' We were talking about the music and Dave was shaking his head saying, 'What we need really is a pulse.' I said, 'I'm a pulse.' And then after that, Alan rang me up inviting me to a practice."

Richard turned up for the rehearsal in Bournemouth, where Alan was living at the time. "Alan was there first and we played together for a bit," recalls Richard. "He said, 'I've never played with a drummer like you before. You're always pushing, all the time.'"

It was now that Richard came up against a new challenge. He'd been told that Hawkwind used a click-track, and he had taped himself playing along with a drum machine to try to gauge his precision. "I thought I had a 79 or 80 per cent accuracy level," he says. "Harvey and Dave turned up and we played for 20 minutes to half an hour, and I played along with this headphone click-track. Dave said, 'Yeah, well, that's sorted then.' Harvey said, 'I'm not so sure about that.'

"By the end of it, they were playing reggae, which they'd never done before. There was me and Al, who were younger, bringing a youthful sort of vibe. The sort of musicians Dave and Harvey and Huw talked about I'd never heard of. I never used to listen to jazz or blues, so I had a new set of influences to bring into the equation.

"Huw wasn't there. He didn't come down to practise with them at that particular time. There wasn't lots of money going round, and because he lived a long way away, it was logistically difficult and expensive for him to come down and rehearse. He was this guy who came and played sometimes but wasn't always in the band. Anyway, that day was Hawkwind auditioning me."

Alan remembers: "I didn't know Richard at all when Dave brought him in. Immediately, we hit it off. He fitted in straight away. I was in Bournemouth at the time. I'd just ended a relationship there – not with

Sally the dancer, this was with someone else. I didn't want to live in Bournemouth any more. Richard lived in Bath and he said he had a room in his squat. I said, 'That'll do for now.' He had a rehearsal room in the cellar, so it was a great opportunity to lock into each other and play together a lot. I moved there for the band!"

Alan, Richard and Dave Brock are still the nucleus of Hawkwind, with Alan enthusing: "We've become best friends. It's like a marriage in a way. Old grudges are never held. We ignore it and carry on."

Richard Chadwick was born on January 30, 1957 in Bromley, Kent, and brought up in Hereford. There, he attended Bishops School, and went on to take a two-year foundation course at Hereford Art College, followed by a three-year degree at Newport College Of Art.

He made a living "shovelling shit for the rich in some form or other" after relocating to Bath, where he moved into his squat and became involved with the alternative musical community. He started his career in an acid-punk band called Demented Stoats, with Bridget Wishart on vocals. After that came the more anarchic Smart Pils. Claire Granger, who sang in the band along with Niki Dark, was the friend Kris Tait made when she was living in Bristol. Both Bridget and Claire later performed together in the all-female Hippy Slags, a much-respected local band, for whom Claire moved to bass. Bridget joined as a replacement for their original singer, "Batty".

Richard lists his influences as Stan Lee and Jack Kirby, the editor and illustrator of *Marvel* comics; punk bands Sedition and Discharge; Bob Calvert; punk-metal crossover groups Amebix and Antisect; Native American ledger art; Don Featherstone, author of the war-gaming book *Battles With Model Soldiers*; The Who; and "pounding grooves".

He is now living "in a reservation cabin in the West Country on the edge of the Vale of Avalon with my love Sophie and a colony of cats".

After joining Hawkwind, he recalls that there was immediately "a lot of playing, a lot of rehearsing and writing material". In November 1988, the new-look group took to the road for a major tour that would run through to Christmas.

That winter also saw the release of the *Travellers Aid Trust* album. It was a compilation put together by Dave Brock and released by Frenchy Gloder on Flicknife. The contributing artists were all free-festival regulars: Hawkwind, The Agents Of Chaos (aka Hawkdog), Nik Turner, Ozric Tentacles, Rhythmites, Tubilah Dog, Culture Shock,

Hippy Slags, Israel Movement, Screech Rock, Radio Mongolia and 2000 DS.

It started out as a lovely idea and it ended in a mass of arguments and recriminations that are still raw today. On March 5, 1989, at Brixton Academy, Hawkwind headlined an all-day tribute concert for Robert Calvert, which doubled as a benefit for his widow Jill. Also playing were Doctor & the Medics, Gaye Bykers On Acid, Pink Fairies, Here & Now, The Starfighters, Atom Gods and Nik Turner's Fantastic Allstars.

Hawkwind were joined by a couple of guests including Martin Griffin, Simon House and poet Alan Ashley who had started making occasional appearances with them. Unusually, Lemmy was not on hand for this particular "special". He was in Brazil. So was Kris Tait, who saw him there with Motorhead.

The trouble was this: Hawkwind took £4,000 for themselves, a sum they claimed as costs. Nik Turner took exception to this and told the audience from the stage that Hawkwind were pocketing four grand. On top of all that, some of the proceeds allegedly disappeared from the venue, leaving Jill Calvert considerably short of the sum that had been raised. And finally, according to Dave Brock, Nik Turner unfairly claimed all the credit for the event.

Nik says: "My band were actually getting paid £400 for the gig, and I heard that Hawkwind were getting £4,000. I thought, 'That's not really very fair,' and so I made a point of announcing during the gig that while my band were doing this benefit for £400, people might be interested to know that Hawkwind were getting £4,000. I thought they ought to know, and they were probably glad to hear a bit of truth about the situation.

"It wasn't a Hawkwind gig, it was a benefit. All these bands were there to raise money for Robert's wife. It would have been different if Hawkwind had donated two-and-a-half thousand back to the cause. Then a lot of money went missing, about three or four grand. I have no idea where that went, and I don't know how much Jill ended up getting."

Richard Chadwick remembers: "It was a brilliant gig. There were all these amazing bands, and it went on for ages. Everyone was having a real gas. We played our set. We were in the dressing room when Nik was haranguing the audience, accusing us of stealing money that we'd generated for Jill Calvert. We'd had to take some money out to cover costs, but that was it. I came from a scene where we'd play hundreds of benefit gigs. You just don't rip off the benefit."

"Turner got the wrong end of the stick," declares Alan Davey. "He made his assumptions and then he spoilt it for everybody. And it had all been going really well. We got paid a fee for doing the show. Four grand. Out of that, we paid for the PA and the lasers and lights, full wages for the crew and diesel for the trucks. A lot of people would've skimped on the show, but we didn't. It's disrespectful to skimp."

Hawkwind say that this left them with £200 each which covered their wages for the two weeks they'd spent rehearsing plus their own diesel.

"Nik thinks we got all this money in our pockets," carries on Alan. "I caught the end of his speech and I just stood there, couldn't believe what he was doing – 'What's wrong with this bloke?' I thought it was a real distasteful thing to do, when we'd worked so hard on getting the set right and arranging it all and spending all the money on the show.

"None of what Nik said was true. It was an awful thing to do at someone's farewell gig. We were seeing someone off. I'll never understand that. Hopefully the audience didn't believe it. We were just furious. Nik's always tried to destroy Hawkwind, right from after he was chucked out.

"Afterwards, Nik disappeared. I was looking for him, believe me. 'Where's that fucking stupid old cunt? I'll tell him exactly what we spent this four grand on.' He was nowhere to be seen. Perhaps he got wind I was after him. My eyes change colour. I'm a very mellow person, but if I'm upset, I change. I'm the Orange Hulk. I hate disloyalty, people saying stuff that's untrue or trying to make problems. I find that unforgivable, and I have rarely let it go. If my eyes change colour . . ."

Dave Brock states: "I was told that the show raised £22,000 for Jill Calvert. We took £4,000 for the costs Alan has mentioned, and the rest of the money went to Jill. She was handed over a piece of paper saying how much she was getting.

"Turner went on after we'd finished our set. He told all the fans, 'All the money from this gig has gone in Dave Brock's pocket.' It was Nik who made the presentation to Jill Calvert. He said, 'This is from me.' She never said thank you to us, and we'd organised the whole thing. It's another black mark against Turner. He got all the accolades for the presentation and for organising everything, and he hadn't even organised it. We thought, 'Bollocks.' "

Dave adds: "After Nik did the announcement, he came back and drank champagne with the band in the dressing room as if nothing had happened." Presumably, that's where he was while the avenging Orange Hulk was searching the building for him.

"I didn't know anything about what he'd said at that time," adds Dave. "I didn't find out until the next day. Later, we heard it all on a tape."

Douglas Smith was involved with Hawkwind but not with the Robert Calvert tribute gig. However, he ventures: "I was under the impression that what they took as band expenses was £4,000. Also, money disappeared that they thought had been in the venue overnight. As far as I know, Jill got about two-thirds of the money that had been promised."

Dave Brock is not aware of any money having gone missing.

Nik Turner adds: "Dave doesn't have any regard or respect. There was a Q magazine interview with Dave which was carried out at the Robert Calvert gig. He stated that I was a very greedy and unscrupulous man who just wanted to play the saxophone over everybody's solos and that I was a thoroughly bad lot. In the next issue, Jill Calvert wrote a letter saying how sad she'd been to read this article by Dave Brock when everything he'd said about me was absolutely true about himself."

In her letter to Q, Jill Calvert declared that "for the privilege of appearing at a benefit, Hawkwind actually saw fit to charge £4,000, directly depriving me and my six-year-old son of that amount, which we could well do with. I find Dave Brock's remarks about Nik Turner, a genuinely dear and kind man, totally appalling. In calling Nik 'a weasel, a very greedy man,' Dave was of course describing himself perfectly. Well done, Dave."

As a direct consequence of the Robert Calvert gig, Huw Lloyd-Langton left the band and violin maestro Simon House returned.

Huw was outraged by the events at Brixton Academy, and for him it was the last straw. He had continued to feel isolated since leaving the Hawkwind partnership, and he had been nursing other grievances since the 1988 winter tour.

Says Marion Lloyd-Langton: "Huw had been given a couple of

hundred quid for rehearsals, but he'd come back at Christmas with not a single penny. Hawkwind had done a very successful tour, but Huw received no merchandising money and he hadn't been paid properly for the gigs. He was supposed to have been paid a session fee. That did get up Dave's nose, 'cos it would have been more than what the band were getting.

"Huw sent £300 back from rehearsals, and £300 he got paid for the first week of the tour. That was all he got – in total, £600. He kept saying to the tour manager, 'When am I getting paid?' At the end of the tour, there was no money for Christmas. Nothing. That, then, was the end for Huw."

Well, nearly. Huw continues: "The very final thing was the Calvert benefit gig. I'd been on the road with my own band at the time and I'd spoken to Dave. He said, 'If you want to do this charity thing, it's up to you. We're not getting paid.' I said, 'I'll do it if it's for charity.'

"Then I heard a rumour the band were getting what they usually got paid, and I was fairly uneasy about that. I found out later on they'd been paid the full fee and I'd been paid this paltry £100 for the roadie and the van hire."

That's when Huw walked out. He elaborates: "At the time I left Hawkwind, things were in a heck of a mess, partly financial. After RCA had decided not to renew the contract with us, there was Flicknife and second-rate record companies, and bootleg albums were coming out right, left and centre. It was just a mess."

However, in a dramatic twist, Huw and Marion much later re-assessed the situation and decided that they'd been unfair to Hawkwind and to Dave Brock in particular.

Says Marion: "I'd misjudged Dave quite a lot, going way back to when everything was so successful, from 1979 on. Everything went into the charts, the tours were brilliant and the audiences were fantastic. But there were a lot of stresses in the band, mainly because of money. After Bronze went bankrupt, rumours started going round that Dave was manipulating the money. Sad to say, I believed some of that and so did Huw.

"I didn't face Dave with this, to my regret. I wish I had. He was certainly aware of what our feelings were, and he did pull me up at one point. He had all the figures and the invoices, and I remember thinking, 'Would he do this if he was guilty?'

"There was so much water under the bridge there was almost a wall between us by the time Huw left the band. We felt really sad, actually. I remember writing a two-page letter to Dave and Harvey and airing my thoughts. Huw hadn't been paid for the 1988 tour, and given that I'd believed all the rumours previously, I was pretty disgusted and I said, 'That's the end of it.' But years later I learnt that Dave didn't know anything about that. [One member of the entourage] was assuring Dave that Huw was being paid his session fee weekly, and this guy, who Dave had trusted, had apparently been pocketing all the money. In hindsight, I should have faced Dave earlier on."

Huw comments: "There's no proof of anything."

Marion would later apologise to Dave Brock, and Huw would again return to Hawkwind. But not for some time. And when it did eventually happen, his luck would change for the worse.

Alan Davey remembers Huw's departure differently. He says: "At the time, he was having a bad drink problem and he was becoming a bit uncontrollable onstage. He'd miss cues and play a lot of bum notes. I can't stand that sort of thing. People are paying £15 to see a band and if you play badly, the fans remember that. They don't want to see bum notes. We tried to help Huw out because he was an old friend, but no matter what we tried, it wouldn't work. We had to relieve him of duty.

"He was in denial. He'd walk around with a Coke can full of gin. Once in a soundcheck, Dave shouted across to Huw, 'Have you got alcohol in that Coke can, have you, Huwie?' Dave was trying to have a dig to try and get him aware of it, but he was doing it with humour. You can't have bad scenes with nice people. It was a mutual thing when he left and there was no bad feeling."

Harvey Bainbridge suggests: "Dave asked him to leave. He was always anti Huw's drinking. I think Huw was getting very poorly with the drink problem."

"That's absolute nonsense," counters Marion. "Harvey and Alan are confused. If that's what the band thought, it was never relayed to Huw. He was not asked to leave. In fact, Dave later called up and said, 'What about our 20th anniversary and America?' Huw told him after the Calvert benefit saga, he'd had enough."

"Everyone used to drink," adds Danny Thompson. "It wasn't just Huw. In all the time I was in the band with him, he was bang on. He was playing some of the best guitar of his life. I think he was treated very unfairly, just for being a worrier. The fact that he left the partnership because he was worried meant that he didn't get any merchandising money off the tours, and if they did really well, he didn't get anything extra. That's a really shitty thing to do to somebody who's been in the band for years."

Just as Huw Lloyd-Langton left, so Simon House was coming back to Hawkwind.

Simon says: "I went for a jam with Nik Turner's band at the Bob Calvert fund-raising gig. Hawkwind were there and I jammed with them as well. I rejoined the band and did an album and a couple of tours. I've always got fond memories of them. We had some great times. Most of the time there was a good feeling of camaraderie and shared adventures. We did get on well most of the time."

"That was great, that was," says Alan of Simon's return. "He turned up at rehearsals and we played the 'hashish song' ['Hassan I Sahba'] straight away. We didn't half miss that violin when we'd been playing it before. That was a magic moment for me. I got on like a house on fire with Simon. After Huw left, we needed a lead instrument, someone to put the icing on the cake. Simon came along and it worked really well. He's a classy musician."

"Great joy!" enthuses Richard Chadwick. "It was great to have Simon in the band. He can really play like hell. I remember at Rockfield when we were doing the *Space Bandits* album, he turned up to play 'Images' and 'Out Of The Shadows' and he'd written the solos down. He recorded three versions and the band, when they were mixing it, had to sort out which violin tracks to use. He can just throw stuff at the canvas and say, 'Use what you want, I don't mind.' Musicians who can't play so well tend to be much more precious. It was that kind of quality. He was really, really good at playing; very fast. He was a good laugh. He had a great capacity for entertaining his mind with drugs. We had a lot in common there."

Another newcomer was entering from the wings: Bridget Wishart was about to become Hawkwind's first and only woman singer, and she wouldn't have an easy ride.

CHAPTER 25

Brighton Ruck

THE Agents Of Chaos were playing intermittent club gigs in the early months of 1989 (they used the name Hawkdog only for festival appearances), after which Hawkwind regrouped for a short tour in June. Many of the artists who'd contributed to the *Travellers Aid Trust* album the year before were invited to support, including the Hippy Slags. They had submitted a couple of tracks for the LP, with 'Cat's Mother' making the final cut.

For Bridget Wishart, the Slags' singer, it had been her first professional involvement with Dave Brock, although the band had solid connections to Hawkwind. They had been part of Richard's circle in Bath and their drummer, Angie Bell, was his girlfriend. They also knew Kris, who had been especially friendly with Claire. In addition, Claire had supplied the lettering for a Hawkwind lyric book years earlier and knew the band from then.

At Nottingham Rock City on June 7, the Hippy Slags were asked to join the headline band onstage. In an email interview with a website called *The Hawkwind Museum*, Bridget reminisced: "We were all invited to sing on a jam that Hawkwind were getting together called 'Back In The Box'. We all said yes and arranged to meet backstage, but when I got there, my bandmates had chickened out and, never being one for being shy, I went for it. I was drunk and haven't a clue what I sang but enjoyed it immensely – and it can't have been that bad as when they were recording the track, they invited me to sing on it. I then went on to sing with them at other gigs and festivals."

Bridget did not consider herself primarily to be a singer at this time. She was a performance artist, which is what she had studied at art college and university, but her personal ambition was to find a platform for combining art and music. Hawkwind was the perfect vehicle.

She told Dave Brock, "I could sing with your band really easily."

Dave remembers: "She also was an art teacher at a boys' school. She was very creative; she had very good ideas."

Richard adds: "She started coming in and doing some stuff. Her whole thing was about the role of the female in society, and a lot of her performances onstage later were extrapolations of that."

The June dates showcased not only 'Back In The Box' but also another new song, 'Treadmill'. Hawkwind later recorded both on a mobile studio at Dave and Kris' farmhouse – by now, they'd moved into the middle of the countryside not far from Exeter, where they still live – and these were the first tracks to incorporate the talents of Richard Chadwick, Bridget Wishart and Simon House. They would surface on *Palace Springs*, a predominantly live album released by GWR two years later.

Lyrically, 'Treadmill' recalls an old Hawklords theme, the regimentation and subjugation of the workforce, although it focuses on offices and the way in which city dwellers' lives are regulated.

The idea for 'Back In The Box' came from a trash novel about a serial killer and the woman he keeps prisoner in a box under the bed. Richard credits Bridget with getting the song together. She says that it had existed already, although she added to it.

It was all going terribly wrong for the travellers. The mutual suspicion between them and the police had been getting worse since 1985's Battle Of The Beanfield.

Dave Brock remembers that at the Aktivator festival in 1988, where Richard Chadwick first played with Hawkwind and where the news of Robert Calvert's death shocked all who had known and admired him, the authorities were maintaining a discreet, or not-so-discreet, surveillance.

"They had a hamburger van or an ice-cream van," he remembers. "Someone set fire to it 'cos they sussed out it was the police keeping tabs.

"We used to have terrible scenes of being stopped by the police, 'cos we were involved in organising lots of free festivals. I was on a blacklist. In the course of three months, we were stopped once a week. One month, they stopped me six times. They'd say, 'We wanna see your MOT documents.' I'd go to the police station and they'd say, 'Hello again, Dave.' I actually got a lawyer to say I was being victimised by the police. It got you down."

On one occasion, having driven to London for a meeting with Frenchy, Dave was stopped and searched and found to be in possession of a truncheon. It was in a fishing bag locked in the boot.

"I used it for hitting trout on the head when I was fishing at Rockfield," explains Dave. "They put me in a police cell for about four hours and when Kris rang up, they wouldn't tell her that I was there. They also found these wrapped sweets from a joke shop. When you bit the sweet in half, a Durex would fall out. They put powder in the sweets. Of course, the police were saying, 'Oh, right, it's cocaine. We'll have to send this off for analysis.'"

Analysis proved that Dave was not in possession of cocaine but, indeed, a few trick sweeties. However, he was fined £150 for possession of an offensive weapon, despite the fact that he wasn't carrying the truncheon, or the bag, when he was arrested and even though the rest of his fishing gear had also been in the bag. Surprisingly, the truncheon, known in the angling world as a "priest", was later returned.

"It was handed to me in a carrier bag by a policeman," Dave recalls. "He told me, 'That young PC who nicked you – he's out to get everybody, to boost his career.'"

Life wasn't any easier for Decker Lin, who recalls: "We were constantly surrounded by helicopters. Even now, if I hear a helicopter over the house, I find it quite disturbing. I remember going out in the morning in the bus sometimes, and my helicopter would follow me all the way to town. I'd do my shopping, and it would follow me back.

"I happened to have one of the very few legal vehicles, so I'd go out and do things that needed doing, taking people to sign on or go to court or go shopping. I got pulled nearly every time."

The travellers' cause wasn't helped by an influx of bandwagon-jumpers who had latched on to the movement after the Beanfield, attracted by the confrontation. The events there had also led to problems at Glastonbury, at one time revered as a natural home for the hippies.

Decker Lin observes: "A lot of people went to Glastonbury after the Beanfield melee. The following year, the message went out that Michael Eavis welcomed Rainbow Village. Everybody who'd been at Molesworth presumed that was an invite to them. After that, Michael Eavis started being a bit funny with travellers, 'cos so many other people were coming in saying, 'I've been at Molesworth.' So instead of 200, there were suddenly 2,000 people.

"The travellers didn't have any management or leaders. It was always very difficult, because you'd have to talk to a hundred or 200 people to see what each individual would want, and Eavis couldn't do that. He'd say one thing or two or three slightly different things to two or three different traveller types, and something totally different to the council. He's always done that. So people would be expecting one thing and then someone would be saying, 'No, you can't.' "

In 1989, Lin – and Hawkwind – turned up at Glastonbury. There had been problems with the local council over the festival licence, and for the first time, the police had been brought into the organisation and planning. Decker Lin helped negotiate with the Chief of Police for a field to be set aside for travellers outside the festival perimeter, on a hill, but then more problems arose.

"The police were doing some of the stupidest things you could imagine before the festival started," she remembers. "They wanted to come in and take the names and addresses of everybody in every vehicle. Eavis was all keen for the police to come in, which would have caused a riot. Then he would've been able to say, 'Look what the travellers do.' Not that all travellers are angels, mind. There are some naughty boys around, as in any society."

After a night of negotiation, a compromise was reached which involved travellers' representatives accompanying police as they walked round the field, simply maintaining a presence rather than taking any personal details. No one wanted any trouble, and peace reigned.

"It's always worth trying the civilised approach with police," remarks Lin, one of the travellers' most skilled negotiators. "You should be nice to start with. You can always be nasty later. Senior police officers were usually quite reasonable. Also, I was brought up not to be cowed by authority. I've always considered myself equal to everybody."

By now, Lin was one of the best-known characters in the travelling community. She says: "I used to do catering, feeding the masses. There were a lot of people who needed feeding. I used to do first aid as well. If there was a problem, people always came and got me. I was good at talking to management and police. I was quite useful."

Up on the hill in the travellers' field, Hawkwind were among many bands appearing on Wango Riley's Travelling Stage – a stage owned and constructed by their friend, Scouse. They played several times over June 20 and 21.

Decker Lin recalls: "One night Eavis and the Chief of Police came up – 'It's too loud. We've had complaints from down the valley.'" The travellers responded by moving the speakers until they were sure that no one else was being inconvenienced by the noise.

"To me," says Lin, "that's being really helpful. We were bending over backwards to help Michael Eavis, but I don't think he realised that."

Richard Chadwick nearly landed himself in the shit at the Treworgey Tree Fayre at the tail end of July 1989. There were big problems all round according to Hawkwind – who were joined for the occasion by Hawkdog guitarist Jerry Richards.

"The promoter thought he could hold a festival on his parents' farm and they wouldn't know when they came back," says Kris. "He panicked halfway through."

Richard continues: "The organisers were threatened by the security there and they went and hid all the money. The people providing services like the bogs, they just said, 'Oh, okay, if we're not getting our money, we're taking our stuff.' They removed the big structure with the toilets, which were round a fucking huge hole. I walked off the stage, out into the blackness and fell straight into the shit pit. It was 14 by 12 feet or more, and about 12 feet deep. As I dropped into it, I realised what I'd done. I saved myself by grabbing the edge before I fell right in."

On September 3, Hawkwind celebrated their 20th anniversary with a gig at Brixton Academy, with Lemmy again turning up for one of his popular guest spots. It was here that Bridget Wishart made her first official appearance with the band, taking the stage for 'Back In The Box'. For now, she too was performing as a guest: she would assume her permanent place in Hawkwind early in 1990.

They squeezed in another free festival – at Clyro Court, scene of Bilbo Baggins' Birthday Party the previous year – and then they were off to the United States and Canada. It had been a long time.

When Hawkwind had last played in America, 11 years earlier, Dave Brock sold his guitar to Marc Sperhauk and split the band. Clearly they had to recover a lot of ground, and the 1989 tour was the first step in a long-term project.

Dave says: "We were quite successful in the Eighties and we'd formed our own little company. We were all directors. We decided to invest all our money into going over to America. We knew we'd lose money on the first tour. The idea was that we'd break even on the second tour and, on the third or fourth, we'd make a profit."

Some years later, Nik Turner would stand accused of blowing Hawkwind's carefully laid plans right out of the water.

For now, though, Dave Brock, Harvey Bainbridge, Alan Davey and Richard Chadwick were in the best of spirits as they flew out in September to set about the job as a four-piece, complete with an exceptional light-show run by Pogle Stowell and his AnArc Illuminations.

"The fans were amazing," raves Alan. "They hadn't seen Hawkwind for so long. They were so happy to see us there and hear us playing well – 'You sound like Hawkwind should do.' They must've thought it was going to be different, but it was all there. It was as powerful and heavy as it always was – a big, flashing bass, and Dave's solos and Harvey's madness on the keyboards."

All of the band except for Dave were seeing America for the first time. "Ah . . . cocaine!" grins Richard, flashing into instant-memory mode before quickly changing the subject: "Me, Al and Harvey spent most of the time glued to the windows of the bus."

New York, on September 28, was the fourth gig in, and it was an important showcase. Unfortunately, someone had interfered with the memory on Dave's drum machine and Richard couldn't hear his click-track through the headphones. Dave believes that it was a roadie called Adie, Pogle's lighting protégé, who accidentally made the mistake while trying to fix a malfunction.

"Dave couldn't remember how the machine worked, and Harvey couldn't," says Richard. "It wasn't playing a tight, hi-hat sound. It was like playing in time to the sea. The gig was ruined because I couldn't play in time with the electronics properly. It was awful."

At the same time, agreeing with Alan, he states: "We discovered a fantastic network of Hawkwind fans out there. Right across America, every gig we'd play at was like a science-fiction convention where all these experts in a highly specialised genre get together and meet for the first time. The concerts were very special in terms of atmosphere. Everywhere we went, we bumped into people who'd met Dave years ago.

"We were grinding around these industrial towns and we got to the Great Lakes. We were playing in this quite big venue with a capacity of 1,000 to 1,500, in Cleveland, Ohio [the Phantasy Club on September 30], and it was full. I remember whacking away playing some really intense thing. Most of the time, I couldn't see much of what was going on; Pogle was really good at dense, acid-rave, psychedelic, trippy light. But this time, across the front of the stage I could see about five guys with really short hair banging their heads on the actual stage and thumping their faces.

"They turned out to be involved with the Orbital Church Of Rock'n'Roll. They'd found their own version of Christianity. They'd built a place where they could worship together. They had a temple and a sound system."

The members of the Orbital Church were committed to opening the "doors of perception" through music and hallucinogenic drugs. "A lot of them worked for the Cleveland Fire Department," says Dave. "They were very nice people, very hospitable."

Hawkwind have always attracted their fair share of bonkers fans. Says Brock: "There was the Hawkwind Ranch. A few years ago, we played a gig in Atlanta, Georgia, and we met these people who had the book *The Knowledge Of Love*, and they were reading hidden meanings into our songs because they thought they could make them go through the doors of perception."

A bit like the Orbital Church, then. "It's all pretty interconnected," agrees Dave. "They take magic mushrooms, put on music and go into higher realms. I should actually feel like a great guru and have all these Rolls-Royces, but it doesn't seem to be the case . . ."

Some fans offer an even more disturbing devotion.

"If you really wanted to manipulate them, they would do whatever you ask," asserts Dave. "I seriously mean that. I could say, 'I think I'll have to get rid of this person or that person, and I know so and so who will go and do it if I say the word.' They are around. But I've always believed in karma, and of course it would be a bad thing for us to do.

"I'm aware of three prisoners who have written to us. One of them murdered six people. He writes a lot of poetry and books and things like that. I've got a big folder of his stuff. He also writes about how the killings all happened, and it's quite frightening. He wishes he could turn the clock back. Hawkwind give him hope, funnily enough. Some of the words in our songs are really helpful to people – not just prisoners. They actually help lots of youngsters. We do try and give lessons, I suppose."

Richard and Alan remember one particularly outrageous hanger-on from their first trip to America: Snowface! "From his nose down, he had this fine film of powder," chuckles Richard. "He was in a terrible mess. We shouldn't have encouraged him."

"He was a walking avalanche," avows Alan. "He just turned up and emptied this bag on the table – about eight ounces of sherbet. He used to just bury his head in it. He was like Al Pacino in *Scarface*, and that's why we called him Snowface."

The tour wound up on the west coast, and Hawkwind met up with a perhaps unlikely friend in San Francisco. Jello Biafra, the Dead Kennedys singer and political agitator, arrived at their gig expressing huge enthusiasm for psychedelia and garage music. According to Harvey, "We spent quite a bit of time with him."

The final date of the tour took place in San Diego on October 12. The band then stayed on for a holiday, at which point they were joined by Harvey's wife Anne and Richard's girlfriend Angie.

Dave and Kris went to Arizona to explore the desert. Harvey, Alan, Richard, Anne and Angie stuck together and hired a car. They returned to San Francisco where one morning at 7am, Alan woke with a feeling of dread.

"I went down to the bay and I felt really awful," he recalls. "I heard the fishermen saying, 'Where have the sea lions and the pelicans gone?' They were nowhere to be seen. I still didn't click it. I had this gut feeling, and when I get a gut feeling like that, I never ignore it. I just wanted to get out of Frisco there and then. I was waking everyone up in their hotel rooms saying, 'I wanna go. I wanna get out.' They all wanted to go thrift shopping."

Eventually, it was decided that the party would go to visit a friend who lived about 40 miles outside San Francisco, up in the hills. Says Harvey: "We were driving out of the city on our way there when the earthquake hit. The road was going a couple of feet up and down, rapidly. We were being shaken around in the car like eggs in an eggbox. Then the radio went dead."

"We'd driven across that famous flyover," adds Richard. "A few minutes after that, it collapsed."

Alan jokes: "I should never have played my bass in San Francisco – a few days later there was an earthquake. Sorry, folks! The road started moving like the sea, and trees were going backwards and forwards. There was a motorcyclist and the road went up with him – he went flying over the trees. The most horrific thing was, I saw a dog get run over 'cos it panicked and ran out in the road. The whole thing lasted 40 seconds. I was actually enjoying it. It was like, 'Wow! I'm in an earthquake.' Feeling the earth going up and down underneath you, the power of it. I forgot about it being dangerous."

The party were directed off the highway and into a little town. "We went and had a cup of tea in a café," recalls Alan. "The tables and the roof were shaking and, outside, the road had all come up. But we were very blasé with the aftershocks and stuff. You're not bothered by it. It was a fantastic experience."

They were told by a policeman that the mountain road they intended to take was now impassable. Plan B was to head straight to Los Angeles. "We travelled down to LA overnight, straight down the highway," remembers Harvey. "Alan took a lot of speed. We ended up at a guy's house at about five in the morning. We had to give Alan some Valium to calm him down."

Dave Brock, who had seen the earthquake on the TV news, reveals: "Someone had given us a speed crystal – strong, pure speed of the worst order. I didn't want it. I'd given it to Harvey. I told him, 'Be very, very careful with this.' They all snorted it and they were up for two days."

"We might have had 'crystal powers' to get there," agrees Alan. "We'd phoned up this Apache Indian, Michael St Thomas, a really nice guy who we'd met in LA, and he'd said, 'You can come and stay here.' We thought, 'We'll just drive to LA then.'"

After LA, the adventurers pointed the hire car towards the Grand Canyon. Arriving there, they walked into the gift shop and by sheer chance bumped straight into Dave and Kris.

Arriving back in the UK, the band went to Rockfield to mix the tapes of the gig they'd played at LA's Palace Theater. The live material was to be released as *Palace Springs*, along with 'Back In The Box' and 'Treadmill'.

"I was in the studio with Paul Cobbold," says Alan. "There was a rumbling under us, and the ground shook a bit. I thought, 'A lorry's gone past.' Then, 'Hang on a minute, it's another earthquake.' Strangely enough, we were doing my bass at the time."

Hawkwind, with Simon House back in the ranks, finished the year with a UK tour, again including two nights at Hammersmith Odeon. The entourage included Lin Lorien, her family and a bunch of friends, all travelling together in the familiar, gaily painted double-decker bus. Lin had been invited along so that she could sell copies of the *Travellers Aid Trust* album at the gigs. Dave and Hawkwind asked for nothing in return.

"So many other bands would have wanted their cut," says Lin. "Hawkwind supported us so much. We didn't get enough copies of the album to sell. There was a problem with the printing of them. So we bootlegged them on to tapes on the machine in my bus. We were taping them as we were going along so we'd have a couple of dozen to sell each night. We printed up the cover to do it properly.

"We bucketed [collected money in buckets] and sold badges and anything we could think of, and we put everything into the Travellers Aid Trust funds. All we took out was our diesel expenses. My bus went along with the stage bus and the crew bus. The crew were saying – 'Your bus will never make it through all these dates.' Their smart Skania bus broke down and my bus didn't."

The tour was a great success for Decker Lin. She reveals: "One of the funniest things when we got back was that we had something like £3,000 in small change in a box in the cupboard. We had to go back to Andover afterwards, and I'd got to go and weigh this money and get it into the bank account. I had a taxi at the time, and I had to find a shopping trolley, fill it up with bags of money and load it into the taxi just to get it all to the bank. They were loath to accept it to start with. I had to get all the charity paperwork out before they would take it.

"The taxi was one of the archetypal Sixties black ones. I could get a double twin pram in there, and all my other children. I had a truck engine put into it, so it was more powerful, but it went no faster than 40 miles an hour. We could tow trucks with it, and we put town and country tyres on it so it could plough across fields."

Lin had also accompanied the band on the June tour; they'd become firm friends through the festival scene. She says: "Hawkwind [and Hawkdog] played whenever they could at all the free festivals. It was just what they did, and it wasn't just a little five-minute set either. They would play and play. Band members from before or somebody from another band would come along and play. They gave their all every time.

"Hawkwind to me never had really just been a music band. They were more of a lifestyle, almost. That's what we believe in, the freedom to think what you want to think and, most of the time, to be able to do what you want to do so long as it doesn't clash too badly with anybody else's ideas – 'good' anarchy."

Unfortunately, "bad" anarchy was breaking out across the travelling world, which was in meltdown. Dave Brock, Kris Tait, Decker Lin and

Scouse would all come to regard 1990 as the year that the free-festival scene died, or was killed.

Simon House left the band again. "Holly, my daughter, got leukaemia and that kind of changed everything," he explains. "I re-mortgaged my house, bought some studio equipment and started doing my own stuff. She's 18 now. She still has to go for a check twice a year. She's just handed in her notice at a solicitor's down in the West End somewhere. She was so fed up and wants to go travelling. She passed her driving test first time, and she's got a little car."

Simon would come back to Hawkwind some years later.

His last show for the time being was in January 1990 at a Channel 4 TV recording in Nottingham, where the band played a full live set. Coincidentally, this was the occasion on which Bridget Wishart stepped in as a full-time member, contributing vocals, dance and performance.

Hawkwind, with Bridget, went into Rockfield to record a new studio album, *Space Bandits*, and ventured out only rarely in the first half of the year. They travelled to Somerset for the Glastonbury Festival on June 23 and 24, and it was the last time that Dave, Kris or Decker Lin would set foot anywhere near Michael Eavis' Worthy Farm.

The organisers had severed their links with CND and had created a new billing. It was now the Glastonbury Festival For Contemporary Performing Arts. However, this year's event would be remembered not for the name change but for the full-scale fighting that erupted between travellers and site security after the festival had officially finished.

The travellers say they were attacked by security thugs. There were 235 arrests, and the next year's Glastonbury was cancelled. Michael Eavis accused the travellers of looting the empty site, although the BBC reported a significant police finding: the security teams had prepared petrol bombs and weapons.

Decker Lin comments: "Michael Eavis should have blamed his security for what happened. They were out for a fight. I've never seen human beings being treated quite so badly."

The travellers, from then on, were no longer welcome at Glastonbury. At the same time, an undesirable element had entered their numbers. "There was violence, thieving and mugging," says Kris. "And it was the weekend hippies that used to be mugged. We were starting to feel that we didn't want to be the bait, bringing people in so they could be robbed."

Decker Lin remarks: "I first put a padlock on my fuel tank in 1990."

Dave likens the situation to a Wild West movie: "The outlaws ride into town, take over the saloon and say, 'We'll help ourselves to guns and food.' At festivals, the outlaws would say, 'I want those tricycles for my kids.' The easy-going people would reply, 'Yes, let the children have a ride.' And when they went to get the tricycles back when they were leaving – 'Well, they're ours now. If you're going to take them back we'll smash your bus up.'

"This greed and nastiness is hard to explain unless you've lived in these places and been involved in it all. It was quite often connected with heroin and Special Brew. A lot of these no-hopers were from the city. They were going out into festival life and getting out of it, and not putting anything back in. You're talking about maybe 10 per cent of people causing problems for the 90 per cent. And so what was camaraderie and unified strength became separated.

"A lot of the old boys were quite easy-going, but when they spoke out, they'd get all their windows smashed at night. There was a guy we knew called Mike The Mechanic. He had a double-decker. He used to supply generators at festivals. He'd fixed the engine of somebody's bus and asked for money, because that was his skill and that's how he made a few quid on the road. They told him to fuck off and they set fire to his bus. His kids were in it at the time. This sort of thing was happening more and more. One woman running a first-aid tent had her tepee burnt down. A guy that we knew was beaten up. It's an overall picture of escalating violence, and we wanted to stop it."

Behind all this was the suspicion that many of the problems involving drugs and violence were being planted there deliberately by the authorities, that some of the "travellers" were infiltrators or addicts paid with heroin, booze or cash to discredit the movement publicly. Similar tactics, it's alleged, were used to instigate the Poll Tax riots and other protests which had started out peacefully; to remove their original power.

Says Kris Tait: "It went a bit peculiar at the end, the free-festival scene. When it kicked off, it really kicked off properly, uncontrollably, with mob riots. It was a deliberate act by someone who wanted to destroy everything. They used violence in the mid-Eighties and then they resorted to tactics. The whole scene was getting too scary, too big and too powerful to be allowed to continue."

"They had to stop the festival scene from the inside," agrees Lin Lorien. "I went off the road because I didn't want my kids growing up in that atmosphere of serious, nasty drugs. There were some very, very good bits and some very bad bits, mostly all at the same time."

One observer, who prefers to remain anonymous, sums it up: "The best way of controlling people is to destroy the society in the same way that the Americans did to the Indians by giving them whiskey. Put heroin into the site to get people to do bad things. Use drugs to pay people to do your bidding. The undercovers were using people."

Against this background, Hawkwind turned up for a free gig on a stretch of public ground outside Brighton on August 19, 1990 – the eve of Dave's 49th birthday. It was anything but a celebration.

"I didn't really want to do it," confesses Dave. "I had this feeling that something bad was going to happen. I wanted to go off to Cropredy in Cambridgeshire, Fairport Convention's festival, which was good fun, kid-orientated."

Instead, he ended up getting shot onstage in East Sussex.

There are differing stories about what triggered the mayhem. Some say that Dave was "egged" onstage in a traditional travellers birthday ritual. What is not disputed is that there was an anti-Hawkwind contingent in the audience, determined to demonstrate its displeasure.

"We'd been speaking out against heroin dealing at festivals," says Brock. "Heroin is problematic. Lots of schoolkids had been coming down to festivals to see what was going on and they were being plied with bad drugs. I'd been going on about this for quite a while, and so had a few other people. The trouble is that if you speak out, sometimes you become a target, and they decided I was a target. There were a lot of weird scenes going on there. I got shot in the leg with an air rifle onstage."

Dave confirms reports that after being attacked, he retaliated by lashing out at his assailant with a spanner. And then: "There was chaos. A lot of Hawkwind fans who were on our side were trying to stop all these things, and it got worse and worse and escalated into a big bundle. It was the end of the festival. A lot of good people got injured. Some terrible things occurred, and the repercussions were so serious. Someone threw our dogs through the window of our bus . . . and they did get their come-uppance. It was the decline and fall. We stopped doing free festivals after that."

Scouse was there, providing his Wango Riley's stage for the gig. He shakes his head: "It was all very messy. The travellers had a lot of skag. It was coming to the end of the season, and I had the sense that they were a little bit jealous that we had somewhere to go.

"Dave hadn't done anything. Something went up over his head on the stage. It was a ridiculous thing for someone to do – it was very, very stupid of them – and everything just went completely tits up. The catalyst was Dave attacking the guy back. There was horrible, horrible violence. Some people in the audience whipped up this crazy fervour and it turned into a real nightmare. Everybody was scared, and the police were just sitting around in their riot vans laughing. It was really hideous, the thing that happened there.

"When we pulled out, someone had loosened up the bolts of the two-bar and my trailer came off 10 miles down the road. It had been sabotaged."

Scouse was at the same time splitting up with his partner, Marge, and the Brighton incident was one trouble too many. He says: "It was the nail in the coffin. It was a very, very black day, the next day, very disappointing. I gave up all the free festivals. I thought, 'What's the point?' I did one more gig with the stage, a show in Waltham Abbey, and I put the whole business on the market and sold it."

Alan Davey rages: "That was the end of it, really. That's what finished the whole travelling scene at the time. I felt angry that it could have happened, that something so bad could have gone on. The most vivid memory I have of that day is of two policemen standing by a car watching, smiling and laughing. They should have stopped it. Awful."

Kris Tait later wrote a poem about the whole disillusioning experience. She says: "I wrote it as a catharsis. I was so pissed off after that had happened, I couldn't get it out of my head. I never write when I'm happy. I write when I have a need. I've got to get these feelings out of my head, put them in a box and throw them away."

Her words weren't thrown away. They were used as the lyrics to a Hawkwind song, 'Festivals', which would appear on the album *Alien 4*. "*I thought that it would be destroyed from the outside . . . not from within/ By the closed-minded Fascists, not by our own kith and kin.*"

"I wish I'd gone to Cropredy," says Dave, rounding out his thoughts. "It was a bad mistake to have gone to Brighton. There's fate for you. That's why we decided to get our own festivals together."

CHAPTER 26

Female Trouble

ROCKFIELD was Richard Chadwick's first experience of a large, professional studio. Going in to record *Space Bandits*, he found everything really exciting, but by the time they'd recorded the first track, he was already disillusioned.

"It was a big, long, very fast song called 'Images' that, lyrically, Bridget had got together," he relates. "It went at 174 beats per minute. I found it very difficult. I listened back and I realised I wasn't staying in time with the click track. That was a let-down for me. I was then faced with the prospect of programming the drums, which I'd never done ever before. I was like a Stone-Age man with his technology."

Then there was the overdubbing.

"That was a big depression," recalls Richard. "I thought, 'Blimey, there's a whole album here where it doesn't feel like I'm playing on it. Oh shit! You need to get a proper drummer who can play properly.' I was in a deep trough of despair."

He remembers taking a phone call from Simon House, who played on the album: "Simon was asking, 'What's happening about the money?' I was despairing about whether I should even be in the band. I was, 'I don't know, ask somebody else.'

"Then I thought, 'I've got two options here – learn how to play the drums properly or get into electronics.' So what I did was I got into electronics. Most of our recordings have been made using midi drumpads. Live, I just use the kit, although I do use the electronics as well."

Hawkwind were also venturing further into technology, including sampling, at this time. Harvey spent hours compiling samples from the television for 'TV Suicide', and Dave was collecting everything from car-horn sounds to animal noises and spoken word. Alan Davey was mastering new skills too.

Says Richard: "He bought a beautiful little fretless bass guitar and taught himself to play it while we were in the studio, just to put the performance on 'Wings'."

Some of the album ideas were more ambitious than others.

"For 'Out Of The Shadows', we tried to get this effect of listening to music outside while the sound is moved by the wind," recalls Richard. To this end, the band attempted to record music coming out of speakers in the yard outside the studio – but there was no wind. They resorted to effects.

Despite his teething problems in the studio, Richard now looks back proudly on *Space Bandits*, if not its cover artwork. He enthuses: "I listened to it about two weeks ago and it sounds pretty amazing. I think it's really expressive and flowing, and beautifully recorded. He was good at that, Paul Cobbold. The band sound really loose, but powerful."

Richard is even impressed by 'Images', complete with the drum program that had caused him so much anxiety. He adds: "The track 'Black Elk Speaks' sounds like a really, really good mix-worthy kind of track. You could use it to DJ with. Bridget does this fantastic poem – *'In your throat is a living song, a living spirit song.'* That's what lifts that track up. Even the girl vocal sound, which was a shock to listen to initially, I think, sounds really bright."

Asked for his assessment of the album, Dave Brock replies, characteristically: "I haven't listened to it." But he reveals that all of the publishing proceeds from 'Black Elk Speaks' were donated to the Sioux Pine Ridge reservation.

He explains: "A lot of the Sioux had been protesting about their treatment and they'd barricaded the reservation. The American government sent sheriffs in to break down these obstacles across the roads, and there was a big shoot-out. There were bad scenes going on over there. They shot a few Indians. The proceeds went to the mothers and the children of the people who had been killed. Nothing really changes over there. The same old thing goes on and on."

'Wings' is another track which has raised cash for charity. It was written by Alan Davey after the Exxon Valdez oil spill and its devastating effect on the bird population.

"It was horrific seeing those images on TV," remembers Alan. "All those birds just struggling to get out of the oil . . . it really hit me big-time. This song just poured out, literally in 15 minutes, the words and the music. I recorded it as a demo, and then we did it for the album. The Royal Society For The Protection Of Birds gets a percentage of royalties."

'Realms' was an equally spontaneous contribution from Alan. "I did it when I was on acid," he confides. "It was deep-space noise, but I can't remember how I did it now."

Asked if he had considered taking acid again to see if he could rediscover his muse, he replies: "I did! I took another tab of acid and I tried to back-engineer it, to figure out what I could have done. I started with the original bass and vocal thing, but I could never do it again. The moral of the story is, always be ready with that 'record' button."

Like Richard, Alan is a fan of *Space Bandits*: "This was an extremely inventive period, and we were coming up with very strong material. We had some strange experimental stuff on there, and we knew when we finished it that it was going to sound really good."

Bridget Wishart isn't convinced. She told *The Hawkwind Museum*: "It's hard to be realistic about it. I was really proud at the time, but it's not my favourite kind of music and it's not the best Hawkwind record."

At the same time, she confessed that she wasn't particularly a fan of the band before she joined and that she didn't have a favourite Hawkwind album.

They spent three months preparing for a UK tour in the autumn and a return trip to America immediately afterwards. The rehearsals took place at Dave and Kris' farmhouse, while Harvey, Alan, Richard and Bridget roomed in a holiday let – part of a big manor house in a country estate nearby.

There, Bridget shared a room with her old friend Richard. She recalled: "He would draw an invisible line down the room and forbid any of my junk to cross it. I did try . . . When we weren't rehearsing, there was a lot of flying of polystyrene aeroplanes."

"We were usually the only ones there," recollects Harvey Bainbridge, whose personal life would be turned upside down by what transpired that summer.

"Most of the time was spent sunbathing," smiles Dave. "That's when Alan fell in love with Alice – and Harvey fell in love with Alice."

Alice Futter was a festival regular who had met Alan at Glastonbury 1989. "We all hung around together in the free field for a while," says Harvey of that first encounter. "I think she was a fan of the band. Alan, as far as I know, tried very hard with her. I didn't know what was going on between them, but I think she did eventually turn him down. She came down to Devon and spent the summer with us the next year when we were rehearsing down at Dave's. Her truck broke down and she parked it at the country house where we were all staying. As the summer progressed, I ended up running off with her. It was all very naughty. It was the summer of love, as Richard keeps telling me . . ."

Harvey got "cold feet" and returned to his wife, Anne, although the reconciliation didn't last for long: "When we came back from the American tour at the end of the year, my wife and I split up. She went off to Australia to visit her brother just before we went into rehearsals for the European tour in the spring of 1991. When we came back from that tour, I lived with Alice in our big truck. After a couple of months or so, I decided I was doing the wrong thing. I had to go and fix my old life up, but that didn't work. I shouldn't have looked back. I should have carried on regardless and realised that my old life was gone. I suppose it was vanity on my part that I thought I could fix it.

"Alice was terribly upset. She was a very nice girl. I just felt that there was no possible way I could go back to her a second time, although I wanted to. I felt it wouldn't have been right. I think she was pretty hard done by. It makes me feel sad to think about it."

In the relatively short time that Harvey and Alice spent together, they conceived a son, Jay. Harvey also has two grown-up children, Matthew and Louis, from his marriage to Anne.

"Alice and I used to get on all right," says Alan, telling his side of the story. "Then after a couple of weeks, we realised it wasn't working out between us. We weren't suited. I went off to Germany to see someone else, a teacher that I'd met in Washington. She was just a friend. I quite often meet women that just end up as friends. Some men meet a woman and that's it, they've gotta bed them. But they don't end up with any female friends, do they?

"I came back and Alice and Harvey had got together. I suppose I was a little surprised, but then, I know Harvey . . . I think it was a mid-life crisis thing, going off with a young girl. I think he was about 40 and she was about 20. She was considered a very young girl for him to be with. Then his wife found out, or she had suspicions, and I think he just lost it with everything, really. Anne, his wife, she was really nice. He probably felt so bad about that."

Space Bandits reached its highest chart position of number 70 in October 1990, and Hawkwind toured the UK in support of it. They played almost all of the new material onstage, usually opening with 'Realms', which found Bridget preparing for take-off in a radiation suit. Elsewhere, she appeared in a skeleton suit and mask for 'Angels Of Death', and transformed herself for 'Back In The Box' with a bald head and a white boiler suit and goggles. At the end of the set, she changed into a new costume for the encore of 'Reefer Madness', coming on like a dapper young gentleman in a suit and tie, accessorised with a hat and gloves – and a beard.

With Bridget, Pogle's extravagant light-show, mime and dancing displays from new girl Julie Murray and Kris Tait's spectacular fire-blowing, Hawkwind had rediscovered the art of theatre in a big way.

"This was the first full tour where I did fire," says Kris. "You can't do it every night 'cos it messes your lungs up. You can get pleurisy if you don't give your lungs a break. It's easy to make it look scary, but it can actually be dangerous. It took quite a long time to make it look dangerous while actually being in control of it."

Kris would from now on concentrate on fire, only returning to dancing when absolutely necessary. She would sometimes be joined in her flaming exploits by Scouse. He may have sold his travelling stage, but he was still happy to perform with Hawkwind from time to time.

Scouse had left school and gone on the road with a clown company when he was 15 and quickly learnt fire-eating, unicycling, juggling – all the circus skills. The clowns began working at festivals, and Scouse remembers being "blown away" watching Hawkwind.

Progressing into staging in 1986, he continued performing too and at one point was running his own Wango's Circus. He also had a troupe called Circus Bong while touring the festivals with the travelling stage. Scouse met Hawkwind properly in 1988 at Wick Tip and he declares: "I very soon got roped into fire-eating with them by Kris."

Kris and Scouse would plan ever-more-elaborate displays for Hawkwind gigs as time went on, sometimes choreographing or synchronising their fire-eating and utilising props and costumes and even trapeze artists. Says Scouse: "Normally when you get to the front of the stage and start spitting fire over the audience, they pull back. I remember once at Glasgow Barrowlands it was the opposite. They were cramming forward. It was mental."

Scouse is now the owner of a company called Wango's, travelling all over Europe supplying festival stages. Three years ago, he finally moved into a house (as has Decker Lin) after years on the road living in a trailer.

Hawkwind had become very tight musically after their months of rehearsal in Devon, and it was generally agreed that Bridget Wishart was an asset. The audiences seemed to approve too, once they'd got over the shock of Hawkwind having a female frontperson. "My major contributions were visual," she told *The Hawkwind Museum*. "I designed all my outfits and linked them to specific songs. I felt the costume and the movement added another dimension to the songs. I also worked on videos for 'Back In The Box' and 'Images' [which she storyboarded and directed]. I also wrote lyrics and melodies, usually for the spacey sections of existing songs."

Bridget's personal tour highlight was being onstage at the Hammersmith Odeon on November 6 (the usual two nights now dropping to one), but she would rather forget the show where she had to perform in agony after tripping over Harvey's monitor. On another occasion, in America, Harvey was indirectly involved in another of Bridget's tumbles: "His roadie fell offstage just as I was coming on, bowling me over into my flight case, knocking it over and shutting me inside." They couldn't have planned it better.

"She was very theatrical," comments Harvey. "She was energetic, full of ideas, and she was good company. She was a bit of a loony, as we all are."

In America, Bridget simply shone. Hawkwind took a couple of weeks off after the UK tour finished, and travelled to the States for a month of dates across November and December 1990. "That was the tour that Bridget got really, really good," says Richard Chadwick. "She discovered and perfected the art of taking on different personae. She concentrated not so much on bizarre, outlandish costumes but on changing herself so that she felt different. Like a long wig gave her the confidence to sing really well. She was singing marvellously. She could really project her voice.

"She had this material that she hitched to a pole, and she spun round and it wrapped round her bit by bit. She'd be wrapped up onstage like a mummy, so that she couldn't move. I can't imagine what that would feel like, with hundreds of people watching, with flashing lights, and if you lose your balance . . .

"She did some really provocative imagery when we played 'The

Golden Void'. And for 'Wings' she looked like a very quaint little girl with a feminine kind of vibe. She had a black shawl over her head. She pulled it off and made it into a tiny little ball, and she was caressing it affectionately. All of a sudden, she ripped it to pieces really aggressively. I thought it was incredible. You draw the audience's attention to this small thing and then start to destroy it."

Dave adds: "She wrote a few numbers that were really good, and some great poems, like 'The Seventh Star' [later released on *Live 1990*]."

"Bridget was quite a big hit in America," agrees Harvey. "Especially with the boys who came to the gigs."

"There were some fans who didn't like us having a female singer," concedes Dave. "Others did. But you can't keep doing the same thing all the time. It would be boring. That's why we only go forwards. We don't live in the past. In fact, our next show is all about androids and that . . ."

But despite the artistic success of the tour, an atmosphere was building up between Bridget and the rest of the entourage as they criss-crossed the United States. "She had this problem with talking to people," recalls Dave. "We accept people, all these different members of the band and their personalities. We know each other so well, all our problems in life. But with Bridget, the roadies used to really dislike her. She'd say, 'Put that here, would you!' or, 'I want that over there!' No please or thank you. 'And when you've done that . . .' Poor old Bridget. And the thing is, she was in a man's world too, which was quite difficult for her. She was living in the bus with us. Angie [Richard's then girlfriend and Bridget's former bandmate] came over too, and Kris was there as well, so it weren't so bad."

Harvey remarks: "It was very hard for a girl in terms of the chauvinism that was probably shown."

Bridget had been used to the friendly informality of Demented Stoats and the Hippy Slags; the Hawkwind touring operation was on a different scale altogether, and she found it at once exciting, professional, chaotic and disturbing.

The tour bus was certainly a step up from the "Slagmobile", a Bedford CA van in which the girls had travelled from gig to gig. But Bridget missed the fun and the companionship of her old band, saying pointedly: "We all got on and no one had ego problems."

Similarly, she had mixed feelings about hotels. They were a luxury and she appreciated them, but they were ultimately lonely places for her. On checking in, she would immediately litter her room with personal items to create some sense of familiarity, some comfort. She maintained her friendship with Richard but she didn't feel particularly close to anyone else in the band, and she found touring exhausting.

Bridget told *The Hawkwind Museum*: "There was always a lot of 'Hurry up and wait' with Hawkwind. It drove me mad sometimes . . . Touring was very tiring and after a few weeks, the only time that we were really focused was when we were onstage. The rest was a blur of meeting people, driving from place to place, and setting up and taking down . . .

"Hawkwind is really a male world. I worked hard when I was with them and enjoyed the creative opportunities. There was a hierarchy that I didn't agree with and a sense of humour that was 'all boy', and it wasn't really my thing. I don't regret the time I spent with them – I was very proud to be in the band – but I guess I was a little disappointed that it didn't work out the way I imagined it would."

Asked for her best Hawkwind memories, Bridget tellingly replied that she didn't have any because "it wasn't that kind of life".

Kris Tait says of Bridget: "She was all right. I was pleased when she first came along. I'm always pleased when there are other women around, because it's so lonely being on the road as the only girl. But she was quite cold towards me, not matey. She felt happy not being one of the lads. I suppose I'm one of the lads, but in a different way. It was strange, actually. We never argued. We were both there at the same time and we were civil to each other, but we never became close friends."

One key character who was missing on that American tour was Pogle, the lighting god. He'd been busted at his home in Reading. Unfortunately for Dave Brock, his van had been parked at Pogle's house at the time of the raid. He went to pick it up, and as he was driving back along the A303, there was a "terrible clunk".

"The police had undone some of the bolts on the drive shaft," he says. "They'd practically disconnected it. It was a punishment. This was all because of our involvement with free festivals."

In Pogle's absence, the illuminations were being controlled by Adie and another lighting technician called Jenny. At the end of the tour, the band and their entourage were in LA. Dave and Kris had been planning to stay on in the States for a little while. Says Dave: "We were in one of those hotels that had a swimming pool and was decorated in pink and turquoise green. It had something like two storeys. I went downstairs and left my credit card at the desk to pay for the hotel bill. The guy at reception took my card and said it was out of date. He cut the fucking thing up and threw it away.

"I was leaning across the desk. I wanted to grab him and clock him one – 'What do you think you're fucking doing?' He called the police. All I would have had to do was make a phone call to sort out any problems over the card. It was hard luck for me and my credit card, and my holiday had gone down the drain."

Dave stormed off upstairs to see the rest of the band. Richard says: "I hadn't witnessed the credit card-cutting but, knowing Dave, I could tell something was seriously wrong. Now was not the time for one of the members of the staff to ask, 'Please may I have a wage rise?'"

It was Adie who misjudged the moment for requesting a pay rise. Asked if he got it, Dave jokes, "No, he got the sack." He later adds, "He didn't get the sack then. He did years later, and he then went on to do other light-shows."

Meanwhile, Hawkwind had to find the cash to pay for the hotel. Dave remembers organising a whip-round. Douglas Smith says, "They got into trouble and I put down a credit card in LA to pay to get them out of the hotel. It was a battle to get the money back again. I was always trying to get money out of them."

Douglas had become a little more involved with the band by this time, having left GWR. Hawkwind had picked up an American manager called Greg Lewerke who set up their deals for *Space Bandits* and *Palace Springs* with Legacy Records (which had taken over GWR, and released both albums on that label). Greg had asked Douglas to look after Hawkwind's interests in the UK for him. Smith stresses that then, and in all future dealings with the group, he was representing rather than managing them.

He says, "Greg Lewerke had been their product manager at United Artists in LA when they had the success in the early days, from 1970 to 1973. They sold a lot of records. But after those two albums, Greg packed up, he had enough, and we continued with them.

"Eve [his wife] and I had got rid of the office – we started working on our own in 1986, and we just focused on consulting to a few clients, taking care of the business only from that point on.

"We cleared up a VAT problem for Hawkwind – Dave, Richard, Alan and Harvey. They had let VAT assessments build up over 18 months, and payment was being demanded. All we were given to work from was a big box of receipts and cheque stubs and a few statements from a roadie who'd been looking after their affairs prior to Greg getting involved. From this, we rebuilt the accounts for the 18 months concerned, getting them out of a very large amount that was being demanded. We only charged them £1,000 for it. We've done many favours for Hawkwind.

"We still administer most of the catalogue for 95 per cent of past Hawkwind members, protecting it from abuse, which is sad. We talk to them all, still. We make sure the royalties are paid correctly and on a regular basis and we got the majority of the catalogue back under all the members' control. This was something we did eight or nine years ago. We got back the catalogue that had been signed away, apart from EMI and most of Cherry Red. The members control all their copyrights of the individual albums and tracks that they are on themselves. It's the most ethical way of doing it.

"GWR and Legacy were sold to Castle after I left GWR. I got two album deals for Dave, Alan and Richard with Castle Communications – one for *Electric Tepee* and the other for *It Is The Business Of The Future To Be Dangerous*. When we got the catalogue that Castle controlled back – these two albums and all the GWR albums and the Legacy albums and three albums of tracks that Dave had signed to a previous manager, Jim White – there was a settlement of a substantial amount of money. The catalogue was reinstated to the members. Once we'd settled with Castle, they were bought by Sanctuary, who respected that the agreed albums and tracks belonged to the members. Getting the albums back was worth more than they ever realised."

Things were trickier with Cherry Red and EMI, which had taken over the United Artists catalogue.

Says Douglas, "Dave had signed agreements with Flicknife. It got into trouble financially, and Cherry Red bought the catalogue. We tried to challenge it and get the catalogue back, but Ian McNay at Cherry Red decided he was going to fight it. The albums sell very little numbers. The royalties of those would add up to very little a year between all of them, and we decided it wasn't worth putting money up to fight Ian McNay. But we did tidy up the deals with Cherry Red, and everyone is getting royalties.

"EMI has a perpetuity deal, but we got the royalties upgraded and a settlement. That was an unrecoupable settlement, as was Castle's. To challenge EMI and get the catalogue back would have cost a lot of money, so we decided to be pragmatic and leave it there."

Douglas first had to sort out Mick Slattery and Terry Ollis, who were insisting on certain conditions in return for agreeing to a settlement with EMI. Says Smith: "Mick was not on any of the original albums, but he's on three tracks, early recordings, which have since appeared on a CD reissue."

These are the demo recordings of 'Hurry On Sundown', 'The Kiss Of The Velvet Whip' and 'Cymbaline', which were included in the digipack CD version of 1970's *Hawkwind*.

"What Mick wanted," continues Douglas, "was that the money would not be involved with Hawkwind's money. He wanted direct payment from EMI and a small settlement.

"Terry Ollis, on the other hand, had lent the band his drums years earlier. Shortly after he left the band, all their equipment was stolen. Terry said that Dave had promised him money for a new drumkit, which he never got. Terry wanted a drumkit, and then he would sign. We got them both sorted, we went forward with EMI, and a deal was done."

Douglas never felt that his work on behalf of Hawkwind was appreciated by Dave Brock. He says: "We'd worked really hard for them, getting this sorted out and that sorted out, getting them out of debt. And then, two months later, I'd read an interview in some magazine and it would be Dave just slagging me off, accusing me of ripping them off, which has never been the case. Dave has constantly inferred that. When challenged about what he was quoted as saying in these articles, he would just say, 'You know, Doug, how all these journalists just misquote you.'

"If you're going to steer a band, as Dave does, you have to be honest and stop telling the world that everybody's ripped you off when it's not the truth, as far as we're concerned. However, I can't confirm that has not happened with other agreements that Dave has signed. It's happened so many times over the whole period that you just begin to wonder, 'Why does he do it?' Why does he have to tell the world that he's this poverty-stricken rock star who everybody has taken money off when he lives on a large and comfortable farm in Devon? Dave likes people to think that he's a struggling, poor old lad, but he's savvy, with lots of horses and property.

"Any ripping off that has been done is because the others have not kept their eyes on the ball and allowed themselves to be ripped off. If albums are licensed with just one signature of a member of the band on the contract, you can guarantee that in the future, questions will be asked. If you do these things honestly, with all the stream rights in place, they don't come back to haunt you. I'm not saying that Dave's done anything dishonest – but the perception by others may be that he has."

Dave says: "Doug, over the years, has had his freak-outs. He's very volatile. He makes a lot of noise sometimes and shouts and freaks out – 'I don't manage you any more, I'm just your consultant.'

"I took my camper van to his house in London. I wanted to catch him in. I wanted to see the accounts. Over the years, we've asked Douglas so many times to send us deals he's done with record companies. We still haven't seen any of them. He says, 'Okay, I'll email them down.' They never arrive. Time and again, I've asked for copies of all the contracts. We never receive them."

"Absolute rubbish," Douglas retorts. "We've made copies of all agreements that we've been involved in and have given them to Dave. In fact, when they sign any agreement, they get a copy. We have made copies for him when he has asked again for a copy. There is a point when it just gets too busy to copy 20 to 40 page agreements all over again. Dave also seems to be under the impression that we've signed deals that we've never told him about, which is something we have never done for any artist.

"And if he did come here in his camper van, it's not something I remember. There's always someone in, so why didn't he just knock on the door? He doesn't have to catch us. Dave has visited us here on many occasions, both socially and for business meetings, and has been given whatever accounts he requested."

"He wasn't in," snaps Dave, insisting on the last word. "But I've got it on video."

Despite the ongoing spats with Dave, Douglas at the time of writing was again working on behalf of Hawkwind – this time on a deal to benefit everyone, past and present. The task of representing and unifying all of the members over one common goal was proving troublesome but, hey, this is Hawkwind. It was nothing new.

The band returned from America in time for Christmas. It had been an eventful year for everyone, not least Dave Brock. For it was in 1990 that he was approached by a young lady claiming to be his 25-year-old daughter.

The first that Dave heard of Jane was when she sent a letter to his PO box address. He dismissed it as a joke. Jane then phoned and left a message on the answering machine. Dave suspected he was being pursued by a crank, and his first thoughts were for his parents: this woman might find their number in the phone book, they were getting on in years, and he didn't want them to be on the receiving end of any upsetting phone calls. Dave and Kris decided to return Jane's call.

"She seemed nice," says Kris. "Quite young and happy."

Dave recollects the story that Jane had to tell: "She said she was born in 1965 and that she was adopted at birth. She traced her mother through her birth certificate, and her mother said I was the father. So then she contacted me. We didn't believe her, although she does look uncannily like me. I went to her wedding."

There, Dave met Jane's birth mother. He says: "I couldn't remember this woman for the life of me. I still don't. She said she lived with me for three months, and she never did. She didn't know any of the people I was talking about. It was quite strange."

Kris adds: "Whoever she was, she'd never actually told Dave she was pregnant. He'd had no idea, so he never had any choice in what happened. At the time we met Jane, she was living in Exeter with her boyfriend, who was a Hawkwind fan. Before she was told Dave was her dad, she'd seen videos of the band, and she'd read my book. It just seemed odd. Of all the people to be born to and have no idea . . ."

"I'm not convinced," says Dave. "Perhaps until we have a proper test, who knows? So I *may* have a daughter. Jane always assumes she's my daughter. But anyway, she came into our life. She's spent time with our horses. She works hard, and she's got two kids herself now."

Kris Tait has been supportive in welcoming Jane into the family, adding: "I wouldn't have been so understanding if she'd been five!"

Dave quickly remarks: "I've been very loyal to Kris. I'd never have done anything like that while we've been together, which is a long period of time. I'm very honest and trusting and trustworthy. We're still in love."

In March 1991, Hawkwind played a European tour and, almost unthinkably, the captain was not at the helm. Dave Brock elected to stay at home in Devon, officially because he was mixing material. In reality, he didn't fancy four weeks of gigs in minor venues.

"I had bronchitis for three months without knowing it," claims Dave. "The thought of having to do another load of dates in small, smoky places . . . You must remember, I was coming up 50 then. I was getting on a bit. They're all younger than me. But I could have been doing something in the studio too. As we speak now, I've got two, three albums I've gotta mix."

Harvey saw it another way: "Dave didn't want to go on a tour bus. He didn't want to mix with everybody else. He was trying desperately hard to persuade me and Alan not to go. Personally, I thought we ought to. There wasn't much money involved, but we hadn't been over to Europe for a while. Alan wanted to do it."

Harvey, Alan, Richard and Bridget were augmented by a guitarist friend of Richard's called Steve Bemand. They'd played together since the days of Demented Stoats. The five-piece rehearsed near Bath and the tour began. As it progressed, Richard noted the effects of Dave's absence with amusement.

"It was great," he laughs. "It was fabulous anarchy – burgeoning egos tottering higher and higher. Bands have a chemistry, and if one element of it is missing and you bring in a new element that's not so pushy or strong a character, the other elements start to reorganise, like a pack of wolves. You get a reconstructing of the hierarchical structure, like being in a fight or an intense game. You can instantly sense your partners' weaknesses in that situation.

"Without Dave's leadership, we had Harvey and Alan getting bigger, as it were. The keyboard solos and bass solos would become longer, and I'd be there, drumming away, and all this for hours on end. The jams and instrumentals would go on longer."

Alan Davey disputes that there were any "burgeoning egos", but he admits: "I remember we jammed out for longer. If Dave thinks something's going on too long or getting boring, he'll put a stop to it. I remember me and Harvey doing our best to make sure things ran properly. It may have looked like we were taking over. You have to have someone in charge to make executive decisions on the tour.

"But it wasn't as good without Dave. I did miss him, in all aspects of it. We didn't get any boos or hassle 'cos he wasn't there, but it's like

Motorhead going on without Lemmy: it ain't gonna happen. I suppose we may have done things we wouldn't have if Dave was there, but I wouldn't say there were a lot of big egos going on."

Harvey says: "Dave's guitar sound is unique, and he's got a distinctive singing voice. We kind of missed that, really."

Both Harvey and Bridget remember the tour more for the places they went and the things that happened there. Bridget's abiding recollection is the mad beach party they enjoyed somewhere in Italy after a gig cancellation, drinking the tour bus dry and then the local café, after which she received an unwelcome proposition from the driver.

Harvey suggests that it was a "big mistake" to start the tour in Amsterdam, where the first gig took place on March 12 at the Paradiso club. A bag of speed was soon procured, and after a couple of gigs in Holland, the band were crossing the border into Germany.

Says Harvey: "Alan was running up and down the bus with his bag of speed as we approached the border. Steve Bemand said, 'I'll look after it.' I said, 'No, don't give it to *him*!' The road crew wouldn't look after it."

The precious powder ended up being sent flying out of the air vent in the bus – quite unnecessarily as it turned out, since the band were waved straight through at the border.

Alan remembers: "We all went into panic mode. Everyone suddenly jumped up and started throwing everything out of the bus. You know what the Germans are like – you have to be like them to be accepted. Richard told me that I consciously got out of my bunk, collected everyone's passport and went straight up to the customs guys and had everything ready. Efficient. They just accepted that this was a bus full of efficient people and let us through. Someone had to take control and look together, and it worked."

In Germany, where Hawkwind played quite a few dates, Steve Bemand caused Harvey more than a few chuckles. "He's a lovely man, Steve," laughs Bainbridge. "He's brilliant. It might have been in Nuremberg or somewhere like that, he went off with some girl and nearly missed the gig. We waited and waited for him. The gig was very odd. It was in something like a cattle auction market, out in the country. My eldest son, Matthew, was a guitar roadie on the tour. It was the first time he'd come out with the band. He'd just returned from Australia where he'd been working at the Sydney Opera House as part of the stage crew, and he'd been out with bands before too. We were going through the road crew saying, 'Who can play the guitar and who knows the songs?' Matthew could have stood at the back strumming along, but he didn't get the chance because Steve turned up just before we went onstage.

"Another story from that tour was in Frankfurt where Steve was a bit out of it. Two of the crew were holding him up at the back of the stage 'cos he was almost falling off. He was just out to lunch."

The dates in what was then Yugoslavia took place just before the war broke out, and the bus driver didn't want to go there. The band, encouraged by the British Embassy, insisted on pressing ahead but found themselves surrounded by tension – and soldiers – in what Harvey felt was "a very edgy place". They played one gig and called off the other because the venue was too small for the gear.

Leaving Greece after shows in Athens, they proceeded to Italy via a ferry across the Adriatic Sea. They weren't carrying any drugs, but the Italian customs nevertheless took a special interest in the band.

"They put the dogs on the bus," says Harvey. "They went through all our gear, and it was really annoying. Then we had a gig in Paris [on April 9]. The driver had been given instructions by his firm just to dump us and our equipment on the pavement in Paris and leave us there because no bills had been paid to the bus company. I had to freak out on the phone with Doug, who was acting as an agent for us in those days. It did get sorted out, and the driver did take us to Belgium for the last gig of the tour. I remember that I had to put my money in the kitty so that the road crew could be paid, and all that kind of stuff. I was on the phone for quite a long time to Douglas from Belgium."

Douglas doesn't remember the incident clearly, but he says: "These sort of things don't happen very often and when they do, it's usually because of other people's mistakes. You pay the bills, but things can go wrong somewhere along the line. The driver's money probably would have been coming out of the Paris fee. Maybe the record company or promoter was supposed to pay the band and 'cos they didn't get paid, the driver didn't get paid. It's not something you can control."

Harvey: "When we got back to England, I spoke to Dave and his first words were, 'Where's all the merchandising money?'"

Harvey left Hawkwind after that tour for various reasons.

"I should've left a lot earlier than I did," he says. "I remember on one occasion, Alan Davey phoned me up. He said, 'We're rehearsing for a couple of days.' I said, 'I've got no money. I'll come down when I've got some.' I was stuck in north Devon. They said there wouldn't be any money until the first gig. I said, 'I can't make it, then.' They were rehearsing at Brock's farm, and most of the money was going to pay off the bills at Dave's studio."

Returning from Europe, Harvey was confronted with the prospect of another American tour. "Dave had brought all the dates forward," he claims. "I didn't understand why." Brock has no recollection of this.

"I was going through problems in my home life at the time," continues Harvey. "I'd split up with my wife and I was moving back in with Alice. I really wanted time off. I didn't want to go out on the road again."

"That European tour was very hard for Harvey, living on a bus," remarks Richard Chadwick. "He's very tall, and he couldn't stand up straight in it. He'd wake early in the morning and go to bed the latest at night. It's very difficult in that kind of environment. He was a big guy in a small space. He left to go off with Alice 'cos she was about to have a baby."

Says Alan Davey: "I was really sorry to see him go. We all love Harvey. He's a really nice old boy. I'd love to play with him again. I had my own little band a few years ago and we always used to invite him along. He's great company, Harvey. One of those ones you always give a hug to when you see him."

Harvey moved to the north of England, although he would continue to see Hawkwind. Through the Nineties, he supported them as a solo artist, and sometimes stayed onstage to play in their show too. In 2000, he would rejoin the band for an eventful tour of Australia and New Zealand.

He is currently living with his partner in Longridge, just outside Preston, and working with children who have extreme behavioural problems. And: "At the same time, I'm trying to work out how I can afford a lawyer to sue Hawkwind. There's lots of money that ought to be coming my way."

Bridget also opted out of the American tour. "She had problems with her boyfriend," says Dave. "He didn't want her to be away touring and doing weeks and weeks of rehearsal."

And so, early in May 1991, Dave Brock, Alan Davey and Richard Chadwick set off to America as a three-piece. It was the third tour in their four-step US plan. The next would be the one in which they expected to start showing a profit.

At the beginning of July, Bridget returned to Hawkwind for a couple of special shows at Glasgow Barrowlands and Brixton Academy, where they were joined by their old keyboard wizard, Tim Blake. They played the Cullompton Festival in the same month, and in August, appeared at the Mildenhall Speedway Stadium, followed by a gig in Exeter.

These were Bridget's last gigs with Hawkwind. As she puts it, "I was asked to go. Someone said they'd go if I didn't."

Alan says that he and Richard invited Bridget to leave, while Dave Brock remembers: "Alan had a major freak-out with her. She'd started singing out of tune. She had problems with her boyfriend and became a bit insecure. The thing with Bridget – she was a lovely girl, very artistic, but she was delicate, quite easy to upset. When she was upset it affected her confidence, and when her confidence was affected, or she was nervous, she couldn't sing in tune properly, which was quite awkward. It used to bug Alan somewhat."

Richard: "He'd be trying to sing harmonies with her."

"I got on very well with her, actually," carries on Dave. "I like her. Always have done. I thought she was really good, very delicate in her artistry. I said, 'Tell you what, Bridget, why don't you go to singing lessons?' It would have been a good idea, to learn to breathe in time. She couldn't handle it really. If someone said, 'For fuck's sake, why can't you sing in tune?' she'd be upset, but she'd try.

"The same thing had happened to me years earlier in Hawkwind. You become insecure and you can't do things right. You lose confidence. Unless you've got people to boost you back up again, it becomes hard to push through. You can't seem to get in, and it's very difficult."

Alan comments: "Rich and I had to tell her, 'It's time for you to go.' She didn't take it very well. It must have been hard for her. Sometimes you have to be a bit ruthless, I suppose, for the good of the band."

After leaving Hawkwind, Bridget returned to alternative, free-festival culture. She formed a duo called Daze with 2000 DS guitarist Danny and played gigs in the south west. She then became a choreographer, costume designer and dancer for Techno Pagan, an outfit involving Alan Davey's former roadie, Clive Cursor. After this, Bridget began working with UV décor company Temple Décor, which provided drapes for a number of Hawkwind gigs.

At 40, Bridget gave birth to a daughter, Hannah, and when last heard of, she was living in Bath and planning to marry Hannah's dad. Hawkwind, meanwhile, were back down to three, and they would stay that way for quite some time.

CHAPTER 27

A Dangerous Business: Alien Abducts Tree!

PALACE SPRINGS, with its mixture of live and studio material, didn't exactly storm the chart when it was released in June 1991. The critics weren't too keen either. *Classic Rock* later assessed it as "a very disappointing odds and sods affair" compared to its predecessor *Space Bandits*, which, according to writer Daniel Letch, exemplified "just how much Hawkwind have succeeded in moving their acid rock roots into the modern Ecstasy-fed cyber age, particularly the sprawling anthems 'Images' and 'Out Of The Shadows'".

Hawkwind, however, had already moved on. They were writing material for their next studio album, *Electric Tepee*, and were working on ways of achieving a big sound with only three musicians. Dave and Alan were sharing lead vocals and were both playing keyboards in addition to their usual guitar and bass. Drummer Richard Chadwick was also singing.

By the time the trio embarked on their September/October tour of Scandinavia and Europe, three new songs had entered the set. They'd been playing 'Snake Dance' all year, and 'Blue Shift' since May. Now they were also performing 'LSD'.

Back in the UK for a handful of December shows, a fourth number, 'Mask Of Morning', was introduced. It was a new version of 'Mirror Of Illusion', the song which had been on the B-side of 1970's 'Hurry On Sundown', Hawkwind's first-ever release. The new material slotted into a selection that most nights included 'Master Of The Universe', 'The Golden Void', 'Hassan I Sahba', 'Levitation', 'Arrival In Utopia', 'Night Of The Hawks' and, from *Space Bandits*, 'Realms' and 'Out Of The Shadows'.

Coming into 1992, Hawkwind began to think about recording –

and their circumstances led them into a world of new possibilities, via the computer. "I remember the thing about *Electric Tepee* was that we thought we had to make a record," says Richard. "We hadn't got an advance or a deal or something at that time, so we said, 'Let's record it here with Paul Cobbold.' "

"Here" was Dave's studio, a converted milking shed at his farmhouse in Devon. "It was the first time we'd done an official studio album in anything other than a proper studio," recalls Richard. "I bravely stepped up and said, 'Don't worry, we'll program the drums.' There was a massive, 4,000-mile learning curve on a Roland R8 drum machine. Steve Bemand came along and helped us suss out the manual. He helped me get going on the drum machine until I was good enough to bring it into sessions and drop the programming into the Atari computer, which was running Cubase, a sequencer program.

"The other thing about *Electric Tepee* is that 'cos there were only three of us, we worked out quite a lot of the music together. We actually played the songs live and worked them out as arrangements and made the machines conform to our arrangements. We'd put them in the machine and program all the drums for them. I acquired drum pads and learnt the procedure of playing into the sequencer so we could capture more of the feel of live performance.

"The three of us look back on that as being quite an achievement for us. We got an entire flow of ideas. We all seemed to be playing at the same speed. We were working together very well, and we became very tight."

Alan agrees that the album was a great challenge, although he was initially quite intimidated by the *modus operandi*. He says: "Paul Cobbold, who was engineering it, was in control of the computer that was driving the 16-track tape machine we were recording on. None of us knew anything about that at the time. Paul was there being the brainy one.

"It was the first time I saw a computer used for recording music, personally. It was quite weird; an instant 'don't-want-to-know' reaction came out of me. But I could see the benefits and I learnt just by being inquisitive. I was watching Paul working and I'd say, 'What did you just do?' He's a good teacher; he's now teaching blind children how to use mixing desks. I learnt a lot from Paul whether he knows it or not. He's the great Bhagwan. A wise Bhagwan."

Onstage, Alan particularly enjoyed creating the layers that the three-piece needed to bulk out their sound. He recalls: "You'd have thought there were six people onstage. I used to have foot pedals that would trigger off sequencers or key changes or effects on the keyboards. It got to the point where I didn't have enough feet left. I had a Jupiter 6 keyboard that was great for sound effects, typical Hawkwind oscillations. I was hitting the keyboard with the end of my bass. If there was an appendage, I used it.

"We did this for a couple of years and it was really enjoyable to do a gig and make a wall of noise like people expect to hear and there's just three of us."

Douglas Smith secured an album deal with Castle Communications, and when *Electric Tepee* was released on the Essential label in May 1992, it climbed to number 53 to become Hawkwind's highest-charting album since *Choose Your Masques* 10 years earlier.

One of the tracks, 'Right To Decide', involved the true story of a shooting near Consett in County Durham, and it landed Hawkwind in trouble with the regional newspapers: "Sick Rock Band Cash In On Dryden!"

"My mother saw the press coverage and she rang me up," says Kris. "She said, 'What's Dave done now?'" Albert Dryden was a former steelworker who had been in dispute with the town council over planning permission for a bungalow.

Kris adds: "He was an eccentric and an inventor. He lived right in the middle of nowhere. He asked for planning permission to build a bungalow in the garden for his mum, and they said no. But if the structure's not more than five feet high, you don't need permission, so he dug a big hole and built the bungalow in the hole. The town planner, Harry Collinson, had a real reputation for being a bastard, and he wasn't having it. Dryden said, 'It'll be over your dead body or mine.'"

In June 1991, the council brought in bulldozers to flatten the bungalow. Reacting furiously, Dryden killed 46-year-old Collinson, the chief planning officer, by shooting him twice in the chest and once in the head while he was on the ground. Dryden also shot and wounded a policeman and a BBC reporter who had turned up to cover the planned demolition.

"People had been doing their jobs too much to the letter, tipping Dryden over the edge," says Kris. "Nobody liked the town planner. Nobody ever spoke a good word about him, even when he was dead. People were outside the court with banners supporting Dryden when he was up for trial."

Dryden was jailed in 1992. He received a life sentence for killing Collinson, and a second life sentence for the attempted murder of a council solicitor. He was also given two seven-year concurrent sentences for shooting the policeman and the BBC reporter. The bungalow was finally razed after Dryden had been incarcerated. He has since made two parole bids.

The incident was referred to in 'Right To Decide', which was set to be released as a single. Dave isn't quite sure how it happened – he thinks an advance copy or a promo version may have found its way to the media or the radio – but somehow, Dryden's family got to hear the record, or at least hear *about* it.

"Then Dryden's sister got in touch with us," says Dave. "She was really upset over what had occurred. She felt we were cashing in. I said, 'No, we were just commenting.' It wasn't done in any nasty way. But out of respect, we cut out the offending verse." The single was withdrawn and the track appeared, minus the Dryden passage, on *Electric Tepee*. Much later, in November 1993, various mixes would be included on the *Decide Your Future* EP.

Hawkwind played a UK tour to promote the album in April and May 1992. *Melody Maker*'s David Bennun turned out for the second date at the Brighton Event club on April 24. He reported a gathering of hippies, crusties and spliffheads "of every hue and haircut", described Hawkwind as "an endearing anachronism" and prepared to take the piss. But he ended up surprising himself.

Noting the three-man line-up, he wrote: "This means they're too busy to crank out their patented Bikerdelia and ace space noises simultaneously, effectively dividing the set into well rockin' speed charges alternated with Tangerine Dreamscapes." He loved the light-show.

The review concludes: "A decade or so from now, when they visit your town again – and they will, they will – and your three-year-old asks, 'Mummy, why are Hawkwind?' you'll be as stuck for an answer as I am now. This much I can tell you: nobody in their right mind would want to see this band. Get wasted and go."

The itinerary included one night at the Hammersmith Odeon, and the band followed on with another London gig on August 15 at Brixton Academy. This was an extravaganza billed as "12 Hours Of Psychedelic Madness", and the line-up included Planet Gong, Back To The Planet, Senser and the Spiral Tribe Sound System.

"We had back and front projections, which looked quite weird," says Dave before admitting to scenes of classic *Spinal Tap* hilarity: "I think we had flying saucers. We had these big, transparent tepees onstage, about nine or ten feet high. Pogle came up with the idea of the tepees, and each one of us was inside one."

It had to go wrong. "We were playing onstage and my tepee started to collapse," confesses Richard. "I know it sounds cheesy . . ."

Two people joined the band onstage that night. They were techno/trance duo Salt Tank, who used guitars and drums as well as synthesisers. They had listened to Hawkwind as youngsters and they would pay respect to their elders by producing a remix of 'Master Of The Universe'. The presence of Salt Tank at Brixton was both a tribute to Hawkwind's influence on the dance generation and an acknowledgement that they remained relevant to it.

"When we first saw Salt Tank, they were smartly dressed young men," remembers Richard Chadwick. "By the time they got onstage, one of them had painted the top of his body red and tied his hair into some sort of neanderthal top knot. They jammed with us, playing electronic noises and samples and stuff."

In 1992, Kris enrolled at the University Of Exeter, studying drama. She would graduate in 1995 and would go on to spend another year taking a post-graduate PGCE.

Hawkwind wound up a busy year with another clutch of UK dates.

Sam Fox had been the nation's favourite Page Three girl but, at heart, she'd always been a rock chick. She'd known Lemmy for years and had written a song with him: 'Beauty And The Beast'. It was inspired by Abba.

Early in 1993, Sam was approached by EMI Records, asking if she would like to take part in a recording and video project for the homeless charity Putting Our House In Order. Jon Beast, the London promoter who fronted the charity, was organising a dozen different versions of the Stones' 'Gimme Shelter'. Some were straightforward renditions by bands such as Thunder. Others involved unusual collaborations – and Sam Fox was delighted to team up with Hawkwind.

She says: "I thought they would be a great band to do it with; it would be a nice contrast. It was the first time I'd ever recorded vocals in a studio with a microphone. I normally go in a booth. But Hawkwind know what they want and they definitely know what they're doing. I think we made a really good version of 'Gimme Shelter', really raw. I like it a lot."

The original session took place in a day in London, where the filming was done. Richard recalls: "She was wearing a leather jacket and a rock-chick outfit whereas we were all in jeans and baggy jumpers. She soon realised, 'Oh, right . . .' and it sort of relaxed after that. She was very image-conscious and she was constantly trying to get me to take my jumper off under the heat of the studio lights. She was a good lass. She had a good sense of humour. She's got a rich background, I'd say."

Sam later travelled down to Devon to Dave's farmhouse. She says the purpose of the trip was to work on song ideas. "I played them a few songs I'd written and they played me a few of theirs. We've still not put them down. We might do it one day." Hawkwind remember, rather, that the reason for Sam's visit was to redo some of the vocals for 'Gimme Shelter'. But despite their differing memories of the occasion, Sam, Dave, Kris, Alan and Richard all got on really well, and they would collaborate again.

Says Sam: "I loved working down there. It was a great situation. They've got farmland, and everything's organic. They're very free and easy people; very loving. As much as you think of them as old rockers, it's like working with a lot of kids. They're a very tight-knit group, very spiritual, very lovely people."

Kris remembers: "We were like, 'Oh, God, she's going to be like this horrible little Page Three bimbo, a girlie.' Alan Arthurs [the artist] and a lot of other people came round, and they'd all washed, and I remember them all standing by the wall waiting for the car to arrive. It was like 'the peasants' waiting there. Sam had this guy, Nigel, a minder, with her. He followed her everywhere, even to the toilet. The first thing she wanted to do was get rid of him."

"And smoke a joint and get stoned," chips in Dave.

Kris continues: "She was brilliant, instantly like, 'Let's go and see the horses. Let's escape from them [the men].' We had some little foals at the time, and we were looking at them when we heard this terrible commotion going on. The dogs had got Nigel. We had five dogs, and they had him against the kitchen door. She said, 'Leave him.' When it came to the recording, she kept borrowing cough sweets off me. I was watching her and I thought, 'Gosh, she's got a really good voice.'"

Alan Davey says that he too had expected "this dippy, blonde-headed plastic toy bimbo". He adds: "I never had her pinned on my wall. Don't you think she looks like Sharon out of *EastEnders*? She was really quite intelligent and articulate and likeable. This was quite a shock, a really nice surprise. We got stoned together and had a bit of a laugh."

The various versions of 'Gimme Shelter' were bunched together in groups of three and released on 12-inch vinyl and CD. Hawkwind and Sam Fox appeared alongside the bluesy rock'n'roll band Thunder and hair-rockers Little Angels.

"I even played my harmonica, and I hadn't played it in years," says Dave.

"He got this superb harmonica sound by lying on the floor to get the right acoustic feedback," recalls Richard. "It sounded like the old blues guys. Musicians totally surprise each other sometimes, and it was one of those moments."

Dave is not at all sure that he lay on the floor, and he changes the subject abruptly: "Years back, I played with Sonny Boy Williamson . . ."

Hawkwind were getting the hang of all the technology at their disposal, and loving it. In the first half of 1993, they played a scattering of British and European gigs, but they were for the most part immersed in their new recordings.

Dave was taking care of vocals, guitar, keyboards and synthesisers, Alan is credited with bass, vocals and wave-sequencing synthesisers, while Richard contributed drums, percussion and vocals.

The resulting album – *It Is The Business Of The Future To Be Dangerous* – would surprise many Hawkwind fans: it's almost entirely a keyboard LP and its titles are often straightforward proclamations or descriptions. They include 'Space Is Their Palestine', 'Tibet Is Not China (Parts 1 and 2)', 'The Camera That Could Lie', 'Techno Tropic Zone Exists' and, extraordinarily for a Hawkwind name, '3 Or 4 Erections In The Course Of A Night'.

"The three of us were using banks of electronics," recalls Richard. "It was an experimental album for us. We'd almost completely sussed out the electronic side. All three of us were using sequencers by then, and writing on them, and we were jamming along with each other much like what was happening in acid house and techno. That was the era of no vocals. Quite a lot of what we did was instrumental, although a few things were organised numbers.

" 'Space Is Their Palestine' was built around samples and sequencers. 'Letting In The Past' – by the end of the track, we were really jamming like hell. In other parts of the music, we literally patched stuff together using technology. 'Tibet Is Not China' was patched together as opposed to us playing it live and working out the arrangements. We also included a version of 'Gimme Shelter' without Sam's vocal on there. I can't remember why we did that. I thought it was better with her singing."

Alan Davey states that, in keeping with its title: "That was a daring album. I thought this was the sort of direction we needed to be going in now. We got all these keyboards and worked them all out. We made really good music, it still had Hawkwind stamped all over it, but it was totally different. That's what the fans like about us. We don't pander to what's expected or to what's in fashion.

"There are only three rock songs on the album. I enjoyed doing it. It was a whole new thing for us to just do keyboards. I listened to it a year ago, and I was amazed how good it was. People didn't like it at first. The reviews were saying, '12 minutes into the album and still no guitar.' But it's become a very popular one."

Classic Rock declared that it "wandered off down a road littered with Ozric Tentacles outtakes and B-sides".

Considering its radical approach, *It Is The Business Of The Future To Be Dangerous* did well to chart at number 75 after its release in October 1993, again on Essential through Castle, with Douglas Smith's help.

Hawkwind, of course, were touring throughout the winter to support it, accompanied by a dancer named Hilary. She had arrived for a tour meeting with her friend Heidi, who turned out to be an old mate of Richard's and the singer of a band called Stagnant Bile. "We've always been inventive with our band names in the West Country," jokes Richard.

Hilary, whose surname no one can remember, performed some intriguing Eastern dancing on the tour, and Adie and Jenny handled the light-show. Says Richard: "It was a post-acid house sort of thing. Jenny was designing slides and projections and stuff, painting things on to the slides. It was more projection rather than just strobes."

In a Radio 1 interview broadcast during the tour, Richard told presenter Mark Radcliffe: "Our music is about trancing and it's about sort of sliding into another world, really . . . There's an external view of it, which is outer space, and there's an internal view of it, which is inner space. And hopefully, the music is a soundtrack that allows you to look into both those places."

They played the UK first, and recorded a gig at Hastings Pier Pavilion on November 27. It would later turn into a live album, *The Business Trip Live* – a perfect title neatly coined by Alan. Then they went to Europe for a couple of weeks in December.

But despite their excitement over the album and their increasing self-sufficiency, certain dissatisfactions were growing within the group. Richard explains his worries: "We'd done a big gig in Brixton [on August 14]. I was looking at a film of it and I thought, 'Christ, it looks really boring. There's a huge space in the middle of the stage where nothing's going on.'"

As far as Alan was concerned, it was time for Hawkwind to return to their more identifiable rock roots but, unfortunately, he was the only band member who thought so. These were problems which would remain unresolved for more than a year.

1994 marked their milestone 25th anniversary, but Hawkwind held no special celebrations. Indeed, they were in a particularly militant frame of mind in February, when they instigated a legal action against their former saxophonist, who had been touring in America as Nik Turner's Hawkwind.

Douglas Smith, on behalf of Dave, Alan and Richard, contacted Maureen Baker, a Los Angeles attorney, asking how the band could protect their name in the States, and at what cost. It was decided that she would write to Nik's booking agent, Todd Cote, insisting that Turner was not in Hawkwind and had no right to use the name.

At the time, Hawkwind had been arranging the fourth tour in the American recovery plan they'd set in motion some years earlier. Says Kris: "We'd been putting a lot of the band's money into it. Over three years, we invested £56,000. The first tour, we played shitty gigs in clubs for not much money, and the hardcore Hawkwind fans came. The second time, we were better billed and we played better venues. The third time, we played big venues and we had lots of people. Everything was looking rosy. The next tour was going to be the one where we actually made some money."

"So guess who goes over there?" rages Brock. "Nik Turner as Hawkwind, and he fucked this whole project that we'd done. He managed to ruin our American trip, and he blew a record deal down the drainhole. We had to cancel our tour. He was playing for half the fee."

"Undercutting our price," explains Kris. "He saw a niche in the market. So Doug's lawyer in LA wrote to the agent and said, 'If you put Nik Turner on as Hawkwind, we'll injunct the clubs.' "

This would backfire on Hawkwind themselves: "Then the promoters didn't want to know us," says Kris.

Dave adds: "In the music business, you're just another name quite often. They were thinking, 'Which Hawkwind is it? What's going on? We can't book them – we might get injuncted.' What Nik did was ruin a lot of our hard work."

Douglas Smith recalls: "Dave asked us to make an attack on Nik in the States. We took advice from a copyright and trademark lawyer. This lawyer said that Dave had more right to use the name than anybody else because he, with different members, has consistently traded under it for the last 35 years. He has a perfect right to use it.

"We then trademarked it for him in the UK, which just protects him against other people using it. He's re-trademarked it since. It takes in all the factors – T-shirts, memorabilia and music, specifically.

"However, people like Nik Turner do have the right to trade under the name of 'ex-Hawkwind'. He can go out under his own name or the name of a band and in smaller letters underneath have 'ex-Hawkwind member'. What got up Dave's nose, and Kris', was that Nik was out there with other ex-members apparently playing as Hawkwind. He wasn't really. He was out there as Nik Turner, and the promoters or the agency were calling it 'ex-Hawkwind' in bigger letters, or even 'Hawkwind', because it sold more tickets."

There has been no move to trademark the name in America since that would mean having to do so separately in every state, at an estimated cost of $50,000 plus.

Nik Turner says: "At one time before this, I'd said to Doug Smith, 'I don't see why everybody who was in the band doesn't have a Hawkwind. There could be Nik Turner's Hawkwind, Huw Lloyd-Langton's Hawkwind, Simon King's Hawkwind . . . He was saying, 'That's a great idea.' "

(Over in the Brock camp, the mind-boggling possibility of something like 50 different Hawkwinds playing across Britain at any given time is met with incredulity: they say that any other use of the Hawkwind name would obviously devalue the currency; damage the goods.)

Nik continues: "I did a tour of America and I was going out as Nik Turner's Hawkwind as a result of this conversation I'd had with Douglas Smith. Then we had the legal problem, so I changed the name of the band to Nik Turner's Space Ritual, but it didn't stop the agents or promoters advertising it as Nik Turner's Hawkwind. Doug was on my side at the outset, and I'd spent some time with him before I went to India for six months in 1993. When I came back, I guess he'd got more involved with Hawkwind and he was helping them to threaten me with this legal action. I should have just told them to fuck off. They hadn't trademarked the name in any state.

"Dave was claiming the inalienable right to use the name, and around this same time, Douglas helped him to trademark it in the UK. That to me is an unethical thing to have done. I could say that Hawkwind was the nickname *I* was given originally, but I believe everybody that was in the band has a right to use the name.

"People expect the old mythological, abstract output from the band, but Dave hasn't actually been perpetuating anything like that. People like Barney Bubbles and Robert Calvert were responsible for that mythology. I think Dave is now trading on the myth that they created in the first place along with other members of the band, including myself."

This all dates back to the original misconception, the one that arose when Dave Brock formed the band perceiving himself, the captain, to be at the tiller, while Nik Turner viewed Hawkwind widely as a "people's band" and more specifically as the property of all those who would pass through its ranks.

Douglas Smith comments: "What this is all about is that some of the early members of Hawkwind are very bitter. They were part of the 'incredible, important' years, and those years are what the band has lived off since. They believe that if they had not created that success, then Hawkwind now would not be selling any records at all. They say they have as much right to the Hawkwind ethos as Dave has.

"You can look at it from both points of view. Nik says it's everyone's property. Dave says it's his band. Because Dave's always been there, he is the person responsible for Hawkwind over the succeeding and subsequent years. But where the bitch comes into it . . . you have to have lived through it to understand Nik's point of view, and Harvey's and the others', and I do see it."

Turner had been invited to America in the first place by rhythm guitarist and Inner City Unit fan Tommy Grenas, who'd previously been part of the London squat scene. Now he was living in the States where he had organised Nik's tour as well as recording sessions to "rehash" the Sphynx album, retaining the original recitations and the flute recordings from the Great Pyramid.

Most of the band members were LA-based musicians: Tommy Grenas, keyboard player Len Del Rio, drummer Paul De Lapella, bassist Paul Fox and guitarist Helios Creed. Nik had also recruited some of the old Hawkwind members for the live shows, since he had the express intention of "recapturing the early sound of the band" and hoped to create a sort of "Space Ritual 1994". Del Dettmar joined up, and Turner thinks that Alan Powell and Simon House played too.

Del Dettmar comments: "The main thing that was upsetting was that Dave was getting solicitors to write to the promoters of the different gigs. I remember Nik talking to Douglas on the phone from Washington. I had a word with him too. I said, 'Hi, Douglas, I'm in America,' and then I probably gave him back to Nik. I've no idea what they were saying to each other."

Del would tour the States with Turner again the next year, with Simon House playing support, and they would both travel to Japan with him too. It was the beginning of the band now known as Space Ritual, whose members are all from early line-ups of Hawkwind.

The dispute over the name was over for the time being – but some years later it would reignite, escalating into a full-scale war in which Nik Turner almost went to prison and everyone involved lost a lot of money.

"Alan had a few problems, stress and these things, where he went a bit nutty," says Dave Brock, looking back on Hawkwind's first gigs of 1994. These were in April in Dublin and Belfast, launching a short spring tour. (Back on the mainland, Simon House would guest at a couple of shows.)

"We were in Dublin airport," continues Dave, "and Alan's sitting there with his head in his hands crying. He wanted to commit suicide. Everybody was looking, horrified. I saw a priest sitting with four nuns. I went over and I said, 'Oh, Father, do you think you can come and talk to this friend of ours?' The priest came over and said to Alan, 'What can I do for you?' He said, 'You can fuck off.'"

Alan has no recollection of this incident. He replies: "I don't even remember the day or the gig or the airport. It's a really bizarre one, that. I can't remember being in that state. I must have just totally repressed it. I'm not a suicidal person – God, no! The only thing I can think of is that I might have had a blackout.

"I once took STP by mistake. I was told it was acid. If I don't know what something is, I wouldn't touch it. I wouldn't touch heroin, pills, anything I don't know. I haven't done acid since 1994. I just smoke these days. Anyway, for six months after this STP, I kept blacking out with no warning at all. It was quite a weird period. Once I was getting up off the settee at home and the next thing I knew, I was waking up shaking on the floor. I think I was having a fit."

Alan does, however, remember getting himself and Brock banned by British Midland after a heated argument on a plane. The band were travelling to Europe for a tour, and they had booked their seats well ahead. However, because of snow in Belgium only one flight out of the two scheduled was going to go, and it was the one Hawkwind had booked.

"So we got on the plane and then they asked us to get off," says Alan. "It seemed obvious to me that the first-class passengers from the other flight were going to be stuffed on our plane. I just refused to get off. I'm very strong in my principles. I think they ended up calling the airport police to try to remove me. Dave was getting involved as well. There was just Dave and I left on the plane."

Much to-ing and fro-ing and shouting ensued, with Dave and Alan being taken off and returned to the plane twice. "We were within our rights," says Alan. "I had my ticket and my seat. They had to get the British Midland top guy there. I wasn't going to have any snotty little stewardess or fat pig from British Midland telling me that we couldn't travel. It was all held up for about 40 minutes, but Dave and I made sure Richard was on and we did get the flight. We were then banned by British Midland."

Dave comments: "I'm in charge of the band. I'm the captain, the one who has to suffer the consequences of the actions, whoever has done them. Alan's done a few naughty things in the past. He's smashed things up. I saved him from getting beaten up in Italy, in Milan, by some blokes in a club. He had a major freak-out at somebody. I said, 'I'm very sorry, he's suffering from jetlag and he's had a bit of a break-down.' He just goes off the wall sometimes, Alan does."

Alan's anxieties over Hawkwind would continue through 1994,

especially after the release of *The Business Trip Live* in September on Emergency Broadcast System – the band's own label, set up with the help of Douglas Smith. They had created an outlet not only for official releases, archive recordings and even other artists but for side projects which Dave felt "weren't suitable for Hawkwind *per se*".

In February 1995, they released an album, *White Zone*, under the *alter ego* of Psychedelic Warriors. It was an ambient/techno enterprise, indicative of Brock's policy of continuous change and ongoing interest in the musical world outside.

This was all more than enough for Alan. "I thought Hawkwind should drop the keyboard thing – 'Done that'," he explains. "I said, 'This ain't gonna work. Let's do the complete opposite to what people expect and get rocky again.' But they wouldn't. They wanted to continue with this keyboard stuff. I had all these songs I played to them, and they weren't interested, really. It made me feel a bit outside of it all."

Hawkwind, who had signed off 1994 with an October/November European tour, were more concerned about the empty space at the front of the stage, first identified by Richard. In the spring of 1995, they recruited a fourth member, the wild and crazy Ron Tree, who would bring his own particular brand of lunacy to the band as a vocalist and theatrical performer.

"They found me in the gutter!" declared Ron in an interview shortly after joining Hawkwind. "We met at festivals. I've just been playing in lots of different bands and doing a few support gigs. I wrote to Dave to see if he needed a singer and he gave me a go, and so far it's been going all right."

Ron, a bass player turned singer, was talking in St Catharines, Ontario, in April 1995. In another interview the same month, he stated: "They were a three-piece and a bit sparse. I just said to Dave, 'I'll do a good job for you.'"

Hawkwind had finally made it back across the Atlantic for a month-long tour of Canada and the States, the press were interested and Ron, a long-time Hawkwind admirer, was being hailed as the nearest thing to Robert Calvert that the group could have hoped to find.

Kris Tait admits that he was "quite like Calvert". And Jerry Richards, Dave's guitar partner in Hawkdog/The Agents Of Chaos, comments: "Ron was perfect – fabulous mime, wonderful comic. He's

Performance artist Tony Crerar in the part of Elric, the albino emperor, during the Black Sword tour in November and December 1985. He says: "The show had been very well prepared. Dave had taken the best visual aspects - which were also the heart of the tale." *(Dave Brock Collection)*

"Don't drop the towel!" Nik Turner covers his assets at the Aktivator festival in Tewkesbury on August 14, 1988. Later that day he would hear that Robert Calvert had passed away. "His death was very sad," says Nik. "I was always a very good friend of his."
(Dave Brock Collection)

Hawkwind set up camp in the travellers' field at Glastonbury in June 1989. The area had been set aside for travellers after a tense period of negotiation with the police.
(Dave Brock Collection)

Bridget Wishart, the band's only female vocalist, on stage in San Francisco in December 1990. She didn't always enjoy the long-haul touring. Dave Brock comments, "She was in a man's world too, which was quite difficult for her."
(Dave Brock Collection)

Kris Tait blows a spectacular plume of fire during a Hawkwind show
(Rik Richardson)

Hawkwind's lightshow has always been a crucial part of their performance.
(Mick Hutson/Redferns)

Singer Ron Tree at Aldershot on April 1, 2001. Ron brought new theatrical ideas to the band. "I was into it, just giving my all," he says. Dave Brock comments: "He looked quite amazing, and he was a charismatic kind of guy, a bit like Calvert." *(Rik Richardson)*

Ron Tree wearing his alien head in 1995. He was quite an innovator. "He built a robot out of bits and pieces," says Dave. "He had part of a cement mixer, part of a vacuum cleaner and an alarm bell on it, and all these weird gadgets."
(Brigitte Engl/Redferns)

Ron on stage at the Shepherd's Bush Empire, October 31st, 1997.
(Linda Nyland/Redferns)

When Hawkwind set off for Australia and New Zealand in February 2000, the line-up comprised, left to right: Dave Brock, Harvey Bainbridge, Richard Chadwick, Simon House, Jerry Richards and Steve Taylor. "It was a wild and crazy adventure, good and bad," says Simon, somewhat understating the chaos. *(Bob King/Redferns)*

Alan Davey, who rejoined the group in 2000, salutes the spirit of Lemmy with heavy, pushing basslines. A long-time fan of both Hawkwind and Motorhead, he says: "We play real music. There are no gimmicks or flashy edges... It's all about feel." *(Steve Gillett)*

Nik Turner at the great Hawkestra disaster on October 21, 2000. He says of the ambitious reunion of past and present members: "It was seen as a really cool concept... but the whole thing was very political." *(Awais Butt)*

Huw Lloyd-Langton greets the Hawkestra audience. He says: "It was fairly complicated because there were so many people involved in it. I found it quite enjoyable seeing people I hadn't seen for some time, like Del Dettmar." *(Awais Butt)*

Dave Brock and Sam Fox during the latter's controversial Hawkestra performance of 'Master Of The Universe', which became 'Mistress Of The Universe'. Says Lemmy: "I know Sam Fox, I love her to death, but she doesn't sing 'Master Of The Universe' when Nik Turner's onstage." *(Awais Butt)*

Lemmy played five or six songs on the night, but he states now that the Hawkestra was "horribly disorganised" and marred by financial squabbling. He says: "I thought it was all crap. As usual, the cosmic warriors were arguing about a few bucks. I don't get it." *(Awais Butt)*

Hawkwind and special guests at the Royal Festival Hall in London on October 10, 2001. They are, left to right: Simon House, Alan Davey, Tim Blake, Huw Lloyd-Langton, Dave Brock, Richard Chadwick and Keith Kniveton. *(Melvyn Vincent)*

Arthur Brown, the former "god of hellfire", takes on a brighter persona on the road with Hawkwind in 2003. Arthur now regularly writes, records and tours with the band. *(Rik Richardson)*

Dave Anderson, one of the first bass players, now performs with Nik Turner's Space Ritual alongside other ex-members of Hawkwind. Pictured in 2003, he says: "There's something unique about the chemistry of the band... I have no doubts in my mind that we're probably much more Hawkwind than Hawkwind." *(Mark Flowers)*

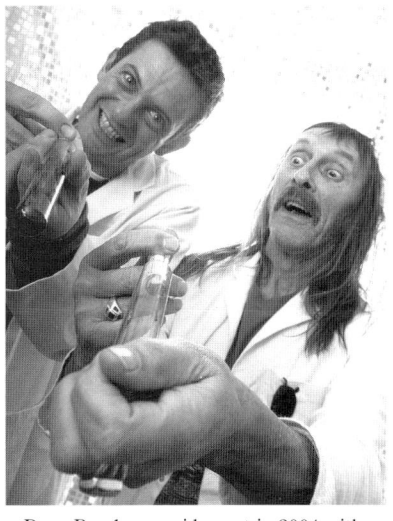

Dave Brock on a video set in 2004 with Hawkwind's latest unlikely collaborator, fan and TV personality Matthew Wright. Matthew says: "It was the most surreal day of my life, wearing the white lab coat and all that." *(Alicia Clarke)*

"I'm the captain of the ship," says Dave Brock, who has steered Hawkwind through some often turbulent waters for the last 35 years. "You have to have a captain otherwise nothing could ever be done." Nik Turner's opposite view of Hawkwind as "a communal thing, a community project" has led to bitter arguments and court cases. *(Melvyn Vincent)*

got such an imagination. Without drawing a Calvert comparison, he was like a flipside of that kind of thing. He'd always come up with an unexpected line, usually a bit dark and twisted."

"Dave had known Ron from the north of England," adds Richard Chadwick. "He'd been badgering Dave – 'I can fucking sing. I can have a go.' He was a really good frontman. He had a really powerful voice. He'd do all the singing parts Dave or Alan couldn't or wouldn't do, and it worked very well for a while. He had a fascination with aliens, and Al was into the same sort of thing. Ron said, 'Let's make an album about alien abduction.'"

In the summer, Hawkwind did just that. "Ron dived into it with gusto," continues Richard. "He had an effects pedal for his vocal. It could make it weird, mimic the effects of squeaky, demonic, giggling aliens. He did revitalise and invigorate the band."

"I got on really well with him," says Alan. "We wrote really well together. 'Xenomorph' I wrote with Ron. I found him so easy to write with. He was full of ideas – so much so that on my first solo album, I got him to sing on three of the tracks."

Davey says of *Alien 4*: "It didn't seem to me like it was one of those stunning turning points although, again, it was a good album and there was some unusual stuff on it. 'Kapal' sticks out, a Hawkwind instrumental. I thought the album was meant to take a more rocky direction – 'Here we go, this is great.' I was writing more rocky songs already, but the band didn't seem to be interested in them. They wanted to go back to this sequencing keyboards and all that sort of stuff."

Jerry Richards was called in to play some guitar at the sessions for *Alien 4*. He'd already played a handful of gigs with Hawkwind over the summer, and was well used to playing with Dave.

"At the time," says Jerry, "they were looking for more flexibility, and taking a lot of the load off Dave. They were getting me in to play bits and pieces. By the time I came in for *Alien 4*, it had been pretty much mapped out, but I did some stuff for that and I was helping out, computer-wise, on the production side of things."

Jerry is credited with playing on 'Death Trap', 'Wastelands' and 'Are You Losing Your Mind?'

The big UK tour took place in October, the month of the album release, with European dates following into November. It was one of Hawkwind's big visual productions. Says Kris Tait: "I'd just graduated from university, I'd done lots of stage management in my degree, and I was full of creative ideas. We wanted to try them out and do something spectacular. I was stage manager on that tour and Colin Rowell was the tour manager. He'd tour managed us back in the early Eighties.

"The '95 tour was almost like a belated 25th anniversary celebration, 'cos we hadn't done anything special the year before. We got two dancers in, Michelle Gaskill and Liam Yates, and I was doing fire. I was also cueing the lights and looking after the band and doing a lot of driving. It was a really busy tour, that. We got Colin and Val from Flying Saucers back to do our catering."

"There was a lot of mime and dance in the show," reflects Dave. There were costumes and masks, too, and a storyline running through the performance.

In keeping with this rediscovered spirit of adventure, Hawkwind overhauled their set. It was obviously plump with new compositions such as 'Sputnik Stan', 'Xenomorph', 'Alien I Am', 'Abducted', 'Blue Skin', 'Vega', 'Kapal', 'Death Trap' and 'Wastelands', plus three songs yet to be recorded: 'Elfin', 'Photo Encounter' and Dave's 'Love In Space'. However, many of the evergreen favourites had been dropped with only 'Silver Machine', 'Welcome To The Future', 'The Golden Void' and 'Hassan I Sahba' surviving the cull. Other oldies such as 'Lord Of Light' from *Doremi*, 'Robot' from *PXR5* and 'The Iron Dream' from *Quark*, were selected for their suitability in the story, and *It Is The Business Of The Future To Be Dangerous* was represented by 'Space Is Their Palestine'.

"We were working very closely with Ron Tree," says Kris. "We choreographed him into the dance. The whole thing was about alien abduction, with Ron being abducted. We had him spread-eagled at one point, and we acted out tattooing and branding him, 'cos the aliens branded the people. It was quite ritualistic. The fire was also choreographed to the dance. It all worked together.

"Ron used to do some spontaneous things, in the way that Calvert used to do. He used to go into skips outside the gigs to see what he could find. He once found a big Fifties hairdryer, the sort they had in salons, and he came running across the road with it just as a police car appeared. He used to come onstage with that on. It looked like a big alien head.

"There were lots of different elements in the story, like Sputnik Stan collecting rubbish in space. Liam and Michelle worked fantastically well together. We didn't know until the end of the tour that they didn't actually get on very well personally. They never showed it. They were very professional. It turned out that Liam didn't like working with Michelle.

"He was a very strong martial arts dancer. Michelle was very elegant. He could pick her up and throw her around. It worked really well, her grace against his strength. They got more and more into it, and we'd gather more props. We did a lot of mask work, with big alien masks. Liam would wear a big red skirt in 'Hassan I Sahba', and he'd do a cart-wheel onstage.

"We did a fantastic show at the Brixton Academy [on October 21]. Scouse brought these circus performers to work with us. We outnumbered the band. We had this girl Sylvie doing trapeze; we had a guy doing ropework and he had some big silver balls that he could roll up his arm. For 'Love In Space' he did this wonderful build-up in the air. Then there was Liam and Michelle, me and Scouse. That was fantastic. It all came together."

"I always liked doing Brixton Academy," nods Scouse, who performed as Wango Riley. "They have a big, big stage for the fire show."

It was a triumphant phase of Hawkwind's career, even though *Alien 4* failed to make the Top 75. The band were always happiest when they were testing their own creativity, meeting challenges and presenting fans with concerts they would never forget.

The next year would see them broadening their horizons musically with the addition of a second guitarist, Jerry Richards. And that was when Alan Davey really got fed up.

CHAPTER 28

The Adventures Of The Fantastic Four

RON TREE was well into heroin when he joined Hawkwind, and he would wrestle with his habit throughout his six years in the band. It was, he says, a stressful environment and not one in which he was ever likely to beat his addiction. It was only in 2004 that he was finally able to clean up, after four months in rehab and a near-fatal overdose.

Ron was born in Leeds on April 8, 1963. He attended Green Lane and Castleton primary schools, then Armley Middle School and West Leeds Boys' High before leaving the education system at 16. He took on a variety of jobs, from labouring to working with mentally handicapped people painting garden gnomes, but from the earliest days, he knew: "I was an artist."

Ron learnt to play bass, and his first band was Plato's Jacuzzi. By the time he was playing in his next band, Bastard, he had come to know Hawkwind quite well, having met them on the festival circuit. He would turn up to see them whenever they played locally, and when Bastard split, he talked endlessly to Richard Chadwick about needing to find another band. At Richard's suggestion, he teamed up with the West Country group 2000 DS after meeting them at Glastonbury. Still based in Leeds, he worked in Germany and London with 2000 DS but soon became fed up and "escaped". Returning to his home town, he started a noise-guitar group called Lizgizzad and at this time began taking smack.

"I dropped out of things," he recalls. "But then there was a moment of clarity." Ron was hugely inspired by punk: "I formed this other band called The Sewer Suckers, really high-energy, fast, psychedelic punk – but not punk. We were a bit like a more insane Inner City Unit. It was great."

Ron had already suggested to Dave Brock that Hawkwind needed a frontman and that he was just the person for the job, having tested out his vocal skills with the Suckers. He had loved the Lemmy-era Hawkwind and felt that the three-piece line-up could do with a rocket up the arse – which, to varying degrees, is what the members felt themselves.

"Dave said yes," relates Ron. "But I waited a year before they even gave me a rehearsal to try me out. Dave was probably thinking, 'We don't want Ron singing on it – he's a punk.' He assumed I was just going to yell. Then, eventually, they got so bored they decided to try me, by which time I'd got into heroin. If I'd gone down to Devon when Dave said yes originally, I'd probably have got out of smack because, then, I was only just getting into it."

Ron was accepted into the band in March 1995 and, in his enthusiasm, he vowed to meet his responsibilities head-on. He says: "Of course I didn't want to screw Hawkwind up, so I'd take Methadone, the heroin substitute, and do my best. I always did the job right, the audiences loved it, and I was always there for rehearsals. I lived in Leeds and I used to scoot up and down on the train. Then Richard got me a place in Frome [where Ron still lives] through his girlfriend's parents. I had to get away from the smack scene in Leeds.

"Then it all fucked up down here with my girlfriend at the time. She couldn't get off the shit. We'd had a daughter, Teneesha (an Indian name), who was taken off us in Leeds after I'd joined Hawkwind. I was fighting a court battle, I was signing on and I was struggling to keep my habit together. On the other hand, I was becoming famous in this band and everybody probably thought I was well sorted. It was like heaven and hell."

Despite his early worries that Teneesha would be adopted, Ron still regularly sees his daughter, who is nine and living near to him at the time of writing.

All of these personal problems were gnawing away at Ron during his appearances with Hawkwind in 1995 – the American tour and the UK Alien outing, which had made him such a vividly popular character with the fans. Still, he looks back on these days as his favourite Hawkwind period, saying, "I was into it, just giving my all."

"Ron had some fantastic ideas," enthuses Dave Brock. "He built a robot out of bits and pieces. He had part of a cement mixer, part of a vacuum cleaner and an alarm bell on it, and all these weird gadgets. He would do the support slot. He used to play his bass riffs and the machine used to rattle away in time and talk to him. It got a bit boring after 15 minutes . . . We did use the robot on and off. I think we used it onstage on the Alien tour. When it worked, it used to leap forward.

"Ron was a very visual character. He looked quite amazing, and he was a charismatic kind of guy, a bit like Calvert, funny enough. He was also a good bass player, which may have affected Alan's confidence. Ron's downfall was bad drugs."

For his part, Ron had believed in Hawkwind: "I thought I'd be a real part of it, and that it would be a powerful thing to be in a band like that. I didn't realise I would be powerless. I thought I would be connected and that I'd get spirituality from it.

"I've found out a lot in rehab. My triggers are spirituality, connectedness, joy, power and security. I had the illusion that these things were in Hawkwind when I first started. But there were things happening in the band, and I got seriously disillusioned. I had been pretty blind to what was going on."

By 1996, Ron had identified his disappointments although he would not address them for a long time, and then not to the group. He claims that Hawkwind restricted his artistic freedom and also tried to mould him into some sort of Calvert-esque character, picking up from where the departed poet had left off. He felt "crushed".

"I was disconnected, you see," says Ron. "Obviously, that cramps your creativity. And the heroin habit – that's just going to carry on."

All things considered, it was a turbulent year.

Alan Davey, who'd been in the line-up for 12 years, stormed out of Hawkwind controversially and, to this day, he and his colleagues give differing accounts of his departure.

At least the dancers had resolved their problems. Liam Yates had left the band after the flamboyant tour attending *Alien 4* and he'd been replaced by Pebs, from a dance centre in Bristol.

The spring and summer months were fairly encouraging. In May, Hawkwind kept up their prolific programme of album releases with *Love In Space*. Issued by Emergency Broadcast System, it immortalised the Alien tour with live material recorded at Cardiff's St David's Hall and Bristol's Colston Hall on October 18 and 19, 1995.

In July, a fascinating compilation came on to the market, also on the EBS label. *Future Reconstructions: Ritual Of The Solstice* contains a collection of Hawkwind remixes by the likes of Utah Saints, Knights Of The Occasional Table, Astralasia, Zion Train and Salt Tank, who contributed 'Master Of The Universe' and whose Malcolm Stanners had coordinated the project. The LP tightened the band's close links to the dance world.

Jez Willis of Utah Saints, who remixed 'Silver Machine' for the album, declares: "We definitely did it out of respect for Hawkwind, and the chance to work on a classic track. We were given a choice, and 'Silver Machine' was the really obvious one. It had that big, brilliant 'whoosh' in it, an incredibly exciting noise."

Utah Saints were known for weaving all sorts of influences, from rock to pop and funk, into their bedrock of house/techno, and Jez was no stranger to Hawkwind.

He says: "They are one of those bands who are just always there. I've seen them several times over the years. They're like a travelling Glastonbury, which is really nice. Also, Lemmy had been in them and Motorhead were always one of my favourite bands. The best time I saw Hawkwind was at Loughborough University. There were about 800 people there, and there was just this barrage of noise and lights. Talking as someone who's never done hallucinogenic drugs, they seemed trippy even when you hadn't taken any drugs. It definitely worked for me.

"When I was in The Cassandra Complex, an electronic punk band, we used to cover 'Orgone Accumulator'. Even as an electronic band, you can just jam it. When I was in the band MDMA, we played what we now find has become this legendary Treworgey Tree Festival [in 1989], and Hawkwind were headlining that. It was probably the only festival that MDMA did. It was just full of crusties and techno crusties. The promoters got really scared, packed up and ran away, and let everyone get on with it. It was just like true anarchy."

Richard Chadwick would certainly testify to the chaos, at least as far as the toilet pit was concerned.

Utah Saints were presented with a live version of 'Silver Machine'. Jez recalls: "All we could lift off it was the chorus. We played everything else ourselves. It's a funny thing with remixes. Quite often you end up doing a lot of it yourself. We overdubbed some guitar and I think we had a guy called Mike from the band Skin playing some guitar on it. I wanted it to just go whooshy, and we felt like it did go whooshy. It's very rare you get a remix that stands the test of time, and

I don't know if that one does. If I were doing it again, I'd probably do it differently."[*]

Despite his series of close encounters with Hawkwind, Jez Willis didn't actually know anyone in the band apart from Ron Tree; they'd met previously in Leeds. And he had little personal contact with them when Utah Saints supported Hawkwind at a "swirly" gig at Brixton Academy, an invitation extended because of the remix.

This was the show which had taken place on October 21, 1995, complete with the circus performers. Titled "Techno Trips And Psychedelic Dreams", it brought together Salt Tank, Electric Groove Temple, Back To The Planet, RDF, Porcupine Tree, Optic Eye, Cybernaut, Captain Rizz and Techno Pagan along with Utah Saints.

Jez says: "The Hawkwind fans are far less hostile than a lot of rock audiences. They're more open to different sounds and ideas. Almost by definition, they're not bothered by whether something's cool or not cool. They just want to have a good time."

Hawkwind had by now established a tradition for "swirly" support acts, as Jez might describe them. Ozric Tentacles were just one of the names often seen alongside that of Hawkwind on gig posters and flyers. Many other contemporary artists also fitted into the spirit of the gigs, from Salt Tank and the Spiral Tribe crew at 1992's "Psychedelic Madness" show to Aphex Twin, the industrial Test Dept and Transglobal Underground, with their world beats, at the "24-Hour Technicolour Dream", also held at Brixton Academy on August 14, 1993.

Michael Dog was another invited to submit a remix for *Future Reconstructions* in collaboration with Future Loop Foundation. Says Michael: "I picked 'The Golden Void'. I was all excited, thinking, 'Great, there's a violin part on it, a nice mellotron part,' having all these ideas of how I'd do it. I got the tape of the parts, and the parts were a few seconds of vocal and some rough guitar lines and I'm thinking, 'Hang on, this is not the "Golden Void" that I remember.'

"I listened more closely and on the vocal part, I could hear guitar in the background, really quiet. The tape had come straight from Dave Brock, and the penny dropped that he'd taken these parts off a four- or eight-track reel to reel.

"If the heads aren't aligned properly, you get bleed – one track slightly bleeds into another so you get a ghost sound, which accounted

[*] Much later, Jimmy Cauty from The KLF would also remix 'Silver Machine'.

for this little bit of guitar on the vocal track. He sent these bits out of a ropey live version. I ended up using one line of vocal and wrote a whole other track.

"Basically, UA had the rights to all the music from that era, so Dave couldn't send us parts from the original version 'cos he'd have to pay UA for the use of it. I was just sitting in the studio thinking, 'Oh God, this is so dodgy.' But we did a great track which, as far as I know, was never released."

Michael doesn't work in the music industry any more: "I had enough of it. Almost everyone was like Dave although, to be fair to him, he was no worse than about 95 per cent of the other people in the business."

1996 wasn't a big touring year for the band. There was a major London show at Brixton Academy on June 21 under the banner of "Future Reconstructions Of The Solstice", with Ozric Tentacles, Loop Guru, Tribal Drift and Captain Rizz also on the bill. Hawkwind continued on with a handful of UK gigs and a European tour to follow the release of *Love In Space*. By now, they had recruited a new theatrical performer, Hazel the belly dancer, who'd made a guest appearance on the previous Alien tour.

"We did some wonderful choreographed things, with Michelle and Pebs dressed in big evening dresses and giant cups and saucers," says Kris. "It was very stylised, moving across the stage as if it was a giant chess board. Hazel, this larger-than-life character, would sort of shimmy through it, belly dancing. She actually teaches it."

Unfortunately, Pebs didn't like Hazel too much. "All the girls arguing . . ." sighs Dave Brock. "It's temperamental behaviour, isn't it?"

All three dancers left at the end of the tour, although Hazel would continue to guest with Hawkwind from time to time.

In August, Jerry Richards was once again invited to join the line-up, this time at a big bikers' festival in Clermont-Ferrand, France. He remembers: "There were about 50,000 Angels there, and Iron Maiden."

The Hawkwind member who enjoyed it most was Alan Davey, and that's because he wasn't there. He insisted he didn't want to do the gig and Ron Tree slung his bass back on to take his place.

Kris Tait says: "This was Lord Phil again [the Rt Hon Philip Harvey]. His girlfriend's son, Danny, had got involved with Hell's Angels and we got roped into doing the gig."

"It was a culturally different thing to what we were used to," adds Richard Chadwick. "It was like a Euro biker festival, just pretty straight and weird. It didn't seem as interesting."

Dave: "We were stuck in a yellow caravan at the back of the stage. We were sitting there for hours wishing we could go home. We had no crew, nothing. Johnnie Allan, who used to work as a roadie with us, and Motorhead too, was there. He was working with Iron Maiden."

"They were packing all their stuff," recalls Richard. "They were just about to fly out to Mexico. We were thinking, 'It's a different bloody world.' Ron played really well that day, but we felt like, 'We can't be arsed with this. Fuck it, let's just knob off home after the gig.'" Which they did.

Jerry went on to play a couple more "exploratory" shows with Hawkwind in Holland in September, and he would soon join up full time.

In yet another sign of the changing times, Kris had taken on the role of tour manager, driving the band around in their minibus, checking them into the hotels, ensuring that their backstage rider was fully provided and picking up the fee at the gigs.

"I'd kind of worked my way up," she remembers. "I'd taken over the merchandising, I'd helped out on the lights, I'd been stage managing – I'd done a bit of everybody's job. It was just a natural development, especially since our previous tour manager couldn't drive and I was doing it anyway." Eventually, Kris would take the logical next step and become the manager of Hawkwind. But not for a while.

Jerry Richards' phone rang one day and Dave Brock was on the line. "We're going to Greece," Dave told him. "Do you want to come and play some guitar?" Jerry was more than happy to leave the gloom of the English late autumn for a few days abroad.

It turned out to be an extraordinary trip although the shows, in Thessaloníki and Athens on November 8 and 9, were the least memorable aspect of it. "After the gigs, Alan had a nervous breakdown, he took the band's money and left," says Dave Brock. "He reckoned he could go off and be a star in his own band."

"He knobbed off in Greece with our expenses and went off to form Bedouin," agrees Richard Chadwick.

Jerry remembers a different scenario. He says: "Alan left the band in a big huff 'cos he said Dave had been doctoring the books. We said to

Alan, 'We've seen the books. They're all right.' He said to Dave, 'I've accused you now of doing things you obviously haven't been doing. I can't stay. I have to leave now.' We said, 'Don't worry, man. It's not a problem.'

"At the same time, there were a lot of political considerations going on. Doug Smith was making headway with a group called Chumbawamba. They'd started to garner a lot of support from within the music industry, even though they'd started out as a bunch of anarchists. Within a year, they would find themselves being cosseted by major record companies [EMI]. Douglas is a famous entrepreneur, and he can take advantage of situations at the drop of a hat. After all, he did give us Hawkwind and Motorhead and Girlschool. He was starting to work more closely with Chumbawamba, and the management of Hawkwind began to suffer. That's what happens. I think Alan had pretensions to go off and do his own thing. So off he went and did that for a while."

Alan is horrified at the suggestion of any financial impropriety on his part. "I wouldn't ever take money from the band," he insists. "I didn't do that. It would be unforgivable. I don't know why Dave or Richard would say that. I couldn't stay in Athens 'cos it was so smelly, hot and polluted. I wanted to go back to Thessaloníki. I just hired a car and went, really. I may have gone quickly, and maybe they thought I'd run off with the money because of that. But when I left Athens, all the tour money was still there. I was skint. When I got home, I had to go straight on the dole. We were all broke at that point."

"Everybody has some sort of problem," remarks Dave cryptically, adding that Alan had been behaving strangely throughout the trip: "He'd brought his girlfriend, Anne, to Greece because he wanted to have a holiday with her. She was a nice girl. He was trying to avoid her coming into the dressing room. He left her surrounded by Greeks at the gig. She said, 'Alan doesn't want me coming in.' He had this thing about the 'inner sanctum' of the dressing room.

"He didn't travel with us on the bus either. It was a very nice 30-seater bus and there were only about 12 people on it, but he didn't want her mixing with us. Then we met them at the airport and they tried to avoid us by hiding behind a pillar. He was definitely on some weird sort of thing then. He's probably embarrassed now."

Alan does confirm: "My worst time in Hawkwind was in Greece, 'cos everything was getting on top of me. The band was off in the wrong direction altogether. I had to watch something I loved so much going down the drain."

This was all to do with Alan's belief that Hawkwind should be taking it easy with the keyboards and reacquainting themselves with their rock roots. He adds: "I thought I knew what I was talking about. I know what's good for the band, but they wouldn't listen. Then they got Jerry, and his playing – it's not Hawkwind. I used to call him Huw Lloyd-Hillage. Whatever he played sounded like either of them [Huw Lloyd-Langton and Steve Hillage]. I couldn't see him bringing anything to the band.

"He'd be playing lead in the wrong key. I kept hearing bum notes. He didn't get me off at all. If you play with someone like Dave, he gets you off. Richard sometimes does things and it gets me off, and vice versa. That's what you've got to have in the band.

"Jerry used to whinge onstage 'cos I was too loud, but I was never any louder than I was before. No one had ever complained before this. He'd be saying, 'Turn down.' I'd say, "No. Buy a bigger amp or join another band. I'm not turning down for you after all these years.'

"In the end, I had to say, 'Either he goes or I go. I can't play with this guy.' For some reason, they wanted to keep him in. I did leave after the Greek gigs. I said, 'I'm off.' I took all my rock songs and I did Bedouin."

"We all knew what Alan wanted to do," responds Dave. "Sometimes people go off in different directions. If we listened to his songs and we didn't particularly like them, we'd say so, and he'd get a bit upset. You can sometimes start feeling like it's 'them' and 'me'."

"I couldn't understand why they'd keep a semi-professional," continues Alan. "Jerry's not a professional like I am. I don't dislike him – offstage he's a nice chap – but I couldn't stay in a band with him. He didn't have what we needed at the time.

"I'm so passionate about Hawkwind, I didn't like to see it going in the wrong direction. I got upset a lot. My point was proven later on with the *Distant Horizons* album. It was the biggest disaster they'd ever done. Dave did admit to me later that I was right all along. He'd come to see me about four times a year, trying to get me back in the band. He'd be all jolly and jokey, just like how it seemed to be in the old days. He'd tell me what they were doing. Then he'd say, 'Do you want to come?' I'd ask, 'Is Jerry still there?' 'Yes.' 'Then, no.' I had an awful lot of letters from fans saying, 'There's a big hole in the band now.'"

Jerry responds: "I can't say I remember asking Alan to turn down onstage. I would've been more likely to favour him turning up. Alan has his own reasons for doing what he does. As far as I know, he left to pursue avenues that he thought were open to him with his own band. He got frustrated with the sequencers, and he decided this would give him more scope to do what he wanted with his music. I don't know how successful that's been in terms that he's now back playing with Dave. Alan has his own idiosyncrasies which one either learns to live with or puts into the box that demands attention at the time.

"He does have something of a reputation with PA crews and lighting people and management for being rather forthcoming with his emotions. He is prone to the classic Zappa phrase of 'petulant frenzy'. As an example, one day a box of new CDs from Douglas at Emergency Broadcast System was delivered to the farm. Alan's name had been neglected in some of the credits, and he was last seen jumping up and down on the smashed remains of the CDs that had been sent from London. As usual, everything was right as rain the next day. Over the course of months, it can get extremely wearing.

"Working in close proximity with people, there are bound to be things that rise to the surface and cause some conflict. A bit of conflict and stress within any organisation is probably good for it. It's important to try and keep things fresh. Hawkwind has always been about experimentation, and they must have that."

Ron Tree recalls: "I wasn't really surprised when Alan left because of the way he was being. He was freaking out a lot. Apparently, he's not really changed today. I don't know what happened in his childhood, put it like that. And I feel for him. He told me he couldn't express himself in the band. He just slagged Dave off totally – 'I'm going to do it with my band.' Then he went off and did that and nothing really happened."

Dave Brock remarks: "We'd known Jerry Richards for quite a few years and he's quite a gentleman in his way. Al didn't like his guitar playing at all. He thought it was fucking awful. Jerry, when he joined the band, helped us quite a lot."

Richard says that Jerry was particularly conscientious in the studio, where he was completely at home with the new technology and went out of his way to see that things were done properly: "He's a very hard-working person. He sets himself to do something and he just fucking does it. He loved playing live as well. Where he really helped us a lot was in keeping the band going after Alan left. At that point, the whole writing structure of the band changed too."

Alan had already recorded a solo album, *Captured Rotation*, before he quit Hawkwind, with Ron Tree singing on three of the tracks. It was released by Emergency Broadcast System in 1996.

"Douglas sent it to *Aardshock*, a big monthly magazine in Holland," says Alan. "They did a rating of maybe 100 CDs and mine got the highest score, over Nirvana and Motorhead and Cheap Trick. The next month, they did a three-page article. I thought, 'I'm on the right track here.' I remember Douglas saying, 'Why can't Hawkwind make an album that sounds as good as yours?'"

A year later, Alan released another solo album, *Bedouin*, on EBS and formed a touring band, also called Bedouin, which reunited him with former Hawkwind drummer Danny Thompson. They recruited Captain Rizz guitarist Sean Massett.

The band were founded on the principle of "hard rock with Arabic overtones", and were also described as "a psychedelic Motorhead". They played European dates in the summer of 1997, including a German Hawkfan festival which Hawkwind couldn't make. "We did that two years in a row," says Alan. "A lot of people who saw us said we were far superior to Hawkwind. They were going through a bad patch."

In 1998, Al – now officially known as Alan "The Elf" Davey – was invited by the Italian label Black Widow to compose an album of sci-fi rock music. Working on his own, he produced *Chaos Delight*, which emerged early in 2000. Next came another solo project, *Al Chemical's Lysergic Orchestra*, a mail-order-only release.

Bedouin were still on the road and gathering a following. "I set the tours up myself," says Alan. "We used to do 20 gigs over the course of two months. I learnt all about how to run a band, and I can appreciate what Dave goes through now. We used to go down a storm wherever we played. To begin with, I was doing all the vocals. It was very liberating. Some people used to say it was the perfect mix between Motorhead and Hawkwind. That's what I am, I suppose. They're my two favourite bands. I was just glad people liked what I was doing."

Two especially committed fans and friends, twins called Andy and Clive, paid for the group to record an album. They went into the studio for two weeks and came up with *As Above So Below*, later issued on the Salahadin label.

By now, Sean had been fired. He had been opposed to the idea of

Bedouin playing occasional Motorhead tribute gigs in the guise of Ace Of Spades. Alan also says he was unreliable. Sean was replaced by Glenn Povey, who'd been on the same joinery apprenticeship as Alan in Ipswich. The group had also expanded, with Starfield's Danny "Bash" Faulkner coming in on vocals.

He was asked to leave after the album recordings, since it was felt his vocals weren't aggressive enough, and the band continued as a three-piece. At the same time, Alan was working on another album, with his cousin Nigel Potter. They were sprucing up some old 1993 recordings of Nigel's songs, and the result was *Alien Heart*, a mail-order release. Says Alan: "The quality isn't that good because they're very old, four-track recordings."

A live Bedouin album, *Live And Beyond*, was recorded in 2000, just before Alan's return to Hawkwind. Still, Davey has never disbanded Bedouin and is currently mixing another live album.

Jerry Richards was born on November 13, 1962 in Warwickshire – "the home of The Bard". Growing up, he moved "all over the place" with his family, arriving in Coventry in the early Seventies.

He was "comprehensively educated" at secondary school, after which he attended sixth-form college and Lanchester Polytechnic, where he was a student in the Faculty Of Art.

Says Jerry: "I did a Fine Art in ceramics on the job, as it were, with a fine potter, Peter Illesley. I can throw a pot with the best of them. I sold lots of pottery. As a sideline, to raise a few hundred quid when I needed to, I'd go off into the countryside, find a groovy house I liked the shape of, knock on the door and say, 'I'll make you a replica model of your house in fine stonewear – handmade, hand-glazed, totally unique. It'll be a one-off. I can do that for £500 for you.' I'd choose houses that were architecturally interesting and a bit of a challenge to make and design. There's nothing like getting your hands stuck into a mud pie. You don't mind getting a bit messy when you end up with beautiful results."

Jerry was in a few "pick-up bands" with friends in the years before Tubilah Dog, which was run along the lines of a cooperative. They played "dance-driven, tribal stuff, using the earliest samplers and bits and pieces we had lying around".

He adds: "People were all piling in saying, 'Love the drums!' and 10 years later, that's what we've got. People have been doing music for mind and body forever. All these things are recycled. Now we've got

The Darkness – rehashed Queen and Be Bop Deluxe. It's just so old it's brand new again."

It was, of course, in Tubilah Dog and the free-festival scene that Jerry met Dave Brock and became a member of Hawkdog and The Agents Of Chaos. Through the same connections, Dave met Hawkwind's future lighting engineer Adie, who had started out as a roadie for Tubilah Dog.

Now in Hawkwind and with Alan gone, Jerry felt perfectly at home. He says: "We were getting on fantastically. Good heavens! We were the fantastic four!"

The fantastic four – Dave, Richard, Ron and Jerry – now had to find the way forward. Richard Chadwick: "Dave and Alan used to write lots of stuff together. Without Alan, there had to be a restructuring. Ron had been around with us and he'd got this relationship with Dave in terms of writing."

"Dave used to think Alan's songs weren't that much cop," offers Ron. "They used to have a bit of a sifting through. It weren't just, 'That's a good 'un.' Alan would always be pushing for his songs. It was funny, really. I don't think I had any better opportunities after Alan left. It didn't help that there wasn't a lot of budget. The band was really exciting still, but it was more difficult to get things together."

Richard comments: "Ron was beginning to suffer from his self-inflicted illness."

"Heroin addiction," declares Dave.

"He hid it from us for a long time," continues Richard. "He became erratic. He wouldn't turn up for rehearsal. At other times, although he was motivated to do things, it was difficult for him to manifest them. Ron is a really hands-on, do-it-in-the-here-and-now kind of person, but sit him in front of a computer and say, 'Write your tune,' and he'd be stumped. Dave, Jerry and I were deeply into sequencers. Ron would sit around for hours and hours with not very much to do. And there was this burgeoning thing going on which he was keeping hidden from us."

"And he had problems at home, don't forget," adds Brock.

"Jerry held it all together," concludes Richard. "He would do all this boring stuff to make things happen." The boring stuff involved administration, paperwork and liaison. Before long, Jerry would take over the tour management.

No one saw anything of Hawkwind during the first half of 1997. They were in retreat, working on new material and planning the next stage of their campaign.

"I was on the farm for four months without going home," says Jerry. "You write beautiful poems home to your loved ones, you telephone and send postcards. The band becomes very much a family, a unit. Usually, trouble only starts when outside influences start coming in and upsetting the apple cart."

The first gig of the year was a charity benefit for the homeless, organised by Marion Lloyd-Langton. Held at Blackheath Concert Hall on June 7, it was the climax of a series of events taking place over more than a week.

It was a noteworthy Hawkwind gig thanks to Scouse, who joined Kris in the fire displays. "I nearly set fire to the venue," he laughs. "A droplet of lit petrol from my fire torch touched the paper cone in the monitor. It burst into flames instantly. There were flames about two or three feet high along the front of the stage. All the lights went on in the venue. They were about to start evacuating the building. I rushed off-stage and threw my fire sticks into the hands of Max Splodge from Splodgenessabounds, who happened to be there. I grabbed the fire extinguisher and dashed back onstage to put out the fire.

"It was the right type of extinguisher, a powder one. But when I came on, the girl doing the monitor mix rushed up to me yelling, 'Don't!' She thought it was a water one and I was going to cause an electrical problem. I had to tell her to bugger off. I put it out in a big puff of powder, there was coughing and spluttering in the front row, the lights went back down and everybody roared. They loved it.

"It was purely an accident, we got away with it, and there were no serious *post mortems* with the band. I thought they should have written it into the set for the audience reaction alone. There were no other dangerous occurrences that I can remember."

Dave Brock remembers one: "There was a gig once in Windsor and the Windsor chapter of the Hell's Angels were there. These plastic Christmas decorations caught fire and started dropping down. The guy who was running the venue went bananas. He had a big freak-out and he wasn't going to give us our money. Of course, we did get it in the end . . ."

The next month found Hawkwind out on the road again, this time in Spain and America. In Spain, they drove across the Pyrenees as part of a convoy travelling to the village of Escalarre for the Dr Music festival on July 12 and 13. It took place in a large, green stretch of meadowland surrounded by majestic peaks.

Within two weeks the band had landed in the United States, where they opened with gigs in Chicago, Cleveland and New York's Coney Island. The last show, and the highlight, was their July 31 appearance at the Strange Daze festival in Sherman, located in the south-western part of New York state.

"We had a wild party," says Dave. "It was a whole festival built around Hawkwind. It was a wonderful place to be if you were in the band. The promoter was Jim Lasko, who was from the Orbital Church Of Rock'n'Roll. We'd known them for years. It was the first space-rock festival in America."

"It was beautifully organised," remembers Richard. "We got lots of people who were used to festival culture in America. Unlike English festivals where people turn up with a bedroll under one arm and a tent under the other, they have camper vans with proper cooking stuff, and they go round and follow bands on tour. It's all incredibly well organised. Each campsite would have a major installation of facilities and water. We'd be wandering around and people would be saying, 'Hey, hey, do you want to come for dinner?'

"There was a big drum circle and all the earth-magic characters. After drumming away for a while, they were taking their clothes off and chanting."

"It was a fabulous festival," confirms Jerry. "Hardcore Hawkwind fans were springing out from everywhere. With Jim Lasko and his Strange Trips set-up, we could plug into a network that existed there but was not very well known. It's now the stoner-rock circuit, but that was before all those groups like Queens Of The Stone Age. There was a healthy interest, and it took a name band like Hawkwind to put it back on to the agenda."

It was in this natural environment that Hawkwind were joined onstage by an old acquaintance – Nik Turner.

Says Richard: "He was guesting with a band called Far Flung, playing some of the Hawkwind numbers he'd written. I thought they played well. I really liked them. We were the headline act, and we played just as the sun was going down. I remember Dave saying he'd carefully explained to Nik, 'Don't play over this part . . .' I listened to a recording of it, and it sounds great. We did a reggae improvisation over one of the songs that Nik used to do, 'Master Of The Universe' or 'Brainstorm'."

This was undoubtedly due to the presence of Captain Rizz, a half-Irish, half-Jamaican Rastafarian with impressive dreads who had often supported Hawkwind with his own band and was now making occasional appearances onstage with them. He was beginning to develop an intuitive rapport with Ron Tree.

Richard carries on: "I thought that with Nik coming on with us, things might get better in the future, that maybe we could get back together and do things. He did actually come and play with us later on at St Austell and Croydon."

Dave: "I made sure Nik couldn't go on for hours with his saxophone. It was quite a tight band, and we knew exactly what we wanted. Nik was on his best behaviour."

"It was really good fun," remembers Jerry. "It was another element from the Hawkwind arsenal – bring on the big guns. There was the usual banter, the odd quip. Dave said to the audience, 'Of course, you realise Mr Nik Turner is old enough for his bus pass now.'"

"When we finished the set," says Dave, "we had a couple of encores. Then Nik said, 'Come on, everybody, I want Hawkwind to come back onstage.' He went on all by himself and played a half-an-hour saxophone solo. 'Well,' he announced, 'They're a bunch of cunts. They won't come back.'"

Dave had hoped that after all of the band's frustrated efforts to rebuild their profile in America, this short but effective trip might be "the start of something really wonderful". With this in mind, Hawkwind arranged a return visit in August the next year for another Strange Daze event in Ohio.

Typically, they were doomed to disappointment. Dave Brock and Ron Tree would suffer some rough justice courtesy of US immigration officers who didn't much like their previous convictions and they would be stranded on the opposite side of the Canadian border from the rest of the band. That border never did smile on Hawkwind, as Lemmy would undoubtedly agree.

Kris Tait was not around for a lot of 1997. She was studying for her PGCE, and when Hawkwind embarked on a major UK tour stretching from the end of September through to November (with a handful of gigs in the Netherlands tacked on to the end), she relinquished the reins of responsibility. Jerry Richards, having built up an extensive knowledge of the organisation, took on the task of tour managing the group as well as playing in it, although Kris would still turn up when she could.

She was on hand for the first gig at a Dracula commemorative festival in Whitby on September 27, but it wasn't an auspicious start.

"It was quite cold for September," she states. "I remember arguing, trying to get the cash before the band went onstage. I think we only got £7,000 – which was more than most of the other bands did. The Stranglers were playing, and they got their full fee. I remember thinking, 'Whoever handles them, he must be pretty good.' Arthur Brown was there too, and it was the first time Dave had seen him for a long time. We met him in the car park up above Whitby, and Dave had a chat with him. At the gig, he did 'Fire'. We went on after him and I did my fire show. He got filmed for Tyne Tees and we didn't."

Jerry was outraged by some of the problems he faced on the road. He recalls: "There was so much sabotage going on by various promoters along the way, not honouring the contracts properly, trying to change the terms of contracts after they'd been signed, trying to withhold VAT. It was shocking. It was a considerable production, it cost a lot of money and you have to know exactly what's going on. There are plenty of people willing to take advantage at the drop of a hat.

"Apollo Leisure were underwriting some part of the tour. We spoke to them and they pulled in the big guns and told these regional promoters to get a grip because the way they were treating us was wrong.

"It was down to me to try to make a success of the tour and turn a reasonable profit on it to invest back into the next bunch of projects. It was a very, very busy time. On a day-to-day basis, I was responsible for making sure we had somewhere to stay, that we could book a restaurant in the evening, that everyone got paid. The way I like to run things is that people feel empowered in their jobs. I was a conduit between the band's aspirations and the logistics on the road.

"There were always ups and downs, things that niggled and rankled with people, and not everybody has a good day every day. A band like Hawkwind has a heavy tradition of doing things in its own way, and inevitably there were some conflicts, but nothing we couldn't get around."

Looking back on this period, Kris Tait thinks that Jerry was probably too nice to be a tour manager. "You have to be quite aggressive to do this," she considers. "It wasn't Jerry's fault. I don't think he even wanted to be tour managing. He got thrown into it because there was nobody else.

"There seem to have been lots of problems. You have to be willing to get nasty. Jerry just wasn't aggressive. If you let anybody get away with something at a gig, the word goes round – 'Hawkwind are easy to rip off.' I go in and I say, 'Right, we'll leave everything in the truck until you've fed the crew and got the things that are on the rider. I'm not unpacking it.'" When they worked together, Jerry and Kris would make a formidable "good cop, bad cop" duo.

Douglas Smith comments: "I had suggested that Hawkwind manage themselves and turn to us for advice when they needed to. We said we'd get an agent for the tour, and they were supposed to be managing the whole thing. They got Jerry Richards to do it. The tour turned into a disaster, but Eve got all their money out for them in the end, even though there were problems with a few promoters. She stayed on top of it the whole time and all she got was abuse from certain people in and around the band. I've never heard so much rudeness in my life to a woman."

Asked about his involvement with Chumbawamba and the feeling around Hawkwind that they were being abandoned by him, Douglas replies: "My time was more devoted to Chumbawamba. They sold six or seven million albums and when a band starts selling records like that, you work very hard on it. So I wasn't around that much for Hawkwind. A tremendous amount of jealousy went down about it, and the situation deteriorated.

"The only contract I had with Hawkwind was dated from the Seventies, and they've never paid me on it. When they ever lost money on a tour, I'd cut our commission to help them. Sometimes we'd only charge them five per cent to help them out. I helped Alan with a couple of his solo albums, I lent money to him, and I've never had any back.

"Science fiction is the core of the band. People make up stories. I had a lot of things said about me, like I was 'buying drugs'. Pete Frame did his family tree and it was written that, 'Douglas came into the office with one of his suitcases full of drugs.' The last thing I ever did was get myself in a situation where I could be busted for drugs.

"I worked with Chumbawamba because they're honourable people. They're honest. They pay their bills. They're pro-active. Sometimes

I'd have to beg Dave to turn up at an interview in London. He'd say, 'Get someone else to do it.' Then they'd get all the glory and Dave would be pissed off.

"Chumbawamba were the first band that's ever thanked me for their success. We got a deal, we made them a lot of money and I have a note in a drawer upstairs with a little heart on it – 'Doug and Eve – thank you. Chumbawamba.' "

Douglas is still managing the Chumbas, along with two or three acts as yet unknown in this country.

The 1997 autumn tour was timed to promote the release by Emergency Broadcast System of the new Hawkwind album, *Distant Horizons*, which had been recorded earlier that year. And in line with Alan Davey's opinion of the album, few of the band were happy with it.

Dave Brock says: "The keyboards with the weird, spacey, dancey things – some of those didn't work. It sounded a bit wishy-washy, but you have to try."

Jerry comments: "That album was constantly being interrupted by having to go off and do gigs. It was unbelievably distracting. I really like doing gigs, but the band were contractually obliged to deliver something and being stretched in a million different directions into all kinds of strange shapes. When the management structure isn't all that it could be, it's very difficult to keep things running smoothly.

"It was a very difficult album to make. I like bits and pieces of it. We didn't have as much editorial control over it as we should have had. What was released was not actually what we prepared. The rest of the band were fairly hacked off about it."

The album included a guest appearance by Steve Smith on audio generator in 'Phetamine Street'.

There was much more of a buzz around *In Your Area*, part of which was recorded live on the last date on the 1997 tour, at the Brussels Ancienne Belgique on November 20. The rest of the album contains material recorded at Dave's studio. It was released in America first on Griffin Records and then in the UK by Voiceprint in 2000.

"I really liked that album," says Jerry. "It's more exploratory."

Malcolm Dome, reviewing *In Your Area* in *Classic Rock*, agreed. He wrote: "Vibrant, coherent yet also adventurous and madcap, this is exactly the sort of album that reaffirms Hawkwind's perennial pre-eminence."

Ron Tree had by now moved on to bass full-time at his own request, replacing Alan, and although he continued as the vocalist, his opportunities for outrageous theatre were limited. As he says himself, "I couldn't change my costumes all the time."

An extra visual interest was supplied by Captain Rizz, who had been making guest appearances with Hawkwind since the Strange Daze festival. "He was brilliant, I've gotta say," smiles Ron Tree. "I really enjoyed working with him. He should've been kept in the band."

A doubtful Kris Tait opines: "At the start of the tour, he came on and did the odd bit of reggae singing. Towards the end of it, he was staying onstage a lot longer, and he started doing this jamming thing with Ron. The fans either loved him or hated him, and some of them *really* hated him. But he was great on the things that he did well.

"He's a character. He once stood for Parliament against Glenda Jackson. His band, Captain Rizz, had supported us all the way through one of our tours. I think it might have been the Alien tour. They were managed by a friend of ours, Simon Tepee, and they were crazy people. We used to call them the Rizlas. They were all black except for the keyboard player."

Hawkwind welcomed two other guests onstage during the 1997 dates. One was Crum, the keyboardist who had joined The Agents Of Chaos after sending Dave a succession of tapes which sounded "quite spacey". Finally, Hawkwind roadie Mr Dibs – who still works with the band – played a series of guest spots on bass.

"It got a bit chaotic, that tour," says Kris. "I remember going to see a few of the gigs, and I wasn't very impressed."

"That was Dave getting as many people in as he could to make a show of something happening," says Ron Tree. "He was covering angles. But it was good to work with them all."

Ron was still happy enough to be in Hawkwind, but the honeymoon was nearly over.

CHAPTER 29

Peace, Love And GBH

THEY'D come up with the novel wheeze of Hawkwind "passports" for fans. These would be supplied free of charge to applicants who would then be eligible for special offers and privileges. It's a scheme that is still working well for the band and fans alike, with passport holders gaining access to exclusive CDs and private gigs and parties.

One such CD, limited to 500 copies, was *Hawkwind Live 1997*, compiled by Jerry Richards and Ron Tree. "It's the Hawkwind album I'm most proud of," says Ron today. "It catches the feeling of what we were like."

Importantly, Hawkwind were working towards a new type of festival experience, one in which they could guarantee the safety and enjoyment of everyone who attended. They had been shocked by the scale of the violence at Brighton in 1990, they had witnessed the decline of the free-festival scene, and they wanted to create an alternative: the Hawkfest. The passports were crucial to this venture.

Kris Tait explains: "We thought it would be good to be able to do some things privately. It's a nice idea that you're part of a club. We wanted to hold festivals without having to try to get licensing for big public events.

"The fans have to put their photographs on the passports, and it means that Hawkfests are completely safe festivals. They are for passport holders only. They are at liberty to buy tickets for friends and family, but these tickets are invalid unless they are presented at the door by the passport holder who bought them, the idea being that you're responsible for your guests. It's a bit like a social club where you sign people in. We can do things more cheaply this way too, and we know exactly who's coming.

"The result is that there's zero crime. Children can wander around at night and be totally safe, because we have the name, address and photograph of everybody who's on that festival site. The police love it because there are no security problems."

Hawkwind audiences are as fanatical as ever, if smaller than they once were, and a great part of the devotion stems from their feeling of belonging. Many fans have flown the flag for years, and decades.

Superfan Bernhard Pospiech, 44, from Gelsenkirchen, Germany, has been a loyal follower since 1974 when, at the age of 14, he heard 'Silver Machine' on the radio. He was initially attracted by "the mixture of rock and electronics and the driving rhythm in their sound," and was further captivated by their adventurous science fiction. He has since seen the group live around 30 times, travelling as far afield as Holland and England.

Bernhard has collected more than 150 Hawkwind albums and CDs as well as posters, T-shirts and tour programmes. He has also compiled detailed information archives about the band, and is regarded by Dave and Kris as an authority.

Asked what he most enjoys about Hawkwind these days, Bernhard replies: "The music and the close contact to the band members. We – the fans and the band – are a huge family."

In this context, the passports made perfect sense. It would take a few years to get the Hawkfests off the ground; the first would take place in Devon in 2002, followed by another in Blackpool a year later. But the passport system was up and running by 1998. It's a shame, perhaps, that no gigs took place that year. There was an attempt at one but it turned into a shambles, ironically because of real passport problems (Dave's and Ron's).

Hawkwind were, as usual, at work on new material, but they no longer had a UK outlet for it. Douglas Smith had blocked any more releases on Emergency Broadcast System.

He claims: "It just got to the point of stupidity. I set it up as a limited company that we're all part of. It created a cash flow for Hawkwind on a regular basis, but you couldn't talk to them. Alan would ring up and ask for an advance and then Dave would want to know, 'Why has Alan got all this money?' If they'd taken it seriously they'd have a nice little earner there.

"The amount of money they got out of the company was quite substantial. Then along comes somebody else and offers them £3,000 to release something. Hawkwind are looking for the £3,000.

"The plan with EBS was to get everybody involved. Many of the ex-members would release new product through this vehicle, and some old product was released too. The artists were getting decent royalties and returns. But we ended up putting albums out that probably sold 500 copies. We put out Simon House's album, a couple of Alan's albums, Harvey had an album out, and Dave's albums didn't sell. All the sales were down. The last one we put out was Hawkwind's *Distant Horizons* in 1997. I called it a day. I just didn't want to do it any more. But EBS still exists, and the albums are still part of the company."

By 1998, Kris was back with the band full time, having finished her studies. She slipped back into her tour managing role, even though there wasn't much touring to worry about, and for the next year or two, could rely on practical and administrative back-up from Jerry Richards, the good cop. The relationship with Douglas Smith had become so distant it was almost non-existent.

Kris recalls: "I didn't mind tour managing, but I didn't want to manage the band. I didn't want to do all the record deals and everything." She was anxious to find a reliable manager, and Hawkwind got through two candidates relatively quickly.

"They were both only interested in getting their hands on the back catalogue," says Kris. "And they were charging us 20 per cent for that. Basically, we felt like we were being ripped off. They were pretty much crap and we didn't have them for very long."

Kris would end up in the role of caretaker manager, and would only take on the job officially when Hawkwind ran out of takers that they trusted.

The next Strange Daze festival was to be held on August 15 in a park not far from Cleveland, Ohio. This was the day after the 10th anniversary of Robert Calvert's death and Hawkwind intended to pay tribute at the festival, having rehearsed a set that contained lots of Calvert material.

The band, and Captain Rizz, were flying to Cleveland via Toronto because it was the cheapest route. But Dave and Ron were travelling without immigration clearance because their applications had not been processed in time for the gig. Their problems were to do with their police records.

Ron had a couple of previous convictions for possession of cannabis and one for possession of heroin. "They were small amounts," he says, "but the convictions were enough to stop you being free."

Dave's record was varied. There was his old cannabis-plant conviction, which he had admitted from the outset. Other prosecutions lurking in the background were for possessing an offensive weapon (the fishing truncheon) and for pinching a bottle of milk. Says Dave: "The milk bottle was a silly thing when I was very young." Then there was a conviction for GBH.

Douglas Smith comments: "It was many years ago that we first applied for immigration into America so that Hawkwind could tour there. We were asked if we had any previous convictions. Being a manager, I'm pragmatic and I realised that sooner or later, with a band that are well known for their representation of the drug life, some inspector is going to take a look at the realities.

"So I did it properly and the immigration people allowed for all the drugs to be taken into account. We did a procedure to get a waiver for them all, and they've continued to be able to go into America on any occasion."

Obviously, this was long before Ron Tree joined the band.

"Dave didn't admit all his convictions," continues Douglas. "As far as I can remember, his only admission was this one cannabis plant, and so he's been investigated many times. Every tour I was involved with, Dave had problems with immigration because of the incidents that he didn't admit. They've played games with him all his life. He was called in for interviews, and they brought up the subject of him nicking a bottle of milk – petty larceny. Later on, this other criminal conviction for GBH came into it, and Dave's lawyers had to take care of the situation.

"Lemmy has immigration clearance. I have one as well. I have a 'not ineligible for entry into the United States of America due to the Lennon ruling'. That's how Lemmy has been able to stay in America, because he's always been open about convictions he had in the past. With Dave, eventually I got a senator in Cincinnati to help us out. He sent a letter to the embassy, and that got Dave his immigration in the end."

Brock contends that his problems stemmed from Douglas' declaration of the cannabis conviction: "I got busted for having a cannabis plant. I was a dangerous criminal in the American Government's eyes.

Douglas Smith had declared it, so I had to apply for a waiver every time I went to America."

Dave explains the background to the GBH charge, which dates back to the mid-Eighties: "I caught some bloke who was trespassing on my property sticking his head in our recording studio. When I asked him what he thought he was doing, he was quite stroppy towards me. I laid into him, really. I gave him a big whack, and he went to hospital and had a lot of stitches in his head. I had to go to court over it. I got a £250 fine although the judge seemed to agree that I was in my rights to defend my property. Even the police said, 'It might be a stupid thing to say but you can't attack people – you have to wait for them to attack you.' Some of these characters are aggressive and if you back down, they might give you a terrible beating.

"We're not peace-loving hippies. When we lived in Seaton, we had our house broken into. I found out who'd done it – four burglars. I went round this guy's house with a mallet and a can of petrol. His girl-friend opened the door, I shoved her out of the way and he jumped out the back window and ran away, actually. So I didn't do anything. I said, 'Look, if I get hold of him . . .' I'd have burnt his place down.

"Another of the burglars I saw in the high street and he ran to the police station. The day after it happened, two of Satan's Slaves, who are affiliated to the Hell's Angels, drove into Seaton. They were looking for me 'cos they wanted to know if we'd be interested in doing a gig at the St George's Hall in Exeter. One of the guys who broke into my house saw them – Seaton's a small place – and thought they'd come to get him.

"All four burglars got caught and they got in terrible trouble. They told the police I had huge amounts of drugs in my house. The police searched the place from top to bottom and they didn't find a thing. They apologised.

"I tell you what . . . I had to go and MOT our camper recently. I took it to the bus station where the heavy vehicles go. It's a big place. One of the people working there was the guy who did the lights at the Phoenix Arts Centre in Exeter. He'd helped us once when we had some problems with our light-show.

"Then another bloke came up to me and said, 'Are you still playing?' It turns out he's in Satan's Slaves, who we did the gig for at St George's Hall. He knows my son Pascoe, who's in prison at the moment."

Pascoe has been in trouble with the law on and off for many years, and his latest sentence was for burglary. Dave confides: "He has a heroin habit. It's a real shame. He's got a lovely girlfriend and a lovely daughter. We've been trying so hard with him for many years, but it's just impossible. He's been in prison before, but he didn't learn his lesson. In these little country towns, dope smokers and heroin takers all know each other. It's very hard to break out of it. Pascoe would get out of jail and come back to the same area. He'd be all right for a while but he'd end up back on heroin, stealing stuff. It's never-ending. There's nothing I can do now. He's in his thirties. He's an adult, not a child.

"A few friends of ours, they had similar problems. You think, 'Oh, God, is this happening because I'm a musician?' "

In 1998, Dave had sent his passport off as usual and applied for the waiver to get into America.

"It was issued," he confirms. "But it hadn't arrived, and we'd booked the flights. We had to go, so I went on my other passport. As we went through the US immigration at the airport in Toronto to get the connecting flight to Cleveland, the officers were looking at all these weird-looking characters. Captain Rizz had a rucksack on his back, and he was pretending he wasn't with us.

"When you get convictions, they print these numbers in your passport, and the immigration people can immediately check. I went through and they obviously saw 'drugs, violence and theft'. They thought, 'Aye, aye.' I got past and then I got called back and that was it. They wouldn't let me or Ron into the country."

The rest of Hawkwind travelled on as planned to Cleveland. Ron Tree stayed in Canada for a night and got blitzed. He says: "Dave gave me 200 gilders to walk through the airport with. I went into Toronto, changed the gilders up and blew the money on cocaine. I flew back home the next day."

At the time Dave was called back, Kris had already gone through immigration and had her green card stamped. She says: "This meant that I'd officially entered America and then I'd left it again and I hadn't come back out properly. After three months, I'd be classed as an illegal immigrant." It was another complication that would have to be ironed out later.

Dave and Kris went first to the embassy in Toronto and then found a place to stay in Niagara. From there, Dave made contact with the Strange Daze organisers. The band had arrived a few days ahead of the gig, and there was still time for Dave to straighten out his problems. This depended on his passport arriving in Devon. Kris' mum Margaret Tait and her friend Rose, dog-sitting at the farmhouse, were watching and waiting, ready to have the passport flown out to Dave immediately it was delivered. Infuriatingly, it turned up too late, on the morning of the gig.

"I was really down in the dumps," says Dave, who was nevertheless working on a contingency plan. "I said, 'I'll get on a mobile phone while Hawkwind are playing, I'll be able to hear what's going on and I'll sing on the phone.' It could have gone through the PA."

Richard Chadwick, Jerry Richards and Captain Rizz, across the river, were becoming more panic-stricken as the gig approached. "There were all these bands, beautiful weather and all these people saying, 'Where's Dave?'" recalls Richard. "At the same time, I was thinking, 'Shit, these people are all going to turn round and say to Jim [Lasko], 'We want our money back 'cos Hawkwind aren't playing.' Jim was saying, 'You've got to go on.'"

As an emergency measure, two American musicians – Steve Taylor and Steve Hayes – were recruited and hastily rehearsed. (Bassist Taylor would later join the line-up for a tour of Australia and New Zealand when Ron Tree was indisposed.)

Richard carries on: "We were in a tent going through this stuff which Jerry, Rizz and I knew really well, but these other two Americans had no idea of. By the evening, it had got frantic. People were freaking out and saying, 'What's going to happen?'"

Dave, meanwhile, was on standby in Canada with a mobile phone, but he never did get his chance to do his long-distance singalong.

"Nobody came up to us and said, 'We've got Dave on the phone,'" says Richard. "We had to start without any of the electronics working. We just had to do it. You're thinking, 'Christ – Dave and Ron can't come so all we have got is us. This is it.' It was very hard work, but the audience cheered and everything was all right. We got away with it."

The way Dave Brock sees it, Voiceprint Records saved his bacon. The way Nik Turner sees it, Brock had no right to get his bacon saved by issuing archive material on Voiceprint without consultation.

The nightmare scenario that Huw Lloyd-Langton had predicted, leading to his decision to quit the Hawkwind partnership, had finally happened – to Dave.

Peace, Love And GBH

"We formed a couple of companies for different line-ups of the band," Dave explains. "Some of the members in one of our companies hadn't paid their income tax. We were responsible for our own earnings because we were self-employed. I'd paid mine, but the Inland Revenue were chasing me for the rest of the money that was owed by other partners. Being a householder, I'd become liable. They didn't know where the rest of the band were. They didn't want to know anything about them. They said, 'You're responsible.' So I was lumbered with paying the bill."

He needed to raise some money, but Hawkwind were no longer able to release material through Emergency Broadcast System. Then, just at the time of the financial emergency, Voiceprint Records expressed an interest in the band.

Dave arranged for the release on Voiceprint of some old material, including CD reissues of the Weird Tapes series. He was also pleased to shake hands with Voiceprint over forthcoming Hawkwind product, hence *In Your Area* (2000), *Yule Ritual: London Astoria 29.12.00.* (2001), *Canterbury Fayre 2001* (2002) and *Spaced Out In London* (2004).

He says: "The [tax] money came back out of the publishing on the records." Once the tax debt had been paid off, says Dave, the contributing musicians on the albums received full accounting and royalty cheques.

At the time of writing, the Voiceprint website was advertising 19 Hawkwind albums for sale. They comprised all but *Spaced Out In London* from the above titles plus *Atomhenge, Dawn Of Hawkwind, Family Tree, Hawkfest 2002, Live At Glastonbury 1990, Live 1990, Masters Of The Universe: Complete '79 – Collector Series Vol 1, Live 1982: Collector Series Vol 2, Spacebrock*, and seven Weird Tapes albums. The band's new studio collection, *Take Me To Your Leader*, was also due to be released on Voiceprint.

Nik Turner is not the only member of the band to take exception to the archive releases, although he is the most vociferous. He blasts: "Dave has instigated the release of quite a lot of albums through Voiceprint, some of which I am on. I gave my permission for none of these releases.

"I think they're all of a really shite standard. A few years ago, I was in Scandinavia and somebody showed me a review of this Hawkwind album that Voiceprint had put out. The review said it was crap and whoever released it should be ashamed of themselves. I've had several royalty statements, which I've sent back to Voiceprint, about these albums I'm on.

"If you hit people when they're poor and give them money and they accept it, they're accepting the terms and conditions that go with it. I'm not going to let them get away with preying on my poverty. I haven't accepted any money from Voiceprint. I wrote them a letter saying, 'I'm returning your statements. Before I accept any money, I'd like to see a copy of the agreement that allows you to release material I'm on without my consent and for a rate which I never agreed to.' Until then, I won't accept any royalty payments from them. It's my standing on a principle of not accepting a hand-out from a record company. People should be seeing these arseholes as they are."

Although Nik is not alone in his protest, he is the only one to have turned down the money. All his former colleagues have, it appears, cashed their cheques while still castigating Brock and Voiceprint.

Douglas Smith observes: "This has raised the hackles of a number of the ex-members who have granted nobody the right to sign on their behalf and who put Voiceprint on very stern notice. It has seemed to stop Voiceprint from making any further moves on the archive material, but they're still selling almost every one of the albums that Dave gave them. I think it's wrong. As a human being and as a manager, I have to have the permission of all the artists involved before I would do a deal."

"You've got to remember that Hawkwind is Hawkwind," retaliates Dave, who says he sees the group as an evolving entity needing continuous investment rather than a succession of individuals: "The money goes to keeping the band going. It doesn't go to me. There's a band that's continuing to fly the flag. A lot of the things that we do go to 'the all'.

"If we've got some tapes and they need remixing, I don't get paid for doing that. I do it for love and for the good of the all. Everybody will get a bit of money out of it, it keeps the band going, and that's what we want.

"A lot of people have been earning plenty out of this band. Alan and Richard have been working with us for quite a few years and they're selling records Nik Turner was on. It's for the good of the all, not for my pocket. We utilise our money in ventures. We spent all that money on the American project and Nik went and blew that down the drain.

"You have to think for the good of everybody. It's like The Three

Musketeers. All these different artists that came in and out of the band – they are all good in certain ways, but there's no one person who's a great star. Hawkwind operates as an entity. You've got to have a captain, of course, but it's not like there's ever been any guitar hero. It's always been a unit where people come and go. They all give something, they paint their picture with sounds and then they go and do something else. Quite often, a lot of them come back to us.

"These records on Voiceprint aren't selling thousands of copies. We're just about scraping by. We have to get all the artwork together ourselves for a nice cover – whatever we have to do . . .

"Voiceprint send accounts out to every person and everybody gets paid direct. I know exactly what they all get. And Voiceprint did support us when nobody else did. Rob Ayling, who runs the label, is also involved with Tim Blake. He puts out Tim's records, Huwie's records, Alan's, Jerry's . . . When you look at their catalogue, it's huge. It's not the pissy little record company Nik Turner portrays it as."

The Voiceprint controversy is only the latest of many uprisings against Dave Brock by former Hawkwind members. Since the earliest days of the Weird Tapes, through Flicknife and beyond, he has been accused time and again of plundering his personal archives for commercial gain without seeking the permission of the former members and sometimes without crediting the songwriters. He has also come under suspicion of releasing sub-standard bootlegs through a plethora of tiny labels across the UK and Europe, thus diminishing the reputation of the band.

Dave retorts that in the early days, his colleagues were usually too stoned to remember hearing and agreeing to his plans for record releases. He denies any involvement in rubbishy bootlegs, insisting that he would not endanger the good name of the band he has led for 35 years and therefore his own living. He counterclaims that the real damage to Hawkwind's legend has been done by Dave Anderson's release and licensing of *Bring Me The Head Of Yuri Gagarin* from the tapes originally supplied by Nik Turner.

The total eclipse of the sun on August 11, 1999 enthralled the nation. For new-agers, old hippies and all the travelling types who observe the solstices and know their astronomy from their astrology, it was a special cause for celebration.

It was expected that Cornwall would be swamped by pilgrims eager to be the first in the country to view this rare celestial spectacle, and a series of eclipse parties and festivals were arranged across the county. In the event, the anticipated crowds stayed at home, discouraged by warnings of traffic jams and over-priced accommodation and camp sites.

Some festival organisers never recovered from the disappointing attendances. Michael Dog says: "Megadog ran until 1998 as a touring show, and then Bob [Dog] did three festivals, the last of which was the Eclipse. It was affected by the thing of lots of people theoretically going to the West Country and not in reality. It was under-attended. A lot of money was lost. So that was the end of it, really."

Hawkwind were among those who did make the effort to go to Cornwall, and they played twice on the day of the eclipse in the grounds of a farm outside the village of Carleen.

It was a cloudy morning, but just after 11am, the spectators thrilled to the sudden darkness, the plunging temperature, the dropping of the wind and the silence of the birds as totality approached. An hour later, Hawkwind played their first set.

It was a chilled, ambient performance with lots of improvisation in keeping with the spirit of the occasion and the time of day. Richard, coming out from behind the drums, unusually took lead vocals in a song dedicated to the sun, and the set finished with what's thought to be the first-ever live rendition of 'Hippy'.

The night-time show, by contrast, was a total assault on the senses, summed up by one member of the audience writing on the Hawkeye website: "This is what Hawkwind are masters of: conjurers of chaos, frenzied sounds and sonic energy."

Jerry Richards says the live recording sounds wonderful and hopes to release it in the near future.

It was only a matter of months after the eclipse that Ron Tree began to feel really miserable. He says: "My situation in the group – it did crush my spirituality. It took my joy away. It made me feel powerless, disconnected. I weren't allowed to express myself 100 per cent creatively in the band. I couldn't blossom fully. You were only getting bits of me there. I was really in Dave's band.

"It's not particularly Dave's fault. It's just the way he works. He was doing what he normally does. I'm just as much to blame because I didn't speak up to him. Perhaps if I'd said, 'I feel restricted, I need to express myself more,' it might have helped. I'll give him the benefit of the doubt there.

"I did try to say, 'Let's do an album like this, let's work together as a band.' He'd say, 'All right, then,' and just come out with an idea of his own. I had to sing my lyrics all over music that was already written. It's always written for you. I used to get maybe two or three songs, including the melodies, on an album. It's more than most people got, and it's better than one. But he'd have most of the royalties from the songs. It would have been nice to have written the tunes with him.

"Then again, how would I feel if I'd been in it for 30 years? You've gotta look at it both ways. I'm not moaning. I think it would be better if people could just find a happy medium where they all work together rather than one man controlling the whole thing. I like Dave and what he does. He's done well so far, although it doesn't seem to be making him very happy with it. If he could just let go a bit more . . ."

Ron's other problem was the ongoing Calvert connection. He recalls: "I felt I was being channelled by people, like I were being put in his shoes and that didn't feel good. It weren't intentional, but it used to really fucking piss me off. They'd get me singing songs like 'Robot' [a Brock/Calvert co-write]. It's weird. There was a funny similarity, and it weren't purposely done. I could mimic anyone. I used to keep saying, 'I'm me and I don't really want to keep singing these songs.' I respect the guy and his family, but I didn't want to put it on and pretend for them. It just seemed like it were going wrong."

Ron also accepts: "I could have been a hell of a lot better if I'd been in my right mind and not fucked up on that shit [heroin]. Dave did talk to me about smack. He was pretty good to me on that level. He never tried to pressure me; he never said, 'You'd better get off that or you're out of the band.' He'd give sort of family advice. He'd stick things in for me, try and say the right things. He'd say, 'You know, you have to change everything when you get off it.'"

For the time being, Ron saw no way out of his unhappiness. He says: "I was ready for just getting out of the band. Things started getting slowly worse over the next year or so. I just carried on because I did like playing to a lot of people. And it was going well, but I didn't know why." Ron is sure he would have left Hawkwind eventually, if he hadn't been sacked first.

For the second year in a row, the band kept a low profile. Prior to the eclipse performances, they'd played only two gigs, a motorcycle event at Pentrich Coneygrey Showground on July 30, where they were joined by bikers favourite Dumpy, and a private party in Honiton, Devon, on August 4.

They were quiet again until November when a string of UK dates in Oxford, Norwich, Milton Keynes, St Austell and Croydon brought some familiar characters back on to the stage.

Violinist Simon House and keyboardist Harvey Bainbridge had returned to Hawkwind. Captain Rizz was still cropping up at the odd date. And at St Austell and Croydon, Nik Turner was welcomed back as a guest.

"It was prearranged," says Nik of this surprising development. "Dave phoned. He's got the gall of the devil. He's a Leo, probably in his own world. I'm easy-going, I forgive people very easily, and I'm hard-up so I'll do anything for money. No, that isn't strictly true . . .

"I thought Hawkwind were great at those two gigs. We were just getting to know each other again. It was vaguely a prelude to the reunion concert which happened the next year. I really enjoyed myself. I was trying to get people enjoying themselves and the band. I'd bought myself a radio microphone and I walked around in the audience playing in this wacky latex suit that a mate of mine designed for me. It's confrontational music, really – bringing music close to people and bringing people close to me."

There was a new face, too, at St Austell where Hawkwind introduced Keith Kniveton, an audio generator player who would stay with them for quite some time. "Keith buys up old synthesisers," says Kris Tait. "We first got to know him when he asked us if Dave wanted to sell his old EMS synthesiser. Then he started mending gear for us, and there was always plenty of work for him."

A fan of Hawkwind, Keith enjoyed the ultimate privilege of ending up with the group.

It was a thoroughly suspect set-up, and the members of Hawkwind are reluctant to go into too much detail about it even now. Suffice to say that the February 2000 tour of Australia and New Zealand was not organised through the usual professional channels.

Says Dave Brock: "We got involved with this guy who wanted to be an impresario and who had contacts in New Zealand. We didn't realise that all his contacts were his cocaine-dealing friends. Everyone looked at the tour like it was going to be a paid holiday. Fantastic! We met up with this guy and everything looked jolly wonderful."

Harvey Bainbridge claims: "I said to Dave, 'Are you sure it's not a cocaine dealer's pipedream?' I went to rehearse and found this guy had been paying them in cocaine rather than money."

"I wasn't paid in cocaine," retorts Dave. "The band all got bags of grass given, including me, I might add. But that wasn't until we got there. I didn't have any cocaine, if that's the case."

Douglas Smith ventures: "The story I got is that there was some big kerfuffle about a large amount of money – 'Wouldn't it be a good idea if it went with the band?' There were lots of stories about Dave carrying big amounts of money."

Whatever the motivations and shortcomings of the "promoter", Hawkwind were in for an outrageously eventful tour, and none more so than Simon House.

Simon was in the line-up alongside Dave, Harvey, Richard and Jerry. Ron Tree was unable to make the trip. Alan Davey says that Dave tried unsuccessfully to persuade him to stand in on bass. The band eventually recruited the American Steve Taylor, who had come to the rescue at the Strange Daze festival when Brock and Tree had been stranded in Canada.

Steve Taylor was a member of Far Flung, the band that Nik Turner had been playing with in the States. Far Flung were also involved in Pressurehed, some of whom – including Taylor – had helped Turner to re-record the Sphynx album.

Both Harvey and Simon had asked for money upfront before they left the UK.

Harvey: "I said to Dave, 'I'll do it for two months' rent,' because I knew there was going to be no money from the tour. I said, 'As long as I can get £800, fine.' He said, 'Oh yes, that'll be there.' I went to rehearse at Dave's place and there was no money to be had. Then I was told I would get the money at the airport. I missed out on mine, although I think Simon House managed to grab his. I ended up in New Zealand and I hadn't got any money. I had to phone the landlady up and tell her that I would be back and I would have my rent then."

"Harvey gets suckered again," nods Douglas Smith.

Dave answers: "Before Harvey left the country, we had to pay his rent into his bank account, and we've got a receipt for doing it. Kris was tour managing then, so we've got the receipts for all these things. Harvey has a temporary memory loss. Harvey and Simon were the two that got the most."

Simon House agreed to join the tour on condition that his daughter Holly, then 14, would come too.

He explains, "This was shortly after I'd moved into my flat in Finchley. I'd just managed to get a residence order for Holly to come and live with me. She'd been suffering terribly for years at the hands of her mother, and I'd been trying to do something about it for all that time. I'd finally managed it and I couldn't leave her behind."

It was agreed that Holly should join the entourage. Simon recalls, "I was thinking, 'Not only has she escaped from her mother but she's going to go on the trip of a lifetime.' It was her first trip out of England.

"The return tickets to Auckland in New Zealand were paid for in cash by this promoter, which must have looked a bit iffy down the ticket office. I'd met him, and he wasn't a particularly nice guy. The whole thing sounded extremely dodgy."

But the problems for Simon and Holly started before they even arrived in New Zealand, falling foul of US immigration officers in a swoop that brought back bad memories for Dave in particular.

Simon had not known until the last minute that the flight involved a long stopover in LA. He'd expected to fly in the opposite direction around the world. Therefore, he had not applied for the waiver which entitled him to enter America despite a conviction for possession of cannabis dating back to 1969.

He remembers: "We got on the plane one cold, wet Saturday morning at Heathrow. Some 12 hours later, we got off at LA for seven hours. We were going to wait in the transit lounge. A lady from United Airlines asked if we wanted to go out. I said, 'I've got a bit of a problem with visas and stuff.' I gave her my passport. She came back in and said, 'It's all right, fill in this form and you can go through passport control.' I wanted to go and drive round LA in a taxi for a few hours to show Holly a bit of America.

"I filled the form out, but then as soon as we went through, this guy said, 'Mr House, please come into the office.' Me and Holly went into this office and he locked the door – 'It looks like you and your daughter are going to be on the next flight back to London.' They'd seen in my passport a previous visa which had this code number on it relating to my conviction."

At the same time: "Holly was coming down with tonsillitis, getting a temperature. It was awful, really awful. I felt powerless. They took our cases off the plane and they drove me and Holly for miles in this van with an armed guard to the other side of the airport to immigration control, through all these checkpoints. We saw cameras and guns everywhere.

"They banged us up in this room which was half-glass, half-wall with these mainly young, oriental-looking people. We were sitting there for hours and we could see what was going on in other offices. One guy deliberately left his office door open so that we could see him body searching men and women. I was thinking, 'They're going to do that to Holly. They're going to do that to me.' "

Luckily, they didn't. And when Simon and Holly went to have their mugshots taken in another part of the office complex, a woman employee took an interest in the pair – "because we were the only people who weren't Malaysian", Simon reasons. She made a couple of calls and arranged that rather than being sent back to England, Simon and Holly should travel on to New Zealand. Three guards escorted them back to the transit lounge with their luggage just in time for the plane.

"There was a 13-hour flight to Auckland," says Simon. "About half way there, a guy just a couple of seats away from me and Holly had a heart attack, and so we diverted to Honolulu – which is still America. He didn't die.

"Holly and I were put in a different van with guards and taken to a different part of the hotel in Honolulu where everyone was staying until the flight was rescheduled. At any given time, four armed guards were sitting outside our rooms in the hotel. If we went to the pool or the drinks machine, they came with us. It was totally unreal. The whole thing was a terrible, traumatic experience."

Finally, three days after they'd set off, the entourage arrived in Auckland, where Holly slept for 16 hours straight and managed to shake off her illness. But the drama wasn't over yet for Simon.

The band arrived in Auckland to newspaper headlines about their journey. They were whisked off to what seemed like a commune run by the travellers – or "housetruckers" – who were friends of the "promoter".

Richard Chadwick and Jerry Richards found their hosts extremely creative and generous, opening up their home and their fridge to the newcomers for free, while Harvey remembers being broke and Simon talks about being hungry, "scratching around" for food and having whip-rounds for trips to the supermarket. Kris Tait was dubious about the whole set-up.

She says, "We only stayed in this house in the beginning. Then we were in their garden in the camper van." Dave shared Kris' doubts and had insisted on hiring a camper rather than living in anyone's home or indeed in the motel chalets that followed as the tour got under way.

Harvey's interpretation is this: "Dave kept himself to himself. It would've been nice if we could all have had little camper vans. 'All hail the king!' How tacky that we all had to lumber along with nothing and pay for his bloody camper van as well." Dave insists: "I hired it on my credit card and I never got paid for the fucking thing."

Serious problems arose almost immediately. Hawkwind arrived in New Zealand to find the tour structure in chaos: "We had to rebook the gigs, sort out the posters, everything," says Dave.

Richard explains: "These people in New Zealand weren't very good at organising things. They were useless, but they meant well, and I can never thank them enough for what they did for us. We were all pretty broke there. But Kris and Dave spent a week on the phone prior to the first gig, reorganising the tour."

Nerves were already strained when Hawkwind left Auckland after two gigs and drove on to New Plymouth. Dave and Kris travelled in the camper; the rest of the band took in a spot of sightseeing on the scenic route and arrived late at the venue, where Dave – in "a terrible mood" according to Simon – fired everyone.

Dave recalls: "They came in all hot and perspiring at seven o'clock after the doors had opened. I said, 'Look, you should have been here at 3pm. You're all sacked.' Tempers were fraught at that gig."

Reinstated once the moment of anger had passed, the band members moved on to Wellington, where the peculiar financial aspects of the tour became even more extraordinary.

Dave says: "There was a husband and wife team who were handling things. They took their money out of the gig every night, but something was going on there that we never got to the bottom of. The band were being paid for with bags of marijuana."

Kris adds: "The guy was taking the money on the door. One night I saw him taking a couple of thousand dollars out of the gig. He said he had to hide it somewhere 'cos he didn't think it was safe. The money we took in didn't match with the money we were given."

Dave takes up the tale: "One morning in Wellington, there was a knock on the door of our camper van. These two people who were working for the promoter were saying, 'Can you come into the motel? Something awful's happened.' The woman said, 'The money's all gone. Last night it was on this shelf in our chalet and now it's gone. We saw a figure come in.' We all had a meeting."

Kris: "And this mad promoter was going demented because the money had disappeared."

"He went nutty and he blamed me for it as well," adds Dave. "Being the band leader, I got the blame for everything that went on. He's blaming me for not making any money. He was paranoid. Taking these drugs makes people like this. It's a weird story. He owes us money for the trip.

"We had all the accounts for the tour written out. I said, 'Tell you what we'll do – we'll have a meeting with this guy. There's been no fiddling going on. It's been honest.' All I've got out of it was a couple of hundred quid. Simon got about £500 before he left and Harvey got £400 because he wanted his rent. He probably pocketed about £800 all told."

Kris carries on: "Then the money was found in Holly's room. It was nothing to do with Holly, obviously."

Neither Simon House nor Holly remember this happening, although Simon ventures: "Maybe it's true. The whole thing was just so dodgy that it wouldn't surprise me, although it couldn't have been that much money. We did five or six gigs in New Zealand altogether, and they were only in small clubs. Some of the gigs, there were only 60 or 70 people there. Maybe the guy took the money himself because he'd laid out a lot to start with. It just doesn't add up, really. We were spending money on hotels and travelling around, which isn't cheap when you've got 13 people."

Things improved greatly when Hawkwind changed the itinerary and looked instead to Australia. Kris says, "We were supposed to be doing South Island in New Zealand. We saw that it was not a viable tour. It was going to cost £2,500 to get everybody and the equipment there, and even if every man, woman and child in the area came to the gig, we still wouldn't break even."

The band were in touch with a consortium of Hawkwind fans in the state of New South Wales, Australia, who said: "Blow out the South Island dates and we'll get you gigs in Australia."

Kris obtained the necessary visas, and Simon then had to negotiate his daughter's passage: "The guy in Australia wasn't prepared to pay for Holly. I agreed that if they paid for her, I'd reimburse them later. So I ended up owing them money, which I repaid a few months after I got back."

In Australia, Hawkwind were treated like royalty. They were wined and dined and booked into fine hotels, and the gigs were sold out. Once again, the obligatory bag of grass was dished out to everybody.

Dave says: "Simon took mushrooms and anything else that was given to him."

"So did I," grins Richard. "There was a lot of time off. Plenty of research to be done, I thought."

For Simon, the fortnight in Australia was "like a dream". He says: "They looked after us something rotten. I took lots of drugs and I fell in love with someone who broke my heart a few months later. I met her in Byron Bay. I'd had some mushrooms and after the gig we got talking and ended up walking on the beach. She was a very interesting, very intelligent person. We got on really well and she stayed with me for the rest of the trip. Then she flew over to England a couple of months later – she was actually English.

"I went back over to visit her in September and it all went down the toilet. She'd been with someone else. It was awful. She said, 'I don't want you staying in the house any more.' I had to go and stay with these people I didn't even know. Then she changed her mind and I moved back. Then it all blew up again. It's bad enough having your heart broken when you're at home, but 11,000 miles away . . .

"We spent the last night together and everything was fantastic. A couple of days later, I phoned up and she was with this other bloke. I suppose it's one of the hazards of being on the road. The same thing happened to me the first time we went over to the States in the Seventies."

Simon's whirlwind romance was interrupted briefly when he took ill: "I had a duodenal ulcer and it was getting worse and worse. I was lying on the back seat of the minibus groaning. Then Jerry's back went out. So there were two invalids by the time we got to the doctor. He sorted us both out and just as we arrived in Sydney, I was starting to feel human again."

At the end of the Australian idyll, Hawkwind returned to Auckland for a final gig.

"We had to sort this crap out," sighs Dave. "There was a lot of violent threats and things like that. Everybody else was paranoid about getting beaten up, and I had to threaten the promoter."

Hawkwind arrived back in the UK with differing feelings about the tour.

Simon: "It was a wild and crazy adventure, good and bad. We had some good times, saw some amazing scenery. We did decent gigs. I'm glad I went. Oh yeah. It was pure rock'n'roll."

Jerry: "I'd really love to live in New Zealand. Unlike Australia, there are no deadly snakes or spiders or crocodiles. You're perfectly safe. It's absolutely wonderful. What I remember is the fabulous energy and the effort that was put in by the people that got it all together. They had an incredible commune where they owned the land. I do remember a big freak-out . . ."

Harvey: "We had a nice time in Australia. The people there put $1,000 into my bank account and I got a few hundred out of merchandising as we went around, but it still didn't add up to the £800 I'd been promised. It was a shitty situation.

"I was dubious about going in the first place, although I'd never been to Australia and New Zealand. I thought it was an opportunity not to miss. I was just dismayed that the same things were going on with the band. I thought perhaps it would be a bit more grown-up. We got back here and I thought, 'They're still a bunch of shysters. It's a dead end. There's no point in even arguing over it all. It's only money, and if someone wants to behave like that, then let them do it.'"

Harvey left Hawkwind for the last time, although he would continue to turn out for special gigs. At the same time, another much-loved character was appearing over the horizon. Huw Lloyd-Langton had been playing with Nik Turner. Now he was fastening his seat belt in readiness for his return to Hawkwind. And it would be a bumpy ride.

CHAPTER 30

The Great Hawkestra Disaster

IN 1994, Del Dettmar, still living in Canada, had an amusing idea. He'd just been sent a four-CD Hawkwind compilation, *25 Years On* – not to be confused with Hawklords' 1978 album of the same name. Released as a box set by Griffin in America, it covers the years 1970 to 1994 and was presented in picture-disk format with a booklet titled *Further Extracts From The Hawkwind Log* and a comic-book version of Michael Butterworth's *Ledge Of Darkness* novel.* Del read the accompanying literature.

"It said there had been 35 people in the band," he remembers. "I was thinking, 'Wow! There's enough people to form the I Used To Be In Hawkwind Orchestra.' You couldn't be in it until you'd left the band. I went happily around telling people I was in the Hawkwind Orchestra, and it was just a joke, like a fantasy."

Six years later, the fantasy became a reality and the joke turned sour. The grand reunion of numerous past and present members of Hawkwind at Brixton Academy on October 21, 2000 degenerated into chaos, ending in furious arguments and, finally, in court.

The idea of a reunion had been bandied about for some time, but the project finally got off the ground after a conversation between Douglas Smith and promoter John Curd, who was staging Motorhead's 25th anniversary gig the next night, a Sunday, at the Academy. John suggested that if Douglas could round up the people needed for a classic Hawkwind concert, he could make a weekend of it.

It all hinged on Dave Brock and Nik Turner being prepared to play together, which they were. With the addition of Lemmy, the foundation stones were laid and the rest of the line-up would be built easily

---

* This was the comic book which had so impressed Dave Brock at the time of The Mad Professor's Laboratory tour.

around them – or so it was thought. The event was described as Hawkestra.

This was an exceptionally exciting proposal in many ways. It was a chance for younger fans to see the original members in action and for older fans to revel in a night of starfaring nostalgia. The different generations of musicians would meet each other and play together for the first time, which many were looking forward to. The show would obviously sell out, and there would be spin-offs to benefit everyone, not least the merchandising and the audio and video recordings.

Douglas Smith also reckons that the follow-on opportunities could have been enormous: "If they'd pulled together, they could have cleaned up. They could have had a year of headlining festivals. They could have got away with it."

Realistically, there was no chance of Dave Brock and Nik Turner pulling together while both were taking prominent roles in the organisation. They were working at cross purposes as they had always done, and any hope of a united front, any prospect of agreement, had collapsed before the players got anywhere near the stage of the Academy.

Dave, in Devon, was taking charge of the rehearsals and the set, which Nik believed was unfairly biased towards the contemporary Hawkwind line-up. Nik was recruiting as many former members as possible, including Del Dettmar in Canada, and undertaking to have their travel paid, which infuriated Dave. He also refused to recognise Turner's right to be part of the financial consultations with Douglas Smith and Helter Skelter, the agency. Dave favoured a sliding scale of payments which guaranteed larger amounts for the people who had done the most work for the gig or had been in the band for long periods of time (Lemmy, whose membership was relatively short-lived, was a star and therefore an exception). Nik's proposals insisted on more equal payments.

By the time the cleaners were sweeping the fag ends out of Brixton Academy, the live recordings had been kidnapped and locked away in a lawyer's office, where they remain. Douglas Smith saw trouble brewing and walked out of the project soon after setting it in motion.

He says: "Nik was a fundamental part of the whole arrangement along with Dave and everyone else who was taking time to make it work. Then Dave decided to change the plan by having his Devon mafia as the central unit and bolting the other former members on to that. That's not what the punters wanted. We had about 5,000 people emailing in their favourite tracks, their favourite line-ups, everything. We knew exactly what the fans wanted. A lot of people thought that Dave hijacked the event.

"It was difficult to get Dave to do anything. He wanted this and that, and a guarantee that all his big expenses would be covered. The proposal that Dave was putting forward is not what the understanding was from the very beginning. It was beginning to look like it was a money gig for Dave Brock and a lot of the other older members would get the odd hundred quid for coming along.

"Dave didn't sign the contract. That was automatic for him. Often in the past, he would either not sign or he would sign on behalf of everybody. There was no agreement on the percentages. There just wasn't an understanding between all of them. Nobody knew what was going on or how much money they were getting. I called Dave up one day and suggested we should get this sorted out. I raised my voice. He said, 'You don't raise your voice at me!' He slammed the phone down and we didn't talk for a long time.

"Nik was contacting a large number of band members to come and join, where Dave Brock didn't really care. He was only concerned that Lemmy was on the show so he could sell out the concert.

"I rang the agent up and said, 'I suggest you tell John Curd to cancel this 'cos it's turning into a major mess.' At the time they started rehearsing, none of the agreement was settled, none of the show was settled, none of the lighting was settled. And I thought, 'Forget it.' I got fed up and I walked out. And I stopped looking after the business affairs of Dave, Alan and Richard.

"Then these silly stories started happening about how someone was threatening to beat me up at the gig because I'd 'stolen Lemmy's life'. I decided to go just to see this whole scenario of this guy trying to have a go at me." In the event, Douglas couldn't make it to Brixton because he was delayed on a flight back from Germany.

Nik Turner reveals that he took a front role in the concert organisation so that Lemmy would not know his former manager – Douglas – was involved, otherwise he might not have agreed to take part.

Lemmy says today: "Douglas I think was a good man corrupted by a scheming woman. He was always in love with Eve and she married this other geezer. Then she was available again and he got together with her again, and I think it ruined him. At the time I joined Hawkwind, he was the man at the top. He seemed like a right geezer. That's how he gets away with it, isn't it? Rose-tinted underpants."

Douglas leaps to the defence of his wife: "Eve told Lemmy to fuck off once. She was forthright, always told him the truth. She wouldn't put up with his tantrums and, because of that, she was a woman who in his mind should be despised. That's the only thing you can put this down to. I've been with the same woman for dozens of years. No one in the world is as honest and straight as Eve is. She's considered by everybody to be one of the nicest people you could ever meet. I'm told I'm a very lucky person. Lemmy is wrong."

Dave Brock has photographs to prove that on the concert tickets, the posters and the billing at the front of Brixton Academy, it was plainly advertised as a Hawkwind gig. And he felt that it was up to Hawkwind, the existing group, to make the night a special one. Hawkestra was a name given to the event, not the superband.

Accordingly, Dave assumed responsibility for the performance, although he adds that Douglas asked him to be the musical director. He decided to split the show in two. The regular line-up – with Alan Davey returning to the fold – would play the first half on their own, and then they would provide the musical foundation for most of the second section when various combinations of guests would be introduced. The bulk of the rehearsals were done in Devon – three weeks with the core band and three weeks with various extra players – and later came three days' practice in London. Many of the musicians only attended the city sessions.

Dave states: "The idea was for us to supply a tight backing band for all these people, some of whom weren't professional musicians any more. We worked out exactly what we were doing. We started off with 'Hurry On Sundown', going through all the eras, just mapping out pieces. In fairness to all the people who'd been in the band, I had to select the songs they would shine on. We wanted to try and get everybody involved in doing certain bits and pieces. Thomas Crimble only came on for 'Hurry On Sundown' 'cos he wasn't in the band when we did the other numbers."

Brock professes that in the original discussions about the gig, it had been agreed with Helter Skelter that he and Lemmy would each receive a flat fee of £1,500, with the other musicians paid according to their service records, how long they would spend onstage and/or how much they would contribute to the show.

"Why should someone who is onstage for five minutes be given the same amount as somebody who's onstage for three hours?" he asks, indignantly.

According to Dave and Kris, the agreements included: Harvey Bainbridge (£1,000), Tim Blake (£300), Richard Chadwick (£1,000), Thomas Crimble (£50), Alan Davey (£1,000), Martin Griffin (£300), Simon House (£500), Huw Lloyd-Langton (£700 – later reduced to £500), Terry Ollis (£200), Jerry Richards (£400), Steve Swindells (£250), Danny Thompson (£400), Ron Tree (£500) and Nik Turner (£800).

Alan Powell, Keith Kniveton and producer and engineer Raymond Steeg were also provided for in the official list of 19 musicians, but there was no allocation for Mick Slattery, Dikmik or Del Dettmar, who would all arrive at the invitation of Nik Turner. Additionally, the cast list expanded to take in Sam Fox, Scouse and Kris on fire displays, dancers and props specialists.

The above figures were never made official in a contract, but they were the basis upon which Dave says he proceeded with the rehearsals and the gig.

"The contracts we were sent didn't have a fee on them," says Kris. "We said we wanted a contract that specified how much we were going to get. Stupidly, we went ahead and did the show without a contract, on trust."

Dave, flipping through his paperwork, says: "The more we read this stuff, the more cross we get. John Curd sent me a letter – this is September 28, not much more than three weeks before the gig – with a list of everyone's names on. And I've got to sign a piece of paper saying I guarantee all these people will play or else he will pull the gig. He says he's not prepared to refund or give discounts at the door. I refused to sign it. I've got Lemmy's letter to me, where he says he would do the gig if I was doing it. I've got faxes from Douglas. I've got emails from Helter Skelter.

"We wouldn't have agreed to do the show in the first place if we'd known Nik Turner was doing some secondary deal and being put in charge of the money."

Kris adds: "Normally, we get an advance on a gig. We asked Douglas for expenses. Those were £100 a week wages, petrol as per receipts and £75 a day for our studio, including gear hire, electricity and so on. We had to hire a PA to do the rehearsals down here, microphones and that sort of stuff. A rehearsal studio anywhere else would cost a lot more. We paid for band members' hotels. We were told, 'No.' We did get all that money back in the end, but it took a long time."

"We were working here for six weeks for nothing," says Dave. "Various people came down to do their bits. Then we had to hire the rehearsal room in London – a proper big studio, with the dancers and the light-show and everything, and we had to pay all of this out of our money."

Nik Turner: "Hawkestra was seen as a really cool concept. The billing might have said Hawkwind, but the night was about everybody who was there, about Hawkestra, whether that's the name of the show or the name of the band. John Curd wouldn't have been interested in promoting Hawkwind. As far as he's concerned, that's Dave Brock and his two little mates. People like John Curd were interested in the concept of the Hawkestra. It was the legacy of all the people who had been in Hawkwind that was generating the popularity of the event.

"The whole thing was very political. I had said I'd only do the gig if I had some sort of involvement rather than just being a bit of confetti. I insisted on becoming involved in the business aspect of it. I was somebody pretty straight who would take control of the finances so they didn't fall into Dave's hands. I agreed my role with Doug initially, then John Curd and Paul Bolton from Helter Skelter. My goal was to make sure everybody got a fair deal rather than just being paid £10 and told to fuck off, which is what might have happened. Dave was trying to get control of the money.

"At the beginning, I felt that everybody should get exactly the same amount, which is what Lemmy said too, but that was unrealistic. If you're talking about certain people that did very little and other people that did a lot, it wouldn't perhaps be very fair."

Lemmy was eventually signed to a contract for £1,500, but Nik persuaded him to take a reduction to £1,000.

"Doug Smith, Paul Bolton and I then propounded a fair payment scenario which was relative to how long people had been in the band and what their importance was," continues Nik. "Of course, it was all dependent on how much was taken and what everything cost. The figures that we projected weren't what Dave wanted. It seemed to me that as far as he was concerned, a few people should get a lot and nobody else was getting much. He's saying he agreed these amounts. I don't know anything about that, but it doesn't mean that the rest of us agreed."

And also: "I wanted the highest quality control in the merchandising, the design of the image and the logo and stuff like that," says Nik, "with the money shared out fairly among everybody. But then it was agreed that the merchandising would be supplied by Voiceprint [the label].

"When it came to the rehearsals, Dave just tried to hijack the whole thing. He was telling everyone, 'These are the songs we're going to play. You're going to play on this one, not on that one.' It was very controlled. It wasn't at all democratic, and I didn't feel very at ease. He directed the whole thing to his liking without reference to anyone in a very cavalier fashion. He's a law unto himself with no regard or respect for other people. That's how he's always been.

"The story of Hawkwind is truly Machiavellian. People, mostly band members' wives, would say, 'Cor! Nobody would do something as mean as that.' But Dave would. They were appalled at the way Dave treated their husbands or boyfriends."

Keyboard player Steve Swindells was one of the musicians who went to Devon for the rehearsals.

"The idea appealed to me," he explains. "Doug had rung me and said I'd be the main keyboard player. I spoke to Dave on the phone. I was promised a sum of money, and a percentage, which made it also appealing. I thought, 'When it comes out on an album, it'll be a nice little earner, especially with Lemmy and Nik Turner involved.' I hopped on a train with my keyboard and Dave picked me up. I hadn't seen or spoken to him for 20 years. He looked just the same, just a bit more wizened. He took me to his farmhouse, which is pretty remote, up a muddy track. There were lots of mangy dogs running round in the yard biting everybody, including me."

"They might have barked at him," says Kris. "But I'm sure he would have told us if he'd been bitten. They're actually very well-kept dogs and their injections are up to date. They get bathed and groomed regularly."

"Dave and Kris really looked after me," continues Steve. "They brought out some vintage wine and some nice food and said I could stay the night there. I'd been promised about £650 and I was paid some expenses for the train fare and stuff. And then the goalposts moved.

"I was staying in a room in this horrible pub with a carvery where they kept this three-day-old meat warm under lights. The rehearsals went really well, but I was getting more and more cross.

"Dave was saying that everybody should be paid according to how long they'd been in the band. I'd only been in the band for one bloody album and one tour. Suddenly I was in a situation where I was being offered two-and-a-half per cent of proceeds as opposed to the guaranteed sum of £650 against a percentage profit on the door on the night. Dave was falling out with Douglas, who was trying to be sensible – 'You can't suddenly say Steve's going to get less. He's one of the few people actually rehearsing.' I did five weeks and I was one of very few. Ron Tree arrived for the last few days at the farm. Most people just turned up for the London rehearsals.

"I thought it was an appalling way to treat me when I'd done all that work. I got £150 expenses for my entire rehearsals. There was a dispute and eventually I got another £120. I'd come into the thing thinking, 'Maybe Dave and I can write together and revitalise the band.' The combination of him and me could have been quite powerful songwriting-wise. It wasn't a masterplan, just a vague idea.

"I understand Dave is basically Hawkwind, and he has held them together over the years. I have the greatest respect for him. He has a great voice, fantastic range. He has a very distinctive style. No one else in the world has that. No one plays guitar like Dave. It's so powerful, that sort of scrubby jugga-jugga-jugga. He can be an absolutely charming person when it suits him. But as a result of Hawkestra, I realised I couldn't possibly work with him again."

Kris answers: "Dave didn't change the goalposts. I don't remember Steve being offered £650. We were working from the figures we'd agreed with Helter Skelter. Steve was offered a fixed fee and, if there was any money over on the night, which there wasn't, the percentage was going to be worked out *pro rata*. The figures were nothing to do with us anyway. Nik Turner was the one handling the money. If Steve thought he didn't get what he was entitled to, he could have gone to a small claims court. That's what we had to do. Dave definitely didn't change Steve Swindells' money in the middle of rehearsals."

"What did happen was that we asked Douglas for expenses money and we didn't get it," adds Dave. "We wanted £100 a week each for rehearsals which he refused. It caused a big argument. We used our own money covering people's hotels and other expenses. We're easy-going and amiable. Steve Swindells, all these people . . . they've stayed here and we got on wonderfully well. Nik Turner stayed with us only a few years ago and we got on with him fine.

"I don't remember any big problem with Steve during the rehearsals. He was saying it was good fun. He was as matey as could be. He was telling us about some friends of his who were going to record a dance version of 'Master Of The Universe'. He was perfectly all right; he had a great time. Everybody enjoyed it."

"I was the uninvited guest," says Del Dettmar. He was uninvited as far as Dave was concerned, and he wasn't the only one. Dave objected to funding major travel expenses out of the gig.

"Nik paid to fly Del and Alan Powell in from Canada and America," says Dave. "It had been agreed not to do that, but he did it anyway."

"Who agreed not to do it?" challenges Turner. "Dave and Kris did, that's all. These sweeping statements! They're taking the stance that it's Dave's band, that he has the decision about everything. I would say they were the only people that didn't agree to it, probably."

Turner persuaded Del: "Be a rebel and come."

Del flew door to door, from his home in Canada to the venue: "I left here, this brave little porch upon which I stand now, on the Friday. I landed in London on Saturday morning, I went straight to the gig and I had wonderful jetlag. I met Dave. I gave him a big hug and I noticed how terrible he looked – really tired, totally frazzled. Poor, haggard Dave.

"I went out to the thrift store and I bought some jeans, and some orange juice and bananas. I went back to Brixton Academy and I never did find a room to sleep in, 'cos I'd keep meeting somebody I knew. I had a chat with Dikmik. I saw Terry Ollis and his kids – that was quite amazing. I met a bunch of people I didn't know. I didn't have any rehearsal. I was talking to the person who was doing the cooking about making icing out of honey and cream cheese. It's a very nice icing.

"Dave didn't make me any great invitations or offers. There was an unnamed bass player, as I stood there in the small backstage corridor upstairs, approaching. He recognised me and said, 'Hi,' and abruptly he turned round and walked away as if I could infect him with some form of embarrassment."

Adrian Shaw felt so uninvited he didn't go. He says: "I felt that Dave had a problem with me for some reason. I'd always got on well with him. I was asked to do the Hawkestra, and I said, 'Yeah, of course, it'll be fun.' Then I was told about the rehearsals and I wasn't sure what format it was taking. It seemed various people would get wheeled on and off. I thought I'd better find out what songs I was meant to be brushing up on.

"Dave was weird with me, very evasive. I realised he didn't want me to play at all. He said, 'By all means come along and you can get on the stage.' I said, 'No, I don't think so.' If he'd explained his reasons to me I would've understood. I don't think he feels required to give explanations. Never explain yourself – part of his dictatorial stance in the band."

For some of the Hawkwind clan, it was a marvellous night. Others thought differently, including Dave Brock.

"We had Dave on one side of the stage and everybody else on the other," laughs Turner. "We were having a great time and Dave was scowling at everybody, giving black looks. One guy was talking about having a T-shirt printed that said, 'Sacked!' and everybody would have been wearing them."

Says Dave: "The fans probably thought it was fantastic, but I found the Hawkestra a real task, really hard-going, really wearing. I wouldn't say I enjoyed it, no. I don't think Lemmy did. I was done in, exhausted. We'd been doing it for six weeks. The stress and strain of organising all this, wanting it to be so good and professional . . . At the end of it, I went upstairs and fell asleep, and I'd never in my life done that after a gig.

"Onstage, the sound quality was so bad you couldn't hear what was going on half the time. People were out of synch with each other. We had a power failure and everything went off. Where was Nik? He was in the dressing room drinking champagne. When things went wrong, they weren't there to salvage it. All the people who should have been out front making it look groovy were just standing around like a bunch of dummies. I thought, 'Fucking great.' Sam Fox was one of the few people who put something into the performance. She was dancing around and enjoying it. A lot of bad things happened . . . the looks people were giving us onstage. Nik Turner turned his back on Sam and wouldn't cue her.

"John Curd had this disco playing loud music in the foyer while we were onstage and when things were quiet, you could hear it blaring away. Alan got the man of the match award. He was onstage for three hours, and he was right on the case. I was on the stage for two-and-a-half hours because there was half an hour when Alan, Danny Thompson and Huwie played, and I didn't.

"It was nice to see Mick Slattery. He's an old buddy. And Dikmik. But some of them were miserable, whingeing, not even saying thank you to Alan and Richard who've flown the flag for all these years. Some of these guys shook their hands, but there was all this moaning. I thought, 'What a miserable bunch of cunts.' "

"I call them Whingewind," quips Alan.

Dave continues: "Tim Blake shook my hand and said, 'It's been a real pleasure.' A few others. But, overall, they had very bad grace."

Lemmy chortles: "The Hawkestra gig was horribly disorganised. They brought Dikmik from somewhere and Del over from Canada and when they went onstage, their shit wasn't plugged in. Hawkwind were a world-class band, or they used to be, but they didn't have it together at all. Our show the next night was very well arranged.

"They're like a fucking cabaret act now. They played a medley of their greatest hits. That band Nik Turner has [Space Ritual] is probably more like Hawkwind than Dave's is. I played about five songs – 'Silver Machine', 'Down Through The Night', 'Space Is Deep', 'Master Of The Universe' and 'Brainstorm'.

"Dave Brock – he's lost the plot. He brought on a guest singer, and who he brought on was in magically bad taste – Sam Fox. 'I'm the mistress of the universe . . .' I know Sam Fox, I love her to death, but she doesn't sing 'Master Of The Universe' when Nik Turner's onstage. What is wrong with this picture? Everything. I don't get along all that well with Nicky, but it's his number. It ain't right. Nik was there dressed as a lizard with spikes sticking out of his costume. Actually, I think he might be some kind of a lizard."

Nik remarks: "Sam Fox is not particularly a friend of mine, but I don't have anything against her. I was told that she was going to be singing 'Master Of The Universe'. Well, it's a song that I wrote. I don't really have any objection to her singing it, but I would have liked her to be more involved with me rather than just coming on and forgetting all the words. We could have sung it together."

It had been years since Lemmy had seen some of his old bandmates. He reflects: "Dikmik looked exactly the same. Del did too. He didn't have his checked blanket with him, but I think he would have if he could've found it. Terry Ollis sounded just like he used to. He kept his clothes on. He's beat up by then. Like it does, the world had asserted itself on him."

Asked about the financial disputes going on behind the scenes, Lemmy says: "I thought it was all crap. As usual, the cosmic warriors were arguing about a few bucks. I don't get it. Such fucking arseholes. I thought, 'Fuck it.' I couldn't give a shit what way they were paying the fees. I was earning my own money."

"They're all as bad as each other," agrees Danny Thompson. "They're all greedy, conniving bastards, the lot of them. There never was any peace and love. The funny thing is that nobody actually says anything when they're all together. They all get stoned and no one's got the guts to say anything to anybody.

"The actual playing was great. I did four or five numbers. Everyone was milling about, and there was lots going on. The rehearsals were interesting. Dave was telling people to do it this way and that way so it wouldn't be a mishmash. I could see his point. He wanted it to be good and not some lame jam.

"It was fantastic to hear Lemmy playing, never having seen them live with him. That, to me, is what the Hawkwind sound is. It's *Space Ritual* and *Warrior*. Lemmy didn't give a fuck. He was taking the piss out of everybody and Dave doesn't like that, so he'd disappear. Lemmy said, 'Dave Brock's got his empire, but I've got my empire, and my empire's bigger.'

"The place was packed out, and we didn't get any fucking money for months and months. When we did, it wasn't what we were told we were going to get, but it never is."

Ron Tree agrees with Lemmy's assessment of the gig. He says: "It was awful. It was a joke, a shambles. All the people involved were thinking of themselves. The show was bloody disastrous. I was just flobbed on at the end to do a little bit of Calvert stuff."

Mick Slattery states: "I'd spoken to Nik on the phone. He said, 'Come and do a couple of numbers.' I went along to Brixton and Dave wouldn't let me play because I hadn't come to the rehearsal. No one had told me there was a rehearsal."

Mick and Dikmik – "very straight and grown-up these days," according to Douglas Smith – did take a bow onstage, even though they didn't perform.

The eternally upbeat Martin Griffin makes a mild complaint: "There was an element of organisation that was lost. I was kind of indignant that Dave wouldn't let me drum. I ended up playing percussion. I felt the thing tended to be regimented, maybe a little much. It could have been truer to the Hawkwind vibe.

"A year later, Nik did a [smaller] reunion at the Astoria. It was so easy, fluid and democratic. I think the optimum would have been somewhere between the two. The Hawkestra gig was a bit anal-retentive. The Astoria was a little shambolic. Backstage at Brixton, there were guys from the band I'd never met, early people like Mick Slattery and Thomas Crimble, and a couple of young guys who post-dated me. The atmosphere was so relaxed and good – with certain exceptions. The old and the young got on well.

"I did enjoy the gig. Both there and at the Astoria, there was a tangible freedom of spirit evident among all the Hawks. Despite irritations and personality clashes, predictable among a tight-knit collection of artistic individuals, that freedom is the essence of the band."

Steve Swindells might not agree. He winces: "I was going to sing 'Shot Down In The Night' and Dave was going to sing it with me onstage. In rehearsals, it was sounding really, really good.

"By the time of the gig, I was barely speaking to Brock over what I perceived to be his total disrespect for my contribution. He lost my guest list. Five minutes before the gig, I had to go down and plead at the door for members of my family to come in.

"Brock locked himself in his dressing room with Kris. No one was allowed in there except Lemmy. He was taking the piss out of Dave anyway. It was hilarious. The whole event was tense, but the show was great. There was a lot of power and passion.

"I did the gig through gritted teeth, even though it was exciting and the audience was all singing along, which was fabulous. Then Dave did the dirty on me in 'Shot Down In The Night'. He was supposed to come in to sing the high bits – it's an octave thing – and suddenly, where's Dave? He'd walked offstage. I was doing the low octave and I had to switch and sing the high bit in the second and third verses. It was a nightmare. He didn't play guitar either. Maybe he really did break a string . . . I left immediately after the concert with my friends and family 'cos I was so furious."

However, Steve did make two new friends at Hawkestra. One was guitarist Jerry Richards. "He's a Scorpio like me," says Steve, "and we got on absolutely great." The pair are now working together on the Emoticon project with Jon Moss, Winston Blissett and Dale Davies.

He also met Nik Turner for the first time: "He and I formed an instant rapport," says Swindells. "He's an old hippie and I'm an urban sophisticate. He's a very nice bloke, he's a fair bloke, and he was concerned that everyone should be recompensed."

Sam Fox could not have known about the bad blood that was flowing just below the surface of the Hawkestra show. She was never a party to the internal feuds, and she experienced only the warmest welcome. She loved it.

"I didn't believe how many people had been in that band," she gasps. "They'd come from all over the world. I'm not being funny, but there were people there who looked about 100 years old.

"I went to a rehearsal studio under a bridge in Putney and we went through the song they wanted me to do – 'I'm the mistress of the universe . . .' Yeah, it's a concept! It was quite an easy song to learn. We went onstage at Brixton a couple of days later. I did an unplanned duet with Lemmy. We were talking in the dressing room and I said I'd really love to do 'Silver Machine'. He said, 'Come on, then, let's do it,' and brought me on to the stage. I knew the words from memory.

"It was a great reunion but it was quite confusing 'cos there were so many people going on and off. Normally, I have my stand with a wireless mic. When I got on, I was in the middle of the stage, I tried to move the mic stand and all the wire from the mic wrapped round it and then it got caught round my leg. So I chucked it, made it look like I meant to. Anything goes, which is great.

"We partied at the gig until the early hours. I remember Krissy doing plenty of fire-eating backstage. She nearly set us all alight at one point. She was trying to teach me. I thought, 'Nah, nah, nah, I'll give it a miss.' It was great to see Lemmy. He always shows me lyrics he's written. We hadn't seen each other since my father died. He said he was really sorry about it. He'd just written a song about his dad. I read it and it made me cry. Amazing lyrics, very deep. We had a nice night."

Tim Blake, who'd travelled from France, was another happy bunny. "I considered I was well paid for that gig," he announces, rather surprisingly. "I put in a good half of it. Other people put in even more."

Jerry Richards remarks: "With Nik Turner and Simon House in the band, we had the balance of the orchestra pretty well right. It sounded harder, faster and more dense than at any time since *The Space Ritual*."

Alan Davey had finally agreed to have another whirl with Hawkwind, and he was welcomed back despite the circumstances of his departure.

Dave says: "It was an example of our gentlemanly behaviour. We said, 'It was a good idea that you took some time off to sort your brain out.'"

Alan remembers: "Dave said to me, 'You really should do the Hawkestra.' It seemed to me I should be there. It was quite upsetting not being with Dave during the previous years. We'd been friends for a long time and I missed his company.

"Ron Tree was still about. He was able to function, but he was on his last legs at that time. Soon after the Hawkestra, he disappeared. Jerry Richards was still in the band, but Dave had made it clear to me that he was on the way out, 'cos Huwie was coming back in. I didn't have to worry about it."

"Alan came back 'cos obviously he was skint," offers Ron Tree. "He's a bit of a poison dwarf. As soon as he got back in the band, it wasn't long 'til I were out of it. He told me, 'That Jerry, he's going, but your place is safe.' Jerry's a nice guy. He weren't really right for it, Jerry, but he tried to be right."

For Alan, the Hawkestra gig was something of a test. "It all went a bit funny when the monitors blew up in something like the second number," he says, with understatement. "That was the worst thing that can happen. There were points when Lemmy was playing and couldn't hear Richard's drumming, so he couldn't play along with it. I kind of took over, 'cos my pair of monitors were the only two that were working.

"I started getting everybody in the monitors there so I could hear what they were all doing. I was counting and doing the changes and conducting almost. It was the first gig back for years. To get lumbered with that sort of responsibility . . .

"Richard did most of the set. Alan Powell and Danny Thompson did a few numbers. I didn't get to speak to Alan much, or Dikmik. I know Dikmik quite well, actually. I've always been very good friends with him. He didn't play. I think they wanted everything including instruments provided for them. If you're a musician, you've got your instrument, haven't you? If someone asks you to come and play a gig, you don't tell them they have to get you an instrument, not in this day and age.

"For me, the highlight was when me and Lemmy did that bass duelling bit on 'Psychedelic Warlords'. I know Lemmy's style inside and out. We went up and up and up."

Lemmy was, of course, Alan's early hero. Reciprocally, he has named Alan as his favourite bass player of those who succeeded him in Hawkwind. By now, they had played together several times.

Says Alan: "I'd only been in the band six months and I was blasting out 'Brainstorm' with Lemmy at the anti-heroin gig at Crystal Palace. It's the only time 'Brainstorm' has ever sounded like 'Overkill'. At Reading Festival, we rubbed our bass strings up against each other – 50,000 watts of corrugated iron being dragged across a floor. I remember, also at Reading, Lemmy turning himself full up. He was drowning out Huwie. Huwie kept going up to Lemmy's plug on his amp and pulling it out. The roadie would put it back in. Huwie would go over and unplug it again.

"At the Hawkestra, I was more than happy to stay off while Lemmy was doing his bit. He kept saying, 'Come on for this one, and this . . .' and insisting on me going onstage with him. He said to me, 'How on earth did you manage to stay in this band with Dave for so long?' How do you answer a question like that? I said, 'We just get on. There's no big mystery. We want the same things for the band.' Dave is not a young man any more. He doesn't need that bullshit."

Huw and Marion Lloyd-Langton have mixed memories of the concert. "It was fairly complicated because there were so many people involved in it," says Huw. "I found it quite enjoyable seeing people I hadn't seen for some time, like Del."

"It was fantastic to see all these people you'd never expect to see together all under one roof," enthuses Marion. "There were queues outside. They couldn't all get in. Huw was asked to do two or three numbers, but he ended up doing the whole set, which Jerry Richards was supposed to have done. He shook Huw's hand afterwards and said he was marvellous. He was very humble, Jerry.

"Huw was offered £500 initially. What he and other artists got on the night was £100. There was a hoo-ha. It was outrageous. I put it on my website I was so disgusted."

Huw prefers not to talk about the figures. "Anything to do with business," he declares, "and a safety curtain comes down in my brain."

Nik Turner tried to ensure that everybody who played went home with £100 each, plus expenses. Since he wasn't in a position to issue any additional cash on the night, the final payments would be sorted out later.

He explains: "The rest of the money was all in pre-sold tickets and ticket agencies, and it wasn't in hand. They had to do their accounts."

Dave points out that certain people received no money on the night from Nik, namely Keith Kniveton and a team of people who had made sculptures for the stage, including giant heads. Dave also claims that Lemmy missed his £100.

Turner responds: "Keith Kniveton was not, as far as I knew, a member of the Hawkestra. I'd seen him prior to this in the Coliseum in St Austell. He was playing onstage and not getting paid. He was one of those fans who did it as a labour of love. He came to the Hawkestra gig and Dave had given him the impression he was going to get paid, but to me, he wasn't part of what the thing was about – all the people who had been in the band.

"There was him and the sculptors, who Dave hadn't told me about. If I'd known, they'd have been a legitimate expense. They were personal friends of mine too. When I realised Dave hadn't done anything about arranging for them to be paid, I told them that if they presented Paul Bolton from Helter Skelter with a receipt or a bill or whatever, they would get their money. I thought I gave Lemmy his money. He was going off nightclubbing with Samantha Fox after that. It wasn't me intentionally not paying people. I gave Dave his £100 on the night. He didn't question it at the time. There wasn't any of this backbiting and bullshit."

"Paul Bolton gave Nik Turner a big pile of cash before we came offstage," says Kris.

Among the services and expenses Nik paid for on the night were those of the video and sound crew who were filming the gig. Dave had already arranged for a company called SPV to record and film the event, at a cost of £10,000. The company was also due to film the next day's Motorhead gig.

"I objected and wouldn't go along with it," says Nik. "I thought, 'Because the equipment's there, I could do it myself.' I arranged for us to hire the mobile that was there, a 48-track digital, for £3,000 and have somebody engineering and producing it. Then I got Steve Swindells' brother-in-law and a digital camera crew to shoot the thing. So I recorded it and filmed it and then I arranged for the tapes not to be available to Dave 'cos I didn't want him bootlegging the whole thing. If that happened, none of the band would make any money out of it.

"The tapes are still locked away. They will be released only if we can get a really good deal that is agreed by everybody. Then everybody will benefit. Dave doesn't own the tapes. They're owned collectively by all of us."

Swindells elaborates: "There was a legendary German producer, Zeus B Held, who lived near me in Willesden Green. He did the recording for free for us, expecting he would be producing it and getting points. I called my brother-in-law, who's a film-maker. He was studying at the London Film School. We asked him if he could hire four digital cameras and grab three of the students to shoot the gig. My brother-in-law got paid £150, and the students were paid too, plus they got work experience. My brother-in-law will be on a percentage if the tapes are released.

"At Brixton, I said to Zeus and my brother-in-law, 'Once we've finished, the minute it stops, get these videos out of here, and the recordings.' All those tapes are now with lawyers."

Dave Brock and Kris Tait are emphatic that, "Nik didn't have any right to take the tapes," and have been pressing hard for their return. At the very least, they believe they are entitled to the footage and recordings of the first half of the gig during which Hawkwind played without guests.

Nik Turner replies: "I say these tapes are all part of the whole event and that they belong to everybody. If Dave and Richard and Alan are on the first half, they probably have more of a right to those ones than perhaps everybody else, but the whole thing was a project. It wasn't a piecemeal thing. I'll give them to Dave if everybody's agreeable to that. I'd say they are a jewel in the skull or, rather, the crown of the band's back catalogue."

The next development, according to Kris, was that, "Nik decided Dave wasn't getting his £1,500."

Nik sent a letter to Paul Bolton in October 2000 which he copied in "weird, handwritten faxes" to everyone playing at the Hawkestra event. It says, "This is to confirm that I have been asked to represent the majority of the Hawkestra." The letter goes on, "I wish therefore to undertake this responsibility and authorise you (Paul) to distribute the money."

"But," says Kris, "it wasn't to be distributed in the way that had been agreed with us."

Dave swiftly wrote to Bolton: "Dear Paul, I have been asked by these people, who are part of the Hawkestra line-up, to confirm that Nik Turner does not represent them. Harvey Bainbridge, Richard Chadwick, Ron Tree, Alan Davey, Jerry Richards, Huw Lloyd-Langton, Danny Thompson, Keith Kniveton and Simon House. I also confirm that he does not represent me."

Nik Turner comments: "I only know that the people I spoke to said if I was involved in the financial aspects, they would do the gig. If I wasn't, they wouldn't. Most of the people were there because they'd been in the band, and the reason they were no longer in the band was 'cos Dave had sacked them. My only agenda was wanting everybody to be treated fairly."

The dispute dragged on for more than a year. Sources close to Paul Bolton confide that since there was no unanimously elected representative for the musicians, and certainly no agreement on how the collective should share the money, he was being put in an almost impossible situation.

"Then," says Kris, "Paul Bolton sent this new thing out setting out the way everybody was going to get paid, and we said no. It had to be true to the original agreement we had, or paid *pro rata*. We were pissed off about the fact that Alan and Richard were not being treated with the respect they deserved."

Dave was being offered £629.

"Paul Bolton was the one who'd agreed to pay Dave £1,500 in the first place," carries on Kris. "They had no truck with paying Lemmy his money, but the attitude was that, 'It doesn't really matter about Dave.' Dave had done six weeks of solid rehearsals, plus we'd been holding back on other gigs on Douglas' advice so as to make this one special. The actual core of the band worked through all of the rehearsals, they were onstage for most of the set, and it didn't seem fair that they should have their entitlement reduced so much when payments were being made to Dikmik or Mick Slattery, who just walked on and gave a wave to everybody."

"Dikmik and Mick were there and they were part of everything," Turner bites back. "Who cares if they played or not? They deserved to be paid."

Kris continues: "We sent an invoice to Helter Skelter for £1,400 [taking into account the £100 cash payment at the gig] and we said, 'If you don't pay it as agreed, we're going to take you to the small claims court.' So we did. We went out there to test the water for everybody else.

"If Nik had kept his nose out, we'd have got what we were all promised with the recording deal on top. Everybody would have got a percentage of that. We were going to do a touring show, then a Hawkfest and everybody could have come along. Nik can be charming; he can be lovely. But I get emotional and angry because of the hurt and the bad things he's caused us."

Dave adds: "It should have been a wonderful occasion. But the whole camaraderie, the idea of this fantastic show that we could take to Europe, with as many different people as we could in the Hawkestra, was smashed to pieces by Turner. He turned people against us. He got everybody backbiting – 'I've got 15 members on my side and you've only got four on yours.' When I phoned everybody up, they said, 'It's a load of bollocks.' All these old boys get money out of the Hawkwind records. At the end of it all, it's a shame."

Dave sent a letter to Helter Skelter stating: "I'm objecting to any cheques being paid out which accord to Nik Turner's suggested breakdown until you receive an agreement in writing from myself. May I remind you that there are legal proceedings pending in the county court relating to this matter."

Paul Bolton, in an email dated February 23, 2001, suggested to Dave: "Why can't you and Nik talk? Then all this crap can be finalised. Forget your ego and ring him."

It was way too late for that, but Dave offered a concession. In a letter to Bolton, he wrote: "If I'm offered the same fee that Lemmy has accepted, £1,000, I will be prepared to drop the case, otherwise the case will proceed."

Meanwhile, various members were querying the whole-band allocation from the takings of the gig.

According to figures supplied to Dave Brock, the gross income was £75,519. The net income, after VAT, was £64,271.49. The costs allegedly amounted to almost £30,500, and they included hall rental,

PRS, PA, lights and trucking, stage crew, tour manager (Kris says she was the tour manager, and didn't get paid for it), advertising, PR, artwork and design, handbill printing and distribution, security, staffing, catering, towel hire and cleaning, insurance (public liability and cancellation), telephone, decks, risers, staging and mics, supports and DJs, miscellaneous expenses and theatre dressing. The net takings after costs were recorded as £30,835.70.

Some Hawkwind members, including Dave, assert that the money they were being expected to accept was inconsistent with the scale of the revenue.

"Someone had a good night," remarks Alan Davey. "But it wasn't us."

Nik Turner, meanwhile, was taking issue with the merchandising share-out. He says: "It had been verbally agreed that the profits would be shared out equally. A while after the gig, I received a cheque from Voiceprint saying, 'Here's your share of the merchandising.' I was being paid according to how Dave wanted it paid. I wouldn't accept the cheque, because I would then have been accepting the terms and conditions that went with it. I sent it back, saying that I never agreed to the breakdown.

"I got a reply from Rob Ayling at Voiceprint. He said, 'If you can send me a copy of any agreement, I'll act upon it. But perhaps you should talk to your solicitors about it.' Him talking about a solicitor is like rattling a sabre at me. He's not threatening me, 'cos I'm completely in the right. Unfortunately, everybody else accepted the money, as has also been the case with the Voiceprint album releases."

Dave Brock's court case against Helter Skelter was due to be heard in Taunton. It was then rearranged: it would take place at the London County Court at 10.30am on November 21, 2001, while Hawkwind were on tour. An adjournment was refused. Coincidentally, it was in that same month that Dave Brock initiated the first strike against Nik Turner in a legal campaign that would also lead to the courtroom.

Far away in Canada, Del Dettmar, the first person known to have spoken the idea of the "Hawkwind Orchestra", looks back on the gathering that he had imagined as a fantasy and finally attended in the real world as "the uninvited guest".

"I believe I was there," he chuckles. "I played on the Dave Brock famous-old-track medley. I would have played for nothing, but I would have preferred an invitation to be involved from the very beginning and have a say in what was going on musically. My hundred pounds and my air fare? Well, what can you say? I'm glad I did it. Sure. It was a riot."

CHAPTER 31

Fallout

DAVE describes the Hawkestra debacle as "a nightmare of weird things, skulduggery and deviousness". As if to prove that a reunion really was possible, and that it could be run smoothly and effectively, he immediately organised another, albeit with a more manageable number of guests.

"It was Dave's answer to the fact that the Hawkestra ever happened," says Harvey Bainbridge. "He wanted an in-party, with just the people he had chosen himself."

It was staged as a Christmas celebration at the London Astoria on December 29, 2000. Dave, Alan, Richard, Simon, Jerry and Ron were joined by Harvey, Huw Lloyd-Langton, Tim Blake, Captain Rizz, Keith Kniveton and Michael Moorcock, who was not there in person but gave readings over the phone of 'Warrior On The Edge Of Time' and his signature 'Sonic Attack' – the same tactic that Dave had planned for the Strange Daze festival in Cleveland. Also playing was saxophonist Jez Huggett, who had taught Kris Tait to play the sax and had also appeared at the Hawkestra. Jez would continue to perform occasionally with the band in the ensuing years.

The event was commemorated on the album *Yule Ritual: London Astoria 29.12.00.* which was released in October the next year by Voiceprint. *Classic Rock*'s Mick Middles would be complimentary about the group's "anarchic glory", remarking that "it's strangely comforting to know that Hawkwind are, in every sense, 'out there' . . ." while also noting "moments where the sound stretches too far to the edge and you're left to wonder what on earth is going on".

Jerry Richards enjoyed working with Tim Blake. "What a character," says Jerry. "He's larger than life. I think he's absolutely beautiful. He has spent a little too long in France."

At the time of going to print, Tim was said to be recovering from injuries sustained in a car accident there.

At the Astoria, Tim was thrilled to be back onstage with the band. "I love playing with Hawkwind," he says. "I've done my best to be present when I've been invited to be. I've been very lucky. Every time I come to one of these reunions, I find myself very welcome with the fans.

"I probably get on best with Richard Chadwick, although that in no way diminishes my friendship with Dave. Dave is someone I like, and I like to play with. I like Richard as a person and he's the kind of musician one particularly needs to know. This is a drum musician who is completely at ease in the world of electronic sequences, drum machines and time clocks and everything. You can be playing electronic music or electro-acoustic music or rock'n'roll. No problem." It would not be Tim's last invitation from Hawkwind.

In March and April 2001, the band played a handful of gigs, with and without guests, and on June 22, headlined an open-air bikers festival at Castle Donington, with Huw Lloyd-Langton and Keith Kniveton guesting. It was the end of the line for Ron and Jerry.

Jerry arrived at the race track straight from Stonehenge, where he'd been celebrating the summer solstice with Richard. The authorities had reopened access to Stonehenge the year before, 15 years after the Battle Of The Beanfield, and were again allowing free gatherings.

"There must have been up to 10,000 people," remembers Jerry. "The Ozrics and Joey from Eat Static were there. We stayed up all night and at midday, we trundled back and went up to the gig at Donington. I really enjoyed the soundcheck there. Everybody was in a good fun mood.

"It was a visual performance, what with the light-show and the 747s flying over the stage on their way to East Midlands Airport. They looked pretty spectacular as we were doing the old 'Silver Machine'. It was magnificent, a great one to bow out on, really."

Jerry was not informed that he was out of the band, and neither was Ron Tree. "I was a full-time member of the band," says Jerry, calmly. "But every now and again you need a big shake-up and people are no longer asked to come and do things. A new crew of people come in and try and do something different. Ron and I were just not invited to do anything more."

Dave comments: "Jerry wasn't actually sacked from the band. He was edged out in a gentlemanly way. No one wants to sack people sometimes. Alan was back, and Alan didn't want Jerry involved. It was a difficult situation. Jerry was a friend of mine when we used to do festivals. He's an amiable character and a hard worker. But at the end of the day, Alan did put us in a position – 'It's him or me.' I decided, 'We'll have to be polite about this and basically distance ourselves from Jerry.' You leave it to him to think, 'Well, okay, perhaps I'll go back to doing my foley.'* Then, foolishly, Jerry went and did something with Nik Turner."

"There was a kind of ultimatum," carries on Kris. "We asked Jerry to do one of the Hawkfests. He chose Nik instead."

Richard Chadwick, who had been pursuing side projects with Jerry, intercedes on his behalf: "He said he didn't see it as, 'I'm playing with Nik' or 'I'm playing with Hawkwind.' "

"It's ridiculous," confirms Jerry. "If any of my old mates calls me up and says, 'We're doing a gig just down the road from you, do you fancy coming to play?' I'll always say, 'Yep, I'll see you there.' Nik operates a very open-door policy, and he really does embody that free spirit that the band's famous for – being the people's band. Playing with Nik didn't endear me to certain people. I was a bit disappointed. I thought they were bigger than that, had a bit more vision."

Jerry carried on with his soundtrack work, supplying music and sound effects for TV, radio and film. He has worked with some of the Monty Python crew, and played on a variety of sessions. He has a project called the Earth Lab with one of his old buddies from Tubilah Dog, and he is still writing and playing in Emoticon with Steve Swindells.

"There are lots of things going on," he says. "It's a case of trying to keep on top of them. It stops you getting bored at the weekend."

Jerry now lives on the outskirts of Coventry with his partner Karmen and their cat, Merlin. He says: "Our little spot is called Fish Pond Bottom. It's residential round here. We have nice bits and bobs out the back of the house – foxes and squirrels and all sorts of creatures doing the rounds."

Ron Tree is less philosophical about his dismissal from Hawkwind. He wasn't upset at being fired. On the contrary, he'd been discontented for

---

* Soundtrack work.

ages and in time would probably have left. He was, however, unhappy not to have been informed that he was dumped.

"I really liked Ron, but later on he totally changed," remarks Alan Davey. "I wondered, 'Who is this guy now?'"

Richard adds: "I myself said to Ron, 'You can't do this any more. You've gotta stay at home and be a full-time parent. You're a legal guardian. You're going to have to do it.'" By now, Ron had fathered a son, Calum, who was six at the time of writing.

"Ron had a bad drug habit," says Dave. "All of us had had enough of propping him up and we couldn't tolerate it any more. There were suggestions that he should go away and get himself together, but he never did. It was the same as Jerry – he left in a gentlemanly way."

Ron didn't see anything gentlemanly about the fact that he was expected to sit around wondering what was going on. He recalls: "It must have been a strain on Dave with me on drugs. He did put up with a lot. But I didn't get any vibe off him that I needed to leave, although now I think it was Dave, with a little help from Alan, who wanted to get rid of me. I didn't mind being thrown out of the band. It's just that he didn't tell me. I was waiting to go to rehearsals and no one came and picked me up.

"A few days later Richard turns up. He has a calming, chilled-out vibe in the group, even though he plays like a fierce lion. He's like the Charles Hawtry of it. Richard realises – 'Oh, Dave hasn't rung you, then.' He goes, 'You're not doing it. You're not in the band.' That was the shock – that Dave didn't say anything to me. I felt let down. I'm Dave's friend, I have no animosity towards him, and I've enjoyed the time I spent with him, so whatever his reasons were, I respect them. But I thought he was my *friend* friend, and it made me think about that. I still think he's my friend. He perhaps found it difficult to say. Perhaps he didn't want to hurt me that much by telling me. Again, apparently, he's done that to other people.

"I tried to talk to him but he could see the phone numbers of the people who were ringing him and he wouldn't take my calls. Then I phoned from a call box. He says, 'You're not being sacked. We're just doing a different style. We're going to use you later on.' I should have asked him, 'Why didn't you tell me you just wanted to change the band?' I spoke to some people saying they asked Dave and Kris, 'What happened to Ron?' and they said, 'Oh, we don't know. He just went away. He were out of his head on drugs.'"

Of his heroin problem, Ron confirms: "Dave tried to help, but I wasn't ready for it. Nik [Turner] also has been a good friend to me. He's tried to help me by saying, 'Do you want to live or do you want to die?' He felt sorry for me, the way I ended up out of Hawkwind."

After realising he was no longer in the band, Ron says: "I didn't do much. I went into a heroin miasma, and struggled, and my partner Mitzy and my little boy Calum backed me all the way through it."

Ron carried on struggling until 2004, when he finally received the right help. He reveals: "I've been in drug rehab for four months. It was a spiritual programme. It was good. I found a spirituality, not like in worship but inside myself, realising it's in everything outside including stones, twigs, trees. It's a microcosm within a microcosm. I'd been taking LSD and mushrooms in abundance 'cos they were spiritual and they put you close to nature. I didn't realise you could use meditation or visualisation to get into plants and trees without having to take mind-altering drugs. I don't really need to do that.

"What happened was quite horrendously frightening. I went through this rehab. It would've been the only time it would have worked – the right counsellor, the right people, the right time. I worked hard at it and it changed me and I came out and still I had trouble out here. Something made me take heroin, and I didn't know why.

"I took three quid's worth and nearly died and was brought round. The near-death experience and the pain of my young one and my partner now . . . the pain of letting them down, and myself, after all that, and the realisation that that was the last chance I had and if I do it again, I really will die . . . It was such a shock to my body I shook all night. It brought me back to reality with a real crack, to really know not to ever do it again. Now the door is shut on it. I can look at myself in the mirror and say, 'I'll never take that again.' "

Ron emerged from the darkness with a positive energy which he has been channelling into his family and a new group called Mother Of All Bands. "Everybody in the world who wants to be in it is in it," he announces. "It mirrors what humanity is and what it has ever been from the beginning of time. It's giving you the picture of who you are back at yourself. There's a nucleus, and everybody who wants can join in – fire, dancers, circus. Sound sculpture is involved, and all the different types of music there are on the planet. There's no rehearsal and no structure. We play for free. We just ask for donations."

And as for Hawkwind, Ron acknowledges that he did take

something valuable from the experience: "I suppose I learnt that maybe I should communicate properly."

It had been decided that Jerry Richards was leaving, and Huw and Marion Lloyd-Langton were invited to visit Dave and Kris in Devon. Marion doesn't remember this starting out as anything other than a social occasion.

"We weren't even thinking of Huw rejoining," she relates. "We were just talking over dinner. That's when I said sorry to Dave about my misconception of him. I said, 'Dave, I have to apologise to you. There were so many rumours. I should have faced you with them. Instead, I chose to believe what was being said. I have since learnt that most of it was lies and misunderstandings.' It had been worrying me for a long, long time. I felt bad about it. Huw's always had a soft spot for Dave, and so have I. Dave was across the table. He looked at me and he said, 'Listen, it doesn't matter.' And then he said, 'Jerry's a great player, but I miss Huw. He's the man.' We started talking about Huw coming back into the band."

Huw had been playing with Nik Turner in an outfit called The Hawkwind Isle Of Wight Reunion Band. The idea was to recapture the sound and spirit of the band around the time of the legendary 1970 festival. Nik had renewed his friendships with drummer Terry Ollis and bassist Thomas Crimble at the Hawkestra, and he invited them into the line-up along with Huw. All four had played at the Isle of Wight: indeed, that had been the scene of Huw's catastrophic acid trip.

Turner had also been back in contact with an old friend, Chris Hewitt. They'd both been on the free-festival scene, and Chris was the organiser of Yorkshire's 1978 Deeply Vale festival where Nik's Sphynx band had performed. Nik had accepted Hewitt's offer to release some live material from that concert on his own Ozit Morpheus Records. Chris Hewitt was now giving Nik advice and practical help with the new band, and he would soon become their manager.

They appeared at a big community festival in Wales and at Liverpool Stairways. Dave Brock was invited to come and play, and didn't. Then came a gig at a dancehall in Blackpool, where the band were billed as 2001: A Space Rock Odyssey. Harvey Bainbridge turned up to that one. They followed on with a show in Crewe.

In collaboration with Hewitt, the band would go on to experiment with variations of the name xhawkwind. This would quickly lead Nik

Turner into open warfare with Dave Brock.

Chris Hewitt alleges that at the time of the Blackpool gig, things started getting dirty. He claims he received abusive phone calls from Dave Brock and Alan Davey and adds: "The Hawkwind Isle Of Wight Reunion Band were fairly successful. The gigs were packed out. That's when you were automatically forced to take sides in this division between Dave and Nik. I'd been a real fan of Hawkwind and what they stood for in the Seventies, and it was pretty awful to have to be on one side or the other. The first casualty was really Huw. He was told that if he was playing with Nik, he couldn't play with Dave."

Kris Tait responds: "We tried every way to stop them using the Hawkwind name before we were forced to go to court. We wrote to them, we sent solicitors' letters. We did talk to Chris Hewitt quite reasonably on the phone and tried to reason with him."

Says Dave: "We were firm but not abusive."

Other trouble had blown up between Nik, Huw and Marion.

Says Nik: "I was managing the band at this point and paying everybody very fairly. I picked up the money, paid everybody's expenses, took a little bit for my own administrative costs and shared the rest out.

"The Blackpool gig came along and Huw's wife got involved – 'Well, Huw wants lots of money.' He wanted £600 when everybody was supposed to be getting about £350 each. This would mean the rest of us would have to take a drop to about £270 each so that Huw could have his £600. Marion insisted on it. Huw was more easy-going.

"Maybe he's had this relationship with her where he plays at being the guitarist who's a bit of a nice little lad and she's like his mum, I suppose, and has to manage his affairs. She came on very heavy on his behalf, so we all said we would pay the £600, just for an easy life.

"Then she complained about a record that had been released which was a mixture of live material from these gigs. She said Huw had never given his permission. Huw *was* asked. He did agree to it and it was released with his consent.

"I got this terrible phone call – 'Well, you know Huw wouldn't allow that to be released.' At that point, Huw left the band, although not because of any personal falling out – I've always been on good terms with him in spite of all this peripheral negativity that's been going on around him."

Marion is adamant that Huw did not give his permission for the album release. She says: "It was a bloody awful CD. I rang Nik and said, 'What the hell is this crap?' He said, 'It's only a low-key thing.' He said, 'Talk to Chris Hewitt.' Chris Hewitt said Huw had signed a contract. I said, 'Produce that contract.' It was very naughty. It cost us nearly £1,000 just to get a lawyer's letter out."

Chris Hewitt responds: "Four out of five people wanted to get the live material out. Huw got paid more money than anyone else for the gigs because of Marion."

For Huw, however, the problem was all in the name. He contends: "The trouble was that Nik was almost calling it Hawkwind. It was just impossible to carry on with that situation and also work with the real Hawkwind. It was, 'Take your pick.' It was either Hawkwind or Nik's band, and there's only one Hawkwind. I'd prefer to work with them than a scrappy sideline band. I was quite happy to go out and do a few gigs with Nik and the rest of them. There's no reason they couldn't go places really, as long as they use a different name and don't go out pretending to be Hawkwind. I haven't really spoken to Nik since I did those couple of gigs with him."

Huw was replaced by Mick Slattery, Hawkwind's original guitarist, who doubled up with Huw in Blackpool. Mick recalls: "Nik phoned me up and I went on a couple of gigs. Just being back with him again . . . I was really quite nervous and keeping my eyes on the equipment. At one point after the second number, I looked up and thought, *'There's Terry Ollis and there's Nik Turner!'* We've been playing ever since."

After a short period of time as Spaceritual.net, the group would settle on the name of Space Ritual, and they now comprise Nik (sax and flute), Mick Slattery (guitar), Thomas Crimble (guitar), Dave Anderson (bass), Terry Ollis and his son Sam Ollis (both drums), Del Dettmar (signals and noises) when possible, and keyboardist John Greves. There are dancers and special guests, with Robert Calvert's son Nick occasionally putting in an appearance on vocals.

Dave Anderson says: "It's amazing we're all still alive. We've had a wealth of experience since we played together in the Seventies. Terry Ollis is my soul brother. We'll always be very good friends.

"At one time, we hadn't seen each other for at least 15 years. One of the clients at my studio rang me and said, 'I've just arrived at the village. I'm at the Goat Hotel. Do you fancy coming down for a drink?' I don't drink much and I don't know why I said it but I said, 'Okay then, I'm in bed at the moment, but I'll come down and meet you at the pub.'

Just as I was taking my first sip of a pint, there was a tap on my shoulder. I turned round and it was Terry Ollis. I'm saying, 'Fucking hell, what on earth are you doing here?'

"He'd been coming up every summer to look after a farm for some friends of his that went on holiday in the summer. Just by chance we bumped into each other. Sam, his son, is the same age as my son, Ross. They were both into fishing. After that, every time he came up, he'd spend all his time up at the studio with me. And now we're playing together again.

"There's something unique about the chemistry of the band. It's more than the sum of the individuals. I have no doubts in my mind at all that we're probably much more Hawkwind than Hawkwind. We're the true Hawkwind, and Dave wouldn't agree, but what the fans are saying speaks volumes."

"We're all older but not much wiser," says Thomas Crimble. "When we get together, we make that particular noise which is early Hawkwind noise. When there's enough money from the tour to pay for Del Dettmar's expenses, he comes over from Canada and plays with us and makes spontaneous noises. He still plays his axe and he manages to get it through customs. I don't know how he does that. He's a lovely chap."

Mick Slattery takes a slightly different view of the group: "People are beginning to accept that we're our own band, we've got our own sound and we haven't got much to do with Hawkwind. Obviously there's a connection there in the music, but I think it would be a good idea to get away from it a bit. Things change all the time on the stage anyway. The audiences have been fantastic."

Dave Brock followed up on the Devon dinner discussion by inviting Huw to rehearsals for the next Hawkwind gigs. Huw accepted, despite his previous experiences in the band and his alarm that many of the past and present members were dividing so bitterly into two camps, supporting either Brock or Turner.

"It was horrible," he declares. "I didn't want anything to do with it. It's just a damn shame. The reason I'd left the previous time . . . it was all business and money and rubbish. It was water under the bridge. At this point, I was just happy to be invited to play. I was, 'Sod the money.' I just shrugged off anything to do with the financial aspects of it. Different people were shouting about different things. Some of it you might listen to and believe but then half of it's probably rubbish anyway. The financial thing just gets in the way of the enjoyability of it, and the artistic aspect. Hawkwind was always an enjoyable band to go up and play with, and I didn't mind the idea of a few gigs."

A few gigs turned into many, and his arrival stabilised the band as a five-piece comprising Dave, Alan, Richard, Simon House and Huw. At the Canterbury Sound Festival on August 18, they were joined onstage by Keith Kniveton and Sixties 'Fire' legend Arthur Brown, who was MC at the event. The set was immortalised on *Live At Canterbury Festival 2001*, released the following Christmas by Voiceprint.

Says Kris: "Dave just thought it would be a great idea to get Arthur to sing 'Silver Machine'. He just made up the words and got it all wrong." This would be the first in a series of collaborations with Arthur Brown.

Keith Kniveton, Tim Blake and Jez Huggett augmented the line-up at the Royal Festival Hall on October 10. Touring the UK and Ireland throughout November, Hawkwind were occasionally accompanied by Kniveton and Captain Rizz. It was an eventful tour, especially for Simon House and Huw Lloyd-Langton.

By now, Marion Lloyd-Langton was co-managing the band with Kris Tait. Kris was successfully working towards restoring Hawkwind's performance fee to a realistic level, due to the shortcomings of a previous manager who had lowered the asking price by £3,000. She had decided that the only person who could run the band was herself, and she recruited Marion to form another "good cop, bad cop" alliance in which Kris, this time, was the good guy.

"Marion's really good at getting things together, sending 200 people a press kit," says Kris. "She was also the 'nasty policeman'. She'd ring up and be nasty. She's used to coming at things from a business point of view. It was quite good to have somebody like her working with me."

Dave speaks out in praise of Kris: "It's been real difficult on her, being involved in Hawkwind for all these years. It's a very male-orientated thing. She's been ostracised lots of times, even here in the milking shed [home studio]. She'd say, 'Oh, I feel like I shouldn't come in. No one talks to me.' I soon put a stop to that. But it is a gentleman's club. It's been ever so difficult for her on and off.

"She integrated herself so much, from when she started doing the merchandising. It's the only way she could cope with things. That's why she went off and did her courses. She had the courage to go off and do things. We had mime artists – she'd go and study mime so she could do a lot of these things I used to talk about. She ends up being manager of the band. She knows everybody in the business."

The first couple of dates passed without incident but at Nottingham Rock City on November 7, 2001, Simon House sprang a big surprise on the audience – and the band.

"He came out of the closet!" trumpets Dave. "He started wearing women's clothes onstage – and offstage. He's a transvestite, I'd say. He wears these horrible things. As this tour progressed, he was seen going into ladies' clothes shops. He started brushing his hair back. I think he wanted to explore the female sexuality of himself. Prior to this, he never used to wear anything unusual, and he never said anything to us about it. He just suddenly started wearing these clothes.

"You just accept that's the way he is. The fans used to whistle. I always used to make a joke or a silly remark to defuse it. Simon likes to get a reaction."

"That's all true," says Simon. "Some people get very shocked by things like that. I don't understand it. What people wear is up to them. Earlier on, I mentioned my previous partner. She has Huntington's disease. We lived together for a long time, from 1970 until 1993, during the course of which we had two children."

They are Holly and Thor, who was 31 at the time of writing. Thor is now a musician with a studio in Stoke Newington, London. He teaches music technology in Highgate and he loves techno.

Simon returns to the subject of the children's mother: "She was getting progressively demented as a result of the disease. Her central nervous system was destroying itself. She became more and more bad-tempered, violent and demanding, 24 hours a day. In the middle of the night, she'd start throwing things around.

"The result of that was I didn't have my own life. For, say, 20 years, I was completely controlled and repressed and I wasn't really living. In the late Eighties, things started getting really bad. I was trying to get help. I went to the GP, the social services, the Huntington's Disease Association, and I even went to the police. She'd lock me in the house. Sometimes the neighbours phoned the police when they heard the screaming and yelling.

"There was nothing anyone could do. People with the disease can pretend not to have it and the police think it's just a bit of domestic. My priorities were protecting my children all that time. That was my sole purpose in life. I did other things as well, but at the back of my mind was the thought of my children getting emotionally and physically tortured by their mother. My own feelings didn't come into the picture at all until my relatively recent freedom – that was Holly coming to live here. I suppose, also, my parents are both dead now, so I don't have to answer to them. Really, I'm free to do anything that I want."

Simon discovered that what he wanted to do was to dress up.

"I'm not gay," he sets out. "I just get a really nice buzz from it. One of the reasons is that I've got nice legs! I'd like to do some adverts for Pretty Polly . . . You can get really aggressive reactions sometimes, especially from men. I think they may feel threatened. At the same time, they'll quite happily watch Lily Savage or Eddie Izzard and that's okay, or go to a pantomime. The band were fine about it. I was wearing a gold shirt and some green sequinned hotpants and tights.

"We were in my home town of Nottingham, actually. Everyone said, 'Let's go to this music shop.' So we did, and next door was this clothes shop. I saw these hotpants, and green is one of my favourite colours, so I thought I'd try them on. I wore them onstage. I wasn't being totally female. I wasn't wearing make-up. I did wear a wig once at a Hawkfest, but that was because it was so bloody cold. I've got quite a few wigs . . . It's not like a mad obsession. I don't do it that much. I've been to a club a couple of times dressed up. The woman from Australia who I mentioned earlier – that's how I discovered that."

Simon has been working on a solo project, a concept called Gene Warp, which is an exploration of sexuality. "The album is taking ages," he sighs. "It'll probably never get finished."

Describing Gene Warp on his website, he writes: "Yes, God gave us sex energy . . . the most powerful stuff in the galaxy . . . be careful! Male and Female, not one or the other, but a mixture of both . . . an oscillation between the two . . .

"Anyway, one day a couple of years ago, while my erstwhile girlfriend was in the bath, I saw her dress lying on the floor. 'Mmm,' I thought, and put it on. 'God, it looks better on you than it does on me,' she exclaimed, somewhat disgruntled, but I had to agree. So, Gene likes dressing up . . . Mmm!!!

"And there's nothing quite like being feminine and a bit outrageous . . . even a bit of a tart . . . come on guys, why should women have all the fun! . . . go down to that charity shop and find something nice and frilly!"

Kris Tait tells the story of the dressing room in Dublin on November 26. She says: "Marion and I went in to clear the room to put the buffet out. In the middle of the room was a carrier bag and in it were all these little miniskirts and tarty tops, all new with the labels still on.

"I said, 'Oh my God, Marion, there's only two of us here. Either Huw's bought them for you or Dave's bought them for me.' We were laughing about how neither of them usually had such bad taste. We put the bag in the corner and all the time I was hoping, 'He wouldn't. He *wouldn't* have bought me that stuff.'

"Later on in the evening, having the buffet, Simon's going, 'Has anybody seen a carrier bag?' Me and Marion were going, 'Ooooh!' trying not to laugh. 'Is this yours?' 'Yes, that's the one.'"

Dublin was the scene of a much more serious event involving Huw Lloyd-Langton. He'd been feeling really ill for four days, since the gig at Brighton's Concorde 2.

"I started feeling terrible, very fluey in Brighton," Huw remembers. "We had a day off after it and I thought I might recover from what they call the 'tour flu'. We got to Ireland, I went to a doctor and he thought it was double pneumonia. I was still feeling very dicky, but I did the Dublin gig. Somehow, they got me home. I thought at one point I'd been spiked I was hallucinating so badly."

Marion adds: "We flew into Bristol and he thought we were on a train. He was acting really weird."

Huw continues: "Next thing I knew, I was in hospital on a drip and oxygen and all the rest of it. It turned out to be legionnaires' disease, which is a strain of pneumonia. You can just catch it, and I caught it on the 2001 tour. Marion and I were due to fly out to Australia. I'd cancelled going 'cos Hawkwind had a few things in the pipeline that conflicted with it. As it turned out, it was a darned good job I did, 'cos I couldn't have gone anyway. I was in Barnet General Hospital."

"Kris went with me instead," says Marion. The Australian trip was a present from her boss Andrew Briggs. Marion had known Andrew for ages; Huw had been his guitar tutor for years, when Andrew was an estate agent. He changed career and rose to become the chairman of Pocket Phone, selling it to One 2 One, which then became T-Mobile.

Marion went to work for him as a PA and business administrator. She says his willingness to allow time for her activities with Hawkwind and his gift of return tickets to Australia are typical of his generosity. She still works for him.

"Unfortunately, when Huw came out of hospital, he gradually went downhill, from quite a reasonable weight to skeletal," recalls Marion. "He had no appetite. He got iller and iller. He couldn't walk more than a few yards. The doctor said to me that he'd been quite a long period without oxygen going into his brain, so he was completely disorientated. Things were just not real, were they?"

"I don't know whether it was an offshoot of legionnaires' or what," replies Huw. "I wasn't eating properly, that's for sure. I was drinking too many alcohol beverages and generally not looking after myself. Marion was starting to be away a lot. She'd always looked after me and told me off when I was naughty."

Marion was travelling backwards and forwards from Spain, where Andrew was a tax exile until 2002.

Huw would not recover his health for a long time. Indeed, it would worsen as his whole world fell apart in a succession of personal crises. But he struggled on with Hawkwind for another year, and he was back onstage for their end-of-year show at the London Forum on December 20, an occasion which found Tim Blake once again revelling in his guest spot at the keyboards.

Dave Brock, however, was probably glad to see the back of 2001. At the same time that Huwie was starting to suffer the symptoms of legionnaires' disease in Brighton on November 21 and Kris and Marion were giggling over the contents of Simon House's carrier bag, a small claims court in London was ruling against Dave in his legal dispute with Helter Skelter over the Hawkestra. Dave and Kris received the news via mobile phone in an on-the-spot report from their representatives – Kris' mother Margaret Tait and her best friend Rose.

"Kris Tait's mother was in tears 'cos the judge gave her a roasting," declares Nik Turner, echoing at least one other account of the hearing. "The upshot of it was that the case was thrown out of court and the money was shared out at the rate we'd originally agreed."

A resolutely tearless Margaret Tait, while conceding defeat, claims a moral victory and attests to a wonderful day in court: "We had the most gorgeous judge," she confides. "We knew we wouldn't win but he was super, and he was very nice-looking as well. He was a High

Court judge who was standing in, and I still follow his progress in *The Times.*"

Margaret had offered to represent Dave in court since Hawkwind would be away on tour. Entrusting the care of Brock's dogs and horses to another animal-sitter, Margaret travelled to London with Rose and a sheaf of documents. Paul Bolton was there to represent Helter Skelter, accompanied by a solicitor.

"We enjoyed the surprise on their faces when they saw two elderly ladies walking in," laughs Margaret. "I'd never been to a court. I didn't know what to expect. Rose knew as much about it as I did. She was acting like my clerk. We were asked if we had any witness statements and we didn't even know what witness statements were. We just wanted to go in so they wouldn't get it done without anybody being there to support Dave and Kris. It gave Rose and me a presence in the courtroom. We also felt strongly about the injustices – that the case was transferred from Taunton to London and that an adjournment was refused, especially since it was Dave who had brought the case.

"The judge said to me that I didn't have any right of audience, but he decided I could have my say. I explained that the original agreement with Paul Bolton had been that Dave and Lemmy would each get £1,500 and that they were now only offering Dave £629. The judge said that he couldn't find for us because the original agreement hadn't been written down. It had been a verbal contract.

"I said to him that I didn't feel this should be heard when Hawkwind were on tour. I also said that as a matter of principle, Lemmy and Dave should be paid the same figure."

Margaret produced the fax from Lemmy, complete with flurries of swearing, in which he described Hawkwind as "a legend of monstrous proportions", agreed to play the gig providing Dave did and implied that, financially, he would be on equal standing with Brock.

"I said to the judge: 'Lemmy is only getting £1,000, and Dave should get the same amount.' The judge said, 'Could you give Dave Brock the same thousand pounds you're giving Lemmy?' Paul Bolton said he couldn't do that.

"I said to the judge – by this time I thought of him as rather a good friend – 'Excuse me, your honour, but this Hawkestra . . . Nik Turner took so much from each person to have a video made and he took the tapes. Would you ask Mr Bolton to get them back for us, please?' The judge asked Mr Bolton if he'd help to get them back. His reply was,

'I'm not in a position to do that.' I got quite carried away. The judge asked him if he would try to get them and he said he would try.

"The judge didn't have to do any of this, but he did it. This is what impressed me about him."

According to Margaret, Helter Skelter asked for costs and were refused. She adds: "The hearing wasn't as scary as it could have been. Another judge mightn't have been as nice. He's just a fantastic man. We stayed behind because we wanted our papers back, and he said, 'Are you really the dog- and house-sitters?'

"We were quite euphoric when we came out. I wouldn't think twice about doing it again. We got on to our mobiles. We felt it was a moral victory and we went and had a big celebration. We thought it was a good day out in London."

Paul Bolton comments: "I don't find it sexy dragging all this up again. I've already defended myself in a court of law and been victorious."

Kris Tait remarks, "We knew that because there wasn't any official agreement in writing, we would lose the case, but we did want to make a point. We had just trusted them. We were a bit greener then. We wouldn't allow that to happen now."

Douglas Smith says: "I understand certain members' points of view sometimes. When Nik was a bad boy, using the Hawkwind name in America, I understood the others' feelings. When Dave started mistreating the others from the reunion on, I saw the others' point of view. I thought Dave was starting to become silly."

Dave and Kris contend that their fall out with Helter Skelter has cost them certain career opportunities, having received an email from Paul Bolton on July 9, 2003 in which he informed them that he would not recommend any of the acts he represented to "get involved in an event organised by Hawkwind".

In a final surprise, the Hawkestra members – who had been paid according to the figures authorised by the court – received a second cheque from Paul Bolton, sent out in April 2004. The figures represented "remaining monies". None of the band members had been aware there were remaining monies.

Dave Brock was granted the largest amount of £172. Lemmy, Nik Turner, Alan Davey, Steve Swindells, Tim Blake, Richard Chadwick, Harvey Bainbridge, Simon House and Huw Lloyd-Langton all received £103.48. Danny Thompson, Martin Griffin, Thomas Crimble, Terry

Ollis, Jerry Richards, Ron Tree, Keith Kniveton, Alan Powell and Raymond Steeg were paid £68.99.

As for Margaret and Rose – they have now embarked on a new career as "rock chicks", helping out on the gates and with security at Hawkfests.

CHAPTER 32

The Hawkwars

NIK TURNER was inaugurating a series of reunion gigs under the banner of Greasy Truckers Party Featuring Members Of The Hawkestra. The first took place at the London Astoria on October 21, 2001 – the anniversary of Hawkestra at Brixton.

In an email sent out to every Hawkestra participant, including Dave Brock, he promised: "We can all be onstage together, having fun, going wild, living dangerously, having a good old knees-up together." Needless to say, Dave Brock declined the invitation.

"It was all very scuzzy and a bit low-rent," says Steve Swindells. "There were about 600 people there. I didn't want to do any more after that and I haven't and I don't intend to."

The next year's event would take place at the London Mean Fiddler on November 8, and the Greasy Truckers would also take to the road for a string of special gigs.

Chris Hewitt recalls: "In London I was presented with a guest list of 95 people – and there I was trying to get a decent fee out of the promoter."

"I did both of those gigs," says Adrian Shaw. "I met a lot of people I'd never met before. Jerry Richards, he's a very nice guy and a good guitarist too. Judging by what I've heard of the Hawkestra one, it certainly was the opposite. There weren't any egos involved. It was complete chaos. Nik was the lynchpin that held it together, although he's enormously democratic and was leaving it to everyone to put forward ideas and do whatever they wanted. At one point, we had three drummers and four bass players. One of the drummers was Jon Moss from Culture Club. I was talking to Steve Swindells and we found out we had things in common, like Hepatitis C. I was trying to convince Steve to undergo the treatment, having been through it and found it worked." Ron Tree was one of those who played with Nik during this era.

In November 2001, Nik received a legal letter on behalf of Dave Brock, warning him to stop using the name xhawkwind. He made some alterations to his advertising and the storm clouds subsided – for a while. Margaret Tait wouldn't have to wait long for her next encounter with the British judicial system.

"xhawkwind didn't sound like an idea that would offend anybody or delude anybody into thinking we were anything other than ex-members of Hawkwind," reflects Nik Turner.

In May 2002, he received another warning letter for using the name, and threw it away. He explains: "I didn't take it very seriously. I thought it was a lot of shit. Who is Dave Brock to say I can't use the name of Hawkwind as an ex-Hawkwind member? I didn't have any problem about using the name because Hawkwind had originally been my nickname. I hadn't realised Dave and Douglas had trademarked the name."

Nik went to Glastonbury and was preparing to take the stage with xhawkwind on Thursday, June 27, 2002 when he was served with a writ. It summoned him to attend court in Exeter on July 2, the next Tuesday, to answer to Dave for continuing to use the name. Nik didn't attend, and Dave got an interim injunction.

"It was such short notice," says Turner. "At that point I didn't have any representation. I didn't realise Dave was so desperate he was willing to take me to court. I believe that the people who had the right to the name were the members who signed to United Artists as Hawkwind and were credited with jointly writing the tracks on the first album. If you trademark something, you own it, and I don't feel that Dave owned the name. I still didn't think the thing was very serious. Had I known it was, I would have had representation and perhaps taken a different tack."

Dave and Kris had once again enlisted the support of Margaret Tait, who holds copies of all the relevant documents. She describes a series of hearings and adjournments carrying the case through to August, during which time it was alleged that Nik had committed contempt of court by publishing material about his latest battle with Dave, in contravention of the injunction.

On August 9, a "telephone hearing" was held, this time in a Plymouth court, between Dave's solicitor, the judge and Nik's barrister. Nik was not in attendance because he was still in the process of gathering his defence. Dave, Kris and Margaret, with an entourage of around a dozen people including Richard Chadwick, Alan Davey, Keith Kniveton, a broadsheet journalist and a fanzine writer called Trevor Hughes, did make it to the courthouse, where Dave handed in the evidence of what he considered to be Nik's contempt of court, allegedly including emails and material from the internet. The case was adjourned to August 28.

There was a certain despondency in the camp, especially for Kris when the entourage dispersed after leaving the court. It was her birthday and nobody, apparently, wanted to hang around for a drink. She hadn't rumbled the surprise party . . .

Nik had faxed a handwritten letter to 19 former members of the band, the writer Michael Butterworth and Robert Calvert's widow Jill, explaining that he had been injuncted by Dave, who was "demanding a £4,000 out-of-court settlement". In the letter, Nik set out his beliefs that he was not misleading anyone or threatening the mothership by using the name xhawkwind.

The letter – titled *Re: The Hawkwars* – told its recipients: "Dave has letters of affidavit from Huw Lloyd-Langton, Simon House, Richard Chadwick, Alan Davey, fans, Trevor Hughes, Rob Godwin and Rob Ayling of Voiceprint Records."

According to Nik's correspondence there were small labels both in America and the UK releasing "a lot of shite Hawkwind product, gleaning absolutely awful reviews". He contended that this devalued the band's original catalogue, the subsequent official product and "all the creativity, work and love put into the band by all of us, plus many more". He added that Hawkwind had been "run downhill".

Nik wrote: "I'm not saying that I am Hawkwind any more than anyone else, but the original band that signed the UA deal were Hawkwind, and were then manipulated out . . . Hawkwind was a communal band, never Dave's band. He just thought it was because he fucked everyone off, but it is still ours."

He signed off by appealing for comments and, preferably, affidavits. Dave Anderson was among those who obliged. Michael Moorcock sent a letter back to Nik, who explains: "Michael expressed his sympathy with me. He said he felt he'd been ripped off. He thought what was happening to me was shocking and he would support me right down the line during the court case. He said I could use his letter however I wanted. It somehow got on to some website or other. Later, I think Dave Brock got in touch with Michael Moorcock and he retracted his letter, having already told me I could do what I liked with it.

"It was hopeless, really. They were all saying, 'Yes, we'll back you up,' and then very few did. I guess people are quite happy to go along with it as long as I'm doing the legwork. When it comes to being in the frontline, they've all disappeared. Some people are movers and some people are sitters-still. They would be happy to receive any positive result that I achieved, but not to stand up with me and be in the firing line."

Chris Hewitt adds: "Michael Moorcock, Jill Calvert and Lemmy all agreed that Nik could represent them. And then Dave got at them and they became neutral or changed side."

As far as the allegations of contempt are concerned, Nik says: "Probably what other people consider contempt, I wouldn't. I don't know where the line is drawn. What is the ruling? They're saying I was writing things on the internet. I don't think I put anything on anybody else's website."

The next hearing was on August 28, in Bristol. The night before had been filled with frantic negotiations. Says Margaret: "Nik kept saying he was going to agree to everything and he'd fax the document back within half an hour. Kris was in negotiation with the barrister, who kept emailing stuff to her because Dave wouldn't talk to Nik. She was the middle person. It was nothing to do with her personally. It was between the two barristers. The barrister was emailing it in and she was having to print it off and fax it to Nik. He didn't bother sending the agreement back that night – and we all went to bed before midnight.

"The following morning at 8am, Nik sent through a copy of the agreement which he'd said he was going to sign and send back, but it was totally altered and it wasn't signed. We went to Bristol and our barrister gave it to the judge. The court official said, 'We've had a fax from the defendant's solicitor, saying they are all "physically unable" to come 'cos they've been negotiating well into the night.' This letter came into the court at 9.11am."

Margaret says that more negotiations were set up straight away and someone was sent to stand over the nearest fax machine, in a different building, to wait for Nik's signed document. It didn't come.

Nik: "They wanted me to agree to something. I wanted them to agree to something else. Basically there was no compromise. Their agreement was that I would pay £4,000 damages to Dave Brock, promise not to use the Hawkwind name and also promise not to use the name of a bird and an element together, for instance Sparrowearth. They tried to tie me down to that. I found myself out of my depth. I eventually acknowledged that they'd trademarked the name, but I didn't feel they had the right to. I had two immoveable objects on either side of me. I don't know about being 'too tired' to come to court. I thought there was going to be an adjournment and we didn't need to be there."

Says Margaret: "The judge said, 'I'm sorry but I'm not adjourning it and I'm awarding costs to Mr Brock.' "

Nik then applied to have set aside the order in which he had to pay Dave's costs. Brock's team said no to that application, and so Nik then had to jump through some fairly mind-boggling legal hoops. The upshot was that everybody returned to court in Exeter on November 22, 2002 – the day that the original spirit of Hawkwind, to whatever extent it now existed, was finally extinguished.

"Nik went into court to apply to have his defence put in late," says Margaret. "We said we wanted to apply to have him committed for contempt of court. The judge said we could both make our applications and adjourned for 20 minutes. He advised us to try to sort it out between ourselves. We filled this form out for contempt and we showed it to Nik's barrister."

By now, Dave's team were armed with posters and other items of merchandise incorporating the word Hawkwind which had allegedly been purchased at Nik's gigs. Turner, declaring that he had stopped using the xhawkwind name and had by now adopted the Space Ritual moniker, concedes it's possible that such merchandising had been obtained at his shows: "The fact I had been in Hawkwind does give me the right to use the name in a certain context, so that's probably quite true. At all these points we quite likely did have the name on our posters. I'm not the director of everything that goes on in my name."

Nik also states that his application to quash the order of a £4,000 payment to Dave was successful, while denying all knowledge of the contempt-of-court form filled out by Brock's team. He says: "I don't remember any form. It sounds quite dramatic, but it might have been something just passing."

Dave, Nik and their two legal representatives on the same day met privately to work out a settlement. He says: "I was rather at a disadvantage. I said we should split the costs. That's what I shouldn't have said. I should have turned to my barrister and said, 'What's the deal?' I knew we'd paid out several grand. Dave and Kris were claiming they'd incurred £20,000 costs. We added the two figures together and split it and I ended up with a bill of £7,500. I should have said my costs were twenty grand and then I wouldn't have had to pay them anything. I did end up paying £7,500 to the court. All the gigs I did for a while after that were going towards it."

It was also part of the agreement that in every aspect of Nik's career, he would not make prominent the word Hawkwind. He could use it with an "ex" prefix, but only in smaller lettering than his own name or that of his band.

Margaret: "We could have pursued the case for the full costs but we decided that rather than continue to trial, Dave would accept the agreement. We were just quite happy it was all over. It was taking up so much time and money for absolutely no reason. The more Nik continued with the adjournments, the more we had to ask for. At the beginning, it would have been practically nothing. And £7,500 didn't cover Dave's expenses, nowhere near. Barristers and solicitors don't come cheaply. It wasn't a case of Dave and Kris wanting to take an action, but with Nik passing himself off as Hawkwind, getting promoters and agents confused, you have to say, 'Don't do it.' Dave was only defending his reputation. It didn't have to happen. Just 'cos someone comes along and says, 'I want your name and I'm going to have it . . .'"

Nik would have loved to take the case further. He asserts: "If I'd had £50,000 to spare, we'd have been able to go to the High Court and appeal that xhawkwind wasn't confusing people with the name of Hawkwind. The example set by Liberty, who ended up as Liberty X, is a case of how people can work together. We had a case where people weren't working together.

"Dave said I was confusing fans. I was passing myself off as Hawkwind when I hadn't the right to because Dave owned the name, and I was trading on the goodwill Dave had supposedly generated. My feeling was that I had every right. It was me who had generated most of the goodwill. I don't think Dave generated any. I found myself in a position where I couldn't go any further.

"I'm not passing the buck. I feel that the whole thing is my fault, but the reason that I actually went down that road is because of my own ineptitude and my own naivety and I thought, 'The truth will out.' I didn't realise that justice is for the rich.

"Hawkwind in theory was the antithesis of everything that's gone down in this respect. It was always supposed to be about the alternative, but this was about being part of the system and using it against members of the band who thought they were not part of the system."

Chris Hewitt, who supported Nik throughout the case, claims: "I was getting death threats on the phone from anonymous callers. And when we went to court in Exeter, Alan Davey was threatening physical violence towards me."

Kris Tait answers: "Chris Hewitt made himself so unpopular with a lot of fans who thought he was going to destroy the band that I can quite believe he got death threats. They were nothing to do with us.

"Alan did not threaten him with violence. We were in the grounds of the court, and my mum would not have let anybody behave like that. We'd have been taken in for contempt of court. We called Hewitt 'The Puppetmaster'. People were lining up to shout abuse at him, he did have a hard time, but nobody threatened him." Alan simply calls him a "liar".

Hewitt continues: "This court case was all about idealism turning into reality, futility, over the course of 30 years. It's all about nothing. People are instantly disposable. There shouldn't even *be* any sides. The whole thing is an awful mess. I now know why Doug Smith detached himself, since the people who stood for so much have spent their whole lives squabbling. Although if Doug had been acting in the interests of every band member and ex-member fairly, why did he help Dave to trademark the name for his own use? Dave Brock seems to have been singled out as the major player, and all the others are seen as whingeing ex-members. Because Nik is so *laissez faire* and lets everybody do what they want, then part of the mess is his fault. It ended up being two sad old geezers rattling it out in court with money they haven't got. The whole Hawkwind ethos has gone."

Hewitt gave up managing Space Ritual in 2003 amid angry scenes. He has branded them "as unmanageable as Hawkwind . . . a lot of 60-year-old blokes who think the world owes them a living." They have retaliated by declaring a loss of confidence in Hewitt. They now manage themselves.

Nik has changed the name and line-up of his other band, the

Fantastic Allstars. They are now Nik Turner's Galaktikos, and they play a mixture of "groovy Latin jazz and Afro-Cuban rave".

He says: "We welcome everybody to play with us if they have the nerve to come onstage. I try to get people performing, to lose their inhibitions. My advice to people who get stage fright is to have a good time and don't give a fuck. You can't please everybody, so please yourself. Don't worry about other people."

Nik, who jealously guards the privacy of his family, will only admit to "living as a recluse in Wales with some animals and humans". He is closely involved in community work, sharing his musical experience with the local school, the youth club and various children's workshops and festivals. He still does a lot of busking, claiming it pays better than most gigs. "I can play any tune in any key," he declares. "People ask me to play 'Stranger On The Shore', and I play it in every key just to make it last longer."

He often travels 80 miles on a Saturday night to Cardiff, where he has shot footage for a documentary film about his busking life.

"I could get away with playing 'The Pink Panther' all night there and earn about £300," he reveals. "At midnight, when people are on their way home, the whole street starts performing if I play 'The Pink Panther'. Girls in very sexy dresses, boys all pumped up on steroids . . . even the police like me. I'm doing a service, defusing fights – taking the music to the people.

"I don't present myself as anybody but just a busker. Sometimes people recognise me. Sometimes they tell me they saw Hawkwind gigs that changed their lives. I'm really happy that people have had very good experiences of things I've been involved with."

Douglas Smith's favourite quote is one of Hunter S Thompson's: "The music business is a cruel and shallow money trench, a long plastic hallway where thieves and pimps run free, and good men die like dogs. There's also a negative side."

Smith says of the court case: "It's so petty. This ended up as a stupid waste of money. Nik would ring for advice. Dave would say, 'Nik's ripping us all off.' I'd think, 'There's 16 albums on Voiceprint.' There are 20 or 30 labels in this country recycling material by Hawkwind and other bands of their era. Some musicians are receiving only two or three pence an album. It's servitude. I have often thought about writing the truth of the music business."

The court case further polarised the Dave Brock and Nik Turner camps, although there are some ex-members who prefer not to take sides. Martin Griffin says: "Nik was the first person I knew and he was very much the vibe of Hawkwind. He is a personification of post-hippiedom in the UK. He asked me and others if we wanted to join the camp to see if we couldn't get a fairer slice of the royalties. And I couldn't set against Dave. I had no qualms saying to Dave, 'Where's the royalty on that?' but I couldn't join a legal movement against him. Hawkwind don't exist without Dave, and any value of the back catalogue was being generated by his endeavours.

"At the same time, I can see the other side of the coin. The Hawkestra [Greasy Truckers] put together by Nik was more fun than the Hawkestra put together by Dave. And again, Dave is a friend of mine. He's a man I think highly of and count as a friend. I managed not to get involved."

Harvey Bainbridge also wanted to avoid any legal commitment. He comments: "Nik was trying to get me to jump on Voiceprint releasing Hawkwind stuff. They'd handed out quite a lot of money on the advance and Dave kept most of it. I had a long chat with Nik and always tried to keep away from the legal side of things. It's pointless spending money on lawyers to recoup relatively piddling amounts of money.

"Dave was trying to get people to say Nik was a complete rotter. And a few people I've spoken to really regret doing that. I just thought it was all a bit silly – much ado about nothing."

Dave has explained that the first money from Voiceprint was used to settle tax bills for two Hawkwind members. Since then the musicians have been receiving regular cheques.

Adrian Shaw was also willing to side with Nik but not to become legally entangled. He says: "Nik's a lovely guy. He's a man of principle and I respect him for that. It would be very nice if everybody got what they deserved. I was quite prepared to go along with him so long as I didn't have to appear in court or spend anything. I was very sorry that it got him into financial problems. He did get stung quite badly. That's exactly the reason I wouldn't have invested any time or money in it. I was only on two albums."

Dave Anderson was more forthcoming in his support for Turner. He fumes: "Dave has no bloody right to think he's Mr Hawkwind. He's one of a bunch of people that happened to bump into each other. Nik had as much right to use the name Hawkwind as Dave did. Nik was the frontman, while Dave would not turn up at gigs and I'd have to play guitar. Nik would always be there beside me."

Steve Swindells avers: "If Nik Turner is taking any further action, I will support him."

Thomas Crimble accompanied Nik to court in Exeter where he acted as a go-between for Turner and Brock, succeeding in getting them together for the settlement. He says: "Up until Glastonbury, when Nik was given the piece of paper ordering him to come to court, I thought it was a joke about Dave not being happy about us using the name xhawkwind, especially as we were partly to do with the fame that Dave has been trading on for the last 30 years. We set it up.

"We came to an out-of-court settlement whereby Nik had to pay about £7,000. If we'd gone on to the High Court, we may have won – but I just figured it wasn't worth someone's house. In the winter of 2003, we did about 30 gigs, raised the money, paid Dave off and that was it. It's been tough."

Among Dave's defenders is Huw Lloyd-Langton, who comments: "I was lying here one night and the thought went through my brain that Nik, myself, Thomas Crimble and Terry Ollis – if you add up the years that us four had been part of Hawkwind, it wouldn't amount to anything like the length of time that Dave's seen it through. So who's really got the right to the name? Dave has carried it on through the years. Whether people are happy about that is another thing, but he has been the thread."

"There'll always be a Hawkwind while Dave's around," says Marion. "He's the driving force."

Looking back on the case today, Dave says: "What Nik did was ruin our reputation and all our hard work. A lot of close friends of mine, they actually believed the things he was saying. When it was all found untrue, the damage had been done.

"Michael Moorcock and me were really great friends. Nik had this letter from him. What actually happened there – Nik's so plausible. He's an amiable character. We got on well until we really got to know him. Michael has apologised for what he said about us, but the friendship is damaged.

"With Turner at the court case . . . he was pretty lucky. We saved him from going to prison, 'cos he was in contempt of court so many times. He said, 'Can I shake your hand?' Then he wanted to know, 'Is there any chance of me playing with the band again?' I wanted to knock him out of his chair."

Hawkwind's first gig of 2002 was in Hastings, at the Pier Pavilion, on July 18, and it saw the return of drummer Danny Thompson, playing in tandem with Richard Chadwick. He lasted a record two days before leaving again, and Simon House went with him.

Danny recalls: "Because of Bedouin supporting at some of the Hawkwind gigs, Dave had heard me playing, and I'd become a much better drummer than I was when I was in Hawkwind. Dave wanted to do a big drum thing, like tribal drumming, and he knows I love the band. We rehearsed for a week and I didn't get any money. He said we'd get money for the two gigs we had coming up. Hastings was packed out."

The second gig, on July 20, was the first-ever Hawkfest, which was held at Seaton in Devon. This was the private festival which the band had been planning ever since issuing the Hawkwind passports, and they were joined onstage by Tim Blake, Keith Kniveton, Jez Huggett and Captain Rizz.

Says Dave: "I was riding around on my bicycle, I'd stop and talk to people, kids would go, 'Give us a ride.' That's how it should be. At gigs the band are working – we're onstage playing. Often we allow fans in in the afternoon to listen to what's going on. We're quite accessible. We like all that. That's why we got the passport system together.

"You can be aloof and create this mystery about yourself, but at the end of the day, when you do something like the Hawkfest, that's the joy. People don't make nuisances of themselves. They're the same as us, and they're only there to have a good time and say, 'Well, thank you very much.' It's great to have lots of people shake your hand to say, 'Thank you very much. Keep it going.' All this sort of thing is really good. It does make you feel like you've achieved something."

Danny and Simon were less happy. Simon complains: "I drove down to Devon to rehearse for a couple of days, back up to London, down to Hastings to do a warm-up gig, back to London, and back to Devon to do the Hawkfest and then back to London – all in a week. I drove about 1,000 miles and it ended up costing me money.

"Alan said we were guaranteed a few hundred each on the Hastings gig. I saw Dave disappearing with the money bag from that. At the same time, we'd been offered £14,000 by Secret Records to do a video of the festival. We would have got a couple of grand each, which would have been something. We all have to pay the rent. At the last minute, Dave decided not to sign the contract because it was for perpetuity. As far as I'm concerned, so fucking what?

"Then Dave said, 'We've only sold 400 tickets for Hawkfest, so we're not going to make any money.' It was forbidden to ask about money. Kris was saying, 'I don't know anything about money. Talk to Dave.' Dave would say, 'You're not going to ask me about money as well, are you?' So I was feeling guilty about asking to be paid.

"We could have had a couple of hundred quid from the Hastings gig or a couple of grand from the video deal. It would have been better than nothing, but I got nothing."

Danny Thompson says: "There was no money from the festival, which they arranged themselves. They sell lots and lots of merchandise. You don't get fucking any of it. I got £100 for the whole fucking lot. For rehearsing and doing the gigs, and that's because we didn't have any petrol money to get to the festival. 'Oh, it's locked away in the flight case.' 'Unlock the fucking flight case and give me my money.' I got £100 to get to Devon.

"Things were no different. There was money in the pot, but everyone was just getting fobbed off as usual. Dave's really moody all the time. It's the same old thing. It's all down to money. As long as everyone's getting the same, I don't mind, but it seems to be more about a pension fund than anything. I just said, 'That's it, stuff it, see you later.' It was nowhere near the fun it was back when I first joined them."

"He couldn't have stayed even if he'd wanted to," Kris retaliates. "It wasn't his choice to walk away. He wasn't offered any more gigs.

"At Hastings, Danny left after the gig. We found him at the end of the pier kissing this blonde girl. We gave him his money, and we had him sign for it. Everybody got paid that night."

Kris adds that nobody was under any illusions about the prospect of earning anything from the Hawkfest, since the band had to pay for the licences, land, stage and PA hire, truck hire, crew, lights, support bands, toilets, police and even AA road signs, and ended up out of pocket.

"It was a kind of experiment to see if we could do it," she contends. "There wasn't lots of merchandising getting sold. We all worked for nothing. But Danny was so nasty that weekend. He's six feet four, and he was throwing his weight around. It was intimidating. And his drumming wasn't great."

"He played very well at the rehearsals," adds Dave. "Everybody was well aware that we weren't going to make anything from the Hawkfest – it cost me a lot, personally – but when it came to it, Danny was hustling all the time, knocking on the door of the van demanding money. If he got £100, that's a lot more than I got.

"Also, Bedouin were playing. Alan was keeping them going as a sideline, and they got paid, so Alan must've paid Danny, who was drumming with them too. There's a bit more than meets the eye with this. Alan's activities with Bedouin were growing less and less, and the other two guys were pissed off. A problem had developed between Bedouin and Danny.

"When we did the next Hawkfest, we printed up some free, four-track CDs to give to the fans, with one Hawkwind track. Danny phoned Alan up complaining he hadn't got paid for it. You've got the publishing problem, but if you're giving stuff away for free, that doesn't come into it."

Addressing Simon's complaints, Kris states that if he drove 1,000 miles in a week, so did the rest of the band. And the proposed Secret Records video, she says, had been in negotiation for a year, with the deal crashing because it would have barred Dave from playing the set onstage again.

"Simon just didn't know what was going on," she says. "It wasn't just Dave deciding something for no reason."

A compilation album including many of the artists appearing at the festival was released later by Voiceprint, titled *Hawkfest 2002*.

Hawkwind followed on with an appearance at Wembley Arena on October 19, supporting their old bandmate Lemmy and Motorhead. They welcomed Lemmy, Tim Blake and Arthur Brown on to the stage as guests.

Arthur and Tim were then invited to take part in the band's UK tour in the first half of December. "Arthur was doing vocals and we did two of his songs as well as our own," says Kris Tait. "We didn't do 'Fire'. Half the fans thought he was fantastic. The others were pissed off 'cos he'd get the words wrong. Old Hawkwind fans don't like anything different. He could do the Calverty numbers very well."

Tim Blake was his usual enthusiastic self, and he describes the last gig, at Walthamstow Assembly Hall on December 13, as "an apogee, a high point". "Curiously," he adds, "I haven't played with them since. They had a very nice tour lined up for spring 2004 but I wasn't involved.

They did it as a three-piece, and that line-up is probably the best Hawkwind I've seen. In the old days, Douglas made it very easy for me to come and go, and this is no longer the case."

Tim's "apogee" in Walthamstow has been captured for posterity with the 2004 release by Voiceprint of *Spaced Out In London.* "It's a bit strange because it has no names on it," he remarks. "There are a lot of live records with me playing with Hawkwind and I don't find them particularly satisfying. I find this one very satisfying.

"The thing is this. Hawkwind don't really need a synthesiser player because Dave plays all the synths. Quite a few guitar players I've played with have slowly disappeared behind more and more synthesisers. Steve Hillage, Dave . . . they're all doing it. Finally I came to the conclusion, 'Well, let them.' If you let them do this, you're playing guitar parts on keyboards. That's what I really enjoyed doing with Hawkwind and that's what I'd like to continue to do.

"There was a certain point on the tour where Huwie had split with us, and I had this job of being the main soloist. I enjoyed that very much. This had been suggested to me in 1979, and now I think it's very good. Perhaps I'm a bit slow . . ."

Hawkwind played the Northampton Roadmender's on December 10, there were only two more dates left on the tour, and Marion Lloyd-Langton received a call from Dave: "I've put Huw on a train, Marion."

Huw's health problems had become so serious he simply couldn't carry on. He returned home, and things went from bad to worse. The Lloyd-Langtons had two daughters, with Kirsty having come along in April 1984 as a sister for Louise.

In February 2003, at the age of 39, Louise committed suicide with an overdose of paracetamol. For Huw and Marion, the continuing heartbreak is that she didn't really mean to do it.

"It was a cry for help," reveals Marion. "She'd never really got over the break-up of her marriage. She got married at 21. She was really happily married for two or three years, she had a little boy, and then she found out her husband had been having an affair before he married her. The woman was a teacher and she was pregnant. Louise had had alcohol problems ever since.

"Her new boyfriend, a guy she'd lived with for two or three years, went to prison for attempting to murder her. He was an absolute maniac. He was arrested trying to put a petrol bomb through the letter box of her flat. The court case lasted for days. She was living under protective custody. He got five years, and they let him out after 18 months.

"After the overdose, she was in a coma for six weeks. The doctors said she hadn't taken enough paracetamol to kill her, but she was so weak that her lungs, liver, everything collapsed. She came round. I tried to persuade her to go into a clinic. She said, 'Yes, I will, Mum. It's just so stupid. I was too proud.' She went back into the coma and died. It was just awful. She was such a loving girl, very artistic, but she had such bad luck."

"She was attracted to the wrong type of person all the time," says Huw. "She never had a good relationship with anyone. I think that took its toll on her, whether it be drugs or alcohol or not."

Marion was so distraught that the next month she left Huw, who was then doubly devastated. They had been renting a cottage in Henley-on-Thames while the house they live in now was being done up.

"Huw stayed in the cottage and I moved into the house here," says Marion. "I went round every week to clean the cottage and make sure Huw had food and money. He wasn't looking after himself. I was cracking up. I needed help. I ended up having a breakdown."

That happened in August. "I destroyed the house without even knowing it. I was upstairs and the police were knocking on the door. I went downstairs and there was Huw and Kirsty. The police said, 'Can we come in?' I said, 'What's happened?' I looked around. I was just terrified. I said, 'What? *What?*' The cupboards were ripped off in the kitchen. All I could see was blood everywhere. The policeman said, 'Come and sit down. We think you've had a bit of a breakdown.'"

Marion saw a doctor immediately. Then she went to stay for a while with her sister in Ireland. About returning to Henley, she said, "I realised I couldn't live without Huw. I said to him, 'Please will you move into the house with me?' Perversely, the breakdown brought us back together. Throughout that bad period, we couldn't communicate, and that made everything worse. We'd been together since we were young adults, really."

It was Marion who now needed help, and she turned to Huw, telling him that he had to start taking care of himself to be able to look after her. "He completely turned his life around," she reveals. "He eats a real healthy diet and he's stopped drinking the hard stuff. He'll have a couple of pints, maybe, and that's it. It'll always be volatile between us because I'm Irish and Huw's Welsh, but we're closer than ever now."

Huw had lost so much weight and energy that it took a long time to rebuild any strength, and he still has some way to go. After contracting legionnaires' disease, he broke his arm four times, most recently in November 2003 in a freak accident involving Marion and a burst of gymnastics in the living room.

"She went to go flying over the couch," grimaces Huw. "My arm went and she didn't."

Returning to Hawkwind for their Christmas show at the London Astoria on December 21, Huw would play a solo acoustic set with a cast on his arm.

Few would guess that Matthew Wright, the journalist turned TV and radio presenter, is a long-time fanatical Hawkwind supporter.

"Looks can be deceiving," chuckles Matthew, whose devotion to the band dates back to 1979. A 14-year-old living in Croydon, he was introduced to the world of time, space and Hawkwind by his best friend's older brother and was immediately converted. In 1980, around the time of *Levitation*, he saw them live for the first time and has been in the audience of just about every tour since then.

One of his most memorable and life-changing experiences was the 1984 Stonehenge Festival, where Hawkwind surrounded themselves with vestal virgins and presented Alan Davey and Danny Thompson in the line-up for the first time.

"I went in a boy and came out a cosmic man," declares Matthew, whose next big excitement came along in the summer of 1986 when Hawkwind played a gig in Exeter. "It was my 21st birthday," he relates. "I got my mate to give Dave Brock this note, asking him to say happy birthday to this fan out the front." Dave did his duty.

"Fast forward to 2003," says Wright. "I had my now defunct Saturday radio show on LBC. It was supposed to be a news and current affairs show, but due to the fact we had no real news or current affairs input, it became very much 'what Matthew wants to talk about this week'. So I talked about Genesis P Orridge, Daevid Allen and Dave Brock."

Dave and Kris travelled to London for an interview on the show, and they were astounded at the depth of Wright's knowledge about the band.

"I sang half his songs over the airwaves," remembers Matthew. "I think I knew some of his old songs better than he did. He felt like he was amongst friends, which he most definitely was. Then he said, 'Why don't you come and do it on the stage for real?' I said, 'All right then.'"

Dave and Kris first became aware of Wright's fascination with the band when his PA asked if he could come along to the first Hawkfest. On that occasion, he couldn't make it down to Devon, and he finally met Brock for the first time at LBC.

"We went to his house afterwards, briefly," says Kris. "We all got on really well. We kept saying, 'We'll be at the Astoria. We'll see you onstage.'"

Kris is referring to the Astoria gig that Hawkwind were due to play on May 25 as part of their forthcoming mini-tour.

"We texted him and he texted us and said something about how good it was to meet a hero who lived up to your expectations," continues Kris. "We sent one back saying, 'We weren't joking about the Astoria.' He replied to say, 'I'd be made up.'"

Kris sent Matthew a CD containing two versions of 'Spirit Of The Age', one with vocals and one without, so he could practise it. True to his word, he then performed it with the band at the Astoria. "He came along and he brought his flying helmet," says Kris. "He was raving all week about it on his TV programme. He was brilliant."

"I walked onstage and it was just fucking awesome," remembers Matthew. "The audience probably had no idea who I was. There was a stunned silence, but there was a big cheer for the song, a surge of energy. From the second verse, it went really, really well. I couldn't believe it. I loved it – 'When can I do it again?'"

Matthew was subsequently invited down to Devon to supply the vocals for a new recording of 'Spirit Of The Age' in the milking shed. "I was really surprised by how well it turned out," he laughs. "I've never been a singer. From a fan's point of view, this has all been like a dream come true for me."

'Spirit Of The Age' would eventually be released as a single in the summer of 2005 – along with a second CD version featuring as its lead track Wright's live Astoria version of the song.

"He's a laugh," says Alan Davey of Wright. "He's a man who likes a joke. He's been good."

The next part of Matthew's personal dream come true was the making of the video, which finds him singing in a test tube: "It was the most surreal day of my life, wearing the white lab coat and all that."

"Lene Lovich is on it too," says Kris. "She's a friend of Arthur Brown's."

Lovich, the renowned Seventies new-wave warbler, contributed vocals to 'Angela Android', another track recorded around this time.

Dave, Kris and Matthew Wright have since become the best of friends, meeting up socially in London and Devon, while Matthew has continued to make sporadic appearances with Hawkwind.

In return, he promises: "It's payback time. I want to help them get the profile they deserve. I'll do whatever I can to raise awareness and get the band out there to claim their proper place in history.

"Some people might dismiss Hawkwind as a three-chord band, but Dave is a brilliant guitar player and songwriter, and he's always doing stuff. The hippie lifestyle is all well and good. I hope that it's a very comfortable hippie lifestyle for Dave when he retires."

The May 2003 mini-tour, with Arthur Brown still singing vocals, found Simon House making another of his returns to the band.

Hawkwind played through the summer with a private party in Newquay and an appearance at a bikers' Rock and Blues Festival held at Pentrich Coneygrey Showground on July 25. "Simon turned up there with his girlfriend," recalls Dave. "There was a silly scene at the hotel 'cos they had a twin room and not a double. Kris and me were in the middle of parking our camper van in the rain on the camp site. She gets a call – 'Oh, we're leaving. We're not staying here. We're not having this.' That was Simon. Then Alan phones up and says exactly the same thing. I had a big freak-out with him. Kris was really upset, 'cos she didn't book the rooms anyway. I said to Alan, 'I'm fucking fed up with you.'

"They turned up at the gig and I said, 'Right, everybody. I'm going to have a meeting. If you want to start moaning, tell us to our faces what's the problem.' Of course, there was no problem. It was nothing really. They just got het up about having twins instead of doubles."

Simon, however, did have a problem. He would play one more gig – the second Hawkfest, which took place at St Michael's On Wyre, not far from Blackpool, on August 9 – and then he would quit the band. He has not, so far, gone back.

Dave Brock remembers the Hawkfest as a "fantastic day", adding, "I really enjoyed myself there." The group were joined onstage by Keith Kniveton, Huw Lloyd-Langton, road crew members Mr Dibs and Keith Barton (who had a band of their own in which they played bass and guitar respectively), and Harvey Bainbridge.

Classic Rock's Dave Ling travelled north to review the gig. He remarked upon the safe and friendly atmosphere that the band had been trying to promote with their private festivals and described Hawkwind's three-hour set as "an absorbingly informal trawl through a three-decade-plus career".

Harvey has not played with the band since. He says: "After Australia and New Zealand, I swore that if I did anything for Hawkwind again, I would have to have money in my hand first. Then I had long-standing fans phoning me up about the Hawkfest asking if I was going to be there. It was only down the road from where I live. Dave phoned me up in the end and asked if I'd like to come.

"While we were talking, he said, 'Well, of course, there'll be no money.' I said, 'I didn't expect there would be.' It was quite a nice gig, really. All these other bands were playing as well. I rather hoped that I would be thanked for turning up and offered a T-shirt or something, but no.

"They were charging £50 a ticket and they were selling merchandising as well, and Dave's giving me all this argy-bargy about how it's non-profit making, while all the time they're drinking champagne. Where's all the money going?"

Kris Tait responds: "Everybody, including Harvey, got paid for that second Hawkfest, and they all enjoyed it. I do believe that Harvey was drinking champagne too. It was on the rider for everybody."

"We haven't spoken since then," continues Harvey. "Alan sent me a text message before they did the Astoria gig in December. Would I like to be the support band and do a few numbers with them for an all-in fee of £500?" After an exchange of text messages, Harvey heard back from Alan, who now said, "Sorry, Harv, logistically we can't do it."

Alan explains: "We had a plan to do something that didn't work out. Then we had another plan that was going to be more expensive and we just couldn't afford Harvey, which was a shame. Dave, Richard and I really like what Harvey does and I'm sure there'll be more slots for him in the future."

"That was my last contact with Hawkwind," says Harvey. "It was quite bizarre. Previously, I'd been invited back to do gigs and I was always short-changed from what I'd been promised. No more now. No more at all."

Simon House was expected to travel with the band to Amsterdam for their next gig, on August 17. "He didn't turn up," says Dave. "Kris' mum had paid for the flights on her credit card. We'd booked Simon's flight and his hotel room, and it was all non-refundable. The day before we were leaving, Simon decided he didn't want to go." Dave, Alan and Richard did the gig with the help of Mr Dibs and Keith Barton.

There were no more shows for two months. Hawkwind were due to appear at the Exeter Phoenix Arts Centre on October 25. "I spoke to Simon," says Dave. "I said, 'You've cost us an airfare and a room.' He didn't turn up. No one said, 'You're sacked,' or anything like that. He just didn't play with us again. I don't know why he left the band. He never told us. He is on the new album, though. He came down and recorded in Devon." Keith Barton and Pete Pracownik, the fantasy artist and guitarist, played with Hawkwind in Exeter.

Simon tells his side of the story: "I wasn't going to get any money from the Amsterdam gig. On the mini-tour previous to that, Dave had said I'd get £400 a gig. I ended up with £200 a gig. Expenses never got paid. It was just getting to the point where I wondered, 'Is it worth all the stress for next to nothing?' I didn't know they'd booked the rooms and all that. It hasn't made any difference to anybody in the big picture. It was just a little club."

Dave is emphatic that Simon did know his fares and accommodation had been booked, and on the subject of the mini-tour, Kris stresses: "£200 a night is the equivalent of £1,400 a week plus expenses, food and transport."

Simon confirms: "I never said to Dave I was leaving the band. I think my last words to him were something to do with the album. I told him I'd moved to Cornwall and that was about it. He asked me to do a gig in Exeter for no money, so I said, 'Maybe.' Bollocks. I didn't do it. I've been doing gigs with Astralasia and I get the same money playing in these little clubs as I did with Hawkwind. I find it physically painful to play loud music, and Hawkwind is loud."

Kris argues that Simon would have been paid for the Exeter gig.

"If the money was all right I suppose I would play with them again," continues Simon. "It depends on what happens in the rest of my life. There's a lot of things changing at the moment. I'd very much rather do my own stuff."

He has been shuttling between London and Cornwall, where his girlfriend lives, since 2003, and also trying to sell a house he owns in Muswell Hill.

Alan Davey comments: "I think Simon lost his fire for the band. We were going through a period where we weren't earning a lot of money. I think he is a little bit money-orientated. There's nothing wrong with that. Dave, Richard and I will put work into the band for nothing to keep it running. That's what you have to do in Hawkwind. You carry on regardless."

The lines of communication between House and Hawkwind remain open. Says Alan: "I get odd texts from Simon saying, 'Hello darling, how are you?' "

Hawkwind finished the year with a London Astoria gig on December 21, where Lene Lovich appeared with them onstage.

They had already recorded the bulk of the album that would soon create new waves of excitement around the band.

CHAPTER 33

Keys To The Future

IN April and May 2004, Hawkwind played a dozen "straight rock'n'roll" gigs as a three-piece across the UK and Ireland. They were supported by the ever-popular Huw Lloyd-Langton, who delivered a solo acoustic set each night to great acclaim.

Hawkwind took the opportunity to introduce some more material from their forthcoming album, *Take Me To Your Leader*. 'Angela Android' had been in the set for a year or so, along with an updated version of 'Spirit Of The Age', but the audiences were now hearing Alan Davey's 'Out Here We Are' for the first time.

The band were joined on stage by familiar faces Crum and Pete Pracownik at Cardiff Coal Exchange on April 29 – but one friend, fan and sometime Hawkwind member was noticeable by his absence throughout the tour. There was no sign of Keith Kniveton.

Keith had made the big mistake of falling out with Alan, and he has not played with Hawkwind since. "He got all funny," says a typically direct Davey. "He started insulting me for some reason. I have no idea why. People started telling me, 'Keith's been saying this about you.' I picked him up on it immediately. He just denied it all and I could tell he was lying. Later on, he admitted it as well. He tried to make up, but I was still a bit, '*Wooarrrh!*' I thought we were best mates.

"Keith's afraid to come down here [to the milking shed]. He knows if he does, I'm going to have to confront him and ask him what all that was about and why did he do it?"

"It caused a hiccup in the planetary universe of Hawkwind," jokes Dave Brock. "It was a triviality that Alan blew out of all proportion. He was behaving like a brontosaurus. I find Keith all right. He's got a good ear. He's a good musician. He's good at playing synthesiser. He's very good technically, on the computer and as an engineer. He does a lot of weird things with my guitar. Keith occasionally rings me up and I'd love him to come and play again, which is quite difficult because unfortunately we've got the Alan problem. It's a weird old thing between him and Alan, and they should stop this fucking stupid nonsense, but in their world it's a major thing."

The rift with Alan was the last in a series of problems for Keith Kniveton after he became involved with Hawkwind. According to Kris Tait, "Keith did not like playing live. He couldn't handle it. He's a tiny little fellow and he's very shy, very nervous, like a mouse."

"He reminds me of a bird," decides Dave. "He's a strange, bird-like character. And also his personality is quite fragile. He likes to have a woman who dominates him and tells him what to do, to keep things together for him."

Kniveton was reportedly with such a woman – a girlfriend called Tone – when he first went on the road with Hawkwind.

"Keith's a nice bloke," declares Kris. "And Tone was very helpful, she was a good friend to us and she did a lot of hard work for Hawkwind. She wasn't frightened of rolling her sleeves up. I wouldn't say she was a nasty person, but she wouldn't stand any nonsense from anybody. She could be scary. She was *big*. She was in charge of the Hawkwind passports."

Dave continues: "You've gotta remember that they'd all be on the tour bus together. It's quite hard to fit in for a while until you get the gist of who's who. Tone felt totally out of place 'cos she's quite a demanding sort of woman. So in the bus, they had the downstairs sleeping room and they were isolated from the rest of the crew who were above them."

Storm clouds eventually gathered over the winter tour of 2001. Kris: "We were doing a gig in the West Country and Keith packed up and walked out because Tone told him to. We were really pissed off."

This happened due to a misunderstanding over Keith's onstage sound – or rather, the lack of it. "Tone was plugging all Keith's stuff in," says Kris.

"But it seems she didn't flick over the switch on his DI [direct input] box," continues Dave. "And they blamed Tim [Sunderland, who was mixing the sound]."

"They said that Tim hated Keith and had cut his sound off from the show so that it wouldn't come out front," adds Kris. "Tim would never in a million years do something like that. He's a total professional."

It's probable that Keith's dramatic exit happened at Torquay on November 20, 2001, since he did not appear with the band again until July the next year, at the Seaton Hawkfest. All was then forgiven, and Keith made sporadic appearances with Hawkwind through to the autumn of 2003, after which he fell foul of Alan Davey through a chain of Chinese whispers.

Hawkwind had been working long and hard for months to master the computer programs necessary to complete *Take Me To Your Leader.* "Keith was quite on the case with the computer and we weren't," explains Dave Brock. "He was giving us lessons. Alan was still learning – he's very good at it now, by the way – but at the time he felt threatened in a way, a bit resentful of Keith's knowledge. Alan likes to be the boss of that sort of situation.

"I was talking about this to Keith, and I said, 'Alan is not an engineer yet. He's still learning his trade,' as it were. Unfortunately 'cos they're all a lot of old fucking gossips, Alan got to hear about it and had a major freak-out. That caused the problem between Alan and Keith, and Tone seized upon it to weave a bit of intrigue and make Alan look a bit smaller than he should be."

"Dave hadn't said anything maliciously," points out Kris. "Alan had one of his fits of rage and he rang up Keith and Tone and threatened them. Tone then erased the whole passport database. She said, 'We'll not have anything to do with Hawkwind any more.' We said, 'If you have a row with Alan, it's between you three.' But they walked out. And my mum had to retype the names and addresses of 2,000 passport holders, all from paper copies in the files.

"It was just a really petty argument, and Dave and I got caught in the crossfire. I was upset. I'd been friends with Tone. I think they took it out on the wrong people. It created more workload for me, Dave and my mum, but it didn't affect Alan the slightest little bit."

As a postscript to the story, Kris reveals: "Tone and Keith split up on Christmas Day [2004]. He's been devastated ever since and lost loads of weight.

"A few months ago, he realised the damage that had been done. He started ringing up and apologising to everybody. Dave said, 'No hard feelings,' but Alan wouldn't accept his apology."

The summer season arrived, and after a couple of dates in Greece in May, Hawkwind set out for some of the big European festivals.

In Sweden's Solvesborg on June 11, they were joined onstage by two devoted fans – rhythm guitarist Phil Caivano and singer/guitarist Dave Wyndorf from New Jersey's stoner-rock band Monster Magnet, who have covered personal Hawkwind favourites such as Robert Calvert's 'The Right Stuff'.

A month later, at Finland's Ruisrock Festival, Hawkwind again welcomed Caivano to the stage, along with Lemmy. Wyndorf, on this occasion, was sick with a stomach upset – and also sick with disappointment at missing his opportunity for such an exciting guest appearance.

The three-piece Hawkwind followed on with a performance at the Burg Herzberg Festival in Germany on July 17 before returning to Devon to prepare for a major UK Christmas tour.

Just as Keith Kniveton was leaving, another keyboard player was about to enter into the ranks of Hawkwind – and he would become a major influence on the direction of the band.

Jason Stuart was not a replacement for Keith. There could have been room for both, in the same way that Kniveton and Tim Blake succeeded in playing complementary roles at the Royal Festival Hall in October 2001. Alan: "Keith was mainly an EMS [synthesiser] player giving us sound effects like Dikmik. He's not a great keyboard player like Jason is, but he was good on the EMS. We had all this great backing stuff like always, but we needed some icing on it again. There was definitely room for a keyboard player to tinkle about, and tinkle Jason does."

The new boy had supported Hawkwind on various occasions since the mid-Nineties as a member of Captain Rizz, and he had come to know the band members socially after moving to Devon. He was born on December 20, 1968, in Detroit and after only a few months moved to England with his parents. Growing up in Salisbury and London, he first became aware of Hawkwind at the age of around 10 when his mother took him to Stonehenge for the summer solstice and walked him round the stone circles.

"I don't remember seeing Hawkwind play on that occasion," admits Jason. "But I just knew that they were there. They were on the festival scene."

Another decade or so later, Jason was seeing them in the line-up of every festival he went to. "It's part of your childhood," he asserts. "It's part of history. They were sort of like heroes, really. Now I'm privileged enough to play with them.

"The first time I actually *loved* their songs was in 1995 when we [Captain Rizz] did a tour with them. One night we were all watching at the back of the venue, Hawkwind were playing 'Love In Space', and we all just suddenly looked at each other at the same time and went, 'Brilliant!' That's when I think I was hooked."

Towards the end of the Nineties, Jason relocated from London to Honiton, Devon, where his family have owned a restaurant and bar for nearly 20 years. "I used to come down here to get away from London," he says. "It's such a magical place I ended up staying. I live on a ley line. That might have something to do with it. I used to bump into the guys from Hawkwind regularly because we were from the same general area, and we'd say hello."

Jason's first visit to the milking shed was unconnected to the band. "Dave was kind enough to let me play in the studio," he recalls. "I came over to try some music by myself. Dave said, 'Help yourself, plug in . . .'"

In 2004, Jason was invited to come and have a play with Hawkwind, who in fact were trying him out for a job. "We were already aware that he was a good player," explains Alan.

"I was hoping it would lead to something more," admits Jason. "I was scared shitless. Luckily, I'd known the guys for a few years and they're nice people. They made me very welcome as friends first, so I didn't have any real angst.

"I didn't know all the music, but they made me feel comfortable. I understood after the first half an hour of playing with them that I had a lot to learn from their experience and their professionalism and their sheer musicianship. I realised that what sounds simple can sometimes be very complex. It's what you *don't* play that counts. That's where they're professionals – they make it look very easy."

Despite his comparative inexperience, Jason passed his audition with flying colours. He was invited to join the band as a full-time member and was immediately put to work. "They're sticklers for rehearsing," he remarks. "You put effort in, and that's what our job is.

"All their arrangements are very, very musical. Forgetting all the modern technology and all the software, it's a band that's very focused on playing live. You can only learn from experienced musicians and it's a learning curve for me. People who know their craft and have been in the business for years and years, it's the most natural thing for them, but I'm learning every day I play with them. They're my teachers. I'm growing and progressing, and we're all looking forward.

"It feels like a family, which is what I think the band are all about. The Hawkfests are very family orientated. That really attracted me as well. Things have got too commercialised these days, but Hawkwind have kept to the spirit, it's still living strong and that's why they're still here. The music is just part of what we do."

Jason made his live Hawkwind debut with a brace of autumn gigs, prior to the start of the tour proper in December. Also taking their first steps with the band at Cheltenham Town Hall on October 23 and Bournemouth BIC Pavilion (28) were a pair of costumed dancers – the first of a succession of dancing teams hired to dramatise the themes of cloning, androids and technology inhabiting the new and at that time still unreleased album *Take Me To Your Leader*.

With all of the band members except for Richard Chadwick dressed in white lab coats, Hawkwind set out to recreate the album's setting – a space laboratory – aided by Mr Dibs, who delivered recitations, and guest performer and old pal Dumpy, stepping up both nights for 'Master Of The Universe'.

The projections and lights further illustrated the lyrical content of the songs, which saw four additions: Alan Davey's high-energy 'Greenback Massacre', Richard Chadwick's 'Digital Nation' (a cautionary tale about the addictive nature of online video gaming), Dave Brock's 'To Love A Machine', an early audience favourite, and the controversial 'Ode To A Timeflower', which was built around the voice of Robert Calvert reading poetry from beyond the grave.

Fans at both gigs were thrilled to see that Brock was now out front with a lead guitar, not hidden behind banks of keyboards – and he is still maintaining this position at the helm.

The main Take Me To Your Leader Tour, opening at Newcastle Journal Tyne Theatre on December 4 and winding up just before Christmas at Birkenhead Pacific Road Arts Centre, offered a similar set list and presentation, although there were a few disappointments along the way. Here and there, there were imperfections in the sound quality, and certain venues were too small to accommodate the full production, specifically the dancers.

Hawkwind had hoped to enlist Arthur Brown as the narrator, but in the event he opted out of the tour, and he has not performed with the group since then. "Arthur seems to have become very busy with his own band," explains Alan. "It's like my own situation with Bedouin. Bedouin are lost in the desert somewhere."

It was then agreed that Matthew Wright would make a great narrator, but he was unable to commit to much of the tour. The speaking parts and poems were finally undertaken in some style by Dave Brock and Mr Dibs, both reading from clipboards in their lab coats.

Matthew did, however, make it to the London Astoria on December 19, 2004, when he took to his reading role with relish before a jam-packed audience. "At one point," says Alan pointedly, "we were told that we'd never sell out the Astoria again."

That night in central London was the scene of the most triumphant Hawkwind gig in many years. Some of their longest-serving fans vow that they have rarely heard the group play with such power and sense of purpose, and there was huge acclaim for a set that so dynamically brought together the old and the new. Yet, for a minute there, it looked like Hawkwind might be staring disaster in the face.

Babyshambles had been due to play the Astoria the night before, but their leading man, Pete Doherty, characteristically failed to show up. The fans responded by smashing up the PA and the lighting system, and it was only through the efforts of the venue's own crew, working round the clock, that normal service was restored in time for Hawkwind's show.

Says Jason: "As soon as we went in to soundcheck, I felt electricity running through my veins. The hairs on the back of my neck stood up. The Astoria was a place I had respected for many years and to actually play there was really special. It's home. London's home. There was a wonderful vibe and I felt very proud and happy."

"The Astoria is always special," adds Alan. "The new material went down really well at that gig. Normally, you get this delay before the audience cheer, but 'cos we've got Fleece doing the sound out front and he's such a good engineer, people could hear it all properly, the tunes and everything, straight away."

It was Hawkwind's annual Christmas party gig, and some of the fans had answered the call to come fancy-dressed as androids, robots, scientists and clones. Also enjoying the festive cheer, the dancers and the giant screen projections (showing such diverse images as bacteria, wriggling sperm, dollar bills and planet Earth) were former band members Mick

Slattery, Martin Griffin and Paul "Twink" Noble, who was drafted in to replace Tim Blake in 1980, only to break his foot a few days later.

Onstage, Dumpy – a solo support act on the tour, playing guitar, bass pedal and effects – joined the band for 'Brainstorm' and, as usual, 'Master Of The Universe'.

The evening found Hawkwind in clear command of a vigorous and thoroughly atmospheric performance of contemporary – yet timeless – space rock, all four members locked in tightly and visibly enjoying every moment. The reaction was predictably ecstatic, not only from the fans but from various members of the press, including two extremely enthusiastic young blades from a daily tabloid.

Something seemed to be happening; it had been in the air for a while. Suddenly, people were buzzing, wanting to know about Hawkwind again, to see them and to write about them, to hear their new album. Events had taken on a momentum of their own. The ball was rolling in the right direction, and it still is.

The second part of the Take Me To Your Leader Tour hit the road several months later, in May 2005, and still there was no sign of the album. Kris and Dave were continuing negotiations with several labels who wanted to release it, although in the end they would stick with Voiceprint.

The dates, in the UK and Europe, opened on May 4 at a festival in Bergen, Norway, carrying on through Middlesbrough, Blackburn, Sheffield, Wolverhampton, Nottingham, Helsinki and Tampere in Finland, and Croydon. There followed a short run of festivals at Giessen and St Goarshausen in Germany (June 17 & 18) and the Dour Festival in Belgium (July 15).

"At Bergen, we played with one of my favourite bands, Enslaved," remarks Richard Chadwick. The annual Bergen festival goes on for about a week with international artists playing at large and small venues across the town. Two Norwegian bands – Enslaved and We – are particular fans of Hawkwind, which is why they were chosen to play with them. Members of We were invited to join in on 'Brainstorm' and 'Masters Of The Universe'.

Enslaved are musically rooted in Norway's black metal scene, although they have developed progressive qualities. Richard, emerging from a 10-year romance with hard techno and drum'n'bass to embrace the various close relations of death metal, enthuses: "I love all that stuff – the passion in music is coming back. It's all part of an emotive thing. People want that after a decade of techno and hip hop. They want that human sort of action.

"I've been talking to Ivar [Bjornson], the Enslaved guitarist, on email. He gave us a lot of Enslaved stuff and we gave him a lot of Hawkwind stuff. We traded! I discovered they were keen fishermen, so Alan had a lot in common with them.

"At the Dour Festival in Belgium, we were sandwiched between a lot of heavy metal bands such as Anthrax. The response and the vibe I got was, 'Oh, this is a breath of fresh air.'

"Initially people think, 'What's this?' But it [the Hawkwind set] has the edge and attack of rock music and it's got all that space and atmosphere that goes with it. Our forays into Europe, that we can fit into different kinds of festival bills, I think is significant."

Alan Davey says it's his proudest achievement with Hawkwind. *Take Me To Your Leader* was a long time coming – it had been eight years since the band's last proper studio set, the disappointing *Distant Horizons* – but the fans had waited with patience and optimism. As the release dates approached, both *Take Me To Your Leader* and its lead single, 'Spirit Of The Age', were at number one in Amazon's pre-release charts. At the time of writing, their highest placings in the commercial charts had not been established.

The album had changed and changed again in the making as Hawkwind worked away for months in the milking shed, intent on getting every detail right. This was no problem for Alan. He lives near South Molton – not far from Dave and Kris – so the travelling was easy, and he was unshakeably committed to an album that he engineered, mixed and produced with Brock.

"We've done the whole thing ourselves," he declares. "We learnt a new studio program called Logic. That's why it took so long to do. You start mixing and then you learn something else which can improve it, so you have to go back and apply it. Ten or 11 times we mixed it. I think we got as far as we could without going into the overkill zone. It sounds big and lush and quite raw – a Seventies kind of production that's still edgy.

"When we'd finally finished it, I played it to my brother Andy. He really likes the old Hawkwind, and he couldn't find fault with it, so that was a good test. It's just as good to listen to stoned as the old albums, I'd say. There's some stuff on it that's really different because with the new digital studio we can do things that we couldn't do with tape. Then again, it's got Hawkwind stamped all over it."

As time went on, some songs – 'The Reality Of Poverty' and 'Cyberspace' – were dropped in favour of stronger ones, a wise move considering that their replacements, 'Greenback Massacre' and 'To Love A Machine', have already become firm fan favourites. A short piece, 'Sighs', was also slotted in.

"It's an album of warning," continues Alan. "It's all about cloning and androids, about the bad decisions we're taking in society that's going nowhere but to destruction. Say if you're 20 now, you'd get a mortgage for 25 years. In 25 years, there might not be a house left. People are more interested in their back garden than in the rest of the world, and they have to start thinking seriously about this."

Jason ventures: " 'Greenback Massacre' is very pertinent to the political situation in America at the moment. An inexhaustible amount of money is being spent on the wrong things."

"If our leaders don't start acting civilised, why should we?" demands Alan. "That's the problem with what's going on now. Teenagers see their leaders as these corporate war types. There's no example being set. There's one particular piece on the album that's very controversial, a spoken-word thing from Arthur Brown. It will spark a few conversations. That's the idea; get people talking about things."

The track he refers to is 'A Letter To Robert' (referring to Calvert).

Dave: "When Arthur was down here, he made up this track off the top of his head. It was one of those wonderful, magic moments – inspirational."

There are lighter ideas too. 'Angela Android', for instance, tells the whimsical story of a lonely guy in a spaceship with only an android replica of his girlfriend for company.

The album title itself was suggested by a toy alien given to Dave in Cleveland. A small, speaking doll, which he has kept, it squeaks, "Take me to your leader!"

Given the album's extended gestation period, it's hardly surprising that some of the tracks feature musicians and contributors who have already flown away. Simon House is responsible for the keyboards on 'Angela Android' and the violin on 'Sunray', Arthur Brown performs 'Sunray' and 'A Letter To Robert', and Lene Lovich flexes her extraordinary vocal cords on 'Angela Android'.

Matthew Wright takes the microphone for 'Spirit Of The Age', not only on the album cut but on the studio and live versions issued as companion singles at the end of August 2005. (The live tracks across the two singles were recorded at the Astoria on May 25, 2003.)

Guest Jez Huggett endows 'Out Here We Are', 'Digital Nation' and 'Angela Android' with sax, trumpet and flute, while some sympathetic organ playing by James Clemas distinguishes 'Spirit Of The Age' and 'Sunray'. Bringing things bang up to date, Jason Stuart is the keyboard man on 'Greenback Massacre' and 'To Love A Machine'.

The album, dedicated to the late and much-loved DJs John Peel and Tommy Vance, was launched with a short, impromptu Hawkwind performance and a Spacehead set featuring Richard Chadwick at a crowded party in London's Borderline club on September 1. It was released four days later.

Dave Brock, however, had already moved on: "I listened to the album a couple of weeks ago. Well, it's all right, but it's like doing a painting. Once you finish it, you put it on the wall and do another one. After we finished *Take Me To Your Leader*, I started doing the Calvert project."

Dave had lots of old Robert Calvert material on tape, much of it recorded in the early Seventies, and he decided to pick out a selection of poetry readings and surround them with up-to-date music. The result is a 12-track album provisionally titled *The Calvert/Brock Project*, which Dave completed in August 2005. It's likely to be released by Voiceprint some time in 2006.

"It's been interesting, especially after doing the Hawkwind album which was quite difficult, learning how to operate the computer," says Dave. "This was totally different to anything else I'd been working on. I'd have maybe 50 seconds of Calvert doing one of his poems and I had to put three minutes of music behind it. I had to cut things up. Maybe four lines and a bit of music, then another four lines, so it all sounds good and interesting."

That was the big challenge: creating variety. "A lot of his stuff was very clever and funny," says Brock. "There's one where he gets locked in a cupboard – *'What's going on in here? I think I must be drugged. How did I get in this cupboard?'* Another is about a kid on a swing in a playground. At the same time, all you've got is that monotone poetry, so I tried to do everything in steps. I put a singer on, and I tried different rhythms and instruments. There's one with an EMS synthesiser which builds up into a big rock number. The one about the boy on the swings – Alan plays string bass on that, and it sounds a bit like Grateful Dead. With each one, you've gotta do something totally different to the other. I just did it all myself and got Alan and Richard to put their parts on afterwards."

But would Calvert approve? "He'd love all this because it's different. I worked with Bob for years and years. He would write words and I'd supply the music. I knew him really well, I knew his problems. As a team we were quite on the case. But I must admit it was quite weird working with his voice again."

Another album release is in the offing – a live one from Hawkwind. Alan Davey reveals that the band are keen to immortalise the *Take Me To Your Leader* show, not only because some of the songs have changed since they were originally recorded but also because this has proved their strongest set in years.

"It would be a shame to lose it," says Alan. "We'd like to have a proper recording of it. I'm looking forward to mixing it. I spoke to Paul Cobbold about doing the next Astoria show [the annual Christmas party on December 21, 2005]."

After playing their last show of the summer, the Off The Tracks Festival at Castle Donington, Derbyshire, on September 3, Hawkwind took a holiday, intending to regroup later in the year in the studio.

The next mission is to give some of their old songs a spring-clean – or, rather, a total make-over – having already reinvented 'Spirit Of The Age' and 'Paradox'. The latter had first appeared on the single 'You'd Better Believe It', and in its new, studio format, is now a partner track to 'Spirit Of The Age (Live)'.

The evergreen 'Silver Machine' has also undergone a facelift. "We kept Lemmy's vocal on it, and Dave's original vocal," says Alan Davey. "Richard put another vocal on. We chopped out anything Nik's done. Me and Dave put a new bass and guitar on it and a new drum track. It builds up on the end, with Dave playing a 12-string and harmonica. It's a pleasure to listen to him. He's a real blues player, Dave. Richard always gets really excited when he gets his harmonica out."

The revamped classic made its debut on Total Rock Radio on March 11, 2005, along with a dedication by Dave to Tommy Vance who had died five days earlier of a stroke. The song has also been heard flying out, sideways through time, at various racing tracks, as a fitting anthem for the Oxford Silver Machine speedway team.

Hawkwind are now considering other back-catalogue songs that they feel would benefit from an update. One candidate is Brock's 'We Took The Wrong Step Years Ago' from *X In Search Of Space*. Others are 'The Demented Man' (*Warrior On The Edge Of Time*) and 'Infinity' (*PXR5*). "They're all sort of mellow numbers that we could completely rock up or rearrange," says Alan. " 'Psi Power' was almost folk rock when it started out and a couple of years later it was a punky sort of number. We'll get to all these and see if they work or not."

There will be new material too.

Dave: "*Take Me To Your Leader* is over and next year [2006] we'll probably do something else. Alan and me aren't keyboard players, and now we've got Jason, what we'll be doing next will be probably a bit different."

Jason's presence, it's hoped, will usher in a new era in Hawkwind's songwriting. "It's significant that he's joined us," explains Richard, "because he is essentially a live player rather than a sequence-ist. So it's encouraging a shift towards a more organic, rhythmic approach."

"He's the 'anti-sequence'," cracks Alan. "Jason played some piano on 'To Love A Machine', and it made it into a much more musical piece."

"This is appearing in the reworking of old songs," continues Richard. "Because of the way he's able to play this hands-on approach, it enables us to bring back things I really like, like dynamics and tempo changes, allowing the music to breathe in an organic kind of way, and hopefully this will evolve in our songwriting.

"I really feel we need to break away from the sequencer in our writing and build structures in a more traditional way – playing together in real time and making the sequencer conform to our ideas. I think we've been through a decade of music that was utterly, rigidly controlled by a sequencer. But what's really popular at festivals now seems to be this anthemic, slow-moving kind of music that gets people emotively involved."

"This band is based on musicianship," adds Jason. "We can get up there with the instruments and just play and that's what's important. We don't have to rely on technology. It's getting back to the feel of people doing it live and for real."

"We've been trying hard for a long time," declares Richard. "Our big, tortuous thing was overcoming the recording sessions for *Take Me To Your Leader*. We got over that initial learning curve to the point where we can use the equipment fairly intuitively. It's changing the flavour of the music, becoming more human.

"What we've been heading for is to try and get the intuitive dynamics that we get onstage on to our recordings. We've now worked out how to do it. There's new things, different dynamics, working in the band, like the shift in the membership. I think that's probably why there's this new energy and perkiness. We're able to aim at musical goals and achieve them to some extent."

With plans being made for another Hawkfest next year and the latest dancers, Stripey and Snail, preparing some spectacular fairy routines complete with showers of glitter, Hawkwind are looking to the future with confidence and a new sense of support.

"We seem to be appearing in a lot more magazines these days," notes Alan Davey. "Our name keeps cropping up – and we're not paying anyone to do it! It seems that people just want to write about us, which is the best thing. Hopefully, that'll be a springboard for something good.

"That court case stuff could've destroyed any band, but we keep ploughing through. I'm sure Dave and Kris had a lot more stress about it than Richard or I did. We had our fair share of it as well, but it's just irrelevant to me now.

"The band is getting better all the time, it's getting tighter and tighter, the gigs are getting better, and we're having fun with it. We have a laugh onstage. There's a lot of joking and taking the mickey out of each other over the microphone. We're getting on with it and enjoying it and the crowds are seeing that. There are a lot of smiling faces."

CHAPTER 34

Dave Brock: God, Satan . . . Or Just The Captain Of The Ship?

ALAN DAVEY sometimes thinks it's like being in a movie, a sort of *Carry On Dr Brock*. Whenever there is a controversy, a disagreement or a major tumult in or around Hawkwind, Dave is usually at the centre of it.

His name, more than that of any other member of the group at any time, inspires extreme reactions from the people around him. Those who like him love him, and will defend him fiercely against any criticism. Those who don't, and there are many, loathe him and will attack him vehemently, sometimes so viciously that their allegations cannot be published.

Some ex-Hawks including Tim Blake, Martin Griffin, Jerry Richards and Adrian Shaw are more balanced in their views of Dave, which also infuriates his detractors.

The thorny issue at the source of all the problems is control: Dave's perception of Hawkwind as his band, his grip on it, his hiring and firing and the way in which he does or doesn't do it, his collection of archive recordings from which he compiles albums, his business methods and his apparent wealth. "He's a control freak who doesn't have any time for anybody," declares Nik Turner.

One of the most frequently heard complaints is articulated here by Harvey Bainbridge: "I'm sitting here with no money while Dave is selling records he's no right to sell."

These records include the Weird Tapes cassette series, later released by Voiceprint along with other albums that the former members object to. As stated earlier, these same members, with the exception of Nik Turner, are cashing the cheques they now receive from Voiceprint.

Dave also stands accused of issuing bootlegs on a variety of small labels around the world.

Brock retorts: "Bootlegs are bad recordings. They have bum notes, people singing out of tune and bad presentation. I would never allow things like that to go out. For one thing, it makes you look stupid. I'm trying to protect my catalogue. A lot of live stuff has come out where the performances are good. For instance, *Spaced Out In London* we released ourselves. Tim Blake's keyboard playing was all over the place, the volume was going up and down, and we were able to iron these little things out. Now it's a good performance. I wouldn't have put it out as it was.

"Kris and I see Hawkwind bootlegs on the internet. People are doing it all the time. I get sent some. I've got a recording from the Roundhouse that I never even knew was being recorded at the time.

"There's a guy who worked for us as a sound mixer, and a lot of the stuff he recorded is available. I did object, 'cos none of us like bootlegs. Sometimes you're singing out of tune a bit, or having a bad day. You think, 'Fucking hell, this is awful and they've gone and released it.'

"I've turned up at places, seized tapes and taken them away. I've seen tapes at record fairs. People are still doing it. People are doing this all over the bloody place, and it's nothing to do with me.

"We try to stop people bootlegging us. I've got stuff here that the fans would love. Rockfield, with Calvert right on form. Bob and I talking in silly [mock posh] voices to each other. Simon King's drumming is spectacular. I'm contemplating releasing some of that. I really don't see what difference it makes to the artists when it shows the band in a good light."

Brock considers a list of some of the labels releasing Hawkwind product: "Samurai was to do with Jim White, and then the records were re-licensed. They crop up everywhere, they do. Obsession I think was Dave Anderson and Nik Turner's label. Thunderbolt I have no idea. Receiver Records was run by the accountant who was in charge of Trojan Records. We did try to get some money out of them. I don't know where they got their material from.

"Action Replay and Knight Records I know nothing about, or Elite. Some of these companies did licensing deals for a couple of years. Then it reverts to whoever puts these records out, who you never know. Marble Arch was put out by Castle. Anagram might have been a Frenchy sub-licence. Cyclops – that's a guy in America. Emporio I've never heard of. Snapper Music was a Douglas sub-licence from Emergency Broadcast System.

"Repertoire and Dressed To Kill might be something to do with Dave Anderson. Mausoleum is connected with Receiver. Lake Shore Records I have no idea. Burning Airlines I think is Dave Anderson. Shakedown Records might be Anderson and Turner. None of these have been anything to do with me."

Douglas Smith reasons that "if Dave is releasing music on small labels, then that has to be proved. And the difficulty about the proof is that if you go through the lists of records that have been released in this country, there are dozens of labels that don't exist. So it's very hard. Most pressing plants have to report to MCPS on all pressings. But there are one or two plants who will get vinyl and CDs pressed, no questions asked. It's possible to get a run of 500 records done.

"Dave has certainly been responsible for the release of all the records on Voiceprint. There may be an issue with the others at some point, because they have been released without the permission of everybody else.

"Many years ago, we had a meeting with Hawkwind to try to resolve all these people who weren't on the contracts not getting their royalties from EMI. It turned into a really big argument. Bob Calvert had jumped on the table and was attempting to smack various members round the head. Their accountant at the time said, 'Why don't you ask Douglas to come up with a solution?'

"I came up with a formula to work out how much each person – 11 of them – should get as a percentage from the total sales of Hawkwind on EMI. They've worked to that diligently ever since. When I renegotiated the EMI contract, Dave decided they would stick to that, even though only four original people signed the contract. Everybody gets paid. Absolutely 100 per cent. My only official title should be long-time arbitrator."

Steve Swindells is one of the members who alleges that Dave has released material from jams without crediting him as a co-writer. He admits, "It's offensive to me, although I couldn't be bothered asking Dave about it because I only found out very much later and it's such small fry in terms of finance."

Dave replies that by the very nature of jams, it's difficult in retrospect to ascertain who was responsible for what ideas.

It's often pointed out that Dave owns a big farmhouse, acres of land, horses and a studio, the suggestion being that he has acquired these things at the expense of the former members. Nik Turner says: "Dave's the only person who made any money out of Hawkwind, and everybody else is broke."

Brock replies: "Nik Turner lives in a big farmhouse in Wales. Douglas Smith has two houses, one in Spain, with acres of fruit trees and a swimming pool. What people tend to forget is that I got a mortgage with the advance on the publishing contract with United Artists. I wrote my own reference on their headed notepaper. That's how I got the old police house when I first moved to Devon. It was a run-down place. I did it all up, dug the garden, painted it and sold it. The money I got from that got the next mortgage, and so on. Lots of friends of mine did the same thing. It took quite a few years and a lot of hard work to get to where I am today.

"I've done a huge amount of work on this place myself and it's still a run-down farm. Nik's got more land than us. He had a three-storey house with a shop underneath it in Belsize Park. He does travel around a lot. I know what they all get . . .

"If you work hard, you can get things. I know exactly how much money Harvey's had over the years, and he's wasted it away. He was living in a place called Lake, and he had the opportunity of buying the house. It must have been in the Eighties. We did some record deal and we got an advance. He couldn't decide what to do. I said, 'You should buy it, Harvey,' but he didn't. Then he moved to a tithe cottage and he had the same opportunity there. He never did it. He will always moan about never having money, but he's one of these people who cannot get anything together.

"Just recently Alan and Richard were denying having any money, but I know they did. They just frittered it away. It's the same old thing about smoking dope. They always smoke it straight away and it's gone.

"We're doing pretty well now, 'cos Kris is our manager and she's honest. We know where everything's going. A lot of money used to be squandered on extra people and drink riders, when half of us don't drink. Other people used to drink it all. We started tightening up."

Turning to the subject of his tape archives, Dave says: "Yeah, I've got a huge amount of stuff. I've got lots of stuff from RCA Active, Kingsley Ward's label, which he gave me. We've been friends for years. I've got lots and lots of live stuff. That's where the Weird Tapes came from, and we used that money to support the fanzines. One was Brian Tawn's, and there were others around Britain and in Europe. I used to send them a few hundred quid here and there to keep them going over a period of maybe two or three years.

"Nik was aware that we were releasing these tapes years ago. They all knew what was going on. You say, 'We're going to put some tapes out, get some money in to cover the cost of the fanzines,' but they just forget. Two years later – 'No one's told me.' Richard gets told things and he forgets them. He never listens. They all get stoned and forgetful. Harvey's the same. We did a radio thing with him recently and he was nice as pie to me.

"As far as Voiceprint are concerned, Nik's an old fool, basically. They're holding his money for him, hundreds of pounds." Turner is refusing to accept the money, claiming that he never gave his permission for any releases.

"Has Dave Anderson got Dikmik's permission to release *Bring Me The Head Of Yuri Gagarin*?" raps Dave. "And another thing – there have been Nik Turner escapades where he said that he wrote songs he didn't. He released an album and he put his name to three or four numbers. 'Silver Machine' was on it. He'd changed the words. 'Psychedelic Warlords' – I'd written that.

"A lot of the stuff was being bootlegged, basically, like *Live Seventy Nine*. All the fans wanted the whole of the show with Tim's Crystal Machine bit in the middle, which wasn't on the original release. Rob Ayling from Voiceprint got in touch with Tim and he said he'd be highly delighted to have his bit on there. It was released as *Complete '79*. The fans loved it. Rob has got permission from Jill Calvert for all Bob's stuff. And these albums recoup the money, which is more than Dave Anderson's ever do, apparently. Hawkwind fans like these interesting things, and they still go out and buy the major releases, so it doesn't affect sales. That's why RCA weren't bothered by the Flicknife releases. A small company releasing a *Friends And Relations* album isn't going to upset anybody.

"The one that caused the biggest damage to us was *Yuri Gagarin* coming out under different labels and in different box sets with different bands. That to me is taking the piss out of us."

Answering criticisms that he has tried to take the lion's share of the writing credits, Dave says: "I didn't write everything. They've all had an opportunity of doing things. Harvey's done a lot of stuff. Calvert wrote a lot of stuff. Alan Davey is one of the main songwriters in the band. You see, there's lots of other people doing things."

Nik Turner further alleges: "Everybody in the band when we signed to United Artists had jointly written a lot of the material on the first album. When the album was re-released I suddenly saw that rather than the titles in the songs being credited to Hawkwind, they were credited as having been written by Dave Brock. He'd hijacked the credits without anybody knowing. I think he thought because he owned the name, he owns the rights to everything."

"No, that's not the case," insists Dave. On the latest EMI reissue CD, all songs are credited to Hawkwind/Dave Brock.

Several members including Danny Thompson and Harvey Bainbridge have complained about not being paid for gigs, with Danny stating that he is "upset and annoyed about the bootlegs and not knowing who's getting the money". Other musicians such as Del Dettmar say they failed to receive due royalty payments after leaving the band.

Dave raises an eyebrow: "We've had all these people working with us over and over again. If they don't like us, why have they kept coming back? And why has it taken them 30 years to complain?"

Many Hawkwind members have expressed displeasure at Dave's habit of getting rid of band members. Harvey Bainbridge suggests that Dave liked to use other people to carry out sackings for him, or else would cold-shoulder people out of the group.

"He'll work behind someone else," says Harvey. "He'll get someone else to do it. He got Bob Calvert to get myself and Martin Griffin in. Then he would wind me up to speak up against other people. He'll decide that he doesn't want to have people around that aren't producing any more, but he can't be seen to be the nasty person, the one that pushes people out."

"We haven't had that many sackings," replies Dave. "I've sacked Huw. He knows the reasons why. Turner was sacked twice. People sometimes play badly. You can't say, 'They're no use.' Sometimes you put up with bad playing for long periods of time. If you were working in an office with people, you asked them to do something and they fucked it all up, it would be, 'Wrong again, wrong again! Can't this person get it together?'

"In this band we've always given people huge amounts of time to pull themselves together and do something. At the end of it all, you get to the point where you just can't handle it any more.

"Ron faded away. Jerry faded away. It's far better to fade away and then they might pop up one day and we might play somewhere else. Ron has been in rehab. He might come back and be really together and sing for us again. And we can say, 'Come on then, Ron.' So I'd like people either to pay a bit more attention to what they're doing or else to leave and be gentlemanly about it without me having to say, 'You're fucking sacked.' Then they always think you're the one. Sometimes, we'll all have a meeting about someone. In a couple of weeks' time you want to give them another try, 'cos these guys are mates of yours. Once you sack them, they hate you. You don't want to end up hating each other. I'd rather them say, 'The time's come for me to go.'

"With Martin Griffin, I probably said, 'You do it, Harvey. Your turn.' Why should I always have to be the one? Occasionally, we shared the duties around. People were usually 'gentlemanly' about leaving. They'd get a little bit of a push, but it's better to use a bit of discretion, to 'decide to leave to pursue other activities'. It's better to be a gentleman."

Harvey maintains it was also difficult to work with Dave because of his propensity to keep people guessing, change plans suddenly and undo arrangements that other people had made.

"Sometimes things truly happen at the last minute and sometimes some people never bother to find out," states Dave. "We aren't deliberately mysterious. People can't be bothered half the time. They won't listen. It's like a school trip. Every member of the band has to be told what they're doing and then they have to be told again."

It's said by some that Dave's approach to life is at odds with the love, peace and anti-materialism that Hawkwind once represented. Doug Smith says: "The biggest disappointment is that the philosophy they presented more often than not they couldn't live by themselves. It wasn't always financial. It's more ephemeral than that. They don't practise what they preached. One thing was said and then something different would be said, perhaps behind your back. Yet, all of them are very pleasant people, including Dave. He's a very great charmer."

Harvey adds: "Dave's attitude is, 'Peace and love and . . . money.' Eventually you got involved in this whole thing about keeping tabs on what's going where, having to make sure you got your fair share. That was why I was quite happy to let it go."

"How do you live in a world without money?" wonders Dave. "You have to earn a living. The band have to earn a living, otherwise we wouldn't be able to function. Everything would be wonderful if it was all free. They're living in the past, some of these people. Our road crew, they do these outings at low prices for us. We've got a lot of loyal people who've worked with us because of what we stand for. I've refused to do gigs for the amount of money it costs us to hire a bus or a truck. The trucking companies are getting more than I'm getting on a tour.

"The rock'n'roll business being so corrupt, all these different people, trucking companies, bus companies – the guy who's driving the bus wants £10 food and £50 per diem, plus he's paid to drive the bus. It's all these things around the periphery which piss me off.

"You know how much it costs to actually play per night, to move the light show and crew. We've gotta move 20 people around. It's a business. We're running a business, but we're trying to make it a pleasant business."

"Dave Brock is a very good businessman and he doesn't miss one trick in the book," says Thomas Crimble.

"I don't think I'm a very good businessman," disagrees Dave. "If I was, I'd be living somewhere lavish. I wouldn't be where I am now. He's another one, Thomas. He was only in the band five months. Why does he say these things? Jealousy. The boys who weren't in it very long were jealous. They were always jealous of Bob too. If he were alive now, they'd be sniping at Bob. It's only 'cos he's dead he's a great hero."

Douglas contends that, in his experience, Dave was not hospitable to band members when they were working in the milking shed. "They weren't welcome to come in for dinner," elaborates Douglas.

Dave says simply: "Like I was saying to Richard – he's been in the milking shed for 15 years. He said he wouldn't come down here if he didn't like it – 'It's my escape from reality.' Unfortunately, it's my home."

Harvey offers: "Richard and Alan and Jerry were all camping out in various parts of the studio, and Dave was having all his bills paid. Yet he falls all over himself when Lemmy's about. And there were Richard and Alan and Jerry trying their best. He was taking the piss."

On a roll now, Harvey adds: "One of the things Dave used to do years ago. He got his little girlfriend Kris to go round hotel rooms to find out what we were talking about. He used to make me laugh."

"That's all sour grapes," responds Dave. "They smoked too much dope. Kris wasn't ferreting information. She's always a chatty person. That's the way she is. The other thing is with Kris, she's really been a great support for this band. Nobody realises it half the time. Over the years she's always been very helpful, very fair. I remember Harvey accused us of stealing the merchandising money, 'cos Kris is my girlfriend. She got paid for printing T-shirts up, 'cos she was working for the band. Then she got the accounts together – 'Right everybody, I've got the accounts here. Do you want to see them?' Nobody bothered to read them."

Most intriguingly, an anonymous former member of Hawkwind whispered on the phone: "Don't forget to ask about Pink Floyd and the million pounds."

Dave responds: "I don't know anything about it. I couldn't tell you." Nor can anyone else in the band.

Asked about his reputation as the "bad guy", Dave answers: "It doesn't bother me. Of course I get pissed off with being blamed for everything, but that's the way they all seem to do it. It's a shame really. We had a guy, Trevor Hughes, who'd been working on and off with us for years. He does these little magazines. He was at all the court cases with us. He wanted to print all this stuff about what Nik was doing. We said, 'We don't want to go into all that.' We said, 'No, just don't do it.'

"We were doing a gig in Birmingham a couple of years ago and we didn't have any money up front to pay for the crew. We wanted people to buy the official merchandising to cover the costs of the crew's wages. We had an outside PA coming in and we had to pay cash on the night for that too. I said, 'Trevor, can you not sell your magazines at the gig?' He took real umbrage at not being able to do this. Richard was saying, 'Trevor's pissed off 'cos he wants to sell his magazines.' I said, 'I'm not fucking interested.'

"After the show, Trevor had packed up all his stuff and gone. We suddenly found out he'd started working with Nik Turner, which I find quite strange. He travelled free with us. He had his own bunk with us, he got fed by us, he stayed in hotels with us. We never took any money from him. He was working for himself and selling his magazines at gigs for £1 or £2 and he does quite well. He takes up to a couple of hundred quid a night. He's been to all the gigs. It just goes to show you. I got fucking offended. [Turner, for his part, claims to have been wary of Trevor because he'd supported Dave against him in the xhawkwind case.]

"All these people – Harvey, Lemmy, Dikmik, Nik. They wouldn't have been in the band if I didn't enjoy working with them. I enjoy working with Alan and Richard. We've been together for all these years and we've got the best rhythm section probably this band ever had. I enjoy working with Jason. The worst time was the court case. All that was fucking terrible. It really wore us down. It was like all Turner wanted to do was damage us as much as possible."

Nik Turner alleges: "A lot of people are actually frightened of Dave. There's a wall of silence around him to a large degree. I've been broke enough to not give a fuck."

"I wouldn't say people are afraid," counters Dave. "You get older and mellower. Whereas earlier on, I'd like everything to be right. All of us did. Sometimes the crew would jump to attention when things were happening. It's just if you're running things and you want it all to be right, you've got to be aggressive rather than easy-going. It's no different, really. I've never clocked anyone in the band but I've threatened them all."

Turner continues: "He's an arrogant, unhappy, discontented person who's always trying to get something up on someone else. He never smiles."

Dave Brock smiles.

"You can never be his real friend," adds Frenchy.

Harvey asserts: "He's a strange bloke, Dave. I used to think he was okay. He's a charming, charming man, but he liked to give the impression he was very put-upon. Everything was everyone else's fault, never his. After a while you get to see that he's just dissatisfied with what everybody else does. There's a wonderful story that at Steve Took's funeral, Simon King was there and Dave Brock turned up. Someone said, 'I didn't realise Dave Brock knew Steve Took.' Simon said, 'I didn't either.' This other person said, 'There are two things I don't like about Dave Brock.' Simon said, 'What's that?' 'His face.'"

Alan Davey fights Dave's corner relentlessly. He says: "People who don't give Dave the time of day are missing out. It's quite a treat getting close to Dave. He's a funny man. He's always been really honest with us on the finances. Everyone gets an equal share. The things that are said about Dave come from pure jealousy, 'cos he is The Man. All the songs he's written – it's about time Dave had a Grammy award for influencing so many bands over the years. He deserves it if anyone does."

Asked about Dave's reputation for ruthlessness, Alan replies: "I don't see that as being true at all. If he's portrayed as an ogre, it's because he forges ahead and leaves people behind. He's always gone ahead of everyone else and done something different. If you can't keep up, you get left behind.

"I've run my own band and I know you have to be callous for the good of the band. It's like in Bedouin when I had to sack Sean, even though Danny Thompson was really angry about it. Sean was letting us down."

Kris Tait says she feels "very defensive and protective" when Dave comes under fire. "Any woman probably does if someone slags off their man," she reasons. "It's hurtful. It's hard. 'I can say that about him, but you can't.' A lot of times, it's just water off a duck's back, but sometimes you can see Dave is really hurt. He was hurt about Michael Moorcock. He was hurt about what Nik did.

"It does annoy me when the criticism is unfair. A lot of people don't know Dave. He can seem a bit brusque, but if you actually get to know him, he's a really nice person. I don't get protective in every band argument. I don't side with Dave automatically. We squabble quite a lot. But I've got this great sense of justice and sometimes Dave doesn't look as though he cares, but underneath he does.

"We stick together. We're quite a good team, really, but we're not a team to try and exclude other people. We're a team to try and keep things going and, hopefully, I've been a support to him. You've gotta talk to somebody . . ."

Huw Lloyd-Langton states simply: "There is no such thing as Hawkwind without Dave Brock."

Jerry Richards comments: "There's always been a piratical aspect to the band, even in the lyrics. Sometimes things will go on which might seem a bit weird, but there may well be a reason behind it which may not necessarily be clear.

"It could be argued that Dave has stood at the tiller of the band for years regardless of the personalities who have come and gone and given the world an amazing back catalogue of music. Dave's quick to smile and you have to like him. We're all likeable. None of us are real bad people. I learnt a lot from Dave Brock. You can't grumble, really. You've gotta have fun while you can."

Adrian Shaw says: "I don't have a big problem with Dave. He's a nice guy. He's a laugh. You can't dispute his importance within Hawkwind. He *is* Hawkwind now, and it wouldn't have been the same band without him.

"The Weird Tapes, Voiceprint – this is the only real bone of contention with Dave. I get an occasional small royalty for them, which was probably due to other people causing a fuss about it. It would have been nice to have been informed that the stuff was coming out.

"I do understand that if Dave wants to put this stuff out and was doing it correctly, he'd be having to contact everybody on it, which would make it virtually impossible. He just goes ahead and does it anyway. It may be unethical, but it doesn't bother me very much. If he hadn't done it, the recordings wouldn't exist. At least the stuff's out there in the public domain. If anyone is going to reap the benefits, better him.

"Douglas Smith has always said, 'Don't cash the cheques 'cos that's accepting the status quo.' But a penny in the hand is worth more than a pound in the bush. Life's too short, really. I'm quite relaxed about things."

Martin Griffin is equally relaxed. He says: "I got no royalty cheque for 10 years after leaving Hawkwind. Not a penny. It went somewhere. I don't particularly resent it. I always assumed the money went to the band. Perhaps if I was a songwriter I would feel differently. I wrote one song, 'Psychosonia' on *Sonic Attack*. The credit disappeared, strangely. There are albums I've played on that I haven't even been sent a copy of. The last four or five I've had to buy in shops. But I can't just bang my fist – 'Oh, that Dave Brock, what a rotter.' I think some of them do."

Tim Blake chooses his words carefully: "Now Hawkwind is working as an independent enterprise, it could be good, but I haven't found it personally beneficial.

"Groups like Hawkwind go through a lot of extremes. It's quite normal. And they navigate in extreme forms of hyperspace, not all the time but they certainly have, and people have moments of weakness, moments of greed. I don't know if we should be blaming people for them. Psychedelic hard rock is a pretty extreme experience. Space rock sounds very good too, of course. There's a lot of opportunism in there. It's a frustration for me, but I think it could always get better."

Dave Brock sums up his feelings about his former colleagues: "I'm the captain of the ship," he confirms. "When the ship's in port, they're all trying to get on board – 'Hi, where are you going to this time?' Sometimes people go off on their lifeboats, they land on an island, and later we go and pick them up off their island and they're all glad to come back and do something. When we went to Australia, I just picked up the phone and said to Simon, 'Want to come to Australia?' 'Yes.' It's quite a nice existence. They all get paid reasonable fees, they have a nice time, they're comfortable. We're not nasty people."

DISCOGRAPHY

Due to the sheer volume of Hawkwind albums, official and unofficial, which have been released over the years, and the extensive duplication of songs, it is impractical to provide tracklistings here.

OFFICIAL ALBUMS

Hawkwind
August 1970 Liberty

In Search Of Space
October 1971 United Artists

Doremi Fasol Latido
November 1972 United Artists

Space Ritual Alive
May 1973 United Artists

Hall Of The Mountain Grill
September 1974 United Artists

Warrior On The Edge Of Time
May 1975 United Artists

Astounding Sounds Amazing Music
August 1976 Charisma

Quark Strangeness And Charm
June 1977 Charisma

25 Years On
October 1978 Charisma

PXR5
June 1979 Charisma

Live Seventy Nine
July 1980 Bronze

Levitation
October 1980 Bronze

Sonic Attack
October 1981 RCA Active

Church Of Hawkwind
May 1982 RCA Active

Choose Your Masques
October 1982 RCA Active

Zones
October 1983 Flicknife Records

Stonehenge: This Is Hawkwind Do Not Panic (double LP)
November 1984 Flicknife Records

The Chronicle Of The Black Sword
November 1985 Flicknife Records

Live Chronicles (double LP)
November 1986 GWR Records

Out And Intake
April 1987 Flicknife Records

The Xenon Codex
April 1988 GWR Records

Space Bandits
September 1990 GWR Records

Palace Springs
June 1991 GWR Records

Electric Tepee
May 1992 Castle Communications

It Is The Business Of The Future To Be Dangerous
October 1993 Castle Communications

The Business Trip Live
September 1994 Emergency Broadcast System

Alien 4
October 1995 Emergency Broadcast System

Love In Space
May 1996 Emergency Broadcast System

Distant Horizons
November 1997 Emergency Broadcast System

In Your Area
April 2000 Voiceprint Records

Yule Ritual
October 2001 Voiceprint Records

Live At Canterbury Festival 2001
December 2002 Voiceprint Records

Spaced Out In London
March 2004 Voiceprint Records

Take Me To Your Leader
September 2004 Voiceprint Records

COMPILATIONS, LIVE RELEASES, CURIOSITIES, RARITIES AND REISSUES

Greasy Truckers Party (Various Artists)
April 1972 United Artists

Glastonbury Fayre (Various Artists)
June 1972 Revelation

BBC In Concert
September 1972 BBC

Dragon Fly (Various Artists)
September 1974 American Forces Radio

Roadhawks
April 1976 United Artists

Masters Of The Universe
February 1977 United Artists

Rock On (Various Artists)
March 1977 Phillips

Sonic Assassins / Dave Brock (Cassette)
March 1980 Weird Records

Repeat Performance
September 1980 Charisma

Hawkwind Live / Hawklords (Cassette)
October 1980 Weird Records

Hawkwind Free Festivals (Cassette)
October 1980 Weird Records

Hawklords Live '78 (Cassette)
June 1981 Weird Records

Hawkwind 1976/7 (Cassette)
September 1981 Weird Records

Hawkwind Friends And Relations (Various Artists)
March 1982 Flicknife Records

Hawkwind 1970/3 (Cassette)
October 1982 Weird Records

Dave Brock Demos (Cassette)
October 1982 Weird Records

Hawkwind Friends And Relations (Twice Upon A Time) (Various Artists)
April 1983 Flicknife Records

The Text Of Festival
July 1983 Illuminated Records

Hawkwind 1966/73 (Cassette)
November 1983 Weird Records

Independent Days (10-inch mini LP)
June 1984 Flicknife Records

Bring Me The Head Of Yuri Gagarin
January 1985 Demi Monde Records

Hawkwind Friends And Relations (Volume 3) (Various Artists)
April 1985 Flicknife Records

Hawkwind Friends And Relations (Volume 1 & 3) (Various Artists) (Cassette)
April 1985 Flicknife Records

Hawkwind Friends And Relations (Volume 2 & 3) (Various Artists) (Cassette)
April 1985 Flicknife Records

Space Ritual (Volume 2 – double LP)
May 1985 American Phonograph

Live '70–'73
July 1985 Castle Communications / Dojo Records

In The Beginning
July 1985 Demi Monde Records

Anthology (Vol. I)
November 1985 Samurai Records

Ridicule
November 1985 Obsession

Anthology (Vol. II)
June 1986 Samurai Records

Anthology (Vol. III)
June 1986 Samurai Records

Hawkfan 12
June 1986 Hawkwind Feedback

The Hawkwind Collection
October 1986 Castle Communications

Independent Days (Volume 2)
November 1986 Flicknife Records

The Approved History Of Hawkwind
November 1986 Samurai Records

Bristol Custom Bike Show (Various Artists)
March 1987 GWR Records

British Tribal Music
November 1987 Start Records

The Official Picture Log Book
November 1987 Flicknife Records

Early Daze (The Best Of Hawkwind)
November 1987 Thunderbolt Records

Spirit Of The Age
April 1988 Virgin Records

Zones / Stonehenge
November 1988 Flicknife Records

The Best Of Hawkwind Friends And Relations (Various Artists)
November 1988 Flicknife Records

Travellers Aid Trust (Various Artists)
November 1988 Flicknife Records

Levitation / Hawkwind Live
December 1988 Castle Communications

Acid Daze (The History Of Hawkwind)
April 1990 Receiver Records

Stasis (The UA Years 1971–1975)
April 1990 EMI Records

The Best Of And The Rest Of Hawkwind Live
July 1990 Action Replay

Night Riding
July 1990 Knight Records

BBC Radio One Live In Concert
October 1991 Windsong

Masters Of The Universe
October 1991 Marble Arch

Spirit Of The Age
October 1991 Elite Records

Anthology
December 1991 Castle Communications

3 Originals
February 1992 Castle Communications

The Friday Rock Show Sessions (Live At Reading '86)
March 1992 Raw Fruit Records

Mighty Hawkwind Classics (1980–1985)
April 1992 Anagram Records

Tales From Atomhenge (The Robert Calvert Years)
October 1992 Virgin Universal

The Best Of Hawkwind Friends And Relations (Various Artists)
March 1993 Anagram Records

The Best Of
February 1994 Castle Communications

Silver Machine
December 1994 Spectrum Records

California Brainstorm
December 1994 Cyclops Records (box-set)

Undisclosed Files Addendum
February 1995 Emergency Broadcast System

White Zone (by Psychedelic Warriors)
February 1995 Emergency Broadcast System

Hawkwind Friends And Relations (The Rarities) (Various Artists)
March 1995 Anagram Records

Independent Days (Volume 1 & 2)
November 1995 Anagram Records

Space Is Deep
November 1995 Receiver Records

Hawkwind Friends And Relations (Cosmic Travellers) (Various Artists)
April 1996 Anagram Records

Emergency Broadcast System Samples (Various Artists)
April 1996 Emergency Broadcast System

Future Reconstructions: Ritual Of The Solstice (Various Artists)
July 1996 Emergency Broadcast System

Live And Rare (Onward Flies The Bird)
March 1997 Emporio Records

The Ambient Anarchists
September 1997 Snapper Music

The 1999 Party (Live At The Chicago Auditorium)
November 1997 EMI Records

Welcome To The Future
December 1997 Dressed To Kill Records

Sonic Boom Killers
July 1998 Repertoire Records

Anthology 1967–1982
September 1998 Castle Communications

Hawkwind 1997
January 1999

Dawn Of Hawkwind (Various Artists)
June 1999 Blueprint Records

Epocheclipse – 30 Years Anthology
August 1999 EMI Records

Epocheclipse – The Ultimate Best Of
August 1999 EMI Records

Year 2000: Codename Hawkwind (Volume One)
September 1999 New Millennium Communications

Live At Glastonbury 1990
November 1999 Voiceprint Records

Choose Your Masques Live 1982: The Collectors Series Vol. 2
November 1999 Voiceprint Records

Complete '79: The Collectors Series Vol. 1
November 1999 Voiceprint Records

Year 2000: Codename Hawkwind (Volume Two)
August 2000 New Millennium Communications

Weird Tapes 1 (Sonic Assassins / Dave Brock)
September 2000 Voiceprint Records

Weird Tapes 2 (Hawkwind Live / Hawklords Studio)
September 2000 Voiceprint Records

Weird Tapes 3 (Hawkwind Free Festivals)
September 2000 Voiceprint Records

Weird Tapes 4 (Hawklords Live 78)
September 2000 Voiceprint Records

Weird Tapes 5 (Hawkwind Live 76 & 77)
September 2000 Voiceprint Records

Weird Tapes 6 (Hawkwind Live 1970–73)
September 2000 Voiceprint Records

Weird Tapes 7 (Dave Brock Demos)
September 2000 Voiceprint Records

Family Tree (Various Artists)
October 2000 Voiceprint Records

Atomhenge '76
October 2000 Voiceprint Records

Spacebrock (Various Artists)
October 2000 Voiceprint Records

Live 1990
June 2001 Voiceprint Records

Hawkwind Friends And Relations (Very Best Of Rarities) (Various Artists)
December 2001 Anagram Records

Masters Of Rock
April 2002 EMI Records

Live In Nottingham 1990
June 2002 Voiceprint Records

Cosmic Overdrive
November 2002 New Millennium Communications

Doremi Fasol Latido / In Search Of Space
March 2003 EMI Records

Complete Set
March 2003 Lake Shore Records

Oscillations
May 2003 Burning Airlines Records

Live In Nottingham
October 2003 Classic Rock

Hawkfest 2002 (Various Artists)
October 2003 Voiceprint Records

Welcome To The Future
November 2003 Shakedown Records

SINGLES

Hurry On Sundown c/w Mirror Of Illusion
July 1970 Liberty

Silver Machine c/w Seven By Seven
June 1972 United Artists

Urban Guerilla c/w Brainbox Pollution
July 1973 United Artists

Psychedelic Warlords (Disappear In Smoke) c/w It's So Easy
August 1974 United Artists

Kings Of Speed c/w Motorhead
March 1975 United Artists

Kerb Crawler c/w Honky Dorky
July 1976 Charisma

Back On The Streets c/w The Dream Of Isis
January 1977 Charisma

Quark Strangeness And Charm c/w The Forge Of Vulcan
July 1977 Charisma

Psi Power c/w Death Trap
October 1978 Charisma

25 Years c/w Only The Dead Dreams Of A Cold War Kid
May 1979 Charisma

25 Years c/w Only The Dead Dreams Of A Cold War Kid / PXR5
May 1979 Charisma

Shot Down In The Night c/w Urban Guerilla
June 1980 Bronze

Who's Gonna Win The War c/w Nuclear Toy
November 1980 Bronze

Hawkwind Zoo EP (12-inch)
May 1981 Flicknife Records

Motorhead c/w Valium Ten
July 1981 Flicknife Records

Motorhead c/w Valium Ten (12-inch)
August 1981 Flicknife Records

Angels Of Death c/w Trans–Dimensional Man
October 1981 RCA Active

Sonic Assassins EP (12-inch)
December 1981 Flicknife Records

Who's Gonna Win The War c/w Time Of
July 1982 Flicknife Records

Silver Machine 10th Anniversary EP
August 1982 RCA Active

Your Last Chance EP (Various Artists)
February 1983 Flicknife Records

Quark Strangeness And Charm / PXR5 (Cassette)
April 1983 Charisma

Motorway City c/w Master Of The Universe
October 1983 Flicknife Records

Night Of The Hawk c/w Green Finned Demon
March 1984 Flicknife Records

The Earth Ritual Preview EP (12-inch)
March 1984 Flicknife Records

Needle Gun c/w Arioch
October 1985 Flicknife Records

Needle Gun c/w Song Of The Swords / Arioch (12-inch)
October 1985 Flicknife Records

Zarozinia c/w Assault And Battery
April 1986 Flicknife Records

Zarozinia c/w Assault And Battery / Sleep Of A Thousand Tears (12-inch)
April 1986 Flicknife Records

Silver Machine c/w Magnu
July 1986 Samurai Records

Silver Machine c/w Magnu / Angels Of Death (12-inch)
July 1986 Samurai Records

Motorhead c/w Hurry On Sundown
August 1986 Flicknife Records

The Early Years Live EP (12-inch)
December 1990 Receiver Records

Gimme Shelter (Rock EP) (Various Artists) (12-inch)
April 1993 EMI Records

Spirit Of The Age (Solstice Remixes) (Various Artists) (12-inch)
June 1993 4 Real Communications

Decide Your Future EP (Various Artists) (12-inch)
November 1993 4 Real Communications

Quark EP (12-inch)
September 1994 Emergency Broadcast System

Area S4 (12-inch)
October 1995 Emergency Broadcast System

Love In Space EP
September 1997 Emergency Broadcast System

Spirit Of The Age (Radio Edit) c/w Angela Android and Assassins Of Allah (both Live) and Spirit Of The Age (Live) c/w Paradox 2005
August 2005 Voiceprint Records

INDEX

Index

567

6/07 (62553)

THE SAGA OF
HAWKWIND

THE SAGA OF
HAWKWIND

CAROL CLERK

OMNIBUS PRESS

LONDON / NEW YORK / PARIS / SYDNEY / COPENHAGEN / BERLIN / MADRID / TOKYO

Cover designed by Fresh Lemon

ISBN: 1.84449.832.8
Order No: OP 50809

Exclusive Distributors:
Music Sales Limited,
8/9 Frith Street,
London W1D 3JB, UK.

Music Sales Corporation,
257 Park Avenue South,
New York, NY 10010, USA.

Macmillan Distribution Services,
53 Park West Drive,
Derrimut, Vic 3030,
Australia.

To the Music Trade only:
Music Sales Limited,
8/9 Frith Street,
London W1D 3JB, UK.

Every effort has been made to trace the copyright holders of the photographs in this book but one or two were unreachable. We would be grateful if the photographers concerned would contact us.

Typeset by Galleon Typesetting, Ipswich.
Printed by Mackays of Chatham plc, Chatham, Kent.

A catalogue record for this book is available from the British Library.

www.omnibuspress.com